W9-CAY-853

Frommer's®

Belgium, Holland & Luxembourg

Here's what the critics say about Frommer's:

"Amazingly easy to use. Very portable, very complete."
—Booklist

♦

"The only mainstream guide to list specific prices. The Walter Cronkite of guidebooks—with all that implies."
—Travel & Leisure

♦

"Complete, concise, and filled with useful information."
—New York Daily News

♦

"Hotel information is close to encyclopedic."
—Des Moines Sunday Register

Other Great Guides for Your Trip:

Frommer's Amsterdam

Frommer's Irreverent Guide to Amsterdam

Frommer's Europe

Frommer's Europe from $50 a Day

The Complete Idiot's Travel Guide to Planning Your Trip to Europe

Frommer's®

6th
Edition

Belgium,
Holland &
Luxembourg

by George McDonald

MACMILLAN • USA

ABOUT THE AUTHOR

George McDonald is a former contributing writer and deputy editor of the KLM Royal Dutch Airlines in-flight magazine *Holland Herald,* and he has written extensively about the Netherlands for various international magazines and guidebooks.

With additional material by Patrick Flynn.

MACMILLAN TRAVEL USA

A Pearson Education Macmillan Company
1633 Broadway
New York, NY 10019

Find us online at **www.frommers.com**

ISBN 0-02-862601-X
ISSN 1044-2413

Editor: Jeff Soloway
Production Editor: Lori Cates
Photo Editor: Richard Fox
Design by Michele Laseau
Staff cartographers: John Decamillis, Roberta Stockwell
Additional cartography: Mark Reilly
Page creation by Toi Davis, Laura Goetz, Natalie Hollifield, and Linda Quigley

SPECIAL SALES

Bulk purchases (10+ copies) of Frommer's and selected Macmillan travel guides are available to corporations, organizations, mail-order catalogs, institutions, and charities at special discounts, and can be customized to suit individual needs. For more information write to Special Sales, Macmillan General Reference, 1633 Broadway, New York, NY 10019.

Manufactured in the United States of America

Contents

List of Maps

AN INVITATION TO THE READER

In researching this book, we discovered many wonderful places—hotels, restaurants, shops, and more. We're sure you'll find others. Please tell us about them, so we can share the information with your fellow travelers in upcoming editions. If you were disappointed with a recommendation, we'd like to know that, too. Please write to:

Frommer's *Belgium, Holland & Luxembourg*
Macmillan Travel USA
1633 Broadway
New York, NY 10019

AN ADDITIONAL NOTE

Please be advised that travel information is subject to change at any time—and this is especially true of prices. We therefore suggest that you write or call ahead for confirmation when making your travel plans. The author, editors, and publisher cannot be held responsible for the experiences of readers while traveling. Your safety is important to us, so we encourage you to stay alert and be aware of your surroundings. Keep a close eye on cameras, purses, and wallets, all favorite targets of thieves and pickpockets.

WHAT THE SYMBOLS MEAN
✪ Frommer's Favorites

Our favorite places and experiences—outstanding for quality, value, or both.

The following abbreviations are used for credit cards:

AE American Express	EC Eurocard
CB Carte Blanche	JCB Japan Credit Bank
DC Diners Club	MC MasterCard
DISC Discover	V Visa
ER enRoute	

FIND FROMMER'S ONLINE

Arthur Frommer's Budget Travel Online (**www.frommers.com**) offers more than 6,000 pages of up-to-the-minute travel information—including the latest bargains and candid, personal articles updated daily by Arthur Frommer himself. No other Web site offers such comprehensive and timely coverage of the world of travel.

The Best of Belgium, Holland & Luxembourg

The Benelux nations aren't very large, but they offer the visitor a huge number of wonderful experiences. Below are my choices for the very best.

1 The Best Travel Experiences

- **Traveling Through Time in Bruges:** Without a doubt, Bruges is one of Europe's most handsome cities. Its almost perfectly preserved center sometimes seems more like a film set or museum exhibit than a living city, because it throws your sense of time so out of joint. Its historic buildings run the gamut of architectural styles from medieval times to the 19th century. The city's picturesque canals are the icing on Bruges's cake. See chapter 6.

- **Riding the Kusttram (Coast Tram):** Riding the modern and comfortable Kusttram still seems like an old-fashioned adventure. The 2-hour journey takes you all along the 43½-mile Belgian coast, from De Panne on the French border to ritzy Knokke-Heist near the Dutch border. Along the way, you can stop at a number of inviting resorts or even smaller places, such as a stretch of beach or a horse-riding trail—whatever takes your coastal fancy, the Coast Tram can get you there. See chapter 8.

- **Touring the Ardennes:** The Ardennes, which covers the eastern third of Belgium, beyond the River Meuse, and on into Luxembourg, is unlike any other landscape in the Benelux countries. Its steep river valleys and thickly forested slopes make it a place apart. This is a historic land of castles, stone-built villages, and farmhouses, but that's not all. The region also has famous resort towns like Spa and Bouillon, unequaled cuisine based on its fresh produce and game, excellent winter skiing, nature and fresh air in abundance, and towns like Bastogne and Ettelbruck, which recall the sacrifice American soldiers made for victory in the Battle of the Bulge. See chapters 10 and 23.

- **Skating on the Dutch Canals:** When the thermometer drops low enough for long enough, the Dutch canals freeze over, creating picturesque highways of ice through the cities and countryside. At such times, the Dutch take to their skates. Joining them could be the highlight of your trip. See chapter 14.

- **Following the Tulip Trail:** The place to see the famous Dutch tulips in their full glory is the Keukenhof Gardens at Lisse, where vast numbers of tulips and other flowers create dazzling patches of color in the spring. Combine your visit with a trip through the bulb fields between Leiden and Haarlem. See chapter 15.

- **Checking Out the Windmills on the Zaanse Schans:** In flat Holland, wind is ever present, so it's not surprising that the Dutch have used windmills to assist with their hard labor, from draining polders to sawing wood. At one time the industrious people around the Zaan, northwest of Amsterdam, had almost 500 windmills working for them. Today, of the twelve that survive, four have been reconstructed in the Zaanse Schans, together with other historical buildings reminiscent of the Zaan region's bustling past. See chapter 15.

- **Celebrating Carnival in Maastricht:** Holland never seems so divided by the great rivers as it does during carnival season. Southerners declare that their celebrations are superior, and if you ever run into a southern carnival parade, you'll have to admit that they know how to party. In Maastricht the festivities are especially boisterous. On the Saturday before Ash Wednesday, the mayor officially hands over the keys of the city to Prince Carnival, who will reign for the next 3 days. During this time, people parade the streets of Maastricht in an endless procession of outrageous outfits and boundless energy. The atmosphere is always high spirited, but it never gets out of hand. See chapter 19.

- **Driving the Wine Trail in Luxembourg:** Follow the Route du Vin along the peaceful banks of the Moselle River from Echternach to Mondorf-les-Bains. Here, the low hills of Luxembourg are covered with vineyards. Several wineries open their doors to visitors, offer guided tours, explain how their wine is produced, and treat you to a little of what they have stored in their vats. See chapter 23.

2 The Best Castles & Stately Homes

Luxembourg is the castle capital of Europe. In this fairy-tale landscape, turrets and moats straight out of picture books seem to appear around every corner.

Belgium still has examples of the tough-minded approach to castle building, in which pathways for boiling oil take precedence over graceful turrets. This is a reflection of the country's position at the crossroads of Europe and of its traditional role as a battleground for bigger and stronger neighbors to settle their quarrels.

There aren't many real castles (square and imposing ones, built for defense rather than simply to live in) left in Holland. One of the reasons is that in the prosperous and relatively peaceful years of the 17th century, these ungainly buildings were completely reconstructed to create more habitable dwellings and fashioned to the French taste, which was starting to become the rage all over Europe.

- **Beersel** (near Brussels, Belgium): This 13th-century castle just 5 miles south of Brussels looks to be the ideal place for pulling up the drawbridge and settling in for a siege—and if the owners have had the foresight to amply stock the rustic Auberge Kasteel Beersel restaurant inside, the proceedings need not be too burdensome. This is a castle just like Disney makes them, with turrets, three towers, a drawbridge, a moat, and the spirits of all those who have, willingly or unwillingly, resided within its walls. See chapter 5.

- **Het Gravensteen** (Ghent, Belgium): Even more than 900 years after it was built, the castle of the Counts in Ghent can still summon up a chilly feeling of dread as you look at its gray stone walls. It's a grim reminder that castles were not all for chivalrous knights and beautiful princesses; this one was intended as much to cow the independent-minded citizens of Ghent as to protect the city

The Benelux Countries

North Sea

Waddenzee

Ijsselmeer

Groningen
Leeuwarden ○   ○ Groningen

Friesland

○ Assen

Drenthe

North Holland

Lelystad ○   ○ Zwolle
Haarlem ○ ★   **Flevoland**
Amsterdam   **Overijssel**

The Hague   **Utrecht**   **NETHERLANDS**
South Holland   Utrecht ○   **Gelderland**
Rotterdam   ○ Arnhem

's Hertogenbosch
North Brabant

○ Middleburg

Zeeland   ○ Antwerp   **Limburg**

Bruges ○   **Antwerp**   **GERMANY**

West Flanders   ○ Ghent   **Limburg**
East Flanders   ○ Hasselt
Brabant   ○ Maastricht
★ Brussels
BELGIUM
○ Liège
Hainault   **Liège**
○ Mons   ○ Namur
Namur

Luxembourg

LUXEMBOURG
FRANCE   Arlon ○
★
Luxembourg

from foreign marauders. Inside are the tools of the autocrat's profession: torture instruments that show that what the Middle Ages lacked in humanity they made up for in invention. See chapter 7.

- **Bouillon** (near Dinant in the Ardennes, Belgium): This was once the home of a genuine hero, although a hard-handed and ruthless one: Godfrey of Bouillon, who led the First Crusade in 1096, and in 1099 took Jerusalem by storm (massacring its Muslim inhabitants in the process). Meanwhile, back in Bouillon, his castle was being taken over by the Prince Bishop of Liège. It still stands today, 38 miles southeast of Dinant on the River Meuse, atop a steep bluff overlooking the town, the bridge over the River Semois, and the road to Paris. You can tour its walls, chambers, and dungeons. See chapter 10.
- **Het Loo Palace** (near Apeldoorn, Holland): William III, who became King of England, had a royal hunting lodge built here, in the forests surrounding Apeldoorn. Subsequent members of the House of Orange made alterations to the palace, especially in the 19th century, but recent renovations have revealed much of the original decoration, and what couldn't be saved has been redesigned according to the original plans. Don't miss the gardens, which have once again been returned to their 17th-century splendor. See chapter 18.
- **Ammersoyen Castle** (near 's-Hertogenbosch, Holland): This is a magnificent example of a moated fortress with sturdy towers at its corners, an architectural type that was introduced into Holland in the second half of the 13th century. The Ammersoyen's history was turbulent—it burned down in 1590 and was left in ruins for half a century before being rebuilt. See chapter 19.

3 The Best Museums

- **Musées Royaux des Beaux-Arts** (Brussels, Belgium): Paintings by many of the finest Belgian artists are assembled in the exceptional setting of this twin museum's neoclassical Museum of Historic Art. You'll find an entire section devoted to Brueghel, as well as works by Rubens, van Dyck, Hieronymus Bosch, and many others. Go underground to the Modern Art Museum for works by Magritte, Delvaux, Ensor, Rops, Alechinsky, and others. See chapter 5.
- **Koninklijk Museum voor Schone Kunsten** (Royal Fine Arts Museum; Antwerp, Belgium): Brussels's art museum may be the more conveniently placed for most visitors, but if you want to see the Flemish masters in all their glory, you should head north to Antwerp, where the Fine Arts Museum has the best collection of their works in the world, including the largest group of Rubens masterpieces in existence. See chapter 7.
- **Musée de la Vie Wallonne** (Museum of Walloon Life; Liège, Belgium): Set in a 17th-century convent, this museum rambles through the history and culture of the French-speaking (and Walloon dialect–speaking) region of Belgium called Wallonia. Its exhibits also ramble through the building that houses them, covering everything from popular arts and crafts to industry and agriculture; there's even an interesting section on theater marionettes. See chapter 9.
- **Rijksmuseum** (State Museum; Amsterdam, Holland): The Rijksmuseum houses some of the Netherlands's most important works of art: Rembrandt's world-famous *Nightwatch,* four of Vermeer's beautiful miniatures, and numerous works by Frans Hals. All in all, this is one of the most impressive collections of Old Masters in the world. There's also an extensive collection of antique furniture, sculpture, and applied arts, as well as the extraordinary Asian and Oriental art

collections, displayed in the South Wing overlooking the recently relandscaped Museumplein. See chapter 14.

- **Vincent van Gogh Museum** (Amsterdam, Holland): This museum has an extensive collection of its namesake's work: a total of 200 paintings and 500 drawings, ranging from the famous *Sunflowers* to ear-less self-portraits. The permanent collection also includes important works by van Gogh's 19th-century contemporaries, and there are often temporary or visiting exhibitions concentrating on the same period. A modernistic extension, designed by Japanese architect Kisho Kurokawa, will be completed in 1999 and will provide more space to properly display the museum's holdings, including its print collection. See chapter 14.
- **The Mauritshuis Royal Cabinet of Paintings** (The Hague, Holland): This wonderfully intimate museum is set in the 17th-century palace of a Dutch count. Its collection of Golden Age art treasures is small but unrivaled. See chapter 16.
- **Museum Boymans Van Beuningen** (Rotterdam, Holland): This museum features a range of art forms, from visual to applied arts, covering a period of over 7 centuries. Here you'll see paintings by everyone from Brueghel and van Eyck to surrealists like Magritte and Dalí. See chapter 16.
- **Museum Het Catharijneconvent** (St Catherine's Convent; Utrecht, Holland): This museum, which is appropriately housed in a former convent, will give you a clear picture of Holland's Christian heritage. The collection of medieval art and illuminated manuscripts is particularly impressive. See chapter 18.
- **National Museum of Military History** (Museum of the Battle of the Bulge; Diekirch, Luxembourg): Luxembourg has many museums devoted to the peaceful aspects of life, but there's something special about this tribute to the heroes of the Battle of the Bulge (1944–45), something gritty, immediate, and real that sets it apart from other war museums. Its centerpiece is a series of dioramas that give you an eerie sense of being there in the battle, in the snow, with danger all around. The display is bound to inspire both sympathy and admiration for the men who really were there, who fought and died for freedom all over the beautiful Ardennes region that is now so peaceful. See chapter 23.

4 The Best Cathedrals & Churches

- **Onze-Lieve-Vrouwekerk** (Church of Our Lady; Bruges, Belgium): The soaring 122m (396-foot) spire of this church can be seen from a wide area around Bruges. As a magnificent bonus, the church also holds a beautiful marble *Madonna and Child* by Michelangelo (one of his few works outside Italy); a painting by Anthony van Dyck; and the 15th-century bronze tomb sculptures of Charles the Bold and Mary of Burgundy. See chapter 6.
- **Onze-Lieve-Vrouwekathedraal** (Cathedral of Our Lady; Antwerp, Belgium): You can't miss this towering example of the Flemish Gothic style if you visit Antwerp, or even pass close to the city. Its 123m (400-foot) spire dominates the area. This is in fact the biggest church in the Benelux countries, with seven naves and 125 pillars. But oversized statistics are not Our Lady's only attraction—there are no fewer than three Rubens masterpieces inside, as well as paintings by other prominent artists. See chapter 7.
- **Cathédrale Notre-Dame** (Cathedral of Our Lady; Tournai, Belgium): This cathedral is a harmonious blending of the Romanesque and Gothic styles. It has five towers and a magnificent suite of stained-glass windows, as well as paintings by Rubens and Jordaens. Equally interesting are the opulent pieces in the

Treasury, especially the gold-and-silver reliquary, The Shrine of Our Lady, dating from 1205. See chapter 11.

- **Westerkerk** (West Church; Amsterdam, Holland): The Westerkerk's 277-foot tower, the Westertoren, is the tallest in Amsterdam, providing a spectacular view of the city. Anne Frank could hear every note of the carillon's dulcet tones while in hiding from the Nazis in her nearby house. See chapter 14.
- **Cathedral of St. Bavo** (Haarlem, Holland): Walking to the town center from Haarlem station, you catch only glimpses of the church, but the moment you reach the market square it is revealed in all its splendor. This cathedral, which was completed after a relatively short building period, has a rare unity of structure and proportion. Regular concerts are given here on the famous organ built by Christian Müller in 1738. The young Mozart once played on this instrument. See chapter 15.
- **Sint-Janskerk** (Gouda, Holland): At 400 feet, this is the longest church in Holland. It also has some of the most magnificent stained-glass windows in Europe. See chapter 16.
- **The Domkerk** (Utrecht, Holland): This magnificent cathedral was begun in the 13th century. Its 365-foot tower, which dominates old Utrecht's skyline, offers a great view of the city. See chapter 18.
- **Notre-Dame Cathédrale** (Luxembourg City): The cathedral of Luxembourg City was built late for the Gothic style—in the early 17th century—but is nevertheless a great Gothic monument, albeit clearly influenced by Renaissance ideals. The Octave of Our Lady of Luxembourg takes place here every year before the statue of the Virgin, which is said to have miraculous powers. See chapter 22.

5 The Best Offbeat Trips

- **Walking on the Wadden Sea** (Holland): At low tide, the Wadden Sea, between the northern coast and the Wadden Islands, virtually disappears, and if you're up for a walk in the mud, you can join a Wadden Walking (*Wadlopen*) trip and plow your way over land to one of the islands. Several companies, both in Groningen and Friesland, organize guided trips from May through early October. If you're lucky you might encounter some seals gallivanting in pools left by the retreating tide or sunbathing on the flats. See chapter 17.
- **Riding White Bicycles in Hoge Veluwe National Park** (Holland): It was tried once in Amsterdam—providing free white bicycles for everyone to use—but the bikes mysteriously disappeared and turned up in private hands with fresh coats of paint. The scheme has worked much better in this beautiful national park (which apparently doesn't shelter as many bike thieves). Just head to Hoge Veluwe's parking lot, pick up a bike, and explore the traffic-free scenery to your heart's content. See chapter 18.

6 The Best Outdoor Activities

- **Sand Yacht Racing at De Panne** (Belgium): Conditions on the beach at De Panne are ideal for this exciting, unusual sport. See chapter 8.
- **Skiing in the Ardennes:** Quite a few ski and winter sports shops in the Belgian and Luxembourg Ardennes have bet the farm and lost their shirts by banking on snowfall each winter. Some years it snows and some years it doesn't, and some years it does but by the time skiing enthusiasts arrive hotfoot from Brussels the

covering has melted and the ski slopes are as green as a golf course. Still, when it does snow enough, the Ardennes is a pleasant place to ski. There are a dozen or so downhill centers but most skiing in the Ardennes is cross-country. A particularly good location is the Hautes Fagnes Nature Reserve between Eupen and Malmédy, but you can ski only on the designated trails, as this is a protected landscape. See chapter 10.

- **Cycling in Holland:** In this nation with a population of 15 million people, there are some 11 million bicycles, so you can believe that the Dutch are all but born in the saddle. To fully engage in the Dutch experience you positively have to board a bicycle and head out into the wide green yonder. The tourism authorities have marked out many cycling tour routes and have published descriptive booklets and maps to go along with them, available from VVV offices. A few suggestions for longer tours: cycling around the IJsselmeer, the big lake north of Amsterdam, which you can do in anything from 2 days to a week; cycling along the coast from Zeeland to Zandvoort; touring the beautiful countryside of the "green province," Drenthe; and following the course of the River Maas down into hilly Limburg. Many train stations around the country have bikes for rent.

- **Strolling Along the Dunes of the Amsterdam Sea Defenses (Zandvoort, Holland):** If, on a sunny day, you feel like being at the seaside but want to avoid the crowds at the beach, head to a quieter alternative a few miles south of Zandvoort—the extensive dunes system (called *Kennemer Duinen* and *Amsterdamse Waterleiding Duinen*) that backs up the sea defenses. You can have an active fresh-air experience here, strolling along the paths through the woods on the eastern side and across the dunes leading west toward the sea. You'll find quite a variety of flora in this relatively small area, and the beach is never far away if the call of the sea proves too strong. See chapter 15.

- **Canoeing in the Biesbosch:** This unique natural park of marshland, meadows, and willow woods was formed during the St. Elizabeth floods of 1421, when 16 villages were submerged and the former polders became an inland sea. There are several possibilities for exploring the Biesbosch, including by tour boat, but paddling your own canoe is the best way to get close to nature. See chapter 19.

7 The Best Romantic Getaways

- **Château Vacations in Wallonia:** The French-speaking region of Belgium is noted for its beautiful châteaux, dating from the 17th, 18th, and 19th centuries, set in the countryside amidst ornamental gardens and often surrounded by moats. Nowadays, some of these venerable, stately homes have been transformed into hotels or restaurants, offering guests luxurious living and fine dining. There are châteaux in the suburbs of Brussels, along the steep valley of the River Meuse, among the rolling hills of the Ardennes, and set amidst the wide-open green spaces of Hainaut on the French border. A weekend in one of these châteaux is surely among the most romantic getaways imaginable. For further information, contact the Wallonia-Brussels Tourist Office (☎ **02/504-0200;** fax 02/513-6950). See chapters 9 and 10.

- **Kasteel Wittem** (Wittem, Holland; ☎ **043/450-1208**): This romantically idyllic 12th-century castle is also a hotel, and the perfect place to stay after exploring the south of Holland's Limburg province. In summer you can dine or have breakfast on a magnificent terrace overlooking the garden and moat. See chapter 19.

8   The Best Hotels

- **Métropole** (Brussels, Belgium; ☎ 02/217-23-00): This century-old hotel in the heart of Brussels maintains the belle époque splendor of its first days and combines it with modern furnishings and service. Its L'Alban Chambon restaurant is one of Brussels's best. See chapter 5.

- **Art Hotel Siru** (Brussels, Belgium; ☎ 02/203-35-80): This is one of the most surprising—even shocking—hotels you'll find anywhere. Its art-aficionado owner had the innovative idea of inviting Belgium's top artists each to "decorate" a room with a painting, sculpture, or installation on the theme of travel. Many of them took up the challenge, with the result that each room is a miniature single-exhibit art gallery. The art is, obviously, contemporary, so the response from guests can vary. Some regulars ask for a different room each time so that after a hundred visits they'll have toured the full "gallery"; some always ask for the same room; others, shaken by an unsettling image, ask for a room change in the middle of the night. One thing is certain: The Siru is unforgettable. See chapter 5.

- **'t Bourgoensche Cruyce** (Bruges, Belgium; ☎ 050/33-79-26): If all the virtues and character of the splendidly preserved, gloriously medieval city of Bruges could be encapsulated in a single hotel, this would be the one. You won't find a better welcome anywhere than in this polished little gem of a place. See chapter 6.

- **Sint-Jorishof** (Ghent, Belgium; ☎ 09/224-24-24): Everything that was said of Bruges's 't Bourgoensche Cruyce can be said with equal justification of Ghent's Sint-Jorishof Hotel, which dates from 1228. Like Ghent itself, this hotel is less pretty than Bruges's champion, with an exterior blackened by the centuries (don't worry—the interior is spotless), but, if anything, that only makes it seem more at home in its surroundings. See chapter 7.

- **Hotel Pulitzer Sheraton** (Amsterdam, Holland; ☎ 020/523-5235): Walking down the elegant Prinsengracht, admiring the historic canal houses, you might well be taken by surprise when you see the Hotel Pulitzer's entrance hall. This hotel was built within a block of no fewer than 24 adjoining properties, most of which are between 200 and 400 years old. Your room will overlook the greenery of the inner courtyard, or one of two canals, and if you stay in a deluxe duplex room, you may even get a key to your own canal-side front door. See chapter 14.

- **Hôtel des Indes Intercontinental** (The Hague, Holland; ☎ 070/363-2932): Within this opulent hotel, you can lean over the balustrade on the first-floor landing to watch the cream of The Hague's society having tea in the lounge, the lights of chandeliers reflecting in the polished marble pillars. The rooms are equally grand and comfortable. See chapter 16.

- **Hotel Lauswolt** (Beetsterzwaag, near Leeuwarden, Holland; ☎ 0512/358-1245): This 19th-century country house has been converted into a luxury hotel equipped with the latest amenities and leisure facilities. Some 2,700 acres of woods and heather offer ample opportunity for walking or horseback riding. You can also play golf or tennis, and there are even two swimming pools. All this activity will surely stir your appetite—luckily, the cuisine is of the same high standard as the other comforts in the hotel, and dinner in the elegant 19th-century dining room will be an unforgettable experience. See chapter 17.

- **De Campveerse Toren** (Veere, Holland; ☎ 0118/501-291): This ancient inn guards the harbor of Veere. With the Veerse Meer (Lake Veere) lapping at the walls below your room, you can look over the entire length of the lake and to the harbor where pleasure boats are moored. Little is as calming to the spirit as a walk through the old streets of Veere at dusk, when most of the tourists have gone for the day. Later, back in your room at the inn for the night, you'll be gently lulled to sleep by the murmuring waters of the lake. See chapter 19.

- **Grand Hôtel Cravat** (Luxembourg City; ☎ **052/22-19-75**): The Grand Hôtel Cravat has been a Luxembourg institution for nearly a century. And for fine dining nearby, you won't need to look much further than its own Le Normandy. See chapter 22.

9 The Best Restaurants

Citizens of Belgium and Luxembourg have always prided themselves on the quality of their cuisine, which they claim is clearly superior to that of France. Not so the Dutch, whose kitchens have been traditionally characterized more by a satisfying stolidity than by any pretensions to delicacy or invention. Nowadays, however, influenced by the many cultures living within their borders, Dutch chefs work their own culinary wonders.

- **Comme Chez Soi** (Brussels, Belgium; ☎ **02/512-29-21**): If Michelin were to introduce a 4-star category, Comme Chez Soi would undoubtedly be one of the first to collect the extra star. The irony about this culinary holy-of-holies is its name: "Just Like Home." I definitely don't eat gourmet fare at my home, but perhaps this is standard stuff at owner and Master Chef Pierre Wynants's place. A hallowed silence descends on diners as they sample their first mouthful of his French specialties with added Belgian zest. This being Belgium, the silence doesn't last long, but the taste and the memory linger. See chapter 5.
- **In 't Spinnekopke** (Brussels, Belgium; ☎ **02/511-86-95**): For a different kind of Brussels eating experience, try this down-home restaurant dating from 1762. Here, traditional Belgian dishes are given the care and attention expected of more refined—though not necessarily more tasty—cuisine. See chapter 5.
- **Le Sanglier des Ardennes** (Durbuy, Belgium; ☎ **086/21-32-62**): This restaurant, located in a hotel in one of the prettiest of Ardennes villages, has the rustic looks and ideal location to go along with its fine country food. Walking in the surrounding wooded hills is the perfect preparation for lunch or dinner here. See chapter 10.
- **La Rive** (in the Amstel Intercontinental Hotel, Amsterdam, Holland; ☎ **020/622-6060**): If two prestigious Michelin stars don't make your mouth water, then what will? La Rive even has a special table where you can watch how the chefs actually do it. While dining, you can enjoy the view through tall French windows to the broad Amstel River. The service and wine cellar are in the finest modern French traditions. See chapter 14.
- **Le Restaurant** (in the Hotel des Indes Intercontinental, The Hague, Holland; ☎ **070/363-2932**): The Hague's nickname "Dowager of the Dutch East Indies" could well apply to the elegant Hotel Des Indes. The food it serves is refined and delicious, combining European and colonial flavors. See chapter 16.
- **Restaurant de Echoput** (Apeldoorn, Holland; ☎ **057/691-248**): Game features prominently on the menu at this restaurant, set amidst the forests near Apeldoorn, on the edge of the Royal Wood. During the hunting season you can have wild boar, venison, and any kind of fowl, always succulent and prepared

with flair. In spring and summer the menu is just as delectable, and in fair weather you can dine on the terrace in the fresh forest air. See chapter 18.

- **Château Neercanne** (Maastricht, Holland; ☎ 043/325-1359): "To live like a god in France" goes the Dutch proverb expressing the pinnacle of earthly pleasure. You might imagine yourself to be both a god and in France if you dine at this château, which was designed following French models. What's more, in true French culinary style, the food here is seductively elegant and the wine cellar is unique and impressive—the wines are kept under perfect conditions in the marlstone caves behind the château. See chapter 19.

- **Saint-Michel** (Luxembourg City; ☎ 352/22-32-15): The Saint-Michel occupies a little side street in the Old Town, but lights up the entire city with classic French cuisine that makes no concessions where quality is concerned. See chapter 22.

10 The Best Moderately Priced Hotels

Dutch businesses have a well-established ability to extract money from people's pockets; they must, however, reckon with Dutch consumers, who are not exactly spendthrifts. Belgians and the appropriately named Luxembourgeoisie may have a less well-advertised attachment to their liquid assets, but believe me, they know the value of a franc. When traveling in these three countries, it's always possible to do as the natives do and find a good deal for your money. The following moderately priced hotels have got their quality/price ratios just about right.

- **Hôtel Welcome** (Brussels, Belgium; ☎ 02/219-95-46): This is the best little hotel in Brussels. With only six rooms, it's tiny, but the welcome's a big one, and the standard of the rooms is high. As an added bonus, you have only to trip down the stairs to find yourself in one of the best seafood restaurants in the city, La Truite d'Argent. Try to get Michel to tell you about the hotel and restaurant's history, preferably over a glass or two of Kwak beer—but be careful: it's a long story and Kwak is strong beer. See chapter 5.

- **Hôtel Egmond** (Bruges, Belgium; ☎ 050/34-14-45): You can think of the Egmond as your own country mansion, for not much more than a hundred bucks a room. There's just one problem with this image: The Egmond is not actually in the country. In compensation, it has its own grounds and gardens, and is located next to the Minnewater (Lover's Lake) and the Begijnhof. See chapter 6.

- **Hôtel la Falize** (Durbuy, Belgium; ☎ 086/21-26-66): If you only have the time to visit one place in the Ardennes, Durbuy should be it, for the unsurpassed beauty of its hill-enclosed setting and the tranquil charm of its cobbled streets and stone houses. And the perfect inn for your stay is Hôtel la Falize, which just about encapsulates all the town's old-fashioned, homey virtues. See chapter 10.

- **Ambassade Hotel** (Amsterdam, Holland; ☎ 020/626-2333): This hotel occupies ten neighboring canal houses on the "Golden Bend"—for centuries the city's most fashionable address. Here, you really feel that you're in the home of a rich 17th-century merchant. Most of the individually-styled and spacious rooms have large windows overlooking the canal, as does the split-level chandeliered breakfast room. If you need some modern—in fact, new-age— relaxation, you can take to the flotation tanks or relax into a deep massage at the hotel's Koan Float center. See chapter 14.

- **Hotel Seven Bridges** (Amsterdam, Holland; ☎ 020/623-13-29): There are some hotels where you realize that the owners aren't just running a business, but doing what they love. The Seven Bridges is that kind of place—Pierre Keulers and Günter Glaner have found both their hobby and their profession in this fine hotel in Amsterdam. It's no exaggeration to say that all the furniture, fixtures, and fittings have been selected with loving care, and guests receive the same conscientious attention. See chapter 14.
- **Hotel du Casque** (Maastricht, Holland; ☎ 043/321-4343): Maastricht, in the south of Holland, is where the cold-blooded northern Dutch come to get lessons in how to have fun. Though Maastrichters do their best, you can generally see them shaking their heads sadly, as though their less-talented brethren never will learn the lesson. The Hotel du Casque overlooks the Vrijthof, which basks in its reputation as the liveliest square in the liveliest city in the country. Despite its prestigious address, this hotel is as moderately priced as you'll find in Maastricht. See chapter 19.
- **Grand Hôtel du Parc** (Clervaux, Luxembourg; ☎ 352/9-10-68): The northern Luxembourg town of Clervaux is one of the most dramatic in the Ardennes; it's situated in a plunging valley, watched over by a castle on the mountain heights. The Grand Hôtel du Parc offers old-fashioned charm with all the benefits of modern facilities, including a sauna and solarium, at a downright affordable price. See chapter 23.

11 The Best Cafes & Bars

- **Le Falstaff Cafe** (Brussels, Belgium): In some ways I hate to put Le Falstaff at the head of Brussels's best cafe list, because its self-satisfied, of-course-we're-the-best attitude can occasionally get on your nerves. Nevertheless, fair reporting compels me. Le Falstaff deserves the highest accolades for its marvelous sense of style, its eclectic and beautiful mix of art nouveau and art deco, its consistently good food and extensive drink list, and even its often-infuriating waiters. This is self-satisfied, bourgeois Brussels at its best and worst. For a unique, less pretentious alternative, try A la Morte Subite instead. See chapter 5.
- **De Engel** (Antwerp, Belgium): There are cafes in Antwerp with a lot more action, but for a real Antwerpenaar brown cafe–style pub, it's hard to beat De Engel. Its location at a corner of the Grote Markt adds to the attraction, but to experience De Engel's crowning glory, order a glass of Antwerp's own, lovingly poured De Koninck beer—a golden brown liquid in a glass called a *bolleke* (little ball) that glows like amber in the sunlight streaming through De Engel's windows. See chapter 7.
- **'t Dreupelkot** (Ghent, Belgium): Ghent has no shortage of fine cafes, and you can just about guarantee that any one you enter will provide pleasant memories. 't Dreupelkot adds a particularly warm glow of appreciation, however; its stock-in-trade is *jenever*, one of the most potent alcoholic liquids known to humankind. Actually, some of 't Dreupelkot's 100 varieties are fairly mild, while others have been flavored with herbs and spices. The atmosphere in the cafe is great—it's filled with cultured *jenever* buffs rather than with drunks. See chapter 7.
- **'t Smalle** (Amsterdam, Holland): This cozy, crowded brown cafe on Amsterdam's Egelantiersgracht is usually thick with cigar smoke, *jenever* vapor, and lively

conversation. You can escape the crush on the splendid water-side terrace, a perfect place to watch cyclists and cars rushing past while resting your legs on the terrace railing. See chapter 14.

- **In den Ouden Vogelstruys** (Maastricht, Holland): This friendly, popular Maastricht watering hole was already well-trodden territory when it came under artillery fire in some war or another in 1653, and took a hit from a cannonball that remains lodged in one of its walls. The place attracts a broad—in some cases very broad—cross-section of Maastricht society. See chapter 19.

12 The Best Shopping

- **Diamonds** (Antwerp, Belgium): One thing is for sure, you'll be spoiled for choice in Antwerp's Diamond Quarter, which does six times as much diamond business as Amsterdam. Much of the trade here is carried on by the city's Orthodox Jewish community, whose conservative ways and traditional black clothing make a striking contrast to the glitter of their stock-in-trade. See chapter 7.

- **Lace** (Belgium): There are two kinds of Belgian lace: exquisitely handmade pieces and machine-made stuff. Machine-made lace is not necessarily bad—indeed some of it is very good—but this is the form used to mass produce pieces of indifferent quality to meet the demand for souvenirs. The highest-quality lace is handmade. Brussels, Bruges, and Ghent are the main, but far from the only, points of sale. See chapters 5, 6, and 7.

- **Pralines** (Belgium): The Swiss might argue the point, but the truth is that Belgian handmade chocolates, filled with various fresh-cream flavors, are the best in the universe. You can't go wrong if you buy chocolates made by Wittamer, Nihoul, Godiva, Leonidas, and Neuhaus, available in specialist shops all over Belgium (and in Holland and Luxembourg too). See chapter 5.

- **Delftware** (Holland): Originally, the pottery made in the factories at Delft was white, imitating tin-glazed products from Italy and Spain. But during the 16th century, blue Chinese porcelain was imported to Holland, and this was soon recognized to be of superior quality. So the Delftware factories started using a white tin glaze to cover the red clay and decorating the pottery in blue. This Delft Blue became famous the world over, along with Makkumware, which is pottery produced in the Dutch town of Makkum. Delftware and Makkumware are for sale in specialized shops all over the country, but it's far more interesting to go to one of the workshops in the towns themselves and see how it's made. Little has changed over the centuries, and all the decorating is still done by hand. See chapters 16 and 17.

- **Flower Bulbs** (Holland): Nowadays many growers offer bulbs with a health certificate clearing them for entry into foreign countries, so you'll have no problem buying some bulbs for home. You might not know what kind to buy though, as it is difficult to choose from the incredible variety of shapes and colors offered in Holland. Some bulbs flower early in January, others wait until the warmer months of May or June. Knowing this, you can choose bulbs with different flowering times, so you can enjoy their bloom over a long period in spring. Check before buying, however, as not all bulbs are certified for entry into the U.S. Packages must have a numbered phytosanitary certificate attached to the label, allowing you to import the bulbs. In Amsterdam, you can't do better than buying them from the Floating Flower market on the Singel canal. See chapter 14.

- **Wine** (Luxembourg): Holland's tiny output notwithstanding, Luxembourg is the only real wine producer in the Benelux countries. The vintage in question is the highly regarded Moselle wine, perhaps not as well known outside the Grand Duchy and its immediate neighbors as German and French wines, but fine stock nonetheless. See chapter 23.

2

Planning a Trip to the Benelux Countries

Perhaps nowhere else in all of Europe are there so many points of interest compressed into such a small area as there are in Belgium, Holland, and Luxembourg. Topping the list are such purely aesthetic attractions as lyrically beautiful scenery, artistic masterpieces, cultural events, and intriguing reminders of a long and colorful history. There are also the more mundane (but essential) advantages of convenience, economy, and friendly populations, not to mention a host of other travel delights—the exquisite food and drink of Brussels, the exuberant sociability of Amsterdam, and Luxembourg's sidewalk cafes.

Below is some practical information you should know before leaving home.

1 Visitor Information, Entry Requirements & Customs

VISITOR INFORMATION

The official tourist agency for each country maintains overseas branches that provide excellent in-depth information on a vast array of subjects, including special interests. You'll find national and local tourist office addresses given in the appropriate chapters; useful overseas addresses for all three countries are given below:

BELGIAN TOURIST OFFICE U.S. (covering **Canada** also): 780 Third Ave., Suite 1501, New York, NY 100017 (☎ **212/ 758-8130;** fax 212/355-7675); **U.K.** (covering **Ireland** also): 31 Pepper St., London E14 9RN. Telephone and fax numbers for the U.K. office depend on whether you want information on Dutch-speaking Flanders or French-speaking Wallonia (you can get information in English in either case). Flanders: (☎ **0171/458-0044;** fax 0171/458-0045); Wallonia: (☎ **0171/458-2888;** fax 0171/ 458-2999); Brussels information is available at both of these contact points.

NETHERLANDS BOARD OF TOURISM U.S.: 355 Lexington Ave., 21st Floor, New York, NY 10017 (☎ **212/370-7360;** fax 212/370-9507); 9841 Airport Boulevard, Suite 710, Los Angeles, CA 90045 (☎ **310/348-9339;** fax 310/348-9344); 225 N. Michigan Ave., Suite 1854, Chicago, IL 60601 (☎ **312/**

819-1636; fax 312/819-1740); **Canada:** 25 Adelaide St. E., Suite 710, Toronto, ON M5C 1Y2 (☎ **416/363-1577;** fax 416/363-1470); **U.K.** (covering **Ireland** also): 18 Buckingham Gate, London SW1E 6LB (☎ **0171/828-7900;** fax 0171/828-7941).

LUXEMBOURG NATIONAL TOURIST OFFICE U.S. (covering **Canada** also): 17 Beekman Place, New York, NY 10022 (☎ **212/935-8888;** fax 212/935-5896); **U.K.** (covering **Ireland** also): 122 Regent St., London W1R 5FE (☎ **0171/434-2800;** fax 0171/734-1205).

ENTRY REQUIREMENTS

If you're a citizen of the United States, Canada, Britain, Ireland, Australia, or New Zealand, or of most European countries, the only document you'll need to enter Belgium, Holland, or Luxembourg is a valid passport. None of the three Benelux countries requires a visa unless you plan to stay longer than 3 months within its borders. If you're a citizen of another country, be sure to check on your country's status before you leave. Health or vaccination certificates are also not required. Drivers need only produce a valid driver's license from their home country.

CUSTOMS
WHEN ENTERING . . .

BELGIUM & LUXEMBOURG   Travelers over the age of 17 with passports from overseas or non-EU countries may bring in free of duty 200 cigarettes or 50 cigars or 250 grams of tobacco, 2 liters of still wine and 1 liter of spirits, and 50 ml (1.75 ounces) of perfume. Other goods must not exceed a value of 2,000 BF ($55.55). Citizens of EU countries are allowed to bring in 800 cigarettes, 400 cigarillos, 200 cigars, 1 kilogram of tobacco, 10 liters of spirits, 90 liters of wine (with a maximum of 60 liters of champagne), and 110 liters of beer. Other products and amounts of currency are not limited.

HOLLAND   Visitors 17 years and older from non-EU countries may bring in 400 cigarettes or 100 cigars or 500 grams of tobacco, 1 liter of alcohol over 22 proof or 2 liters of alcohol under 22 proof or 2 liters of liqueur plus 2 liters of wine, and 50 grams of perfume. Other goods must not exceed a value of Dfl 500 BF ($250). Those from an EU country may import the same as mentioned above for Belgium and Luxembourg.

WHEN RETURNING TO . . .

THE UNITED STATES   You can bring back into the United States $400 worth of goods (per person) without paying a duty on them. There are a few restrictions on amounts: 1 liter of alcohol (you must be over 21), 200 cigarettes, and 100 cigars. Antiques over 100 years old and works of art are exempt from the $400 limit, as is anything you mail home. Once per day, you can mail yourself $200 worth of goods duty-free; mark them "for personal use." You can also mail to other people up to $100 worth of goods per person, per day; label each as "unsolicited gift." Any package must have on its exterior a description of the contents and their values. You cannot mail alcohol, perfume (it contains alcohol), or tobacco products.

You pay a flat 10% duty on the first $1,000 worth of goods over $400. Beyond that, it works on an item-by-item basis. For more information on regulations, check out the **U.S. Customs Service** Web site at **www.customs.ustreas.gov** or write to P.O. Box 7407, Washington, DC 20044, to request the free "Know Before You Go" pamphlet.

To prevent the spread of diseases, you can't bring any plants, fruits, vegetables, meats, or other foodstuffs into the U.S. This includes even cured meats like salami (no matter what the shopkeeper in Europe says). You may bring in the following: bakery goods, all but the softest cheeses (the rule is vague, but if the cheese is at all spreadable, don't risk confiscation), candies, roasted coffee beans and dried tea, fish (packaged salmon is OK), seeds for veggies and flowers (but not for trees), and mushrooms. Check out the USDA's Web site at **www.aphis.usda.gov/oa/travel.html** for more information.

CANADA   Duty-free allowances are limited to $300 a year and a maximum of 200 cigarettes, 50 cigars, 2.2 pounds of tobacco, and 40 ounces of liquor. Gifts mailed from abroad should be plainly marked "Unsolicited Gift, Value Under $40."

UNITED KINGDOM   Duty-free allowances depend on whether your goods were bought in a duty-free shop within these three EU countries or in other non-duty-free shops. If you live in the United Kingdom, your duty-free purchases may include 800 cigarettes, 400 cigarillos, 200 cigars, 1 kilogram of tobacco, 10 liters of spirits, 90 liters of wine (with a maximum of 60 liters of champagne), and 110 liters of beer. Other products and amounts of currency are not limited. The customs regulation most rigidly enforced is the prohibition on importing animals or pets of any kind; any violation incurs stiff penalties.

2 Tips for Travelers with Special Needs

TRAVELERS WITH DISABILITIES   Many hotels and restaurants now provide easy access for people with disabilities, and some display the international wheelchair symbol in their brochures and advertising. It's always a good idea to call ahead to find out just what the situation is before you book. Holland's Schiphol Arrivals Hall (North) has a service to help the disabled through the airport, and the Netherlands Board of Tourism issues a *Holland for the Handicapped* brochure. There's also comprehensive assistance for travelers with disabilities throughout the Netherlands Railway system. In Luxembourg, contact **Info Handicap,** rue de Contern 20, 5955 Itzig (☎ 352/36-64-66; fax 352/36-08-85). Inquire also at the national tourist board offices in Belgium and Luxembourg for specific details on the resources in those countries.

A particularly helpful organization is **Mobility International USA,** P.O. Box 10767, Eugene, OR 97440 (☎ 541/343-1284; fax 541/343-6812), which charges a small annual fee and provides travel information for those with disabilities.

An organized tour package can make life on the road much easier. One well-established firm that specializes in travel for the disabled is **Flying Wheels Travel,** Box 382, Owatonna, MN 55060 (☎ 800/535-6790; www.flyingwheels.com).

FOR SENIORS   Many major hotel and motel chains now offer a **senior citizen's discount,** and you should be sure to ask for the reduction when you make the reservation (there may be restrictions during peak days) and carry proof of your age when you check in (driver's license, passport, etc.). If you fancy organized tours, **AARP Travel Service** (see below) puts together terrific packages at moderate rates.

Membership in the following senior organizations also offers a wide variety of travel benefits: The **American Association of Retired Persons (AARP),** 601 E St. NW, Washington, DC 20049 (☎ 202/434-2277), and the **National Council of Senior Citizens,** 8403 Colesville Rd., Suite 1200, Silver Spring, MD 20910-3314 (☎ 888/3SENIOR).

Major sightseeing attractions and entertainment spots also often offer senior discounts—be sure to ask when you buy your ticket—but many such places abroad offer these reductions only to their own citizens, on production of an appropriate ID card.

FOR FAMILIES   One of the most economical travel choices for families is to stay in **self-catering cottages** or apartments, which cost less per person than hotels and B&Bs, and have the added advantage of retaining more of a sense of home for children.

An increasingly popular choice is a **farmhouse holiday.** Children and parents alike usually enjoy walking the fields and, more often than not, helping with farm chores. Although opportunities for farm stays are not as numerous in the Benelux countries as in some others, the national tourist offices for all three can help you locate possibilities.

As for keeping the children amused, what child wouldn't be happy exploring the castles that are scattered across the Benelux landscapes? Give your youngsters a head start with a short run-down on the people who built these fascinating structures and what happened within their walls, and you'll soon find their imaginations running wild. In the cities, small towns, and villages, the colorful pageantry of past centuries as depicted in numerous festivals will surely delight the younger set. In Holland, watch faces light up at the lilliputian "Holland in a Nutshell" miniatures at Madurodam. In Belgium, Brussels's Manneken-Pis statue, a famous national monument of a little boy urinating, is usually a winner. And look for wildlife centers in all three countries. Virtually every sightseeing attraction admits children at half price, and many offer family ticket discounts.

FOR STUDENTS   Before setting out, use your high school or college ID to obtain an International Student Identity Card from the **Council on International Educational Exchange (CIEE)** (☎ **800/2COUNCIL;** www.ciee.org) or from a branch of its travel agency, **Council Travel,** the biggest student travel agency in the world. This card entitles you to many student discounts. **American Youth Hostels,** P.O. Box 37613, Washington, DC 20013-7613 (☎ **202/783-6161;** fax 202/ 783-6171), will, for a fee of $13.95, send you a directory of youth hostels worldwide. This organization also issues Youth Hostel membership cards priced at $25 for ages 18 to 54, $10 for those under 18, and $15 for those over 55.

3 Special-Interest Travel Programs

EDUCATIONAL/STUDY TRAVEL   There are few more exciting or satisfying travel experiences than a period spent abroad pursuing studies while totally immersed in the day-to-day lifestyle of a foreign culture. To help you decide among the many study programs offered in Belgium, Holland, and Luxembourg, contact the **Institute of International Education,** 809 United Nations Plaza, New York, NY 10017 (☎ **212/883-8200;** fax 212/984-5452). In Holland, the **Foreign Student Service,** Oranje Nassaulaan 5, 1075 AH Amsterdam (☎ **020/671-5915;** fax 020/673-9531), can provide general information about study in that country.

WORK CAMPS   A vacation spent as a work-camp volunteer can also be a rewarding experience. In most cases, you pay your own transportation costs but are furnished with accommodations and meals in exchange for labor. A leading recruitment agency for American volunteers is **Volunteers for Peace,** 43 Tiffany Rd., Belmont, VT 05730 (☎ **802/259-2759;** fax 802/259-2922). Your $15 annual contribution brings you its newsletter and the *International Work Camp Directory.* There's another $195 charge for arranging a western European work-camp stay.

CYCLING   Belgium, Holland, and Luxembourg are all ideal cycling countries. In Holland, especially, and in parts of Flanders, there are often special cycle tracks in towns and cities, and well-signed long-distance routes. You can also take your bicycle on a train. Rental bikes are usually available at major train stations, and often at smaller ones, and some even have arrangements that allow you to pick up and return bikes at stations at either end of a particular route. All three national tourist boards can help you plan an itinerary best suited to your physical condition and time restraints. Holland's excellent *Cycling in Holland* publication is especially useful. Organized bike tours can be arranged through **International Bicycle Tours,** P.O. Box 754, Essex, CT 06426 (☎ **860/767-7005;** fax 860/767-3090); and **Cycletours,** Keizersgracht 181, 1016 DR Amsterdam (☎ **20/627-4098;** fax 20/627-9032).

4 Getting There

BY PLANE

Many major airlines charge competitive fares to Benelux cities, but price wars break out regularly and fares can change overnight. Tickets tend to be cheaper if you fly midweek or off-season. High season on most routes is June through early September—the most expensive and most crowded time to travel. Shoulder season is April through May, mid-September through October, and December 15 to 24. Low season—with the cheapest fares—is November through December 14 and December 25 through March.

You can get the best fares simply by planning ahead and buying low-cost **advance-purchase (APEX) tickets.** Usually, you must buy APEX tickets 7 to 21 days in advance and must stay in Europe 7 to 30 days. The downside is that APEX locks you into those dates and times, with penalties for trying to change them.

A more flexible but more expensive option is the **regular economy fare,** which allows for a stay shorter than the 7-day APEX minimum. You're also usually free to make last-minute changes in flight dates and to have unrestricted stopovers.

In addition to structured fares, airlines often introduce special promotional discounted fares and attractive fly-drive packages. Always check the travel sections of your local newspapers for advertisements about these.

OTHER GOOD-VALUE CHOICES

CONSOLIDATORS   Consolidators, also known as bucket shops, act as clearinghouses for blocks of tickets, on regularly scheduled flights, that airlines discount during slow periods.

One of the biggest U.S. consolidators is **Travac,** 989 Sixth Ave., New York, NY 10018 (☎ **800/TRAV-800** or 212/563-3303; **www.travac.com**). Also try **TFI Tours International,** 34 W. 32nd St., 12th Floor, New York, NY 10001 (☎ **800/ 745-8000**); **Euram Tours,** 1522 K St. NW, 4th Floor, Washington, DC 20005 (☎ **800/848-6789** or 202/789-2255; **www.flyeuram.com**); and **Travel Avenue,** 10 S. Riverside Plaza, Suite 1404, Chicago, IL 60606 (☎ **800/333-3335** or 312/876-6866; **www.travelavenue.com**).

In addition, **Cheap Tickets** (☎ **800/377-1000**), **1-800/FLY-4-LESS,** and **1-800/FLY-CHEAP** all specialize in finding the lowest fares out there. You can often get discounted fares on short notice without all the advance-purchase requirements.

Trailfinders (☎ **0171/937-5400** in London) is a consolidator in the United Kingdom that offers access to tickets on major European carriers. There are many

Cyberdeals for Net Surfers

More savvy travelers are finding excellent deals on everything from flights to whole vacation packages by searching the Internet. Although Web sites tend to change as fast as the Internet itself, a good beginning is to engage your favorite search engine, such as Yahoo or AltaVista, and search for the keyword "travel." Here are some particularly useful sites.

Microsoft's **www.expedia.com** features a "Fare Tracker" that allows you to search for the cheapest flight to a certain destination and even to subscribe to an e-mail service that gives you updated information on the cheapest flight every week. **www.travelocity.com** offers a similar service. **www.travelcom.es** allows you to search travel destinations to decide on that perfect vacation and offers links to travel-agency sites all over the world and in all 50 states. **www.previewtravel.com,** featured prominently on America Online, is the most user-friendly and one of the best of these sites. It offers incredible vacation, airline, and hotel deals, and its offerings are updated every day. **www. moments-notice.com** promotes itself as a travel service, not an agency. New vacation deals are offered every morning—many of them are snapped up by the end of the day. A drawback is that these vacations may require you to drop everything and go almost immediately.

other bucket shops around Victoria and Earls Court in London. **CEEFAX,** an information service included on many home and hotel TVs, runs details of package holidays and flights to continental Europe and beyond.

CHARTER FLIGHTS   In a strict sense, charters book a block of seats (or an entire plane) months in advance and then resell the tickets to consumers. Always ask about restrictions: You may have to purchase a tour package and pay far in advance and pay a stiff penalty (or forfeit the ticket entirely) if you cancel. Charters are sometimes canceled when the plane doesn't fill. In some cases, the charter company will offer you an insurance policy in case you need to cancel for a legitimate reason (such as hospitalization or a death in the family).

Council Travel, 205 E. 42nd St., New York, NY 10017 (☎ **800/226-8624** or 212/822-2800; www.ciee.org), arranges charter seats on regularly scheduled aircraft. One of the biggest charter operators is **Travac** (see "Consolidators, above"). For Canadians, good charter deals are offered by **Travel CUTS** (☎ **888/ 838-CUTS;** www.travelcuts.com), which also has an office in London (☎ **0171/ 255-1944**).

PACKAGE TOURS   For those travelers who feel more secure if everything is prearranged—hotels, transportation, sightseeing excursions, luggage handling, tips, taxes, and even meals—a package tour is the obvious choice, and it may even help save money.

A good travel agent can tell you about the many excellent bus tours offered in the Benelux region, with all-inclusive rates well below any you could manage on your own. Three leading reliable operators that include the Benelux countries in many of their reasonably priced European tours are: **Globus-Gateway/Cosmos Tours,** 150 S. Roblos Ave., Suite 860, Pasadena, CA 91101 (☎ **800/556-5454** or 818/339-0919); **American Express Travel Service,** P.O. Box 5014, Atlanta, GA 30302 (☎ **800/241-7000**); and **Maupintour,** P.O. Box 807, Lawrence, KS 66046 (☎ **800/255-4266**).

FLYING TO BELGIUM

Belgium is easily accessible from almost any point around the globe through **Brussels National Airport,** at Zaventem, 14.5km (9 miles) northeast of the city center. A shiny new terminal has opened in recent years, and this has greatly improved passengers' experience of landing at and departing from Brussels. The airport has good duty-free shopping. See "Orientation" in chapter 5.

AIRLINES   Some 30 international airlines fly into Brussels's National Airport; among them the national airline, **Sabena,** which flies direct from New York, Chicago, Atlanta, Boston, and Montréal. For schedules and reservations in the U.S. and Canada, contact your travel agent or Sabena Belgian World Airlines (☎ **800/ 955-2000**).

Other airlines flying from the U.S. to Brussels include **American Airlines** (☎ **800/433-7300**) from Chicago, and **United Airlines** (☎ **800/538-2929**) from Washington Dulles Airport.

London and many smaller British cities have flights to Brussels by **Sabena** (☎ **0181/780-1444**), **British Airways** (☎ **0345/222111**), and **British Midland** (☎ **0345/554554**). Low-cost carriers such as **Virgin Express** (☎ **0800/891199** or 0171/744-0004) also fly to Brussels from various British airports.

FARES   Airfares are one of the most volatile of all travel expenses, and the following fares are meant purely as a guide—be sure to check all available flights when you book. As we go to press, Sabena and U.S. airlines' round-trip fares—New York/Brussels—were averaging $300 and up for APEX, $1,566 for unrestricted coach class, $2,546 for business class, and $3,562 for first class (Sabena's own flights have no first class but some of its partner airlines do). Tax and Customs fees run to about $30. These fares all have seasonal and promotional variations.

FLYING TO HOLLAND

Amsterdam's **Schiphol Airport,** 12.5km (8 miles) southwest of the city center, is served by airlines from around the globe and is the home base of KLM, Holland's national airline. Schiphol is consistently rated the best in the world when international travelers are polled (it certainly gets my vote as the most efficient!). The terminal itself is a wonder of efficient organization, with signs in English, streamlined Customs and Immigration checkpoints, and quick, direct rail links to Amsterdam's city center, Rotterdam, and The Hague. For more information on Schiphol Airport, see "Orientation" in chapter 14.

AIRLINES   Although most major airlines fly from North America to Amsterdam, my personal choice is Holland's national airline, **KLM Royal Dutch Airlines.** Since its 1920 flight from Amsterdam to London (the first regularly scheduled air service anywhere in the world), KLM has grown to offer flights to more than 130 cities in 80 countries around the world. KLM's close partnership with Northwest Airlines, with full code-sharing, means that there are direct flights or easy connections from most U.S. and Canadian cities. For information and booking, contact your travel agent or Northwest Airlines (☎ **800/447-4747,** in Canada 800/ 361-1887).

Other airlines flying from the U.S. to Amsterdam include **American Airlines** (☎ **800/433-7300**) from New York (via London), and **United Airlines** (☎ **800/ 538-2929**) from Washington Dulles Airport.

Also offering a comprehensive schedule of service between North America and Amsterdam is **Martinair** (☎ **800/MARTINAIR**), which has nonstop flights year-round from Miami, Orlando, Tampa, and Denver; and from May through

September from Newark, Los Angeles, and Oakland. Martinair's regular fares are often less expensive than those of the larger, better-known airlines.

London and many smaller British cities have flights by **British Airways** (☎ **0345/222111**), **KLMuk** (☎ **0990/750900**), and **British Midland** (☎ **0345/ 554554**).

FARES   Round-trip fares between New York and Amsterdam average around $370 and up for APEX, $1,483 for coach, and $4,628 for business class (no first class). Add tax and Customs fees of about $30. All fares are subject to seasonal and promotional variations.

FLYING TO LUXEMBOURG

Luxembourg's **Findel Airport** is 6km (4 miles) northeast of Luxembourg City. See "Orientation" in chapter 22.

AIRLINES   For years, **Icelandair** (☎ **800/223-5500**) led all other airlines in providing the most direct and inexpensive way to reach Luxembourg from the U.S. and Canada. Icelandair offers departures from New York, Baltimore/Washington, Boston, Minneapolis, Orlando, and Halifax; flights stop in Iceland (Reykjavik) on the way to Luxembourg. Stopovers in Iceland of up to 21 days are allowed for no additional airfare.

Luxembourg's small national airline, **Luxair** (☎ **352/47-98-42-42**), operates a limited scheduled service within Europe, mostly to prominent capital cities and popular Mediterranean tourist destinations. Luxair has regular flights from London and Manchester in the U.K. (☎ **0181/745-4254**), as well as from Berlin, Copenhagen, Paris, Prague, Rome, Vienna, and Zürich, among others. **British Airways** (☎ **0345/222111**) has regularly scheduled service from London, **KLM** (☎ **020/474-7747**) from Amsterdam, and **Sabena** (☎ **02/723-23-23**) from Brussels. Connections at these airlines' hubs open up a great number of destinations in Europe and around the world.

FARES   Round-trip fares between New York and Luxembourg average around $585 and up for APEX, $1,459 for coach, and $5,035 for business class (no first class). All fares include taxes and are subject to seasonal and promotional variations.

BY TRAIN

TO BELGIUM   Britain and Belgium are connected via the 50km (31-mile) Channel Tunnel. On the high-speed **Eurostar** train, which has a top speed of 300kmph (190 m.p.h.), the travel time between London Waterloo Station and Brussels is 3¼ hours (a figure that will be cut substantially when the high-speed train lines in Belgium and Britain become operational). For Eurostar reservations, call ☎ **0345/303030** in Britain. Departures from London to Brussels are at approximately hourly intervals at peak times. Fares from London to Brussels are $183 one-way for unrestricted first class, $123 one-way for unrestricted second class, and $107 return for the nonrefundable restricted second class Super Saver fare (tickets must be purchased 14 days in advance). In the United States, call BritRail for all train information at ☎ **800/677-8585.**

The new Thalys high-speed train, connecting Paris, Brussels, Amsterdam, and Cologne, has cut travel times from Paris to Brussels to 1 hour 25 minutes. For Thalys information and reservations in France, call ☎ **08-3635 3536;** in Belgium, ☎ **0900/95-777.** One-way weekday business class fares from Paris to Brussels are $90; weekend returns cost $98. Tourist-class returns start at $80. Thalys trains run every hour or so between Paris-Nord and Bruxelles-Midi stations.

TO HOLLAND The new Thalys high-speed train has cut travel times from Paris to Amsterdam (via Brussels) to 4¼ hours, a figure that will be reduced to around 4 hours when the high-speed train lines in Holland are operational. For Thalys information and reservations in Holland call ☎ **0900-9296;** tickets are also available from main train stations and travel agents. One-way weekday business-class fares from Paris to Amsterdam cost $115; weekend returns cost $140; tourist-class returns start at $75. Four Thalys trains run between Paris and Amsterdam every day (via Brussels).

TO LUXEMBOURG There are direct, though relatively slow, train connections from Belgium, France, and Germany. None of the high-speed services—TGV, Thalys, and Eurostar—serves Luxembourg City. The service from Brussels, via Liège, links with trains from Amsterdam and London.

RAIL PASSES

Rail service to the Benelux countries from major European cities is frequent, fast, and mostly inexpensive compared with air travel. See the planning chapters for each country for more details. An important consideration for anyone planning to travel a lot by train is an appropriate pass allowing reduced-rate travel.

EURAIL PASSES All Eurail passes must be purchased **before leaving the United States** and are available through travel agents. The **Eurailpass** allows unlimited first-class travel on the trains of 17 countries (including Belgium, Holland, and Luxembourg) at a cost of $538 for 15 days, $698 for 21 days, $864 for 1 month, $1,224 for 2 months, and $1,512 for 3 months; the **Eurail Saver Pass** offers discounts for from 2 to 5 people traveling together, so that the rates for the previous options are $458, $594, $734, $1,040, and $1,286, respectively. The **Eurail Flexipass** offers 10 days of travel for $634 and 15 days for $836, both within a period of 2 months; the related **Eurail Saver Flexipass** for from 2 to 5 people costs $540 and $710, respectively.

The **Eurailpass/Youth** allows unlimited second-class travel on the trains of 17 countries (including Belgium, Holland, and Luxembourg) at a cost of $376 for 15 days, $489 for 21 days, $605 for 1 month, $857 for 2 months, and $1,059 for 3 months. The **Eurail Flexipass/Youth** offers 10 days of travel for $444 and 15 days for $595, both within a period of 2 months. There are (at the time of writing) no Saver options for the Youth pass.

BENELUX TOURAILPASS If all or most of your travel within Belgium, Holland, and Luxembourg will be by train, a good investment is the **Benelux Tourailpass,** available from travel agents. It gives you unlimited travel in all three countries on any 5 days in a 1-month period. The pass costs $217 for first class, $155 for second class, and $103 for ages 4 to 25 in second class only. For two people traveling together, the rates are $326 for first class and $233 for second class. The pass offers discounts on certain Eurostar and Thalys high-speed train services, but is otherwise not valid on the high-speed trains.

INTERRAIL If you're a resident of Europe, consider buying the **InterRail Pass.** Europe's rail network has been divided into 8 zones, each one identified by a letter from A to H. Belgium, Holland, and Luxembourg belong to Zone E West, which also covers France. You can buy a pass for 1, 2, 3, or all zones, with the price varying according to the number of zones and the age of the traveler. For Zone E travel only, the pass is valid for 22 days (multiple-zone passes are valid for a month), and costs about $350 for adults, $250 for ages 5 to 25, and $175 for ages 4 and under. It can be bought at most train stations and many travel agents.

BY BUS

Eurolines operates the most comprehensive bus network in Europe. Its reservations number in Holland is ☎ 020/560-8787; in Belgium ☎ 02/203-0707.

TO BELGIUM   There is **Eurolines** coach service between London Victoria Bus Station and Amsterdam Amstel Station (via ferry), with two departures daily. Travel time is around 8 hours. For reservations, contact Eurolines (☎ 0990/808080) in Britain.

TO HOLLAND   There is **Eurolines** bus service between London and Amsterdam, with four departures daily. Travel time is around 11½ hours. For full details, contact Eurolines (☎ 0990/808080 in Britain).

TO LUXEMBOURG   Luxembourg City can be reached by Eurolines coaches from London and Amsterdam, both via Brussels. The journey time is around 13 hours from London and 7 hours from Amsterdam. See above for contact numbers.

BY CAR

The Benelux countries are crisscrossed by a dense network of major highways connecting them with other European countries. Distances are relatively short. Road conditions are excellent throughout all three Benelux countries, service stations are plentiful, and highways have good signs. Traffic congestion in both Brussels and Amsterdam, however, can cause monumental tie-ups—in these two cities, it's best to park your car at your hotel garage and use local transportation or walk (the best way, incidentally, to see either city).

VIA THE CHANNEL TUNNEL FROM THE U.K.   If you want to drive from Britain to Belgium, Holland, or Luxembourg (and you don't mind missing out on the fresh sea air and the view of the white cliffs of Dover), you can use the fast and efficient **Le Shuttle** auto-transporter through the Channel Tunnel from Folkestone to Calais (a 35-minute trip), and continue from there. Le Shuttle has departures every 15 minutes at peak times, every 30 minutes at times of average demand, and every hour at night. Fares for a passenger car and its passengers (the number of passengers is not a factor) range from £109 ($174.40) to £169 ($270.40), depending on day, time, and other variables; special promotional fares can be as low as £50 ($31.25). The cheapest transits are usually midweek between 2 and 5am. For Le Shuttle (Eurotunnel) reservations in Britain, call ☎ 0990/353535. Reserving in advance makes sense at the busiest times, but the system is so fast, frequent, and simple that you may prefer to retain travel flexibility by just showing up, buying your ticket, waiting in line for a short while, and then driving aboard.

BY BOAT FROM BRITAIN

In the United States, detailed information is available from travel agents and Brit Rail Travel International (☎ 800/677-8585).

TO BELGIUM   **P&O North Sea Ferries** (☎ 0148/237-7177) operates a daily car ferry service between Hull (also known as Kingston-upon-Hull) and Zebrugge; overnight journey time is 14 hours. A second-class single ticket for a foot passenger in an economy cabin costs £48 ($76.80). **Hoverspeed** (☎ 0990/595-522) operates a frequent (5 to 7 times daily) fast-catamaran ferry service from Dover to Ostend; journey time is under 2 hours. A second-class single ticket for a foot passenger costs from £25 ($40) to £30 ($48).

TO HOLLAND   **P&O North Sea Ferries** (☎ 0148/237-7177) operates a daily car ferry service between Hull (also known as Kingston-upon-Hull) and Rotterdam

Europoort; overnight journey time is 14 hours and a second-class single ticket for a foot passenger in an economy cabin costs £48 ($76.80). If you're coming from the north of England or Scotland, you can travel by **Scandinavian Seaways** (☎ 0125/524-0240), which has a daily car ferry service from Newcastle-upon-Tyne to IJmuiden on the North Sea coast, west of Amsterdam; overnight journey time is 14 hours and a second-class single ticket for a foot passenger costs £40 ($64). **Stena Line** (☎ 0990/707070) sails four times a day between Harwich in southeast England and Hoek van Holland (Hook of Holland) near Rotterdam; journey time is 3 hours 40 minutes and a second-class single ticket for a foot passenger costs £48 ($76.80).

5 Getting Around

BY PLANE   The Benelux cities are so close together that air travel is really not worth the added expense unless time is a vital factor (and even then it might still be quicker going by train). Air service among the three countries is provided by **KLM Cityhopper, KLM Exel,** and **Sabena.** The KLM associates fly frequent scheduled services between Amsterdam, Rotterdam, Eindhoven, Maastricht, Groningen, and Enschede in Holland; as well as to Brussels and Antwerp in Belgium; and to Luxembourg City. Sabena flies from Brussels to Amsterdam and Luxembourg City. For current schedules, fares, and reservations, call **KLM** at ☎ 020/474-7747 in Holland; and **Sabena** at ☎ 02/723-23-23 in Belgium. See "Getting There" earlier in this chapter for KLM, Sabena, and Luxair contact numbers in the U.S., Britain, and Canada.

BY TRAIN   One of the best train systems in the world operates in these small countries. There is virtually no spot so remote that it cannot easily be reached by trains that are fast, clean, and almost always on time. Furthermore, rail travel is a marvelous way to meet the locals, because the people of the Benelux countries spend as much time riding public transportation as they do behind the wheel of an automobile. Schedules are exact—if departure is set for 12:01pm, that means 12:01pm precisely, not 12:03pm—and station stops are sometimes as short as 3 or 4 minutes, which means you must be fleet of foot in getting on and off.

For information on convenient, money-saving rail passes, such as the **Eurailpass** and the 5-day **Benelux Tourail pass,** see "Getting There," above.

Belgium, Holland, and Luxembourg also have discount train passes for travel within their own country's borders. In each country there are many lower-cost options, including cheaper weekend and day returns, and reductions for multiple journeys and more than one passenger (not all options are available in each country). You should always ask about lower-cost options before buying. You'll find more details in the planning chapters of each country.

BY BUS   Intercity bus service is poor or nonexistent throughout the Benelux countries. This is not as bad as it sounds, because the train network is among the best in the world and fast, comfortable intercity trains do all the work. If you really want to, you can travel intercity by bus, but the buses stop a lot en route, so journey times are long, and you'll often have to change at an intermediate town—for example, a trip from Brussels to Liège is two journeys: Brussels–Leuven and Leuven–Liège. Tourist offices and bus stations can furnish schedule and fare information.

The exception to the avoid-the-bus rule is in sparsely populated places where there is little or no train service, such as Zeeland in Holland and the Ardennes in

Belgium. In such areas there are more regional bus services, although the buses still may be few and far between. In general, unless you have a specific reason for wanting to go by bus, you'll always find it better to go by train.

All cities have excellent bus and/or tram (or trolleybus) service and some have metro (subway) service, which means you can easily deposit your car at the hotel and avoid city driving woes.

BY CAR   While getting around by train is relaxing and fast and touring by bike is healthier and more human in pace, traveling by car still gives you the most freedom to ramble at your own speed, either on or off the beaten path. You'll find information on specific requirements, rules of the road, gasoline prices, maps, automobile clubs, and other driving assistance resources in the appropriate chapters for each country.

There is a major proviso to this, however. The Benelux countries have a high density of population in relation to their size, so roads are busy. In addition, many drivers in the region have a high density of road-aggression, so driving can descend into a struggle for survival. The major roads are often busiest precisely at the most popular vacation times, and accidents are not uncommon.

Virtually all major **car-rental** companies have offices in the three capital cities and some other large cities, although arranging a rental outside of a metropolitan area can present problems. Names and locations of rental companies are listed in the appropriate chapters for each country.

HITCHHIKING   Hitchhiking is permitted (not encouraged!) in Belgium and Luxembourg, although prohibited on highways (you can, however, stand on the approach road). It's officially forbidden in Holland, but many a blind eye is turned by officialdom to those standing in a safe spot to hitchhike.

SUGGESTED ITINERARIES

These itineraries are based on taking in some of the possibilities of all three Benelux countries. In the "Planning" chapters for each individual country, there are specific itineraries for a vacation spent in one country alone. So you might want to consider those suggestions as well.

The sheer diversity of historical, cultural, and entertainment attractions in Belgium, Holland, and Luxembourg is a strong argument for spending your entire vacation in the Benelux region, no matter how much or how little time you have available. But let's start by assuming that visiting Benelux is just a part of your vacation plans.

The Highlights in 3 Days

You need to be really pushed for time, and really motivated, to do this. Spend one complete day in Amsterdam. On the second day take the train to Brussels and spend the rest of the day there. On day 3 take the train to Bruges. You *can* do this, because journey times by train are short and departures frequent, but it's a bare minimum, reconnaissance-type exercise.

The Highlights in 5 Days

You could stick to an itinerary similar to the one above, but do things at a more human pace, without having to pack and unpack so often. Spend the first 2 days in Amsterdam; on day 3 head for Brussels; then spend day 4 in Bruges. That leaves 1 day. Luxembourg is too much of a stretch for a single day, so you could choose instead to visit the Belgian coast, Ghent, or Antwerp on day 5. If you're traveling by car, there would be time for a look at the Meuse Valley or one of the towns in the Ardennes instead.

If You Have 1 Week

This time scale brings other options within range. Three days based in Amsterdam means you not only get to see the sights but also start to get a feel for this outstanding city. For a side trip on 1 of the 3 days, you have as many colorful choices as a bee in a botanical garden. Visit the tulip fields if it's spring; visit Haarlem or The Hague, or rent a bike and take a spin along the lake called the IJsselmeer to Hoorn. You could even drive north and take the ferry from Den Helder across to Texel island. On day 4, instead of going straight down to Brussels, take the train to the southern Dutch city of Maastricht. From here, on day 5, you can easily get by train to Liège in Belgium, or if you're traveling by car, you have the Meuse Valley or the Ardennes at your feet. Try to be in Brussels by night on day 5. The last 2 days should be for Brussels and Bruges.

The Whole Shebang in 2 Weeks

This amount of time allows you to experience the Benelux countries in surprising depth, by allotting 5 days each to Belgium and Holland and 3 to Luxembourg, with a total of 1 full day for travel from one capital to another. You'll still have to make some choices, though, from the suggestions listed below.

No fewer than 2 full days should be allotted to the attractions and charms of Amsterdam. During the next 3 days, take your pick of day trips to: The Hague, Rotterdam, Utrecht, Haarlem, Maastricht, Delft; the bulb fields and famous Keukenhof Gardens; the former fishing villages of Volendam and Marken, with their traditionally garbed populace; the medieval town of Edam and the nearby concentration of picture-postcard windmills at the Zaanse Schans; or a tour of the Enclosing Dike and the IJsselmeer.

In Belgium, most of your sightseeing can be done in easy day trips from a Brussels base, but I recommend also spending a night in Bruges, if possible. After devoting your first 2 days to the Brussels sightseeing attractions and a side trip to Waterloo, spend 1 of the next 3 days in Bruges and the other 2 on day trips to your choice of the following destinations: historic Ghent; Ostend, Knokke, and other resorts along the Belgian coast; Tournai, with its historic churches and museums; Mons and its nearby ruined castles and abbeys; Antwerp and its diamond cutters (via Mechelen, with its famous bell ringers); and Liège (home of Europe's oldest street market, held every Sunday). Or alternatively, let Bruges give you a taste of Flanders and then go to the Ardennes, making Bastogne a stopping point, to see its World War II Battle of the Bulge memorials.

In Luxembourg, spend your first day exploring Luxembourg City, with its unique network of cliffside casemates and fortress remains, its impressive cathedral, and the Grand Duke's Palace. On one of the remaining days, take a daylong bus tour of the Luxembourg Ardennes region to see Wiltz, or one of the other scenes of action in the Battle of the Bulge, and the feudal castles at Esch-sur-Sûre, Clervaux, Vianden, and the Sûre Valley. On your second day, take a half-day tour to the Moselle Valley and the famous Bernard Massard Wine Cellars at Grevenmacher.

6 Tips on Accommodations

Belgium, Holland, and Luxembourg established the Benelux Hotel Classification System back in 1978 and updated the standards in 1994. Each establishment that accepts guests must publicly display a sign indicating its classification (from "1" for those with minimum amenities to "5" for deluxe, full-service hotels). The national tourist boards do an excellent job of providing full accommodations listings and advance booking for visitors. The Belgian and the Netherlands tourist offices (see "Visitor Information, Entry Requirements & Customs," earlier in this chapter), as well as the **Netherlands Reservation Center,** P.O. Box 404, 2260 AK Leid-schendam, (☎ **070/419/5500;** fax 070/419-5519), will reserve accommodations for you at no charge before you leave home. The Luxembourg Tourist Office can furnish a complete list of accommodations in the Grand Duchy.

HOTELS

In all three countries, you can choose among luxury hotels in city or rural locations, smaller urban hotels with moderate rates and somewhat limited facilities, and charming, family-run country inns. No matter what end of the price scale it's on, each lodging will be spotlessly clean and will feature a staff dedicated to personal attention and excellent service. The rates quoted include the service charge (usually 15%), tax, and, in most cases, breakfast.

Be sure to inquire about discounts when you book your room. Many hotels have a variety of room rates. It's sometimes possible to pay less if you'll settle for a shower instead of full bath facilities. Also, weekend or midweek rates are often available.

BED-AND-BREAKFAST (B&B)

In virtually every region of Holland, it's possible to stay with private families. Because there's no national listing of such homes, however, you'll have to check with local tourist offices for names, addresses, and prices (inexpensive in most cases). One word of warning: If you plan to travel in July or August and would like this kind of accommodation, you'd better make arrangements several months in advance. The Netherlands tourist offices in the United States, listed in "Visitor Information, Entry Requirements & Customs" earlier in this chapter, can help with addresses of local tourist offices.

In Belgium and Luxembourg, a B&B means a small hotel or pension.

YOUTH HOSTELS

The Benelux countries are filled with high-grade hostels, in both urban and rural settings. Prices for a dormitory bed run around $10; with breakfast, about $12.

The first thing to be said about hostels is that, although they're called "youth hostels," you'll be welcomed whether you're 6 or 60. The second thing to note is that in order to use many of them you must have an **International Youth Hostel Card,** which should be purchased before you leave home. It's available from **American Youth Hostels, Inc.,** P.O. Box 37613, Washington, DC 20013, and costs $10 for those under 18, $25 for those ages 18 to 54, and $15 for those over 55. For an additional $13.95 you can purchase the organization's *International Youth Hostel Handbook* (Vol. I, *Europe and the Mediterranean*).

IN BELGIUM   For a list of the hostels in Belgium, write directly to **Infor-Jeunes,** rue du Marché-aux-Herbes 27 (☎ **02/514-41-11**), 1000 Brussels.

IN HOLLAND   For details on the more than 45 hostels in Holland, contact **Stichting Nederlandse Jeugdherberg Centrale (NJHC),** Prof. Tulpplein 4, 1018 GX Amsterdam (☎ **020/551-3155**).

IN LUXEMBOURG   Hostels are located in Beaufort, Bourglinster, Echternach, Ettelbruck, Grevenmacher, Hollenfels, Lultzhausen, Luxembourg City, Trois-vierges, Vianden, and Wiltz. Standards are exceptionally high in all. For complete details, including extra services available, get the "Youth Hostels Guide" from the **Luxembourg Youth Hostels Association,** place d'Armes 18, Luxembourg (☎ 352/22-55-88).

CAMPING

There are outstanding camping grounds throughout Belgium, Holland, and Luxembourg. Prices run between $10 and $20 per night, depending on location and facilities. Each country can furnish a directory of its campgrounds.

IN BELGIUM   Belgian tourist offices can supply a brochure listing camping facilities, or you may write for a directory and other information to: **Royal Camping and Caravanning de Belgique,** rue de la Madeleine 31, 1000 Brussels (☎ 02/513-12-87).

IN HOLLAND   Netherlands tourist offices can supply a directory of all camping facilities, but all bookings must be made directly. Bikers should inquire about the special 8-day "Hospitable Bike Camping" package available during spring and summer: Contact **Gastvrije Fietscampings Foundation,** P.O. Box 93200, 2509 BA Den Haag (☎ 070/14-71-47). Again, summer reservations must be made well in advance.

IN LUXEMBOURG   Luxembourg's camping grounds are numerous and well equipped. The government rates each one and requires that the rating be shown at the entrance. Be advised that it's illegal to park a vehicle used for lodging on public roads or in public places. For a free guide listing all camping facilities in Luxembourg, contact the tourist offices listed in "Visitor Information, Entry Requirements & Customs," earlier in this chapter.

FARM HOLIDAYS

Although this is a fairly new trend in the Benelux countries, more and more farm families are offering home stays to tourists. This is a marvelous way to experience life inside both modern farm complexes and those that still retain their medieval, farmyard-centered architecture. Breakfast is provided, and it's often possible to arrange for a home-cooked evening meal. Arrangements (including prices) must be made directly with farm families; for detailed information on the many possible locations, contact the tourist offices at addresses given in "Visitor Information, Entry Requirements & Customs," earlier in this chapter.

7 Tips on Dining

If I were asked to give one unconditional guarantee for your Benelux visit, it would be this: You will eat well, and you'll never be far from a good place to eat. Standards of ingredients, preparation, presentation, and service are extraordinarily high throughout Belgium, Holland, and Luxembourg—and the number and diversity of restaurants are nothing short of staggering. This is perhaps the one single area in which you'll get the best value for your dollar in every price range, from budget to deluxe.

To some degree, dining out in the Benelux countries takes on the aspect of entertainment. Whereas many Americans view dinner as a prelude to the evening's entertainment, for people here dinner *is* the evening entertainment. They would no more tolerate rudeness or being rushed through their meal than they would bad food poorly prepared. And therein lies a caution—be sure you allow enough time for each meal. That impeccable service may not be indifferent, but to Americans it can sometimes seem slow. My advice is to do as the natives do and give yourself over to the occasion. Relax, enjoy your surroundings and your companions, and you may even find that the wait between courses enhances your appreciation of each new dish.

In all three Benelux countries, sidewalk cafes are as numerous as blooms in a Dutch tulip field—and it's a safe bet that you will quickly become as fond of them as are the locals. What may come as a surprise is that these charming eateries lining city streets and village squares have the same high standards as the upscale restaurants.

Beneluxers like to drink as well as eat, and it's not hard to guess their favored beverage: in a word, beer. Beer is Belgium's national drink, and it's no less popular in Holland and Luxembourg. Imported beers are freely available, but you won't want to miss sampling at least a few of the local brews, more than 300 of which are produced in Belgium alone.

Wine lovers will find the best vintages from France widely available. As for local products, Luxembourg's Moselle Valley wineries produce outstanding riesling, rivaner, auxerrois, and several sparkling wines that rival champagne (but are less expensive).

Holland's native *jenever,* a deceptively smooth, mild-tasting gin, rivals beer in the affections of the Dutch. It comes in a colorless *jonge* (young) form or the amber-colored *oude* (old) version—either can be lethal if not sipped slowly.

8 Tips on Shopping

While the Benelux countries are not known for bargain prices, they do constitute one of the best marketplaces in the world when it comes to the variety of goods for sale. After all, it was trade that built and sustained these nations from their earliest times.

IN BELGIUM   Look especially for antique lace—a bit pricey, but good value. Also, European antiques may be found in Brussels shops and street markets. Excellent galleries in Brussels offer paintings by recognized masters of the past, in addition to budding masters of the future. Antwerp is the diamond-cutting center of Europe and offers excellent shopping for these precious stones. And don't forget that some of the best chocolate in the world comes from Belgium.

IN HOLLAND   Serious shoppers in Holland will be attracted to Delftware from Delft and Makkum, the antiques shops of Amsterdam and The Hague, and diamonds from master cutters in Amsterdam. There's also an abundance of charming, old-fashioned clocks, crystal, and pewter. Less-serious (and less-expensive) choices include chocolates, cheeses, liqueurs, flower bulbs, and wooden shoes.

IN LUXEMBOURG   Many fine galleries in the city of Luxembourg feature paintings by artists from the Grand Duchy and around Europe. For an excellent souvenir of your Luxembourg visit, pick up a porcelain plate decorated with a painted local landscape or one of the cast-iron wall plaques produced by the Fonderie de Mersch depicting castles, coats-of-arms, and local scenes.

3

Getting to Know Belgium

Belgium is a small country. Not quite so small that if you blinked you'd miss it, but small enough that a couple of hours of focused driving will get you from the capital, Brussels, to any corner of the realm you care to mention. Yet the variety of culture, language, history, and cuisine crammed into this small space would do credit to a country many times its size. Belgium's diversity is a product of its location at the cultural crossroads of Europe. The boundary between the continent's Germanic north and Latin south cuts clear across the country's middle, leaving Belgium divided into two major ethnic regions, Dutch-speaking Flanders and French-speaking Wallonia.

The stresses and strains of living on such a cultural fault-line show up in regional antagonisms that might tear another country apart. That they haven't has as much to do with Belgians' good sense as anything else. Belgians are, of course, proud of their Flemish or Walloon origins and of their Dutch or French mother-tongue, but while some politicians are constantly pushing the separatist agenda, ordinary citizens are for the most part too busy getting on with the good life to pay too much attention. Not much of the talk in the multitudinous cafes and restaurants across the land is of the minutiae of regional politics. It may turn out to be Belgian Railways that saves the country in the end, as the trains are filled with Walloons heading for the beaches and seafood restaurants of Flanders, and Flemings going the opposite way, to the rolling hills and country eateries of the Ardennes.

1 The Regions in Brief

Belgium covers some 11,800 square miles (about the same as Maryland) and is only 150 miles across from the sea to the Ardennes. Water is a crucial part of the Belgian landscape. Rivers that run from south to north carve out the great Meuse and Scheldt basins, then hurry to empty into the North Sea in estuaries that form Belgium's fine natural harbors. Major highways trace river routes. In the Ardennes, heavy rain swells rushing mountain streams most years. Annual rainfall in Belgium, in fact, is almost double that in Holland (and Holland certainly gets more than enough of the stuff).

Belgium

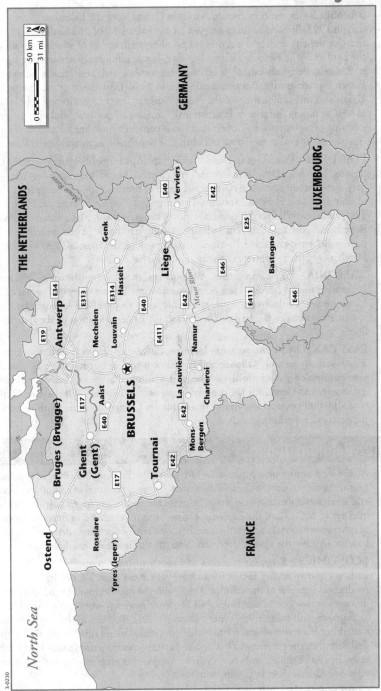

BRUSSELS *Bruxelles* in French; *Brussel* in Dutch. Since the federalization of the state in 1993, Brussels has been a region on its own, a kind of Brussels D.C. Its area includes the city itself and a rim of surrounding territory, all of which lies within the borders of the Flemish Brabant Province, but is administratively separate from it. Brussels, Belgium's capital, is officially bilingual, Dutch and French, although French is predominant. But because this is also the *de facto* capital of the European Union and the headquarters of the North Atlantic Treaty Organization (NATO), as well as of any number of international commercial, political, diplomatic, and lobbying organizations, the streets of Brussels contain a multilingual cacophony of languages that evokes the Tower of Babel. The population is around one million.

FLANDERS *Vlaanderen* in Dutch. For a graphic picture of Belgium's two ethnic regions, Dutch-speaking Flanders and French-speaking Wallonia, draw an imaginary east-west line across the country just south of Brussels. The northern provinces of East and West Flanders, Antwerp, Limburg, and Flemish Brabant are Flemish. This is where you'll find the medieval cities of Bruges, Ghent, Mechelen, and Ypres (Ieper); the port and diamond industry of Antwerp (home of the great Flemish painter Rubens); and some 40 miles of beaches along the coast of West Flanders. Flanders is home to approximately five million inhabitants.

WALLONIA *Wallonie* in French. Wallonia consists of the provinces of Walloon Brabant, Hainaut, Namur, Liège, and Luxembourg. The art cities of Tournai and Mons, historic castles by the score, and scenic resort towns of the Ardennes are the tourist attractions of this beautiful region, which has a population of about 4 million.

EAST CANTONS *Ostkantone* in German; *Cantons de l'Est* in French. East Cantons is actually part of Wallonia, and not its own region, but it's where Belgium's German-speaking minority lives. The East Cantons have considerable political autonomy, and German is the country's third official language. Of the East Cantons' 100,000 population, around two-thirds are German speakers, with most of the remainder speaking French.

2 Belgium Today

After a long history of occupation by foreign troops, Belgium has emerged as a site for the coming together of European nations. Its many centuries of accommodation and its strategic location have made Belgium the natural choice to host the headquarters of NATO and the European Union, both of which are in Brussels. Scores of other international organizations are headquartered in Belgium; Brussels is home base for possibly the world's largest concentration of international diplomats.

ECONOMICS Belgium's tradition as a center of trade continues as well; it's a leading exporter among industrial nations, with more than 50% of its industrial production sent out of the country. Along with the high-technology industry, traditional crafts—such as lace making and tapestry weaving—continue to flourish.

Together with most other western European nations, Belgium has experienced something of a recession and relatively high unemployment (10%) in the 1990s. To deal with this, the government has imposed certain spending restrictions and raised taxes. In 1993 Belgium embarked upon a multiple-year program to transfer certain state-owned businesses to private ownership.

GOVERNMENT Politically, modern Belgium is a parliamentary democracy under a constitutional monarch, Albert II, who succeeded his brother Baudouin as king in 1993. The legislature is composed of a senate and chamber of representatives, both of whose members are elected for 4 years. The government exists in a more-or-less permanent state of crisis due to the cultural and linguistic divide, with ambitious regional politicians, particularly in Flanders, often pushing the country to the brink of dissolution. Still, rumors of Belgium's demise have been heard before and have always proven greatly exaggerated, and it seems likely that the federation of autonomous regions will remain stable enough to see the country through.

LANGUAGE   In the northern provinces, some 5½ million inhabitants speak a derivation of German that evolved into Dutch and its Flemish variation (sometimes called Vlaams, but more often just referred to as Dutch). To the south, about 4½ million Walloons speak the language of France. In Brussels the two languages mingle. So strong is the feeling for each language in its own region, however, that along the geographic line where they meet it's not unusual for French to be the daily tongue on one side of a street and Flemish on the other. And throughout the country, road signs acknowledge both languages by giving multiple versions of the same place name—Brussel/Bruxelles or Brugge/Bruges, for example. There's also a small area in eastern Belgium where German is spoken. Belgium, then, is left with not one, but three, official languages: Dutch (a.k.a. Flemish), French, and German.

Note: A side-effect of Belgium's cultural divide is that while Flemings are mostly willing enough to speak French to anyone who doesn't speak Flemish, they generally prefer to speak English instead of French to native English speakers who also speak French. Confused? Welcome to Belgium.

REGIONAL DIFFERENCES   History has left its stamp on more than just language in Belgium. In both Flanders and Wallonia people cling as tightly to their traditions and customs as they do to their language. Religious lines are sharply drawn as well, with little mingling of Catholics, Protestants, and anticlericalists. In the area of public life that will most affect you as a visitor, you'll find three separate national tourism agencies offering assistance: one for Flanders, another for Wallonia, and yet another for that special case, Brussels. If that sounds complicated, it's not, for there's very little overlap, and the three agencies work together almost seamlessly.

In short, far from being a homogeneous, harmonious people with one strong national identity, Belgians take considerable pride in their strongly individualistic attributes. Do they get along with one another? Well, in a manner of speaking. After all, for hundreds of years both the Flemish and the Walloons were forced to adopt an outward appearance of compatibility with all sorts of alien rulers, yet time and again events revealed their strong inner devotion to independence: Thus the Flemish accept the fact that Brussels (located in their geographic territory) conducts the country's business in French, and Walloons head for the beaches of Flanders without a second thought. Virtually every Belgian is bilingual, with English thrown in for good measure. So they not only get on fairly well with each other, but they also make it easy for the visitor. Belgians are quite willing to adapt their language to the occasion, all the while fiercely protecting and preserving the heritage that is uniquely their own.

Impressions

Belgium suffers severely from linguistic indigestion.
                                    —R. W. G. Penn, *Geographical Magazine* (March 1980)

The "Typical" Belgian

Defining a "typical Belgian" is not easy, because Belgians go to great lengths to make sure that there is nothing typical about them. Housing is a good example. Whereas neighboring Holland has row after row of houses identical in design, most Belgians would be horrified to live in such a straitjacket. Belgian houses are gloriously and often eccentrically diverse. Ordinary townhouses in Brussels often have the architect's name inscribed proudly in stone on the facade.

Belgians are, however, typical in some respects. Most are quite happily bourgeois in their work and daily life, in their pride in their homes, and in providing for their families. They have a connoisseur's enjoyment of the good things in life and the self-discipline to work hard enough to earn them. Any Bruxellois can tell you that Brussels has more Michelin Star restaurants per head than Paris—if you doubt it, count them and see.

A "typical" Belgian speaks both French and Flemish, not to mention excellent English, and passable German. Owning a home is a passion for every Mr. and Mrs. De Keuster, as is driving a respectably big car. Their children attend a state school, but will be moved to a private one if there is the slightest suspicion that the school's standard is slipping. Their annual 2-week holiday in France is supplemented by a week at the Belgian coast, probably at ritzy Knokke-Heist, or if the kids are still young, at tranquil De Haan.

RELIGION   The vast majority of Belgians are Catholic, though there's a smattering of Protestants and a small Jewish community. Throughout the centuries, Belgians—nobles and peasants alike—have proclaimed their faith by way of impressive cathedrals, churches, paintings, and holy processions. The tradition continues today. For example, the lay sisterhoods known as *beguines,* which date back to about 1189, are still flourishing. Within these communities, widows and disadvantaged women enjoy a pious community life that's both a refuge and a source of companionship. Beguines usually consist of quiet streets, small houses, a church, and a community hall. You'll find these oases of peace right in the center of such cities as Bruges and Ghent.

FOLKLORE   Folklore still plays a large part in Belgium's national daily life, with local myths giving rise to some of the country's most colorful pageants and festivals, such as Ypres's Festival of the Cats, Bruges's pageants of the Golden Tree, and the stately Ommegang in Brussels. Antwerp owes its very name to the myth of a gallant Roman centurion who slew a despotic giant and cut off his hand, giving the city its "Red Hand of Antwerp" symbol (*Hand-werpen* is Dutch for "to throw a hand"). In Belgium's renowned puppet theaters, marionettes based on folkloric characters identify their native cities—Woltje (Little Walloon) belongs to Brussels, Schele to Antwerp, Pierke to Ghent, and Tchantchès to Liège.

THE BELGIAN CHARACTER   Courtesy based on mutual acceptance of differences is the prevailing rule among Belgians, and it's the thing you'll notice most on your first encounters, whether with salespeople in the shops, restaurant personnel, taxi drivers, or railway station porters. This courtesy, however, is dispensed with a healthy dollop of reserve. Now, that sort of cautious courtesy could appear to be a cool aloofness that is rather off-putting. But don't be misled. If there is one characteristic all Belgians have in common, it's the passion with which they pursue any special interest—be it art, music, sports, or that greatest of all Belgian passions, food. Show your own interest in the subject at hand and coolness evaporates as you're welcomed into an affectionate fraternity.

Undoubtedly, the Belgian's appreciation for the good things in life springs from this passionate nature. Indeed, appreciation is at the bottom of a national insistence on only the best. Standards are high in every area of daily life, and woe betide the chef who tries to hoodwink patrons with less-than-fresh ingredients, the shopkeeper who stocks shoddy merchandise, or any service person who is rude—their days are surely numbered. Belgians—Flemish or Walloon—are eminently practical, and none will spend hard-earned money for anything that doesn't measure up.

Ah, but when standards are met, to watch Belgian eyes light up with intense enthusiasm is nothing less than sheer joy. Appreciation then moves very close to reverence, whether inspired by a great artistic masterpiece, or a homemade mayonnaise of just the right lightness, or one of Belgium's more than 300 native beers. If you have shared that experience with a Belgian companion, chances are you'll find your own sense of appreciation taking on a finer edge.

3 History 101

EARLY HISTORY Julius Caesar first marched his Roman legions against the ancient Belgae tribes in 58 B.C. For nearly 5 centuries thereafter, Belgium was a tranquil backwater of the empire, shielded from the barbarians by the great Roman defense line on the Rhine, but subject to periodic incursions.

From the beginning of the 5th century, Roman rule gave way to the Franks, who held sway for nearly 200 years. In the year 800 the great Charlemagne was named Emperor of the West; he instituted an era of agricultural reform, setting up underling local rulers known as counts. In 814, after Charlemagne's death, these counts rose up to seize more power. By 843 Charlemagne's son had acceded to the Treaty of Verdun, which split French-allied (but Dutch-speaking) Flanders in the north from the southern (French-speaking) Walloon provinces.

Then came the Viking invaders, who attacked the northern provinces. A Flemish defender known as Baldwin Iron-Arm became the first Count of Flanders in 862; his royal house eventually ruled over a domain that included the Netherlands and lands as far south as the Scheldt in France. Meanwhile, to the south, powerful prince-bishops controlled most of Wallonia from their seat in Liège.

As Flanders grew larger and stronger, its cities thrived and its citizens wrested more and more self-governing powers. Bruges (Brugge) emerged as a leading center of European trade; its monopoly on English cloth attracted bankers and financiers from

Dateline

- **58 B.C.** Julius Caesar marches against Belgae tribes.
- **A.D. 800** Emperor Charlemagne introduces agricultural reform and creates the title of count.
- **843** Treaty of Verdun splits Flanders from the Walloon provinces.
- **1302** Philip the Fair of France defeated at "Battle of the Golden Spurs" in Flanders.
- **1328** Beginning of Hundred Years' War in Flanders.
- **Mid-1400s** Philip the Good, Duke of Burgundy, gains control of Low Countries.
- **1500s** Era of "Flemish Primitives"—artists Van Eyck, Bosch, van der Weyden, and Memling.
- **1555** Philip II of Spain introduces Inquisition persecution against Protestants.
- **1568–1648** William the Silent leads Protestants' rebellion to regain control of seven northern provinces.

continues

- **1713** Spanish Netherlands (including Belgium) comes under rule of Hapsburgs of Austria.
- **1795** French rule of Belgium begins.
- **1815** Napoléon defeated at Waterloo. Belgium becomes part of the Netherlands.
- **1830** Belgian War of Independence breaks out.
- **1831** Belgium becomes a constitutional monarchy headed by King Leopold.
- **1914** German forces invade Belgium.
- **1918** End of World War I.
- **1940** King Leopold III surrenders Belgium to Germany at outset of World War II.
- **1944** Benelux Union with Holland and Luxembourg signed in London by governments in exile.
- **1945** World War II ends.
- **1950** Leopold III returns to throne.
- **1951** Leopold III abdicates in favor of his eldest son, Baudouin.
- **1971** Moderate constitutional reforms are introduced, granting some regional autonomy.
- **1992** Both branches of the legislature vote to ratify the Treaty on European Union.
- **1993** King Baudouin dies. He is succeeded by his brother, Albert II (b. 1934).
- **1993** Constitution is amended to create a federal state composed of the autonomous regions of Flanders and Wallonia, and Brussels-Capital, with the German-speaking communities a largely self-governing part of Wallonia.
- **1995** The government is forced to impose unpopular budget cuts and tax increases to meet the strict financial

continues

Germany and Lombardy. No one could have foreseen that Bruges's fine link to the sea, the River Zwin, would eventually choke with silt and leave the city high and dry, forever landlocked. Ghent (Gent) and Ypres (Ieper) prospered in the wool trade. Powerful trade and manufacturing guilds emerged and erected splendid edifices as their headquarters. In Liège, great fortunes were made from iron foundries and the manufacture of arms.

THE 12TH TO THE 15TH CENTURIES

This era was one of immense wealth, much of which was poured into fine public buildings and soaring Gothic cathedrals that survive to this day. During the 15th century, wealthy patrons made possible the brilliant works of such Flemish artists as Van Eyck, Bosch, van der Weyden, and Memling.

As cities took on city-state status, the mighty Count of Flanders, with close ties to France, grew less and less mighty; in 1302, France's Philip the Fair made a bold attempt to annex Flanders. However, he had not reckoned on the stubborn resistance of Flemish common folk. Led by the likes of Jan Breydel, a lowly weaver, and Pieter de Coninck, a butcher, they rallied to face a heavily armored French military. The battle took place on July 11, 1302, in the fields surrounding Kortrijk. When it was over, victorious artisans and craftsmen scoured the bloody battlefield, triumphantly gathering hundreds of golden spurs from slain French knights. Their victory at the "Battle of the Golden Spurs" is celebrated to this day by the Flemish.

But this valiant resistance was crushed by 1328, and Flanders suffered under both the French and the English during the course of the ensuing Hundred Years' War. When Philip the Good—Duke of Burgundy in the mid-1400s and ally of England's King Henry V—gained control of virtually all the Low Countries, he was able to quell political troubles in Ghent and Bruges but unable to prevent extensive looting in Dinant or the almost total destruction of Liège. His progeny, through a series of advantageous marriages, managed to consolidate their holdings into a single Burgundian "Netherlands." Brussels, Antwerp, Mechelen, and Louvain attained new prominence as centers of trade, commerce, and the arts.

By the end of the 1400s, however, Charles the Bold, last of the dukes of Burgundy, had lost the Duchy of Burgundy to the French king on the field of battle, and once more French royalty turned a covetous eye on the Netherlands. Marriage to Mary of Burgundy, the duke's heir, appeared a sure route to bringing the Netherlands under French rule, and a proposal (in reality an ultimatum) was issued to Mary to accept the hand of the French king's eldest son. To the French prince's consternation, Mary promptly wrote a proposal of marriage to Maximilian of Austria. The Austrian's acceptance meant that the provinces became part of the extensive Austrian Hapsburg Empire.

THE 16TH & 17TH CENTURIES A grandson of that union, Charles V—born in Ghent and reared in Mechelen—presided for 40 years over most of Europe, including Spain and its New World possessions. However, he was beset by the Protestant Reformation, which created dissension among the once solidly Catholic populace. It all proved too much for the great monarch, and so he decided to abdicate in favor of his son, Philip II of Spain.

Philip ascended to power in an impressive ceremony at the Palace of the Coudenberg in Brussels

- criteria for the European Monetary Unit (EMU).
- **1996** The nation reacts with horror to the deaths of four girls (two children and two teens), kidnapped by an alleged pedophile ring. Two other children are rescued by police following their kidnap and sexual assault, and the names of other missing children are linked to the ring. The public reacts with anger and mass street demonstrations amid allegations of police and official incompetence and cover-ups.
- **1999** Belgium joins ten other European Union countries in launching the new European currency, the euro.
- **2000** Brussels is European Capital of Culture.

in 1555. An ardent Catholic who spoke neither Dutch nor French, he brought the infamous instruments of the Inquisition to bear on an increasingly Protestant—and increasingly rebellious—Netherlands population. The response from his Protestant subjects was violent: for a month in 1556 they went on a rampage of destruction that saw churches pillaged, religious statues smashed, and other religious works of art burned.

An angry Philip commissioned the zealous Duke of Alba, his most able general, to lead some 10,000 Spanish troops in a wave of retaliatory strikes. The atrocities committed by order of the Duke of Alba and his "Council of Blood" as he swept through the "Spanish Netherlands" are legendary. The Duke was merciless—when the Catholic counts of Egmont and Hornes tried to intercede with Philip, he put them under arrest for 6 months, then had them publicly decapitated in the Grand-Place in Brussels.

Instead of submission, however, this sort of intimidation gave rise to a brutal conflict that lasted from 1568 to 1648. Led by William the Silent and other nobles who raised private armies, the Protestants fought on doggedly until finally independence was achieved for the seven undefeated provinces to the north, which became the fledgling country of Holland. Those in the south remained under the thumb of Spain and gradually returned to the Catholic church. As an act of revenge, Holland closed the River Scheldt to all shipping, and Antwerp, along with other Flemish cities, withered away to just a shadow of their former prosperity.

THE 18TH & 19TH CENTURIES At the beginning of the 18th century the grandson of Louis XIV ascended to the Spanish throne, thereby bringing French domination to Spain's possessions in the Low Countries. That domination was short lived, however; in 1713 the Spanish Netherlands was returned to the Hapsburgs of Austria. A series of revolts against reforms instituted by Joseph II, Emperor of Austria, helped to consolidate a sense of nationalism among the

Low Country natives, who—for the first time—began to call themselves Belgians. Austrian-Belgian conflicts raged fiercely until 1789, when all of Europe was caught up in the French Revolution.

In 1795, Belgium wound up once more under the rule of France. It was not until Napoléon Bonaparte's crushing defeat at Waterloo—just miles from Brussels—that Belgians began to think of national independence as a real possibility. Its time had not yet come, however; under the Congress of Vienna Belgium was once more united with the provinces of Holland. But the Dutch soon learned that governing the unruly Belgians was more than they had bargained for, and the 1830 rioting in Brussels was the last straw. A provisional Belgian government was formed with an elected National Congress. On July 21, 1831, Belgium officially became a constitutional monarchy when a relative of Queen Victoria, Prince Leopold of Saxe-Coburg, became king, swearing allegiance to the constitution.

The new nation soon set about its own version of the industrial revolution: developing its coal and iron natural resources, and rebuilding its textile, manufacturing, and shipbuilding industries. The country was hardly unified by this process, however, for most of the natural resources were to be found in the French-speaking Walloon regions in the south, where prosperity returned much more rapidly than in Flanders.

The Flemish, while happy to be freed from the rule of their Dutch neighbors, bitterly resented the greater influence of their French-speaking compatriots. Many viewed the acquisition of a French-speaking Belgian colony in the African Congo region as further evidence of domination by an oppressive enclave, and there were increasing signs of trouble within the boundaries of Belgium itself.

THE 20TH CENTURY   It took yet another invasion to bring a semblance of unity. When German forces swept over the country in 1914, the Belgians mounted a defense that made them heroes of World War I—even though parts of the Flemish population openly collaborated with the enemy, hailing them as "liberators" from Walloon domination. Still, tattered remnants of the Belgian national army—led by their "soldier-king," Albert I—held a tiny strip of land between De Panne and France for the entire 4 years of the war.

With the coming of peace, Belgium found its southern coal, iron, and manufacturing industries reeling, while the northern Flemish regions were moving steadily ahead by developing light industry, especially around Antwerp. Advanced agricultural methods yielded greater productivity and higher profits for Flemish farmers. By the end of the 1930s the Flemish population outnumbered the Walloons by a large enough majority to install their beloved language as the official voice of education, justice, and civil administration in Flanders.

With the outbreak of World War II, Belgium was once more overrun by German forces. In the face of overwhelming military superiority, King Leopold III decided to surrender to the invaders, remain in Belgium, and try to soften the harsh effects of occupation. By the war's end he was imprisoned in Germany; a regent was appointed as head of state. His controversial decision to surrender led to bitter debate when he returned to the throne in 1950, and in 1951 he stepped down in favor of his son, Baudouin.

Impressions

Our country has the unique advantage of lying at the crossroads of the great cultures of Europe.

—The late King Baudouin (1990)

❷ Did You Know?

- The world's first diamond engagement ring was bestowed on Mary of Burgundy by Archduke Maximilian in Bruges in 1477.
- The manufacture of playing cards has been a Belgian specialty for over 100 years, with the largest factory in Turnhout exporting between five and seven million packs a year.
- The "Little Blue People" known as Smurfs were the creation of Belgian artist Pierre Cuilliford, who named them *Schtroumpf*, which translates—loosely—as "whatchamacallit."
- There *are* famous modern Belgians—Hergé (Georges Rémi) created Tintin; Adolphe Sax invented the saxophone; Georges Simenon wrote the Inspector Maigret books; Belgian-American Leo Baekeland invented bakelite. Also, the great singer Jacques Brel was Belgian, as was the surrealist painter Magritte; so too was Agatha Christie's fictional detective Hercule Poirot.
- A bar in Ghent, Dulle Griet, requires customers to deposit a shoe when they order a glass of Kwak beer, which comes in an expensive—and highly collectible—wooden-framed glass.
- Until 1870, live cats were thrown from the Belfry in Ypres (Ieper) during an ancient festival, the *Kattestoet* (Cat-Throwing Festival). Toy pussies are now thrown (Top Cat would never have stood for it).
- Among the many solemn Belgian fraternities devoted to some age-old drink or food product is one that honors what is in effect a toasted ham and cheese sandwich.
- At the last reenactment of the Battle of Waterloo, in 1995, the actor playing Napoléon was so overcome by stress that he suffered a heart attack and was removed from the battlefield by ambulance. Fortunately he survived to "fight" another day.

During Baudouin's 42 years as king, much progress was made in achieving harmony among Belgium's linguistically and culturally diverse population. During the 1970s efforts were made to grant increasing autonomy to the Flemish and Walloons in the areas where each was predominant, as well as to apportion power to each group within the national government and the political parties. Finally, in 1993, the constitution was amended to create a federal state, made up of the autonomous regions of Flanders and Wallonia, together with the bilingual city of Brussels and autonomous German-speaking communities.

The downside of this constitutional tinkering aimed at keeping the country intact was that it also brought the country perilously close to splitting up, as each regional government went its own way, leaving the increasingly marginalized federal government walking a tightrope between them. With so many layers of government—federal, regional, provincial, city, and communal—all of which needed an impressively outfitted administration, taxation and bureaucracy were coming dangerously close to choking the life out of the economy.

As the 1990s progressed, ordinary Belgians became increasingly disenchanted with their governance. Simmering resentment boiled over in anger in 1996 with the deaths of two little girls and two teenage girls, and the abduction of others, at the hands of a pedophile ring. The belated arrest of the prime suspect, a convicted sex offender who had been released early from prison, lifted the lid on a tale of official incompetence that destroyed people's already shaky faith in their institutions, and brought hundreds of thousands into the streets of Brussels in protest.

It was unclear how far the subsequent impulse for reform would carry. Still, much was achieved on other fronts. Most notably, Belgium hit, more or less, the strict financial targets that allowed it to participate in the European Monetary Union. What this will mean for the Belgium's economy is anyone's guess, but the achievement was undeniably encouraging.

4 Rubens, Brueghel & Magritte: Belgium's Influence on Art

Despite its small geographic size, Belgium has exerted a significant influence on the Western art world. The works of Hieronymus Bosch, Brueghel, Rubens, Van Dyck, the brothers Van Eyck, and Magritte represent only a fraction of the treasures you'll see gracing the walls of Brussels's Musée Communal and Musée d'Art Ancien, the Museum of Fine Arts in Tournai, the Groeninge Museum in Bruges, and Ghent's Museum of Fine Arts.

The Golden Age of Flemish painting occurred in the 1400s, a century dominated by the so-called "Primitive" artists, whose work was almost always religious in theme, usually commissioned for churches and chapels, and largely lacking in perspective. As the medieval cities of Flanders flourished, more and more princes, wealthy merchants, and prosperous guilds became patrons of the arts.

In the 15th century, the function of art was still to praise God and illustrate religious allegory, but **Jan Van Eyck** (ca. 1390–1441), one of the earliest Flemish masters, brought a sharp new perspective to bear on traditional subject matter. His *Adoration of the Mystic Lamb,* created with his brother Hubert for St. Bavo's Cathedral in Ghent, incorporates a realistic landscape into its biblical theme.

The "Primitives" sought to mirror reality, to portray both people and nature exactly as they appeared to the human eye, down to the tiniest detail, without classical distortions or embellishments. These artists would work meticulously for months—even years—on a single commission, often painting with a single-haired paintbrush to achieve a painstakingly "lifelike" quality.

The greatest Flemish artist of the 16th century lived and worked for many years in Antwerp. From 1520 to 1580 the city of Antwerp was one of the world's busiest ports and banking centers; as such it eclipsed Bruges as a center for the arts. Many of the artists working here looked to the Italian Renaissance masters for their models of perfection. **Pieter Brueghel the Elder** (ca. 1525–69), who had studied in Italy, integrated Renaissance influences with the traditional style of his native land. He frequently painted rural and peasant life, as in his *Wedding Procession,* on view at the Musée Communal in Brussels.

Brueghel painted fewer than 50 oils (although he finished another 250-plus drawings and etchings), but he is still considered one of the greatest 16th-century artists. His works are filled with allusions and allegorical references to the politics and culture of the period, as well as with many plausible and explicit period details. Much of Brueghel's symbolism is obscure to us today, but it would have been clear to the contemporary Flemish audience full of hatred for their Spanish masters. The artist also had a fabulous, grotesque side, clearly influenced by the artist Hieronymus Bosch; see *The Fall of the Rebel Angels* in the Royal Fine Arts Museum (Musées Royaux des Beaux-Arts), Brussels.

In 1563 Brueghel moved to Brussels, where he lived at rue Haute 132. Here his two sons, also artists, were born. **Jan Brueghel** specialized in decorative paintings of flowers and fruits; **Pieter Brueghel the Younger** became known for copying his father's paintings.

Peter Paul Rubens (1577–1640) was the most influential baroque painter of the early 17th century. The drama in his works, such as *The Raising of the Cross,* housed in the Antwerp cathedral, comes from the dynamic, writhing figures in his canvases. His renditions of the female form gave rise to the term "Rubenesque," which describes the voluptuous women who appear in his paintings.

Portraitist **Antony van Dyck** (1599–1641), one of the most important talents to emerge from Rubens's studio, served as court painter to Charles I of England, though some of his best religious work remains in Belgium. Look for the *Lamentation* in the Museum voor Schone Kunsten in Antwerp, and the *Crucifixion* in Mechelen Cathedral.

Belgium's influence on the art world is by no means limited to the old masters. **James Ensor** (1860–1949) was a late-19th-century pioneer of modern art. One of his most famous works is the *Entry of Christ into Brussels*. Ensor developed a broadly expressionistic technique, liberating his use of color from the demands of realism. He took as his subject disturbing, fantastic visions and images.

Surrealism flourished in Belgium, perhaps because of the earlier Flemish artists with a penchant for the bizarre and grotesque. **Paul Delvaux** (1897–1989) became famous, but the best known of the Belgian surrealists was unquestionably **René Magritte** (1898–1967). His neatly dressed man in the bowler hat, whose face is always hidden from view, became one of the most famous images of the surrealist movement. Many of these modern works can be seen at two sections of the Royal Fine Arts Museums (Musées Royaux des Beaux-Arts) in Brussels—the Museum of Historic Art and the Museum of Modern Art—and the Royal Fine Arts Museum (Konikljke Museum voor Schone Kunsten) in Antwerp. The fine arts museums in Ghent, Tournai, and Liège, and the modern art museums in Antwerp and Ostend are also major sources.

5 Architecture Through the Ages

It's not until after A.D. 1000, when the Romanesque style appeared, that we can really begin to discuss Belgian architecture per se. Even then it's difficult to talk about a Belgian style, because the history of the area that was Belgium— that is, Flanders and Wallonia—does not lend itself to an easy architectural definition or history. If a general statement can be made about Flemish architecture (as distinct from that of Holland) it is that it drew its inspiration from the south and was more often directly influenced by France, whereas Holland's was influenced by Germany.

The greatest example of the Romanesque in Belgium is Tournai's magnificent black marble cathedral, which actually contains a hodgepodge of styles. Its nave (dating from 1110) retains the original Romanesque fenestration; the east end is Gothic; and the transepts are in a transitional style. Belgium also has a number of castles that exhibit Romanesque traces, such as the one in Antwerp's port, the Steen, and Ghent's Gravensteen Castle, which was the seat of the counts of Flanders.

During the Gothic period Belgian architecture was greatly influenced by French Gothic, especially in the 14th century. The basic floor plan of a Gothic cathedral is like a cross, with the long beam running from west to east. The interior is divided into the nave, where worshipers would sit, and the choir. Behind the choir there's generally a rounded apse, and an aisle called the ambulatory. The "crossbeam" of the cross is called the transept.

The entire structure is punctuated with pointed arches and spires, and pointed Gothic vaults in place of rounded ceilings—everywhere points stretching upward to the heavens. The exteriors are covered by a filigree of stone and statuary.

The greatest ecclesiastic examples of the Gothic style in Belgium are St. Michael's Cathedral, in which the choir is in fact Belgium's earliest Gothic work, and the churches of Notre Dame in Mechelen, St-Pierre in Louvain, and St. Bavo's in Ghent. Antwerp Cathedral is perhaps the most imposing example of late Gothic; it was begun in 1352 at the east end and the nave was completed in 1474.

Examples of great Gothic civic architecture also abound. In the 15th century Bruges became a center for the Hanseatic League, while other important commercial centers emerged in Ghent, Antwerp, Louvain, and Ypres. Each town has a rich heritage of civic buildings from the period—guild halls, exchanges, warehouses, and wealthy merchant residences. Among the finer examples of this richly ornate architecture are the Cloth Hall at Ypres (built 1200–1304), the Cloth Hall in Mechelen, the Grande Boucherie in Ghent, and the Vieille Boucherie in Antwerp. Gothic style continued until the early 16th century when Renaissance decorative elements began to appear. The outstanding example of this Flemish mannerism is the Antwerp Town Hall, built in 1561–65 by Cornelius Floris.

During the 18th century Belgium developed a baroque, richly decorated style best exemplified by Brussels's Grand-Place. After 1750, neoclassicism took over, influencing such urban designs as Place Royale in Brussels, which was laid out by the French architect Barre.

Much Belgian civic architecture in the 19th century was classical, such as the Théâtre de la Monnaie (1819). Again, architecture and urban planning were influenced by France. A stroll along boulevard Anspach will reveal iron grillwork, mansard roofs, and other elements of this style. Two buildings remain from the period, the colossal and classical Palace of Justice, by Joseph Poelaert, and the neobaroque Stock Exchange.

Another style appeared briefly at the turn of the 20th century. It was called "art nouveau" in England and the United States but called "jugendstil" (coup de jouet) in Belgium and Holland. Art nouveau's prime materials were glass and iron, which were worked with decorative curved lines and floral and geometric motifs. Belgium produced one of its greatest exponents in Victor Horta (1861–1947); his work can be seen in Brussels where the Tassel House (1893) and the Hôtel Solvay (1895) are forerunners of the ambitious Maison du Peuple (1896–99), with its concave, curved facades and location within an irregularly shaped square. His most famous building, though, was the Innovation department store (1901) which, unfortunately, was destroyed by fire.

Modern architecture was largely introduced to Belgium by Henry van der Velde (1863–1957), who was interested in functionalism and had studied architecture in Weimar at the school that eventually developed the Bauhaus style (under Gropius).

6 A Taste of Belgium

Belgian chefs are often influenced by the French, but they add their own special touches. Native specialties in Wallonia include *jambon d'Ardenne* (ham from the hills and valleys of the Ardennes) and savory *boudin de Liège* (a succulent sausage mixed with herbs). Almost every menu lists *tomates aux crevettes* (tomatoes stuffed with tiny, delicately sweet North Sea shrimp and light, homemade mayonnaise), which is filling enough for a light lunch and delicious as an appetizer. A very special treat awaits visitors in May and June in the form of Belgian asparagus, and from October through March there's endive, which is known in Belgium as *witloof* (white leaf).

Flanders has added its own ingredients to the mix of Belgian cuisine. The Flemish share the Dutch fondness for raw herring, generally eaten with equally raw onions, while *sole à l'Ostendaise* and the small, gray North Sea shrimp are also firm favorites. River fish used to be the main ingredient of the Flemish soup-like stew called *waterzooï,* but today's rivers being increasingly polluted, chicken is now a more familiar ingredient.

If you're basically a potatoes person, you're in good company, for Belgians dote on their *steak-frites,* available at virtually every restaurant—even when not listed on the menu. Lest you think that *frites* in Belgium are the same as American french fries, let me hasten to enlighten you. These are twice-fried potatoes, as light as the proverbial feather. They're sold in paper cones on many street corners and (in my opinion) are best when topped with homemade mayonnaise, though you may prefer curry or even your usual catsup. Frites will also accompany almost anything you order in a restaurant.

Seafood anywhere in Belgium is fresh and delicious. *Moules* (mussels) are absolutely addictive and are a specialty in Brussels, where you'll find a concentration of restaurants along the Petite rue des Bouchers that feature them in just about every guise you can imagine. (Ironically, Belgian mussels actually come from Zeeland in Holland and may, in fact, be the only Dutch products Belgians will admit to being any good.) *Homard* (lobster) also comes in a range of dishes. Don't miss the heavenly Belgian creation called *écrevisses à la liègeoise* (crayfish in a rich butter, cream, and white-wine sauce). Eel, often swimming in a grass-green sauce, is popular in both Flanders (where it's called *paling in 't groen*) and Wallonia (*anguilles au vert*).

No matter where you eat, you should know that **service** will be professional but not exactly speedy. Belgians don't just dine; they savor each course—if you're in a hurry, you're better off heading for a street vendor or an imported fast-food establishment.

Finally, a word on **Belgian chocolate.** Whatever the Swiss or anyone else might say to the contrary, Belgian chocolates are the world champs; they're so lethally addictive that they ought to be sold with a government health warning. They can also be wonderful gifts for friends back home. Those made by Wittamer, Nihoul, Neuhaus, Godiva, and Leonidas ought to do the trick. Buy them loose, in bags weighing from 100g to boxes of 2kg or more. Take a prepared box, or simply point to those you want, or ask the assistant for a mixture. Made with real cream, they do not keep well—but then you weren't planning on keeping them for long anyway, were you?

Note: Most Belgian restaurants are open 7 days a week from noon to 2:30pm for lunch and from 7 to 10pm for dinner. These hours may vary, however.

BELGIAN DISHES

Aside from virtually any of your own favorite French dishes, you'll find Belgian specialties on every menu. The following are especially noteworthy:

Asperges à la Flamande   Lovely local white asparagus served with sliced or crumbled egg and melted butter for dipping.

Stoemp   Mashed potatoes and vegetables accompanied by sausage or meat.

Cheese   There are more than 300 varieties of artisanal cheeses, each of which has a local following but is often little known outside Belgium. Try cheesy marvels such as Corsendonk, Passendale, Maredsous, Petrus, Château d'Arville, Wynendale, Rubens, and Le Regalou.

Chicon/Witloof   Chicory, or Belgian endive, is wonderful when served wrapped in thin slices of ham with a topping of cheese sauce.

Crevettes/garnalen   Tiny shrimp from the cold waters of the North Sea, served in a variety of ways (at Oostduinkerke some fishermen still fish them from horseback). Look for *tomates aux crevettes* (tomato stuffed with shrimp and mayonnaise) and *croquettes de crevettes* (crusty, deep-fried shrimp cakes).

Frites/frieten   The scandalously misnamed "french fries" are in fact a Belgian specialty, twice-fried, lighter than any you've ever encountered. They're served with steak or moules or in paper cones and topped with homemade mayonnaise or catsup.

Game   The eagerly awaited autumn game season in the Ardennes usually brings to the menu wild boar, venison, hare, and wildfowl.

Gaufres   Those wonderful Belgian waffles; try them with sugar, fruit, and/or whipped cream.

Gaufres aux Fruits   Small, thin waffles filled with prune, apricot, or other fruit mixtures.

Gaufres de Liège   A heavy waffle topped with caramelized sugar.

Hareng/Haring   Herring is eaten raw at the Flemish coast (where it's called haring) and is often served with raw onions.

Jambon d'Ardenne   Smoked ham from the Ardennes—positively addictive.

Lapin à Bière   Rabbit cooked in beer—inexpensive, hearty, and delicious.

Marcassin   Wild boar from the Ardennes, usually served roasted.

Moules/mosselen   Mussels, a Belgian national dish.

Oie à l'Instar de Visé   Goose that has been boiled, then sautéed.

Paling in 't groen/anguilles au vert   Eel in a grass-green sauce.

Ragoût liègeois   A stew of potatoes, vegetables, and veal.

Salade liègeoise   A mixture of smoked bacon, potatoes, onion, parsley, and French beans.

Steak   Comes in many forms: sautéed, served with butter or béarnaise sauce; with marrow (entrecôte à la moelle); and with cracked black pepper (steak au poivre).

Waterzooï op Gentse wijze   A freshwater-fish stew originating in Ghent (although nowadays chicken is more often used).

BEER & WINE

What to drink with all those tasty dishes? Why, beer, of course! Belgium is justly famous for its brewing tradition, and there are more than 300 brands produced within its borders (some believe it's as many as 1,000). Some are pilseners, like Stella Artois, Jupiler, Maes, Primus, and Eupener. The majority, however, are local beers, specialties of a region, city, town, or village; some are made by monks. Each beer has a distinct, and often beautiful, glass, which is why you can instantly tell what everyone is drinking in a Belgian bar. Needless to say, with so many choices it may take quite a bit of sampling to find a favorite. Among names to look for that you won't find outside Belgium (except in Holland) are Duvel, Chimay, Hoegaarden,

De Koninck, and Kwak; those still brewed by Trappist monks, Orval and West-malle; and Faro, Krieklambiek, and Lambiek from the area around Brussels.

If, by chance, you're not a beer drinker, or want a change, the finest wines from France, Italy, Spain, Portugal, Luxembourg, and Germany are always available at prices way below what you'd pay in the United States.

For a digestif, you might try a gin, in Flanders known as *jenever* (or, colloquially, as *witteke*), and in Wallonia known as *genièvre* (colloquially as *pèkèt*). This stiff grain-spirit is often served in glasses little bigger than a thimble. Belgium's 70 jenever distilleries produce some 270 varieties, some flavored with juniper, coriander, or other herbs and spices. Among notable brands are Filliers Oude Graanjenever, De Poldenaar Oude Antwerpsche, Heinrich Pèkèt de la Piconette, Sint-Pol, and Van Damme. Jenever in a stone bottle makes an ideal gift.

4

Planning a Trip to Belgium

While Belgium is not a difficult country to come to grips with thanks to its widespread use of English, relatively small size, and excellent tourist infrastructure, a little forethought can still save you precious time and effort. This chapter will give you the practical information you need to plan your trip.

1 Visitor Information & Money

VISITOR INFORMATION

For contact details of the Belgian tourist offices in the U.S., Britain, and other countries, see "Visitor Information, Entry Requirements & Customs" in chapter 2.

In Belgium, the **Belgian Tourist Office** is at rue du Marché-aux-Herbes 63, 1000 Brussels (☎ **02/504-03-90;** fax 02/504-02-70). All cities and towns, and even some villages, have their own tourist offices, many of which are listed in this book under the appropriate destination. A complete list of addresses and telephone numbers is available from the main office in Brussels.

MONEY

The **Belgian franc** (abbreviated BF; you also sometimes see FB and BEF) is made up of 100 centimes. Notes are issued in 100-, 200-, 500-, 1,000-, 2,000-, 5,000-, and 10,000-franc denominations. Coins come in 50 centimes, and 1, 5, 20, and 50 francs. It's a good idea to keep a small supply of 5- and 20-franc coins on hand for tips, telephone calls, parking meters, and the like. You may occasionally be given Luxembourg francs (LF); although strictly speaking not legal tender in Belgium, these are universally accepted and have the same value as their Belgian equivalents.

CURRENCY EXCHANGE   Change your money at a bank, or if you carry American Express traveler's checks, at **American Express,** bd. du Souverain 100, 1000 Brussels (☎ **02/676-21-11**). Another good option is **Thomas Cook,** Grand-Place 4, Brussels (☎ **02/513-28-45**). The currency exchange offices (*bureaux de change*) at Brussels's three main railway stations—Gare du Nord, Gare Centrale, and Gare du Midi—also offer good rates for cash and traveler's checks. The worst deals are at Brussels Airport, where exchange rates at all currency exchange offices in the Arrivals area are lousy; and at street currency exchange offices throughout the

The Euro

During the lifetime of this edition of *Frommer's Guide,* the new European currency, the fabled if not necessarily fabulous **euro,** will move from being a theoretical unit of money to being a reality. The symbol of the euro is a stylized "E," which actually looks like an upper-case "C" with a horizontal double bar through the middle; its official abbreviation is "EUR." Belgium is one of the first wave of 11 countries that are establishing the new currency; this means that in time the Belgian franc will disappear and be replaced by the euro. The changeover will not happen all at once, however. Below is the timetable for introducing the euro.

- **January 1, 1999.** The euro becomes a currency in its own right, but at this introductory stage there are no banknotes or coins in circulation. The conversion rates of the euro against other currencies, such as the U.S. dollar and the British pound, are established by the European Central Bank. Banks and other financial institutions begin trading in euros and accepting payment in euros. The Belgian franc remains the only currency in Belgium for cash transactions (although, of course, some businesses may choose to accept payment in other currencies, such as the U.S. dollar and the German mark).

- **Until December 31, 2001.** The introductory process continues. More and more businesses start posting their prices in euros alongside Belgian francs. There are still no euro banknotes or coins in circulation—payment in euros can be made only by check, credit card, or some other bank-related system.

- **January 1, 2002.** Euro banknotes and coins are introduced. Over a maximum 6-month transition period, Belgian franc banknotes and coins are withdrawn from circulation. The euro becomes the official currency of Belgium.

country, which often combine poor exchange rates with high commission charges—but remember that these are often open when the banks are closed.

CREDIT CARDS   These are almost universally accepted by hotels, restaurants, shops, and gas stations, and for travel by plane and train (and even some taxis). The smaller the business and the smaller the community, the less likely they are to be accepted.

ATMS   Cash machines are widespread in Belgian cities and towns, and you even find them in bigger villages. Most are called "Bancontact" or "Mister Cash" and are identified by a logo with one or both of these names. They accept cards linked to the Cirrus and Plus networks, in addition to Eurocheque cards; many also accept Visa and MasterCard, less often American Express and Diners Club. There are a few ATMs at Brussels Airport, and using them is a way to avoid bad deals at the airport's currency-exchange offices.

2 When to Go

"In season" in Belgium, as in the other Benelux countries, means mid-April through mid-October. The peak of the tourist season is July and August, when the weather is at its finest. If you're one of the growing numbers who favor shoulder- or off-season travel, you'll find Belgium every bit as attractive during those months. Not only are airlines, hotels, and restaurants cheaper and less crowded during this time (with more relaxed service, which means you get more personal attention), but there are also some very appealing events going on. For example, Brussels swings

The Belgian Franc

At this writing $1 = approximately 36 francs (or 1 franc = 2.8¢) and £1 = approximately 55 francs (or 1 franc = 1.8 pence); these were the rates of exchange used to calculate the dollar and pound values given in this book and in the table below.

BF	U.S.$	U.K.£	BF	U.S.$	U.K.£
1	.03	.02	500	13.89	9.09
5	.14	.09	750	20.83	13.64
10	.28	.18	1,000	27.78	18.18
20	.56	.36	1,250	34.72	22.73
25	.69	.45	1,500	41.67	27.27
30	.83	.54	1,750	48.61	31.82
40	1.11	.73	2,000	55.55	36.36
50	1.39	.91	2,500	69.44	45.45
75	2.08	1.36	3,000	83.33	54.55
100	2.78	1.82	3,500	97.22	63.64
125	3.47	2.27	4,000	111.11	72.73
150	4.17	2.73	4,500	125.00	81.82
200	5.56	3.64	5,000	139.89	90.91
250	6.94	4.55	6,000	166.67	109.09

into its rich music season in April, and Tournai turns out for the colorful thousand-year-old Plague Procession the second Sunday in September.

CLIMATE Belgium's climate is moderate, with few extremes in temperature either in summer or winter. It does, however, rain a lot, although there are more showers than downpours. (It's a good idea to pack a raincoat.) Temperatures are lowest in December and January, when they average 42°F, and highest in July and August, when they average 73°F.

HOLIDAYS Public holidays are January 1 (New Year's Day); Easter Monday; May 1 (Labor Day); Ascension Day; Whitmonday (The Monday after Whitsunday, the seventh Sunday after Easter); July 21 (Independence Day); August 15 (Assumption Day); November 1 (All Saints' Day); November 11 (Armistice Day); and December 25 (Christmas).

BELGIUM CALENDAR OF EVENTS

Several festivals in Belgium take place in the days leading up to Shrove Tuesday, which falls on February 16 in 1999 and on March 7 in 2000.

January

- **Festival of Fools,** Ronse. *Zotte Maandag* (Crazy Monday) festivities, with masked characters called "Bommels," actually takes place on a Saturday. Contact **Ronse Tourist Office** (☎ 055/21-25-01). Saturday after the Epiphany (January 6).

- **Antiques Fair,** Palais des Beaux-Arts, Brussels. Contact **Palais des Beaux-Arts** (☎ 02/507-84-66). Second week of January.

What Things Cost in Brussels	U.S. $
Taxi from the airport to the city center	34.00
Train from the airport to the city center	2.50
Local telephone call	.55
Double room at the Royal Windsor Hotel (very expensive)	306.00
Double room at the Hotel Arlequin (moderate)	117.00
Double room at the Sabina (inexpensive)	67.00
Lunch for one at Falstaff (moderate)	28.00
Lunch for one at 't Kelderke (inexpensive)	17.00
Dinner for one, without wine, at Maison du Cygne (very expensive)	83.00
Dinner for one, without wine, at Falstaff (moderate)	42.00
Dinner for one, without wine, at the 't Kelderke (inexpensive)	28.00
Glass of beer	1.20
Coca-Cola	1.20
Cup of coffee	1.65
Roll of ASA 100 color film, 36 exposures	5.00
Admission to the Brussels City Museum	2.20
Movie ticket	8.35
Theater ticket to the Opéra National	15.00–100.00

- **Brussels International Film Festival,** at Cinema Porte de Namur, Brussels. Contact Tourist Information Brussels (☎ **02/513-89-40**). Late January.

February
- **Carnival,** Eupen. Five days of pre-Lenten revelry in the capital of Belgium's German-speaking district. Highlight is the Rosenmontag (Rose Monday) Procession. Contact **Eupen Tourist Office** (☎ **087/55-45-45**). Thursday to Shrove Tuesday (the day before Ash Wednesday).
- **Carnival,** Malmédy. The Cwarm festival brings good-natured mayhem to the streets of this otherwise sober town. Sunday is the day of the big parade, when costumed characters called Banes Courants chase people through the streets and others called Haguètes snare passers-by with long wooden pincers. Contact **Malmédy Tourist Office** (☎ **080/33-02-50**). Saturday to Shrove Tuesday.
- **Carnival,** Aalst. Three days of pre-Lenten festivities, including the Giants' Parade with the horse Bayard, onion-throwing from the roofs of the Grote Markt, and the parade of Vuil Jeannetten—men dressed as women. Contact **Aalst Tourist Office** (☎ **053/73-22-62**). Sunday to Shrove Tuesday.
- **Carnival,** Binche. One of Europe's most colorful street carnivals, led on Shrove Tuesday by the sumptuously costumed Gilles of Binche. Contact **Binche Tourist Office** (☎ **064/33-40-73**). Sunday to Shrove Tuesday.

March
- **Bal du Rat Mort,** Ostend. This outrageous fancy-dress event takes its grisly name from a chic Paris cafe. Proceeds go to charity. Contact **Ostend Tourist Office** (☎ **059/70-11-99**). First Saturday in March.
- **Carnival,** Stavelot. The Blancs Moussis, characters with long red noses and hooded white costumes, are the stars of the town's Laetere procession. Contact

Stavelot Tourist Office (☎ 080/86-23-39). Refreshment Sunday (3 weeks before Easter).

- **Carnival,** Fosses-la-Ville. Costumed characters called Chinels parade through the streets. Contact **Fosses-la-Ville Tourist Office** (☎ 071/71-14-68). Refreshment Sunday (3 weeks before Easter).

- **Brussels International Fantasy Film Festival,** Auditorium du Passage 44, Brussels. Screens science fiction and fantasy films. Contact **Tourist Information Brussels** (☎ 02/513-89-40). Late March.

April

- **International Folklore Festival,** Leuven. Contact **Leuven Tourist Office** (☎ 016/21-15-39). Easter weekend. April 2–5.

- **Sablon Spring Baroque Music Festival,** Place du Grand-Sablon, Brussels. Open-air concerts in the square. Contact **Tourist Information Brussels** (☎ 02/513-89-40). Third week of April.

- **Flower Show,** Ghent. Contact **Ghent Tourist Office** (☎ 09/225-36-41). Belgium's top flower show, the biennial Ghent Floraliën, next takes place from April 22 to May 1, 2000.

- **May Day's Eve Festival,** Hasselt. Participants in the *Meieavondviering* plant a May Tree in the Grote Markt and burn dummies representing winter, while witches dance. Contact **Hasselt Tourist Office** (☎ 011/23-95-40). April 30.

May

- **Queen Elisabeth International Music Competition,** Brussels. For young musicians. Contact **Tourist Information Brussels** (☎ 02/513-89-40). May and June.

- **Festival of the Cats,** Ypres (Ieper). During the traditional Kattestoet, velvet cats are thrown from the town Belfry. Contact **Ypres Tourist Office** (☎ 057/20-07-24). Every third year on the second Sunday in May; next in 2000.

- **Procession of the Holy Blood,** Bruges. The Bishop of Bruges carries a relic of the Holy Blood through the streets, while costumed characters act out biblical scenes. Contact **Bruges Tourist Office** (☎ 050/44-86-86). Ascension Day (fifth Thursday after Easter).

- **Chariot of Gold Procession,** Mons. Religious procession of guilds and the reliquary of St Waudru. Followed by a street performance, the Lumeçon, in which St George slays the dragon. Contact **Mons Tourist Office** (☎ 065/33-55-80). Holy Trinity Sunday (first Sunday after Pentecost).

- **Brussels Jazz Marathon,** Place du Grand-Sablon, Brussels. Various venues around the city. Contact **Tourist Information Brussels** (☎ 02/513-89-40). Last weekend of May.

June

- **Day of the Four Processions,** Tournai. Features flower-decked floats, a military band, and the highlight, a procession of "giants" representing historical characters, including King Childeric of the Franks and France's King Louis XIV. Contact **Tournai Tourist Office** (☎ 069/22-20-45). Second Sunday in June.

- **Carillon concerts at St Rombout's tower,** Mechelen. Contact **Mechelen Tourist Office** (☎ 015/21-18-73). Saturday to Monday evenings, mid-June through August.

- **Cartoon Festival,** Knokke-Heist. Contact **Knokke-Heist Tourist Office** (☎ 050/63-03-80). June through September.

July
- **Ommegang,** Grand-Place, Brussels. Dramatic historic pageant and procession, representing the entry of Emperor Charles V into Brussels in 1549. Contact **Tourist Information Brussels** (☎ **02/513-89-40**). First Tuesday and Thursday in July.
- **Brosella Folk and Jazz,** Théâtre de Verdure, Brussels. Contact **Tourist Information Brussels** (☎ **02/513-89-40**). Mid-July.
- **Entertainment,** Grand-Place, Brussels. Concerts, theater, dance, exhibitions, and other forms of entertainment animate the Grand-Place. Contact **Tourist Information Brussels** (☎ **02/513-89-40**). Entire month.
- **Belgian National Day,** Brussels. Marked throughout Belgium but celebrated most in Brussels, with a military procession and music at the Royal Palace. Contact **Tourist Information Brussels** (☎ **02/513-89-40**). July 21.

August
- **Carpet of Flowers,** Grand-Place, Brussels. The historic square is carpeted with two-thirds of a million begonias arranged in a kind of tapestry. Contact **Tourist Information Brussels** (☎ **02/513-89-40**). Mid-August in even-numbered years.
- **Marktrock Rock Festival,** Leuven. Rock and jazz in the square in front of the Town Hall. Contact **Leuven Tourist Office** (☎ **016/21-15-39**). Mid-August.
- **Outre-Meuse Folklore Festival,** Liège. Music, dance, and theater performances. Contact **Liège Tourist Office** (☎ **04/221-92-21**). Mid-August.

September
- **Liberation parade,** Brussels. The Manneken-Pis statue is dressed in a Welsh Guard's uniform in honor of the city's liberation in 1944. Contact **Tourist Information Brussels** (☎ **02/513-89-40**). September 3.
- **Procession of the Plague,** Tournai. Contact **Tournai Tourist Office** (☎ **069/22-20-45**). Commemorates the epidemic of 1090. Second Sunday.

October
- **Ghent International Film Festival,** Ghent. Contact **Ghent Tourist Office** (☎ **09/225-36-41**). Mid-October.

December
- **Walnut Fair,** Bastogne. Traditional matchmaking market. Contact **Bastogne Tourist Office** (☎ **061/21-27-11**). Mid- to late December.
- **Christmas Market,** Grand-Place, Brussels. Includes an open-air ice-skating rink. Contact **Tourist Information Brussels** (☎ **02/513-89-40**). Throughout the month.
- **Nativity Scene and Christmas Tree,** Grand-Place, Brussels. The crib has real animals. Contact **Tourist Information Brussels** (☎ **02/513-89-40**). Throughout the month.

3 Getting Around

Belgium's compact size makes it easy on travelers. The roads are excellent (though often busy), and the comprehensive railway and bus system is one of Europe's best.

BY TRAIN

All major tourist destinations in Belgium can be managed in a day-trip by rail from Brussels. For example, Antwerp is 29 minutes away by train; Ghent, 32 minutes;

Namur, 40 minutes; Bruges, 55 minutes; and Liège, 75 minutes. These times are by the fast inter-city (IC) trains; inter-regional (IR) trains are somewhat slower; and local (L) trains are the tortoises of the system, stopping at every station on the way.

If all or most of your travel will be by rail, your best investment is the **Benelux Tourrail Ticket,** good for unlimited travel in all three countries (for any 5 days in a 1-month period). It's a good buy at 3,230 BF ($89.70) for first class and 2,100 BF ($58.35) for second class; for rail travel throughout Europe, the best value is the **Eurailpass** (see "Getting There," in chapter 2).

Even if you make only one or two day-trips by rail, be sure to inquire about Belgian Railways' **Minitrips**—1-day excursion tickets to major sightseeing destinations at discount prices.

There are also bicycles for rent at major train stations.

BY BUS

In Brussels, Bruges, Liège, and all other major cities, there is good local bus service. Regional buses serve every area of the country, with fares and schedules available from local bus or railway stations, but they're slow, often infrequent, and require transfers at intermediate points to make long-distance journeys.

BY TAXI

To get a taxi in Belgium, you must either wait at the numerous taxi stands found at hotels, railway stations, and shopping areas, or call by telephone. Tip and taxes are included in the meter price—you need not add another tip unless there has been exceptional service (help with heavy luggage, for example).

BY CAR

Driving conditions are excellent in Belgium, with lighted highways at night, roadside telephones connected to the 900 emergency number, and "TS" (Touring Secours) yellow cars that patrol major highways to render emergency service at minimal cost. If you have car trouble, simply pull off the road, go to one of the roadside telephones, and dial ☎ **070/34-47-77,** then wait for the TS. On other roads call TS from the nearest telephone or your cell phone.

Belgian drivers, however, are not so excellent. They're notoriously fast and aggressive and have some of the worst road-accident statistics in Europe, so go carefully.

RENTALS   Rental cars with U.S. specifications are available from **Hertz** (☎ 800/654-3001 in the U.S.), which has offices at bd. Maurice Lemonnier 8 in Brussels and at Brussels Airport (☎ 02/726-49-50); and **Avis** (☎ 800/331-2112 in the U.S.), which has offices at the airport and rue Américaine 145 in Brussels (☎ 02/720-09-44). Rates begin at about 1,800 BF ($50) for a small car with unlimited mileage (the per-day rate is less for longer rentals). Other rental companies include **Budget** (☎ 02/720-80-50) and **Europcar** (☎ 02/348-92-12), whose rates may be slightly less.

AUTOMOBILE CLUBS   Both the **Royal Automobile Club de Belgique,** rue d'Arlon 53, Brussels (☎ 02/230-08-10), and the **Touring Club de Belgique,** rue de la Loi 44, Brussels (☎ 02/233-22-11), have working arrangements with international Automobile Association clubs. Get information from your local club before leaving home.

GASOLINE   Leaded super-grade gasoline (identified by red markings on the pump and pump handle) costs around 38 BF ($1.05) per liter, or 144 BF ($4) per U.S. gallon; lead-free Eurosuper (identified by green markings on the pump and pump handle) costs around 34 BF (95¢) per liter, or 129 BF ($3.60) per U.S. gallon. Most gas stations close at night, except those on main expressways, but many remain accessible by Eurocheque card holders through automatic payment systems.

DRIVING RULES   To drive in Belgium, U.S. citizens need only a valid passport, a U.S. driver's license, and a valid auto registration. The minimum age for drivers is 18. On highways, speed limits are 70kmph (43 m.p.h.) minimum, 120kmph (74 m.p.h.) maximum; in all cities and urban areas, the maximum speed limit is 50kmph (31 m.p.h.). Seat belts must be worn in both the front seats and in the back. One important driving rule is the *priorité à droite* (priority of the right), which makes it perfectly legal most of the time to pull out from a side road to the right of the flow of traffic. That means, of course, that you must keep a sharp eye on the side roads to your right.

ROAD MAPS   Tourist offices provide excellent city, regional, and country maps. Michelin maps nos. 213 and 214 cover the country; they are detailed and reliable, and can be bought for about 300 BF ($8.35) from bookstores, news vendors, some supermarkets, and other outlets.

HITCHHIKING

It's generally an easy matter to hitch a ride on Belgium's main roads, which connect all major cities around the country. Remember that **hitchhiking is illegal on expressways,** although authorities are pretty lenient about access roads.

SUGGESTED ITINERARIES

Belgium is so crammed full of places to go and things to see and do that you'll be hard pressed to decide how to spend your time. I'm going to assume you have a week in the country; if you have more time, you'll have no problem filling it, by staying longer in some places and exploring a wider area from your chosen base or bases; if you have less, that's easy too—cut some of the suggestions completely, rather than cramming several together. It's better to devote a whole day to Ghent, say, than to try to combine it with Antwerp on the same day. Remember, vacations are supposed to be relaxing, which is not necessarily the same thing as lazy!

It might make sense to base yourself in Brussels, which is centrally located, and make day-long forays to historic cities that are at most a little more than an hour away by train. That way, you'll have time to get a feel for this intriguing capital in addition to seeing the highlights of the great centers of art and history nearby. On the other hand, you'll get lot of Brussels this way, and the city isn't all *that* interesting. I recommend staying overnight in Bruges, Antwerp, or Liège rather than just visiting by day and returning for the night to Brussels, especially if you're going by train.

Driving in Belgium is not really essential unless you want to visit the Ardennes, in which case it's the only really viable way of getting around. Drivers should pick up the Belgian Tourist Office's excellent and detailed *Itineraries for Motorists* booklet, which sets out driving routes in every region.

Among the Belgian cities you shouldn't miss are **Bruges,** Belgium's most romantic, well-preserved medieval town; **Ghent,** whose narrow streets and gabled buildings hold traces of an exciting history and bold deeds of the past; **Ostend** and its neighboring coastal towns, each with its own distinctive seaside resort personality; **Tournai,** the country's second-oldest city, with its awe-inspiring cathedral;

Liège, the rebel city with its colorful street market and engaging puppetry; **Namur** and **Dinant,** handsome and scenically sited on the River Meuse; and any of the charming towns and villages in the picturesque Ardennes.

If You Have 1 Week

Days 1 and 2   Don't leave Brussels before you've spent a minimum of 2 days exploring its sightseeing splendors. On the afternoon of day 2, take a side trip to nearby Waterloo, where Wellington and his army gave Napoléon the boot in 1815, settling Europe's fate for a hundred years.

Day 3   Get an early start to allow a full day in Bruges, a fairy-tale medieval city that has been called the most romantic in the world. Start with a boat ride through the canals, then see Michelangelo's *Madonna and Child* at the Church of Our Lady, the Memling Museum, and the busy, colorful Grote Markt and the elegant Burg at the city's center. Spend the night in Bruges.

Day 4   It wouldn't surprise me if you decide to spend another day in Bruges to fill in some of the inevitable gaps from the previous day. If not, you can continue to the coast and either stay at one place, such as Ostend, soaking up some rays (if you're lucky) and sinking some great seafood, or board the Coast Tram (Kusttram) to tour the entire 64km (40-mile) coastline. Maybe you're not a beach kind of person—in that case, take in some more city-based history and excitement in either Ghent or Antwerp. In Ghent, ancient seat of the counts of Flanders, visit St Bavo's Cathedral and view *The Adoration of the Mystic Lamb,* the masterpiece of the van Eyck brothers. Then take time for a boat trip on the canals or the River Leie. In Antwerp, visit the Rubens House and the Cathedral of Our Lady. Return to Brussels for dinner and evening entertainment.

Day 5   Take the train or drive to Liège, the hot-blooded city on the River Meuse. Visit the 11th-century Palace of the Prince-Bishops, the Cathedral of St. Paul, and the fascinating Museum of Walloon Life. If it's a Sunday, don't miss the colorful street market. Later in the day, if you have a car, you might choose to drive along the valley of the Meuse, to Huy, Namur, and Dinant.

Days 6 and 7   If you're driving, the whole of the Ardennes is open to you, with its magnificent scenery and some of the best dining in the country (this region is renowned for its smoked ham—and not recognized enough for its freshwater trout). You can easily make a 2-day run through the Ardennes. Its highlights include Bouillon, with its medieval castle; Bastogne, where the memory of the brave Americans who fought and won the Battle of the Bulge is kept alive; Spa, which gave its name to a whole resort concept; and Eupen, which borders Belgium's biggest national park, the Hautes Fagnes Nature Reserve.

If You Have More than 1 Week

You can take up some of the options you had to abandon, such as visiting both Ghent and Antwerp, instead of just one of them, and both visit Liège and tour the Meuse Valley. Mons and Tournai, historic art cities both, weren't even included in the first week's itinerary; they certainly shouldn't be left out of the second week's. In the Brussels area, you could usefully fit in a side trip to Mechelen, another of Flanders's architecturally wealthy towns. And if you are fortunate enough to have a few more days to play with, spend them at the coast or getting into the nooks and crannies of the Ardennes.

FAST FACTS: Belgium

American Express   In Brussels, the Amex office is at bd. du Souverain 100, 1000 Brussels (☎ **02/676-21-11**). In Antwerp, the office is at Frankrijklei 21, 2000 Antwerp (☎ **03/232-59-20**).

Baby-Sitters   Hotels often have, or can recommend, a baby-sitting service. Local universities and colleges may also offer baby-sitting. In Brussels, contact the **Université Libre de Bruxelles Jobs Service,** av. P. Héger 22, Prefab 4, 1000 Bruxelles (☎ **02/650-21-71**); open Monday through Friday from 10am to 4pm.

Business Hours   Banks are usually open Monday through Friday from 9am to 1pm and 2 to 4:30pm, and some branches are also open on Saturday morning. Shops generally stay open from 10am to 6pm Monday through Saturday, although more and more are also open on Sunday. Most department stores have late hours on Friday, remaining open until 8 or 9pm.

Drug Laws   Belgium has rigid prohibitions against the possession and use of drugs and a strict enforcement policy that virtually guarantees stiff fines and/or jail sentences for offenders. This can be especially important if you are traveling from neighboring Holland, where the rules are more tolerant and enforcement (for soft drugs) is generally lax.

Electricity   If you plan to bring a hair dryer, radio (other than battery oper-ated), travel iron, or any other small appliance, pack a transformer and a European–style adapter plug, since the electricity in Belgium is 220 volts (except for 110-volt shaver outlets).

Embassies   These are all in Brussels: **U.S. Embassy,** bd. du Regent 27, 1000 Brussels (☎ **02/508-21-11**); **Australian Embassy,** rue Guimard 6–8, 1040 Brussels (☎ **02/231-05-00**); **Canadian Embassy,** av. de Tervuren 2, 1040 Brussels (☎ **02/741-06-11**); **Irish Embassy,** rue Froissart 89, 1040 Brussels (☎ **02/230-53-37**); **New Zealand Embassy,** bd. du Regent 47, 1000 Brussels (☎ **02/512-10-40**); **South African Embassy,** rue de la Loi, 1040 Brus-sels (☎ **02/285-44-00**); and **United Kingdom Embassy,** rue Arlon 85, 1040 Brussels (☎ **02/287-62-11**).

   Locations of diplomatic representatives of other countries can be obtained from the **Ministère des Affaires Etrangères,** rue des Quatre Bras 2, 1000 Brus-sels (☎ **02/516-82-11**).

Emergencies   In case of accidents, call ☎ **100.** For day or night emergency medical service, call ☎ **02/479-18-18** or ☎ **02/648-80-00;** for emergency dental service, call ☎ **02/426-10-26** or ☎ **02/428-58-58;** for police assistance, call ☎ **101;** for fire, ☎ **100.**

Fax   Most hotels have fax facilities, as do most local **Belgacom** offices.

Mail   Airmail postage to North America and the rest of the world (except Europe) is 34 BF (95¢) for postcards and normal-size letters weighing up to 20 grams (about 0.8 oz.). The rate for Belgium and the European Union is 17 BF (45¢) for postcards and letters up to 20 grams.

Pharmacies   Each pharmacy has a list of late-night pharmacies posted on the door.

Police   For emergency police assistance, call ☎ **101.**

Safety   Belgium is generally a safe country—even its big cities are low-crime areas. However, like many countries, Belgium has experienced a creeping spread of drug-related crime. In Brussels the metro system has recently been plagued by muggers, and although increased police presence and video surveillance have brought this under control, it's still better not to venture into deserted metro access corridors after dark; with other people around it's generally safe. Similarly, at night in quiet areas, exercise caution in using ATMs.

Telephone   The country code for Belgium is **32.** When calling Belgium from abroad, you do not use the initial **0** in the area code. From example, if you're calling a Brussels number (area code **02**), you dial only the international access code (which is **011** when calling from North America) and then **32-2,** followed by the subscriber number. You dial only the initial **0** of the area code if you're calling long distance within Belgium.

Direct dialing to other European countries in addition to overseas (including the United States and Canada) is available in most hotel rooms in Belgium. **Telephone** boxes that display stickers showing flags of different countries can be used to make international calls with operator assistance. Holders of AT&T credit cards can reach the money-saving **USA Direct** service by calling ☎ **0800/ 100-10** in Belgium. Similar services are offered by **MCI CallUSA** ☎**0800/ 022-9122, PhoneUSA** ☎ **0800/022-0224, Sprint Express** ☎ **0800/022-9119, Canada Direct** ☎ **0800/022-9116,** and **British Telecom** ☎ **0800/022-9944.**

Most public telephones now accept Telecards valued at 200 BF ($5.55), 500 BF ($7.72), and 1,000 BF ($15.45) rather than coins. Cards can be purchased at news vendors and some shops. Coin telephones accept 5 BF (17¢) and 20 BF (67¢) coins, and it's advisable to have a good supply of these coins when you place a call. Most local calls cost 20 BF (67¢). For information in Belgium call ☎ **1207** or ☎ **1307;** for international information call ☎ **1204** or ☎ **1304.**

To send a **telegram** by telephone, call ☎ **1325.** Telegrams can be sent also through **Belgacom,** bd. Emile Jacqmain 166, 10000 Brussels (☎ **02/ 202-31-11**).

Time   Belgium is 6 hours ahead of eastern standard time in the United States (9am in New York is 3pm in Belgium). Clocks are moved ahead 1 hour each year at the end of March and back 1 hour at the end of September.

Tipping   Restaurants and hotels will almost always include the 15% service charge and the whopping 21.5% value-added tax (TVA/BTW). So there's no need to do the quick math in your head and leave an extra tip—unless, that is, you've had really exceptional service and want to add a little more. Taxis include the tip in the meter reading.

Here is a general guide to tipping for other services: give 20 BF (65¢) to ushers in some theaters and cinemas, 20% of the bill for hairdressers (leave it with the cashier when you pay up), and 50 BF ($1.40) per piece of luggage for porters.

Brussels 5

In a way, there are two Brussels. One is the brash new "Capital of Europe," increasingly aware of its power and carrying a padded expense account in its elegant leather pocketbook. The other is the old Belgian city, once the seat of emperors, today more than a little provincial but still tenaciously hanging on to its heritage against the wave of Eurobuilding.

The two cities intersect, of course, often in someone's favorite bar or restaurant, but they sit uneasily together. Most foreigners who live in the city long enough, or even stay on an extended vacation, find that they need to choose between the two. As an outsider, it's easy enough to live in the Eurocity. Getting below the surface to the real Brussels is more difficult, though well worth the effort.

The Bruxellois like things convivial—ignoring, however, the red-clawed aggressiveness that consumes them while driving—and simple yet stylish. If you like deploying assorted items of cutlery over a proud regional specialty, feel at ease contemplating the consumption of a carefully crafted artisanal beer, or think that centuries-old traditions are not only worth keeping alive but also still have meaning today—why, then, you should fit right in.

1 Frommer's Favorite Brussels Experiences

- **See the Grand-Place for the First Time.** There's nothing in Brussels quite like strolling from one of its fairly ordinary side streets into the historic Grand-Place. You'll never forget your first look at this timelessly perfect cobbled square, surrounded by gabled guild houses and the Gothic tracery of the Hôtel de Ville (Town Hall) and Maison du Roi (King's House).
- **Watch the Son-et-Lumière on Summer Evenings in the Grand-Place.** This sound-and-light show in which a series of colored lamps on the Hôtel de Ville (Town Hall) are switched on and off in sequence to a piece of appropriately grand music is admittedly kind of kitsch. But who cares? It's also magical.
- **Shoot Manneken-Pis.** We mean with a camera, of course. Nobody can resist this statue of a gleefully piddling little boy. Should you be any different?
- **Dine at Comme Chez Soi.** This restaurant, with space for just 45 diners, has earned three Michelin stars. It's probably easier to get into the kingdom of heaven than master chef Pierre Wynants's

culinary holy-of-holies. If you do get a seat, though, you'll surely agree that heaven can wait.

- **Stand under the Seven Giant Spheres of the Atomium.** You'll hope that the seven giant spheres of this colossal representation of an atom won't fall on your head. Next to this monstrous model (it's 165 thousand million times bigger than the real thing) you'll be the one who feels like a microscopic particle.
- **Snap up a Bargain at the Flea Market.** Each day, from 7am to 2pm, the Marché-aux-Puces in place du Jeu de Balle offers everything from the weird to the wonderful at rock-bottom prices.
- **Shop for Antiques in place du Grand Sablon.** You'll be lucky if you score a bargain at this weekend antiques market—the dealers here are well aware of the precise worth of each item in their stock and are calmly determined to get it. But it's still fun to wander the market, browsing and haggling, and who knows? You just might stumble on that hard-to-find affordable treasure.
- **Meet with Bruegel and Magritte.** The Historic section of the Musées Royaux des Beaux-Arts (Royal Fine Arts Museums) has Bruegels such as *The Fall of Icarus* and *Winter Landscape with Ice Skaters,* along with works by Rubens, Bosch, Van Dyck, Jordaens, and others. Go underground to the Modern section for works by Magritte, Delvaux, Ensor, Rops, Alechinsky, and others.
- **Pig Out on Belgian Chocolates.** Those devilish little critters—handmade Belgian pralines—are so addictive they should be sold with a government health warning. Try the Wittamer chocolatier in place du Grand Sablon, and eat your fill.
- **Refight the Battle of Waterloo.** They actually do "refight" the battle in a reenactment held every 5 years on its anniversary (the next will be in 2000). Otherwise, settle for climbing the Lion Mound in the town of Braine L'Alleud, near Brussels (see "Waterloo," below), for a magnificent view over the theater of war.
- **Admire Art Nouveau.** Brussels considers itself the world capital of art nouveau. Local architect Victor Horta (1861–1947) was its foremost exponent. The master's colorful, sinuous style can be seen at his former home, now the Horta Museum, and in buildings around the city.
- **Go Underground for Art.** Most of Brussels's Métro stations have been "decorated" with a work of art—painting, sculpture, mosaic, or installation—by leading Belgian modern artists. Taken together, they form an underground museum that you can tour for the price of a Métro ticket.
- **Take a Ferry-Boat Trip.** The ferry in question is a tiny, electrically operated pontoon that makes the 1-minute crossing to Robinson's Island in the pond at the heart of the Bois de la Cambre.
- **Find the Lost River.** Believe it or not, Brussels is built on a river called the Senne. The City Fathers ordered it covered over in the 19th century, but traces of the missing river can still be seen.
- **Enjoy Opera at La Monnaie.** In 1830, Belgium's war of independence broke out during a performance at this graceful neoclassical theater, so you never can tell what an evening at the opera has in store.
- **Shop at the Galeries Royales St-Hubert.** The world's first shopping mall, opened in 1847, is a light and airy triple-gallery enclosing boutiques, bookshops, cafes, restaurants, and a theater and cinema.
- **Visit the Comic Strip Museum.** Thoughts of Superman and Batman should be set aside. Belgian comic-strip art is an altogether more sophisticated product, although its most famous creation, Hergé's *Tintin,* proves it can also be fun.

- **Stroll Around Europe.** Mini-Europe, that is, a collection of emblematic buildings from the European Union's 15 member nations. These include the Leaning Tower of Pisa, Big Ben, the Acropolis, the Arc de Triomphe, and the Brandenburg Gate, all in beautifully rendered 1:25-scale detail.
- **Drink Brussels Beer at Le Falstaff Cafe.** The design of this cafe is a fanciful mix of art nouveau, art deco, and rococo. Falstaff also boasts some of the most self-important waiters in the land. Ask them deferentially for a typical Brussels brew, such as *gueuze*.
- **Take a Hike.** Brussels is a green city, nowhere more so than in the Forêt de Soignes, which stretches from the Bois de la Cambre to Waterloo. This is a great place to escape maddening crowds and fuming traffic.

2 Orientation

ARRIVING

BY PLANE   **Brussels National Airport** is served by the Belgian national carrier Sabena, as well as virtually all major European airlines and many other international carriers. Brussels National is at Zaventem, 9 miles from the city center. There's a direct train service to Brussels's three main stations (Gare du Nord, Gare Centrale, and Gare du Midi), operating between 5:43am and 11:14pm, with a one-way fare of 140 BF ($3.90) in first class and 90 BF ($2.50) in second class. Tickets are available at all railway stations—you pay more if you buy your ticket on the train. The trip to Gare du Nord takes 20 minutes. The trains have wide corridors and extra space for baggage.

Don't hire a taxi from one of the illegal touts who may approach you as you leave the terminal building: You are likely to be overcharged. Go instead to the taxi stand and wait your turn for one of the many legitimate taxis. Those that display an orange sticker depicting a white airplane offer reduced fares from the airport to the city center; others will charge about 1,200 BF ($33.35), while some taxis offer reduced rates for a pre-booked return journey (ask your driver for details).

BY TRAIN   Brussels is well served by high-speed trains—the Eurostar through the Channel Tunnel from London and the Thalys connecting with Paris, Amsterdam, and Cologne. For Eurostar information and reservations, call ☎ **0345/ 303030** in Britain and **020/423-44-44** in Belgium. For Thalys information and reservations, call ☎ **0900/10-777** in Belgium; **08-3635 3536** in France; **0221/19419** in Germany; and **0900/9226** in Holland.

In addition, there are Trans-Europe Express (TEE), International (INT), and Eurocity (EC) international services connecting throughout Europe; and Intercity (IC), Inter-Regional (IR), and Local (L) services within Belgium (Amsterdam is also an IC destination from Brussels). For schedule and fare information on train travel in Belgium and abroad, call ☎ **02/555-25-25.** Tickets are sold at all stations and, in the case of Eurostar and Thalys tickets, at many travel agents. Timetables are available at all stations, and main stations have information and reservation desks.

There are five big railway stations in the Brussels metropolitan area. Travelers arriving from other European countries will probably want to get off at one of the three main stations: **Gare Centrale,** Carrefour de l'Europe 2; **Gare du Midi,** rue de France 2 (which is also the Eurostar and Thalys terminal); and **Gare du Nord,** rue du Progrès 86. Trains traveling within Belgium may also stop at **Gare du Quartier Léopold,** place du Luxembourg; and **Gare de Schaerbeek,** place Princesse Elisabeth 5 (which is also the international auto-rail terminal).

BY BUS   Eurolines operates one daily return service from London's Victoria Coach Station, via the Dover–Calais ferry or the Channel Tunnel's Le Shuttle train, to Brussels. For schedule and fare information on this service and on Eurolines's services from all other major towns and cities in Europe, contact Eurolines at ☎ **0582/404511** in Britain and **02/203-07-07** in Belgium. Most buses from continental destinations arrive in **rue Fonsny** beside Gare du Midi, although some stop at various city center locations around **place de Brouckère.** Many travel agents have schedules and fares. There are few really useful regional bus services within Belgium (trains do most of the work); most of those that do exist stop at **Gare du Nord.**

BY CAR   Anyone thinking of driving into Brussels would be well advised not to, or at any rate to park the car at the hotel parking lot (if it has one) and leave it there. You won't need your car to get around here.

VISITOR INFORMATION

Tourist Information Brussels (T.I.B.) is on the ground floor of the Hôtel de Ville (Town Hall) in the Grand-Place (☎ **02/513-89-40;** fax 02/514-45-38). T.I.B. provides very good tourist information, including the comprehensive visitors' booklet "Brussels Guide & Map." It also makes hotel reservations; organizes paid-for guided walking tours in summer; and has well-trained, multilingual tourist guides who may be engaged by the hour or day. The office is open in summer daily 9am to 6pm; and in winter Monday to Saturday 9am to 6pm, Sunday 10am to 2pm.

The **Belgian Tourism Center,** which covers the whole country, is located at rue du Marché-aux-Herbes 63 (☎ **02/504-03-90;** fax 02/504-02-70). It's open June to September, Monday to Saturday 9am to 7pm, Sunday 9am to 6pm; October to March, Monday to Saturday 9am to 6pm, and also Sunday 9am to 6pm during April, May, and October, and to 5pm November to March.

CITY LAYOUT

The heart-shaped inner city of Brussels—roughly 1½ miles in diameter, lying within the inner ring road that follows the line of the old city walls—is where most of the city's premier sightseeing attractions lie. Still, the 19 separate, self-governing *communes* (municipalities) composing the 62½ square miles of the Brussels Capital Region offer many sightseeing attractions of their own. Some 14% of the total area is occupied by parks, woods, and forest, making this one of Europe's greenest urban centers.

The city center, once ringed by fortified ramparts, is now encircled by broad boulevards known collectively as the **Petite Ceinture.** Brussels is flat in its center and western reaches, where the now-vanished River Senne once flowed. To the east a range of low hills rises to the upper city, which is crowned by the Royal Palace and has some of the city's most affluent residential and prestigious business and shopping districts. The **Grand-Place** (*Grote Markt* in Dutch) stands at the very heart of Brussels, and is both the starting-point and reference-point for most visitors. Brussels's excellent railway system runs almost directly through the middle of the city, with **Gare du Nord** (Noord Station) just across the northern rim of the Petite Ceinture, **Gare Centrale** (Central Station) in the city center not far from the Grand-Place, and **Gare du Midi** (Zuidstation) near the southern rim. The street signs are in both French and Dutch.

STREET MAPS   Go to the Tourist Information Office in Brussels and pick up its *Brussels Guide & Map,* which has a fairly detailed street map of the inner city, with principal tourist attractions marked. If you need a comprehensive street map, you can buy the *Géocart Bruxelles et Périphérie* at most news vendors and bookstores.

NEIGHBORHOODS IN BRIEF

Brussels, a city of nearly one million inhabitants, is divided into 19 *communes* (local government districts)—"Brussels" is both the name of the central commune and of the city as a whole (it's also the name of a larger entity called Brussels Capital Region, a kind of Brussels D.C.). However, from a visitor's perspective, the communes and their boundaries are less useful than a geographic and social slicing up of the city.

The city center itself can be divided into the main central area, around the **Grand-Place** (which includes the restaurant-intensive **Ilot Sacré** district); the **place du Grand Sablon;** and adjacent streets. Central Brussels also includes the **Marché-aux-Poissons** (Fish Market) and the **Haute Ville** (Upper City), east of and uphill from the Grand-Place, which runs along rue Royale and rue de la Régence to place Louise and av. Louise. This area abuts the working-class Marolles district.

Beyond the center things start to get hazier, as Brussels's communes don't have quite as distinct a character as, say, Paris's arrondissements or London's boroughs. On either side of **av. Louise,** which is itself a chic boulevard south of the city center, are the classy districts of **Ixelles** and **Uccle;** they're both good areas for restaurants and shopping and both border the wide green spaces of the **Bois de la Cambre** and the **Forêt de Soignes.**

East of the city center lies a part of Brussels whose denizens are regarded by many Bruxellois with the same suspicion they might apply to extra-terrestrials newly landed from Alpha Centauri. I refer, of course, to the **European Union district** around place Schuman, where the European Commission, Parliament, and Council of Ministers buildings jostle for space in a warren of offices populated by civil servants, journalists, and lobbyists (of course, the area is also home to cafes and restaurants that cater to Euro-appetites). A quaint old neighborhood has vanished to make way for these noble edifices.

North of the city center lies one of the city's three major train stations, **Gare du Nord,** and **place Rogier,** which is a public transportation hub and a home to hotels and boutiques. A big leap northward from here on the public transport network (and something of a leap of the imagination as well) brings you to the suburban **Bruparck** recreation zone. Inside this complex is the Mini-Europe theme park; the 26-screen Kinepolis cinema; an artificial village of shops, cafes, and restaurants; and the Océade water recreation center. Beside it is the Atomium, the Brussels Planetarium, the Heysel Soccer Stadium, and the Parc des Expositions exhibition center.

3 Getting Around

BY PUBLIC TRANSPORTATION

Maps of the integrated public transport network—métro, tram, and bus—are available free from the tourist office, from offices of the **S.T.I.B.** public transport company at Galérie de la Toison d'Or 20 (☎ **02/515-20-00**), and from the métro stations at Porte de Namur, place Rogier, and Gare du Midi. In addition, all stations and most bus and tram stops have maps. The full system operates from 6am to midnight, after which a limited night-bus system operates. If possible, avoid the crush at morning and evening rush hours. Watch out for pickpockets, especially at busy times, and try to avoid walking alone in deserted access tunnels, particularly after dark—the risk of being mugged is minimal but not entirely absent.

BY METRO   While not overly extensive, the dedicated métro (subway) system is fast and efficient, covering many important city-center locations on its 30-mile network, as well as reaching out to the suburbs and to the Heysel/Bruparck conference, exhibition, and recreation zone. Stations are identified by signs with a white letter "M" on a blue background. In this city, a descent underground takes you into an art center—métro stations are decorated with excellent specially commissioned paintings by contemporary Belgian artists. Métro and bus tickets can be used interchangeably (for ticket information, see "By Bus & Tram," below).

BY BUS & TRAM   An extensive network of tram routes offers the ideal way to get around Brussels. Trams are generally faster and more comfortable than buses. Trams and urban buses are yellow in color. Their stops are marked with red-and-white signs and often a shelter as well. You stop a tram or bus by extending your arm as it approaches so the driver can see it; if you don't signal, the bus or tram may not stop. Tickets—which can also be used on the métro—cost 50 BF ($1.40) for a single journey (known as a "direct"); 240 BF ($6.65) for a five-journey ticket bought from the driver; 330 BF ($9.15) for a ten-journey ticket available from métro stations and some other S.T.I.B. stations; and 130 BF ($3.60) for a 1-day ticket valid on all urban services.

You must validate your ticket by inserting it into the orange electronic machines that stand inside buses and trams and at the access to métro platforms. Though the ticket must be revalidated each time you enter a new vehicle, you are allowed multiple transfers within a 1-hour period of the initial validation, so you can hop on and off métros, trams, and buses during that time and only one journey will be canceled by the electronic scanner. If more than one person is traveling on one ticket, the ticket must be validated each time for each traveler.

Inter-Regional bus services, orange in color, operate to points outside Brussels and also stop within the city.

BY TAXI

The minimum rate for taxis is 95 BF ($2.65) during the day and 170 BF ($5.30) at night. Charges per kilometer vary from 38 BF ($1.05) to 76 BF ($2.10), depending on location and time. Tip and taxes are included in the meter price, and you need not add an extra tip unless there has been extra service, such as helping with heavy luggage, although naturally enough drivers won't refuse a tip in any circumstances. All taxis are metered. They cannot be hailed in the street, but there are taxi stands on many principal streets, particularly in the center, as well as at railway stations. To request a cab by phone, call **ATR** (☎ **02/647-22-22**); **Autolux** (☎ **02/411-12-21**); **Taxis Bleus** (☎ **02/268-00-00**); **Taxis Oranges** (☎ **02/513-62-00**); or **Taxis Verts** (☎ **02/349-49-49**).

BY CAR

Don't drive; it's a jungle out there. Good public transportation and the occasional taxi ride will get you anywhere you want inexpensively and hassle-free. Park your car either at your hotel or in one of the many public parking areas—the tourist office or your hotel can furnish the address of the nearest one—and do not set foot in it again until you're ready to leave the city. Belgium has some of Europe's worst road-accident statistics. Normally polite citizens of Brussels turn into red-eyed demons once they get behind the steering wheel. Driving is fast, except at rush hour, and always aggressive. At rush hour (which actually lasts about an hour to either side of 9am and 5pm) it is almost impossible to move on main roads inside the city and on the R0 outer ring road. Sundays and early mornings are better, and evenings are not too bad.

If you must drive, watch out for the notorious "priority from the right" system, whereby traffic merging from your right usually has priority (or right-of-way) to enter the road you're on. And always remember that Brussels drivers take their priority in any and all circumstances—be ready to stop instantly at all such intersections. At rotaries, traffic entering the rotary usually has priority over traffic already on it. Poles with orange diamond signs, which you see mostly on main roads, mean that priority lies with traffic already on the road, so you don't have to stop. This system has caused so much mayhem that it's being changed at some accident hotspots and obvious danger-zones—but not everyone knows about the changes or acts on them, so stay alert and be careful.

On-street parking meters have varying hours of operation and charges. City drivers should keep a supply of 5 BF and 20 BF coins on hand.

RENTALS   Rental cars are available from **Hertz** (☎ **800/654-3001** in the U.S.), which has offices at bd. Maurice Lemmonier 8 in Brussels and at Brussels National Airport (☎ **02/726-49-50**); and **Avis** (☎ **800/331-2112** in the U.S.), which has offices at rue Américaine 145 in Brussels and at Brussels National Airport (☎ **02/720-09-44**). Rates begin at about 1,800 BF ($49.85) for a small car with unlimited mileage (the per-day rate is less for longer rentals). Other rental companies include **Budget** (☎ **02/720-80-50**) and **Europcar** (☎ **02/348-92-12**), whose rates may be slightly less. See "Getting Around," in chapter 4, for more details.

ON FOOT

Brussels's city center is small enough that walking is a viable option—however, it's not tiny and traffic can be both heavy and frantic, adding up to a tiring experience. The best solution if you have several days is to slice your time into segments for walking tours. Otherwise, a combination of walking and using the excellent public transport system is best. Beyond the center, public transport is a virtual necessity.

Be especially careful when crossing roads at the black-and-white pedestrian crossings with no signals. Astonishingly, pedestrians at these crossings were only recently given legal priority over cars! Drivers might not yet be completely used to the new regulations. Also watch out for cars turning (legally) right or left at traffic lights, even when the green "walking man" indicates that you can cross.

4 Special-Interest Networks & Resources

FOR STUDENTS & YOUNG PEOPLE   **Infor-Jeunes Centre,** rue du Marché-aux-Herbes 27 (☎ **02/514-41-11**), is a useful contact point for information and advice. **SOS Jeunes,** rue Mercelis 27 (☎ **02/512-90-20**), is a 24-hour service for young people in emotional distress.

The following colleges have English-speaking staffs and can furnish details of student clubs and associations: **The Open University,** chaussée de Bruxelles 233, 1410 Waterloo (☎ **02/354-90-93**), offers various academic degrees via correspondence courses and tutorials; **Vesalius College,** 2 Pleinlaan, 1050 Brussels (☎ **02/ 629-21-11**), offers undergraduate degrees in 10 majors.

FOR GAY MEN & LESBIANS   For information, contact **Infor Homo,** av. de Roodebeek 57 (☎ **02/733-10-24**). The Brussels section of the *Best Guide to*

Amsterdam & the Benelux for Gay Men and Lesbians lists accommodations, bars, and nightclubs.

For health information, contact **Info AIDS** (☎ **02/5132-26-51**); or **CETIM** (Hospital Universitaire St-Pierre), rue Haute 322 (☎ **02/535-31-11**).

FOR WOMEN   Contact the **International Inner Wheel**, rue Royale 33 (☎ **02/219-30-60**), for information on weekly public meetings and other information of interest to women.

FOR SENIORS   For **urgent social assistance,** call ☎ **02/425-57-25.** See "Fast Facts: Brussels," below, for medical and safety emergency numbers.

FAST FACTS: Brussels

American Express   American Express International, Inc., is located at bd. du Souverain 100, 1000 Brussels (☎ **02/676-21-11**).

Area Code   Brussels's telephone area code is **02.** The country code for Belgium is **32.** If you're phoning a Brussels number from the United States or from any other country, you don't dial the first **0** of the area code; you dial only **32-2** followed by the subscriber number. You don't need to dial the area code at all if you're phoning a Brussels number from within the city; the subscriber number alone is enough. You dial the full area code only if you're phoning a Brussels number from elsewhere in Belgium.

Baby-Sitters   Many hotels can provide reliable baby-sitting service. A student baby-sitting roster is maintained by U.L.B. Service, "Jobs," CP 185, av. F. D. Roosevelt 50 (☎ **02/650-26-46**).

Business Hours   Banks are open Monday to Friday from 9am to 1pm and from 2 to 4:30pm. Shopping hours Monday to Saturday are from 9 or 10am (some shops, such as bakers and news vendors open earlier) to 6 or 7pm, with some shops also open the same hours on Sunday. Many shops stay open until 8 or 9pm on Friday.

Cinema   English-language films (mostly American) are rarely dubbed, but instead shown in English with French and Dutch subtitles.

Currency Exchange   All banks and major train stations have currency-exchange facilities. Banks generally offer the best rates, but the station exchanges come close. Street *bureaux de change* offer poorer rates and may charge high commissions, but unlike banks, these are open in the evenings and on weekends. **American Express** (see above) and **Thomas Cook,** rue de la Montagne 6 (☎ **02/503-31-38**) offer fair rates. Most hotels will also exchange currency but usually at poor rates.

Dentists   For emergency dental care, you can reach a local dental referral service at ☎ **02/426-10-26** or 02/428-58-58. The staff can locate an English-speaking dentist for you.

Doctors   For emergency medical service in the Greater Brussels area (around the clock), dial ☎ **02/479-18-18.** Be sure to explain that you want an English-speaking doctor.

Embassies/Consulates   See "Fast Facts: Belgium" in chapter 4.

Emergencies   In case of accident, call ☎ **100.** For day or night emergency medical service, call ☎ **02/479-18-18** or 02/648-80-00; for police assistance, call ☎ **101;** for fire and ambulance, ☎ **100.**

Language   Many Belgians speak fluent English, and almost all speak at least some. And unlike Parisians, for example, most are happy to speak English. Shops, restaurants, and hotels are usually staffed by at least one or two fluent English-speakers.

Lost Property   The baggage office in the arrivals hall of Brussels National Airport can help if you have lost luggage or other property aboard an aircraft (☎ **02/723-60-11** or 02/723-39-29); for property lost within the airport, go to the Brussels Terminal Company (B.T.C.) office (☎ **02/753-68-20**). The bigger railway stations have lost-property offices as well; call ☎ **02/555-25-25** if you lose something on a train. Property lost on the métro, tram, or bus may be recovered from S.T.I.B., av. de la Toison d'Or 15 (☎ **02/515-23-94**). If you lose something in the street, try the local police station; many Belgians are honest enough to hand in property they've found.

Newspapers/Magazines   News vendors at railway stations and many other locations have the *International Herald Tribune* and *USA Today* on sale Monday through Saturday; *Time, Newsweek,* and *US News & World Report* are available weekly; and other U.S. business and consumer magazines are also widely available. All national daily and Sunday British newspapers are sold here as well. For English-speaking visitors, the most useful publication is the weekly magazine **The Bulletin,** published each Thursday and filled with news, articles, information on special events, and useful addresses.

Police   In an emergency, call ☎ **101.** For nonemergencies, **Brussels Central Police Station** is at rue du Marché-au-Charbon 30 (☎ **02/517-96-11**).

Post Office   The post office at Gare du Midi, av. Fonsny 48a, is open 24 hours every day. Others are open from 9am to 5pm Monday through Friday and are closed weekends and public holidays; the office in the Centre Monnaie shopping and business center in the city center is also open on Saturday from 9am to 1pm. Conveniently located post offices are at Centre Monnaie, Gare Centrale, Gare du Nord, rue du Progrès 80, the Bourse, and the Palais de Justice.

Radio/Television   You'll hear French, Dutch, and German on television and radio, as well as the occasional imported English-language program. Some American-produced television shows are dubbed into another language, which can be quite entertaining. BBC World Service Radio is broadcast on medium wave throughout the day, while BBC Radio 4 can be picked up with fairly good reception on long wave.

Safety   Brussels is generally a safe city. It came out on top in a recent European Union survey of murders per million inhabitants in various cities, with 4 murders per million, compared with Amsterdam's 77, London's 21, and Washington, D.C.'s 693. There is, however, a growing trend toward crime, particularly pickpocketing, theft from cars, and muggings in places such as métro station foot tunnels. Don't exaggerate the risk, but take sensible precautions, particularly in obvious circumstances such as on packed métro trains or when withdrawing cash from an ATM at night.

Taxes   Restaurants and hotels usually include a 16% service charge, as well as a whopping 21.5% value-added tax (known as TVA and BTW in Belgium). This tax is also an unwelcome addition to any purchase, but you may be able to recover it from some shops by having the official receipt stamped by Belgian Customs on departure and returning the stamped receipt to the shop. Your refund should arrive by check or be credited to your credit card within a few weeks. Not all shops participate in this scheme so it pays to ask first, particularly for major purchases.

Tipping A service charge is included on most, though not all, restaurant bills. In this case, it's enough to round up the bill to the nearest convenient amount, if you wish, rather than leave a full-fledged tip. Otherwise, 10% is adequate, and more than most Belgians would leave.

5 Accommodations

Brussels has good accommodations in every price range, including deluxe hotels of just about every international chain, as well as new or remodeled Belgian establishments. There's actually a glut of hotel rooms, mainly for business travelers, which potentially means special discounted rates on weekends and during July and August—be sure to ask. All rates include the value-added tax, a service charge, and often a complimentary continental or buffet breakfast.

Both Tourist Information Brussels (T.I.B.) and the Belgian Tourism Center (see "Visitor Information," above) will make reservations for the same day if you go to their offices in person and pay a small fee (which is then deducted by the hotel from their room rate). **Belgian Tourist Reservations,** bd. Anspach 111, 1000 Brussels (☎ 02/513-74-84; fax 02/513-92-77), provides a similar service. The T.I.B. publishes an annual *Hotel Guide* with listings organized by price range and can also provide complete information on the **hostels** of Brussels.

When booking, you should confirm your reservation in writing, stating the length of time you expect to stay, the exact date and approximate time of your arrival, the desired number of rooms, the type of bed (single or double), the preferred location in the building (if you require a view of the garden, river, etc.), and whether you require a private bathroom.

The **Hotel Reservation Service** (☎ and fax **02/534-70-40**), located in a tiny booth in the Gare Centrale, near the Meeting Point (and near the steps leading to the restrooms), can make room reservations in Brussels and throughout Europe in one- to five-star hotels for a flat fee of 100 BF ($2.80) per group in Brussels and 200 BF ($5.55) for other European locations. The booth is open 7 days a week, from 9am to 9pm in summer, 10am to 8pm in winter. This is a private firm staffed with English-speaking personnel, who can find you a room even on days when Brussels appears sold out. The métro station is conveniently located around the corner (you don't even have to leave the building to reach it).

Note that all of the recommended accommodations below come with private bathroom unless otherwise noted. For a map of Brussels accommodations, see pages 76–77.

IN THE CITY CENTER
VERY EXPENSIVE

Hôtel Amigo. rue de l'Amigo 1–3 (behind the Bourse), 1000 Brussels. ☎ **02/547-47-47.** Fax 02/513-52-77. www.hotelamigo.com. E-mail: hotelamigo@hotelamigo.com. 185 units. MINIBAR TV TEL. 8,900–11,500 BF ($247.20–$319.45) double; suites from 15,500 BF ($430.55) and up. Rates include continental breakfast. AE, DC, JCB, MC, V. Parking 490 BF ($13.60). Métro: Bourse.

In old Brussels slang, an "amigo" is a prison, and indeed there was once a prison on the site of this hotel. But don't worry—any resemblance to the old amigo is purely in the name. This superb hotel has the most convenient location in town—just 1 block off of the Grand-Place. Although the hotel's Spanish Renaissance architecture is right at home in this ancient neighborhood, the hotel dates back only to 1958. Its flagstone lobby, clubby bar, small restaurant, and other public rooms are the epitome of understated good taste, with lots of Oriental rugs, antiques, wall tapestries, and wood accents. The rooms are fairly spacious and elegantly appointed, and service from the friendly, efficient staff is as deluxe as the hotel itself. Around 120 rooms (two-thirds) have air-conditioning, and all have hair dryers.

Dining/Diversions: A bar and a small restaurant are on the premises.

Amenities: Concierge, 24-hour room service, laundry and dry cleaning service.

✪ **Radisson SAS Hotel Brussels.** rue du Fossé-aux-Loups 47 (close to Gare Centrale). ☎ **0800/333-3333** or 02/219-28-28. Fax 02/219-62-62. www.radisson.com/brussels.be. 281 units. A/C MINIBAR TV TEL. 12,000 BF ($333.35) double; suites from 18,000 BF ($500) and way up. AE, CB, DISC, DC, MC, V. Parking 770 BF ($21.40). Métro: Gare Centrale.

The Radisson SAS is modern but in a way that still seems in keeping with its neighborhood, just a few streets away from the Grand-Place. Despite its modern facilities and design, the hotel retains its classic elements and even incorporates a part of a medieval wall. There's a huge atrium with cafe terraces and fountains, and some of the rooms look out on the atrium rather than the "outside world." The rooms lack nothing that a modern luxury hotel can provide and are designed in a variety of styles. Some are "Scandinavian," chic and modern; some are stylishly "Italian"; some "Oriental," with rattan and bamboo as the decorative motif; and some are plushly upholstered "Royal Club."

Dining/Diversions: The very fine Sea Grill restaurant specializes, of course, in seafood; the Atrium serves Belgian and Scandinavian specialties; and the attached Henry J. Bean's is an American-style bar and grill that has already become an institution among locals and expats alike.

Amenities: Concierge, 24-hour room service, laundry and dry cleaning service, newspaper delivery, twice-daily maid service, baby-sitting, secretarial services, express checkout, valet parking, courtesy car, health club, Jacuzzi, sauna, business center, conference rooms.

✪ **Royal Windsor Hotel.** rue Duquesnoy 5 (between Grand-Place and Gare Centrale), 1000 Brussels. ☎ **0800/203-3232** or 02/505-55-55. Fax 02/505-55-00. 266 units. A/C MINIBAR TV TEL. 11,000 BF ($305.55) double; suites from 18,200 BF ($505.55). AE, CB, DC, MC, V. Parking 490 BF ($13.60). Métro: Gare Centrale.

This sparkling modern hotel, only 2½ short blocks from the Grand-Place, incorporates marble, polished wood, and gleaming brass and copper in its decor. The tone of elegance is set from the very first by the lobby and the huge circular medallion on the wall behind the reception desk that depicts all the Duke of Wellington's major battles. All rooms are luxuriously furnished, but some are a bit on the small side, though none is really cramped. The elegant bathrooms have such extras as hair dryers and scales.

Dining/Diversions: In Les 4 Saisons restaurant, gourmet meals are served in a graceful setting. Then there's the Edwardian-style Windsor Arms, where light lunches and snacks are available amid lots of polished mahogany, etched glass, and leather upholstery. You can drink at the Waterloo Bar and dance until the wee hours at the Griffin's nightclub.

Amenities: Concierge, 24-hour room service, laundry service, newspaper delivery, in-room massage, baby-sitting, secretarial services, express checkout, valet parking, health club, sauna, business center, conference rooms, car-rental desk, tour desk.

EXPENSIVE

Hôtel Bedford. rue du Midi 135 (near place Rouppe), 1000 Brussels. ☎ 02/512-78-40. Fax 02/514-17-59. E-mail: hotelbedfordb@pophost.eunet.be. 297 units. MINIBAR TV TEL. 6,800–8,650 BF ($188.90–$240.30) double. Rates include full breakfast. AE, DC, MC, V. Parking 350 BF ($9.70). Métro: Anneessens.

This modern hotel is an easy walk from the Grand-Place. Its public areas, which include a bar and a restaurant, Le Magellan, are tastefully decorated, the lobby reminiscent of an English country house. Each of the attractive guest rooms has a private bathroom, hair dryer, and radio. More than 100 rooms have been refurbished recently and are furnished in a modern style. Some rooms have air-conditioning, and all have hair dryers. A piano bar, the Bedford Lounge, serves a good selection of Belgian beers. Laundry, dry-cleaning, a gift shop, and a sheltered parking lot are available.

Jolly Hotel Atlanta. bd. Adolphe-Max 7, 1000 Brussels. ☎ 800/221-2626 or 02/217-01-20. Fax 02/217-37-58. 242 units. MINIBAR TV TEL. 9,300 BF ($258.35) double; 14,000–17,000 BF ($388.90–$472.20) suite. Children under 12 stay free in parents' room. Rates include breakfast. Weekend discounts available. AE, DC, JCB, MC, V. Parking 700 BF ($19.45). Métro: De Brouckère.

The prestigious Jolly hotel chain based in Italy has transformed this Brussels landmark into a model of modern comfort and sophisticated decor. Its location couldn't be better for shopping, and the Grand-Place is only a few minutes' walk away. Room amenities include an extra telephone in the bathroom and hair dryers.

Dining/Diversions: An outstanding breakfast is served in the window-walled rooftop dining room overlooking the city, and the cozy lounge off the lobby features piano music as well as light snacks.

Amenities: 24-hour room service, laundry and dry cleaning service; meeting rooms.

✪ **Le Dixseptième.** rue de la Madeleine 25, 1000 Brussels. ☎ 02/502-57-44. Fax 02/502-64-24. 24 units. MINIBAR TV TEL. 6,600 BF ($183) studio; 9,800–13,600 BF ($272.20–$377.75) suite. AE, DC, MC, V. Limited parking available on street. Métro: Gare Centrale.

Le Dixseptième, one of Brussels's delights, is located close to the Grand-Place in a neighborhood of restored houses. Its rooms are big enough to be more like suites than ordinary rooms and some have balconies. All are designed in 18th-century style, with wood paneling and marble chimneys, and are named after famous Belgian painters from Brueghel to Magritte. Two beautiful lounges are decorated with carved wooden medallions and 18th-century paintings.

✪ **Métropole.** place de Brouckère 31 (near the Centre Monnaie), 1000 Brussels. ☎ 02/217-23-00. Fax 02/218-02-20. www.metropolehotel.be. E-mail: info@metropolehotel.be. 400 units, 10 suites. A/C MINIBAR TV TEL. 11,000 BF ($305.55) double; 15,000 BF ($416.65) suite. Rates include full or continental breakfast. AE, CB, JCB, MC, V. Parking 500 BF ($13.90). Métro: De Brouckère.

This classic old-world hotel dates from the late 1800s. Its splendidly ornate interior is a turn-of-the-century showcase of marble, gilt, soaring ceilings, potted palms, and lavishly decorated public rooms. What's more, the Métropole is located right in the middle of the city center, with popular shopping just out the back door and the Grand-Place only a few blocks away. The corridors and the spacious rooms with classic furnishings harken back to former days. Even if you don't stay at the hotel, it's well worth visiting, just for its own precious sense of itself. Approximately 50 rooms have recently been refurbished.

Dining: The elegant L'Alban Chambon restaurant caters to the sophisticated gourmet, and the extravagant Victorian Café Métropole (see "Dining," later in this chapter), complete with gas lamps, is charming. There's also a heated sidewalk terrace, which creates its own sense of occasion, although the outlook on a busy street is uninspiring.

Amenities: Concierge, 24-hour room service, laundry and dry cleaning service, newspaper delivery, twice-daily maid service, baby-sitting, secretarial services, express checkout, valet parking, health club, Jacuzzi, sauna, business center, conference rooms, car-rental desk.

MODERATE

✪ **Arlequin.** rue de la Fourche 17–19 (near the Grand-Place), 1000 Brussels. ☎ **02/514-16-15.** Fax 02/514-22-02. E-mail: arlequin@skynet.be. 70 units. TV TEL. 3,850–4,200 BF ($106.95–$116.65) double; 4,250–6,000 BF ($118.05–$166.65) suite. Rates include buffet breakfast. AE, DC, MC, V. Parking 720 BF ($20) in nearby lot. Métro: Bourse.

Among moderately priced hotels, the Arlequin rates high on several counts. First, it's in the very heart of the city, with the restaurant-lined Petite rue des Bouchers right outside its back entrance. Then there's the fine view of the Town Hall spire (spectacular when lit at night) that overlooks rooftops and narrow medieval streets. The guest rooms are rather plain, but most have plenty of natural light and modern, comfortable furnishings. Hair dryers are available.

IN THE AV. LOUISE AREA
VERY EXPENSIVE

✪ **Conrad.** av. Louise 71, 1000 Brussels. ☎ **02/542-42-42.** Fax 02/542-42-00. 269 units, 15 suites. A/C MINIBAR TV TEL. 15,000 BF ($416.65) double; suites 30,000 BF ($833.35) and up. AE, DC, MC, V. Parking 450 BF ($12.50). Métro: Louise.

Big, bright, and fancy, the Conrad occupies a prime location on stylish av. Louise, set back a little from the road. Its architecture is the latest in luxury hotel design, with enough sparkling white marble to restore the Acropolis. Rooms are spacious, and furnishings maintain a classical feel that would have suited one of the great luxury liners of the past. His-and-hers bathrobes, trouser presses, hair dryers, and ice makers are just some of the additional fixtures and fittings gracing the guest rooms. The bathtubs are uncommonly huge.

Dining: The French restaurant La Maison du Maître offers all the refinements of haute cuisine, while the Café Wiltshire maintains a less formal tone.

Amenities: Concierge, 24-hour room service, laundry and dry cleaning, newspaper delivery, baby-sitting, secretarial services, express checkout, valet parking, courtesy car, health club, Jacuzzi, sauna, business center, conference rooms.

✪ **Stanhope.** rue du Commerce 9 (parallel to av. des Arts), 1000 Brussels. ☎ **02/506-91-11.** Fax 02/512-17-08. 50 units. A/C MINIBAR TV TEL. 9,900–14,900 BF ($275–$413.90) double. Rates include full breakfast. AE, DC, MC, V. Parking 300 BF ($8.35). Métro: Trone.

An old convent in the upmarket shopping district around av. Louise and Porte de Namur has been transformed into a graceful and memorable hotel. The ambiance of the Stanhope seems to combine that of a country retreat with a prime metropolitan location. All the guest rooms are individually decorated in variations of Old English style. The rooms each have two television sets and three telephones, which may not be a typically Old English touch, but is certainly convenient.

Dining/Diversions: The Brighton restaurant (closed on weekends) has a business-lunch menu for 1,350 BF ($37.50). The cuisine here, contrary to the hotel's English image, is French (dinner is also served). In addition there's a tearoom and a bar.

Amenities: Concierge, 24-hour room service, laundry and dry cleaning, newspaper delivery, in-room massage, twice-daily maid service, baby-sitting, secretarial services, express checkout, valet parking, courtesy car, health club, Jacuzzi, sauna, conference rooms, car-rental desk, tour desk.

EXPENSIVE

Bristol Stéphanie. av. Louise 91–93, 1050 Brussels. ☎ **02/543-33-11.** Fax 02/538-03-07. 142 units. A/C MINIBAR TV TEL. 10,200 BF ($283.35) double; suites from 18,500 BF ($513.90) and up. AE, DC, MC, V. Parking 350 BF ($9.70). Métro: Louise.

This sleekly modern hotel looks as if it was designed for the 21st century. Every feature—from lobby design and fittings to furnishings in the kitchenette suites—is streamlined, functional, and representative of the very best in avant-garde planning. The Bristol Stéphanie is located in a pretty section of av. Louise, one of the city's most select shopping streets. Its rooms include a lovely roof-garden suite and the luxurious Connoisseur Rooms, as well as the spacious Classic Rooms, some of which feature kitchenettes.

Dining: The Gourmet Restaurant has both a French and an international menu.

Amenities: Concierge, 24-hour room service, laundry and dry cleaning, babysitting, secretarial services, express checkout, heated indoor pool, health club, Jacuzzi, sauna, business center, conference rooms.

MODERATE

Cascade. rue Berckmans 128, 1060 Brussels. ☎ **02/538-88-30.** Fax 02/538-92-79. 80 units, 1 suite. A/C MINIBAR TV TEL. 3,000–6,000 BF ($83.35–$166.65) double. Rates include breakfast. AE, DC, MC, V. Free parking. Métro: Hôtel des Monnaies.

This new hotel, close to the upmarket shopping district around av. Louise, offers excellently equipped rooms and four-star service, in spite of its official three-star classification. Rooms are outfitted with blue carpeting and light pine furnishings, and the colors of the curtains and bedspreads recall a sunset at sea. Bathrooms are equipped with hair dryers. The hotel doesn't have a restaurant and separate bar, but there are plenty of restaurants and bars in the vicinity. In good weather, breakfast is served on the courtyard terrace.

Clubhouse Hotel. rue Blanche 4, 1050 Brussels. ☎ **02/537-92-10.** Fax 02/537-00-18. 81 units. MINIBAR TV TEL. 4,100–6,900 BF ($113.90–$191.65) double; 12,500 BF ($347.20) suite. Rates include buffet breakfast. AE, DC, MC, V. Limited parking available on street. Métro: Louise.

This small gem near the fashionable av. Louise offers typically English country house decor, down to the fireplace in the lobby. The spacious, attractively furnished rooms all have private bathrooms, hair dryers, writing desks, and trouser presses. Some have kitchenettes. An English-style buffet breakfast is served in a pleasant and intimate dining room—so if you like your ham 'n' eggs done with a touch of class, this could be the place for you.

INEXPENSIVE

Hôtel de Boeck. rue Veydt 40 (a 10-minute walk from place Louise), 1050 Brussels. ☎ **02/537-40-33.** Fax 02/534-40-37. 35 units. 1,600–3,200 BF ($44.45–$88.90) double. Additional person 720 BF ($20) extra. Rates include buffet breakfast. AE, DC, MC, V. Limited parking available on street. Métro: Louise.

This hotel has extra-spacious, adequately furnished rooms. Some have color TV and phone. About half the rooms can accommodate four or five, making the Hôtel de Boeck ideal for small groups and families.

Hôtel L'Agenda. rue de Florence 6, 1000 Brussels. ☎ **02/539-00-31.** Fax 02/539-00-63. 38 units. MINIBAR TV TEL. 3,000–3,600 BF ($83.35–$100) double; 4,100 BF ($113.90) suite. AE, DC, MC, V. Parking 200 BF ($5.55). Métro: Louise.

This exquisite little hotel is just steps away from av. Louise. Its very modern rooms were last redecorated in 1996 with light-colored wood furniture and gold and orange curtains and fittings. All have coffeemakers and come with complete kitchens. The bathrooms are equipped with hair dryers. Ask for a room that overlooks the inner courtyard for the best view.

✪ **Les Bluets.** rue Berckmans 124, 1060 Brussels. ☎ **02/534-39-83.** Fax 02/534-39-83. 17 units. TV TEL. 1,250–2,450 BF ($34.70–$68.05) double. Rates include breakfast. AE, MC, V. Limited parking available on street. Métro: Hôtel des Monnaies.

Les Bluets is a sweet place, a fine old family hotel in a building that dates from 1864. It's run by a proprietress who looks on her guests almost as members of the family. The decor is memorable. Furnishings appear to have been selected from Brussels's fine antiques shops and flea markets, by someone with an eclectic—not to say eccentric—taste in periods, styles, and ornamentation.

IN THE UPPER CITY
VERY EXPENSIVE

Royal Crown Hotel Brussels. rue Royale 250 (adjacent to the Botanique), 1210 Brussels. ☎ **02/220-66-11.** Fax 02/217-84-44. 307 units, 8 suites. A/C MINIBAR TV TEL. 9,300 BF ($258.35) double; suites from 11,900 BF ($330.55) and up. AE, DC, MC, V. Parking 400 BF ($11.10). Métro: Botanique.

This fine luxury hotel has an ideal location for exploring both the "old Brussels" of the city center and the newer "upper city." The public rooms are elegantly modern, with lots of mirrors, marble, and crystal chandeliers. The guest rooms are somewhat smaller than in other hotels of this category, but all are attractively and comfortably furnished. All rooms have hair dryers.

Dining/Diversions: Hugo's, a gourmet restaurant, features French cuisine. Hugo's Cocktail Lounge serves drinks.

Amenities: Concierge, 24-hour room service, secretarial services, dry cleaning and laundry service, baby-sitting, solarium.

EXPENSIVE

✪ **Astoria.** rue Royale 103 (near the Colonne du Congrès), 1000 Brussels. ☎ **800/SOFITEL** or 02/227-0505. Fax 02/217-11-50. E-mail: info.bxl.astoria@sofitel.be. 118 units. A/C MINIBAR TV TEL. 8,000 BF ($222.20) double; 14,000 BF ($388.90) suite. AE, CB, DC, MC, V. Valet parking 600 BF ($16.65). Métro: Botanique.

This gem of a hotel is one of Brussels's premier lodging experiences. From the minute you walk into the belle époque foyer, you're transported into a more elegant, less hurried age. The hotel dates from 1909, just a few short years before Europe's age of innocence ended with World War I, and its plush ambiance recalls the panache of that lost heyday—but is updated with the latest fixtures and fittings. The sumptuous surroundings feature Corinthian columns, antique furnishings, and textured marble. The comfortable Pullman Bar, just off of the lobby, is similarly ornate, its decor based on that of the Orient Express restaurant. The guest rooms are attractively furnished in a style in keeping with the overall character of the hotel, although not extravagantly so. All have hair dryers.

Dining/Diversions: Le Palais Royal serves mostly French fare. The Pullman Bar serves bar food, including cold-cut sandwiches, salads, croques monsieur (toasted ham-and-cheese sandwiches), and smoked salmon.

Amenities: Concierge, 24-hour room service, laundry and dry cleaning service, newspaper delivery, baby-sitting, twice-daily maid service, secretarial services, express checkout, valet parking, health club, business center, conference rooms.

MODERATE

Lambermont. bd. Lambermont 322, 1030 Brussels. ☎ **02/242-55-95**. Fax 02/215-36-13. 43 units. TV TEL. 2,800–3,900 BF ($77.80–$108.35) double. Rates include breakfast. Limited parking available on street. AE, DC, MC, V. Tram: 23.

This is a good choice for anyone with a car who doesn't want to drive into the city center but doesn't want to be out in the boonies either. The Lambermont is on one of the main roads leading to the R0 ring road in the northern Schaerbeek district. You can get to the center on the nos. 65 or 66 buses, and to av. Louise for shopping and to the Bruparck recreation area on the 23 tram. The hotel is modern, with good facilities, including tennis courts, a short distance away. The rooms are relatively small yet are well equipped. There's a small but cozy bar downstairs.

INEXPENSIVE

Hôtel Sabina. rue du Nord 78 (adjacent to place des Barricades), 1000 Brussels. ☎ **02/218-26-37**. Fax 02/219-32-39. 24 units. TV TEL. 2,400 BF ($66.65) double. Rates include buffet breakfast. AE, DC, MC, V. Limited parking available on street. Métro: Madou.

This small hotel is like a private residence. The owners are friendly and hospitable. Although rooms vary in size, all are quite comfortable and simply yet tastefully done in modern style and pastel tones, with twin beds side-by-side against a laminate headboard. Three of the rooms have kitchenettes for 100 BF ($2.80) extra. All rooms have hair dryers. The old grandfather clock in the reception area and the polished wood along the walls of the restaurant give the place a warm, homey atmosphere.

IN THE PLACE ROGIER AREA
MODERATE

✪ **Albert Premier.** place Rogier 20 (beside Gare du Nord), 1210 Brussels. ☎ **02/203-31-25**. Fax 02/203-43-31. 285 units. MINIBAR TV TEL. 3,000–5,000 BF ($83.35–$138.90) double. Rates include buffet breakfast. DC, MC, V. Limited parking available on street. Métro: Rogier.

This grand old duke—king, really, as it bears the name of Belgium's King Albert I—of Brussels's hotels is now fully renovated inside, though it retains its graceful 19th-century facade. The hotel's fortunes have risen with those of its surroundings. Finally, things in this once-elegant, then seedy, neighborhood on the edge of the city center have been turned around—it's now a busy business and administrative area. The rooms are minimalist in terms of facilities, but modern, comfortable, and attractively decorated. There's a fine restaurant on the premises.

✪ **Art Hotel Siru.** place Rogier 1, 1210 Brussels. ☎ **02/203-35-80**. Fax 02/203-33-03. 101 units. MINIBAR TV TEL. 3,900–6,200 BF ($108.35–$172.20) double. Rates include buffet breakfast. AE, DC, MC, V. Parking 425 BF ($11.80). Métro: Rogier.

This is a fascinating mid-sized hotel in an area that was formerly rundown—it used to be a red-light district and still has some peep-show joints and offbeat appliances shops—but has been going upmarket fast since a slew of fancy office blocks were built nearby. What sets the Siru apart is that its owner has persuaded 130 contemporary Belgian artists, including some of the country's biggest names, to "decorate" each room and some corridors with a work on the theme of travel. Given the unpredictable nature of reactions to modern art, some clients apparently reserve the same room time after time, while others ask for a room change in the middle of the night. In any case, this hotel is not easily forgotten, and the rooms themselves are cool and modern. All have hair dryers.

IN THE MARCHÉ-AUX-POISSONS AREA
MODERATE

Hôtel Vendôme. bd. Adolphe-Max 98, 1000 Brussels. ☎ **02/227-03-00.** Fax 02/218-06-83. 106 units. MINIBAR TV TEL. 4,850–6,250 BF ($134.70–$173.60) double. Rates include buffet breakfast. AE, DC, MC, V. Parking 550 BF ($15.30). Métro: De Brouckère or Rogier.

This is one of Brussels's most conveniently located moderately priced hotels, a short walk from good shopping, slightly farther to the Grand-Place. The rooms are rather plain but comfortably furnished. Breakfast is served in the cheerful, greenery-filled winter garden, which has a skylight to shed natural light. "Business Club" rooms are newer and larger and have air-conditioning, and all rooms have hair dryers.

Ibis Brussels City. rue Joseph-Plateau 2 (beside place Ste-Catherine), 1000 Brussels. ☎ **02/513-76-20.** Fax 02/514-22-14. 235 units. TV TEL. 3,600 BF ($100) double. AE, DC, MC, V. Limited parking available on street. Métro: Ste-Catherine.

This large, modern hotel in the fascinating (and central) "fish market" district is a member of one of Europe's leading budget-priced chains. The rooms are brightly furnished, and bathrooms are being fully renovated in the course of 1999. There's also a children's play area.

INEXPENSIVE

George V. rue 't Kint 23 (beside place du Jardin-aux-Fleurs), 1000 Brussels. ☎ **02/513-50-93.** Fax 02/513-44-93. 16 units. TV TEL. 2,200–2,500 BF ($61.10–$69.45) double. Rates include breakfast. MC, V. Parking 250 BF ($6.95). Métro: Bourse.

The "George" is in a less-than-appealing part of the city center, but one that looks more rundown than it actually is. In any case, the place is within fairly easy walking distance of the Bourse and Grand-Place and offers prices that are hard to beat (as well as a free shuttle-bus service to Gare du Midi, the Grand-Place, and the main museums). The facilities are straightforward but clean, and the owner is a genuine enthusiast for his hotel and his guests. A free drink offered to each guest at the nearby In 't Spinnekopke restaurant (see "Dining," below) should be all the excuse you need to visit that unparalleled source of fine traditional Belgian cuisine. With the purchase of the building next door, the George V should add 8 to 12 more rooms during 1999.

Hôtel Pacific. rue Antoine Dansaert 57 (street facing the Bourse), 1000 Brussels. ☎ and fax **02/511-84-59.** 18 units (some without bathroom). 1,650–2,150 BF ($45.85–$59.70) double. Showers 100 BF ($2.80) extra for those in rooms without bathrooms. Rates include breakfast. No credit cards. Limited parking available on street. Métro: Bourse.

This good-value hotel has a friendly, soft-spoken owner, named Paul Pauwels, and an unbeatable location, just a 5-minute walk from the Grand-Place and 2 blocks from the Bourse. Most rooms are large, with plumbing fixtures dating from 80 years ago. Breakfast is served at street level in a fin-de-siècle room eclectically decorated with a zebra skin, a Canadian World War II steel helmet, railway signal lamps, copper pots, and a Buddhist prayer wheel.

✪ **Hôtel Welcome.** rue du Peuplier 5, 1000 Brussels. ☎ **02/219-95-46.** Fax 02/217-18-87. 6 units. A/C MINIBAR TV TEL. 2,700–3,200 BF ($75–$88.90) double. AE, DC, MC, V. Limited parking available on street. Métro: Ste-Catherine.

ⓘ   Family-Friendly Hotels

Ibis Brussels City *(see p. 73)*   This hotel in the fish market area is a member of a European chain known for its affordability and value. This one caters to families especially. It has a children's play area to keep the tots amused while parents are relaxing.

Jolly Hotel Atlanta *(see p. 68)*   This hotel has moderate rates, an excellent location near the Grand-Place, and a policy allowing children under 12 to stay in their parents' room for free.

Hôtel de Boeck *(see p. 70)*   This family favorite near place Louise has huge, well-furnished rooms—they don't necessarily have all the latest amenities, but the whole family can stay in one room in considerable comfort.

Les Bluets *(see p. 71)*   The remarkably hospitable proprietress of this hotel will make your family feel like members of *her* family.

It would be hard to imagine a smaller hotel (it's the smallest in Brussels), or one that inspires fonder memories. Regular guests are loyal enough that the hotel is often fully booked—admittedly not a difficult feat—so you should reserve well in advance. The owners, an enthusiastic couple named Michel and Sophie Smeesters, have created bright, cheerful guest rooms. A superb seafood restaurant, La Truite d'Argent (see "Dining," below), is attached—it's one of the best in the fish-market area. A small tiled dining room is the setting for breakfast and, in the evening, for guests who prefer not to dine in the main restaurant. Amenities include room safes, trouser presses, and hair dryers.

PRIVATE HOMES

Brussels has several excellent bed-and-breakfast organizations that pair visitors with host families who rent rooms in their homes: **Bed & Breakfast Taxistop,** rue du Fossée-aux-Loups 28, 1000 Brussels (☎ 02/223-22-31; fax 02/223-22-32); **Bed & Brussels,** rue V. Greyson 58, 1050 Brussels (☎ 02/646-07-37; fax 02/644-01-14); and **Windrose,** av. Paul Dejaer 21a, 1060 Brussels (☎ 02/534-71-91; fax 02/534-71-92). All will send you a list of host families (the Windrose includes a personal profile of the families) and the rates charged. There's a booking fee of 500 BF ($16.65) per reservation, and rates vary from 1,600–2,200 BF ($44.45–$61.10) for a double. Phone or fax them for more details.

6 Dining

Food is a passion in Brussels, which boasts more Michelin-star restaurants per head than Paris. People here regard dining as a fine art and their own favorite chef as a grand master. It's just about impossible to eat badly in this city, no matter what price range you're operating within.

The city offers no fewer than 1,500 top-quality restaurants. You can spend as much as $100 for a meal in one of the culinary giants or as little as $15 for one prepared with as much loving care in a smaller, more intimate, and informal place. However, it's my firm conviction that even those on a tight budget should set aside the wherewithal for at least one big splurge in one of Brussels's fine restaurants—expensive, but food for the soul as well as the stomach.

Each year, the tourist office issues a comprehensive dining directory entitled "Gourmet," which gives each restaurant's rating in irises, the flower of Brussels, instead of the traditional stars. It's a very good idea to pick up a copy at the beginning of your stay in the city.

The Brussels restaurant scene literally covers the entire city, but there are one or two culinary pockets you should know about. It has been said that you haven't truly visited this city unless you've dined at least once along **rue des Bouchers** or its offshoot, **Petite rue des Bouchers,** both of which are near the Grand-Place. The two streets are lined with an extraordinary array of small, ethnic restaurants (everything from French to Spanish, Italian, and Greek), most with a proudly proclaimed specialty, and all with unbelievably modest prices (under $15). Reservations are not usually necessary in these colorful, and often crowded, restaurants—if you cannot be seated at one, you simply stroll on to the next one.

Then there is the cluster of small restaurants with truly excellent kitchens in the **Marché-aux-Poissons** (Fish Market) section, only a short walk from the Grand-Place, in the Ste-Catherine area. This is where fishermen once unloaded their daily catches from a now-covered canal. Seafood, as you'd expect, is the specialty here. You must book ahead—a delightful afternoon's occupation is to stroll through the area to examine the bills of fare exhibited in windows and make your reservation for the evening meal.

Belgian cuisine is based on the country's own regional traditions and produce, such as asparagus, chicory (endive), and the humble Brussels sprout. A tradition in Brussels is to cook with local beers like gueuze and faro. Also, look for great steaming pots of Zeeland mussels, which have a fanatical local following.

Warning: Many restaurants close on Sunday, so it pays to plan ahead for weekend meals.

IN THE CITY CENTER
VERY EXPENSIVE

✪ **Comme Chez Soi.** place Rouppe 23. ☎ **02/512-29-21.** Reservations required for dinner. Main courses 1,250–2,975 BF ($34.70–$82.65); menus 2,150–4,950 BF ($59.70–$137.50). AE, DC, MC, V. Tues–Sat noon–2pm and 7pm–10pm (closed July and Christmas/New Year's holidays). Métro: Anneessens. FRENCH.

An expedition inside the hallowed portals of Brussels's triple Michelin-star restaurant, whose name means "Just Like Home," is undoubtedly the culinary highlight of any stay here. The welcome from Master Chef Pierre Wynants—one of Europe's most revered chefs—is warm, and his standards are high enough for the most rigorous tastebuds on earth. This is the stellar end of the spectrum, with unforgettable French cuisine presented in an art nouveau–style setting. It may even be possible to get a table in the kitchen, where you can watch the master at work. Reservations generally have to be made well in advance, and this is not the place for people who must look too closely at their per diems. Lunch is usually less fully booked and so makes a more practical short-notice alternative to dinner, as well as being somewhat cheaper. The menu changes seasonally. Sautéed lobster with truffles and chanterelles makes for a memorable main course, as does the roast saddle of lamb. A good dessert option is the soufflé of preserved oranges in Mandarine Napoléon liqueur, a Belgian specialty.

✪ **La Maison du Cygne.** Grand-Place 9. ☎ **02/511-82-44.** Reservations recommended on weekends. Main courses 950–1,600 BF ($26.40–$44.45); fixed-price menu 2,200 BF ($61.10). AE, DC, MC, V. Mon–Fri noon–2:15pm and Mon–Sat 7pm–midnight (closed 3 weeks in August). Métro: Gare Centrale or La Bourse. FRENCH.

This grande dame of Brussels's internationally recognized restaurants has one Michelin star. The place overlooks the Grand-Place from the former Butchers's

Brussels Accommodations & Dining

 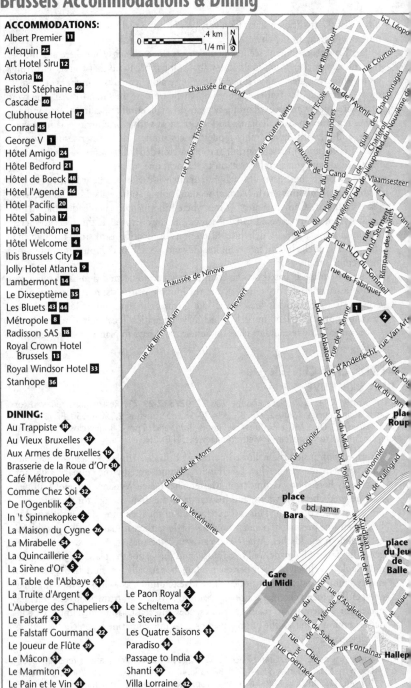

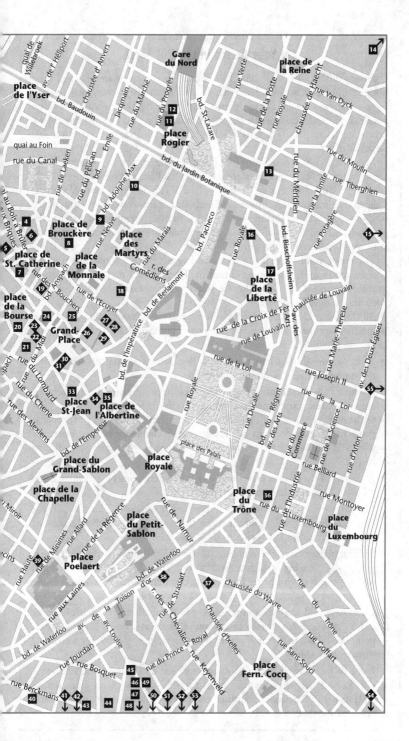

place de l'Yser

quai au Foin
rue du Canal

place de
Brouckère

place de
St. Catherine

place
de la
Bourse

Grand-
Place

place
St-Jean

place du
Grand-Sablon

place de la
Chapelle

Miroir

place
Poelaert

rue Berckmans

quai de Willebroek
av. de l'Héliport
bd. Baudouin

chaussée d'Anvers
Jacqmain
rue du Marché
rue du Progrès

Gare
du Nord

place de
la Reine

rue Verte
rue de la Poste
rue Royale
chaussée de Haecht
Rue Van Dyck

bd. St-Lazare

place
Rogier

rue de Laeken
rue du Pélican
bd. Émile

bd. du Jardin Botanique

rue du Moulin
rue Tiberghien
rue du Méridien
rue de la Limite

bd. Adolphe Max

place
des
Martyrs

rue du Marais
bd. Pacheco

rue Royale

bd. Bisschoffsheim

rue Potagère

place
de la
Liberté

rue Neuve
rue des Comédiens

r. des

rue de l'Écuyer

bd. Anspach
rue des Bouchers

bd. de Berlaimont

rue de la Croix de Fer
chaussée de Louvain
av. des Arts
rue de Louvain

rue Marie-Thérèse
av. des Deux-Églises

bd. de l'Impératrice

rue du Midi
rue du Lombard
rue du Chène
rue des Alexiens

rue de la Loi

rue Joseph II

rue de la Loi
rue de la Science

rue d'Arlon

place de
l'Albertine

bd. de l'Empereur

bd. Royale

rue Royale

bd. du Régent
bd. des Arts
rue Ducale
rue du Commerce

place des Palais

place
Royale

rue Belliard

place
du
Trône

rue de l'Industrie
rue du Luxembourg

rue Montoyer

place
du
Luxembourg

place
du Petit-
Sablon

rue de la Régence
rue Allard
rue des Minimes

rue de Namur

rue Haute
rue aux Laines

bd. de Waterloo
r. des Chevaliers

r. de la Toison d'or

bd. de Strassart

chaussée du Wavre

rue du Trône

chaussée d'Ixelles

av. de la Toison

av. Louise
rue du Prince Royal
rue Keyenveld
rue Sans-Souci

place
Fern. Cocq

bd. de Waterloo
rue Jourdan
rue Bosquet

rue Coffart

77

On Your Guard in the Ilôt Sacré

Opinions differ in Brussels about how acceptable it is to be seen eating in the popular Ilôt Sacré restaurant district, located in the city center between the Grand-Place and rue de l'Ecuyer (particularly the rue des Bouchers and the Petite rue des Bouchers). Some people snootily dismiss this area as a tourist trap. Many others, however, snootily dismiss this dismissal and pile in alongside the tourists. So who's right?

My advice is not to waste time listening to the arguments, but to go there and see for yourself. There are a lot of restaurants in the Ilôt Sacré (which means Holy Islet), representing a veritable United Nations of cuisine styles. Some of the best Belgian restaurants in the city are here, and some of the worst. But the ambiance is always undeniably romantic—on a warm summer evening at a street table, with lanterns and candles all around; or on a cold winter evening in a cozy room with wood and brass in abundance.

The reason you have to be on your guard here is that a few restaurants in the area are known to take advantage of tourists. They figure that by tomorrow you'll probably be on a plane, and if they rip you off in the meantime, well, who cares? You care. So does Frommer's.

All the restaurants listed in this chapter are good ones, and you should have no problems in them. If you prefer the look of another place, however, here are the ground rules:

- A big outdoor display, particularly of seafood on ice, is no guarantee of interior quality. It might well mean the reverse.

- Be wary if the waiter hits on you before you have a decent time to study the menu; be more wary if inexpensive menu items, such as the *plat du jour* (dish of the day), are "sold out"; and be warier still if the waiter offers to "propose you something special" instead. There's a story circulating of two Americans who paid 12,000 BF ($333) for a "special" lunch—you don't want this to be you.

- Be certain of the price of everything you order by checking on a menu or other location, such as a chalkboard, beforehand.

- Check the price of the house wine if that is what you order. This is usually the cheapest wine on the list—but in a few places it is by far the most expensive! The same consideration applies to the house aperitif.

- Seafood platters can cause problems. If you order without checking the price, you may get one big enough to feed Patton's Third Army, with a price tag to match—this is at least better than getting one more suitable for a doll's house yet still with the aforementioned mammoth price tag.

- Check your bill carefully and refuse to pay for anything you didn't order or didn't get. The manager may then mention the magic word "police." At this point you'll have to decide if you have strong enough grounds (or will) to go through with this.

None of the above is meant to discourage you, and it would be a shame if it did. Lots of people come away from the Ilôt Sacré with no more serious complaint than an expanded waistline. But unwary tourists do get ripped off; it happens all the time.

Guild house, La Cygne (The Swan)—where a certain Karl Marx once worked on *The Communist Manifesto* during a 3-year sojourn in Brussels. The interior features polished walnut walls, bronze wall sconces, and lots of green velvet. The service is as elegant as the decor, if possibly a tad stuffy. The menu offers haute cuisine French classics, such as *waterzooï de homard* (a souplike lobster stew), veal sautéed with fresh wild mushrooms, and excellent *tournedos* (filet steak) with green peppercorns. There are also fine chicken and fish dishes, and specialties such as *huîtres au champagne* (oysters with champagne), *goujonette de sole mousseline* (sole mousse), and *dos d'agneau façon du Cygne* (lamb prepared in the style of the Cygne). Because of its location, the Swan is usually crowded at lunchtime, but dinner reservations are somewhat more easily available.

✪ **Les Quatre Saisons.** In the Royal Windsor Hotel, rue Duquesnoy 5. ☎ **02/ 511-42-15.** Main courses 800–1,200 BF ($22.20–$33.35); fixed-price menu 2,290 BF ($63.60). AE, DC, MC, V. Mon–Fri noon–2:30pm; Mon–Sat 7:30–10:30pm. Closed 3 weeks in July–Aug. Métro: Gare Centrale or Bourse. FRENCH.

This quietly elegant and popular restaurant, whose name means The Four Seasons, is done up in soft shades of pink and cream and has an air of romantic intimacy. It was named the best hotel restaurant in Brussels in 1987 by a leading Belgian restaurant guide, and its head chef, Jan Raven, has won several prestigious culinary awards. Menus are seasonal, with different specialties each month. Among the favorites are *crépinette de pigeon* (pigeon in spinach leaves), *rose de saumon au fumet de seiches* (salmon with squid sauce), and *terrine de lotte marin ée à sel marin* (terrine of monkfish). There's an excellent and comprehensive wine list. Highly recommended.

EXPENSIVE

Aux Armes de Bruxelles. rue des Bouchers 13. ☎ **02/511-55-98.** Main courses 600–800 BF ($16.65–$22.20); menu du jour 1,100 BF ($30.55). AE, DC, MC, V. Tues–Sun noon–11:15pm. Métro: Gare Centrale or Bourse. BELGIAN.

This establishment has been a Brussels institution since it opened in 1921. It offers gracious, rather formal service, but a casual, relaxed ambiance. It's an excellent place for your introduction to Belgian cooking, since it offers just about every regional specialty you can think of (including mussels in every conceivable guise). You can sample anything from an excellent beef stewed in beer to a delicious *waterzooï* to a steak with pepper-and-cream sauce, all at quite reasonable prices.

De l'Ogenblik. Galerie des Princes 1 (in the Galeries Royales St-Hubert). ☎ **02/511-61-51.** Main courses 600–900 BF ($16.65–$25); menu du jour 2,000 BF ($55.55). AE, DC, MC, V. Mon–Sat noon–2:30pm and 7pm–midnight (Fri, Sat, till 12:30am). Métro: Gare Centrale or Bourse. BISTRO.

This restaurant offers good taste amid Parisian bistro-style ambiance. Its two-level dining room is filled with wood and brass. The place often gets busy, and the atmosphere is convivial, even if you might find yourself a little too close to other diners. Look for garlicky seafood and meat specialties.

Le Scheltema. rue des Dominicains 7. ☎ **02/512-20-84.** Main courses 650–950 BF ($18.05–$26.40). AE, CB, DC, MC, V. Mon–Thurs noon–3pm and 6–11:30pm; Fri–Sat noon–3pm and 6pm–12:30am. Métro: Gare Centrale or Bourse. BELGIAN.

This is one of those solid restaurants in the Ilot Sacré that keep going day in, day out, year after year, serving up much the same fare but never forgetting that quality counts. Good service and fine atmosphere complement the seafood specialties at this brasserie-style restaurant, which in some ways is similar to others in the district

🎠 Family-Friendly Restaurants

Passage to India (*see p. 85*)   Kids seem to like Indian food, particularly if it's made mild enough not to upset sensitive tummies, as it is here. And there's an intrinsic exotic appeal to an Indian restaurant that can capture the imagination.

La Quincaillerie (*see p. 82*)   This multilayered restaurant in a converted antique hardware store is the kind of place kids enjoy exploring, and the food is good too.

but always goes the extra mile in terms of class and taste. Pâté, *bisque d'homard* (lobster soup), *croquettes aux crevettes* (prawn croquettes), mussels (when they're in season), and a wide range of fish and meat options all grace the excellent menu.

MODERATE

✪ **Brasserie de la Roue d'Or.** rue des Chapeliers 26. ☎ **02/514-25-54.** Main courses 550–850 BF ($15.30–$23.60); menu du jour 1,650 BF ($45.85). AE, DC, MC, V. Daily noon–12:30am. Métro: Gare Centrale or Bourse. BELGIAN/GRILLS/SEAFOOD.

This excellent high-ceilinged brasserie has a décor inspired by art nouveau and Magritte. Fixtures include lots of dark wood and mirrors, and tables have marble tops. The extensive menu caters to just about any appetite. There's grilled meat and a good selection of salmon and other seafoods, as well as old Belgian favorites like *stoemp*—mixed mashed vegetables served with meat or sausage. This welcoming restaurant also has an extensive wine, beer, and spirits list, and a loyal local following. Its owner, Jef De Gelas (who also owns 't Kelderke) is known as the "King of Stoemp."

✪ **Le Falstaff.** rue Henri-Maus 23–25. ☎ **02/511-98-77.** Main courses 450–750 BF ($12.50–$20.85). AE, DC, MC, V. Daily 7am–2am. Métro: Bourse. BELGIAN.

This colorful art nouveau–style tavern and restaurant is located across from the Bourse in what were private mansions in the late 1800s. Huge stained-glass scenes in the style of Pieter Brueghel the Elder depict Shakespeare's Falstaff legend, and the Brueghelian style is carried out in the table settings and in the period dress of the waiters and waitresses. There's even a Brueghelian Menu, featuring Belgian specialties like *melle Beulemans* (chicken with chicory) or rabbit casserole in Gueuze. The à la carte menu is extensive. The prices are so reasonable that Falstaff can be considered either moderate or inexpensive, depending on your appetite.

Le Falstaff Gourmand. rue des Pierres 38. ☎ **02/512-17-61.** Main courses 480–720 BF ($13.35–$20); fixed-price menu 1,000 BF ($27.80). AE, DC, MC, V. Tues–Sat 11:30am–3pm and 7pm–11pm, Sun 11:30am–3pm. Métro: Bourse. BELGIAN/FRENCH.

Le Falstaff Gourmand is the equally notable sister establishment of Le Falstaff brasserie on rue Henri-Maus (see above). Service in Le Falstaff Gourmand is superb, prompt, and friendly, and it's surprising that more people do not take advantage of its charms. In addition to first-class Belgian and French dishes, the restaurant offers one of the best deals in Brussels: the three-course menu gourmand, which includes an aperitif, a glass of wine with a choice of appetizer, and a *pichet* of wine with the main course, all for less than $30 per head.

Le Marmiton. rue des Bouchers 43. ☎ **02/511-79-10.** Main courses 480–720 BF ($13.35–$20); menu du jour 695 BF ($19.30). AE, DC, MC, V. Sun–Thurs noon–3pm and 6–11:30pm; Fri–Sat noon–3pm and 6–12:30am. Métro: Gare Centrale or Bourse. BELGIAN/FRENCH.

The Ilôt Sacré restaurant district in the city center is often dismissed as a tourist trap (see "On Your Guard in the Ilôt Sacré," above). Le Marmiton, however, is quite the opposite. A warm and welcoming environment, hearty servings, and a firm commitment to satisfying customers are the hallmarks of this restaurant. The menu's emphasis is on seafood, but meat dishes are available as well. The seafood cocktail is a massed heap of shellfish and crustaceans which, although only a starter, is substantial enough to be ordered as a main course (or, even better, as a shared starter). All the fish dishes are very carefully prepared. The sole is excellent. The food is complemented by an excellent wine list selected by Le Marmiton's Portuguese-Belgian owner/chef, a man whose love of cooking shows up in his attention to the restaurant's fine cuisine.

✪ **Paradiso.** rue Duquesnoy 34 (off place St-Jean). ☎ **02/512-52-32.** Main courses 300–450 BF ($8.35–$12.50). Tues–Fri noon–3pm and 6:30pm–midnight; Sat–Sun 6:30pm–midnight. Métro: Gare Centrale. ITALIAN.

This great little Italian restaurant is close enough to the Grand-Place to be convenient, but just far enough away to not be immediately obvious to the crowds. As such, it is one of Brussels's best-kept secrets. Owner/chef Santino Trovato has created a little gem, with pasta and pizza just like mamma used to make and a list of fine Italian wines as long as your arm.

INEXPENSIVE

Auberge des Chapeliers. rue des Chapeliers 1–3. ☎ **02/513-73-38.** Main courses 300–635 BF ($8.35–$17.65); fixed-price menus 605–820 BF ($16.80–$22.80). AE, DC, MC, V. Mon–Thur noon–2pm and 6–11pm; Fri noon–2pm and 6pm–midnight; Sat noon–3pm and 6pm–midnight; Sun noon–3pm and 6–11pm. Métro: Gare Centrale. BELGIAN.

This restaurant, housed in a 150-year-old building just off of the Grand-Place, has been serving up bistro food for more than a quarter of a century in a setting accented with dark wood, exposed beams, and checkered tablecloths. The place is popular with locals who live and work in the area, as well as with tourists who are fortunate enough to find it. At the height of lunch hour, it's often packed, so try to come just before noon or just after 2pm. The menu features traditional Belgian pork, chicken, beef, and seafood dishes, some prepared with beer, and an excellent *waterzooï*. Servings are more than ample.

✪ **Cafe Métropole.** In the Hôtel Métropole, place de Brouckère 31. ☎ **02/217-23-00.** Reservations not accepted. Plat du jour 360 BF ($10); light meal 360–450 BF ($10–$12.50). AE, MC, V. Daily 9am–2am. Métro: De Brouckère. SNACKS/AFTERNOON TEA.

Many Brussels visitors never get beyond the pleasant heated sidewalk section of this massive Victorian-style cafe. Inside you'll find a casually elegant decor, highlighted by a marble fireplace, colorful wooden puppets hung from the high ceilings, and comfortable leather seating arranged in cozy groupings. The menu includes sandwiches, soups, quiches, and other light meals. The bar menu fills no fewer than six pages, including some rather exceptional specialties from the head barman.

IN THE AV. LOUISE AREA
VERY EXPENSIVE

✪ **Villa Lorraine.** av. du Vivier d'Oie 75. ☎ **02/374-31-63.** Main courses 1,200–1,800 BF ($33.35–$50); menu gastronomique 3,000 BF ($83.35). AE, DC, MC, V. Mon–Sat noon–2:30pm and 7–9:30pm. Closed 3 weeks in July. By car or taxi is the best way to arrive. FRENCH.

One of the city's top kitchens is located in this renovated château on the fringes of the Bois de la Cambre park. The dining rooms are spacious and have wicker furnishings, flower arrangements, and a skylight. In good weather you may elect to have drinks outside under the trees. Among the classic French offerings are saddle of lamb in a delicate red-wine-and-herb sauce, cold salmon with an herb sauce, partridge cooked with apples, and baked lobster with butter rose.

EXPENSIVE

La Quincaillerie. rue du Page 45 (at rue Américaine). ☎ **02/538-25-53.** Main courses 640–960 BF ($17.80–$26.65); menu du jour 1,750 BF ($48.60). AE, CB, DC, MC, V. Mon–Fri noon–2:30pm and 7pm–midnight; Sat–Sun 7pm–midnight. Tram: 81, 82, 91, or 92 to chaussée de Charleroi. FRENCH.

In the Ixelles district, a part of Brussels where good restaurants are about as common as streetlights, the Quincaillerie manages to stand out as a stylish (if pricey) devotee of good taste and fine ambiance, even though it may be a little too aware of its own modish good looks. The restaurant is located in a former hardware store—which sounds terrible, but this was a traditional old multilevel hardware store, with wood paneling and masses of wooden drawers. It gets so busy here that the waitstaff can be a little harassed and absent minded, but they're always friendly and helpful. Seafood dishes predominate on the menu and are in general better than the meat dishes here. Choices range from a straightforward but tasty salmon steak with vegetables, to more complicated dishes such as seafood cocktails and river trout. You don't need to look much further than a crisp Sancerre as the ideal wine accompaniment to most dishes.

✪ **La Table de l'Abbaye.** rue de Belle-Vue 62. ☎ **02/646-33-95.** A la carte meals 600–980 BF ($16.65–$27.20). AE, DC, MC, V. Daily noon–4:30pm and 7:00–11:00pm. Closed Dec 20–30. Tram: 93, 94 (to top of av. Louise). FRENCH.

This is a restaurant for the French-cuisine enthusiast who likes things done just so and is not too enamored of nouvelle cuisine. The setting is a well-appointed townhouse near the tranquil grounds of the Abbaye (Abbey) de la Cambre. The food here is hard to beat and its prices are not excessive, considering the quality of the fare and its presentation. Look for many French favorites, all best accompanied with a fine wine—from France, of course. Lobster flexes its claws in several interesting ways on the menu here: in pancakes with caviar butter, in a mixed salad, and with a pepper-cream sauce. Lamb marinated in Bourgogne wine is another specialty. In a romantically atmospheric touch, candlelight provides the main illumination for the classic decor, enlivened by sculptures and paintings.

MODERATE

✪ **Au Vieux Bruxelles.** rue St-Boniface 35. ☎ **02/513-01-81.** Main courses 360–720 BF ($10–$20). AE, DC, MC, V. Tues–Sat noon–2:30pm and 6–11pm. Métro: Porte de Namur. BELGIAN/SEAFOOD.

This convivial, brasserie-style 1880s-era restaurant specializes in mussels, which it serves in a wide variety of ways. In Belgium, the personality of the humble but tasty mussel is a staple of conversation as much as of diet, and people assess the quality of each year's crop with the same critical eye that some other countries reserve for fine wines (the fact that the mussels all come from neighboring Holland adds a sharper point to their critical faculties). Au Vieux Bruxelles, a kind of temple to the Belgian obsession with mussels, serves the shellfish in 15 different ways, including raw (accompanied only by a light white wine sauce), baked, fried, grilled, and broiled, as well as in traditional dishes like *moules marinières* (boiled in water with vegetables) and *moules au vin* (boiled in wine).

La Mirabelle. chaussée de Boondael 459. ☎ **02/649-51-73.** Main courses 300–500 BF ($8.35–$13.90); plat du jour 360 BF ($10). MC, V. Daily noon–3pm and 6pm–2:45am. Train: Watermael. BELGIAN.

This brasserie-restaurant in Ixelles is popular both with students from the nearby Free University of Brussels for its "democratic" prices, and with Bruxellois in general for its convivial atmosphere and consistently good food. Plainly decorated, with wooden tables crowded together, La Mirabelle looks more like a bar than a restaurant and often has a boisterous pub-style atmosphere to match. The *steak-frites* (steak with French fries), a Belgian staple, is particularly good here. The garden terrace is good for al fresco dining in summer.

✪ **Le Joueur de Flûte.** rue de l'Epée 26 (beside the Palais de Justice). ☎ **02/513-43-11.** Reservations required. Fixed-price menu 1,200 BF ($33.35). MC, V. Mon–Fri 7–11pm. Métro: Louise. FRENCH.

The choice in this tiny restaurant is nothing if not straightforward—take it or leave it. There's only one fixed-price menu, with a couple of variations for the main course. But don't let that, or the fact that it serves only a dozen diners each evening, put you off. Owner/chef Philippe Van Cappelen has had more than a passing acquaintance with Michelin stars in his time, and now he likes to keep it small, simple, and friendly. Van Cappelen cooks whatever he feels like; but whatever that is, you're virtually guaranteed to feel like eating it.

Le Pain et le Vin. chaussée d'Alsemberg 812a. ☎ **02/332-37-74.** Main courses 450–600 BF ($12.50–$15.65). AE, MC, V. Mon–Fri noon–2pm and 6–10pm; Sat 6–10pm. Tram: 55. MEDITERRANEAN.

The owners of this restaurant were once steeped in the Michelin-star milieu but now have decided to jettison the rigorously controlled bag-and-baggage of that system and concentrate on having some good, clean, tasty fun instead. "Bread and Wine" fits the bill perfectly—and the bill won't be excessive either. The restaurant, located in a converted house, looks out onto a garden. There's a terrace for al fresco dining in good weather. Whether the dish is chicken, fish, meat, or vegetables, the preparation concentrates on bringing out the natural taste, rather than smothering it with over-rich sauces. For interesting variations on common dishes, try the chicken ravioli with basil and parmesan, or the lobster and shrimp lasagna with ginger sauce. Vegetarian dishes are available on request, and vegetables form a big part of the menu offerings.

Shanti. av. Adolphe Buyl 68. ☎ **02/649-40-96.** Main courses 300–450 BF ($8.35–$12.50); fixed-price menus 450–1,000 BF ($12.50–$27.80). AE, DC, MC, V. Tues–Sat noon–2pm and 6:30–10pm. Bus: 71. SEAFOOD/VEGETARIAN.

This restaurant is an exotic-looking place. The decor features lots of greenery and flowers, creating a garden-like feel, as well as crystal lamps, mirrors, and old paintings on the walls. Try "Neptune's pleasure" as a starter—it's crab with avocado and seaweed. As a main course, the shrimp massala with mixed vegetables and coriander is excellent. There's also a good selection of vegetarian menus and dishes, such as eggplant with ricotta in a tomato-and-basil sauce.

INEXPENSIVE

Au Trappiste. av. de la Toison-d'Or 7. ☎ **02/511-78-39.** Main courses 180–600 BF ($5–$16.65). AE, DC, MC, V. Daily noon–midnight. Métro: Porte de Namur. BELGIAN.

This is the best—and perhaps the only—inexpensive dining option in the pricey av. Louise-chaussée de Wavre area. It's a brasserie-style spot with mirrors, chandeliers, and brass railings. The *plat du jour* is usually good; it might be vegetable soup followed by dishes like goulash, fried fish, breaded veal cutlet, or pasta.

Le Mâcon. rue Joseph Stallaert 87. ☎ **02/343-89-37.** Main courses 200–500 BF ($5.55–$13.90), fixed-price menus 345–930 BF ($9.60–$25.85). No credit cards. Daily 10am–2am. Tram: 23, 90. BELGIAN/SWISS.

A little of what you fancy can go a long way, and what your average Bruxellois fancies most of the time is a steaming bowl of moules (mussels), or a user-friendly plate of steak-frites (steak and french fries). Good, uncomplicated dishes like these are Le Mâcon's stock-in-trade. Slightly more exotic dishes, such as *skate au beurre noir* and Swiss fondue, are also available. And all at a price that makes the exercise worthwhile. The restaurant serves a Swiss-style menu on Thursday evenings.

AROUND THE FISH MARKET

The colorful and atmospheric Fish Market (Marché-aux-Poissons), is located beside the now-vanished harbor in the heart of Brussels, where fishing boats used to moor.

VERY EXPENSIVE

✪ **La Sirène d'Or.** place Ste-Catherine 1a (facing the Church of Ste-Catherine). ☎ **02/513-51-98.** Main courses 800–1,200 BF ($22.20–$33.35); fixed-price menus 890–1,300 BF ($24.70–$36.10). AE, DC, MC, V. Wed–Sat noon–2pm and 6–10pm. Métro: Ste-Catherine. SEAFOOD/FRENCH.

This restaurant's specialty is, not surprisingly, seafood. Chef Robert Van Duüren was once chef to the then Prince of Liège, now King Albert II of Belgium, so the dishes have that royal touch. The decor features dark wood walls, overhead beams, velvet-seated chairs, and Belgian lace curtains. Specialties are sole and *bouillabaisse* (a garlicky, mixed-fish soup).

La Truite d'Argent. quai aux Bois-à-Brûler 23. ☎ **02/219-95-46.** Main courses 720–1080 BF ($20–$30); fixed-price menu 1,250 BF ($34.70). AE, DC, MC, V. Mon–Fri noon–2:30pm and 7–11:30pm. Métro: Ste-Catherine. FRENCH/SEAFOOD.

The enthusiastic owners of this restaurant, Michel and Sophie Smeesters (see the Hotel Welcome listing in "Accommodations," above), serve food best described as "superb." Seafood is the specialty here, but meat and fowl dishes are also offered. All the fare is prepared from choice ingredients, and is so pleasing to the eye that you might hesitate to destroy the image by tucking in. The outdoor terrace looking onto the Fish Market is recommended for al fresco dining in good weather.

MODERATE

✪ **In 't Spinnekopke.** place du Jardin-aux-Fleurs 1. ☎ **02/511-86-95.** Main courses 400–780 BF ($11.10–$21.65); plat du jour 360 BF ($10). AE, DC, MC, V. Mon–Fri noon–3pm and 6–11pm; Sat–Sun 6pm–midnight. Métro: Bourse. BELGIAN.

In 't Spinnekopke (which means "In the Spider's Web"), has been a Brussels institution since 1762. Here, hearty standbys of Belgian cuisine, such as *stoemp* and *waterzooi,* are given all the care and attention they deserve—by both the kitchen staff and the diners. You'll eat at simple tables, more likely than not pressed into a small space. But for great food at reasonable prices, getting caught in this web will be well worth it.

INEXPENSIVE

✪ **Le Paon Royal.** rue du Vieux Marché-aux-Grains 6. ☎ **02/513-08-68.** Main courses 360–600 BF($10–$16.65); plat du jour 280 BF ($7.80). AE, DC, MC, V. Restaurant Tues–Sat noon–9:30pm. Tavern Tues–Sat 8am–10pm. Métro: Ste-Catherine. BELGIAN.

"Fish Market" Gems

The good restaurants in the Marché-aux-Poissons area are too numerous to list in this book, but in addition to the very special La Sirène d'Or and La Truite d'Argent (see above), a few more bear special mention. Most serve lunch from noon to 2:30pm and dinner from 6:30 to 10pm on weekdays (call ahead to check). MasterCard and Visa are usually accepted, and reservations can be made but are generally not really necessary. Prices will average about 1,000 BF ($27.80) and up at lunch; 1,600 BF ($44.45) and up at dinner.

Jacques, quai-aux-Brîques 44 (☎ **02/513-27-62**) is a small, rather plain brasserie that's a favorite of many Bruxellois who eat regularly in the Fish Market district. Seafood is the thing to order here, although three versions of steak also appear on the menu. There's also a good list of reasonably priced wines. Other good Fish Market choices include **La Belle Maraichère,** place Ste-Catherine 11a (☎ **02/512-97-59**); **Le Quai,** quai-aux-Brîques 14 (☎ **02/512-37-36**), which specializes in lobster (and even does a lobster takeout service); **La Villette,** rue du Vieux-Marché-aux-Grains 3 (☎ **02/512-75-50**), a real charmer with a good wine cellar and good surf 'n' turf offerings; and **Cochon d'Or,** quai-aux-Bois-à-Brûler 15 (☎ **02/218-07-71**).

This is one of my favorite small, inexpensive restaurants. It's located in a house dating from 1637, with a rustic wood-and-exposed-brick interior and beamed ceiling. You can have just a snack with one of the 65 brands of beer behind the tiny bar (some of which are also used in the cooking) or try the hearty plat du jour (usually a traditional Belgian dish) offered at lunchtime. Specialties are roast suckling pig in mustard sauce, and fillet of cod in a Hoegaarden (white beer) sauce. In fine weather, chairs are sometimes set out under the trees in the little park just across the street.

IN THE UPPER CITY
MODERATE

Le Stevin. rue St-Quentin 29. ☎ **02/230-98-47.** Main courses 600–850 BF ($16.65–$23.60). AE, DC, MC, V. Mon–Fri noon–2:30pm and 7–11:30pm. Métro: Schuman. FRENCH/BELGIAN.

Welcome to Euroland! If you want a chance to rub shoulders with the well-heeled employees of the European Commission—including, on occasion, the august commissioners themselves, and maybe a government minister or two from one of the Union's 15 member states—this is the place to go. True, that's not much of a recommendation, but the food is good anyway, and the Belgian specialties are done in a light, modern way that makes a refreshing change from the usual massive portions in traditional Belgian eateries. The decor puts the emphasis on the past, and features old pictures of Brussels and antique furnishings. Popular dishes here are sole, red mullet, and grilled or roast lamb. Wild mushrooms make a nice accompaniment for any of these meat and fish dishes.

Passage to India. chaussée de Louvain 223. ☎ **02/735-31-47.** Main courses 360–720 BF ($20–$30). AE, DC, MC, V. Daily noon–2:30pm and 7pm–midnight. Bus: 29. INDIAN.

In an enclave of Indian and Pakistani restaurants, Passage to India stands out for its friendly welcome, warm ambiance, and unpretentious yet careful presentation. The decor is bright but restrained, and in the evenings little oil lamps illuminate the room to almost magical effect. Prawn *puri* is a particularly good starter here. *Tandoori* (cooked in the clay oven), curry, and *dhansak* (Persian-style) dishes predominate on the main-course menu. Most are mild to medium in terms of spiciness. If you like it hotter, ask for *Madras* dishes; and for hotter still, *vindaloo*. *Kashmiri* dishes are a light and fruity option for those who don't want so many spices, while *pasanda* dishes, made with red wine, provide a more rounded flavor. Adventurous diners can ask about special Bangladeshi fish dishes.

7 Attractions

Brussels has such a variety of things to see and do that it can sometimes be overwhelming. There are more than 75 museums dedicated to just about every special interest under the sun, in addition to impressive public buildings, leafy parks, and interesting squares. History is just around every corner. Fortunately, numerous sidewalk cafes offer respite for weary feet, and there's good public transport to those attractions beyond walking distance of the compact, heart-shaped city center, which contains many of Brussels's most popular attractions.

Your very first stop should be at the **Tourist Information Brussels (T.I.B.)** office in the Town Hall in Grand-Place to pick up its comprehensive guidebook and city map. The helpful guide is a gold mine of information regarding both tourist sights and the practicalities of your stay in the city. If your visit is a short one, you may want to engage one of its multilingual guides, available at very reasonable rates, to make the best use of your time.

SQUARES & PUBLIC PLACES

The Grand-Place. Métro: Gare Centrale or Bourse

Ornamental gables, medieval banners, gilded facades, sunlight flashing off goldfiligreed rooftop sculptures, a general impression of harmony and timelessness—there's a lot to take in all at once when you first enter the ✪ **Grand-Place** (Grote Markt in Dutch). Once the pride of the Hapsburg Empire, the Grand-Place has always been the very heart of Brussels. Jean Cocteau called it "a splendid stage."

Its present composition dates mostly from the late 1690s, thanks to France's Louis XIV. In 1695, his army lined up its artillery on the heights of Anderlecht and blasted away at the medieval Grand-Place, using the Town Hall spire as a target marker. The French gunners destroyed the square, but, ironically, the Town Hall spire escaped undamaged. Other structures were not so fortunate, however, such as the wood-fronted buildings of the great trading and mercantile guilds.

But the Bruxellois weren't about to let a mere French king do away with their centuries-old corporate headquarters. The guildsmen had the place up and running again within 4 years, on the same grand scale as before but on more solid foundations. The result throws one's sense of time out of joint, as the medieval atmosphere is conjured up mostly in the baroque style known as the Flemish Renaissance. The Town Hall, though badly damaged by Louis's guns, is the real thing, however, dating from the early 1400s.

Your tour of the Grand-Place should include a visit to the Gothic Town Hall, the neo-Gothic King's House (which houses the Museum of the City of Brussels), and the Brewers Museum housed in the brewers' guild house (see "Museums" below). Victor Hugo spent part of his time in exile at No. 26 ("The Pigeon"), firing off broadsides at Napoleon III until the City Fathers asked him to leave for fear the outraged French Emperor would send an army to collect him. At No. 9 ("The

Events in the Grand-Place

Belgium's own royal history is the focus of a dazzling event that brings the 16th century to life in the Grand-Place each July. Called the **Ommegang,** it reenacts the Hapsburg Emperor Charles V's arrival in Brussels in 1549. Some 1,200 participants wearing 16th-century costumes represent members of the imperial family and court, the aristocracy, magistrates, guildsmen, and soldiers. Some parade on giant stilts while others take part in banner-waving demonstrations and displays of horsemanship.

Every second August, the **"Carpet of Flowers"** fills the square with two-thirds of a million begonias "woven" into a delicate tapestry, like an ornamental garden fallen from the sky. Events like the Ommegang and Carpet of Flowers are special, partly because of their rarity. Other interesting events, like the weekly bird market, daily flower market, and frequent summer concerts, are more familiar.

Swan"), Karl Marx created an ideology that would change the world, when he wrote *The Communist Manifesto.*

Don't miss the cafes lodged within the opulent wooden interiors of old guild houses; their upper-floor windows overlooking the Grand-Place give some of the best views in Europe.

place du Grand-Sablon. Tram: 92, 93, or 94.

The Grand-Sablon is filled with outdoor cafes and lined with gabled mansions. Though the traffic passing through it diminishes the cafe-terrace experience, locals consider it a classier place to see and be seen than the Grand-Place. The Grand-Sablon is also antiques territory; many of its mansions house antiques shops or private art galleries with pricey merchandise on display. The dealerships have spread into neighboring side streets as well.

On Saturday and Sunday mornings an excellent antiques market sets up its stalls in front of Notre-Dame au Sablon church. This flamboyantly Gothic church, with no fewer than five naves, was paid for by the city's Guild of Crossbowmen in the 15th century. The statue of Minerva in the square dates from 1751.

✪ **place du Petit-Sablon.** Tram: 92, 93, or 94.

Just across rue de la Régence is the Grand-Sablon's little cousin. This ornamental garden with a fountain and pool is a magical little retreat from the city bustle. The 48 bronze statuettes adorning the surrounding wrought-iron fence symbolize Brussels's medieval guilds. Two statues in the center commemorate the Counts of Egmont and Hornes, who were beheaded in 1568 for protesting the extravagant cruelties of the Council of Blood, the enforcement arm of Spain's Holy Inquisition in the Low Countries.

place Royale. Tram: 92, 93, or 94.

Place Royale is the meeting point of rue de la Régence and rue Royale, two streets that hold many of the city's premier attractions. The square is graced by a heroic equestrian statue of Duke Godefroid de Bouillon, leader of the First Crusade. Its inscription describes him as the "First King of Jerusalem," a title Godefroid himself refused, accepting instead that of Protector of the Holy Places (which amounted to the same thing anyway). Also in place Royale is the neoclassical Church of St-Jacques-sur-Coudenberg.

Brussels Attractions

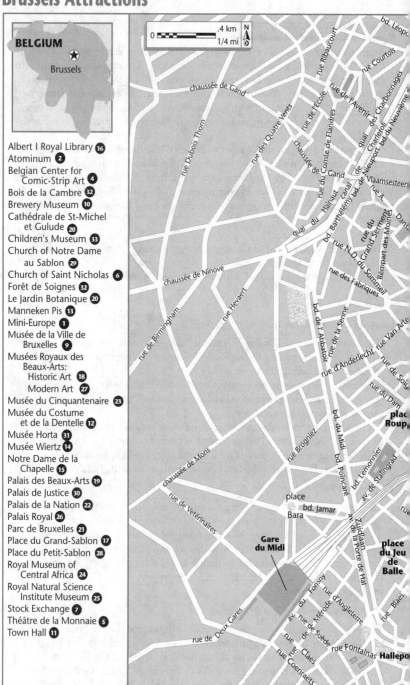

BELGIUM
Brussels

Albert I Royal Library **16**
Atominum **2**
Belgian Center for
  Comic-Strip Art **4**
Bois de la Cambre **32**
Brewery Museum **10**
Cathédrale de St-Michel
  et Gulude **20**
Children's Museum **33**
Church of Notre Dame
  au Sablon **29**
Church of Saint Nicholas **6**
Forêt de Soignes **32**
Le Jardin Botanique **20**
Manneken Pis **13**
Mini-Europe **1**
Musée de la Ville de
  Bruxelles **9**
Musées Royaux des
  Beaux-Arts:
    Historic Art **18**
    Modern Art **27**
Musée du Cinquantenaire **23**
Musée du Costume
  et de la Dentelle **12**
Musée Horta **31**
Musée Wiertz **14**
Notre Dame de la
  Chapelle **15**
Palais des Beaux-Arts **19**
Palais de Justice **30**
Palais de la Nation **22**
Palais Royal **26**
Parc de Bruxelles **21**
Place du Grand-Sablon **17**
Place du Petit-Sablon **28**
Royal Museum of
  Central Africa **24**
Royal Natural Science
  Institute Museum **25**
Stock Exchange **7**
Théâtre de la Monnaie **5**
Town Hall **11**

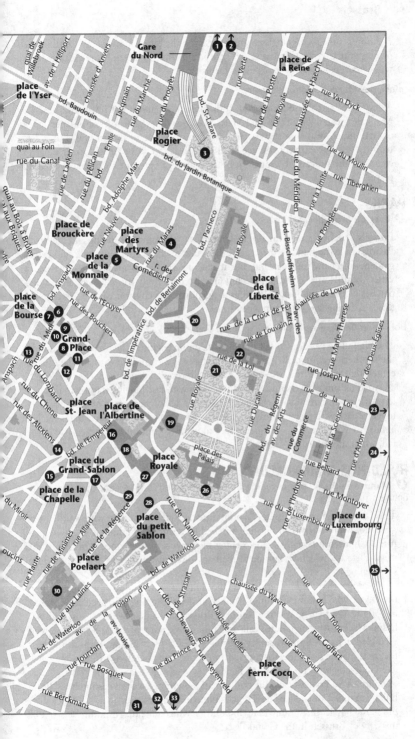

Gare
du Nord

place de
la Reine

place
de l'Yser

quai de Willebroek
av. de l'Héliport
quai au Foin
rue du Canal
quai au Bois à Brûler
ai aux Briques

chaussée d'Anvers
Jacqmain
rue du Marché
rue du Progrès

bd. St-Lazare

rue Verte
rue de la Poste
rue Royale
chaussée de Haecht
rue Van Dyck

bd. Baudouin

place
Rogier

bd. du Pélican
bd. Émile
rue Neuve

❸

bd. du Jardin Botanique

rue du Moulin
rue Tiberghien

rue de la Limite
rue du Méridien
bd. Bischoffsheim
rue Potagère

place de
Brouckère

bd. Adolphe Max

place
des
Martyrs ❹

r. des
Comédiens

bd. Pacheco

rue Royale

place
de la
Liberté

place
de la
Monnaie

❺

rue du Marais

bd. de Berlaimont

chaussée de Louvain
av. des Arts
rue Marie-Thérèse
av. des Deux-Églises

place
de la
Bourse

❻
❼

rue de l'Écuyer

rue des Bouchers

rue de la Croix de Fer
rue de Louvain

rue Joseph II

❾
❿
❽ Grand-
Place
❶❶

bd. de l'Impératrice

❷❶

rue de la Loi

❶❸
Anspach
rue du Lombard
❶❷

rue du Midi

❷❷
❷❶

rue Ducale
bd. du Regent

rue du Commerce
rue de la Science
rue d'Arlon

❷❸→

rue du Chêne
rue des Alexiens

place
St-Jean

place de
l'Albertine

❶❾

rue Royale

❷❹→

❶❻

❶❹
❶❽

bd. de l'Empereur

place du
Grand-Sablon

place des
Palais

rue Belliard

❶❺
❶❼

place
Royale

rue Montoyer

❷❾
❷❼

❷❻

rue du Luxembourg
bd. de l'Industrie

place du
Luxembourg

place de la
Chapelle

❷❽

rue de Namur

place
du petit-
Sablon

du Miroir
rue Haute
rue des Minimes
rue Allard
rue de la Régence

❷❺→

place
Poelaert

bd. de Waterloo

ucins
rue aux Laines
av. de la Toison d'or
r. des 4 Bras
rue de strassart
rue des Chevaliers
rue du Prince Royal

chaussée du Wavre
rue du Trône
rue Goffart
rue Sans-Souci

❸❶

rue Berckmans
rue Jourdan
rue Bosquet
av. Louise

rue Keyenveld
chaussée d'Ixelles

place
Fern. Cocq

❸❷ ❸❸

89

At press time archaeologists were uncovering the foundations of the Royal Palace of Emperor Charles V in the square, but it remains to be seen if the excavated site will be covered over again or put on display.

place des Martyrs. Métro: Brouckère

A few years ago this once-elegant 18th-century square in the lower city near La Monnaie theater, where the "500 Martyrs" of Belgium's 1830 War of Independence are entombed, was in a sorry state, literally crumbling to the ground. But it has recently been extensively restored, and though it lost some of its former raggedy charm in the process, the square is once again an important and attractive public place.

PARKS

✪ **Parc de Bruxelles.** Métro: Parc or Arts-Loi.

Brussels Park lies next to rue Royale between the Parliament building and the Royal Palace. Once the hunting preserve of the Dukes of Brabant, it is now a landscaped garden. The park isn't very big, but it has fine views and manages to combine a variety of different landscaping techniques, from carefully trimmed verges to rough patches of trees and bushes. In 1830, Belgian patriots confronted Dutch troops on this site during the War of Independence.

Bois de la Cambre and Forêt de Soignes. Tram: 92 or 93.

The big public park called the Bois de la Cambre begins at the top of av. Louise in the southern section of Brussels. Its centerpiece is a small lake with an island in its center that can be reached by an electrically operated pontoon. The park gets crowded on sunny weekends. A few busy roads with fast-moving traffic run through the park, so be careful with children. The Forêt de Soignes, south of the Bois, is no longer a park with playing areas and regularly mown grass, but a forest that stretches almost to Waterloo. This is a great place to get away from it all, particularly in the fall, when the colors are dazzling.

BUILDINGS & MONUMENTS

✪ **Manneken-Pis.** Corner of rue du Chêne and rue de l'Etuve. Métro: Gare Centrale or Bourse.

This famous statue is Brussels's favorite little boy, gleefully doing what a little boy's gotta do. More often than not he's watched by a throng of admirers snapping pictures. Children especially seem to enjoy his bravura performance. This is not the original statue, which was prone to theft and "maltreatment" and was removed for safekeeping.

It's known that the boy's effigy has graced the city since at least the time of Philip the Good, who became Count of Flanders in 1419. Among the speculations about his origins are that he was the son of a Brussels nobleman who got lost and was found while answering nature's call, and also that he was a patriotic Belgian kid who sprinkled a hated Spanish sentry passing beneath his window. Perhaps the best theory is that he saved the Town Hall from a sputtering bomb by extinguishing it—like Gulliver—with the first thing handy.

Louis XV of France began the tradition of presenting colorful costumes to "Little Julian" to make amends for the French abduction of the statue in 1747. Since then the statue has acquired more than 500 outfits, which are housed in the Museum of the City of Brussels in the Grand-Place.

Christmas in the Grand-Place

One of the great Brussels Christmas traditions is the kidnapping of the infant Jesus. This is not a case of Belgians reinterpreting the New Testament story, but the handiwork of Christmas pranksters—thieves, if you prefer—who make off with the doll that plays the part of Jesus lying in the crib in the nativity scene at the Grand-Place. Fresh supplies of Jesus dolls have to be kept on hand to keep the Holy Family up to strength, since it is generally agreed that a Nativity scene without the child Jesus is a great disappointment to visitors. So far, no one has stolen any of the animals, but it's probably only a matter of time.

Assuming that all the characters are present, however, the view of the Holy Family in the Grand-Place is a memorable one. The warmly lit windows of the square's 17th-century guild houses, the Town Hall's extravagant Gothic tracery, and the scarcely less fantastic neo-Gothic lines of the King's House make a picturesque backdrop to the "manger-in-a-stable" scene, and the real sheep and goats wandering around the grounds add a charming touch. The stable is dominated by a giant illuminated Christmas tree, which is donated every year by a foreign country.

When freshly fallen snow covers the cobbles, the whole storybook square glows like an icon. In so many ways, and at different times of year, the Grand-Place is the city's showcase. Christmas is no exception.

Two weekends before Christmas is the occasion for the European Union Christmas Market in the Grand-Place. From Friday evening until Sunday evening, the square is a hub of activity, as each country of the EU sets out its stall with traditional foods and other products. There's music, singing, and dancing, and the festive spirit is fueled by mulled wine and typical national drinks. The main problem is that at times the square gets so busy that it is almost impossible to move. Still, this is another colorful and memorable event.

✪ **Town Hall (Hôtel de Ville).** Grand-Place. ☎ **02/279-43-55.** Admission 80 BF ($2.20) for guided tours only. Apr–Sept Tues 11:30am and 3:15pm, Wed 3:15pm, Sun 12:15pm; Oct–Mar Tues 11:30am and 3:15pm, Wed 3:15pm. Métro: Gare Centrale or Bourse.

This spectacular Gothic hall, where the Brussels aldermen meet, is open for visits when the council is not in session. You should begin by examining the outside, however, particularly the sculptures on the facade, many of which are 15th- and 16th-century insiders' jokes. There's a group of drinking monks, a heap of chairs recalling the medieval torture called "strappado," a sleeping Moor and his harem, and St. Michael slaying a female-breasted devil. The belfry is off-center and has an off-center entrance, a flaw that led to tales of how the architect, Jan Van Ruysbroeck, committed suicide by leaping from the belfry when he realized what a terrible mistake he had made (he didn't really).

Inside are superb tapestries dating from the 16th to the 18th centuries. One depicts the cruel features of the Duke of Alba, whose Council of Blood imposed brutal oppression on Belgium; others are scenes from the life of Clovis, King of the Franks. The Aldermen meet in a plush, mahogany-paneled room surrounded by mirrors—presumably so that each party can see what underhanded maneuvers the others are getting up to.

Royal Palace (Palais Royal). place des Palais. ☎ **02/551-20-20.** Free admission. July 22–end September Tues–Sun 10:30am–4:30pm. Métro: Parc or Arts-Loi.

The King's Palace, which overlooks the Parc de Bruxelles, was begun in 1820 and had a grandiose Louis XVI–style facelift in 1904. The older side wings date from the 18th century and are flanked by two pavilions, one of which sheltered numerous notables during the 1800s. Today the palace is used for state receptions. It also contains the offices of King Albert II, though he and Queen Paola do not live there.

Stock Exchange (La Bourse). rue Henri Maus 2. ☎ **02/509-12-11.** Free admission. Mon–Fri 10am–6pm. Métro: Bourse.

The ornately decorated Stock Exchange, a landmark of the Second Empire architecture style, dates from 1873. It's a temple to the venerable religion of making money.

Church of St Nicholas (Église St-Nicolas). place St-Nicolas. ☎ **02/267-51-64.** Free admission. Métro: Bourse.

This delightful little church behind the Bourse is almost hidden by the fine old houses surrounding it, just as its 11th-century Romanesque lines are hidden by a 14th-century Gothic facade and the repairs made after the French bombardment of 1695. The church holds a small painting by Rubens, the *Virgin and Child,* and the *Vladimir Icon,* painted by an artist from Constantinople in 1131.

MUSEUMS

Albert I Royal Library. bd. de l'Empereur 4 (public entrance on Mont des Arts). ☎ **02/519-53-11.** Free admission. Mon–Sat 9am–noon and 2–5pm. Closed last week in Aug, public holidays. Métro: Gare Centrale.

This library museum is an astounding tribute to the history of the written word through the centuries. The Book Museum section contains centuries-old manuscripts and ancient books, as well as current books in all disciplines. The Printing Museum has typographical, binding, and lithographical exhibits. The building also holds the National Library of Belgium.

Brewery Museum (Musée de la Brasserie). Maison des Brasseurs, Grand-Place 10. ☎ **02/511-49-87.** Admission 100 BF ($2.80). Daily 10am–5pm. Métro: Gare Centrale or Bourse.

This museum, operated by the Confederation of Belgian Breweries, is housed in the home of the Brewers' Guild, the Knights of the Mash Staff. A permanent exhibition on modern hi-tech brewing methods has joined the old one on traditional techniques. You'll find numerous paintings, stained-glass windows, and collections of pitchers, pint pots, and old china beer pumps. And you get a chance to sample some of your hosts' finished product.

✪ **Musées Royaux des Beaux-Arts.** rue de la Régence 3. ☎ **02/508-32-11.** Admission 150 BF ($4.15). Historic Art department Tues–Sun 10am–noon and 1–5pm; Modern Art department Tues–Sun 10am–1pm and 2–5pm. Tram: 92, 93, or 94 to place Royale.

Brueghel and Rubens are the stars of the Historic Art part of this show, but the entire history of Belgian painting is well represented, with works by Van Dyck, Bosch, van der Weyden, Memling, Bouts, Jordaens, Ensor, and Rops, among others. International masters on display include van Gogh, Gaugin, and Renoir. Guided tours are available on request.

The adjacent Modern Art department is underground—literally in this case, as you must descend to reach it. You can enter via a connecting corridor from the

Historic part, or from a separate entrance at place Royale 1. Magritte, Dalí, Permeke, Dufy, and Delvaux are all featured, among others.

Musée de la Ville de Bruxelles (Museum of the City of Brussels). Grand-Place. ☎ **02/279-43-50.** Admission 80 BF ($2.20). Mon–Thurs 10am–12:30pm and 1:30–4pm (Apr–Sep until 5pm); Sat–Sun 10am–1pm. Métro: Gare Centrale or Bourse.

This museum is located in the neo-Gothic King's House (which, despite its name, has never housed a king). Exhibits inside document the history of Brussels. Among the most fascinating displays are old paintings and modern scale reconstructions of the historic city center, particularly those depicting riverside activity along the now-vanished Senne. There are also exhibits on traditional arts and crafts, such as tapestry and lace. The pride of the museum, however, is the more than 500 costumes donated to outfit Brussels's famous Manneken-Pis statue—including an Elvis outfit—each equipped with a strategically positioned orifice so that the little sculpture's normal function is not impaired.

✪ **Musée Horta.** rue Américaine 25. ☎ **02/537-16-92.** Admission 150 BF ($4.15) Tue–Fri; 200 BF ($5.55) Sat–Sun. Open Tue–Sun 2–5:30pm. Tram: 81 or 92.

Brussels owes much of its rich art nouveau heritage to the inspired creative vision of Victor Horta, a resident architect who led the style's development. His home and an adjoining studio have been restored to their original condition and are now a museum. They showcase his use of flowing, sinuous shapes and colors in interior decoration as well as architecture.

Musée du Cinquantenaire. Parc du Cinquantenaire. ☎ **02/741-72-11.** Admission 150 BF ($4.15). Tues–Fri 9:30am–5pm; Sat–Sun 10am–5pm. Métro: Schuman or Mérode.

Formerly known as the Royal Museums of Art and History (Musées Royaux d'Art et d'Histoire), the monumental Cinquantenaire traces the history of civilization, particularly, but not exclusively, European civilization. Departments include Archaeology; Antiquity, which features a giant model of Imperial Rome; and European Decorative Arts. Other sections are devoted to lace, tapestry, Far Eastern furniture, toys, stained glass, ceramics, jewels, folklore, and old vehicles, including 18th-century coupes, sedan chairs, sleighs, and royal coaches.

✪ **Royal Museum of Central Africa (Musée Royal de l'Afrique Central).** Leuvensesteenweg 13, Tervuren (suburban commune east of Brussels). ☎ **02/769-52-11.** Admission 80 BF ($2.25) adults, 30 BF (85¢) children 12 and under. Tues–Fri 10am–5pm; Sat–Sun 10am–6pm. Tram: 44 from Métro Montgomery to Tervuren terminus.

Originally founded to celebrate Belgium's colonial empire in the Belgian Congo (now the Democratic Republic of Congo), this museum has moved beyond imperialism to feature exhibits on ethnography and environment, mostly in Africa, but also in Asia and South America. The beautiful grounds of this impressive museum are as much a draw as the exhibits inside. The collection includes some excellent animal dioramas, African sculpture, and other artwork, and even some of the colonial-era guns and artillery pieces that no doubt helped make Belgium's claim to its African colonies more convincing. A more modern perspective is added by environmental displays that explain desertification, the loss of rain forests, and the destruction of habitats.

SIGHTS OF RELIGIOUS SIGNIFICANCE
✪ **Cathédrale des Sts Michel et Gudule.** Parvis Ste-Gudule (facing Gare Centrale). ☎ **02/217-83-45.** Free admission to church; crypt 40 BF ($1.10). Daily 8am–6pm. Métro: Gare Centrale.

Victor Hugo reckoned this magnificent church to be the "purest flowering of the Gothic style." Begun in 1226, it was only officially dedicated as a cathedral in 1961. The 16th-century Hapsburg Emperor Charles V took a personal interest in its decoration, donating the stained-glass windows. In recent years the church's stonework has been undergoing a process of cleaning and restoration, and the dazzlingly bright exterior now makes a superb sight. Inside, the cool and spare decoration focuses more attention on the building's soaring columns and arches. Guided tours of the carillon are available on request Monday through Saturday from May through September; call for information on times.

Church of Notre-Dame au Sablon. rue de la Régence 3B (at place du Grand-Sablon). ☎ **02/511-57-41.** Free admission. Daily 8am–6pm. Tram: 92, 93, or 94 to place du Grand Sablon.

This superb 15th-century church, which has no fewer than five naves, stands at the top end of the square. Inside is a celebrated statue of St. Hubert with an interesting history: It was actually stolen from Brussels and taken to Antwerp but was seized and returned to the Church in 1348, where it has remained ever since.

Notre-Dame de la Chapelle. place de la Chapelle. ☎ **02/512-07-37.** Tram: 92, 93, or 94.

This Romanesque-Gothic church is interesting both historically and architecturally. François Anneessens (1660–1719), a Brussels hero who lost his head for campaigning for civil rights, is buried here. Anneessens was a champion of the freedom of the Belgian communes against the centralist rule of Belgium's Austrian masters. Condemned to death, he refused to plead for forgiveness, saying, "Never! I die innocent. May my death expiate my sins and be of service to my country." He was then beheaded in the Grand-Place. A statue of Anneessens stands in the square named after him—place Anneessens—in the city center, and you'll find a commemorative plaque dedicated to him in Notre-Dame's Chapel of the Holy Sacrament. Notre-Dame de la Chapelle is also the burial site of Pieter Brueghel the Elder and his wife; their epitaph is also in one of the chapels.

MORE ATTRACTIONS

Le Botanique. rue Royale 236. ☎ **02/226-12-11.** Free admission to gardens, main building; admission charged for most cultural events. Métro: Botanique.

This graceful 19th-century glass-and-wrought-iron palace is no longer the Botanical Gardens of Brussels, but it still merits a visit as a monument of 19th-century architecture. There's still a fine ornamental garden outside. Nowadays Le Botanique functions as a cultural center in which theater, music and dance performances, and visiting art exhibitions are held.

Justice Palace (Palais de Justice). place Poelaert (adjacent to place Louise). ☎ **02/ 508-65-78.** Free admission. Mon–Fri 9–11:30am and 1:30–3pm. Métro: Louise.

You may not want to spend too much time here—this is, after all, where Belgians who have run afoul of the law are sent directly to jail. Nonetheless, it's worth seeing architect Joseph Poelaert's extravagant (some would say megalomaniac) 19th-century neo-classical temple dedicated to the might and majesty of the law. The Palace's domed magnificence looms over the rebellious, working-class Marolles district, a none-too-subtle warning that its creators undoubtedly considered salutary.

Palais de la Nation. rue de la Loi 16. ☎ **02/519-81-36.** Free admission. Métro: Parc or Arts-Loi.

The Parliament building opposite the Parc de Bruxelles is quite an elegant place, if you ignore the politicians squabbling in the Chamber of Representatives and the Senate—bickering, after all, is part of the charm of democracy. You can enter only

A Stroll Through the Marolles

The iconoclastic working-class Marolles district, lying beneath the long shadow of the Palace of Justice, is a special place where the old Brussels dialect called *Brusseleir* can still be heard. It's a generally poor community, under constant threat of encroachment and gentrification from neighboring, far wealthier areas—a process the Marolliens seem to want nothing to do with. Locals remain resolutely unimpressed by the burgeoning "Capital of Europe."

Most people get their Marolles "initiation" by visiting the daily flea market in place du Jeu de Balle, which opens at 7am and closes at 2pm. Here the weird-and-wonderful is commonplace. It makes a refreshing change to explore this other Brussels, a simple neighborhood of homes, welcoming cafes, and great, inexpensive restaurants. Simply wander around for an hour or two.

during sessions in either assembly (call in advance; they're usually Monday through Saturday from 10am to 3pm). The entrance to the Chamber is at rue de Louvain 11; the entrance to the Senate is at rue de Louvain 7B. You can also call ahead to arrange a guided tour of the actual building.

Musée du Costume et de la Dentelle. rue de la Violette 6. ☎ **02/512-77-09.** Admission 80 BF ($2.20). Mon–Sat 10am–12:30pm and 1:30–4pm (Apr–Sept until 5pm); Sat–Sun 2–4:30pm. Métro: Gare Centrale or Bourse.

This marvelous museum is near the Grand-Place. Its collection includes some fine examples of historical Belgian lace styles from the once-renowned factories of Mechelen, Bruges, Antwerp, Binche, Turnhout, Poperinge, and Sint-Truiden. In addition, the museum houses displays of costumes, including an array of dresses from the 16th to the 19th centuries.

ESPECIALLY FOR KIDS

Atomium. bd. du Centenaire, Laeken. ☎ **02/477-09-77.** Admission 200 BF ($5.55); reduced-rate combined tickets available for Mini-Europe and the Océade. Apr–Aug daily 9am–8pm; Sept–Mar daily 10am–6pm. Métro: Heysel.

There's nothing quite like this cluster of giant spheres representing the atomic structure of an iron molecule enlarged 165 billion times. It's questionable how many younger kids will be interested in the permanent Biogenium exhibition on genetics and medicine inside, even though it's arranged in a hands-on, interactive fashion, but all will surely want to see the Atomium itself—it's like something from *Close Encounters of the Third Kind.* The view from the viewing deck is marvelous, and you can even wander around inside the spheres. The model was built for the 1958 World's Fair.

✪ **Mini-Europe.** Bruparck (beside the Atomium). ☎ **02/478-05-50.** Admission 395 BF ($10.95) adults, 295 BF ($8.20) children 12 and under. Apr–June and Sept 9:30am–6pm; first 2 weeks of July and last 2 weeks of Aug 9:30am–8pm; mid-July to mid-Aug 9:30am–midnight; Oct–Jan 10am–6pm; closed Feb–Mar. Métro: Heysel.

Kids and adults alike will get a kick out of strolling around such highlights of Europe as Big Ben, the Leaning Tower of Pisa, and the Bull Ring in Seville (complete with simulated sounds of fans yelling *Olé!*), as well as more modern emblems of continental achievement such as the Channel Tunnel and the Ariane rocket. Meanwhile, Mt. Vesuvius erupts, gondolas float around the canals of Venice, and a Finnish girl dives into the icy waters of a northern lake. As the scale is 1:25, the kids will feel like giants.

Belgian Center for Comic-Strip Art (Centre Belge de la Bande Dessinée). rue des Sables 20. ☎ **02/219-19-80.** Admission 200 BF ($5.55). Tues–Sun 10am–6pm. Métro: Gare Centrale.

The center (often called the CéBéBéDé for short) features such popular cartoon characters as Lucky Luke, Thorgal, and, of course, Tintin, yet does not neglect the likes of Superman, Batman, and the Green Lantern. Grown-ups will love this place as well. As icing on the cake, it's housed in a Victor Horta–designed building, the *Magasins Waucquez,* which was slated for demolition before the center took it over.

Children's Museum (Musée des Enfants). rue du Bourgmestre 15 (near the Lakes of Ixelles). ☎ **02/640-01-07.** Admission: 200 BF ($5.55). Wed and Sat–Sun 2:30–5pm. Tram: 23, 90, 93, or 94 to bd. Général Jacques.

Taking its cue from an ancient Chinese proverb, "I see and I forget; I hear and I remember; I do and I understand," this museum brings children face-to-face with aspects of our everyday world. With the help of visual displays, elaborate sets, and role-play games, children can drive a tram, ride in a raft, sit in a space capsule, fight a fire, grow crops, produce a television program, plant a Japanese garden, knead dough, and play the part of a fairy-tale hero. The exhibits change every so often, but revolve around such themes as the Human Body, Water, the City, Communications, Our Fears and Other Emotions, and many others.

Royal Natural Science Institute of Belgium Museum (Musée de l'Institut Royal des Sciences Naturelles de Belgique). chaussée de Wavre 260. ☎ **02/627-42-38.** Admission 150 BF ($4.15). Tues–Sat 9:30am–4:45pm; Sun 9:30am–6pm. Métro: Trône or Maelbeek.

This handsome interactive museum was totally renovated and modernized for its 150th anniversary in 1996. The natural world is on display here, from prehistoric to modern times. There are dinosaur skeletons, a marine tank, and ecology displays and dioramas. The star attractions are the animated dinosaurs, models that move when you press a button.

ORGANIZED TOURS

BY BUS   Coach tours, which last 3 hours and operate throughout the year, are available from **De Boeck Brussels City Tours,** rue de la Colline 8 (☎ **02/513-77-44**). Each tour costs 790 BF ($21.95) for adults and 395 BF ($10.95) for children. Reservations can be made through most hotels, and hotel pick-up is often available. Private tours can also be arranged.

ON FOOT & BY BUS   From June through the end of September, **Chatterbus,** rue des Thuyas 12 (☎ **02/673-18-35**), operates a daily 3-hour tour starting at 10am (also at 2pm during July) from the Galeries Royales St-Hubert, a 19th-century shopping mall next to rue du Marché-aux-Herbes 90, a few steps from the Grand-Place. The tour consists of a guided walk covering the historic center, followed by a bus ride through areas the average tourist would never see. You'll hear about life in Brussels and get a better feel for the city. It's best to make a reservation in advance, but you can also simply show up at the Galeries Royales St-Hubert and hope for the best. The price is 300 BF ($8.35).

SPECIAL & FREE EVENTS

I sometimes feel that simply strolling the streets of Brussels is one of the world's best free attractions. For something a bit more spectacular (but still free), don't miss the festive **Ommegang** celebration in the Grand-Place on the first Tuesday and Thursday in July and the street entertainment around this area during the entire month. On the second Sunday in August, there's the **Planting of the Meiboom** (May Tree), another joyous public occasion. And in mid-August of 2000, the

Grand-Place will be covered by a spectacular **Carpet of Flowers** for all to see at no charge.

WALKING TOUR
Ilôt Sacré to the Marolles

Start: Town Hall, Grand-Place.
Finish: Town center.
Time: About 3 hours.
Best Times: Saturday or Sunday morning, when you can shop in the books-and-antiques market in place du Grand-Sablon.

This walk winds its way through and around the splendid Grand-Place and will help to orient you in the heart of the old city. The tour begins at the Town Hall, which houses the tourist office; after you've picked up some brochures and asked the staff any questions you may have, proceed down Petite rue des Bouchers. This district, called the Ilôt Sacré, is a jumble of streets and passages where restaurants with outdoor terraces, street musicians, and souvenir vendors provide a noisy and colorful atmosphere. On impasse Schuddeveld, a tiny cul-de-sac off Petite rue des Bouchers, is the:

1. **Théâtre Toone VII,** the famous folk puppet theater. A performance at Toone should not be missed. This is a good opportunity to see what shows aren't yet sold out.

Walk farther along the Petite rue de Bouchers to the:

2. **Grand-Place,** which some consider the most beautiful square in the world. This splendid esplanade is surrounded by Flemish Renaissance baroque guild houses from the 17th century, the neo-Gothic King's House, and the 15th-century Gothic Town Hall. The 300-foot tower of the Town Hall bears a spire, on which perches the Archangel Michael, patron saint of the city.

Leave Grand-Place by rue Charles-Buls to the left of the Town Hall. Under the arches of the Maison de l'Etoile is the statue of Everard 't Serclaes, a hero of 14th-century Brussels. Touching the arm of the statue is said to bring you luck. Not far away (about 100 yards behind Town Hall) on rue de l'Etuve and rue du Chêne, standing atop a fountain, is the charming little statue of:

3. **Manneken-Pis** (1619), the "oldest citizen of Brussels." If you're here on a holiday, the little boy will be dressed in one of his 570 colorful costumes kept at the City of Brussels Museum (Musée de la Ville de Bruxelles).

To your left, go up rue du Chêne; along rue de Dinant and rue de Rollebeek you'll come to:

4. **place du Grand-Sablon.** This square, filled with antiques shops, is the place to shop for old curios. An excellent books-and-antiques market is held here on Saturday and Sunday mornings. At no. 40, you can visit the Post Office Museum. Take time to admire Notre-Dame-du-Sablon Church, built in the 15th century by the city's crossbowmen. The church is a superb example of the flamboyant Gothic style, which flourished in Belgium in the 14th and 15th centuries.

Off the larger square, just across rue de la Régence, you'll come to:

5. **place du Petit-Sablon,** designed by the architect Beyaert and laid out in 1890. This garden square is surrounded by a wrought-iron balustrade bearing 48 little bronze statues that represent the guilds of medieval Brussels. Look in the center of the square for the statues of the counts of Egmont and Hornes, who were beheaded in the Grand-Place for their resistance against Spanish tyranny in the 16th century. Behind the garden stands the Palais d'Egmont. On the corner of

rue de la Régence is the Musical Instrument Museum. Go along rue de la Régence toward the majestic:

6. Palais de Justice (Law Courts). This massive building was completed in 1883 after 20 years of construction. From this point, there's a good view of the Marolles quarter.

From behind the Palais de Justice, walk down rue du Faucon and rue des Renards to:

7. place du Jeu de Balle, where a flea market is held every morning (until 2pm). If it's in session when you arrive, take some time to browse among the stalls.

Rue Blaes brings you to place de la Chapelle and the:

8. Notre-Dame de la Chapelle Church, with its remarkable Romanesque-Gothic architecture. This church has always been frequented by famous people—some of whom are commemorated in bas-reliefs and frescoes on the walls. Inside you'll find the tomb of painter Pieter Brueghel the Elder. The memorial "The Velvet Brueghel" was done by the artist's son, Jan. The artist lived and died near here at no. 132 rue Haute. Walking away from the church along the rue d'Or and the bd. de l'Empereur, on your right you'll come to:

9. Mont des Arts, with its Palais de Congrès and the national library. Take rue St. Jean and rue des Eperonniers back to the town center.

8 Sports & Recreation

SPECTATOR SPORTS

✪ **HORSE RACING** There are three tracks in the Brussels area: **Boitsfort,** chaussée de la Hulpe 51 (☎ **02/660-28-39**), reached by tram no. 94 or bus no. 42; **Groenendaal,** Sint-Jansberglaan 4, in Hoeilaart (☎ **02/657-38-20**); and **Sterrebeek,** du Roy de Blicquylaan 43, in Sterrebeek (☎ **02/767-54-75**), reached by tram no. 39 or bus no. 30.

SOCCER The **Maison du Football,** av. Houba de Strooper 145 (☎ **02/477-12-11**), can arrange tickets for international soccer matches if you phone Monday through Friday between 9am and 4:15pm. The local team is FC Anderlecht, which is always in contention for Belgian prizes and usually in the running for European honors as well. During continental tournaments some of the crack European soccer squads can often be seen in action in Brussels.

RECREATION

There's a wide variety of facilities—tennis and squash courts, Olympic swimming pool, gymnasium, and martial arts instruction—at the **Centre Sportif de Woluwe-St-Pierre,** av. Salome 2 (☎ **02/773-18-20**).

BOWLING Leading bowling alleys are **Bowling Crosly Brunswick,** quai du Foin 43 (☎ **02/217-28-01**); and **Bowling Crosly Empereur,** bd. de l'Empereur 36 (☎ **02/512-08-74**).

HORSEBACK RIDING For information on riding stables, contact the **Fédération Royale Belge des Sports Equestres,** av. Houba de Strooper 156 (☎ **02/478-50-56**).

ICE SKATING There's ice skating from September through May at **Forest National,** av. du Globe 36 (call ☎ **02/345-16-11** for hours and fees), reached by bus no. 48 or 54; and at **Poseidon,** av. des Vaillants 4, in Woluwe-St-Lambert (☎ **02/762-16-33**), reached by métro to Tomberg or bus no. 28.

Walking Tour-Ilôt Sacré to the Marolles

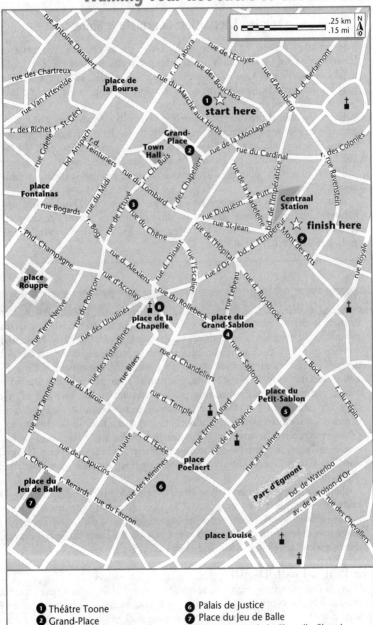

0   .25 km
.15 mi

N

rue Antoine Dansaert
rue des Chartreux
place de la Bourse
rue Van Artevelde
rue du Marché aux Herbs
r. d. Tabora
rue de l'Ecuyer
rue des Bouchers
rue d'Arenberg
bd. d. Berlaimont

☆ **1 start here**

r. des Riches Cl. St-Géry
r. Cdelle Cl. St-Géry
bd. Anspach
r. d. Teinturiers

Grand-Place
Town Hall **2**

rue de la Montagne
rue du Cardinal
r. des Colonies
r. des Ravenstein

place Fontainas
rue Bogards
rue du Midi
rue de l'Etuve
rue du Lombard
rue du Chêne
rue des Chapeliers
rue de la Madeleine
rue Duquesn.
rue St-Jean
Putt.
bd. de l'Impératrice

Centraal Station

3

r. Phd. Champagne
r. Bog
rue d'Alexiens
rue d. Dinant
rue de l'Hôpital
rue d'Or
bd. d. l'Empereur
Mont des Arts

☆ **finish here** **9**

place Rouppe
rue d'Accolay
rue du Poinçon
rue du Rollebeck
rue l'Escalier
rue Lebeau
rue d. Ruysbroek
rue Royale

place Terre Neuve
rue des Ursulines

† **8**
place de la Chapelle

place du Grand-Sablon
4

rue des Vistandines
rue d. Chandeliers
rue d. Sablons
r. Bod

rue du Miroir
rue Blaes
rue d. Temple
rue Ernest Allard

†

place du Petit-Sablon
5

r. du Pépin

rue des Tanneurs
rue Haute
r. d. l'Epée
rue de la Régence
†
rue aux Laines

r. Chevr.
rue des Capucins
r. Renards
rue des Minimes
rue du Faucon

place Poelaert

6

Parc d'Egmont

bd. de Waterloo
av. de la Toison-d'Or
rue des Chevaliers

place du Jeu de Balle
7

place Louise
†
†

1 Théâtre Toone
2 Grand-Place
3 Manneken Pis
4 Place du Grand-Sablon
5 Place du Petit-Sablon
6 Palais de Justice
7 Place du Jeu de Balle
8 Notre-Dame de la Chapelle Church
9 Mont des Arts

Belgian Specialties: Chocolate & More

Belgians know a thing or two about chocolate. Just ask anyone who has ever bitten into one of those devilishly dangerous handmade pralines made and sold by Wittamer, Nihoul, Godiva, Cornez, Neuhaus, Leonidas, and . . . well, it's a long list. Lace is another old favorite that's widely available in the city, particularly in and around the Grand-Place.

Other traditional products of Brussels are beers like *gueuze, kriek,* and *faro,* among the 400 or so different Belgian beers; *geneva* (gin), of which there are some 270 brands produced by 70 distilleries; crystal, particularly superb Val-St-Lambert crystal from Liège; ceramics; jewelry; hand-beaten copper or bronze; and even diamonds, although Brussels is nowhere near as sparkling in this respect as Antwerp.

Finally, sweet-toothed shoppers might like this tip: try **Dandoy** for old-fashioned, spicy speculoos biscuits (traditional Belgian goodies made with cinammon, ginger, and almond) and other treats. The shop can be found at rue au Beurre 31 (☎ **02/511-03-26**).

---

9 Shopping

Brussels is not the place to come looking for bargains. On the whole it's rather expensive, although no more so than neighboring big cities like Paris, Amsterdam, and Cologne. Still, there are reasonable prices to be found, and even bargains. A lot depends on where and when you shop. As a general rule, the upper city around av. Louise and the Porte de Namur is more expensive than the lower city around rue Neuve and the city-center shopping galleries around La Monnaie and place de Brouckère. But this is not a fixed rule. For example, rue Haute, in the upper city, is generally inexpensive, while the Galeries Royales St-Hubert, in the lower city, is generally expensive. In any case, the words to look for are "Soldes" and "Solden" (meaning "Sales" in French and Dutch, respectively), and the even better "Liquidation Totale" and "Totaal Uitverkoop," spreading the good news that "Everything Must Go."

Shopping hours are generally 9 or 10am to 6pm Monday through Saturday. On Friday evening, many city-center stores, particularly department stores, stay open until 8 or 9pm. A useful source of shopping information is the weekly English-language magazine *The Bulletin*, which keeps tabs on the latest shopping ideas and trends, reviews individual shops, and carries advertising.

SHOPPING PROMENADES

Many of Brussels's most interesting shops are clustered along certain promenades or arcades. The **rue Neuve,** which starts at place de la Monnaie and extends north to place Rogier, is practically a pedestrian shopping mall; this busy and popular area is home to many boutiques and department stores, including City 2, a modern shopping complex. **Boulevard Anspach,** which runs from the Stock Exchange up to place de Brouckère, is home to a number of fashion boutiques, chocolate shops, and electronic-appliance stores. The **Anspach Center** (near place de la Monnaie) is a shopping mall.

Europe's oldest shopping mall, the **Galeries Royales St-Hubert,** is a light and airy arcade hosting boutiques, cafe terraces, and street musicians playing classical music. Built in Italian neo-Renaissance style and opened in 1847, architect Pierre Cluysenaer's gallery offers shopping with a touch of class and is well worth strolling through even if you have no intention of even looking in a shop window. The elegant triple gallery—Galerie du Roi, Galerie de la Reine, and Galerie des Princes—was the forerunner of other city arcades such as the Burlington in London. The Galeries Royales St-Hubert is near the Grand-Place, between rue du Marché-aux-Herbes and rue de l'Ecuyer, and split by rue de Bouchers. There are entrances on each of these streets. Métro: Gare Centrale or Bourse.

Av. Louise attracts those in search of world-renowned, high-quality goods from such stores as Cartier, Burberry's, Louis Vuitton, and Valentino.

The **Galerie Agora** (off of the Grand-Place) offers a wide variety of modestly priced merchandise, including leather goods, clothing, souvenirs, records, and jewelry.

OUTDOOR MARKETS

At the **Flea Market** on place du Jeu-de-Balle, a large square in the Marolles district, you can find some exceptional decorative items, many recycled from the homes of the "recently deceased," as well as unusual postcards, clothing, and household goods. The market is held daily from 7am to 2pm.

Every weekend, the place du Grand Sablon hosts a fine **Antiques Market.** The salesmanship is low-key, the interest pure, the prices not unreasonable (don't expect bargains though), and the quality of the merchandise—which includes silverware, pottery, paintings, and jewelry—is high. The market is open Saturday from 9am to 6pm and Sunday 9am to 2pm.

The Grand-Place also has a daily **Flower Market** and a weekly **Bird Market,** which runs from 7am to 2pm and features many varieties of birds (many, sadly, with their wings clipped). Nearby, at the top end of rue du Marché-aux-Herbes, in a square loosely called the Agora, there's a weekend **Crafts Market,** with lots of fine specialized jewelry and other items, mostly inexpensive.

The area around the Gare du Midi is the site of the vast **Sunday Market,** which lasts from 6am to 1pm. It features a large number of Middle Eastern and south European merchants who offer food, clothing, and household goods, as well as unusual items from their home areas. (Don't park in this area on a Saturday evening, planning to leave your car there on Sunday—it will be towed away for sure.)

SHOPPING A TO Z

Here's a short list of my personal recommendations, which is only a small sampling of Brussels's best shopping. The stores mentioned below, however, provide a little something extra in the way of shopping ambiance, as well as value for money.

BOOKS

City Press Center. bd. Anspach 67. ☎ **02/511-11-22.** Métro: Bourse.

This international press shop has a large selection of English-language periodicals and paperback books. Open Monday through Saturday from 8am to 8pm, and on Sunday from 9am to 8pm.

W. H. Smith. bd. Adolphe Max 71. ☎ **02/219-27-08.** Métro: Rogier.

It's not so easy to find a wide selection of English-language books in Brussels, but this major British bookshop chain does have a full-size branch here, which sells magazines and newspapers as well as books. The books, however, usually cost 30% to 60% more than in Britain.

An Affordable Wine Source

If you're planning to buy wine by the bottle, don't be fooled into the idea that you have to go to some expensive wine shop to get something worthwhile. The mid-price **Delhaize** supermarket chain has built up an enviable reputation and a loyal local following for the quality of its wine department. Delhaize's buyers look for good value in all price categories and have an adventurous streak that makes them look beyond just the classic names. There are Delhaize supermarkets all over Brussels (and Belgium). Ask at your hotel desk for the nearest branch and try it out.

CHILDREN

Boutique de Tintin. rue de la Colline 13. ☎ **02/514-45-50.** Métro: Gare Centrale.

Forget computer games and other electronic toys. If you need to buy a gift for the kids, take home some Tintin mementos from this excellent, if somewhat pricey, store.

In Den Olifant. rue des Fripiers 47. ☎ **02/217-43-97.** Métro: Bourse.

This rather cutesy but charming shop specializes in high-quality toys and games for younger children.

✪ **La Trotinette.** rue des Eperonniers 4. ☎ **02/511-00-41.** Métro: Gare Centrale.

La Trotinette reaches back to a kinder and gentler era of children's toys, with tin cars, wooden soldiers, and Barbie dolls from the fifties. One of its more distinguished recent customers was President Bill Clinton.

EURO-STUFF

Eurotempo. rue du Marché-aux-Herbes 84. ☎ **02/502-37-47.** Métro: Gare Centrale or Bourse.

One of the most surprising marketing phenomena of recent years has been the popularity of the European Union's symbol: a blue flag with a circle of 12 stars. At Eurotempo you can find this logo on an astonishing range of products: umbrellas, T-shirts, pens, golf balls, watches, hats, knives, towels—you name it. Where better to buy Eurostuff than in the capital of Europe?

FOOD & WINES

✪ **Dandoy.** rue au Beurre 31. ☎ **02/511-81-76.** Métro: Bourse.

Dandoy is the place for sweet-toothed cookies-'n-cakes fans. Try the traditional Belgian house specialties: spicy speculoos cookies (made with cinammon, ginger, and almond) and pain à grecque, a thin, spicy biscuit.

De Boe. rue de Flandre 36. ☎ **02/511-13-73.** Métro: Ste-Catherine.

Don't miss this small shop near the Fish Market. It has a superb selection of roasted and blended coffee and wines in all price categories, as well as an array of specialty crackers, nuts, spices, teas, and gourmet snacks, many of which are canned, making them suitable for transport home. Open Tuesday through Saturday from 9am to 1pm and 2 to 6pm.

Neuhaus. Galerie de la Reine 25. ☎ **02/502-59-14.** Métro: Gare Centrale or Bourse.

This chocolatier sells some of the best of the dangerously delicious Belgian handmade chocolates. You can buy gift pralines here.

Wittamer. place du Grand Sablon 12. ☎ **02/512-37-42.** Tram: 92 and 93.

Wittamer makes some of the best handmade pralines in the world. Their rolls, breads, pastries, and cakes have also been winning fans here since 1910.

FASHION & APPAREL

Delvaux. Galerie de la Reine 31. ☎ **02/512-71-98.** Métro: Gare Centrale Station or Bourse.

This local company makes and sells some of the best—and priciest—handbags and leather goods in Belgium.

Ganterie Italienne. Galerie de la Reine 3 (off of the Grand-Place). ☎ **02/512-75-38.** Métro: Gare Centrale or Bourse.

This is a glove shop with Italian style, selling attractive handwear that keeps out the winter cold. Open Monday through Saturday 10am to 12:30pm and 1:30 to 6pm.

Kaat Tilley. Galerie du Roi 4 (off of the Grand-Place). ☎ **02/514-07-63.** Métro: Gare Centrale or Bourse.

This fancifully designed boutique stocks chiffon and silk creations. Open Monday 10am to 6pm, Tuesday through Friday 10am to 6:30pm, and Saturday 10:30am to 6:30pm.

Miggerode. rue Haute 158 (Marolles district). ☎ **02/512-62-48.** Bus 34, 95, or 96 from the Bourse.

Buy a gentleman's hat, or have your own blocked, at Miggerode, a ministering angel to a dying art.

Olivier Strelli. av. Louise 72. ☎ **02/511-21-34.** Métro: Louise.

This top-rated Belgian fashion designer is just one of several big names with boutiques in this area. His shop is strong on elegant, ready-to-wear items.

Tie Rack. rue Neuve 53. ☎ **02/217-25-27.** Métro: De Brouckère.

This place is great for those last-minute sartorial emergencies; it stocks a wide range of designer neckwear.

FLOWERS

✪ **Les Fleurs Isabelle de Baecker.** rue Royale 13. ☎ **02/217-26-69.** Métro: Botanique.

This superb flower shop in a superb art nouveau location is just the place for that important bouquet.

LACE

Maison Antoine. Grand-Place 26. ☎ **02/512-14-59.** Métro: Gare Centrale or Bourse.

This lace boutique is one of the best in Brussels and surely has the best location, a former guild house where Victor Hugo lived in 1852. The quality is superb, the service friendly, and the prices decent. Open daily from 10am to 7pm.

Manufacture Belge de Dentelle. Galerie de la Reine 6–8. ☎ **02/511-44-77.** Métro: Gare Centrale or Bourse.

This is a good source for top-quality handmade Belgian lace.

MULTIMEDIA

FNAC. City 2. ☎ **02/209-22-11.** Métro: Rogier.

This good-value books, electronics, and photo chain has a branch in the City 2 multistory shopping mall off of rue Neuve. It also sells concert tickets.

10 Brussels After Dark

Brussels is not known for its nightlife, but that's partly because it's overshadowed by the worldwide reputations of neighboring capitals like Paris and Amsterdam. Nightlife is actually alive and well in Brussels, and if the range is inevitably thinner than in bigger cities, the quality is not.

Nighttime in Brussels can be just about anything you want it to be. Cocktail bars vary from the old, established, almost "clubby" type, to the avant-garde, to the bizarre; and there are also cafe theaters, regular theater in season (September through May), a traditional puppet theater, cafe cabarets, dinner shows, nightclubs, concerts, ballet, opera, and jazz clubs.

For current information on after-dark entertainment during your visit, consult the **Tourist Information Brussels** office in the Town Hall, Grand-Place, Brussels (☎ 02/513-89-40), or buy the weekly English-language magazine *The Bulletin*, which has an extensive "What's On" section.

THE PERFORMING ARTS

OPERA & BALLET The superb and historic ✪ **Théâtre Royal de la Monnaie,** place de la Monnaie (☎ 02/229-12-11), founded in the 17th century, is home to the Opéra National and l'Orchestre Symphonique de la Monnaie. Ballet performances are also presented here. The present resident ballet company is local choreographer Anne Theresa de Keersmaeker's Group Rosas.

CLASSICAL MUSIC The **Palais des Beaux-Arts,** rue Royale 10 (☎ 02/507-84-66), is the home of Belgium's National Orchestra. Concerts are also performed at the **Cirque Royal,** rue de l'Enseignement 81 (☎ 02/218-20-15), which was formerly a real circus, but is now a venue for music, opera, and ballet; and at **Le Botanique,** rue Royale 236 (☎ 02/218-37-32), which generally focuses on small-scale modern and avant-garde performances, not only of "classical" music but also of jazz and other forms.

THEATERS Brussels theater is quite important among French-speaking countries, with more than 30 theaters presenting performances in French, Flemish, and (occasionally) English. Among the most important are **Théâtre Royal du Parc,** rue de la Loi 3 (☎ 02/512-23-29), for classic and contemporary drama and comedies; **Théâtre Royal des Galeries,** Galerie du Roi 32 (☎ 02/512-04-07), with a wide variety of offerings, including drama, comedy, and musicals; the art deco–style **Théâtre du Résidence Palace,** rue de la Loi 155 (☎ 02/231-03-05); **Le Botanique,** rue Royale 236 (☎ 02/218-37-32), which inclines toward the experimental in mostly French theater; and the **Koninklijke Vlaamse Schouwburg,** rue de Laeken 146 (☎ 02/217-69-37), a neo-Renaissance-style building dating from 1887 that brings the world's theatrical highlights to the city in Dutch.

PUPPET THEATER

✪ **Théâtre Toone VII.** impasse Schuddeveld 6, Petite rue des Bouchers 21. ☎ 02/217-27-53. Ticket prices and performance times vary; check in advance.

Look for the small wooden sign in the tiny alleyway—impasse Schuddeveld—to reach this theater, located in an upstairs room in a bistro of the same name. It's the last in the Toone line of puppet theaters, which dates back to the early 1800s—the

Puppet Shows: A Belgian Passion

A special word is in order about a special sort of theater—that of the wooden marionettes that have entertained Belgians for centuries. In times past, puppet theaters numbered in the hundreds nationwide (Brussels alone had 15), and the plays were much like our modern-day soap operas. The story lines went on and on, sometimes for generations, and working-class audiences returned night after night to keep up with the "Dallas" of the times. Performances were based on folklore, legends, or political satire.

Specific marionette characters came to personify their home cities: a cheeky ragamuffin named Woltje (Little Walloon) was from Brussels; Antwerp had the cross-eyed, earthy ne'er-do-well Schele; Pierke, from Ghent, was modeled on the traditional Italian clown; and Liège's Tchantchès stood only 16 inches high and always appeared with patched trousers, a tasseled floppy hat, and his constant companion, the sharp-tongued Nanesse (Agnes).

Today a few Belgian puppet theaters still survive and their popularity has increased in recent years after a decline following World War II, when bombing raids severely damaged many theaters and destroyed many marionettes.

title being passed from one puppet master to the next—and it may be the most popular theater in Brussels. At Toone, Puppet Master José Géal presents his adaptation of such classic tales as *The Three Musketeers, Faust,* and *Hamlet* in the Brussels dialect, Brussels Vloms, but also in English, French, Dutch, and German. In any case, language should present no difficulties since it's easy to follow the action on stage.

ROCK CONCERTS

Forest National. av. du Globe 36. ☎ **02/347-03-55.** Railway station: Forest-Est.

This is the main venue for big rock concerts in Brussels. Smaller-scale shows are likely to go to the Cirque Royal (see "Classical Music," above).

THE CLUB & MUSIC SCENE
CABARET & DINNER DANCING

Le Huchier, place du Grand-Sablon (☎ **02/512-27-11**), open until the wee hours of the morning, features marvelous Hungarian and gypsy music, as well as jazz and just about any other type of music you request, and also offers light snacks and drinks. **Le Pavillon,** in the Brussels Sheraton Hotel, place Rogier 3 (☎ **02/224-32-05**), provides live music for dinner dancing on Friday and Saturday. Burlesque takes center stage at dinner on Saturday at **Moustache,** quai au Bois à Brûler 61 (☎ **02/218-58-77**). Wednesday through Sunday, there's a transvestite dinner show at **Chez Flo,** rue au Beurre 25 (☎ **02/512-94-96**). Night owls can check out **Le Show Point,** place Stephanie 14 (☎ **02/511-53-64**), in the av. Louise area for nonstop "big show" entertainment from 10pm until dawn Monday through Saturday—showgirls, scantily clad or wearing fanciful costumes, strut their stuff in a variety of fetching dance numbers.

JAZZ & BLUES

Jazz has taken a hit in Brussels in recent years. Some of the best-loved spots are now closed—the worst loss of all may be the nightly shindig at L'Estaminet du Kelderke, a cellar bar in the Grand-Place where the music once set the foam flying in the beer glasses. Still, some old places remain, and new ones have sprung up. *Plus ça change, plus c'est la même chose*—the more things change, the more they stay the same, and thank goodness for it.

The **Brussels Preservation Hall,** rue de Londres 3 (☎ 02/511-03-04), lacks some (well, a lot really) of the New Orleans style to which it alludes, but don't let that put you off. It's just a name, after all, and the place itself is quintessential Brussels, the proprietor a genuine enthusiast, the clientele committed, and the music consistently outstanding. Visiting American musicians, some of whom might actually hail from New Orleans, are often on the bill.

A relatively new venue, the **New York Jazz Club,** chaussée de Charleroi 5 (☎ 02/534-85-09), is maybe a little too cool and refined for its own good, but it's willing to be more experimental than the Preservation Hall and is well worth checking out. Sometimes it seems that the thick clouds of cigarette smoke in the dark and lively **Blues Corner,** rue des Chapeliers 12 (☎ 02/511-97-94), have lingered there for decades. Like the blues themselves, this place just goes on and on. Which is how lovers of the heavy licks to be heard hereabouts seem to like it.

DANCE CLUBS

Nothing in life changes quite so fast as the "in" discos. Still, there are some that have stood the test of time—and that of course makes them anathema to genuine disco hounds. Since the turnover rate is so high, be sure to check locally to see if the following are still in operation before setting out for a night of dancing. The most sophisticated dance club in Brussels is ✪ **Griffin's Club** in the Royal Windsor Hotel, rue Duquesnoy 5 (☎ 02/505-55-55), which is in full swing every night except Sunday. The **Mirano Continental,** chaussée de Louvain 38 (☎ 02/218-57-72), is more of a dance hall than a disco, a classy place for those whose wildest years are a few years behind them yet who still like to enjoy themselves. **Nostalgia Club,** rue de la Fourche 49 (☎ 02/513-3291), is something similar, with hits from the 60s and 70s at the top of the bill.

Le Garage, rue Duquesnoy 16 (☎ 02/512-66-22), just off of the Grand-Place, always seems on the verge of going out of style, yet never quite gets there, even if it has lost the wild and wonderful cachet of its earlier days—its location just off of the Grand-Place undoubtedly helps, as does its consistently up-to-date approach to the music. **Cartagena,** rue du Marché-au-Charbon 70 (☎ 02/502-59-08), is as hot as a night in, well, Cartagena, and dispenses drinks and music from all over Latin America. If only techno will do, **Le Fuse,** rue Blaes 208 (☎ 02/511-97-89), is the place—on the first Friday of every month it reinvents itself as the women-only **Pussy Lounge,** and every Sunday as the men-only **La Démence.**

THE BAR SCENE

Now you're talking. Bars are where Brussels lives. It's hard to be disappointed, whether you just pop into a neighborhood watering hole where a *chope* or *pintje* (a glass of beer) will set you back a mere 30 BF (85¢), or whether you prefer to fork out several times as much in one of the trendier places.

Unique, to say the least, is a Brussels favorite, **A la Morte Subite,** rue Montagne-aux-Herbes-Potagères 7 (☎ 02/513-13-18), a bistro of rather special character whose name translates to "Sudden Death," which is also the name of one of the beers you can buy here. Don't worry. The name is just a name, and you'll probably survive in this fine old Brussels cafe, which appeals to an eclectic cross-section of Brussels society, from little old ladies to bank managers, dancers and musicians from the top cultural venues, students—oh yes, and to tourists as well. The decor consists of stained-glass motifs, old photographs, paintings, and prints on the walls, and plain wooden chairs and tables on the floor. Specialties are traditional Brussels beers: *gueuze, faro,* and *kriek,* as well as abbey brews like Chimay, Maredsous, and Grimbergen. The staff's attitude can take a little getting used to; especially if you take more than 3 seconds flat to decide what you want. If you know straight away, you'll have a friend for life, or at any rate, for the evening.

In a quite different vein is ✪ **La Fleur en Papier Doré,** rue des Alexiens 55 (☎ **02/511-16-59**), located in a 16th-century house. From its beginnings in 1846, this bistro and pub has been a mecca for poets and writers. Even now, about once a month, young Brussels poets gather here informally for poetry readings—the dates vary, but you might inquire by phone, or better yet, just drop by and ask in person. This is a wonderfully atmospheric old pub, much like a social club, where patrons gather for good conversation and welcome any and all newcomers. The place also serves what is possibly the best onion soup in Brussels, a great late-night snack.

The following are only a few of the many Brussels pubs and bistros worthy of recommendation. **Au Bon Vieux Temps,** rue du Marché-aux-Herbes 12 (☎ **02/217-26-26**), hidden away at the end of a narrow alleyway, is a gloomily atmospheric old tavern that seems to harken back to a bygone era. You should try the appropriately named Duvel (Devil) beer here—just go easy, that's all. **A l'Image de Notre-Dame,** impasse rue du Marché-aux-Herbes 6 (☎ **02/219-42-49**), is a good, quiet place to drink and read or reflect if you're alone, or to converse with a companion without having to compete with a blaring jukebox.

Le Cirio, rue de la Bourse 18 (☎ **02/512-13-95**), is across the road from the Stock Exchange, and indeed many of the bar's customers look like they've just made a killing on the stock market and have retired to a state of genteel splendor. And what better place to do it in? Le Cirio is a quiet, refined sort of place to sip your beer, in attractive surroundings that make the whole exercise seem worthwhile. **Toone VII,** impasse Schuddeveld 6, Petite rue des Bouchers 21 (☎ **02/511-71-37**), is the home of the puppet theater and an artistic hangout. Art nouveau design and an extensive range of Belgian beers are just two reasons for visiting **De Ultieme Hallucinatie,** rue Royale 316 (☎ **02/217-06-14**), a distinctive cafe that has a kind of sculpted cliffside (a plaster-covered wall that looks like a rockface) for interior decor and a fine, though expensive, restaurant attached. **Le Falstaff,** rue Henri Maus 17 (☎ **02/511-98-77**), first opened in 1904, and with its art-nouveau-with-a-dash-of-art-deco adornment, it's the city's most stylish cafe. It has its drawbacks, though: The waiters are widely considered to have an attitude problem—they act as if they're doing you a huge favor by waiting on you. That can get a bit tiresome, but ironically, a greater problem here is finding a seat—despite the snooty waitstaff this place is popular, and usually packed.

Rick's, av. Louise 344 (☎ **02/647-75-30**), brings a touch of Humphrey Bogart and Ernest Hemingway, accompanied by American and Mexican food, to the stylish av. Louise. The decor might give you the creeps at **Halloween,** rue des Grands-Carmes 10 (☎ **02/514-12-56**), where gargoyles, devils, and other assorted creatures from the darker recesses of the mind help create an unforgettable ambiance. Fortunately, it's also a pretty good bar. Something sad has happened to the painfully chic denizens of **L'Archiduc,** rue Antoine Dansaert 6 (☎ **02/512-06-52**)—they've loosened up a little. Not much, mind you—just enough so that you don't see a hundred lips curling with disdain when you enter wearing clothes that were de rigueur last week instead of today.

MOVIES

Since most movies in Brussels are shown in the original language, you'll always be able to find many English-language films in the theaters. Major cinemas in the city center are: **Actor's Studio,** Petite rue des Bouchers 16 (☎ 02/512-16-96), with two screens; **Arenberg/Galeries,** de la Reine 26 (☎ 02/512-80-63), with two screens; **Aventure,** du Centre 57 (☎ 02/219-17-48), with three screens; **City 2,** rue Neuve 235 (☎ 02/226-6611), with eight screens; and **UGC de Brouckère,** place de la Brouckère 38 (☎ 0900/10-440), with eight screens. **Kinepolis,** bd. du Centenaire 20 (☎ 0900/35-241), is the best equipped and the biggest, with 26 screens, including an IMAX wraparound screen. Part of the Bruparck recreation complex beside the Atomium, Kinepolis is likely to have something for everyone. Most movies shown here are big releases, usually from Hollywood, which is no doubt the main reason why the place is so popular. The **Musée du Cinema,** 9 rue Baron Horta 9 (☎ 02/507-83-70), often features little-seen classic films from the past.

EXHIBITIONS

Exhibitions aren't very high on most visitors' must-see lists, but you might just be in town when one of the big shows, or one that especially interests you, is on at the giant **Foire Internationale de Bruxelles,** place de Belgique, 1020 Bruxelles (☎ 02/477-04-77), at the Heysel. Regular exhibitions include the Home Interiors Exhibition and the Car Show.

OFFBEAT BRUSSELS

It's no accident that René Magritte lived in Brussels. He sat at his easel in a business suit, painting comically unsettling pictures of pipes that aren't pipes and mirrors that reflect the back of someone's head. Forget the myth of Brussels's "sobriety"; Bruxellois are fun-loving people.

For a quirky good time, you can attend a **Bruegelian Banquet** (Kermesse Breugelienne), av. de Madrid 130 (☎ 02/479-78-98), in a former roller-skating arena near the Atomium, and snap up blood-sausages, odorous cheeses, and Brussels beer, while ducking to avoid low-flying falcons (this event is usually attended by a group of falconers, and the falcon flies from one member of the group to another, just above the heads of the diners). Or drink beer from a skull-shaped pitcher in **Le Cerceuil** (The Coffin), rue des Harengs 10–12 (☎ 02/512-30-77), while sitting in purple gloom at a casket-turned-table, being serenaded by funereal music.

For other unconventional diversions, you can arrange to tour the **sewers** by calling ☎ 02/513-8587, or play Russian roulette with falling arrows at vertical archery practice in **Parc Josaphat** (Schaerbeek)—the archers gather at unpredictable times, although any sunny weekend afternoon in summer is a good bet. Otherwise, call the tourist office for possible dates. It may be safer to visit the daily **flea market** in place du Jeu de Balle after its 2pm closing time (it starts at 7am), and hunt around in the leftovers for bizarre things that nobody wanted at any price. Then buy a gentleman's hat, or have your own blocked, at nearby **Miggerode,** rue Haute 158 (☎ 02/512-62-48), the last bastion of a dying art.

Brussels used to have a river called the **Senne.** Last century, the City Fathers had it bricked over and tucked away out of sight. Brussels now has no river, but you can catch a glimpse of where it used to be under the arches behind place St-Géry. The transience of modern authority can be seen at the **Berlaymont Palace,** former headquarters of the European Commission (place Schuman), where the European

Union national flags used to billow proudly until a few years ago, when the building was evacuated as an asbestos-contaminated health hazard (it's currently undergoing a refurbishment process).

Don't miss the transvestite show at **Chez Flo,** rue au Beurre 25 (☎ 02/512-94-96), or the marionette plays in Brussels dialect at **Café-Théâtre Toone VII,** impasse Schuddeveld 6, Petite rue des Bouchers 21 (☎ 02/511-71-37). You might also want to sit amidst aging, genteel splendor at **Café Cirio,** rue de la Bourse 16 (☎ 02/512-13-95), and try to avoid getting bitten by the patrons' poodles; or make funny faces at the too-cool denizens of **L'Archiduc,** rue Antoine Dansaert 6 (☎ 02/512-06-52) to see if you can't get one to crack a smile.

On the way home, take in some **Métro Art**—paintings and sculptures by top modern Belgian artists that grace many métro stations.

11 Side Trips from Brussels

The lovely Brabant countryside around Brussels offers scenic beauty, as well as several sightseeing attractions well worth the short trip.

BEERSEL

The only local example of a still intact ✪ **fortified medieval castle** is at Beersel, only 5½ miles to the south of Brussels, a little off the Mons road (watch for the signpost). The three-towered 13th-century castle is set in a wooded area and surrounded by a moat, which you cross via drawbridge. Pick up the excellent English-language guidebook at the entrance for a detailed history of the castle and its inhabitants, then wander through its rooms for a trip back through time. End your visit with a stop at the magnificent mausoleum that holds the alabaster effigies of Henry II of Witthem and his wife, Jacqueline de Glimes, who lived here during the early 1400s. Visiting hours can vary, so check with the tourist office in Brussels before you go.

Leafy pathways through the castle grounds make this a favorite rural retreat for Brussels residents, especially during the summer months. At the entrance to the park, you'll find **Auberge Kasteel Beersel,** Lotstraat 65, 1650 Beersel (☎ 02/331-00-24), a charming rustic restaurant with a decor of dark wood, exposed brick, and accents of copper and brass. In good weather there's service on the shaded outdoor terrace. Light meals (omelets, salads, soups, and sandwiches) are available, as well as complete hot meals for both lunch and dinner. Prices are moderate. If you don't want a meal, you're very welcome to stop in just for a relaxing draft of Belgian beer.

GAASBEEK

The ancestral château of the counts of Egmont is at Gaasbeek, some 8 miles from Brussels on the Mons highway. The furnishings here are nothing less than magnificent, as is the castle itself. All the rooms are splendid, and far from presenting a dead "museum" appearance, they create the eerie impression that the counts and their families may come walking through the door any moment. Before each guided tour, there's a slide show that will augment your appreciation of the countless works of art, silver items, religious artifacts, and priceless tapestries you'll see in the castle. Check with the Brussels tourist office for opening hours and entrance fees.

WATERLOO

The Battle of Waterloo was Europe's Gettysburg. The battlefield itself remains much as it was on June 18, 1815. To visit it, however, you don't actually go to the town of Waterloo, which, although a pleasant-enough suburb of Brussels, is not really worth going out of your way for—the Battle of Waterloo was not actually fought there. A stretch of rolling farmland dotted with stoutly built manor-farmhouses several miles to the south got that "honor."

At the cluster of buildings beside the **Visitor Center,** you can find "rations" at one of the cafes or restaurants, which have names like Le Hussard, Bivouac de l'Empereur, and Les Alliés. There are also souvenir shops selling everything from Napoleonic corkscrews to hand-painted model soldiers. Beside the crossroads at the Brussels–Charleroi road are monuments to the Belgians and Hanoverians; to Colonel Gordon, Wellington's aide; and to General Picton, shot down at the head of his division. A little way down the Brussels–Charleroi road is La Haie–Sainte, a farmhouse that played a crucial role in Napoléon's defeat by shielding Wellington's center from direct assault.

A pathway beside the Panorama (see below) leads to a memorial to Lieutenant Augustin Demulder, a Belgian soldier who fell in Napoléon's campaign—around this spot Marshal Ney's horsemen surged against unyielding Allied (British, Dutch, Belgian, and Hanoverian) infantry deployed in a "square" military formation. Farther on, a memorial records the position of British artillery that poured grapeshot into Napoléon's Old Guard during their doomed final assault. A stroll of 15 minutes more brings you to Hougoumont Farm, which played a key role in the fighting and still bears the scars of battle. The owners let visitors wander around the grounds.

Visitor Center (Centre Visiteur). route du Lion 252–254, Braine L'Alleud. ☎ **02/385-19-12.** Admission Butte 40 BF ($1.10); Audiovisual and Panorama 275 BF ($7.65); Butte, Audiovisual, and Panorama 300 BF ($8.35). Apr–Sept 9am–6pm; Oct 9:30am–5:30pm; Nov–Feb 10:30am–4pm; Mar 10:30am–5pm. Bus: W from av. de Stalingrad to Centre Visiteur. By car, go south on the R0 Brussels Ring Road (east), then south on the A5, past the Waterloo exit, and follow the signs for Butte du Lion.

Before exploring the battlefield, you should stop here, where an audiovisual presentation on the tactical background plus an extract from a fictional film version of the conflict will give you an idea of the battle's impressive scale.

The view of the theater of war from the top of the great Lion Mound (Butte du Lion) beside the Visitor Center is worth the 226-step climb, although it takes an active imagination to fill the peaceful farmland with slashing cavalry charges, thundering artillery, and 200,000 colorfully uniformed, struggling soldiers.

Also next to the Center is the Battlefield Panorama (Panorama de la Bataille), featuring a painted diorama of the massive French cavalry charge led by Marshal Ney. It was a sensation in the pre-cinema era.

Wellington Museum (Musée Wellington). chaussée de Bruxelles 147, Waterloo. ☎ **02/354-78-06.** Admission 100 BF ($2.80). Apr–Sept daily 9:30am–6:30pm; Oct–Mar daily 10:30am–5pm. Bus: W from av. de Stalingrad to Waterloo.

The well-ordered Musée Wellington (Wellington Museum) is located in Waterloo itself in an old Brabant coaching inn that was the Duke's headquarters. It was from here that Wellington sent his historic victory dispatch.

Bruges (Brugge) 6

Bruges has drifted down the stream of time with all the graceful self-possession of the swans that cruise its canals. To step into the old city is to be transported instantly back to the Middle Ages, when Bruges was among the wealthiest cities of Europe. Unlike so many cities in Europe that have had their hearts torn out by war, Bruges has remained unravaged, its glorious monumental buildings intact. This city is the pride and joy of Flanders and Belgium.

Medieval Gothic architecture is the big deal here. Sure, there's a layer of Romanesque; a touch of Renaissance, baroque, and rococo; a dab of neoclassical and neo-Gothic; and a smidgen of jugendstil and art deco. But Gothic is what Bruges provides, in quantities that come near to numbing the senses—and probably would do so if it weren't for the distraction of the city's contemporary animation.

1 Frommer's Favorite Bruges Experiences

- **Cruising the Canals.** Those open-top canal boats can be scorching in hot weather and bracing in cold, but they're fun and they give you a uniquely satisfying view of the city. There's even a stern-wheel paddle steamer that sails along the canal to the nearby village of Damme.
- **Comparing Codpieces.** Ahem, I really mean admiring the finely carved suits of armor of the statues of Emperor Charles V, Emperor Maximilian of Austria, and King Ferdinand II of Aragon on the Renaissance chimneypiece in the Hall of the Liberty of Bruges in the Burg. (I say Charles's is the biggest.)
- **Climbing the Belfry.** It's only 366 steps to the top—and it doesn't seem like more than about 350. Remembering the view of the city and the Flemish countryside all the way to the sea should compensate for any subsequent muscle cramps.
- **Cycling Everywhere.** Unlike most Belgian cities, Bruges has made cyclists privileged road users, with rights of way that motorists would kill for. You can ride through the city, around it on the ring canal park, and outside it on fresh-air excursions.
- **Sinking a Herring.** These tasty fish are filleted and served fresh and raw with onions at the morning Fish Market in the Vismarkt from Tuesday through Sunday—they won't make you popular with anyone you happen to breathe on for several hours afterward—but the taste is incredible.

- **Stroll the Back Streets.** You don't need to visit the top ten highlights to enjoy Bruges. Shut your guidebook, put away the street map, and just wander, taking time out to make your own discoveries. Bruges's residents live their everyday lives in absurdly beautiful surroundings and don't need to put on a show for the tourists.

2 Orientation

ARRIVING

BY PLANE   Although there is a small airport at Ostend (Oostende) just 24km (15 miles) from Bruges at the Belgian coast, it handles mostly charter and air taxi flights. **Brussels National Airport** is the main airport for Bruges (see "Arriving," in chapter 5).

BY TRAIN   Trains arrive every hour or so from Brussels, Antwerp, and Ghent, and from the North Sea ports of Ostend (Oostende) and Zeebrugge. Journey time is about 1 hour by train from Brussels and Antwerp, 30 minutes from Ghent, and 15 minutes from Ostend and Zeebrugge. A train to and from Lille in northern France connects there with the Eurostar trains through the Channel Tunnel from London to Paris and Brussels. From Paris, you can take the Thalys high-speed trains through Brussels direct to Bruges, or the slower and cheaper International trains, changing in Brussels. International trains from Cologne to London, via Ostend, stop in Bruges. From Amsterdam, you can go via Antwerp or Brussels, either on the Thalys, or the normal International and Inter-City trains.

Although the city is called Bruges in English and French, in Flemish it's "Brugge," and that's what the train station destination boards say. The station is on Stationsplein, about 1 mile south of town, a 20-minute walk to the town center or a short bus or taxi ride. For train information, call ☎ **050/38-23-82** between 6:30am and 10:30pm.

BY BUS   Buses are less useful than trains for getting to Bruges, although there are frequent buses from Ostend, Zeebrugge, and other Belgian coastal resorts, as well as from Sluis in Holland, which is useful if you're coming from Zeeland Province (see "Zeeland," in chapter 19). Bruges bus station adjoins the train station (see above). For schedule and fare information, call ☎ **059/56-53-53** from 6am to 9pm.

Eurolines operates a daily service from London's Victoria Coach Station—via the Dover–Calais ferry or the Channel Tunnel's Le Shuttle train—to Brussels, stopping at Bruges. Bruges can also be reached from all over Britain and Europe on the Eurolines network, via London or Brussels. For schedule and fare information, contact Eurolines at ☎ **0582/404511** in Britain, and ☎ **02/203-07-07** in Belgium.

BY CAR   Bruges is 89km (55 miles) northwest of Brussels and 46km (28 miles) northwest of Ghent on the E40, 92km (57 miles) west of Antwerp on the E17 and E40, and 24km (37 miles) southeast of Ostend on the E40. From Calais and the Channel Tunnel take the E40 east.

For a hassle-free visit to Bruges, drive directly to the large underground car park near the train station at 't Zand and leave your car there until you're headed out of town (see "Getting Around," below). You'll find it all but impossible to use a car in the city center.

VISITOR INFORMATION

The tourist office, **Toerisme Brugge,** at Burg 11, 8000 Bruges (☎ **050/44-86-86;** fax 050/44-86-00), is open April through September, Monday to Friday from

Bruges (Brugge)

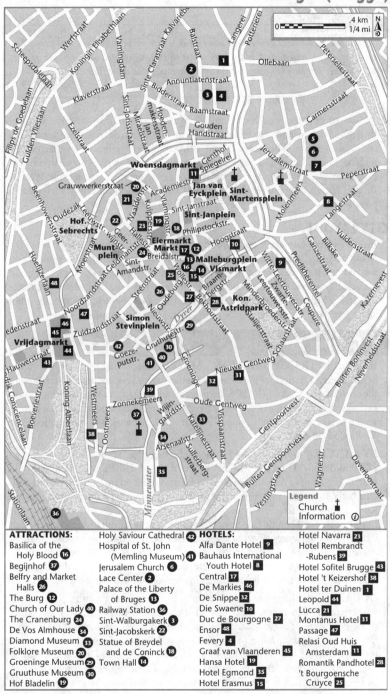

9:30am to 6:30pm, weekends from 10am to noon and 2 to 6:30pm; October through March, Monday to Friday 9:30am to 5pm, weekends from 9:30am to 1pm and 2 to 5:30pm. This friendly and efficient office has brochures that outline walking, coach, canal, and horse-drawn carriage tours, as well as detailed information on many sightseeing attractions. Ask for the complimentary monthly "Agenda Brugge" newsletter and "Exit" brochure, both excellent directories of current goings-on.

CITY LAYOUT

Bruges has two connected centers, the side-by-side monumental squares called the Markt and the Burg. Narrow streets fan out from these two squares, while a network of canals threads its way to every section of the small city. The center is almost encircled by a canal that opens at its southern end to become the Minnewater (Lake of Love), which is filled with swans and other birds and bordered by the Begijnhof and a fine park. On the outer side of the Minnewater is the railway station.

3 Getting Around

BY PUBLIC TRANSPORTATION   Most city buses depart from the bus station beside the train station, or the secondary station at 't Zand, and many buses stop in the center at the Markt. Schedules are prominently posted. A day pass giving unlimited travel on all city buses costs 110 BF ($3.05) and can be bought on the bus, or at the kiosks at the bus stations. For city and regional bus information, call ☎ 059/56-53-53.

BY BICYCLE   You can rent a bicycle at the **Baggage Depot** of the train station (☎ 050/38-58-71) for 325 BF ($9.05) per day, and 250 BF ($6.95) with a valid train ticket; there's a discount on rentals of 3 days or more. In addition, many hotels rent bikes to guests, and there are also at least a dozen bike rental shops around town. Biking is a terrific way to get around Bruges or to get out of town to the nearby village of Damme (see below) by way of beautiful canal-side roads. Recent traffic control measures have made cyclists privileged road users—in more than 50 of the narrow, one-way streets in the city center, bikers can travel in both directions. However, cyclists should always be careful because the streets are filled with pedestrians, many of whom are liable to step in front of you without looking.

BY CAR   Don't drive: Leave your car at your hotel parking lot (if it has one), at one of the six big, prominently labeled underground parking lots in the center (these get expensive for long stays), at one of the four free park-and-ride lots beside the train station, or at a free parking zone outside the city center. It's a short walk into the heart of the old city from any of the parking lots. Driving the narrow streets, many of them one-way, can be confusing. Parking rules are firmly enforced, and unlawfully parked cars will be ticketed, clamped, or towed away.

BY TAXI   There are taxi stands at the Markt (☎ 050/33-44-44) and outside the train station on Stationsplein (☎ 050/38-46-60).

ON FOOT   Walking is the best way to see Bruges. Wear good walking shoes—those charming cobblestones can be hard going.

FAST FACTS: Bruges

American Express   There is no Amex office in Bruges; the nearest is in Brussels (see "Fast Facts: Brussels," in chapter 5).

Area Code   Bruges's telephone area code is **050.** You don't need to dial the **050** area code from inside Bruges or from the suburbs of the city, just from elsewhere in Belgium. Dial **50** (without the initial 0) if you are phoning Bruges from outside Belgium.

Bookstores   The **Brugse Boekhandel,** Dijver 2 (☎ **050/33-29-52**) stocks a fair number of English books, as well as maps, newspapers, and magazines.

Car Rental   Driving is not a good way to see the city's attractions, but if you must rent a car, you'll find **Avis** at Koningin Astridlaan 97/7 (☎ **050/39-44-51**); and **Hertz** at Baron Ruzettelaan 6 (☎ **050/37-72-34**).

Currency Exchange   The tourist office (see "Visitor Information," above) is a good place to change money and traveler's checks, as are banks. Automatic teller machines in the Markt, and at numerous other points in the city center, can be accessed by major credit cards, bank cards linked to the Cirrus and Plus networks, Eurocheque cards, and some also by the major charge cards.

Embassies/Consulates   See "Fast Facts: Belgium," in chapter 4.

Emergencies   For the police, dial ☎ **101;** for firefighters and ambulance, ☎ **100.**

Hospital   For medical problems, go to the **Academisch Ziekenhuis Sint-Jan,** Riddershove 10 (☎ **050/45-21-11**).

Luggage Storage/Lockers   There is a **Left Luggage** department at Bruges train station (☎ **050/38-58-71**).

Post Office   The main post office is at Markt 250 (☎ **050/36-85-97**); it's open Monday through Friday from 9am to 6pm and on Saturday from 9am to 3pm.

4 Accommodations

If a high-rise luxury hotel is your cup of tea, then my best advice is that you stay in Brussels and commute to Bruges. But if you like the idea of a small, atmospheric hostelry (perhaps right on the banks of a picturesque canal) with modern (if not necessarily luxurious) facilities, then opt to stay at one of the hotels reviewed below. You'll find that the accommodations here enhance your visit by enabling you to sink into the timelessness of Bruges. All the hotels listed here are in the old center.

There are several very good budget hotels in Bruges, most with rooms above restaurants on the ground floor. Some come with private bathrooms, but you can save money by opting to share a bathroom down the hall—no real hardship in these establishments.

Try not to arrive without a reservation. Bruges is one of Belgium's premier tourist cities (Brussels has more business and diplomatic visitors), and it's a good idea to make reservations at least 2 weeks before you plan to come. If by some quirk of fate you come into town and have no place to stay, head immediately to the tourist office—like tourist offices throughout Belgium, Bruges has a very good reservation service, and can also book in advance for you. Accommodations are much less heavily booked during the week than on weekends. Rates listed here include service and value-added tax (VAT, or BTW in Bruges).

Note that where hotels have no private parking, there's another option beyond "Limited parking available on street." Bruges's small city center holds six big public parking lots, all clearly marked on access roads. So there will always be at least one within a short walk of your hotel.

EXPENSIVE

✪ **De Snippe.** Nieuwe Gentweg 53, 8000 Bruges. ☎ **050/33-70-70.** Fax 050/33-76-62. 9 units. MINIBAR TV TEL. 5,500–7,500 BF ($152.80–$208.35) double. Rates include full breakfast. AE, CB, DC, MC, V. Limited parking available on street.

De Snippe is set in an early-18th-century building in the town center. It not only holds one of Bruges's leading restaurants (see "Dining," below), but it also offers truly luxurious and spacious rooms, all furnished with restrained elegance. Many rooms have fireplaces. All bathrooms have been fully renovated and are equipped with hair dryers.

Dining: See "Dining," below.

Amenities: Concierge, limited hours room service, laundry and dry cleaning service, newspaper delivery, twice-daily maid service, baby-sitting, secretarial services.

✪ **Die Swaene.** Steenhouwersdijk 1, 8000 Bruges. ☎ **050/34-27-98.** Fax 050/33-66-74. E-mail: dieswaene@unicall.be. 22 units. MINIBAR TV TEL. 5,800–7,200 BF ($161.10–$200) double; 8,950–10,950 BF ($248.60–$304.15) suite. Rates include buffet breakfast. AE, DC, JCB, MC, V. Parking 300 BF ($8.35).

This small hotel overlooking a canal in the town center has rightly been called one of the most romantic hotels in Europe. All guest rooms are elegantly furnished and very comfortable, each with an individual décor. All have hair dryers. The lovely lounge is actually the Guild Hall of the Tailors that dates back to 1779. The hotel is owned by the charming Hessels family.

Dining: The hotel restaurant, which specializes in fish, has won praise from guests as well as critics.

Amenities: Concierge, room service, laundry and dry cleaning service, newspaper delivery, twice-daily maid service, baby-sitting, secretarial services, heated indoor pool, sauna, conference rooms.

Hotel Sofitel Brugge. Boeveriestraat 2, 8000 Bruges. ☎ **050/34-09-71.** Fax 050/34-40-53. E-mail: info.brugge@sofitel.be. 155 units. A/C MINIBAR TV TEL. 5,900–7,100 BF ($163.90–$197.20) double. AE, CB, DC, JCB, MC, V. Limited parking available on street.

You might just get the abbey habit at the Sofitel Brugge, which is housed in a converted 17th-century monastery. This thoroughly up-to-date hotel is located at 't Zand, not far from the railway station in the town center. Its interior is standard "modern," but touches like exposed brick walls and open fireplaces soften the effect considerably. The guest rooms are large and bright, with two queen-size beds; all have hair dryers. Renovations completed in 1998 to 60 rooms brought them up to "Executive" standard.

Dining/Diversions: The Ter Boeverie restaurant serves fine regional cuisine. There's also an atmospheric bar, the Jan Breydel.

Amenities: 24-hour room service, laundry and dry cleaning service, newspaper delivery, baby-sitting, express checkout, heated indoor pool, conference rooms.

⚫ **Romantik Pandhotel.** Pandreitje 16, 8000 Bruges. ☎ **050/34-06-66.** Fax 050/34-05-56. 24 units. MINIBAR TV TEL. 4,990–5,990 BF ($138.60–$166.40) double; 6,990–7,490 BF ($194.15–$208.05) family rooms and suites. Rates include buffet breakfast. AE, DC, MC, V.

The Pandhotel is situated in a very quiet and central area close to the canals, Grote Markt, and museums. This lovely old 18th-century mansion is right in the center of town, yet in its setting among plane trees it's an oasis of quiet and tranquillity. Though the hotel provides modern conveniences such as hair dryers, its exquisite, old-fashioned furnishings lend a special grace to the comfortable rooms. Guests have given Mrs. Chris Vanhaecke-Dewaele their highest praise for her attention to detail and gracious hospitality.

   Amenities: Concierge, 24-hour room service, laundry and dry cleaning service, newspaper delivery, in-room massage, baby-sitting, secretarial services.

MODERATE

Alfa Dante Hotel. Coupure 29, 8000 Bruges. ☎ **050/34-01-94.** Fax 050/34-35-39. 22 units. MINIBAR TV TEL. 3,650–6,250 BF ($101.40–$173.60) double. Rates include buffet breakfast. AE, CB, DC, MC, V. Free parking.

This ultramodern brick hotel is set alongside a lovely canal, a short walk west from the center of Bruges. It's an artful combination of old Bruges style and modern amenities and fittings. The spacious guest rooms are restfully decorated in warm colors like peach and furnished with bamboo and rattan beds. All have hair dryers and most have a view of the canal at Coupure. The hotel has a very good vegetarian restaurant, the Tourmalijn, and a bar. The private parking lot is a real bonus.

De Markies. 't Zand 5, 8000 Bruges. ☎ **050/34-83-34.** Fax 050/34-87-87. 18 units. TV TEL. 2,900–3,200 BF ($80.55–$88.90) double. Rates include buffet breakfast. AE, CB, DC, MC, V. Parking in nearby lot 350 BF ($9.70).

For anyone who wants to experience Bruges's old-world charm while still hanging on to modern comforts, and without paying too steep a price, this relatively new hotel is a good bet. It's located on the corner of the 't Zand square, conveniently close to the old city center. The spacious guest rooms are decorated in black, salmon, and green, and have modern furnishings.

⚫ **Duc de Bourgogne.** Huidenvettersplein 12, 8000 Bruges. ☎ **050/33-20-38.** Fax 050/34-40-37. 10 units. TV TEL. 3,700–5,300 BF ($102.80–$147.20) double. Rates include continental breakfast. AE, CB, DC, MC, V. Limited parking available on street.

The Duc de Bourgogne, which is located in a 17th-century building on a canal, is perhaps the most elegant of the city's small hotels. The fairly large guest rooms here are luxuriously furnished in old-fashioned style, and antiques are scattered all through the hotel. There's a very good restaurant overlooking the canal on the ground floor (see "Dining," below). The canal views from the rooms are superb.

Hansa Hotel. Niklaas Despaarsstraat 11, 8000 Bruges. ☎ **050/33-84-44.** Fax 050/33-42-05. www.hansa.be. E-mail: information@hansa.be. 20 units. A/C MINIBAR TV TEL. 3,500–5,600 BF ($97.20–$155.55). Rates include buffet breakfast. AE, DC, JCB, MC, V. Parking 350 BF ($9.70).

The Hansa, located a short walk from the Markt in a mansion dating from 1869, has a well-established reputation in Bruges. Its rooms are modern and not overly big, but warmly furnished and decorated. All have fold-away ironing boards and hair dryers. The beds are comfortable, the staff friendly, and the ambiance of the hotel welcoming. The ornamental ceiling in the breakfast room is a reminder of the building's respectable origins.

✪ **Hotel Egmond.** Minnewater 15, 8000 Bruges. ☎ **050/34-14-45.** Fax 050/34-29-40. E-mail: egmond@unicall.be. 8 units. TV TEL. 3,200–3,950 BF ($88.90–$109.70) double. Rates include buffet breakfast. No credit cards. Free parking.

The Egmond has only 8 rooms in a rambling mansion next to the Minnewater Park, but the lucky few who stay here will find ample space, plenty of family ambiance, abundant local color, and lots of peace and tranquillity. All rooms have recently been redecorated, and are furnished in an individual style with views of the garden and the Minnewater Park. Every afternoon, free coffee and tea are served in the new garden terrace or in the lounge, which has a 18th-century fireplace.

Hotel Erasmus. Wollestraat 35 (near the Belfry), 8000 Bruges. ☎ **050/33-57-81.** Fax 050/33-47-27. E-mail: erasmus@ap.be. 9 units. MINIBAR TV TEL. 3,750–5,000 BF ($104.15–$138.90) double. Rates include buffet breakfast. AE, CB, MC, V. Limited parking available on street.

This small, cozy hotel is set in a picturesque little square alongside a canal in the town center. The rooms were renovated in 1997, with new carpets and new bathroom fixtures and fittings. All rooms have hair dryers, coffeemakers, and attractive, modern furnishings.

Hotel ter Duinen. Langerei 52, 8000 Bruges. ☎ **050/33-04-37.** Fax 050/34-42-16. www.terduinenhotel.be. E-mail: terduinen@terduinenhotel.be. 20 units. A/C TV TEL. 2,900–4,500 BF ($80.55–$125) double. Rates include full breakfast. AE, CB, DC, MC, V. Parking 300 BF ($8.35).

This charming hotel is an ideal marriage of classical style and modern conveniences. Guest rooms are ample in size, brightly decorated, and have modern furnishings. Some rooms have wooden ceiling beams, and some have a great view overlooking the tranquil Langerie canal, just north of the town center.

✪ **Hotel Navarra.** St-Jacobsstraat 41, 8000 Bruges (near the Belfry). ☎ **050/34-05-61.** Fax 050/33-67-90. E-mail: reservations@hotelnavarra.com. 89 units. MINIBAR TV TEL. 4,750–5,250 BF ($131.95–$145.85) double. Rates include buffet breakfast. AE, DC, MC, V. Parking 350 BF ($9.75).

This was the home of the Prince of Navarre during the 16th century. The Navarra's guest rooms have recently been renovated and are nicely furnished. All have hair dryers. There's a jazz bar and a private garden on the premises, as well as a health club, an indoor pool, and a sauna.

✪ **Montanus Hotel.** Nieuwe Gentweg 78 (between the town center and the railway station), 8000 Bruges. ☎ **050/33-11-76.** Fax 050/34-09-38. www.hotelbel. com/montanus. htm. E-mail: hotel_montanus_brugge@unicall.be. 24 units. MINIBAR TV TEL. 4,400–4,800 BF ($122.20–$133.35) double; 5,600–6,500 BF ($155.55–$180.55) suite. Rates include buffet breakfast. AE, DC, MC, V. Parking 600 BF ($16.65).

The former budget Hotel St. Christophe now has new ownership, a new name, and a whole new, more upmarket ethos. This three-story hotel offers a range of price options for comfortable accommodations. Some of the individually styled guest rooms overlook a big and lovely garden, and all have hair dryers. There's a small bar on the premises.

✪ **Relais Oud Huis Amsterdam.** Spiegelrei 3, 8000 Bruges. ☎ **050/34-18-10.** Fax 050/33-88-91. E-mail: amsterdam@unicall.be. 25 units. A/C MINIBAR TV TEL. 5,100–6,500 BF ($141.65–$180.55) double; 7,500 BF ($208.35) suite. Rates include breakfast. AE, CB, DC, MC, V. Limited parking available on street.

Philip and Caroline Traen have made a hotel out of this large canal-front building, parts of which date back to the 1300s. Rooms are large and sumptuously furnished.

The colors and decorative accents hearken back to the building's origins, based on meticulous research and restoration. Some of the bathrooms feature Jacuzzis. The elegant guest rooms in the front overlook the canal; those in back overlook the garden and picturesque rooftops. The entrance hall, the small salon off the reception area, and the popular bar called "The Meeting" all have a pleasant atmosphere. In the rear, there's a charming little courtyard with umbrella tables and a garden off to one side—the setting for Sunday concerts in June. The famed Traen hospitality makes a stay here in the town center very special.

○ **'t Bourgoensche Cruyce.** Wollestraat 41–43, 8000 Bruges (100 yds. from the Belfry). ☎ **050/33-79-26.** Fax 050/34-19-68. 8 units. TV TEL. 3,500–4,900 BF ($97.20–$136.10) double. Rates include continental breakfast. AE, DC, MC, V. Parking in nearby lot 350 BF ($9.70).

This tiny, family-run hotel, which opens onto a lovely little inner courtyard, provides the very epitome of a Bruges experience. Rooms are adequately large and furnished in a modern style. All have hair dryers, and the more expensive ones have been renovated recently. The hotel's best feature is the wonderful hospitality of Mr. and Mrs. de Flandre, the proprietors. On the ground floor is the hotel's restaurant—one of the best in Bruges (See "Dining," below).

INEXPENSIVE

Central. Markt 30, 8000 Bruges. ☎ **050/33-18-05.** Fax 050/34-68-78. 7 units. 1,500 BF ($41.65) double without bathroom, 1,785–2,600 BF ($49.60–$72.20) double with bathroom. Rates include continental breakfast. AE, CB, DC, MC, V. Parking in nearby lot 350 BF ($9.70).

The aptly named Central is the only hotel on the Markt, Bruges's main square. Its rooms are basic, but comfortable and quite adequately furnished. The entire hotel has been renovated. At the time of writing, 3 of the rooms had a television. One minor drawback is that this three-story hotel has no elevator.

Ensor. Speelmansrei 10. ☎ **050/34-25-89.** Fax 050/34-20-18. 12 units. TEL. 1,960–2,190 BF ($54.45–$60.85) double. Rates include breakfast. AE, MC, V. Limited parking available on street.

It's the canal view at a budget price that makes this hotel a standout. Most rooms are relatively large and all come with bright, modern bathrooms. There's an elevator, and every room has a radio.

○ **Fevery.** Collaert Mansioenstraat 3, 8000 Bruges. ☎ **050/33-12-69.** Fax 050/33-17-91. E-mail: hotelfevery.brugge@unicall.be. 11 units. TV TEL. 2,000–2,400 BF ($55.55–$66.65) double. Rates include buffet breakfast. AE, CB, MC, V. Free parking.

This small family hotel is located on a very quiet side street just north of the center, right off the canal-side Langerei. At the time of writing, the modern and comfortably furnished rooms were not very big, but this was due to change through a program of enlargement during 1999–2000. Each room has a small table and chairs. There's a downstairs lounge and breakfast room. Baby-sitting can be arranged, and reduced-rate bicycle rental is also available.

Graaf van Vlaanderen. 't Zand 19 (along the east side of 't Zand near the railway station), 8000 Bruges. ☎ **050/33-31-50.** Fax 050/34-59-79. 14 units (5 with bathroom). 1,625–2,465 BF ($45.15–$68.45) double. Rates include breakfast. AE, DC, MC, V. Parking in nearby lot 350 BF ($9.70).

This small, three-story hotel provides basic but comfortable accommodations and has a budget-priced restaurant. There's no elevator.

✪ **Hotel Rembrandt-Rubens.** Walplein 38, 8000 Bruges. ☎ **050/33-64-39.** 15 units (11 with bathroom). 1,900–2,300 BF ($52.75–$63.90) double. Rates include breakfast. No credit cards. Free parking.

You won't get much more in the way of genuine Bruges atmosphere, nor much less in the way of facilities, than in this marvelously atmospheric old hotel, right in the heart of romantic Bruges. The welcome is warm and the antique surroundings memorable, so maybe you won't miss the TV and the phone. This hotel's style suits Bruges perfectly and adds a warmth that coldly efficient modern rooms can't equal.

Hotel 't Keizershof. Oostmeers 126 (near the railway station), 8000 Bruges. ☎ **050/33-87-28.** No fax. www.users.skynet.be./keizershof. 7 units (none with bathroom). 1,350 BF ($37.50) double. Rates include continental breakfast. No credit cards. Free parking (for 5 cars).

Despite being one of the least expensive hotels in Brugge, 't Keizershof gets high marks for having clean, comfortable accommodations in a quiet, peaceful location. The young couple who own and operate this hotel speak several languages, and are very helpful to guests in planning their stay in Bruges.

Leopold. 't Zand 26, 8000 Bruges. ☎ **050/33-51-29.** Fax 050/34-86-54. www. hotels-belgium.com. E-mail: hotel.leopold.brugge@skynet.be. 12 units. TEL. 1,600 BF ($44.45) double without bathroom; 2,000–2,600 BF ($55.55–$72.20) double with bathroom. Rates include continental breakfast. AE, MC, V. Parking 360 BF ($10).

The well-run Leopold is located along the east side of 't Zand near the train station. Its furnishings are rather basic but quite comfortable, and there's a bar.

Hotel Lucca. Naaldenstraat 30, 8000 Bruges. ☎ **050/34-20-67.** Fax 050/33-34-64. 17 units, 13 with bathroom. TEL. 1,950 BF ($54.15) double without bathroom, 2,500 BF ($69.45) double with bathroom. Rates include buffet breakfast. AE, MC, V, DC. Limited parking available on street.

This hotel was built in the 14th century by a wealthy merchant from Lucca, Italy, and the high ceilings and wide halls of this mansion convey a sense of luxury even today. The rooms are in excellent condition and sport pine furnishings and pretty flowered wallpaper. The rooms with private bathrooms also have TV. The breakfast buffet is served in the cozy medieval cellar.

HOSTELS

Bruges has excellent hostel facilities, with rates that range from 340 to 480 BF ($9.45 to $13.35) per person. The two recommended here both accept credit cards: **Bauhaus International Youth Hotel,** Langestraat 135–137, 8000 Bruges (☎ **050/34-10-93;** fax 050/33-41-80; e-mail: bauhaus@innet.be); and **Passage,** Dweersstraat 26, 8000 Bruges (☎ **050/34-02-32;** fax 050/34-01-40).

5 Dining

Bruges certainly has no shortage of restaurants. You'll be practically tripping over them in the city center. Most are decent—it's hard to find Belgian restaurants that are consistently bad—even if some have perhaps gotten too used to the "here today, gone tomorrow" nature of the tourists that are their main market. If all you want is to be fed and watered reasonably and put back on the sightseeing trail as fast as possible, you'll have no problem. The restaurants featured below, however, aim to do better: to make dining part of your memorable Bruges experience.

VERY EXPENSIVE

De Karmeliet. Langestraat 19. ☎ **050/33-82-59.** Reservations required. Main courses 750–1,250 BF ($20.85–$34.70); fixed-price menus 2,600–3,200 BF ($72.20–$88.90). AE,

DC, V. Tues–Sat noon–2pm and 7–9:30pm; Sun 7–9:30pm except June through September. Closed January, last week of August, first week of September. BELGIAN/FRENCH.

In 1996, chef Geert Van Hecke became the first Flemish chef to be awarded three Michelin stars. He has described his award-winning menu as "international cuisine made with local products." The result is outstanding, and the decor here is as elegant as the fine cuisine deserves.

✪ **'t Pandreitje.** Pandreitje 6. ☎ **050/33-11-90.** Reservations required. Main courses 1,100–1,400 BF ($30.55–$38.90); fixed-price menus 1,850–3,800 BF ($51.40–$105.55). AE, CB, DC, MC, V. Mon, Tues and Thurs–Sat noon–2pm, 7–9:30pm. FRENCH/BELGIAN.

This restaurant is one of the nicest spots in town. It's located in the shade of the medieval Market Hall's bell tower, just off of the Rozenhoedkaai, one of the most beautiful canal-sides in Bruges. The interior of this Renaissance-era private home has been turned into an elegant Louis XVI setting for a menu of classic dishes. The four-course à la carte meal is superb, and the "menu" of preselected choices is excellent. Try the sea bass served with fennel, parsley sauce, and sautéed potatoes; or the salad of Dublin Bay prawns with artichoke and a truffle vinaigrette.

EXPENSIVE

✪ **Duc de Bourgogne.** Huidenvettersplein 12 (near the Burg). ☎ **050/33-20-38.** Reservations required. Main courses 600–900 BF ($16.65–$25); fixed-price menus 1,275–2,150 BF ($35.40–$59.70). AE, CB, DC, MC, V. Tues 7–9pm, Wed–Sun noon–2pm, 7–9pm. Closed Jan, July. FRENCH.

This large, elegant dining room overlooks a canal, which is illuminated at night. The décor here is just this side of "formal," although in summer no rigid dress code is enforced. The classic menu is a lengthy one. The fixed-price lunch menu changes daily, and the fixed-price dinner changes every 2 weeks. Specialties include *noisettes of veal au Porto.*

✪ **'t Bourgoensche Cruyce.** Wollestraat 41–43. ☎ **050/33-79-26.** Reservations required. Main courses 550–850 BF ($15.25–$23.60); 3-course fixed-price meal 1,400 BF ($38.90) at lunch, 2,200 BF ($61.10) at dinner. AE, DC, MC, V. Thurs–Mon noon–2:30pm and 7–9:30pm. Closed Nov. CONTINENTAL.

You'd be hard put to find a better location, finer food, or a friendlier welcome. The rustic charm of this small dining room overlooking a canal in the town center enhances the culinary delights. The regional specialties prepared by the experienced chef are just simply perfect. The menu reflects the very best in-season ingredients. Regardless of season, a dish not to be missed is the marvelous mosaïque de poissons ("fish mosaic") or any of the other superb seafood dishes. Order from the six-course "gastronomic sampling menu" if you just can't make a decision.

De Snippe. Nieuwe Gentweg 53 (in the De Snippe hotel). ☎ **050/33-70-70.** Reservations required. Main courses 850–1,350 BF ($23.60–$37.50). AE, DC, MC, V. Tues–Sat noon–2:30pm; daily 7–10pm. FLEMISH/FRENCH.

De Snippe enjoys a well-earned reputation as one of Bruges's finest restaurants. Its native dishes are particularly good. Try the crayfish creations, scampi, or sliced wild duck. Nine rooms are also for rent (see "Where to Stay," above).

De Visscherie. Vismarkt 8. ☎ **050/33-02-12.** Main courses 800–1,300 BF ($22.20–$36.10). AE, CB, DC, MC, V. Wed–Mon noon–2:30pm and 7–10pm. Closed mid-Nov to mid-Dec. SEAFOOD.

This attractive restaurant faces the old Fish Market in the town center, and as you might expect, "fruits of the sea" take top billing on the menu. Freshness is virtually a fetish here. Specialties include shellfish in many guises (try the spotted scallops with roe) and Channel sole.

MODERATE

De Gouden Meermin. Markt 31. ☎ **050/33-37-76.** Main courses 450–750 BF ($12.50–$20.85); fixed-price menu 1,550 BF ($43.05). AE, DC, MC, V. Daily 10am–10pm. FLEMISH.

This is my favorite of the many brasseries, tearooms, and cafes that line Grote Markt. This one has both outdoor dining and a glassed-in room that also overlooks the square. The Flemish dishes are made with fresh local ingredients, and the bowls of homemade soup are delicious. Sandwiches, snacks, and crêpes (a large variety, and all good) are available. Service is attentive.

✪ **Kasteel Minnewater.** Minnewater 4. ☎ **050/33-42-54.** Main courses 400–750 BF ($11.10–$20.85); menu du marché 980 BF ($27.20); menu gastronomique 1,600 BF ($44.45). V. Daily noon–2:30pm and 7–10pm. FRENCH/SEAFOOD.

This château-style restaurant occupies a superb location near the Begijnhof, with a terrace on the Minnewater (Lake of Love). Along with its fine food, the place serves up an easygoing charm, making it particularly rewarding to dine here at the end of a long day (or morning) of sightseeing. The fare includes typical Belgian specialties, such as sole Ostendaise, North Sea shrimp, and lamb cutlet with potatoes gratinée.

Restaurant De Stove. Kleine Sint-Amandsstraat 4. ☎ **050/33-78-35.** Main courses 540–725 BF ($15–$20.15); fixed-price menu 1,350 BF ($37.50). AE, DC, MC, V. Fri–Tues noon–1:45pm and 6:30–9:30pm. FLEMISH/SEAFOOD.

This small, family-owned restaurant combines a rustic atmosphere with a more modern style than is the norm in Bruges. The seafood specialties are well worth a try, particularly the Flemish fish stew with fruits de mer.

INEXPENSIVE

Brasserie Erasmus. Wollestraat 35. ☎ **050/33-57-81.** Main courses 300–750 BF ($8.35–$20.85). AE, CB, MC, V. Tues–Sun 11am–midnight. FLEMISH.

This small, popular restaurant is one of the most conveniently located "drop-in" places in Bruges—a great stop after viewing the cathedral and museums. It serves a large variety of Flemish dishes, all prepared with beer. If you need help making a selection, you can ask owner Tom for advice, or try these suggestions: The typically Flemish souplike stew dish *waterzooï* is very good here, and it's served with fish, as it's supposed to be, although they also make it with chicken instead, a style that has become the norm elsewhere. If that doesn't grab you, how about *lapin à la bière* (rabbit in a beer sauce)? About 100 different brands of beer (for drinking) are available.

✪ **'t Dreveken.** Huidenvettersplein 10–11. ☎ **050/33-95-06.** Main courses 360–480 BF ($10–$15). AE, DC, MC, V. Wed–Mon noon–2:30pm and 6:30–10pm. FLEMISH/SEAFOOD.

This charmer, right on a canal in the town center, is in a stone house with flowers blooming in diamond-paned windows. There's a cozy, intimate room downstairs and a pleasant, larger one upstairs. Look out for Flemish specialties such as the souplike stew called *waterzooï* (with chicken), in addition to ham, rabbit, and herring dishes. A notable, and for Flanders, surprising, absentee from the menu is mussels; but the same people also own the De Visscherie seafood restaurant (see above) and a specialist mussels restaurant, De Mosselkelder, also in Huidenvettersplein, so maybe that explains it.

Graaf van Vlaanderen. 't Zand 19 (in the Graaf van Vlaanderen hotel). ☎ **050/33-31-50.** Main courses 375–450 BF ($10.40–$12.50). AE, DC, MC, V. Fri–Wed noon–2pm and 6–9pm. STEAK/SALADS.

This reasonably priced restaurant near the railroad station has an extensive menu and a decor that relies heavily on mirrors and plants. The fare is equally simple, featuring minute steak (steak so thin it cooks in 1 minute), spaghetti, salads, and *steak-frites* (steak and french fries).

't Koffieboontje. Hallestraat 4. ☎ **050/33-80-27.** Main courses 350–650 BF ($9.70–$18.05). AE, DC, MC, V. Daily noon–11pm. SEAFOOD/FLEMISH.

This restaurant has a bright and stylishly modern interior that strikes a noticeable contrast to the often gloomy ambiance of many Bruges restaurants. The extensive menu here is equally cheery; it features seafood specialties like lobster and salmon, as well as such Belgian staples as mussels, steak, and sole.

DINING IN DAMME

Nearby Damme (see "A Side Trip from Bruges," below) has several excellent restaurants on or near its main street, Kerkstraat, that are worth the short drive or canal-boat trip. Among them are **Gasthof Maerlant,** Kerkstraat 21 (☎ **050/35-29-52**), which serves a "market menu" at 950 BF ($26.40); **Restaurant De Lieve,** Jacob van Maerlantstraat 10 (☎ **050/35-66-30**), which specializes in seasonal cuisine, with menus from 900 to 1,950 BF ($25–$54.15); and the atmospheric **Restaurant Pallieter,** Kerkstraat 12 (☎ **050/35-46-75**), which has a specialty of saddle of lamb Dijonnaise and offers menus ranging up to 1,275 BF ($35.40).

6 Attractions

As a leading contender for the title of Europe's most romantic town, Bruges is really one big attraction—a fairy-tale mixture of gabled houses, meandering canals, magnificent squares, and narrow cobblestone streets. But perhaps the most astonishing thing about Bruges is the consistently warm welcome its residents provide to the swarms of visitors. The basis for this is more than mere economics—those who live in Bruges love their city and can well appreciate that others want to experience it.

THE MARKT

In the Markt (Market Square), heraldic banners float from venerable façades. This square, along with the Burg (see below), is the heart of Bruges and the focal point of your sightseeing. Most major points of interest in the city are no more than 5 or 10 minutes' walk away.

✪ **Belfry (Belfort) and Market Halls (Hallen).** Markt 7. ☎ **050/44-87-11.** Belfry 100 BF ($2.80) adults, 50 BF ($1.40) children. Hours for both: Apr–Sept daily 9:30am–5pm; Oct–Mar daily 9:30am–12:30pm and 1:30–5pm.

The Belfry was, and still is, the symbol of Bruges's civic pride. Its magnificent 47-bell carillon peals out over the city every quarter hour, and several times a day in longer concerts during the summer. The tower itself stands 272 feet (84 meters) high. Its lower section dates from around 1240, with the corner turrets added in the 14th century and the upper, octagonal section in the 15th century. If you have the stamina, climb the 366 steps to the Belfry's summit for a panoramic view of Bruges and the surrounding countryside all the way to the sea—you can pause for breath at the second-floor Treasury, where the town seal and charters were kept behind multiple wrought-iron grilles.

From the 13th to the 16th century, much of the city's commerce was conducted in the Hallen. They have recently been brought back into use, as an exhibition center operated by a consortium of local art dealers. Just outside the Hallen, the

Kiwanis Club of Bruges has erected a bronze replica of the Belfry and the Hallen, with descriptions in Dutch, French, German, and English inscribed in braille for blind visitors.

OTHER SIGHTS IN THE MARKT

The **sculpture group** in the center of the Markt depicts a pair of Flemish heroes, butcher Jan Breydel and weaver Pieter de Coninck. The two led an uprising in 1302 against the wealthy merchants and nobles who dominated the guilds, then went on to win an against-all-odds victory over French knights later that same year in the Battle of the Golden Spurs. The small, castlelike building called the **Craenenburg** (it's now a restaurant), located on the corner of Sint Amandstraat at Grote Markt, was used to imprison Crown Prince Maximilian of Austria in 1482. In exchange for that humiliation, Maximilian later on exacted a penalty from the citizens of Bruges that added a note of pure beauty to the city: He obliged them to keep swans in the canals forever. The large neo-Gothic **Provinciaal Hof** dates from the 1800s and houses the government of the province of West Flanders.

THE BURG

The Burg, a public square just steps away from the Markt, holds an array of beautiful buildings, which together add up to a trip through the history of architecture. On this site, Baldwin Iron Arm, Count of Flanders, once built a fortified castle (or "burg"), around which a village grew up that developed into Bruges.

✪ **Town Hall (Stadhuis).** Burg 11. ☎ **050/44-87-11.** Admission 60 BF ($1.65) adults, 20 BF (55¢) children. Apr–Sept daily 9:30am to 5pm, Oct–Mar 9:30am–12:30pm and 2–5pm.

This beautiful Gothic structure was built in the late 1300s, making it the oldest town hall in Belgium. Don't miss the upstairs **Gothic Room (Gotische Zaal)** with its ornate decor and wall murals depicting highlights of Bruges's history. Most spectacular of all is the vaulted oak ceiling, dating from 1385–1402, which features scenes from the New Testament. The statues in the niches on the Town Hall facade are 1980s replacements for the originals, which had been painted by Jan Van Eyck and were destroyed by the French in the 1790s.

Basilica of the Holy Blood (Heilige-Bloedbasiliek). Burg 10. ☎ **050/33-67-92.** Free admission to the basilica; to the museum 40 BF ($1.10) adults, 20 BF (55¢) children. Basilica Apr–Sept daily 9:30am–noon and 2–6pm; Oct–Mar 10am–noon and 2–4pm (closed Wed afternoon).

This Romanesque basilica with a Gothic upper floor has been, since 1149, the repository of a fragment of cloth stained with what is said to be the blood of Christ, washed from his body by Joseph of Arimathea. Legend says that the cloth was brought to Bruges during the Second Crusade by the Count of Flanders, Dirk Van de Elzas—though it's more likely that it came from Constantinople, which was sacked in 1204 by the Crusader army of Count of Flanders Baldwin IX. Every Ascension Day, in the colorful Procession of the Holy Blood, the relic is carried by the bishop through Bruges's streets, accompanied by costumed residents acting out biblical scenes. Normally it's kept in the basilica museum inside a rock-crystal vial which is itself kept in a magnificent gold-and-silver reliquary. Even if you're not interested in the relics, the 12th-century basilica is well worth a visit for the richness of its design and its other treasures.

✪ **Palace of the Liberty of Bruges (Landhuis van het Brugse Vrije).** Burg 11. ☎ **050/44-86-86.** Free admission to courtyard; to Hall of the Brugse Vrije 100 BF ($2.80) adults, 40 BF ($1.10) children age 5–18, free for children under 5. April–September daily 9:30am–12:30pm and 1:15–5pm; October–March daily 9:30am–12:30pm and 2–5pm.

This palace dates mostly from 1722–27, when it replaced a 16th-century building as the seat of the Liberty of Bruges—the Liberty being the district around Bruges in the Middle Ages. It later became a courthouse, and now houses the city council's administration. Inside, at no. 11a, is the Renaissance **Hall of the Brugse Vrije,** the Liberty's council chamber, which has been restored to its original 16th-century condition. The Hall has a superb black marble fireplace decorated with an alabaster frieze and topped by an oak chimneypiece carved with statues of Emperor Charles V, who visited Bruges in 1515, and his grandparents: Emperor Maximilian of Austria, Duchess Mary of Burgundy, King Ferdinand II of Aragon, and Queen Isabella I of Castile.

OTHER SIGHTS AROUND THE BURG

The **Old Registry (Oude Griffie),** built beside the Town Hall as the offices of the Town Clerk, has the oldest Renaissance façade in the city, dating from 1534–37, and now houses the city archives. Facing the Town Hall is the baroque **Provost's House (Proosdij)** from 1665–66, which used to be the residence of the Bishop of Bruges and is now occupied by government offices of West Flanders Province.

OTHER TOP SIGHTS

✪ **Groeninge Museum.** Dijver 12. ☎ **050/44-87-11.** Admission 200 BF ($5.55) adults, 100 BF ($2.80) children. Apr–Sept daily 9:30am–5pm; Oct–Mar Wed–Mon 9:30am–12:30pm and 2–5pm.

The Groeninge ranks among Belgium's leading traditional museums of fine arts, with a collection that covers painting in the Low Countries from the 15th to the 20th century. The Gallery of Flemish Primitives holds some 30 works—many of which are far from "primitive"—by painters such as Jan Van Eyck (there's a portrait of his wife, Margerita Van Eyck), Rogier van der Weyden, Hieronymus Bosch (*The Last Judgment*), and Hans Memling. Works by Magritte and Delvaux are also on display.

Gruuthuse Museum. Dijver 17 (in a courtyard next to the Groeninge Museum). ☎ **050/44-87-11.** Admission 130 BF ($3.60) adults, 70 BF ($1.95) children age 18 and under. Apr–Sept daily 9:30am–5pm; Oct–Mar Wed–Mon 9:30am–12:30pm and 2–5pm.

This ornate Gothic mansion is where Flemish nobleman and herb merchant Lodewijk Van Gruuthuse, who was a counselor to the Dukes of Burgundy, lived in the 1400s. It's now an integral part of the Groeninge Museum (see above). Among the 2,500 numbered antiquities in the house are paintings, sculptures, tapestries, lace, weapons, glassware, and richly carved furniture.

✪ **The Lace Center (Kantcentrum).** Peperstraat 3a. ☎ **050/33-00-72.** Admission 60 BF ($1.65) adults, 40 BF ($1.10) children. Mon–Sat 10am–noon, 2–6pm (5pm Saturday).

This is a fascinating place—the lace of Bruges is, after all, famous the world over. Here there's an abundance of shops offering you the opportunity to take some home. This combination workshop, museum, and sale room is where the ancient art of lacemaking is passed on to the next generation. You'll get a firsthand look at the artisans who will be making many of the items for future sale in all those lace shops. When you purchase lace, ideally you should specify that you want handmade lace, which is more expensive and of higher quality than the machine-made stuff. The most famous laces to look for are bloemenwerk, rozenkant, and toversesteek.

✪ **Memling Museum.** Mariastraat. ☎ **050/44-87-11.** Admission 100 BF ($2.80) adults, 50 BF ($1.40) children. Apr–Sept daily 9:30am–5pm; Oct–Mar Thurs–Tues 9:30am–12:30pm and 2–5pm.

This museum is housed in the former Hospital of St John (Sint-Janshospitaal), whose earliest wards date from the 13th century. To get a sense of the vastness of the wards when this was a functioning hospital, take a look at the old painting near the entrance that shows small, efficient bed units set into cubicles along the walls. The 17th-century Apothecary in the cloisters near the entrance is furnished exactly as it was when this building's main function was to care for the sick.

Nowadays visitors come to see the typical medieval hospital buildings filled with furniture and other objects that illustrate their history, as well as the magnificent collection of paintings by the German-born artist Hans Memling (ca. 1440–1494), who moved to Bruges from Brussels in 1465 and became one of the city's most prominent residents. At this museum you'll find such Memling masterpieces as the three-paneled altarpiece of St. John the Baptist and St. John the Evangelist, which consists of the paintings *The Mystic Marriage of St Catherine,* the *Ursula Shrine,* and *Virgin with Child and Apple.*

De Vos Almshouse (Godshuis de Vos). Corner of Noordstraat and Wijngaardstraat (near the Begijnhof).

This is a fine example of the *Godshuizen* (Houses of God) that were built by the rich in Bruges from the 13th century onward as refuges for widows and the poor. The moneybags weren't being entirely altruistic, however, as the residents had to pray for their benefactors' souls twice a day in the chapel that was an integral part of an almshouse's facilities. The pretty courtyard garden here is surrounded by a chapel and eight original houses, now converted to six, which are owned by the city and occupied by senior citizens. Entrance is not allowed. The complex dates from 1713.

Diamond Museum (Diamantmuseum). Katelijnestraat 93. ☎ **050/33-34-63.** Admission 150 BF ($4.15) adults, 75 BF ($2.10) children. Mon–Fri 10am–noon and 1–5pm, Sat 10am–3pm.

Diamond polishing has been an important local industry for centuries, ever since Antwerp dealers, looking for cheaper skilled labor, brought the craft to Bruges. The technique of polishing diamonds using diamond powder on a rotating disk may have been invented by the Bruges goldsmith Lodewijk van Berquem around 1450. This museum, which opened in 1998, focuses on the history of diamond polishing in Bruges, with demonstrations and displays of equipment.

Folklore Museum (Museum voor Volkskunde). Rolweg 40. ☎ **050/44-87-11.** Admission 80 BF ($2.20) adults, 40 BF ($1.10) children age 18 and under. Apr–Sept daily 9:30am–5pm; Oct –March Wed –Mon 9:30am–12:30pm and 2–5pm.

The Folklore Museum, housed in the low whitewashed houses of the one-time Shoemakers Guild Almshouse, aims to re-create life in Bruges in times gone by. Exhibition rooms depict a primary school class, cooper's and milliner's workshops, a spice store and a candy store, and everyday household scenes. Most refreshing of all is an old inn, De Zwarte Kat (The Black Cat), which has real beer on tap. In summer, children and adults can play traditional games in the garden.

Hof Bladelin (Bladelin House). Naaldenstraat 19. ☎ **050/33-64-34.** Free admission to courtyard and (by prior appointment only) mansion. Apr–Sept Mon–Sat 10am–noon and 2–5pm, Sun 10:30am–noon; Oct–Mar Mon–Sat 10am–noon and 2–4pm, Sun 10:30am–noon.

This 15th-century mansion, which is now a senior citizens' home, was built by Pieter Bladelin, treasurer to Duke Philip the Good. The Medici Bank of Florence took over in 1466 and gave the place an Italian look, particularly in the courtyard, which is thought to be the earliest example of the Renaissance style in the Low

Countries. On the façade are medallions depicting Lorenzo de Medici and his wife Clarice Orsini.

Onze-Lieve-Vrouw ter Potterie (Our Lady of the Pottery). Potterierei 78–79. ☎ **050/44-87-11.** Admission 60 BF ($1.65). Apr–Sept daily 9:30am–12:30pm and 1:30–5pm; Oct–Mar Wed–Mon 9:30am–12:30pm and 2–5pm.

This building, which was founded in 1276 as a hospice, is now a senior citizens' home. Today part of it houses the Potterie Museum, which has a collection of tapestries, 15th to 17th-century furniture, silverware, religious objects, and books, and early Flemish paintings. The adjoining 14th-century church used to be the chapel of the Potters Guild; it has a fine baroque interior.

CITY GATES

The now-vanished city wall once boasted nine powerfully fortified gates dating from the 14th century. The four that survive are (clockwise from the train station) the imposing **Smedenpoort; Ezelpoort,** which is famed for the many swans that grace the moat beside it; **Kruispoort,** which looks more like a castle with a drawbridge; and **Gentpoort,** now reduced in status to a traffic obstacle. Only one defensive tower remains, the **Poertoren,** which was used as a gunpowder store and overlooks the Lake of Love.

WINDMILLS

The park that marks the line of the city walls between Kruispoort and Dampoort in the northeast is occupied by a row of very photogenic windmills. They are (from south to north) the **Bonne Chière Mill,** built in 1888 at Olsene in East Flanders and moved here in 1911; **Sint-Janshuismolen,** built in 1770 and open free to the public from April through September, daily from 9:30am to 12:30pm and 1:30 to 5pm; **Nieuwe Papegaai Mill,** an oil-mill rebuilt here in 1970; and **Coeleweymolen,** dating from 1765, rebuilt here in 1996 and open free to the public from June through September, daily from 9:30am to 12:30pm, and 1:30 to 5pm.

SIGHTS OF RELIGIOUS SIGNIFICANCE

✪ **Beguinage (Begijnhof).** Wijngaardstraat. ☎ **050/33-00-11.** Admission to the Beguine's House is 60 BF ($1.65) adults, 30 BF (85¢) children. The courtyard is free and always open. Apr–Sept 10am–noon and 1:45–5:30pm (Sun 6pm); Oct, Nov, and Mar 10:30am–noon and 1:45–5pm; Dec–Feb Wed, Thurs, Sat, and Sun 2:45–4:15pm, Friday 1:45–6pm.

Through the centuries, since it was founded in 1245 by the Countess Margaret of Constantinople, the Begijnhof has been one of the most tranquil spots in Bruges, and so it remains today. Begijns were religious women, similar to nuns, who accepted vows of chastity and obedience, but drew the line at poverty, preferring to earn a living by looking after the sick or making lace. Today, the begijns are no more, but the Begijnhof is occupied by Benedictine nuns who try to keep the begijns' traditions alive. This beautiful little cluster of 17th-century whitewashed houses surrounding a lawn with poplar trees and flowers makes a marvelous escape from the hustle and bustle of the outside world. One of the houses, the Begijnhuisje, can be visited, as can the convent church during a service.

✪ **Church of Our Lady (Onze-Lieve-Vrouwekerk).** Onze-Lieve-Vrouwekerkhof Zuid. ☎ **050/34-53-14.** Church and Madonna and Child altar free; chapel of Charles and Mary 60 BF ($1.65) adults, 30 BF (85¢) children. Apr–Sept Mon–Fri 10–11:30am and 2:30–5pm, Sat 10–11:30am and 2:30–4pm; Oct–Mar Mon–Fri 10–11:30am and 2:30–4:30pm, Sat 10–11:30am and 2:30–4pm.

It took 2 centuries (from the 13th to the 15th) to build this church, whose soaring 396-foot spire can be seen from miles around Bruges. Among the many art treasures here is a beautiful Carrara marble sculpture of the *Madonna and Child* by Michelangelo. This statue, made in 1504, was the only one of Michangelo's works to leave Italy in his lifetime and is today one of the few that can be seen outside Italy. It was bought by a Bruges merchant, Jan Van Mouskroen, and donated to the church in 1506.

The church also holds a painting of the *Crucifixion* by Anthony Van Dyck, and the impressive side-by-side bronze tomb sculptures of the Duke of Burgundy, Charles the Bold, who died in 1477, and his daughter, Mary of Burgundy, who died at age 25 after falling from her horse in 1482. A windowpane under the tombs allows you to view the 13th- and 14th-century graves of priests.

Holy Savior Cathedral (Sint-Salvatorskathedraal). Sint-Salvatorskerkhof. ☎ **050/ 86-61-88.** Free admission to cathedral; treasury 60 BF ($1.65) adults, 30 BF (85¢) children. Apr–Sept Mon–Fri 10–11:30am and 2:30–5pm, Sat 10–11:30am and 2:30–4pm; Oct–Mar Mon–Fri 10–11:30am and 2:30–4:30pm, Sat 10–11:30am and 2:30–4pm.

This mainly Gothic church with a 100-meter (325-foot) belfry has been Bruges's cathedral since 1834 (its predecessor, Saint Donatian's in the Burg, was demolished by the French around 1800). The 15th-century wooden choir stalls flanking the altar bear a complete set of escutcheons of the Knights of the Golden Fleece, who held a chapter meeting here in 1478. The Cathedral Museum (open Monday through Friday 2pm to 5pm, Sunday 3pm to 5pm) houses the *Martyrdom of St Hippolytus* by Dirk Bouts with a side panel by Hugo Van der Goes, as well as the Cathedral Treasury of gold and silver religious vessels, reliquaries, and episcopal vestments.

OTHER IMPORTANT CHURCHES

There's no shortage of notable churches in Bruges, but as there's also no shortage of other places to see, you probably won't want to spend all your time visiting them. Anyone with a particular interest in churches, however, should try to visit a few of these.

The magnificent **Sint-Walburgakerk (St Walburga's Church)** in Sint-Maartensplein, which dates from 1619–43, is one of the few baroque monuments in this Gothic-fixated city. It has a satisfying amount of marble and a notable altar, pulpit, and communion bench. Sint-Walburgakerk was the Jesuit church of Bruges until 1774.

The **Jeruzalemkerk (Jerusalem Church)** at Peperstraat 3, beside the Lace Center (see above), was built in 1471–1483 along the lines of the Church of the Holy Sepulcher in Jerusalem by the wealthy merchant Adornes family. A replica of the Tomb of Christ can be seen in the crypt underneath the choir.

Also owing much of its of ornamentation to wealthy citizens is **Sint-Jacobskerk (St. James's Church)** in Sint-Jacobplein. This heavy-looking 15th-century Gothic construction has an intricately carved wooden pulpit, with figures at the base representing the continents.

BREWERY TOURS

Straffe Hendrik Brewery. Walplein 26. ☎ **050/33-26-97.** Admission 150 BF ($4.15). Guided visits Apr–Sept daily 10am–5pm; Oct–Mar daily 11am and 3pm.

The brewery here was mentioned in dispatches as early as 1546. Today it produces the famous (in Belgium) Straffe Hendrik beer, a strapping blond brew that can be sampled in the brewery's own brasserie—it has a clean, heavenly taste.

De Gouden Boom Brewery Museum. Verbrand Nieuwland. ☎ **050/33-06-99.** Admission 100 BF ($2.80). May–Sept Wed–Sun, 2–5pm; Oct–Apr open on request only.

Bruges's second major brewery has been operating in this area since 1587. The old malthouse, which holds the museum, dates from 1902, and still has its beer vats and other equipment in place. Exhibits here feature not only the museum's parent brewery, but also the other 31 breweries that were in operation in the city at the turn of the century.

From here it's just a quick shuffle to Langestraat 45, and the **brewery** itself, which can only be visited by guided tour. Here you can see such popular beers as Brugse Tarwebier, Brugse Tripel, and Abdij Steenbrugge being brought to life, and get to taste some of the finished product. Tours are by prior arrangement only.

ESPECIALLY FOR KIDS

The **Boudewijn Theme Park and Dolfinarium** in the southern suburbs at De Baeckestraat 12 is a big favorite with children, who for some reason seem to prefer its rides, paddleboats, dolphins, and orca (killer whale), to Bruges's many historic treasures. Strange but true! Admission is 560 BF ($15.55) for adults, 480 BF ($13.35) for seniors and children age 12 and under, and free for children under 100cm (39 in.). The park is open May through August daily from 10am to 6pm, and during Easter week and on weekends in September from 11am to 6pm.

Zeven Torentjes (Seven Towers) Farm at Canadaring, Assebroek, in the eastern suburbs, is a former manor farm dating back to the 14th century that has been transformed into a children's farm, with pigs, hens, horses, and other animals. Admission is free, and the farm is open daily from dawn to dusk.

Both the theme park and the farm can be reached by bus from the train station and from the Markt.

ORGANIZED TOURS & EXCURSIONS

If you'd like a trained, knowledgeable guide to accompany you in Bruges, the tourist office can provide one for 1,500 BF ($41.65) for the first 2 hours, and 750 BF ($20.85) for each additional hour. Or, in July and August, you can join a daily guided tour at 3pm which leaves from the tourist office; it costs 150 BF ($4.15), children under 14 free. For self-guided tours, "Walkman" guides with taped details in English are available from the tourist office for 300 BF ($8.35) for one or two people.

A "must" for every visitor is a ✪ **boat trip** on the city canals. There are several departure points, all marked with an anchor icon on maps available at the tourist office. The boats operate March through November daily from 10am to 6pm; and December through February on weekends, school holidays, and public holidays from 10am to 6pm (except if the canals are frozen!). A half-hour cruise costs 170 BF ($4.70) for adults, and 85 BF ($2.35) for children 4 to 11, under 4 free. Wear something warm if the weather is cold or windy.

Another lovely way to tour Bruges is by ✪ **horse-drawn carriage.** From March through November carriages are stationed in the Burg every day except for Wednesdays, when they're in the Markt. A 30-minute ride costs 900 BF ($25) per cab, and 450 BF ($12.50) for each additional 15 minutes. There are also two companies operating **horse-drawn trams:** Den Oekden Peerdentram (☎ **050/79-04-37**) has 30-minute tours leaving from 't Zand, starting at 9am and costing 200 BF ($5.55) for adults, 100 BF ($2.80) for children age 4 to 11, under 4 free; Firmin's Paardentram (☎ **050/33-61-36**) has 45-minute tours leaving from the Markt, starting at 9am and costing 300 BF ($8.35) for adults, 150 BF ($4.15) for children age 4 to 11, under 4 free.

Fifty-minute minibus tours with **Sightseeing Lines** (☎ **050/31-13-55**) depart hourly every day from the Markt: January, February, and December 10am to 4pm;

Folklore Events in Bruges

One of the most popular and colorful folklore events in Belgium is Bruges's **Procession of the Holy Blood (Heilig Bloedprocessie),** which dates back to at least 1291 and takes place every year on Ascension Day. During the Procession, the Bishop of Bruges processes through the city streets carrying the golden shrine containing the Relic of the Holy Blood (see "The Burg," earlier in this chapter). Residents wearing Burgundian-era and biblical costumes follow the relic, acting out biblical and historical scenes along the way. The next two processions take place on May 13, 1999 and June 1, 2000.

Every 3 years, the canals of Bruges are the subject and location of a festival called the **Reiefeest.** This evening event is a combination of historical tableaux, dancing, open-air concerts, and lots of eating and drinking. It takes place on 6 nonconsecutive days in August. The next Reiefeest is due in 2001.

The **Golden Tree Pageant** recalls the great procession and tournament held in the Markt to celebrate the marriage of the Duke of Burgundy, Charles the Bold, to Margaret of York in 1468. It's held every 5 years in the last half of August. The next will take place in 2000.

March through June, October, and November 10am to 6pm; July through September 10am to 7pm.

You can get out of town into the Flemish countryside and get some exercise at the same time on a bicycle tour with the Back Road Bike Co. (☎ **050/34-30-45**), which offers three trips of 11, 18, and 25 miles. Phone first to make a reservation; the meeting and departure point is the Burg.

WALKING TOUR
Through the Heart of Bruges

Start: The Burg.
Finish: Lake of Love.
Time: 3 to 4 hours.
Best Times: Saturday and Sunday afternoons from March through October, when you can take in the flea market in the Dijver.

This tour takes in some of Bruges's most stellar sights, as it follows the canals from the city center to the beautiful lake and park to the south. So small is Bruges that you could actually walk this route in less than an hour at a leisurely pace, but you should take time to visit in depth at least one of the places described on the way.

1. From **the Burg,** walk through Blinde Ezelstraat, the vaulted passageway to the left of the Town Hall (as you face it) and cross the canal to Steenhouwersdijk, passing one of the canal boat jetties. To your left are the columns of the covered Fish Market, dating from 1821, where fresh fish from the North Sea are sold on mornings from Tuesday through Saturday. Turn right into the little square called:

2. Huidevettersplein, surrounded by restaurants. One of them is the former Tanners' Guildhouse, the Ambachtshuis der Huidevetters, at nos. 10–11, dating from 1631. Continue through Huidevettersplein to:

3. Rozenhoedkaai, which has a beautiful view across the canal, with the top of the Belfry looming above. Pass by the Sint-Jan Nepomucenus Bridge and its 1767

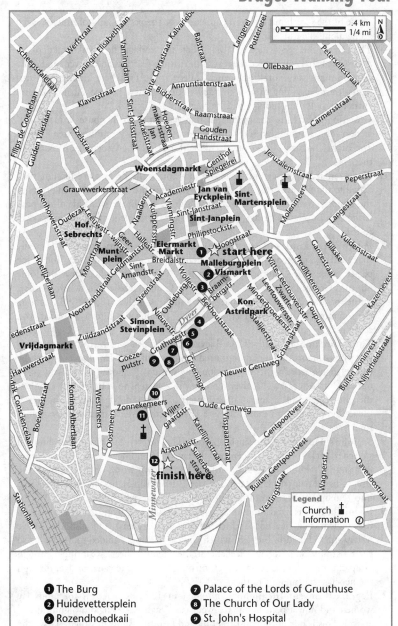

Bruges Walking Tour

Legend
Church ✝
Information ⓘ

1. The Burg
2. Huidevettersplein
3. Rozendhoedkaii
4. The Dijver
5. Groeninge Museum
6. Hof Arents
7. Palace of the Lords of Gruuthuse
8. The Church of Our Lady
9. St. John's Hospital
10. Walplein
11. Beguine Convent (Begijnhof)
12. Lake of Love (Minnewater)

statue of the Czech martyr, who happens to be the patron saint of bridges. Keep going along the canal to:

4. **The Dijver,** the tree-shaded canalside where the weekend flea market takes place. Across the canal you can see the rear of the former Carthusian Convent and some fine old mansions. Note the Europa College at no. 11, where international students learn everything there is to know about the new Europe. At no. 12 is an entranceway leading along a path to the:

5. **Groeninge Museum,** the municipal fine arts museum. It houses a major collection of paintings by the 15th-century "Flemish Primitives" (see "Other Top Sights," above). Cross the Arents Park outside the Groeninge Museum to the:

6. **Hof Arents,** an 18th-century mansion that houses the Brangwyn Museum, dedicated to the English artist Frank Brangwyn. Note the four modern sculptures of the Horsemen of the Apocalypse in the little park. On the west side of the park is the tiny Bonifatius Bridge, which offers a view redolent of Venice; cross over to the:

7. **Palace of the Lords of Gruuthuse,** the stately 15th-century home of the family that held the monopoly on *gruut,* a herbal mixture added to beer. Today the palace houses the Gruuthuse Museum (see "Other Top Sights," above). Come out into Gruuthusestraat and turn left, past Guido Gezelleplein, where there's a statue of the Bruges priest and poet Guido Gezelle (1830–1899), among the foremost 19th-century Flemish writers. Turning left into Mariastraat, you come to:

8. **The Church of Our Lady** (Onze-Lieve-Vrouwekerk), a 13th–15th-century edifice that contains the not-to-be-missed sculpture of the *Madonna and Child* by Michelangelo (see "Sights of Religious Significance," above). When you come out of Our Lady's, make a diversion a few dozen steps to your left, for a look at the pink Jugendstil façade and the murals of Day and Night on the houses at Onze-Lieve-Vrouwekerkhof-Zuid 6–8. Back across Mariastraat is the entrance to:

9. **St John's Hospital** (Sint-Janshospitaal). The history of this former hospital stretches back to the 12th century. Today the building houses, among other things, the Memling Museum, with the best-known works of the 15th-century Bruges-based painter Hans Memling (see "Other Top Sights," above). Continue into Katelijnestraat, then turn right into Stoofstraat, which leads to:

10. **Walplein.** In this handsome square is both a sculpture giving a modern take on the ancient tale of Leda and the Swan (a.k.a. Zeus) and also the Halve Maan/Straffe Hendrik Brewery, which you can visit on a guided tour (you'll also get to sample some of its excellent Straffe Hendrik beer). Continue through Walplein into Wijngaardstraat, then turn right across the canal bridge, through the neoclassical gateway, to the:

11. **Beguine Convent (Begijnhof),** founded in 1245 as a retreat for pious lay women and now a Benedictine Convent (see "Sights of Religious Significance," above). This is one of the most tranquil and beautiful spots in Bruges. Leave the Begijnhof by its southern exit, which brings you to the:

12. **Lake of Love (Minnewater).** On the left side of this idyllic outlook is the leafy Minnewater Park, in which stands the Kasteel Minnewater, a château-style restaurant with a waterside terrace that in fine weather makes the ideal place to end your tour through the heart of Bruges.

7 Shopping

No one comes here for stylish shopping—for that you need Brussels or Antwerp. What Bruges is famous for is **lace.** Most of it is machine-made, but there's still plenty of genuine, high-quality (if expensive) handmade lace to be found. The most famous lace styles are bloemenwerk, rozenkant, and toversesteek. Souvenirs of a more perishable nature include Oud-Brugge **cheese,** and local **beers** such as Straffe Hendrick, Brugse Tarwebier, and Brugse Tripel. The contents of a stone bottle of **jenever** and a box of handmade chocolate **pralines** should also go down well.

Upmarket shops and boutiques can be found in the streets around the Markt and 't Zand, including Geldmuntstraat, Noordzandstraat, Steenstraat, Zuidzandstraat, and Vlamingstraat. There are souvenir, lace, and small specialty shops all over. Most shops are open Monday through Saturday from 9am to 6pm, with late-night shopping to 9pm on Friday. Many also open on Sunday, especially in summer.

SHOPPING A TO Z
ANTIQUES
Antiek Fimmers-Van der Cruysse. Sint-Salvatorskerkhof 18. ☎ **050/34-20-25.**

Sells fine antiques and silverware.

APPAREL
Artlux. Simon Stevinplein 1. ☎ **050/33-60-95.**

For fine leather goods, such as handbags and gloves.

Inno. Steenstraat 11–13. ☎ **050/33-06-03.**

This is Bruges's main department store, which sells a wide range of goods.

BOOKS
Brugse Boekhandel. Dijver 2. ☎ **050/332952.**

Stocks a moderate range of English books, with the focus on travel guides, as well as maps, newspapers, and magazines.

DIAMONDS
✪ **Brugs Diamanthuis.** Cordoeaniersstraat 5. ☎ **050/34-41-60.**

This shop, which is housed in a handsome building dating from 1518, sells a sparkling array of fine diamonds.

FOOD & DRINK
Malesherbes. Stoofstraat 3–5. ☎ **050/33-69-24.**

A French delicatessen, with all that implies in terms of taste and the range of artisanal products.

✪ **Van Tilborgh.** Noordzandstraat 1b. ☎ **050/33-59-04.**

The owner's lip-smacking pralines are made from her own recipe.

Woolstreet Company. Wollestraat 31a. ☎ **050/34-83-83.**

One of several stores in this street selling a wide range of Belgian beers, mainly locally produced.

GIFTS

Callebert. Wollestraat 25. ☎ **050/33-50-61.**

If you tire of the traditional in Bruges, come here for stylishly modern gifts.

LACE

Kantuweeltje. Philipstockstraat 11. ☎ **050/33-42-25.**

You can see fine lace pieces being made by hand in this lace and tapestry specialist, in business since 1895.

Selection. Breidelstraat 10–12. ☎ **050/33-11-86.**

Selection is representative of the better Bruges lace shops in that it offers a good range of handmade lace.

MARKETS

The **Antiques and Flea Market** on the Dijver is a fine show in a scenic location beside the canal. It runs from March through October, on Saturday and Sunday from noon to 5pm. There are also **general markets** in the Markt, every Wednesday from 7am to 1pm, and in 't Zand and nearby Beursplein every Saturday from 7am to 1pm. The **fish market** in the colonnaded Vismarkt dating from 1821 may be less important—although you can buy ready-to-eat prawns and raw herring here—but is still interesting to see. It takes place from Tuesday through Saturday from 8am to 1pm.

8 Bruges After Dark

For information on what to do after dark, get the free monthly brochure **"Exit"** and the free monthly newsletter **"Agenda Brugge"** from the tourist office, hotels, and performance venues. The monthly newspaper *Brugge Cultuurmagazine,* also free and available at these locations, is in Dutch, but its performance dates and venue details are fairly easy to follow.

THE PERFORMING ARTS

The **Royal Municipal Theater (Koninklijke Stadsschouwburg)** at Vlamingstraat 29 (☎ **050/44-86-86**), dating from 1869, is the main venue for opera, classical music, theater, and dance, which take place regularly throughout the year. Another important venue is the **Joseph Ryelandtzaal**, Achiel Van Ackerplein (☎ **050/ 44-86-86**). Smaller-scale events, such as recitals, are often held at the **Prinsenhof**, Prinsenhof 8 (☎ **050/34-50-93**), which used to be the palace of the Dukes of Burgundy, as well as at **Sint-Salvators Kathedraal, Sint-Jacobskerk,** and other churches.

Theater pieces—mostly in Dutch—are performed at the **De Korre Theater,** Sint-Jacobsstraat 36 (☎ **050/34-47-60**), which also has a puppet theater, **Marionettentheater Brugge,** for what is a sophisticated and centuries-old art.

A different kind of theater is on the menu at **Brugge Anno 1468,** Celebration Entertainment, Vlamingstraat 86 (☎ **050/34-75-72**), where actors reenact the wedding of the Duke of Burgundy, Charles the Bold, to Margaret of York in a former Jesuit church, while customers pile into a medieval banquet. Performances take place from April thrugho October, Thursday to Saturday 7:30pm to 10pm; November through March, Saturday 7:30pm to 10pm.

THE CLUB & MUSIC SCENE

The **Cactus Club,** Sint-Jacobsstraat 33 (☎ **050/33-20-14**), presents an eclectic concert schedule Friday and Saturday nights. Try **De Vuurmolen,** Kraanplein 5

(☎ **050/33-00-79**), for a raucous dancing-on-the-tables kind of night; it's open nightly 10pm until the wee hours. ✪ **Ma Rica Rokk,** 't Zand 7–8 (☎ **050/ 33-83-58**), is another bar with dancing; it attracts a young techno-oriented crowd nightly 7pm to 4am (9pm to 6am weekends). A good gay-friendly place is the bar/disco **Ravel,** Karel de Stoutelaan 172 (☎ **050/31-52-74**), open Wednesday and Friday through Monday from 10pm. **Vino Vino,** Grauwwerkersstraat 15 (☎ **050/34-51-15**), somehow manages to successfully combine Spanish tapas and the blues. For jazz, from bebop to modern, you can't do better than ✪ **De Versteende Nacht,** Langestraat 11 (☎ **050/34-32-93**).

THE BAR SCENE

✪ 't **Brugs Beertje,** Kemelstraat 5 (☎ **050/33-96-16**) is a traditional cafe that serves more than 300 different kinds of beer. 't **Dreupelhuisje,** Kemelstraat 9 (☎ **050/34-24-21**) does something similar with *jenever* (gin), stocking dozens of artisanal examples of this deadly art. **Gran Kaffee De Passage,** Dweersstraat 26 (☎ **050/34-02-32**) is a quiet and elegant cafe that serves inexpensive meals.

9 A Side Trip from Bruges

DAMME

This village, just 7km (4.5 miles) from Bruges, was once the city's outer harbor, where seagoing ships loaded and unloaded their cargoes, until the Zwin inlet silted up in 1520. The marriage of Charles the Bold and Margaret of York was celebrated here in 1468—which indicates the important of Damme at the time. Today visitors come to see the picturesque Markt, which holds a statue of native Jacob van Maerlant, the "father of Flemish poetry," and the beautiful canal-side scenery en route from Bruges. It's easily possible to make a day trip to Damme, including lunch at one of the town's restaurants.

ESSENTIALS

GETTING THERE   Getting to Damme is half the delight. One of the nicest ways is to take the small stern-wheel paddle steamer Lamme Goedzaak. Departures are from the Noorweegse Kaai in the north of Bruges, five times daily from April through September. The delightful half-hour trip along the poplar-lined canal takes you past a landscape straight out of an old Flemish painting. Round-trip tickets cost 250 BF ($6.95) for adults, 230 BF ($6.40) for seniors, 180 BF ($5) for children age 3 to 12. For schedules and booking, contact **Rederij Damme–Brugge** (☎ **050/ 35-33-19**).

You can also take one of the minibuses of the **Sightseeing Line** (☎ **050/ 31-13-55**). The 2-hour tours run from April through September, at 2pm and 4pm from the Markt, returning from Damme on the paddle steamer Lamme Goedzaak. Round-trip tickets cost 660 BF ($18.35) for adults and 330 BF ($9.15) for children.

Public transportation buses leave six times daily in July and August, and three times daily from September through June, Monday to Saturday, from the train station and the Markt in Bruges to Damme Town Hall.

You can also drive, cycle, or even walk from Bruges to Damme, along Daamse Vaart Zuid from Dampoort in Bruges.

VISITOR INFORMATION   **Damme Tourist Office** is at Jacob van Maerlant-straat 3, 8340 Damme (☎ **050/35-33-19**; fax 050/37-00-21), facing the Town Hall (Stadhuis) in the Markt.

EXPLORING DAMME

The Gothic **Town Hall (Stadhuis)** in the Markt dates from 1464–68. On its façade are statues of Charles the Bold and Margaret of York, among other historic notables. In front of it stands a statue of the poet Jacob van Maerlant (1230–1296), who wrote his most important works in Damme.

Across from the Town Hall, at Jacob van Maerlantstraat 3, is the 15th-century mansion called **De Groote Sterre.** This was the Spanish governor's residence in the 17th-century, and is now occupied by the Damme Tourist Office, the **Tijl Uilen-spiegel Museum,** and the **Van Hinsberg Forge and Foundry Museum.** Uilen-spiegel is a 14th-century German folk-tale character who came to Damme by a roundabout route and has been adopted by the village. The museums are open from May through September, Monday to Friday 9am to noon and 2 to 6pm, Saturday and Sunday 10am to noon and 2 to 6pm; October through April, Monday to Friday 9am to noon and 2 to 5pm, Saturday and Sunday 2 to 5pm. At Jacob van Maerlantstraat 13, is a 15th-century mansion, the ✪ **Saint-Jean d'Angély House,** where in 1468 Charles the Bold married Margaret of York.

In Kerkstraat, which runs south from the Markt, you'll find the Gothic **St John's Hospital (Sint-Janshospitaal)** at no. 33, a hospital for the poor endowed by Countess Margaret of Constantinople in 1249; and the **Church of Our Lady (Onze-Lieve-Vrouwekerk),** dating from around 1340.

Across the bridge over the Bruges-Sluis Canal, at Dammesteenweg 1, is the 18th-century whitewashed **De Christoffelhoeve (St Christopher's Farm).** Note the ornamental gate and the monumental barn with its mansard roof. A little way to the west along the Daamse Vaart is the **Schellemolen,** a windmill built in 1867.

Beside the jetty where the Lamme Goedzak ties up is a modern **sculpture group** featuring the legend of Tijl Uilenspiegel.

Ghent & Antwerp

7

The cities of Ghent and Antwerp are often linked with Bruges (at least in tourist office propaganda) as the "Three Flemish Art Cities." Though everyone admits that Ghent and Antwerp can't match Bruges for sheer good looks, many Belgians believe them to be the true heartland of Flemish culture. Both cities have a grittier, more "lived-in" feel than Bruges, but neither would yield a millimeter in an argument over relative historical importance, artistic heritage, or contemporary vibrancy.

If time is short, I always advise choosing Bruges ahead of the other two. Just 2 more days, however, bring Ghent and Antwerp within range, and you will miss much if you don't reach out and grab them.

1 Ghent (Gent)

48km (30 miles) NW of Brussels; 51km (31 miles) SW of Antwerp; 46km (28 miles) SE of Bruges

If you were to draw an oval from Brussels to Antwerp to Bruges to Ypres and back to Brussels, Ghent would be almost exactly in the center, and that's fitting, because this magnificent old city at the confluence of the Rivers Leie and Scheldt has always been a pivotal point for this part of Flanders. Ghent was the seat of the counts of Flanders, who built their great castle here in 1180, but local fortifications actually predate their reign, going back to the 900s.

Hands-on rule began very early on here, and the common people—skilled weavers and craftsmen—never learned to live with it. During the Middle Ages, Ghent became as great a manufacturing center as Bruges was a trading center, but it never lacked for turmoil. The artisans rebelled not only against an exploitative nobility but even fought amongst themselves, guild against guild. Over the centuries the people of Ghent clashed with the counts of Flanders, the counts of Burgundy, the king of France, the king of Spain, their rivals in Bruges, and . . . well, anyone else who tried to take power over the town. The fact that they so seldom prevailed for any length of time did not deter them in the least: With each new conquest, they'd settle down for a spell, begin to seethe with indignation, finally reach a boiling point, and then take to the warpath all over again. Small wonder, then, that in 1815 it was Maurice de Broglie, a bishop of Ghent, who sparked the fire of indignation against the rule of Dutch Protestants, a fire that in 1830 would burst into the flame of national independence for Belgium.

After a long history of economic ups and downs, Ghent today has emerged once more as a major industrial center. Her medieval treasures are preserved, not as dry, showcase relics, but as living parts of the city. And to lighten what could be the overpowering grayness of industrialization, there are the flowers—flowers everywhere, creating oases of color as a constant reminder that this is also the heart of a prosperous horticultural industry. In short, Ghent is a busy, lively city, whose reminders of the past are as comfortable in the present as a pair of well-broken-in shoes.

ESSENTIALS

GETTING THERE Ghent is only a 32-minute train ride from Brussels. The main train station, **Gent Sint-Pieters** (☎ **09/222-44-44**), is on Maria Hendrikaplein, a mile or so south of the city center, and is well connected by tram to the center of town.

The **bus station** (☎ **09/210-94-91**) adjoins Sint-Pieters railway station.

By car, Ghent is reached via the E40 from Brussels, the E17 from Antwerp, and the E40 from Bruges.

VISITOR INFORMATION Ghent **Tourist Office** (Dienst Toerisme) is at Predikherenlei 2, 9000 Ghent (☎ **09/225-36-41;** fax 09/225-62-88); open Monday through Friday 8:30am to noon and 1 to 4:30pm. More convenient for personal visits, however, is the **Inquiry Desk** (Infokantoor) in the cellar of the Belfry, Botermarkt 17a, 9000 Ghent (☎ **09/266-52-32;** fax 09/224-15-55); open April through October daily 9:30am to 6:30pm, November through March 9:30am to 4:30pm.

GETTING AROUND Walking is the best way to see the center of Ghent. Farther out, however, it's better to use the excellent and easily understood public transport network, particularly the trams. Most lines travel along Nederkouter and continue to Korenmarkt. For taxis, call V-Tax (☎ **09/225-25-25**).

SPECIAL EVENTS The **Festival of Flanders** is a full program of cultural events that runs throughout Flanders from September through June. In Ghent, international concerts are presented in about 20 settings of medieval splendor. For full details before you come, contact Festival of Flanders Secretariat, Eugeen Flageyplein 18, 1050 Brussels (☎ **02/640-15-25;** fax 02/643-75-37).

The last full week of July witnesses the **Ghent Festivities** (Gentse Feesten), a time of music, dancing, and generally riotous fun and games throughout the city.

The colorful **Begonia Festival** takes place the last weekend in August.

ORIENTATION

The **Korenmarkt** lies at the heart of the city (the *Centrum*). If you arrive by rail at Sint-Pieters, take tram no. 1 to this square. Most of the city's important sights—including the Town Hall, Saint Bavo's Cathedral, and the Belfry—lie within half a mile of the Korenmarkt. The **River Leie** winds through the city center to connect with the River Scheldt and a network of canals that lead to the busy port area. The **Citadel Park,** location of the Museum of Fine Arts, is near Sint-Pieters railway station.

EXPLORING GHENT

Ghent's historic monuments have not all been prettified. Some of them look downright gray and forbidding, which, oddly enough, gives them a more authentic feel.

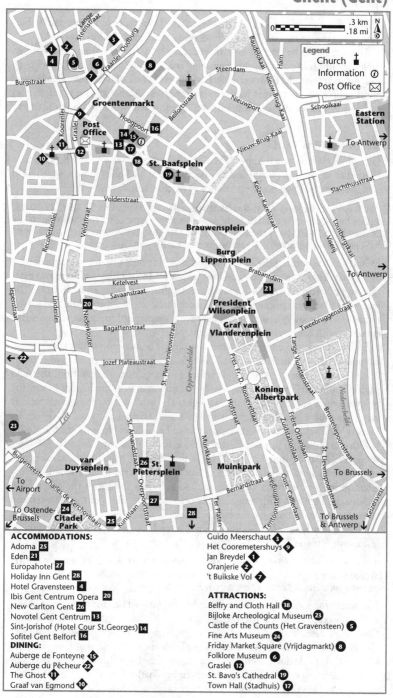

Ghent (Gent)

Legend
Church ✝
Information ⓘ
Post Office ✉

ACCOMMODATIONS:
Adoma **25**
Eden **21**
Europahotel **27**
Holiday Inn Gent **28**
Hotel Gravensteen **4**
Ibis Gent Centrum Opera **20**
New Carlton Gent **26**
Novotel Gent Centrum **13**
Sint-Jorishof (Hotel Cour St.Georges) **14**
Sofitel Gent Belfort **16**

DINING:
Auberge de Fonteyne **15**
Auberge du Pêcheur **22**
The Ghost **11**
Graaf van Egmond **10**
Guido Meerschaut **3**
Het Cooremetershuys **9**
Jan Breydel **1**
Oranjerie **2**
't Buikske Vol **7**

ATTRACTIONS:
Belfry and Cloth Hall **18**
Bijloke Archeological Museum **23**
Castle of the Counts (Het Gravensteen) **5**
Fine Arts Museum **24**
Friday Market Square (Vrijdagmarkt) **8**
Folklore Museum **6**
Graslei **12**
St. Bavo's Cathedral **19**
Town Hall (Stadhuis) **17**

139

The Castle of the Counts of Flanders was actually *meant* to look gray and forbidding, since the citizens of Ghent were so often in revolt against its overlord.

This is a city to be seen on foot. Indeed, only by walking its streets, gazing at its gabled guild houses and private mansions, and stopping on one of its bridges to look down at the canal below, can you begin to get a sense of the extraordinary vigor of the people who have lived here over the centuries. But before setting off, stop in at the tourist office and arm yourself with literature that will help bring the city to life.

THE TOP ATTRACTIONS

First of all, just so you'll know: The "Three Towers of Ghent" you'll often hear referred to are St Bavo's Cathedral, the Belfry, and St Nicholas Church, which form a virtually straight line pointing towards St Michael's Bridge.

✪ **St Bavo's Cathedral (Sint-Baafskathedraal).** Sint-Baafsplein. ☎ **09/223-10-46.** Cathedral free. Open daily 8:30am–6pm. *Adoration of the Mystic Lamb* altar and crypt 60 BF ($1.65) adults, 50 BF ($1.40) children. Open Apr–Oct Mon–Sat 9:30am–noon and 2–6pm, Sun 1–6pm; Nov–Mar Mon–Sat 10:30am–noon and 2:30–4pm, Sun 2–5pm.

Even if you see nothing else in Ghent, you shouldn't miss this massive cathedral on Sint-Baafsplein in the city center. Don't be put off by its rather unimpressive exterior, an uncertain mixture of Romanesque, Gothic, and baroque architecture. The interior is filled with priceless paintings, sculptures, screens, memorials, and carved tombs. About midway along the vaulted nave is a remarkable pulpit in white marble entwined with oak, reminiscent of Bernini.

St. Bavo's showpiece is the 24-panel altarpiece *The Adoration of the Mystic Lamb*, completed by Jan Van Eyck in 1432. Van Eyck's luminous use of oils and naturalistic portrayal of nature and people represented a giant step away from the rigid style of Gothic religious art. But besides its importance in the history of art, the *Mystic Lamb* is spellbinding in its own right. The work was commissioned for this very chapel by a wealthy alderman in 1420. The original artist was Jan's brother Hubert Van Eyck, but the piece was completed by Jan after Hubert's death in 1426.

Other art treasures in the cathedral include Rubens's recently restored *The Conversion of St Bavo*, painted in 1624. It's in the Rubens Chapel, in the semicircular ambulatory behind the high altar. The Romanesque Crypt holds a wealth of religious antiquities, vestments, sculptures, and paintings. Although the church was built in the 14th and 15th centuries, the crypt contains traces of the 12th-century Church of St John. Look for the faint frescoes still to be seen on some of the arches (if, that is, they haven't been cleaned away—several have disappeared in the wake of restorative "progress").

Belfry and Cloth Hall (Belfort and Lakenhalle) Sint-Baafsplein. ☎ **09/223-99-22.** Admission (guided tours only) 100 BF ($2.80) adults, 30 BF (85¢) children 7–16, under 7 free. Tours leave Tues–Sun at hourly intervals from 2:10 to 5:10pm.

Just across the square from the cathedral is the Cloth Hall and the 14th-century Belfry towering above it. Together they form a glorious medieval ensemble. The Cloth Hall dates from 1425 and was the gathering place of wool and cloth merchants during the Middle Ages. The Belfry holds the great bells that have rung out Ghent's civic pride down through the centuries. The most beloved of the bells was a 1315 giant known as "Roeland," destroyed by Charles V in 1540. No fewer than 37 of the 54 bells that now make up the huge carillon are from the remains of "Roeland." The massive "Triomphante"—which was cast in 1660 to replace the favorite—now rests in a small park at the foot of the Belfry, still bearing the crack it sustained in 1914.

If the elevator up to the Belfry's 215-foot-high upper gallery is in operation when you visit, you can see the bells as well as a fantastic panoramic view of the city. A great iron chest was kept in the Belfry's "Secret" to hold the all-important charters that spelled out privileges wrested from the counts of Flanders by the guilds and the burghers of medieval Ghent.

Town Hall (Stadhuis). At the corner of Botermarkt and Hoogpoort. ☎ **09/223-99-22.** Admission (guided tours only, from the tourist information desk in the Belfry cellar) 100 BF ($2.80) for adults, 30 BF (85¢) for children. May–Oct Mon–Thurs 2pm.

This large building turns a rather plain Renaissance profile to Botermarkt, and an almost garishly ornamented Gothic face to Hoogpoort. Its schizophrenic appearance probably came about because its construction started in 1518, was interrupted by Charles V, began again at the end of that century, was halted once more in the early 1600s, and wasn't completed until the 18th century. The changing public tastes and available monies of those years are reflected in the building's styles. In its Pacification Room (Pacificatiezaal), the Pacification of Ghent was signed in 1567. This document declared to the world the Low Country provinces' repudiation of Spanish Habsburg rule and their intention to permit freedom of religion within their boundaries.

✪ **Castle of the Counts (Het Gravensteen) Sint-Veereplein.** ☎ **09/225-93-06.** Admission 200 BF ($5.55), under 12 free. Daily Apr–Sept 9am–6pm, Oct–Mar 9am–5pm.

"Grim" is the word that instantly comes to mind when you first see this fortress, crouching like a gray stone lion over the city. The lugubrious Gravensteen was clearly designed by the counts of Flanders to send a message to rebellion-inclined Gentenaars. It's safe to say that the castle's very appearance did much to instill the awe and fear necessary to keep the people of Ghent in line.

The castle was built by Philip of Alsace, Count of Flanders, shortly after he returned from the Crusades in 1180, with images of similar crusaders' castles in Syria fixed firmly in his mind. According to local legend—supported to some degree by Gallo-Roman artifacts uncovered in recent excavations—the count built on foundations originally laid down by Baldwin of the Iron Arm back in the 800s. If the castle's 6-foot-thick walls, battlements, and turrets failed to intimidate attackers, the count could always turn to the well-equipped torture chamber inside. Relics of that chamber—a small guillotine, spiked iron collars, racks, branding irons, thumb screws, and a special kind of pitchfork designed to make certain that people being burned at the stake stayed in the flames—can be viewed in a small museum in the castle. On a happier note, if you climb to the ramparts of the high building in the center, the donjon, you'll be rewarded by a great view of the rooftops and towers of Ghent.

MUSEUMS

Bijloke Archaeological Museum. Godshuizenlaan 2 (south of city center). ☎ **09/25-11-06.** Admission 100 BF ($2.80), children 12 and under free. Tues–Sun 9am–12:30pm and 1:30–5:30pm.

This museum, located in a Cistercian abbey that dates from the 14th century, contains an outstanding collection of weapons, uniforms, clothing, and household items from the everyday life of years past. Authentic works of art of Ghent and Flanders are exhibited inside the "House of the Abbess," an exhibit space within the museum.

✪ **Fine Arts Museum (Museum voor Schone Kunsten).** Citadelpark (near the railway station). ☎ **09/222-17-03.** Admission 100 BF ($2.80), under 12 free. Tues–Sun 9:30am–5pm.

This fine museum houses both ancient and modern art masterpieces. Highlights include works by Peter Paul Rubens, Anthony Van Dyck, Jeroen Bosch, and Théodore Géricault, along with such moderns as James Ensor, Theo Van Rysselberghe, George Minne, and Constant Permeke.

✪ **Folklore Museum (Museum voor Volkskunde).** Kraanlei 65. ☎ **09/223-13-36.** Admission 100 BF ($2.80) adults, 50 BF ($1.40) children 12–18, under 12 free. Tues–Sun 10am–12:30pm and 1:30–5pm.

This fascinating museum in the city center is set in almshouses dating from the 1300s and later. Instead of glass-case exhibits, it features authentic replicas of typical rooms in homes of the period and in places where crafts and skills such as weaving, metalwork, and carpentry were practiced. There's also a marionette theater that presents performances on specified days of the week (check with the tourist office for current schedules).

OTHER ATTRACTIONS

This beautiful canal-side street called ✪ **Graslei** is home to a solid row of towering, gabled guild houses built between the 1200s and 1600s, when the neighboring waterway formed the harbor of Ghent. To fully appreciate their majesty, walk across the bridge over the Leie to the Korenlei on the opposite bank and view them as a whole, then return to stroll past each, conjuring up in your imagination the craftsmen, tradespeople, and merchants for whom these buildings were the very core of commercial (and civil) existence.

The building at no. 1 was the House of the Free Boatmen, dating from the 1500s; no. 2, the Annex House of the Grain Measurers, from the 1600s; no. 3, the House of the Receiver of the Staple (Customs), from the 1600s; no. 4, the Staple Warehouse, from the 1200s; no. 5, the Main House of the Grain Measurers, from the 1500s; no. 6, the House of the Free Masons, from the 1500s; and no. 7, the House of the Boatmen. The dramas that unfolded within the walls of each are enough to fill a library of books based on Ghent's independence of spirit. This is an ideal spot for leisurely exploration and for snapping a picture that captures the essence of Ghent.

Throughout the city's long history, when trouble erupted in Ghent, as it so often did, the huge **Vrijdagmarkt (Friday Market Square)** was nearly always the rallying point. The statue of Jacob Van Arteveld that stands in the square is a tribute to a 14th-century rebel leader; its base is adorned with the shields of some 52 guilds. The square is also the location of the building in which Belgium's Socialist Party was born under the direction of Ghent's native son, Edward Anseele. Today this is a major shopping area and the scene of lively street markets on Wednesday and Friday mornings and Saturday afternoons. A short distance away, the smaller **Kanonplein** square is guarded by a gigantic cannon known as Mad Meg (Dulle Griet), which thundered away in the 1400s in the service of the Burgundian armies.

SIGHTSEEING TOURS

The tourist office can arrange qualified guides, or you can contact the guide organization directly (☎ **09/233-07-72**) for private **walking tours,** at a charge of 1,500 BF ($41.65) for the first 2 hours (Monday through Friday), and 600 BF ($16.65) for each additional hour. Also ask them about organized group walking tours sometimes conducted during summer months at a fee of 250 BF ($6.95) for adults, children free (admission to see *The Adoration of the Mystic Lamb* included).

A tour that should be a part of every visitor's itinerary is a ✪ **boat ride** along the canals. Open and covered boats, which feature a narrative commentary in several languages, leave the Graslei and Korenlei every 30 minutes from 10am to 7pm, April through October. The trip lasts about 35 minutes, with fares of 160 BF ($4.45) for adults and 80 BF ($2.20) for children under 12.

On certain days during July and August you can also take a **boat trip from Ghent to Bruges** and back, at 1,000 BF ($27.80) for adults, 750 BF ($20.85) for children 12 and under. Contact Rederij Dewaele (☎ **09/223-88-53**), or Benelux-Gent-Watertoerist (☎ **09/282-92-48**).

Also, **horse-drawn carriages** leave from Sint-Baafsplein and Korenlei between 10am and 7pm from Easter through October for half-hour rides that cost 800 BF ($22.20). Call or visit the tourist office for details.

WHERE TO STAY

Because of its proximity to both Brussels and Bruges, Ghent is often regarded by tourists as a day-trip destination, but several very good hotels, both in the city center and on its perimeter, make it a convenient sightseeing base. However, Ghent has fewer hotels than might be expected. Those in the city center are often full at peak times, so try to book in advance.

The tourist office provides an up-to-date "Hotels and Restaurants" booklet at no cost and will also make hotel reservations for a returnable deposit.

TWO REAL GEMS

✪ **Sint-Jorishof (Cour St-Georges).** Botermarkt 2, 9000 Ghent (opposite the town hall). ☎ **09/224-24-24.** Fax 09/224-26-40. www.hotelbel.com/cour-st-georges.htm. E-mail: cour.st.georges@hotelbel.com. 28 units. TV TEL. 3,700–4,400 BF ($102.80–$122.20) double. Rates include full breakfast. AE, DC, MC, V. Parking 150 BF ($4.15).

This historical treasure has been an inn of quality since 1228. If you stay here you'll be in good company, historically speaking: Mary of Burgundy, Emperor Charles V, and Napoléon Bonaparte have all stayed under its roof. Try to get a room in the old building rather than in the more modern annex across the street. The pleasant and comfortable rooms have plush, antique furnishings. The rates here are quite low for such a great location (one of the most convenient in town for sightseeing) and wonderful atmosphere. Some rooms have minibars, and one has air-conditioning. Reserve as far in advance as possible. The Sint-Jorishof restaurant (see "Where To Dine," below) has terrific food and ambiance.

✪ **Hotel Gravensteen.** Jan Breydelstraat 35, 9000 Ghent (a short walk from Graslei and the Castle of the Counts). ☎ **09/225-11-50.** Fax 09/225-18-50. www.gravensteen.be. E-mail: hotel@gravensteen.be. 46 units. MINIBAR TV TEL. 3,990–4,700 BF ($110.85–$130.55) double; 4,615–5,240 BF ($128.20–$145.55) suite. Rates include full breakfast. AE, DC, MC, V. Parking 150 BF ($4.15).

This lovely mansion was built in 1865 as the home of a Ghent textile baron. You enter through the old carriageway (made up of ornamented pillars and an impressive wall niche occupied by a marble statue), which sets the tone for what you'll find inside. The elegant, high-ceilinged parlor is a sophisticated blend of pastels, gracious modern furnishings, and antiques, with a small bar tucked into one corner. The rooms are attractive and comfortably furnished. Those in front look out on the moated castle, while those to the back have city views. There's a top-floor "Belvedere," with windows offering magnificent views of the city. Afternoon tea is available. There's no dining room, but plenty of good restaurants are within easy walking distance. Some rooms have air-conditioning, and all have hair dryers.

EXPENSIVE

Holiday Inn Gent. Akkerhage 2, 9000 Ghent (3 miles from the city center, at the intersection of E17 and E40). ☎ **09/222-58-85.** Fax 09/220-12-22. 140 units. A/C TV TEL. 3,400–7,000 BF ($94.45–$194.45) double. AE, CB, DC, DISC, MC, V. Free parking.

Drivers who don't want to drive into the city center will find this hotel conveniently situated—it's on the main road, only about half an hour from Brussels, Antwerp, and the Belgian coast. The guest rooms are modern and typical of this chain; each is furnished with two double beds. All rooms have hair dryers.

Dining/Diversions: The De Leie restaurant serves French and Belgian cuisine, and the De Lieve bar serves snacks and drinks.

Amenities: Room service, laundry and dry cleaning service, newspaper delivery, baby-sitting, secretarial services, express checkout, heated indoor pool, tennis court, bicycle rental, health club, Jacuzzi, sauna, conference rooms, car-rental desk.

Sofitel Gent Belfort. Hoogpoort 63, 9000 Ghent. ☎ **09/233-33-31.** Fax 09/233-11-02. E-mail: sofitel_gent@unicall.be. 128 units. A/C MINIBAR TV TEL. 8,000 BF ($222.20) double; 14,650 BF ($406.95) suite. AE, DC, MC, V. Parking 150 BF ($4.15).

The Sofitel Gent Belfort has an enviable location just across the road from the Town Hall and within easy distance of the city's premier tourist attractions. The rooms have all the facilities and services expected by a demanding international business and tourist clientele. The hotel is bright and modern and has been designed to fit at least partly into its venerable surroundings.

Dining: Belgian cuisine and international dishes are served in the Van Artevelde Brasserie.

Amenities: In-room hair dryers, concierge, 24-hour room service, laundry and dry cleaning service, baby sitting, health club, conference rooms.

MODERATE

New Carlton Gent. Koningin Astridlaan 138, 9000 Ghent (close to the E17/E40 interchange near the railway station). ☎ **09/222-88-36.** Fax 09/220-49-92. 22 units. MINIBAR TV TEL. 2,600–2,800 BF ($72.20–$77.80) double. Rates include buffet breakfast. AE, DC, MC, V. Parking 100 BF ($2.80).

This modern-style hotel has rooms with standard decor and furnishings. All have been renovated recently. There's no restaurant or bar on the premises, but there are several in the neighborhood, and there's convenient parking in a garage next door.

Europahotel. Gordunakaai 59, 9000 Ghent. ☎ **09/220-60-71.** Fax 09/220-06-09. 38 units. TV TEL. 2,500–3,300 BF ($69.45–$91.65) double. Rates include continental breakfast. AE, DC, MC, V. Free parking.

This modern hotel is set on the banks of the River Leie in the greenery of the Blaarmeersen suburb on Ghent's outskirts. The rooms are large, with bright, attractive furnishings. The hotel has some facilities associated with more expensive places, such as a concierge, 24-hour room service, laundry and dry cleaning service, newspaper delivery, express checkout, conference rooms, and free coffee in the lobby. There's also a bar, a good restaurant, and easy parking.

Ibis Gent Centrum Opera. Nederkouter 24–26, 9000 Ghent. ☎ **09/225-07-07.** Fax 09/223-59-07. 134 units. TV TEL. 3,345 BF ($92.90) double. Rates include buffet breakfast. AE, DC, MC, V. Parking 300 BF ($8.35).

The rooms in this modern hotel are bright and comfortably furnished. There's a nice bar, and although there's no restaurant on the premises, several good eateries are nearby. The Ibis Centrum Opera Hotel basically offers good accommodations at moderate rates, between the city center and the railway station. A major renovation program was undertaken in 1997–98.

Novotel Gent Centrum. Gouden Leeuwplein 5, 9000 Ghent. ☎ **800/221-4542** or 09/224-22-30. Fax 09/224-32-95. www.hotelweb.fr. 121 units. A/C MINIBAR TV TEL. 5,050 BF ($140.30) double; 6,050 BF ($168.05) suite. AE, DC, MC, V. Limited parking available on street.

This modern hotel has an excellent location, near the Town Hall in the city center, within easy walking distance of all major sights. The modern building has been designed to fit, more or less, into its ancient surroundings. Guest rooms are nicely furnished and have individual heating controls. Facilities include a garden terrace and a heated outdoor swimming pool. There's also a restaurant open daily from 6am to midnight, and an attractive bar that has become a meeting place for local businesspeople. All rooms have hair dryers.

INEXPENSIVE

Adoma. Sint-Denijslaan 19 (behind Sint-Pieters train station), 9000 Ghent. ☎ **09/ 222-65-50.** Fax 09/245-09-37. 15 units. TV TEL. 2,100 BF ($58.35) double. Rates include continental breakfast. MC, V. Free parking.

The facilities and atmosphere at this recently renovated hotel have taken a major leap forward, yet the rates remain reasonable for Ghent. Rooms are spacious and brightly decorated, with modern furnishings. You'll find staying here to be a comfortable, if not luxurious, experience.

Eden. Zuidstationstraat 24, 9000 Ghent. ☎ **09/223-51-51.** Fax 09/233-34-57. 28 units. TV TEL. 2,400–3,200 BF ($66.65–$88.90) double. Rates include buffet breakfast. MC, V. Free parking.

The Eden is a good hotel for its price category. It's located not far out of the city center and has a small parking area in the courtyard. The facilities are straightforward. The bathrooms are often a bit cramped.

WHERE TO DINE

In keeping with the city's tradition as a center of Flemish culture, many of Ghent's restaurants keep the region's culinary traditions alive and well, in dishes such as the thick, creamy *waterzooï op Gentse wijze* (a soup that borders on being a stew), and *lapinà la flamande* (rabbit with beer, vinegar, and currant juice), or if it's the right season, asparagus from the Mechelen area. Prices are generally well below those in Brussels. The helpful, free "Hotels and Restaurants" booklet published by the tourist office lists the more prominent restaurants in all price brackets.

VERY EXPENSIVE

✪ **Auberge du Pêcheur.** Pontstraat 41, Sint-Martens-Latem. ☎ **09/282-31-44.** Main courses 850–1,450 BF ($23.60–$40.30); fixed-price menus 1,650–3,050 BF ($45.85–$84.70), wine included. AE, MC, V. Daily 10am–10pm. From Ghent, take A14 (the highway to Deinze) and follow the signs for Deurle. SEAFOOD/FRENCH.

No listing of restaurants in Ghent would be complete without mention of this one. It's located about 20 minutes away in a country inn at the beautiful riverside village of Sint-Martens-Latem. There are actually two restaurants here, the gourmet Orangerie, and the tavern-grill The Green—I'm recommending the Orangerie here, but The Green is also good, as well as being quicker, simpler, and cheaper.

At The Orangerie, the six-course fixed-price dinner features seafood, lamb, and the freshest local specialties available each day, including Flemish asparagus, grilled turbot with mustard sauce, *sole meunière* with french fries, and scallops. The more adventurous might want to try the pigeon with sweetbreads, eel with cream sauce or fresh herbs, or kidneys with mustard sauce. The daily business lunch is a good buy at 950 to 1,350 BF ($26.40 to $37.50), wine included, and a fine way to combine good eating with a sightseeing foray into the countryside.

EXPENSIVE

✪ **Het Cooremetershuys.** Graslei 12. ☎ **09/233-49-71.** Main courses 750–920 BF ($20.85–$25.55); fixed-price menus 980–1,750 BF ($27.20–$48.60). AE, DC, MC, V. Mon, Tues, and Thurs–Sat noon–2pm and 7–9:30pm. Closed July 15–Oct 15. FLEMISH/FRENCH.

To reach this special little restaurant, you mount the stairs in one of the gorgeous 14th-century gabled houses lining the canal. Your entrance into a rather plain room whose walls are hung with musical instruments is accompanied by the strains of taped classical music. Among the starters are snails (*escargots*) with gorgonzola cheese (go on, try it!). Lamb with thyme is a specialty of the main course menu. You might also consider the fish of the day. The *mousse au chocolat* is excellent for dessert.

✪ **Jan Breydel.** Jan Breydelstraat 10. ☎ **09/225-62-87.** Main courses 675–1,150 BF ($18.75–$31.95). AE, DC, MC, V. Tues–Sat noon–2pm and 7–10pm, Mon 7–10pm. SEAFOOD/FLEMISH.

Top honors go to this exquisite restaurant on a quaint street near the Castle of the Counts. Its interior is a gardenlike delight of greenery, white napery, and light woods. Proprietors Louis and Pat Hellebaut see to it that dishes issued from their kitchen are as light and airy as the setting, with delicate sauces and seasonings making the most of impeccably fresh ingredients. Seafood or regional specialties are all superb. This place is highly recommended.

✪ **Sint-Jorishof (Cour St-Georges).** Botermarkt 2. ☎ **09/224-24-24.** Main courses 550–950 BF ($15.30–$26.40); fixed-price menus 1,250–1,850 BF ($34.70–$51.40). AE, MC, DC, V. Mon–Sat noon–2:30pm and 7–10pm; Sun noon–2:30pm. FLEMISH.

This restaurant is located in the centuries-old hotel of the same name opposite the Town Hall (see "Where to Stay," above). The place is a marvel of dark woodwork and stained glass, dominated by a massive fireplace and encircled by an upstairs balcony. The dazzling visual spectacle is matched by the equally impressive culinary one. The wide-ranging menu features hearty portions of fish and meat dishes. Flemish specialties include *paling in 't groen* (eel with green sauce) and chicken *waterzooï*.

MODERATE

✪ **Graaf van Egmond.** Sint-Michielsplein 21. ☎ **09/225-07-27.** Main courses 475–695 BF ($13.20–$19.30). AE, DC, MC, V. Daily noon–3pm and 6–11pm. FRENCH/FLEMISH.

The Graaf van Egmond is located in a marvelous old 13th-century town house on the River Leie in the city center. It serves Flemish specialties like *carbonnade flamande* (beef stew) and *asparagus à la flamande*, along with French creations. Try to get a window seat, which offers a spectacular view of the towers of Ghent.

✪ **Oranjerie.** Corduwaniersstraat 8, Patershol. ☎ **09/224-10-08.** Main courses 480–640 BF ($13.35–$17.80); fixed-price menu 1,400 BF ($38.90). AE, DC, MC, V. Mon–Thurs and Sun noon–2:30pm and 6–11pm, Sat 6–11pm. FLEMISH.

Patershol (which means the cave—or "hole"—in which monks lived a hermit's existence) is an ancient enclave not far from the Castle of the Counts. The place is fast becoming a gastronomic center, as more and more small restaurants move into renovated old buildings in the area. Oranjerie is one of the most delightful of these. As you might guess from its name, it has the bright, cheerful aspect of a garden. The dining rooms are light and airy, and there's a skylight, a fountain, a lovely small garden, and lots of lush greenery. The dishes here are beautifully prepared and presented. The excellent fixed-price menu might offer *bouillabaisse* (fish soup), followed by lamb with mustard sauce, and *sabayonne* (zabaglione) for dessert.

✪ **'t Buikske Vol.** Kraanlei 17. ☎ **09/225-18-80.** Main courses 495–895 BF ($13.75–$24.85); fixed-price menus 975–1,650 BF ($27.10–$45.85). AE, V. Mon–Tues, Thurs–Fri noon–2pm and 7–9:30pm; Sat 7–9:30pm. BELGIAN/FRENCH.

The 't Buikske Vol is one of the gastronomic gems of Ghent, thanks to its cozy, intimate atmosphere and chef Peter Vyncke's insistence on the best ingredients. In recent times the chef has done even better, delivering the same quality at lower prices. The *terrine d'oie* (pâté) and turbot with salmon in butter sauce make for good choices, but a little more adventure can be found in the *filet de biche* (doe steak—try not to think of Bambi when you take a bite), and the *terrine de faisan* (grilled pheasant).

The Ghost. Korenlei 24. ☎ **09/225-89-02.** Main courses 350–750 BF ($9.70–$20.85); à la carte meals 650–1,500 BF ($18.05–$41.65). AE, MC V. Thurs–Tues 11am–3pm and 6pm–midnight. FLEMISH/BELGIAN.

The Ghost is housed in what is allegedly Belgium's oldest crypt, dating back to the 12th century. This restaurant radiates an authentic Flemish atmosphere and serves some superbly prepared food to match. The favorite dish is roast goose—every second table orders it. Other dishes range from T-bone steak to grilled pike. The wine list is extensive too.

INEXPENSIVE

Auberge de Fonteyne. Gouden Leeuwplein 7. ☎ **09/225-48-71.** Main courses 350–700 BF ($9.70–$19.45). MC, V. Mon–Fri noon–2:30pm and 6pm–midnight, Sat–Sun noon–2am. MUSSELS/FLEMISH.

It would be difficult for the food quality to equal the impressive appearance of this art deco restaurant, but it comes pretty close. *Waterzooï* is a particular favorite here, as are the heaps of big Zeeland mussels that Belgium loses its collective cool over.

Guido Meerschaut. Kleine Vismarkt 3. ☎ **09/223-53-49.** Main courses 320–495 BF ($8.90–$13.75). Fixed-price menu 880 BF ($24.45). AE, DC, MC, V. Tues–Sat noon–2:30pm and 6pm–10:30pm. SEAFOOD/FLEMISH.

The Guido of this restaurant's name owns a fish shop in the Fish Market—so it's no surprise that Guido's specializes in seafood. The dining room is simple yet elegant and has painted scenes from Fish Market history. The fish comes fresh off the boat from the North Sea. Dover sole, sole Ostendaise, and a variety of cod, herring, and other well-prepared fish dishes predominate, along with North Sea shrimp, oysters, and mussels prepared in a variety of ways.

OTHER OPTIONS

For the least expensive eating, stop at any of the small restaurants around Saint Bavo's Square, where you'll find more or less the same main courses for about 360 BF ($10). Most of these places have sidewalk tables, and all offer simple but adequate renderings of Flemish dishes.

GHENT AFTER DARK
THE PERFORMING ARTS

From October through mid-June, international opera is performed in the 19th-century **De Vlaamse Opera,** Schouwburgstraat 3 (☎ **09/225-24-25**). Ghent venues for those marvelous Belgian puppet shows are: the **Folklore Museum,** Kraanlei 65 (☎ **09/223-13-36**); the **Teater Taptoe,** Forelstraat 91c (☎ **09/223-67-58**); and **Magie,** Haspelstraat 39 (☎ **09/226-42-18**).

BARS & TAVERNS

In typical Flemish fashion, the favorite after-dark entertainment in Ghent is frequenting its atmospheric bars and taverns. You'll have a memorable evening in any one you choose, but **Oud Middelhuis,** Graslei 6, which provides a 17th-century setting plus more than 300 varieties of beer, is well worth searching out. The same recommendation applies to **Dulle Griet,** Vrijdagmarkt 50, where if you deposit one of your shoes, you'll be given a glass of potent Kwak beer in an all-too-collectable wooden frame that a Kwak glass needs to stand up—you may also need artificial support to stand up if you drink too many Kwaks. The tiniest building on romantic Graslei is the former Toll House, now a little tavern called **Het Tolhuisje,** Graslei 10.

Groentenmarkt, near the Castle of the Counts, makes for a good pub-crawl in an easily navigable area. Try **Het Waterhuis aan de Bierkant,** Groentenmarkt 9, which has more than 100 different Belgian beers (including the locally made Stopken). A couple of doors along is **'t Dreupelkot,** Groentenmarkt 12, which specializes in deadly little glasses of *jenever.* Ask owner Paul to recommend one of his 100 or so varieties, or walk straight in and boldly ask for a 64-proof Jonge Hertekamp or a 72-proof Pekèt de Houyeu; if they don't knock you down, you may be up for an 8-year-old 100-proof Filliers Oude Graanjenever or a 104-proof Hoogspanning. Across the tramlines is **Het Galgenhuisje,** Groentenmarkt 5, a tiny and perforce intimate place popular with students.

2 Antwerp (Antwerpen)

48km (30 miles) N of Brussels; 51km (31 miles) NE of Ghent

Antwerp (pop: 452,000) owes its life to the River Scheldt (Schelde), its soul to the artist Rubens, and its name to a giant of ancient days called Druon Antigon. Legend has it that Druon levied exorbitant tolls on every Scheldt boatman who passed his castle, and if anyone would not or could not pay up, the big man gleefully cut off the miscreant's hand and threw it into the river. Druon's comeuppance came from a Roman centurion named Silvius Brabo, who slew the giant and (as if that weren't enough) also cut off his hand and threw it into the river, thus avenging the boatmen. The Flemish *handwerpen* (throwing of the hand) eventually became Antwerpen, the city's Flemish name.

Of course, historians who deal only in dry facts tell a different story. They claim that sailors described the port city's location as *aan-de-werfen* (on the wharves). But to the people who live here, the severed, bleeding "Red Hand of Antwerp" is the symbol of their city. You'll find two statues in the town commemorating the Roman's act of revenge, and replicas of the giant's hand appear in everything from chocolate to brass.

When you come down to it, if there were no River Scheldt, there would be no Antwerp by any name. The city's prime location just above the point where the

River Scheldt meets the tidal Scheldt Estuary made it an important Gallo-Roman port in the second century B.C. For many centuries after that, Antwerp attracted a bevy of covetous invaders. In the port's early days, the ships moored beside the city center; nowadays the port has moved downstream to the huge excavated docks that jam up against the Dutch border.

As for Rubens, that master is only one of several artists who left their baroque mark on the face of this city and a great love of beauty in the hearts of its inhabitants. You'll see that love expressed in their buildings, their public works of art, and the contents of some 20 museums.

Antwerp is not only the world's fifth-largest port, but also the acknowledged "Diamond Center of the World." Antwerp's diamond business is worth a sparkling $23 billion a year, which swamps Amsterdam's $1 billion—although you would never guess as much from the noise the Dutch city makes about its jewels and the discreet silence maintained by the Belgians.

ESSENTIALS

GETTING THERE   Antwerp's **Deurne Airport** is about 5.5km (3.5 miles) east of the city at Deurne. City bus service runs between the main road outside the airport and Pelikaanstraat in the city proper. Taxi fare is about 500 BF ($13.40) from the airport to the city center. Few scheduled international flights arrive at Deurne, however—**Brussels National Airport** is really the main airport for Antwerp (see Chapter 5, "Orientation"). There's a long-distance bus between the Brussels airport and the Sabena Airlines office in De Keyserlei in Antwerp.

Antwerp's two train stations are **Centraal Station,** 1.5km (1 mile) east of the Grote Markt, on the edge of the city center, and **Berchem,** 4km (2.5 miles) south of the city center. For schedule and fare information, call ☎ **03/204-20-40.** Antwerp is on the **Thalys** high-speed train network that connects Paris, Brussels, and Amsterdam (and Cologne via Brussels). Most Thalys trains stop at Berchem, but a few serve Centraal Station. Reservations are required for Thalys; the local reservations number is ☎ **03/204-20-40.**

Most long-distance buses arrive and depart from the **bus station** on Franklin Rooseveltplaats, a short distance northwest of Centraal Station. Timetables and fare information are available from a kiosk in Centraal Station, or by calling ☎ **03/ 218-14-06.**

Major highways connecting to Antwerp's Ring Expressway are E19 from Brussels via Mechelen and A12 from Brussels via Laeken; E17 from Ghent; and N49 from Knokke, Bruges, and Zeebrugge, bypassing Ghent.

VISITOR INFORMATION   **Antwerp Tourist Office,** Grote Markt 15, 2000 Antwerp (☎ **03/232-01-03;** fax 03/231-19-37), is open Monday through Saturday 9am to 6pm, Sunday 9am to 5pm.

CITY LAYOUT   Centraal Station serves as a focal point. When you're standing in front of the station, the large square opposite you is Koningin Astridplein; to your right is Antwerp zoo; and to your left is Pelikaanstraat, a major diamond center street. De Keyserlei runs toward the river and joins the Meir, Antwerp's main shopping street. The Meir then leads into Schoenmarkt, a short street that curves around the 24-story Torengebouw to reach a large square known as Groenplaats, where there's a statue of Rubens and the Cathedral of Our Lady. One short block beyond Groenplaats (toward the river) puts you right into the large Grote Markt (Market Square), bordered by its Renaissance Town Hall and 16th-century guild houses. This is also where you'll find a statue of the Roman soldier Brabo. Follow the quaint

Antwerp Accommodations, Dining & Attractions

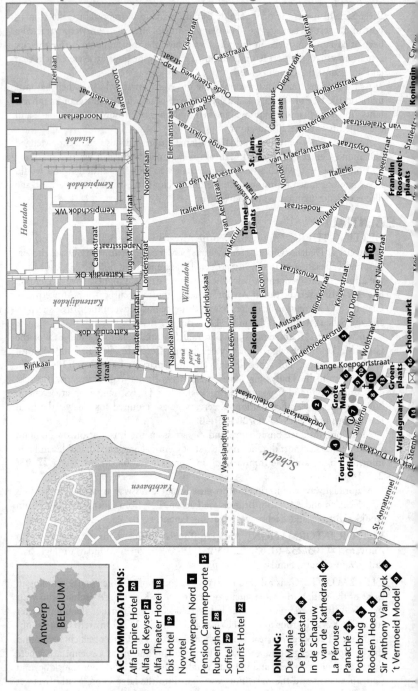

ACCOMMODATIONS:

Alfa Empire Hotel **20**
Alfa de Keyser **21**
Alfa Theater Hotel **18**
Ibis Hotel **19**
Novotel
Antwerpen Nord **1**
Pension Cammerpoorte **15**
Rubenshof **28**
Sofitel **29**
Tourist Hotel **22**

DINING:

De Manie **10**
De Peerdestal **8**
In de Schaduw
van de Kathedraal **16**
La Pérouse **13**
Panaché **23**
Pottenbrug **3**
Rooden Hoed **5**
Sir Anthony Van Dyck **6**
't Vermoeid Model **9**

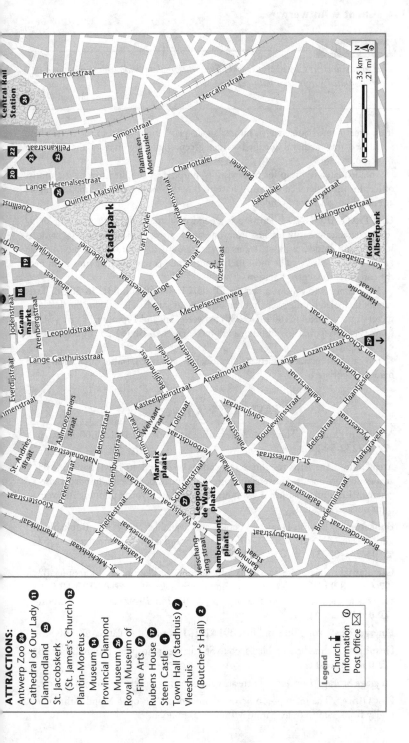

ATTRACTIONS:

Antwerp Zoo **24**
Cathedral of Our Lady **25**
Diamondland **23**
St. Jacobskerk
    (St. James's Church) **12**
Plantin-Moretus
    Museum **14**
Provincial Diamond
    Museum **26**
Royal Museum of
    Fine Arts **27**
Rubens House **17**
Steen Castle **4**
Town Hall (Stadhuis) **7**
Vleeshuis
    (Butcher's Hall) **2**

Legend
Church ✝
Information ⊙
Post Office ⊠

151

This goodly ancient City methinks looks like a disconsolate Widow, or rather some super-annuated Virgin that hath lost her Lover . . .

—James Howell (1619)

little street named Suikerrui (it means "sugar quay") right down to the river, where you'll see the medieval fortified castle, Steen, that now houses the maritime museum.

An adequate **city map** for most visitors' purposes is supplied free by the tourist office; for more detailed use you'll have to buy the "Antwerp A–Z" map, available at bookshops and news vendors.

GETTING AROUND   Antwerp is a good pedestrian city, with its major sight-seeing attractions easily reached from one major street, which changes its name as it goes along. Besides walking, **trams** are the best way to get around the city; a single fare is 45 BF ($1.25). The most useful tourist line is the one that runs from near the cathedral to Centraal Station.

The numbers to call for a taxi are ☎ **03/216-01-60** and **03/238-38-38.** Taxis cannot be hailed on the street but can be found at stands. The fare for the first kilometer or part thereof is 100 BF ($2.80) between 6am and 10pm, or 175 BF ($4.85) from 10pm to 6am; each additional kilometer costs 45 BF ($1.25) throughout the day or night.

You can rent bicycles at Centraal Station; but be warned, traffic can be heavy and hard to negotiate.

FAST FACTS: Antwerp

American Express   There's an Amex office at Frankrijklei 21, 2000 Antwerp (☎ **03/232-59-20**).

Area Code   Antwerp's telephone area code is **03.** You don't need to dial the **03** area code from inside Antwerp or from the suburbs of the city, just from elsewhere in Belgium. Dial just **3** (without the initial 0) if you're phoning Antwerp from outside Belgium.

Bookstores   English-language books are available at **FNAC Bookshop,** Groenplaats 31 (☎ **03/231-2056**), and **Standaard,** Huidevetterstraat 57 ☎ **03/231-0773**).

Car Rental   There are two **Avis** offices, one at Plantin en Moretuslei 62 (☎ **03/218-94-96**) and a second at Boomsesteenweg 560 (☎ **03/829-10-00**). **Hertz** is located at Mechelsesteenweg 43 (☎ **03/233-29-92**) and at the airport (☎ **03/230-16-41**).

Emergencies   For police and fire, dial ☎ **101;** for an ambulance, ☎ **100.**

Hospital   For medical problems, go to St. Elizabeth Hospital, Leopoldstraat 26 (☎ **03/234-41-11**).

Luggage Storage/Lockers   There are coin-operated lockers at Centraal Station.

Post Office   The main post office is at Groenplaats 42, open Monday through Friday from 9am to 6pm, Saturday from 9am to noon.

EXPLORING ANTWERP

Antwerp is a good walking city. Its major sightseeing attractions are easily reached from one major street that changes its name as it goes along: Italiëlei, Frankrijklei, Britselei, and finally, Amerikalei.

The sightseeing treasures of Antwerp are best seen at a leisurely pace—after all, who would want to gallop through Rubens's home at a fast clip? But if time is a factor or if you'd like a good overview before striking out on your own, the city makes it easy by providing guides for walking tours, regularly scheduled coach tours, and a series of boat trips to view Antwerp from the water, as so many visitors through the centuries have first seen her (see "Organized Tours," below).

If you're a dedicated do-it-yourselfer, you can get maps and sightseeing booklets from the tourist office to guide you. Walking trails marked within the city will lead you through typical streets and squares to find the main points of interest. There's even a free ferryboat ride across the Scheldt.

Many of Antwerp's museums and churches are open to the public either for free or at a minimal charge.

THE TOP ATTRACTIONS

✪ **Cathedral of Our Lady (Onze-Lieve-Vrouwekathedraal).** Handschoenmarkt. ☎ **03/213-99-40.** Admission 60 BF ($1.65). Mon–Fri 10am–5pm, Sat 10–3pm, Sun 1–4pm.

This towering Gothic edifice, begun in 1352, is the largest church in both Belgium and Holland. Its architecture is simply stunning—there are seven naves and 125 pillars. The cathedral's original design included five towers, but only one was completed. Its history includes devastation by religious iconoclasts, deconsecration by anticlerical French revolutionaries (resulting in the removal of its Rubens paintings), and a slow rebirth that began after Napoléon's defeat in 1815.

Today, the cathedral houses three Rubens masterpieces: *The Raising of the Cross, The Descent From the Cross,* and *The Resurrection.* Rombouts's *Last Supper,* an impressive stained-glass window dating from 1503, is also outstanding. In July and August, the cathedral bells peal out in a carillon concert on Sundays from 3 to 4pm and on Mondays from 8 to 9pm.

Royal Museum of Fine Arts (Koninklijk Museum voor Schone Kunsten). Leopold de Waelplaats 2. ☎ **03/238-78-09.** Admission 250 BF ($6.95) adults, 100 BF ($2.80) children 12–17, under 12 free. Tues–Sun 10am–5pm. Closed major holidays. Tram: 12, 24.

The collection of paintings by Flemish masters in this impressive neoclassical building is second to none in the world. You'll find more Rubens masterpieces here in one place than in any other. Jan Van Eyck, Roger Van der Weyden, Dirck Bouts, Hans Memling, the Brueghel family, Rembrandt, and Hals are all represented as well. All told, these walls hold paintings spanning 5 centuries, and viewing them is a moving experience. The ground floor holds exhibitions of work by more modern artists, such as Ensor, Magritte, Permeke, and Delvaux.

✪ **Rubens House (Rubenshuis).** Wapper 9–11 (a short walk east of the city center). ☎ **03/232-47-51.** Admission 100 BF ($2.80) adults, 50 BF ($1.40) students. Tues–Sun 10am–4:45pm.

A visit here is pretty much essential if you are to fully appreciate what you'll see elsewhere in Antwerp. Pieter Paul Rubens, whose father was an Antwerp attorney, was brought back to this city at an early age by his mother. By the time he was 32, his artistic reputation was firmly established. In 1610, when he was only 33, his great wealth enabled him to build this impressive home and studio along what was once a canal, the Wapper (about midway down the Meir).

Today you can wander through the reconstructed rooms of the Rubens House, and come away with a good idea of the lifestyle of a patrician Flemish gentleman of that era. There are also examples of Rubens's work scattered throughout, as well as others by master painters of his time. In the dining room, look for his self-portrait, painted when he was 47 years old. Rubens was a lover and collector of Roman sculpture as well. Some of the pieces in his sculpture gallery appear—reproduced in amazing detail—in his paintings.

✪ **Steen Castle.** Steenplein 1. ☎ **03/232-08-50.** Admission 100 BF ($2.80) adults, 50 BF ($1.40) children. Tues–Sun 10am–4:45pm.

The oldest stones of this medieval fortress on the banks of the River Scheldt date from the early 13th century, making this Antwerp's oldest building. Today it houses the National Maritime Museum. There's an extensive library on river navigation and almost every nautical subject, as well as interesting exhibits about the development of the port and maritime history in general. The most eye-catching of all are models of old-time sailing ships, such as East India Company clippers.

Next to the museum there's an interesting industrial archaeological division with the remains of the old Antwerp port; this division is open Easter to November 1.

SIGHTS AROUND THE GROTE MARKT

Grote Markt, while not nearly as dramatic as Brussels's Grand-Place, is no less the focus of the city's everyday activity. In the center of this large square is a huge fountain showing Brabo in the act of throwing Druon's severed hand into the Scheldt.

Town Hall (Stadhuis). Grote Markt. ☎ **03/221-13-33.** Guided tours 30 BF (85¢). Mon–Wed, Fri, Sat 11am, 2, and 3pm (council business permitting).

The Renaissance Stadhuis (Town Hall) was built in the mid-1500s, burned down by the Spanish in 1576, and rebuilt as you see it now. Look for the frescoes by Leys (an important 19th-century painter), some interesting murals, and an impressive 16th-century fireplace in the burgomaster's room.

Vleeshuis (Butcher's Hall). Vleeshouwersstraat 38–40. ☎ **03/233-64-04.** Admission 100 BF ($2.80) adults, 50 BF ($1.40) children 12–18, children under 12 free. Tues–Sun 10am–5pm.

Around the square and in the surrounding streets you'll see excellent examples of 16th-century guild houses. This magnificent Gothic structure, just a short walk from the Stadhuis, is well worth a visit. The Vleeshuis now functions as a museum of archaeology, ceramics, arms, religious art, sculpture, musical instruments, coins, and medieval furnishings. The collections give a good general idea of the daily life in Antwerp during the 16th century, as do the historical paintings (look for the striking *The Spanish Fury*, picturing Antwerp's darkest hour). There's also an Egyptian section.

MORE ATTRACTIONS

✪ **Antwerp Zoo.** Koningin Astridplein 26 (just east of Centraal Station). ☎ **03/201-15-55.** Admission 450 BF ($12.50) adults, 290 BF ($8.05) seniors and children 3–11, free for children under 3. Daily Dec–Jan 9am–4:30pm, Feb and Oct 16–Nov 9am–4:45pm, Mar 1–15 and Oct 1–15 9am–5:15pm, Mar 16–June and Sept 9am–5:45pm, July–Aug 9am–6:15pm. Tram: Centraal Station.

This amazing 25-acre zoo is a real standout among Antwerp's treasures. Its large collection of animals from around the world roam freely through spaces bounded for the most part by artificial reproductions of natural barriers; for example, bright lights instead of closed cage doors keep the aviary bird population at home. There's also an aquarium, winter garden, Egyptian temple (which houses elephants), anthropoid house, museum of natural history, deer parks, Kongo-peacock habitat, and planetarium. The zoo is also something of an art nouveau masterpiece, although whether or not the animals appreciate this is unclear.

✪ **Plantin-Moretus Museum.** Vrijdagmarkt 22. ☎ **03/234-12-83.** Admission 100 BF ($2.80) adults, 50 BF ($1.40) children. Tues–Sun 10am–5pm. Closed major holidays.

In the late 1500s, Christoffle Plantin established an influential printing workshop in this stately patrician mansion in the city center. Its output included an astonishing multilanguage (Hebrew, Greek, Syriac, Latin, and Aramaic) edition of the Bible and translations of other great works of literature. Plantin's name survives in today's publishing world as a widely used typeface. His grandson, Balthasar Moretus, was a contemporary and close friend of Rubens, who illustrated many of the books published by the Plantin-Moretus workshop and also painted the family portraits you'll see displayed here. The museum's exhibits include an antique *Librorium Prohibitorum,* a catalog of books proscribed by the church as being unfit for pious consumption.

St Jacobskerk (St James's Church). Lange Nieuwstraat 73 (a short walk east of the city center, north of the Rubens House). ☎ **03/232-10-32.** Admission 50 BF ($1.40) adults, 30 BF (85¢) children. Apr–Oct Mon–Sat 9am–noon and 2–5pm, Nov–Mar Mon–Sat 9am–noon.

This flamboyant Gothic church with its baroque interior is the final resting place of Peter Paul Rubens. His vault is in the Rubens Chapel, one of seven chapels bordering the opulent semicircular ambulatory behind the high altar. Several of Rubens's works are here, as well as some by Van Dyck and other prominent artists. Rubens is joined in his eternal slumber by a glittering collection of Antwerp's one-time high and mighty, and by a glittering collection of gold and silver and religious objects.

ANTWERP'S PORT

Although it has now been shifted to Zandvliet, some 8 miles downstream from the city proper, Antwerp's port is the very reason for its existence, and is well worth a visit, if only to appreciate its vast size. The entire harbor/dock complex covers 40 square miles. Each year, some 16,000 ships visit Antwerp harbor, transporting an estimated 100 million metric tons of cargo. Port enterprises employ roughly 57,000 people and add more than $6 billion to the national economy.

The Flandria boat cruises and coach tours (see "Organized Tours," below) offer the best view, but the tourist office can also furnish detailed information for those who wish to drive the plainly marked "Havenroute" (if this includes you, keep a sharp eye out for the hazards of this busy workplace—open bridges, rail tracks, moving cranes, and so on).

THE DIAMOND QUARTER

Antwerp is acknowledged as the world's leading diamond center. Some 85% of the world's rough diamonds, 50% of cut diamonds, and 40% of industrial diamonds are traded here annually—together they're valued at more than $23 billion, accounting for roughly 7% of total Belgian exports. The Diamond Quarter, near Centraal Station, is interesting not only for its glitter, but also for the Orthodox Jewish community responsible for much of the trade.

✪ **Diamondland.** Appelmansstraat 33a (near Centraal Station). ☎ **03/234-36-12.** Free admission and free guided tour at 11am. Apr–Oct Mon–Sat 9:30am–5:30pm, Sun 10am–5pm; Nov–Mar Mon–Sat 9:30am–5:30pm. Tram: Centraal Station.

Diamondland provides a fascinating firsthand look at the whole process of transforming undistinguished stones into gems of glittering beauty. The expert cutters and polishers in Antwerp's Diamond Quarter are legendary—the "Antwerp cut" is said to give the stones more sparkle. This luxurious showplace provides a guided tour of its workrooms, and you can also take home a souvenir of lasting value for a price considerably lower than what you'd pay elsewhere.

Provincial Diamond Museum (Provinciaal Diamantmuseum). Lange Herentalsestraat 31–33 (near Centraal Station). ☎ **03/202-48-90.** Free admission (except during major exhibitions). Daily 10am–5pm. Tram: Centraal Station.

Exhibits here examine the history, geology, mining, and cutting of diamonds. Diamond-cutting and -polishing demonstrations take place on Saturday afternoon from 1:30 to 4:30pm.

ORGANIZED TOURS

WALKING TOURS   In July and August, there's a daily guided tour of the city center in English (and French), leaving at 2pm from the tourist office; the price is 150 BF ($4.15), accompanied children under 12 free. The tourist office can also arrange for a highly qualified guide to accompany you on private walking tours around the city at a set rate of 1,500 BF ($41.65) for the first 2 hours, 750 BF ($20.85) for each additional hour. There are also clearly marked self-guided walks, with brochures available from the tourist office.

BY BOAT   The ✪ **Flandria Line,** Steenplein (☎ 03/231-31-00), offers two cruise options. There's a 90-minute excursion on the river, with half-hourly departures during summer months, at a cost of 250 BF ($6.95) for adults and 130 BF ($3.60) for children; and also an extensive trip around the harbor that lasts 2½ hours and costs 400 BF ($11.10) for adults and 250 BF ($6.95) for children. In July and August, there's a delightful harbor dinner cruise from 8 to 10:30pm, costing 1,600 BF ($44.45) for adults and 1,100 BF ($30.55) for children. Most departures are from the city center Steen waterfront.

BY BUS   The tourist office can furnish details of coach tours of Antwerp and its environs as well as some that include such destinations as Ghent and Bruges.

WHERE TO STAY

Rates in Antwerp are generally lower than in Brussels. However, many of the big hotels are on the city's outskirts. The tourist office has a free, same-day reservation service—you make a small deposit, which is then deducted from your hotel bill. The office also publishes a booklet listing all Antwerp accommodations and rates.

A word of warning to budget travelers: The phrase "tourist room" that in other cities means an accommodation bargain in a private home means something rather different in Antwerp—it's a discreet way of advertising very personal services that have nothing to do with a room for the night.

EXPENSIVE

✪ **Alfa de Keyser.** De Keyserlei 66–70 (beside Centraal Station), 2018 Antwerp. ☎ **03/234-01-35.** Fax 03/232-39-70. 123 units. A/C MINIBAR TV TEL. 3,900–5,900 BF ($108.35–$163.90) double. AE, DC, MC, V. Limited parking available on street. Tram: Centraal Station.

This well-located, seven-story, modern hotel has nicely furnished rooms. Some are modern in style, decorated with a pastel color scheme, while others are more classic in tone (done in warmer, wine-red colors). The front lobby is dark and quiet, with plants, a piano, and luxurious sofas. There's good parking nearby, which is important for drivers who want to stay in the city.

Dining/Diversions: Guests can enjoy the fine Chagall restaurant and Paint Pot bar.

Amenities: 24-hour room service, laundry and dry cleaning service, health club, heated indoor swimming pool, solarium, Jacuzzi.

✪ **Sofitel.** Desguinlei 94, 2018 Antwerp. ☎ **03/216-48-00.** Fax 03/216-47-12. 215 units. MINIBAR TV TEL. 3,400–6,500 BF ($94.45–$180.55) double. Children 12 and under stay free in parents' room. AE, DC, MC, V. Free parking. South of the city on the ring road and Singel.

This ultramodern luxury hotel gives you the best of all of Antwerp's worlds. It's in a beautiful park, about 5 minutes from the city's attractions, 10 minutes from the city center, and 15 minutes from the port and the industrial zone. Each room is superbly furnished, with such extras as a hair dryer and trouser press.

Dining/Diversions: Tiffany's is a superb gourmet restaurant. Breakfast and lunch are served in the Park Relais; the Lobby Terras serves snacks; and the Pullman Bar is a cozy, congenial meeting place.

Amenities: Room service, laundry and dry cleaning, baby-sitting, health club, sauna, newspaper delivery.

MODERATE

Alfa Empire Hotel. Appelmansstraat 31 (in the diamond quarter), 2018 Antwerp. ☎ **03/231-47-55.** Fax 03/233-40-60. 70 units. A/C MINIBAR TV TEL. 3,500–4,700 BF ($97.20–$130.55) double. Rates include buffet breakfast. AE, DC, MC, V. Limited parking available on street. Tram: Centraal Station.

This modern hotel has some rooms equipped with a kitchenette and other amenities, including a safe. There's good shopping nearby, as well as several theaters and restaurants, and parking for 400 BF ($11.10) a day.

Alfa Theater Hotel. Arenbergstraat 30, 2000 Antwerp. ☎ **03/231-17-20.** Fax 03/233-88-58. Telex 33-910. 127 units. MINIBAR TV TEL. 2,700 BF ($75) double. Rates include buffet breakfast. AE, DC, MC, V. Limited parking available on street. Tram: Lange Gasthuisstraat.

The location here is convenient to the Rubens House and the theater district. Furnishings are modern and attractive. Some rooms come with kitchenettes. Guests have free use of the sauna and Jacuzzi. The Carousel restaurant—the dish of the day is 400 BF ($11.10)—is open weekdays and Saturday evenings.

Ibis Hotel. Meistraat 39, 2000 Antwerp. ☎ **03/231-88-30.** Fax 03/234-29-21. 150 units. TV TEL. 2,200–3,000 BF ($61.10–$83.35) double. AE, DC, MC, V. Limited parking available on street. Tram: Frankrijklei.

The Ibis is a modern hotel right in the city center, convenient for sightseeing and just across from the weekend bird and flower market (Vogelmarkt). The guest rooms are nicely furnished with a bright decor. There's no restaurant on the premises, but several good ones are in the immediate vicinity.

Novotel Antwerpen Noord. Luithagen Haven 6 (in the docks area, north of the city center), 2030 Antwerp. ☎ **03/542-03-20.** Fax 03/541-70-93. E-mail: nan@novotel.be. 119 units. A/C MINIBAR TV TEL. 3,500–3,900 BF ($37.20–$108.35) double. AE, DC, JCB, MC, V. Free parking.

This modern hotel is set in gardenlike landscaped grounds a bit outside the city center. It has bright, well-furnished rooms, good wheelchair access, good parking, a garden terrace, a restaurant, two tennis courts, and a heated outdoor swimming pool.

INEXPENSIVE

Pension Cammerpoorte. Steenhouwersvest 55 (just off the Vrijdagmarkt), 2000 Antwerp. ☎ **03/231-28-36.** Fax 03/226-28-43. 16 units. TEL. 2,450 BF ($68.05) double. Rates include continental breakfast. AE, MC, V. Limited parking available on street. Tram: Groenplaats.

This pension is very centrally located. The rooms are clean and comfortable; some face the cathedral. This a good inexpensive choice—but note that there's no elevator and the rooms are spread over three floors.

✪ **Rubenshof.** Amerikalei 115–117 (near the Royal Fine Arts Museum), 2000 Antwerp. ☎ **03/237-07-89.** Fax 03/248-25-94. 24 units. 1,500–2,400 BF ($41.65–$66.65) double. Rates include continental breakfast. AE, MC, V. Free parking. Tram: Brederodestraat.

This small family hotel used to be a residence of the Belgian cardinal—perhaps that explains the heavenly atmosphere. The place has a remarkably beautiful interior, with painted ceilings, chandeliers, and a great deal of ornamentation, some of it jugendstil. The rooms are somewhat plainer than the public spaces, but they're still comfortably and adequately furnished.

Tourist Hotel. Pelikaanstraat 20–22 (close to Centraal Station), 2018 Antwerp. ☎ **03/232-58-70.** Fax 03/231-67-07. 134 units (some without bathroom). TV TEL. 1,900–2,800 BF ($52.80–$77.80) double. Rates include continental breakfast. AE, DC, MC, V. Limited parking available on street. Tram: Centraal Station.

The rooms at this reliable hotel aren't fancy, but they're quite modern and comfortable. On the premises is a moderately priced restaurant (closed Sunday and Monday).

HOSTELS

In addition to the conventional youth hostels (see the tourist office for a complete list), there are two reliable hostel-type accommodations (no membership required) with rates of 450 to 1,200 BF ($12.50 to $33.35): **New International Youth Pension,** Provinciestraat 256, 2018 Antwerp (☎ **03/218-94-30;** fax 03/281-09-33); and **Square Sleep-Inn,** Bolivarplaats 1, 2000 Antwerp (☎ **03/237-37-48;** fax 03/248-02-48), which also rents studios with kitchenettes for an amazing 600 BF ($16.65) per person (but you need to bring your own pots, plates, and cutlery).

WHERE TO DINE

The tourist office has a handy restaurant booklet that lists most eateries in town, including long lists of snack bars, pizza parlors, waffle and pancake houses, and tearooms for low-budget eating.

EXPENSIVE

De Manie. Hendrik Conscienceplein 3 (near St. Katelijnevest). ☎ **03/232-64-38.** Main courses 750–950 BF ($20.85–$26.40); prix-fixe dinner, including wines, 2,500 BF ($69.45). AE, DC, MC, V. Mon–Tues and Thurs–Sat noon–2:30pm and 6:30–9:30pm. FRENCH.

This bright, modern restaurant comes up with such originals as an appetizer of quail salad with goat cheese and artichoke, and baked goose liver with bilberries and honey, as well as innovative main dishes. Fillet of hare with cranberries, chicory, and juniper sauce, and grilled wood pigeon with gratinéed brussels sprouts, are both typical of menu specialties, which change every 6 months. The food is excellent, and the setting is very relaxing.

✪ **In de Schaduw van de Kathedraal.** Handschoenmarkt 17–21. ☎ **03/232-40-14.** Main courses 800–1,800 BF ($22.20–$50). AE, DC, MC, V. Wed–Sun noon–3pm and 6–10pm. FRENCH.

This attractive restaurant in the city center features traditional Belgian cuisine gussied up just a bit. Mussels and eel assume several guises on the menu, and beef is also well represented. The specialty of the house is bouillabaisse, which claims to be for two but is actually enough to feed a family of five. If the prices here seem a little inflated, it's probably because of the excellent location; after all, this restaurant lies, as its name says, "in the shadow of the cathedral."

✪ **La Pérouse.** Steenplein. ☎ **03/231-31-51.** Main courses 850–1,450 BF ($23.60–$40.30); fixed-price menus 1,750–2,900BF ($48.60–$80.55). AE, MC, V. Tues–Sat noon–midnight. Closed Aug. FRENCH.

This floating restaurant is moored at the foot of the Suikkerui (during August it abandons its fine cuisine to take on full-time sightseeing voyages). The *waterzooï de poussin* is a model of how this thick, creamy stew should be prepared. Other specialties include lobster salad and monkfish with noodles.

✪ **Sir Anthony Van Dyck.** Oude Koornmarkt 16. ☎ **03/231-61-70.** Main courses 540–680 BF ($15–$18.90). AE, DC, MC, V. Mon–Sat noon–1:30pm and 6:30–9:30pm. Closed most of Aug. CLASSIC FRENCH.

This used to be a Michelin Star–rated restaurant, until its owner tired of staying on the Michelin treadmill and decided to do something less stressful and more fun. The place reopened as a notably relaxed brasserie-restaurant, but still retains its commitment to good food. Its location in Antwerp's delightful Vlaeykensgang courtyard—full of cafes, restaurants, and cheap apartments—all but guarantees a pleasant atmosphere.

MODERATE

✪ **De Peerdestal.** Wijngaardstraat 8 (near the cathedral). ☎ **03/231-95-03.** Main courses 475–575 BF ($13.20–$15.95); fixed-price menu 1,395 BF ($38.75). AE, DC, MC, V. Daily 11:30am–3pm and 5:30–10pm. FRENCH.

In this large, rustic, two-floor restaurant, you can enjoy a light meal of a salad, or indulge in heartier fare such as mussels, fish, or steak (horse meat is a specialty here). Despite its size, there's something almost cozy about the place. Patrons frequently read newspapers as they eat at the long bar.

Rooden Hoed. Oude Koornmarkt 25 (near the cathedral). ☎ **03/233-28-44.** Main courses 450–715 BF ($12.50–$19.85); fixed-price menus 950–1,850 BF ($26.40–$51.40). AE, MC, V. Sun–Thurs noon–3pm and 6–10:30pm, Fri–Sat noon–3pm and 6–11pm. REGIONAL/FRENCH.

This pleasant, old-fashioned restaurant serves good, hearty food at very moderate prices. Mussels, sausages (which come with sauerkraut and mashed potatoes in a delicious "*choucroute d'Alsace*"), *waterzooï,* and fish are all featured on the menu. Try an aperitif, or a snack, in the medieval cellar under the restaurant.

✪ **'t Vermoeid Model.** Lijnwaadmarkt 2. ☎ **03/233-52-61.** Main courses 400–800 BF ($11.10–$22.20). AE, DC, MC, V. Mon–Sat 5–11pm. SEAFOOD.

This rustic Flemish restaurant, built right into the walls of the cathedral, is a delight both aesthetically and gastronomically. It specializes in seafood—smoked trout is a local favorite.

INEXPENSIVE

Panaché. Statiestraat 17 (near Centraal Station). ☎ **03/232-69-05.** Main courses 375–450 BF ($10.40–$12.50). AE, DC, MC, V. Daily 10am–10pm. Tram: Centraal Station. CONTINENTAL.

You have to pass through a sandwich, snack, and delicatessen (*charcuterie*) section to reach this large, busy restaurant. The vast menu features spaghetti, chicken cro-quettes, veal, chicken, steaks . . . if your appetite calls for it, you're pretty sure to find it. Budget watchers can get themselves a satisfying, inexpensive meal by choosing from the long counter loaded with goodies such as sandwiches, herring, cheese, and pastries.

Pottenbrug. Minderbroedersrui 38. ☎ **03/231-51-47.** Main courses 520–690 BF ($14.45–$19.15). AE, CB, MC, V. Mon–Fri noon–2pm; Tues–Fri and Sun 6:30–10pm, Sat 6:30–11pm. FLEMISH/BELGIAN.

The casual, relaxed atmosphere in this place goes well with the sand on the floor and the stove in full view. The menu mainly consists of traditional Flemish dishes, with French additions. Among the best choices here are duck breast with port sauce and a gratin of celery and dates, and salmon or lobster accompanied by fresh pasta with cherry butter.

SHOPPING

Antwerp yields not an inch to Brussels in the style wars—in fact, it could be that Antwerp is the more fashion conscious of the two. Certainly in recent years youthful Antwerp fashion designers have made a major impact within Belgium, and also established a substantial international reputation.

SHOPPING DISTRICTS   Expensive, upmarket shops, boutiques, and depart-ment stores abound in De Keyserlei and the Meir. For haute couture, go to Leopoldstraat; for lace, the streets surrounding the cathedral; for books, Hoogstraat; for electronics and antiques, Minderbroedersrui; and for diamonds, Appel-mansstraat and nearby streets, all near Centraal Station.

SHOPPING HOURS   Most shops are open Monday through Saturday from 9am to 5pm.

MARKETS   Antwerp's famed street markets are fun as well as good bargain-hunting territory. Outstanding among them is the **Bird Market,** a general market that features live animals, plants, textiles, and foodstuffs; it takes place Sunday mornings in Oude Vaartplaats near the City Theater. The **Antiques Market,** at Lijnwaadmarkt (north gate of the cathedral), goes on all day Saturday from Easter to October. At the **Friday Market,** on Wednesday and Friday mornings on Vrijdag-markt facing the Plantin-Moretus Museum, household goods and secondhand fur-niture are put on public auction.

ANTWERP AFTER DARK

Antwerp is as lively after dark as it is busy during the day. To check what's going on while you're in the city, pick up a copy of *Antwerpen,* a monthly publication avail-able at the tourist office.

Main entertainment areas are Grote Markt and Groenplaats, which both contain concentrations of bars, cafes, and theaters; High Town (Hoogstraat, Pelgrimstraat, Pieter Potstraat, and vicinity) for jazz clubs and bistros; Stadswaag for jazz and punk; and the Centraal Station area for discos, nightclubs, and gay bars. The red-light district here, concentrated in Riverside Quarter, is much seedier and less tourist-oriented than the one in Amsterdam.

The Belgian Muppets

Take the kids to the delightful ✪ **Van Campen Puppet Theater,** Lange Nieuwstraat 3 (☎ **03/237-37-16**), where the plot lines are always easy to understand (even if the language isn't).

THE PERFORMING ARTS

Antwerp takes pride in being a citadel of Flemish culture. Two of the region's stellar companies are based here: the **Flanders Opera** (Vlaamse Opera), Frankrijklei 3 (☎ **03/233-68-08**); and the **Royal Flanders Ballet** (Koninklijk Ballet van Vlaanderen), Kattendijkdok-Westkaai 16 (☎ **03/234-34-38**).

To house its vibrant cultural life, the city has no shortage of performance venues. Top of the line for theater and classical music is the **Stadsschouwburg,** Theaterplein 1 (☎ **03/203-77-60**). For music and ballet, there's the classically orientated **Queen Elisabeth Concert Hall,** Koningin Astridplein 23–24 (☎ **03/233-84-44**); and the more modernist **deSingel,** Desguinlei 25 (☎ **03/248-28-28**).

Antwerp has more theaters than any other Flemish city, as well as two excellent theater companies: **Jeugdtheater** and **KNS,** the Royal Flemish Theater. Though most plays are in Dutch, you can often understand the plot regardless of language difficulties, and the quality of these shows merits attendance. For current information and reservations, contact the **Cultural Information Desk,** Grote Markt 40 (☎ **03/220-81-11**).

CINEMA

Antwerp may well lead all of Belgium in foreign films shown, as well as in number of movie theaters, most of which are located along De Keyserlei and its side streets. All films are shown in their original languages, with Dutch and French subtitles. They might be anything from the latest award winner to porn—Antwerp is sophisticated enough to take each type at face value. Lists of current film showings are published in daily newspapers.

THE CLUB & MUSIC SCENE

Along De Keyserlei and its side streets, there's a conglomeration of disco and strip bars—some very classy, others (obvious at a glance) frankly seedy or vulgar. If you're looking for a respectable disco, check the area between Groenplaats and Grote Markt. Look out for **De Blokhut,** Lange Herentalsestraat 6 (☎ **03/226-90-79**); **Opera Café,** Frankrijklei 18 (☎ **03/225-28-20**); **Griffy's,** De Keyserlei 19–21 (☎ **03/233-19-22**); **Hans Christian Andersen,** De Keyserlei 25 (☎ **03/226-48-63**); **Pièce Unique,** Twaalfmaandenstraat 11 (☎ **03/233-55-46**); **Bayside Beach Club,** Groenplaats (☎ **03/227-05-27**); and **Café d'Anvers,** Verversrui 15 (☎ **03/226-38-70**).

THE BAR SCENE

When the sun goes down, the people of Antwerp head for their favorite cafe or bar for an evening of Belgian beer and good conversation—and you'll be very welcome to join their circle. If you don't spend an evening in this manner, it's safe to say that you haven't really seen Antwerp!

Street cafes are generally found in Groenplaats and Grote Markt; "brown cafes" (traditional pubs) and bistros are clustered on Hoogstraat, Pelgrimstraat, Pieter Potstraat, and the surroundings; beer cellars are on Stadswaag; taverns and boulevard cafes are strewn along De Keyserlei; artists' cafes and bars are in Quartier Latin near the City Theater; and gay bars are mostly in the Centraal Station area.

The following are just a few among the hundreds of popular pubs: **De Groote Witte Arend** (The Great White Eagle), Reyndersstraat 12–18, (☎ **03/226-31-90**), a 17th-century cafe in an old abbey where customers are serenaded by classical music; **De Pelgrom,** Pelgrimstraat 15 (☎ **03/234-08-09**), a candlelit cellar with long wooden benches; **De Engel,** Grote Markt 3 (☎ **03/233-12-52**), one of the most atmospheric old cafes in the land, where a *bolleke* (little ball) of Antwerp's own De Koninck beer becomes a work of liquid art; **Elfde Gebod,** Torfbrug (☎ **03/232-36-11**); and **Kulminator,** Vleminckveld 32 (☎ **03/232-45-38**), which displays behind glass a huge selection of beer, including virtually every Belgian brand. **De Vagant,** Reijndersstraat 25 (☎ **03/233-15-38**), offers an altogether different sort of drinking experience: It deals exclusively in *jenever*, of which it offers about 150 varieties.

3 A Side Trip from Antwerp

LIER

16km (10 miles) SE of Antwerp

Lier is a pretty town on the banks of the River Nete, with canal-side scenes reminiscent of Bruges.

GETTING THERE　Lier is best reached by train, departing hourly from Antwerp Centraal Station. There are also buses every half hour or so from the bus station in front of Centraal station, but they take longer. To go by car, take the N10.

VISITOR INFORMATION　Lier **Tourist Office** (VVV) is in the Town Hall (Stadhuis) at Grote Markt 57 (☎ **03/488-38-88;** fax 03/488-12-76).

EXPLORING LIER

Don't miss the ✪ **Zimmer Tower (Zimmertoren),** Zimmerplein (☎ **03/489-11-11**), which dates from the 14th century. It's equipped with the remarkable Centenary Clock and Wonder Clock, which were installed by astronomy enthusiast Lodewijk Zimmer to explain "Life, the Universe, and Everything" to his fellow citizens. The clocks show the sun, moon, signs of the zodiac, seasons, tides on the River Nete, and quite possibly tomorrow's movements on Wall Street. The tower is open daily in July and August from 9am to noon and 1pm to 6pm; the rest of the year it closes at 4pm. Admission is 40 BF ($1.10) adults, 20 BF (55¢) children.

If you have time, also visit the **Municipal Museum (Stedelijk Museum),** Florent van Cauwenberghstraat 14 (☎ **03/489-11-11**), just off of the Grote Markt in the town center. Its art collection includes paintings by Rubens, Jan and Pieter Brueghel, David Teniers the Younger, and local artist Isidore Opsomer. The museum is open from April through October, Saturday to Tuesday and Thursday 10am to noon and 1:30 to 5:30pm. Admission is 40 BF ($1.10) for adults, 20 BF (55¢) for children.

The Belgian Coast & Ypres 8

Belgium's beaches are among the best in northern Europe. The country's 70km (44-mile) North Sea coastline is one continuous vista of fine white sand backed by dunes and dotted with seaside resorts. Unfortunately, to enjoy that vista you have to keep your eyes tightly focused on the beaches. Let your gaze drift inland and it'll immediately bump up against a line of hotels, restaurants, and apartment blocks that sarcastic critics have dubbed the Atlantic Wall. Each of the coast's 13 resort towns is encumbered with an unattractive density of accommodations and other commercial developments that virtually neutralize the coast's natural beauty.

Despite that, most visitors seem relaxed about the situation. Even those who regret the marred natural surroundings find compensation in the superb food, good shopping, and general holiday-making hustle and bustle that the beach resorts offer. Kids love the place. For adults, the Belgian coast offers several different kinds of holiday—sea, sand, and sun; high-flying casino and night-club action; an exercise in sheer gustatory gluttony; or a series of sea-side sightseeing expeditions. With judicious planning, it's possible to cover all these options in an incredibly short amount of time.

The beaches stretch back as much as 500m (542 yards) at low tide, and their gently sloping decline into the sea makes for some of the safest swimming in Europe—although the authorities warn against swimming along isolated stretches. Just remember that this is the North Sea, not the Caribbean—instead of turquoise and sun-warmed, the water is usually gray and pretty darn cold. You can also skim along the beach on wind-blown sail carts (there's no shortage of wind), pedal beach buggies, or join the ever-hopeful sun worshippers in search of the perfect tan.

The visiting gourmand will surely leave frustrated at not being able to gorge at every single one of the excellent restaurants—most of them specializing in seafood—in this small area. Sightseers will be kept busy discovering museums dedicated to fishing, surrealistic paintings, and postimpressionist-era art. Nature-lovers will find some of the region's last scraps of coastal wilderness preserved in a nature reserve tinged with the hue of sea lavender and alive with the whir of bird wings. When the sun goes down, visitors head to the nightclubs that attract top performers during the summer months or to the four casinos (Knokke-Heist, Ostend, Blankenberge, and Middelkerke) that operate year-round.

Transportation Tip

You won't need a car for sightseeing on the Belgian coast if you take the marvelous **Coast Tram** (Kusttram) (☎ **059/56-53-53**), which runs the entire length of the coast, with departures every 10 to 20 minutes in summer, and every 30 minutes in winter. Charges vary from point to point, but if you decide to go the distance—from Knokke-Heist to De Panne (a 2-hour ride)—you'll pay only 250 BF ($6.95). There are also special 1- and 3-day unlimited travel tickets that cost 330 BF ($9.15) and 560 BF ($15.55), respectively. The Coast Tram is not only a great way to get around; it's an attraction in its own right.

Hotels, holiday apartments, and boardinghouses here are plentiful, and their rates are usually less than what you'd expect to pay in such popular vacation spots. This is not to say, however, that you should just drop in without planning—the place is often packed. The smart thing to do is reserve directly or through one of the local tourist offices before you arrive, especially if you're coming on a weekend, since that's when Belgians from the inland cities flock to the sea.

Many foreign visitors combine a trip to the Belgian coast with a visit to the town of Ypres, famous for its associations with World War I.

1 Knokke-Heist/Het Zoute

24km (14 miles) NE of Bruges; 35km (21 miles) NE of Ostend; 60km (37 miles) NE of De Panne

This area, sometimes called "the garden of the North Sea coast," holds five of the classiest Belgian beaches. **Heist,** snuggled up close to the Dutch border, attracts average-income (*classy* average-income) families; **Duinbergen** is chiefly residential and caters to families; **Albertstrand** is more sporty. And *then* things begin to reach the upper levels of "class":

Knokke is fashionable—not as exclusive as it once was, but still fashionable. You can tell by the very look of the place; its main shopping street features upscale jewelers, art galleries, and sporting shops adorned with internationally famous designer names (some designer collections have actually been shown here before Paris!).

The winding residential streets of the nearby suburb **Het Zoute** also fairly shriek "money," and it's big money—the lovely villas proclaim owners of both wealth and what they at any rate consider exquisite taste. Whether or not you fit easily into this monied environment, a drive, cycle, or walk through Het Zoute provides a glimpse of the wealthy lifestyle of its inhabitants—and if that doesn't grab you as a worthwhile way to spend 15 minutes, you can pass right through and arrive at Het Zwin Nature Reserve, where the birds have worse manners but more grace.

ESSENTIALS

GETTING THERE   There's frequent **train** and **bus** service from Bruges. To get here from Ostend and other seafront resorts, take the **Coast Tram** (see above). The combination train/bus/tram stations are located at the south end of Lippenslaan, the main street.

By **car** from Bruges, take the N31 north; from Brussels, take the E40. The N34 runs the entire length of the coast, connecting all the resort towns.

VISITOR INFORMATION   The **Tourist Office** is at Zeedijk 660, Lichttorenplein, 8300 Knokke-Heist (☎ **050/63-03-80;** fax 050/63-03-90).

The Belgian Coast

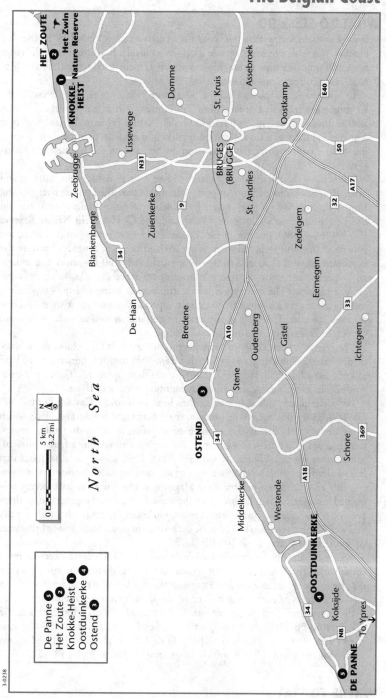

Legend:
- De Panne **5**
- Het Zoute **2**
- Knokke-Heist **1**
- Oostduinkerke **4**
- Ostend **3**

North Sea

N

5 km
3.2 mi

HET ZOUTE **2**
Het Zwin - Nature Reserve
KNOKKE-HEIST **1**

Asseboek
Oostkamp
Domme
St. Kruis
Lissewege
Zeebrugge
BRUGES (BRUGGE)
St. Andries
Zuienkerke
Zedelgem
Blankenberge
Eernegem
De Haan
Bredene
Oudenberg
Gistel
Ichtegem
Stene
Schore
OSTEND **3**
Middelkerke
Westende
OOSTDUINKERKE **4**
Koksijde
DE PANNE **5**
To Ypres

E40
50
A17
32
33
N31
9
34
A10
34
369
A18
34
N8

3-0238

165

WHAT TO SEE & DO

It goes without saying that this area's list of attractions is topped by its five fine beaches, where all manner of seaside sports are available. Beachfront activities range from half-hour sea trips in amphibious vessels launched right from the beach to sand-castle competitions and kite flying.

In Knokke itself you can take a 30-minute ride through the streets in the ✪ **miniature train** that departs from Van Bunnenplein at the promenade. Bikers and/or drivers will enjoy the 48km (30-mile) "Riante Polderroute" that begins in Knokke and takes you through wooded parks and gardens, past the Zwin reserve, into polder farm country, past canals and ditches, and on to Damme and Ooster-kerke.

It was along this stretch of coast that the River Zwin estuary once met the sea and made Bruges a leading European port. After fickle fate silted up the river (leaving Bruges to settle into a land-locked prominence of quite another sort), the old riverbed turned into a salty, sandy marshland: the ✪ **Het Zwin Nature Reserve** (☎ 050/60-70-86), just east of Het Zoute. The reserve covers just 370 acres, but it's one of the most important remaining wetland breeding zones for birds on the northwest coast of Europe. Among the approximately 100 migratory and indige-nous species that enjoy the reserve's facilities are avocets, storks, snipes, plovers, geese, and ducks. The spongy soil here nurtures an amazing variety of vegetation, making the reserve a lovely place to explore, especially in summer, when it's covered with sea lavender. There's an aviary near the entrance as well as a nice restaurant, Châlet du Zwin, and a well-stocked bookshop.

The reserve is open Easter to September from 9am to 7pm; October to the week before Easter, Thursday through Tuesday from 9am to 5pm. Entrance is 165 BF ($4.60) for adults and 105 BF ($2.90) for children up to 12. There's a 2-hour guided tour every Sunday and Thursday morning starting at 10am.

For a completely different kind of fun, head to **Knokke Casino,** Zeedijk 509 (☎ 050/63-05-05), located across from the Albertstrand beach. This place, which dates from the 1920s, is the epitome of elegance, with plush gaming rooms, nostalgic bits of art deco, and glittering chandeliers illuminating a festive, dressed-to-the-nines clientele. There are two nightclubs here, as well as a ballroom that features leading European entertainers. The magnificent Salle Magritte dining room is a tribute to surrealist painter René Magritte, whose paintings have been trans-formed into gigantic murals that adorn the walls. Despite all the glitter—or perhaps because of it—there's a cosmopolitan relaxation about the casino that makes it fun and well worth a visit. You'll need to be decked out in dressy attire and to bring your passport. The entrance fee is 100 BF ($2.80).

A cure for all your ills may be awaiting you at the ✪ **Thalassa Zeecentrum,** a combination spa, fitness center, and gymnasium. In the "thermal institute," you can indulge in hot sea-mud baths and a number of other seawater treatments, work out on a wide variety of exercise equipment, or simply swim in the seawater pool or laze in the sauna. You'll find the Zeecentrum in the Hotel La Réserve, Elizabethlaan 158 (☎ **050/60-06-12**). If you're a guest at the hotel, admission to the fitness club comes with your room rate—others pay 300 BF ($8.35) plus charges based on any additional treatments chosen, which range from 1,000 to 1,200 BF ($27.80 to $33.35).

WHERE TO STAY

Some of the most luxurious (and expensive) coastal hotels are located in this area, but there are many other types of accommodation as well. As in resort regions the world over, rates fluctuate according to the season and even the day of the week, so be sure to ask about reductions. There are several good budget hotels located along Lippenslaan in Knokke that offer no-frills double rooms without private bath for under 2,000 BF ($55.55).

EXPENSIVE

✪ **Hotel la Réserve.** Elizabethlaan 160, 8300 Knokke-Albertstrand (in the town center across from the casino). ☎ **050/61-06-06.** Fax 050/60-37-06. 112 units. MINIBAR TV TEL. 6,500–8,000 BF ($180.55–$222.20) double. AE, DC, MC, V. Free parking.

Although this hotel near the beachfront is quite large, it manages to maintain a comfortable, almost country, air. It's also the home of Knokke's important health spa, the Thalassa Center. The guest rooms, 80 with balconies, are spacious, modern, and comfortable.

Dining/Diversions: The hotel has a very good restaurant, La Sirène, and a lounge bar.

Amenities: Health club, swimming pool, fitness center, sauna, solarium, tennis courts.

MODERATE

Parkhotel. Elizabethlaan 204, 8301 Duinbergen. ☎ **050/60-09-01.** Fax 050/62-36-08. 12 units. TV TEL. 3,000–3,800 BF ($83.35–$105.55) double. Rates include continental breakfast. AE, MC, V. Free parking.

The family-run Parkhotel is just 2 blocks from the beach. Its rooms have recently been renovated and are furnished in a modern style, complete with coffee pots and hair dryers. There's also an excellent restaurant—the owner is the chef—with moderate prices and a quietly elegant decor, as well as an attractive bar.

Pauwels. Kustlaan 353, 8300 Het Zoute. ☎ **050/61-16-17.** Fax 050/62-04-05. 26 units. MINIBAR TV TEL. 4,500–5,100 BF ($125–$141.65) double. Rates include breakfast. AE, DC, MC, V. Parking 375 BF ($10.40).

This elegant small hotel 1 block from the beach rubs elbows with upper-stratosphere shops in Het Zoute. Its guest rooms have recently been refurbished in bright colors, with tartan-style curtains. There's a moderately priced restaurant and an attractive bar. Three of the rooms have kitchenettes. All rooms have hair dryers; most have balconies. Pets are welcome.

INEXPENSIVE

Lido. Zwaluwenlaan 18, 8300 Knokke-Heist. ☎ **050/60-19-25.** Fax 050/61-04-57. 40 units. TV TEL. 1,600–2,000 BF ($44.45–$55.55) double. Rates include breakfast. AE, DC, MC, V. Free parking.

The Lido, about 150 meters from the sea, is modern to the nth degree in both decor and furnishings. Its guest rooms are well appointed and bright. Bathrooms have either a bath with fitted shower or a fitted shower alone. There's also a good restaurant.

WHERE TO DINE

In addition to the restaurants listed below, there are dozens of other excellent restaurants in the area, so explore!

EXPENSIVE

✪ **Aquilon.** Elisabethlaan 6. ☎ **050/60-12-74.** Reservations required. Main courses 600–950 BF ($16.65–$26.40). AE, DC, MC, V. Thurs–Mon noon–2pm and 6:30–9pm (open Wed during school holidays). SEAFOOD.

This ground-floor restaurant on Albertplein in the city center is the most outstanding and most elegant in the area. Allow plenty of time to savor such specialties as veal with mushrooms and truffles or lobster Marguerite.

Ter Dijcken. Kalvekeetdijk 137, 8300 Knokke-Heist. ☎ **050/60-80-23.** Main courses 680–980 BF ($18.90–$27.20); fixed-price menu 2,500 BF ($69.45). AE, DC, MC, V. Wed–Sun 10am–3pm, 6–10pm. FRENCH/BELGIAN.

This elegant, classically decorated restaurant has a solid reputation on the coast. The wide-ranging menu emphasizes seafood. Turbot, grilled lobster, and Iranian caviar are excellent seafood choices, while the lamb cutlets is the best choice among the meats. A fireplace adds to the atmosphere.

MODERATE

✪ **Casa Borghese (Chez Ciccio).** Bayauxlaan 27. ☎ **050/60-37-39.** Main courses 395–580 BF ($10.95–$16.10); average meal 900 BF ($25). AE, DC, MC, V. Summer: Mon–Sat 6pm–1am, Sun noon–3pm and 6pm–1am. Winter: Mon–Wed and Fri–Sat 6pm–1am, Sun noon–3pm and 6pm–1am. Closed Nov. SEAFOOD/ITALIAN.

Excellent Italian and French dishes come at surprisingly modest prices in this modern but cozy place. The pasta is homemade. Italian specialties include cannelloni, lasagna, various spaghetti dishes, and—a firm favorite—shrimp scampi with garlic or tomato-and-cream sauce. This centrally located place is ideal for that late-night meal.

Panier d'Or. Zeedijk 659. ☎ **050/60-31-89.** Main courses 350–525 BF ($9.70–$14.60); Average 4-course meal 1,400 BF ($38.90). AE, DC, MC, V. Thurs–Mon noon–2:30pm; Fri–Sun 6:30–9pm. SEAFOOD/BELGIAN.

Seafood stars at this seaside restaurant, a medium-sized place with traditional decor and long benches along the wall. The fish soup is a local legend. Standard menu items include lobster, cod, sole, and North Sea shrimp, but if you're feeling aristocratic, try the caviar.

2 Ostend (Oostende)

31km (19 miles) W of Bruges; 35km (21 miles) SW of Knokke-Heist; 26km (16 miles) NE of De Panne

Ostend's title as "Queen of the Coast" has long historic roots. The town has seen Crusaders embark for the Holy Land, hosted pirates, resisted Spanish rule from the end of the 16th century into the 17th, been the terminal for sea service to England since 1846, seen her harbor blocked to thwart German submarines in World War I, been bombed during World War II—and has emerged from that long, eventful history as a busy port and lively recreational haven. Today, Ostend offers Belgium's largest casino, a racetrack, an outstanding art museum, a spa, and no fewer than five excellent sandy beaches.

Though queenly, Ostend is very much a queen of the people, welcoming all income levels, with very little of the posh exterior that's so much a part of Knokke-Heist and Het Zoute. Located at almost the exact midpoint of the Belgian coastline, Ostend divides the Oostkust (to the northeast) from the Westkust (to the southwest) and is the ideal touring base for coastal exploration. Its central location, coupled with its mass of entertainment facilities that operate year-round, draws visitors by the thousands.

The elevated Albert I Promenade that runs the entire length of Ostend's 5.5km (3.5-mile) beachfront was, before World War II, lined with elegant private seaside

Ostend

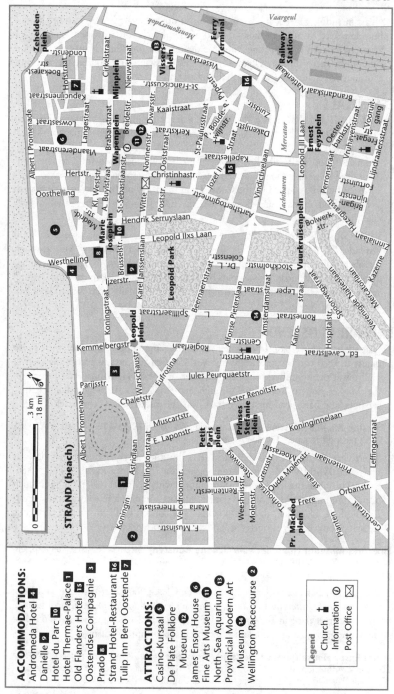

STRAND (beach)

0 — 3 km / .18 mi

ACCOMMODATIONS:
- Andromeda Hotel **4**
- Danielle **9**
- Hotel du Parc **10**
- Hotel Thermae-Palace **1**
- Old Flanders Hotel **15**
- Oostendse Compagnie **3**
- Prado **8**
- Strand Hotel-Restaurant **16**
- Tulip Inn Bero Oostende **7**

ATTRACTIONS:
- Casino-Kursaal **5**
- De Plate Folklore Museum **12**
- James Ensor House **6**
- Fine Arts Museum **11**
- North Sea Aquarium **13**
- Provincial Modern Art Museum **14**
- Wellington Racecourse **2**

Legend
- ✝ Church
- ⓘ Information
- ⊠ Post Office

villas, including several holiday homes of European royalty. After wartime bombings destroyed so many of these fine old houses, hotels and apartment buildings of a purely modern form sprung from the debris. The town also boasts a very good shopping district and an Olympic-sized indoor swimming pool at the seafront. Outdoor pools are filled with heated seawater.

ESSENTIALS

GETTING THERE   Ostend is the main **ferry** terminal for boats to and from Dover, England. The terminal is located very near the town center at Montgomerydok.

There's good **train** and **bus** service from Bruges, and good train service from Brussels. The train station is located next to the ferry terminal (see above).

Ostend can be reached by the **Coast Tram** from any of the other seaside resorts.

By **car** from Brussels and Bruges, take the E40; from any of the seaside resorts, take the N34.

VISITOR INFORMATION   The **Tourist Office** is at Monacoplein 2, 8400 Ostend (☎ **059/70-11-99;** fax 059/70-34-77). It's open from May through October Monday to Saturday 9am to 7pm, Sunday 10am to 7pm; November through April, Monday to Saturday 10am to 6pm, Sunday 10am to 5pm. In July and August, a satellite office is open at the train station, daily from 9am to 1pm and 4 to 7:30pm.

EXPLORING OSTEND

Ostend is the best base from which to explore the entire coast, but there's also plenty to keep you occupied right in town. Carillon concerts ring from the Festival Hall tower periodically through the summer, and there are bandstand concerts on the Market Square from June through September. For late-night dance clubs, cabarets, and bars, head for Langestraat near the eastern end of the beach.

✪ **Casino-Kursaal Oostende.** Monacoplein. ☎ **059/70-51-11.** Admission 150 BF ($4.15); passport required. Gaming rooms, daily 3pm–7am.

There's been a casino at this spot since 1852, but the one you'll find there today was built after World War II, when bombing left the beachfront in ruins. The present Kursaal is one of the largest casinos in Europe, with a concert hall, restaurant (open 5pm to midnight), disco, and, of course, gaming rooms. Here you can play American roulette, blackjack, and punto banco. The concert hall is frequently the venue for symphonic concerts, operettas, and ballet performances.

Fine Arts Museum (Museum voor Schone Kunsten). Stedelijk Feest en Kultuurpaleis, Wapenplein. ☎ **059/80-53-35.** Admission 50 BF ($1.40) adults, 25 BF (70¢) children 14–18, free for children under 14. Wed–Mon 10am–noon and 2–5pm.

Paintings by native sons James Ensor, Jan de Clerck, Constant Permeke, and Leon Spilliaert are featured in this museum on the second floor of the Municipal Festival and Culture Palace in the town center (the Folklore Museum occupies the first floor; see below). It also displays works by Belgian impressionists.

James Ensor House (James Ensorhuis). Vlaanderenstraat 27 (off Wapenplein). ☎ **059/ 80-53-35.** Admission 50 BF ($1.40) adults, 25 BF (70¢) children 16 and under. June–Sept Wed–Mon 10am–noon and 2–5pm; Nov–May Sat–Sun 2–5pm; closed Oct.

The postimpressionist painter James Ensor (1860–1949) lived most of his life in Ostend, and his home has been restored as it was when his aunt and uncle kept a ground-floor shells-and-souvenir shop here. Ensor's studio and lounge are on the second floor. If you're familiar with his paintings you'll recognize some of the furnishings and views from the windows.

North Sea Aquarium (Noordzeeaquarium). Visserskaai (by the old fishing harbor). ☎ **059/50-08-76.** Admission 75 BF ($2.10) adults, 50 BF ($1.40) children 14 and under. Apr–May Mon–Fri 10am–noon and 2–5pm, Sat–Sun 10am–noon and 2–6pm; June–Sept Mon–Fri 10am–12:30pm and 2–6pm, Sat–Sun 10am–noon and 2–6pm; Oct–Mar Sat–Sun 10am–noon and 2–6pm.

This popular attraction features a marvelous display of North Sea flora and fauna, including fish, mollusks, crustaceans, polyps, and anemones, as well as interesting shell and seaweed collections. It's a good sightseeing stop, especially for children.

Provincial Modern Art Museum (Provinciaal Museum voor Moderne Kunst). Romestraat 11. ☎ **059/50-81-18.** Admission 100 BF ($2.80) adults, 50 BF ($1.40) children 16–18, free for children under 16. Tues–Sun 10am–6pm.

The Museum of Modern Art is set in a former department-store building in the town center. Its collection of more than 1,500 items, including paintings, sculpture, graphics, video, and film, gives a complete picture of modern art in Belgium from its very beginnings up to the present. There are also frequent international exhibitions, a children's museum, a workshop for youngsters, slide shows, and educational projects. The museum has excellent facilities for the disabled. The Art Shop sells art catalogs and functional-design art objects, and the Art Café is a pleasant setting for a light lunch or the four-course business lunch.

De Plate Folklore Museum (Heemkundig Museum De Plate). Stedelijk Feest en Kultuurpaleis, Wapenplein (in the town center). ☎ **059/80-53-35.** Admission 50 BF ($1.40). Tues–Sun 10am–noon and 2–5pm.

This museum has interesting displays of Neolithic and Roman artifacts excavated in the vicinity, in addition to exhibits depicting the native dress, folklore, and history of Ostend. There's a re-created fisherman's pub, a fisherman's home, and an old tobacco shop. The Marine section deals with shipbuilding, fishing boats, and the Ostend–Dover ferry line.

Wellington Racecourse (Wellington Renbaan). Koningin Astridlaan. ☎ **059/80-60-55.** Admission to grandstand seats, 350 BF ($9.70) Mon–Fri, 400 BF ($11.10) Sat–Sun, 500 BF ($13.90) public holidays. Free admission to the field opposite the grandstand. May–Sept; call for race times.

You'll find the only racetrack on the coast here, just across from the seafront at the end of the Royal Arcades. There's a grass track for flat and hurdle racing and a lava track for the trotters. The tourist office can furnish a detailed schedule of races.

WHERE TO STAY

Ostend doesn't lack for accommodations, and they're available in every price range, from luxurious hotels right on the beachfront to budget rooms several blocks away from the water. You should not, however, leave your reservations until the last minute; book several weeks ahead during the summer, either directly with a hotel or through any Belgian tourist office. Most hotels have special package rates available: summer midweek stays, winter weekends, and so on. Be sure to ask about reductions.

Note: The tourist office can also book you into inexpensive boardinghouses.

EXPENSIVE

Andromeda Hotel. Kursaal Westhelling 5, 8400 Ostend. ☎ **059/80-66-11.** Fax 059/80-66-29. 92 units. MINIBAR TV TEL. 4,000–6,800 BF ($111.10–$188.90) double. AE, DC, MC, V. Free parking.

The modern Andromeda is one of the best luxury hotels in Ostend and also has a choice location—right on the beachfront and next door to the casino. The guest rooms are the latest word in comfort and decor, with armchairs to relax in and views of the sea through sliding glass doors that open onto balconies.

Dining/Diversions: The Gloria restaurant serves excellent meals in an attractive room overlooking the sea (see "Where to Dine," below). The cocktail bar opens to the sea, with terrace tables for sunny days.

Amenities: 24-hour room service, health club, Jacuzzi, sauna, solarium, swimming pool, baby-sitting.

Hotel Thermae-Palace. Koningin Astridlaan 7, 8400 Ostend. ☎ **059/80-66-44.** Fax 059/80-52-74. 128 units. MINIBAR TV TEL. 4,950–6,950 BF ($137.50–$193.05) double. AE, DC, MC, V. Free parking.

This slightly old-fashioned hotel just off of the beachfront is an integral part of the sprawling thermal-baths complex. The building was constructed in the 1930s, and is still a prominent local landmark today—a reminder of Ostend's previous glory as an exclusive resort. The hotel has comfortable, attractive, fairly standard guest rooms, many with a sea view.

Dining: The art deco–style Périgord restaurant serves high-quality cuisine; the Paddock bistro is more casual.

Amenities: Concierge, laundry and dry cleaning service, baby-sitting.

✪ **Oostendse Compagnie.** Koningstraat 79, 8400 Ostend (on the beachfront near the casino). ☎ **059/70-48-16.** Fax 059/80-53-16. 15 units. MINIBAR TV TEL. 4,500–5,500 BF ($125–$152.80) double; 6,500–8,500 BF ($180.55–$236.10) suite. AE, DC, MC, V. Free parking. Closed Oct and Mar 1–15.

This excellent small hotel in a former royal villa is one of the best on the coast. The place manages to retain an atmosphere of "home," though admittedly, it's home on a grand scale. A pretty terrace and garden face the sea; floor-length windows with the same view line the drawing room; and the dining room is known for its excellent kitchen. The guest rooms are beautifully furnished, much like those in a private home, and the two suites provide such perfect comfort and beauty that they'll tempt you to settle in for a long spell. This is a very popular place, so book as far in advance as possible.

Dining: The high-end AuVigneron restaurant is very popular locally (see "Where to Dine," below).

Amenities: Limited-hours room service, laundry and dry cleaning service, baby-sitting.

INEXPENSIVE

Danielle. IJzerstraat 5, 8400 Ostend. ☎ **059/70-63-49.** Fax 059/70-63-49. 24 units. TV TEL. 2,400–2,600 BF ($66.65–$72.20) double. Rates include breakfast. MC, V. Free parking.

The Danielle is an attractive modern hotel in a very convenient location, near the beach and casino. All the rooms are individually decorated, but the unifying theme is bright colors and light wood furnishings. The staff can arrange baby-sitting, and there's a good restaurant with moderate prices on the premises.

Hotel du Parc. Marie-Joseplein 3, 8400 Ostend. ☎ **059/70-16-80.** Fax 059/80-08-79. 44 units. TV TEL. 2,500–2,900 BF ($68.45–$80.55) double. Rates include full breakfast. AE, CB, DC, MC, V. Limited parking available on street.

This hotel is conveniently located near the casino, the beach, and shopping. Its guest rooms are furnished in a functional, modern style. The art deco–style bar was once frequented by the artist James Ensor and is now a gathering place for writers and artists. There's also a sun terrace, sauna, and solarium.

✪ **Old Flanders Hotel.** Jozef II Straat 49, 8400 Ostend. ☎ **059/80-66-03.** Fax 059/80-16-95. 15 units. TV TEL. 2,300–3,000 BF ($63.90–$83.35) double. Rates include buffet breakfast. AE, DC, MC, V. Parking 300 BF ($8.35).

This centrally located hotel, just a few blocks from the beach, has a cozy, country-house atmosphere. Guest rooms are modern and extensively furnished; each has a floor-to-ceiling, wall-to-wall wardrobe-and-shelves unit, on which the television stands. All rooms have hair dryers. The bar has a cozy, antique feel, with a decor featuring a model sailboat and a model trawler and paintings of country scenes on the walls. The restaurant also has an elegant look, with a marble mantel surrounding the fireplace, a timbered ceiling, and brick arches.

Prado. Leopold II Laan 22, 8400 Ostend. ☎ **059/70-53-06.** Fax 059/80-87-35. 28 units. TV TEL. 2,850 BF ($79.15) double. Rates include buffet breakfast. AE, CB, DC, MC, V. Limited parking available on street.

This modern hotel with wheelchair access is located on a major midtown street a few blocks from the seafront. The rooms are comfortable and nicely furnished in the modern mode. The entry hall has a bar and leather seats. All rooms have hair dryers.

Strand Hotel-Restaurant. Visserskaai 1, 8400 Ostend. ☎ **059/70-33-83.** Fax 059/80-36-78. E-mail: strandhotel@unicall.be. 21 units. TV TEL. 3,300 BF ($91.65) double; 4,000 BF ($111.10) suite. Rates include continental breakfast. AE, DC, MC, V. Limited parking available on street. Closed Dec–Jan.

This pleasant hotel is situated near the yacht harbor and car-ferry terminal. Fresh flowers and plants welcome guests in the entry hall. The rooms are nicely if simply furnished in modern style and have good bathrooms; most also have a harbor view. White wallpaper contrasts with the blue carpets and gray bedcovers. There's a good restaurant, where seafood is a specialty.

Tulip Inn Bero Oostende. Hofstraat 1a, 8400 Ostend. ☎ **059/70-23-35.** Fax 059/70-25-91. 73 units. MINIBAR TV TEL. 2,500–3,200 BF ($69.45–$88.90) double; 4,200 BF ($116.65) suite. Rates include buffet breakfast. AE, DC, MC, V. Parking 400 BF ($11.10).

This modern hotel, a short distance back from the beachfront, has nicely appointed rooms at modest rates. The big, carpeted entry hall has lots of marble. The rooms are furnished in modern style, with a rainbow of colors: salmon-pink wallpaper, pink curtains, blue carpets, and orange chairs. Amenities include a heated indoor swimming pool, Jacuzzi, sauna, and solarium.

WHERE TO DINE

Most Ostend restaurants, not surprisingly, specialize in seafood. Not surprising either is the freshness of the seafood and the expertise with which these coastal chefs prepare it. Fishing boats deliver daily catches to the Visserskaai (fisherman's quay), and the cooks are backed by a long tradition of treating the fruits of the sea with respect. With some 250 restaurants at hand, Ostend is the ideal place for "window shopping" each day for the setting and menu that has the most momentary appeal. Most places serve both a specialty of the day, based on the freshest ingredients available, and a three-course tourist menu, at a set price. And if you're attacked by hunger pangs late at night, many snack bars are open until the wee hours.

Very special indeed are the festive balls and Christmas and New Year's Eve dinners served at the casino. Many Ostend restaurants also feature special dinners and dance music on these occasions.

Below is a very personal list of my favorite Ostend restaurants. Keep in mind that in seafood restaurants, expensive lobster dishes often skew the average price of meals upward; the majority of dishes will actually be priced at the lower end of the scales given below.

EXPENSIVE

✪ **Au Vigneron.** In the Hotel Oostendse Compagnie (on the beachfront near the casino), Koningstraat 79. ☎ **059/70-48-16.** Main courses 745–1,395 BF ($20.70–$38.75). AE, DC, MC, V. Tues–Sun noon–2:30pm; Tues–Sat 7–8:30pm. FRENCH.

This restaurant in the Hotel Oostendse Compagnie (see "Where to Stay," above) features classic French haute cuisine. The menu changes according to the best available ingredients, but you can always depend on their *menu de dégustation* for a memorable meal at a set price. Try the *turbot en croûte* (salted turbot) baked in the oven and served with a light cream sauce, fennel and caviar; or grilled turbot on a bed of spinach, served with sabayonne sauce and accompanied by fried onion rings. Also of good value are the special dinners for two at 4,000 BF ($111.10).

Gloria Restaurant. In the Andromeda Hotel (next to the casino), Kursaal Westhelling 5. ☎ **059/80-66-11.** Main courses 600–1,200 BF ($16.65–$33.35). AE, DC, MC, V. Daily noon–2:30pm and 6:30–10:30pm. SEAFOOD/CONTINENTAL.

This gracious restaurant looking out on the sea is a favorite with locals as well as visitors. Among its specialties are lobster and a variety of North Sea fish, all prepared in innovative, mouth-watering ways; good choices are the lobster soup, smoked salmon, shrimp salad, and fillet of sole. Also look out for the big T-bone steaks and the lamb fillet. Service is as elegant, professional, and polished as the menu and setting. If the weather is fine, the outdoor terrace is a great place to dine.

✪ **Villa Maritza.** Albert I Promenade 76. ☎ **059/50-88-08.** Main courses 450–1,250 BF ($12.50–$34.70); fixed-price menus 1,950–2,500 BF ($54.15–$69.45). AE, DC, MC, V. Tues–Sat noon–2:30pm; Tues–Sun 7–9:30pm. SEAFOOD.

This exquisite restaurant is housed in a seaside villa built in 1885 that was once the holiday home of a Hungarian baroness. Of the many ornate old buildings that once lined the shore, this is one of the few that survived World War II bombings. Inside, Ostend native Jacques Ghaye has created a sophisticated restaurant with an elegant cuisine. Seafood specialties vary with the season; all of them are culinary delights, but especially good options are the lobster with mixed vegetables and saffron, the lobster with red-wine sauce, and the pan-fried sole with green asparagus.

MODERATE

✪ **Old Fisher Restaurant.** Visserskaai 34. ☎ **059/50-17-68.** Main courses 360–600 BF ($10–$16.65). AE, DC, MC, V. Fri–Wed noon–2:15pm and 6–9:30pm. SEAFOOD.

The Old Fisher is one of the best of the many seafood restaurants in this area. It's located right on the fishing quays—about as physically close to fresh seafood as you can get. Menu items include an excellent *bouillabaisse* (fish soup), as well as mussels, shrimps, and prawns in a wide range of dishes, and such standbys as *sole Ostendaise* and turbot. This place isn't posh, but it is highly atmospheric.

Restaurant Tearoom Chopin. Adolf Buylstraat 1a (in the town center). ☎ **059/70-08-37.** Main courses 380–640 BF ($10.55–$17.80); menu of the day 395–425 BF ($10.95–$11.80). AE, DC, MC, V. Fri–Wed noon–10pm. SEAFOOD/FLEMISH.

Monkfish with leek and grilled lobster are standouts on the menu here, but you really shouldn't miss the terrific *waterzooï*. Also look for simple but tasty dishes like *moûles marinières* (marinated mussels) and steak with *frites*. The restaurant is furnished in traditional style, with lots of brown wood.

Villa Borghese. Van Iseghemlaan 65B. ☎ **059/80-08-76.** Reservations recommended on weekends. Main courses 290–630 BF ($8.05–$17.50); fixed-price menus 450–650 BF ($12.50–$18.05). AE, CB, DC, MC, V. Wed–Mon 11am–3pm and 6–10:30pm. Closed last 2 weeks of January. ITALIAN.

There's a real touch of Italy in this centrally located restaurant. The manager personally prepares the lasagnas that are the house specialty, and wicker baskets full of Chianti bottles and bunches of garlic hang from the ceiling. The menu features Italian standards and seafood specialties like seafood *tagliatelle* and shrimp scampi in garlic sauce.

INEXPENSIVE

In addition to the listing below, there are several other attractive restaurants along the Albert I Promenade, which is the best place to window shop for your budget eatery. You'll also find good deals at many of the seafood restaurants on the Visserskaai beside the harbor, especially if you look out for "dish of the day" (*dagschotel/plat du jour*) offers.

✪ **Le Basque.** Albert I Promenade 62. ☎ **059/70-54-44.** Main courses 320–440 BF ($8.90–$12.20). AE, DC, MC, V. Daily 11am–9:30pm. SEAFOOD.

Ostend sole and seafood on the skewer are featured in this pleasant seaside restaurant, which has an outdoor terrace for fine-weather dining. If you're up for eels, try them here in a grass-green vegetable sauce. More ordinary items on the menu include barbecue-grilled cod and salmon, and shrimp croquettes, a good starter choice.

3 Koksijde-Bad & Oostduinkerke

20km (12 miles) SW of Ostend

Oostduinkerke is a small, family-oriented community, but it holds much of interest to art- and nature-lovers. Its 8km (5 miles) of beachfront also encompasses the neighboring resorts of **Koksijde-Bad** and **Sint-Idesbald.** Ostend and De Panne are both within easy reach by auto, bike, or tram.

ESSENTIALS

GETTING THERE   Ostend has the nearest **train** station on the line from Brussels via Ghent and Bruges to the coast. There is frequent **Coast Tram** service from Ostend and all of the other coastal resorts.

By **car,** take the N34, which runs along the coast.

VISITOR INFORMATION   The **Tourist Office** is at Zeelaan 24, 8670 Koksijde (☎ **058/53-30-55;** fax 058/52-25-77).

WHAT TO SEE & DO

Oostduinkerke's chief attraction is its beautiful wide ✪ **beach,** the site of a very special activity you'll find nowhere else along the coast: on days when the weather is reasonable, a group of stalwart, yellow-slickered, oilskin-clad gentlemen mount sturdy horses and wade into the surf at low tide to drag vast nets behind them, ensnaring large quantities of delicious *crevettes*—those tiny, gray shrimp that thrive in the waters of the North Sea. These are the **shrimp fishermen of Oostduinkerke,** and they follow a tradition that dates back several centuries. Much of the catch will go into the kitchens of cafes owned by these same horsemen, but if you go to the

National Fishery Museum's next-door neighbor, the **De Peerdevisser** cafe, soon after the fishermen return, you can purchase the just-caught, just-boiled delicacies by the sackful.

Sand-yachting—a form of overland sailing in a yacht with wheels—is a popular sport at Oostduinkerke. There are several places on the beach where you can rent the colorful vehicles and participate in the fun. Other beach activities include various festivals throughout the summer (ask the tourist office for a complete list to see what's on during your visit), **sand-castle competitions,** and **horseback riding** on the strand. Horses can be rented from Hacienda, Weststraat 9 (☎ **058/51-69-50**) for 600 BF ($16.65) for 1½ hours.

Oostduinkerke's beach is backed by impressive sand dunes, one of which, De Hoge Blekker, rises over 30m (100 feet)—it's the highest dune in the country. **Dune hiking and climbing** are very popular with visitors. Free guided **walking tours** are conducted from mid-June through mid-September, leaving at 9am from the foot of the Hoge Blekker and at 2:30pm from the Hotel La Péniche.

Abbey of the Dunes (Duinenabdij). Koninklijke Prinslaan 8, Koksijde. ☎ **058/51-19-33.** Admission 100 BF ($2.80) adults, 50 BF ($1.40) children 12 and under. Daily 9am–noon and 1:30–5pm.

During much of the 12th century this Cistercian abbey was a center of culture for the region. The abbey lay in ruins for several centuries, but excavations begun in 1949 have revealed archaeological artifacts that shed considerable light on coastal history and the development of this settlement. A small museum on the site presents interesting exhibits displaying these findings.

Near the abbey, the large abbey farmstead (Ten Bogaerde) includes a 12th-century barn that is now an agricultural school. It's typical of the large farm holdings of the ancient abbeys.

✪ **National Fishery Museum (Nationaal Visserijmuseum).** Pastoor Schmitzstraat 5, Oostduinkerke (in a small park at the rear of the Town Hall). ☎ **058/51-24-68.** Admission 80 BF ($2.20) adults, 50 BF ($1.40) students, 30 BF (85¢) children 6–12, children under 6 free. Sept–June Tues–Sun 10am–noon and 2–6pm; July–Aug daily 10am–noon and 2–6pm.

This museum has maps of sea routes followed by local fishing fleets and also displays fishing implements used through the centuries, sea paintings, a fishing-harbor model, a North Sea aquarium, and a wonderful collection of fishing-boat models from A.D. 800 to the present. The interior of a typical fisherman's tavern is another highlight.

✪ **Paul Delvaux Museum.** Paul Delvauxlaan 42, Sint-Idesbald. ☎ **058/52-12-29.** Admission 250 BF ($6.95) adults, 180 BF ($5) students and children. July–Aug daily 10:30am–6:30pm, Apr–June and Sept–Dec Tues–Sun 10:30am–5:30pm.

The nephew of internationally famous surrealist artist Paul Delvaux has turned a Flemish farmhouse into a modernized museum displaying his uncle's works. Delvaux's adulation of the female form is conveyed in many of the paintings, as is his love of trains and train stations.

WHERE TO STAY

Hotel Terlinck. Zeedijk 294 (at Terlinckplein), 8670 Koksijde. ☎ **058/52-00-00.** Fax 058/51-76-15. 37 units. TV TEL. 3,000–4,200 BF ($83.35–$116.65) double. Rates include buffet breakfast. AE, DC, MC, V. Free parking.

This modern hotel in the center of Koksijde offers a friendly welcome and a high level of comfort. Many rooms have a sea view, and all are furnished in a bright, contemporary style. The fine restaurant specializes in seafood and is popular locally.

Grand Hotel Gauquie. Leopold II Laan 251, 8670 Oostduinkerke. ☎ **058/51-10-88.** Fax 058/52-29-36. 64 units (48 with bathroom). 1,720–2,400 BF ($47.80–$66.65). Rates include continental breakfast. MC, V. Limited parking available on street.

This big rambling hotel is in a charming old building about 50m (54 yards) from the sea. The rooms, though far from being lavishly equipped, are clean and comfortable. This place offers good value for people who aim to spend most of their time at a seaside resort out-of-doors.

WHERE TO DINE

Although few of the restaurants here are truly gourmet, many come close, and most have unbelievably affordable prices. Fresh-caught shrimp is the local specialty.

✪ **Bécassine.** Rozenlaan 20, Oostduinkerke. ☎ **058/52-11-00.** 4-course menu 1,250 BF ($34.70); 5-course menu 1,600 BF ($44.45). AE, DC, MC, V. Fri–Tues noon–2pm and 7–9pm. SEAFOOD.

This a homey kind of place that serves great food at very reasonable prices—but only as complete 4- or 5-course menus, not a la carte. Tasty North Sea shrimp are the stars of the show. Try them in shrimp soup or stuffed in potatoes and pastries. The *bouillabaisse* is great too. There are only seven tables here.

4 De Panne

26km (16 miles) SW of Ostend; 7km (4 miles) SW of Oostduinkerke

De Panne, near Dunkirk, is Belgium's closest coastal point to France and England. Its sandy beaches have been the scene of several significant historical events: In 1830 Leopold I set foot on newly independent Belgian soil here to become the first of the country's homegrown kings (though it had certainly seen its share of foreign royalty!); and during World War I it was here that King Albert I and his queen clung to Belgian resistance against German occupying forces.

But the beach's most famous moment came in 1940, when it was the site of the massive evacuation of beleaguered Allied forces carried out by a makeshift armada of small craft gathered from boat owners around England. When "the miracle of Dunkirk" was over, almost all the soldiers were saved, and the 12.5km (7.5-mile) stretch of beach between Dunkirk and De Panne was a mass of military litter. It's a little-recognized fact that the British commander, Lord Gort, was not headquartered in Dunkirk but here in De Panne.

But today, despite the area's tumultuous history, it's the wide beach—0.5km (500 yards) at low tide—and spectacular sand dunes that bring hordes of tourists to De Panne each year. The dunes are made all the more beautiful by vast wooded areas that turn them into a wonderland of greenery banding the white sands of the beach and the gray sea beyond. In July and August, accommodations here can be hard to come by despite the presence of thousands of holiday homes and apartments.

ESSENTIALS

GETTING THERE   Ostend has the nearest **train** station on the direct line from Brussels via Ghent and Bruges to the coast. There's also a train station just south of the town at Adinkerke–De Panne for local trains from Bruges and Ypres. De Panne is the southern terminus of the **coast tram** line that extends north to Knokke-Heist.

By **car,** take the N34 coast road from any of the coastal resorts; from Bruges, Ghent, and Brussels, take the E40 to Veurne and then go north a short distance on the N8.

Sand-Yachting at De Panne

The long, wide beaches, firm sand, and frequent high winds at De Panne make for ideal conditions for sand-yachting, a form of overland sailing on "yachts" with wheels. There are several rental companies on the beach. They outfit you in a wetsuit and a crash helmet, give out a few rudimentary tips on how to handle the machines, push you out into the wind—and off you go. The yachts are unwieldy to handle at first, and heavier than they look, so maintaining stability can be difficult until you get the hang of it. But once you do, it's an exhilarating feeling.

VISITOR INFORMATION The **Tourist Office** is in the Town Hall (Stadhuis), Zeelaan 21, 8660 De Panne (☎ **058/42-18-18;** fax 058/42-16-17). During summer months there's also an **information desk** on the Zeedijk promenade (☎ **058/42-18-19**).

EXPLORING DE PANNE

Outdoor recreation is what people come to De Panne for. With all those dunes to explore and the beach for sunning, swimming, and sand-yachting, no one's ever short of things to do. The tourist office can furnish a series of beautifully illustrated informative brochures on the dunes and forest areas, and it also organizes special **guided tours** periodically during summer months.

A walk through De Panne's tree-lined residential streets, with rows of villas left over from another era, is a delight. There are old fishermen's cottages still in use on Veurnestraat.

There are four nature areas nearby that are all free and always open. The 840-acre ✪ **Westhoek Nature Reserve** (Natuurreservat Westhoek), on the western edge of De Panne, encloses a fascinating dune landscape, with vegetation that varies from full-grown trees to scrubby shrubs. Visitors have the unique opportunity to observe the evolution of sand dunes, which are always changing, though almost imperceptibly. In the middle of the reserve is a bare area of sand known locally as "the Sahara." Signposted footpaths guide you all the way. To the east of De Panne is the 150-acre **Oosthoek Nature Reserve** (Natuurreservat Oosthoek), which has more dunes and woods.

The 230-acre **Cabour Estate** (Domein Cabour), straddling the Belgian/French border, is another area that provides interesting walks. There are frequent guided tours during summer months (check with the tourist office for schedules). **Calmeyn Wood** (Calmeynbos), which covers only 110 acres, is the loving legacy of one man, Maurice Calmeyn, who in 1903 began to plant trees here in order to preserve the dunes. Some 25 varieties of his trees are thriving today.

It's instant enchantment for children at ✪ **Meli-Park,** De Pannelaan 68, Adinkerke (☎ **058/42-02-02**), the famous honeybee-themed leisure park—it's like Disneyland with costumed honeybee mascots instead of mice. A multitude of delightful attractions will appeal to the whole family. There's Apirama (exploring the bees' kingdom by boat), Elfira (a fairy-tale wonderland), the animal park, a jungle fantasy parrot show, a water symphony, Carioca (all sorts of playground activities), and Phantom Guild, with three different fun fairs filled with rides. Meli-Park is a real treat. It's open from April through the first week of September daily 10am to 5pm; and during the rest of September on Wednesday, Saturday, and Sunday 10am to 5pm. The admission charge, which covers all attractions, is 595 BF ($16.55) for adults, 495 BF ($13.75) for children 6 to 12, and free for children under 6 and children less than 1m (39 inches) tall.

WHERE TO STAY

Holiday homes, some built as replicas of traditional fishermen's cottages, are the most popular form of accommodation in this largely family-oriented resort. The tourist office can furnish a complete list of rental agents, but you should know that most places are booked months in advance and for periods of no less than a week. One of the largest of the holiday villages is **Duinhoek,** Duinhoekstraat 123, 8660 De Panne (☎ 058/41-52-08; fax 058/42-04-19). Rates are 8,000 to 24,000 BF ($222.20 to $666.65) for a six-person residence for 1 week. The tourist office can also direct you to private homes, where a double room and breakfast runs about 1,800 BF ($50) per night. No matter what type of accommodation you choose, your best bet is first to contact the tourist office, specify the type of accommodation and price range you're looking for, provide the exact dates of your arrival and departure, and try to be flexible. If you're still unsuccessful, consider an Ostend base for day trips.

Hotel Donny. Donnylaan 17. ☎ **058/41-18-00.** Fax 058/42-09-78. 35 units. TV TEL. 2,950–5,000 BF ($81.95–$138.90) double. Rates include buffet breakfast. AE, DC, MC, V. Free parking.

This modern hotel is casual but still quite classy. It's located in a scenic setting of dunes about 150 meters from the beach. Some of the rooms have balconies facing toward the sea, and all are comfortably furnished in a style that complements the contemporary look of the building. There is a health club, a swimming pool, and a good restaurant specializing in seafood.

WHERE TO DINE

There are nearly 100 restaurants in De Panne, covering a wide range of specialties and prices, though few are really expensive. Seafood, especially shrimp from local waters, is the highlight here. For the least-expensive restaurants, look along the Zeedijk, the beachfront promenade—it's half-tiled, with cafe terraces right on the sand. On Nieuwpoortlaan there's a row of fast-food places selling mussels and *frites* (fries) for next to nothing. The upmarket restaurant below, although a bit pricey, is widely acknowledged to be the best in town. The restaurant of the Hotel Donny (see above) is also good.

✪ **Le Fox.** Walckierstraat 2. ☎ **058/41-28-55.** Main courses 495–995 BF ($13.75–$27.65); fixed-price menus 895–1,800 BF ($24.85–$50). AE, DC, MC, V. Wed–Sun noon–2:30pm, Tues–Sun 7–9:45pm. SEAFOOD.

This leading restaurant just off of the beachfront offers exceptional seafood dinners. The interior is rustic and features an open fire. If you have a taste for lobster, try the 3-course lobster dinner for two, a good deal at 3,600 BF ($100): It includes lobster salad, lobster *bisque* (soup), and a half-lobster. Turbot and salmon-and-asparagus fondue are other good choices. Unlike most of the restaurants along the coast, Le Fox leaves mussels off the menu but makes up for this omission with oysters, scampi, langoustines (spiny lobster), and shrimp.

5 Ypres (Ieper)

110km (68 miles) W of Brussels; 93km (57 miles) SW of Antwerp; 62km (38 miles) SW of Ghent; 60km (37 miles) SW of Bruges

Ypres is set in the West Flanders **Heuvelland** (Hill Country)—an exaggerated label for some low and gentle slopes rising from the otherwise flat polders behind the coast. Because the town is in a hard-to-reach corner of Belgium, many visitors, particularly British ones, combine a visit here with a trip to the Belgian coast.

The town owed its early prosperity to a flourishing textile industry, which reached its pinnacle in the 13th century. Sadly, over the centuries, Ypres was victimized by one war after another, and became a mere ghost of its former self. By far the most devastating event was World War I, when hardly a brick was left standing after three terrible battles. Many visitors, in fact, come to pay homage to those who fell on the surrounding battlefields, many of whom lie buried in the extensive military cemeteries here. Ypres pays its respects at 8pm every day of the year, when traffic beneath the Menen Gate is halted and members of the local fire brigade sound *The Last Post* on silver bugles that were gifts of the British Legion. Perhaps the most poignant tribute of all came from the Canadian colonel and poet John McCrae:

> *In Flanders fields the poppies blow,*
> *Between the crosses, row on row,*
> *That mark our place; and in the sky,*
> *The larks, still bravely singing, fly,*
> *Scarce heard amid the guns below.*
> *We are the dead. Short days ago*
> *We lived, felt dawn, saw sunset glow,*
> *Loved, and were loved. And now we lie*
> *In Flanders fields.*

Homage could also well be paid to the determined citizens of Ypres who have rebuilt, brick by brick, the most important of the city's medieval buildings, exactly as they were, carefully following original plans still in existence in order to preserve their town's colorful past.

ESSENTIALS

GETTING THERE   Ypres is an awkward place to get to by public transport, but can be reached by **train** from Brussels, Ghent, and Bruges, and by **train and bus** from De Panne and Ostend on the Belgian coast.

By car, it's easiest to come from De Panne on the coast, taking the N8 south via Veurne.

VISITOR INFORMATION   The **Visitors Center** is in the Cloth Hall, Grote Markt (☎ 057/20-07-24; fax 057/21-85-89). It's open from April through September Monday to Saturday 9am to 6pm, Sunday 10am to 6pm; October through March Monday to Saturday 9am to 5pm, Sunday 1 to 6pm.

SPECIAL EVENTS   Every year on the second Sunday in May, Ypres celebrates one of Europe's most colorful pageants, the ✪ **Festival of the Cats** (Kattestoet), when hundreds of velvet cats are thrown by the town jester from the Belfry to crowds below. The custom originated centuries ago when the great Cloth Hall, where cloth was stored until sold, attracted thousands of mice, and cats by the hundreds were imported to eliminate them. Once the cloth was sold, however, the cats themselves became a problem. After careful consideration, local officials, clearly unfamiliar with modern concepts of environmental engineering, came up with the brilliant solution of flinging them from the Belfry. How that tradition evolved into today's lively carnival I have no idea, but you won't care once you're caught up in the revelry that surrounds this spectacular procession.

EXPLORING YPRES

In your walks around Ypres, you'll want to look for a few special sights. The **ramparts** that once surrounded the town are among the few structures not demolished

Impressions

What passing bells for those who die as cattle?
Only the monstrous anger of the guns,
Only the stuttering rifles' rapid rattle
Can patter out their hasty orisons.
            —"Anthem for Doomed Youth," Wilfred Owen (1893–1918)

during World War I. You can reach them via stairs at the Menen Gate (see below). You can also walk around to the **Lille Gate** (Rijselsepoort) to explore one of the most beautiful **British war cemeteries,** with a lawn that many local people will tell you is the greenest in Europe. Notice, too, the many streets lined with reconstructed 17th-century facades.

On panels set in the **Menen Gate** (Meensepoort), a 130-foot memorial arch, you'll find the names of some 54,896 British and Commonwealth soldiers who fell near Ypres in World War I and who have no known grave—this famous monument is called the "Missing Memorial." Every evening at 8 o'clock, traffic through the gate is stopped while uniformed Ypres firefighters sound the plaintive bugle notes of *The Last Post,* in a brief but moving ceremony that dates back to 1928.

Ypres's medieval glory is reflected in its beautiful Gothic ✪ **Cloth Hall** (Laken-halle), the original of which was built between 1260 to 1304. Inside is the ✪ **In Flanders Fields Museum** (☎ 057/20-07-24), an interactive museum that views the "Great War" through the eyes of the ordinary people—soldiers and civilians—who experienced it. From the center of the Cloth Hall rises a 210-foot-square **Belfry** (Belfort).

The graceful spire of **St Martin's Cathedral** (St-Martenskathedraal) in St Maartensplein is a landmark in the town. Inside is the tomb of a bishop of Ypres named Jansenius, whose heretical theories wreaked havoc in the 17th century. The cathedral is open to visitors from 8am to 8pm, except during services; admission is free.

The **Merghelynck Museum,** Merghelynckstraat 2 (☎ 057/20-07-24), is a wonderfully lavish manor house furnished with Louis XV and XVI antiques. It also houses a collection of Chinese and Japanese porcelain. Visits are by appointment only, and admission is 50 BF ($1.40) for adults, 30 BF (85¢) for children.

The **Belle Godshuis Museum,** Rijselsestraat 38 (☎ 057/20-48-31), counts among its treasures the *Virgin and Child* by the Master of 1420. Other exhibits include religious paintings from the 16th to the 19th centuries, by such artists as Nicolaas Van de Velde and Gilles Lamoot. In addition, there is a large collection of pewter, lace, and furniture. The museum is open from April through October, Tuesday to Sunday 9:30am to noon and 1:30 to 5:30pm. Admission is 50 BF ($1.40) for adults, 30 BF (85¢) for children.

ALL QUIET ON THE WESTERN FRONT

For visitors from Britain, Ireland, and Canada, Ypres is a place of pilgrimage, just as the Battle of the Bulge memorials in the Ardennes are places of pilgrimage to many Americans. Ypres, like the Somme and Verdun in France, was one of the slaughterhouses of the Western Front in World War I. The 55,000 names on the Menen Gate (see above) are those of soldiers with no known grave; many more died here as well. In fact, in the few square kilometers of the Ypres Salient, more than 250,000 soldiers from Britain and its Empire were killed, and an even greater

A Word of Warning

Farmers plowing their fields regularly turn up some of the thousands of unexploded shells that still lie under the ground hereabouts. You occasionally see rusting clumps of them by the roadside, awaiting the attention of the Belgian army's bomb-disposal squad. Do not touch or otherwise interfere with them, as they are unstable and liable to explode.

number of Germans. The whole area around Ypres is one big cluster of gigantic military cemeteries, 160 of them. It is an immensely sad place. When I visited it, the words of a Scottish lament played time and again in my mind:

> *Did they beat the drum slowly?*
> *Did they play the fife lowly?*
> *Did they sound the Dead March as they lowered you down?*
> *Did the band play the Last Post and chorus?*
> *Did the pipes play The Flowers Of The Forest?*

In addition to the daily attrition of 4 years of trench warfare, four major battles were fought in the salient. During the Second Ypres, in 1915, Canadian soldiers became the first victims of chemical warfare, when a green cloud of poison gas came drifting over no-man's land from the German lines. The greatest battle was the 6-month-long Third Ypres, better known as the Battle of Passchendaele, after the village east of Ypres that was its focus (its Flemish name is Passendale). It was called "Passiondale" by the British soldiers, who suffered 170,000 casualties capturing the village.

To the survivors of those terrible events, and to the descendants of the young men swept away by shells, bullets, and poison gas, Ypres can never be forgotten. Each spring, the blood-red poppies bloom in wild profusion in Flanders's fields, and each year tens of thousands of visitors come to Ypres, to keep vigil with the Lost Generation.

In addition to the excellent **In Flanders Fields Museum** in Ypres (see above), you can also visit the preserved stretch of trenches at nearby **Sanctuary Wood.** Amazingly, there is otherwise almost no remaining sign of the vast network of trenches—the once-tortured landscape has been reclaimed by agriculture.

Also, in the gently rolling countryside around Ypres, you'll find—if you have the heart to visit them—a multitude of tranquil and often beautiful **military cemeteries** and **monuments.** The Ypres Visitors Center can provide itineraries, but for an independent 1- to 2-hour excursion by car, venture out along the N8, past **Hellfire Corner,** to the preserved stretch of trenches at **Sanctuary Wood** and the nearby **Canadian Monument** on **Hill 62.** From there, cross to the N332 and N303 through Zonnebeke, to the **Tyne Cot Commonwealth Military Cemetery** and its 12,000 graves surmounted by a Cross of Remembrance in white Portland stone. Finally, to be evenhanded, head for nearby Langemark and the 44,000 headstones of the **German Military Cemetery.**

A THEME PARK

If you are traveling with children you may be glad to escape to the peaceful, if not exactly tranquil, pursuits of ✪ **Bellewaerde Park,** Meenseweg 497, Ieper-Zillebeke (☎ **057/46-86-86**). This theme park combines the familiar white-knuckle rides with a wildlife reserve and various re-created natural environments. Ironically, it's set in what was once the wasteland of the front lines of World War I. The park is open from April through June and during the first week of September daily 10am to 6pm; July and August daily 10am to 7pm; second week of September through mid-October Saturday and Sunday 10am to 6pm. Admission is 670 BF ($18.60) adults, 600 BF ($16.65) children, free for children under 1m (39 inches).

WHERE TO STAY & DINE

Hotel Old Tom. Grote Markt 45, 8900 Ypres. ☎ **057/20-15-41.** Fax 057/21-91-20. 17 units. TV TEL. 2,000–2,200 BF ($55.55–$61.10) double. Rates include continental breakfast. MC, V. Free parking.

This small family-owned hotel offers a prime location in the center of town and reasonable rates. With only nine rooms, it fills up fast in summer. The building, like most of Ypres, has been rebuilt, but still has plenty of antique style. The rooms are comfortable and nicely if simply furnished. The cafe-restaurant on the ground floor has an outdoor terrace and serves regional specialties, such as eels prepared in a variety of ways, as well as more ordinary dishes.

Hotel-Restaurant Regina. Grote Markt 45, 8900 Ypres. ☎ **057/21-88-88.** Fax 057/21-90-20. www.hotelregina.be. E-mail: info@hotelregina.be. 17 units. MINIBAR TV TEL. 3,250 BF ($90.30) double. Rates include buffet breakfast. AE, MC, V. Free parking.

This is an excellent small hotel in neo-Gothic style. Some of the rooms have a view of the fountain on the Grote Markt. The rooms are stylishly furnished and equipped, and the hotel has what might well be Ypres's best restaurant right on the premises.

9

Liège & the Meuse Valley

The steep-sided valley of the River Meuse has long been one of Belgium's premier tourist areas. The river rises in northern France, takes an L-shaped course through Belgium, and then crosses into Holland, where it finally empties into the North Sea south of Rotterdam. Along its Belgian banks are historic towns and cities, beautifully situated châteaux and abbeys, resorts, casinos, and some of the country's most striking scenery—as well as big industrial plants whose aging smokestacks spoil some of the views. The river is generally considered to be the western boundary of the Ardennes region, which you'll be able to see to the left as you head upstream.

It's best to do the Meuse Valley as a driving tour, beginning at Liège and heading upstream along the river to Namur, Huy, and Dinant. But it's also quite possible to tour the area by train and bus, as connections are frequent and fast. In that case, you should base yourself in Liège or Namur, both of which are also gateways to the Ardennes.

1 Liège

112km (69 miles) SE of Brussels; 33km (20 miles) NW of Huy; 66km (41 miles) NE of Namur

Fervent, lively Liège is the big city in these parts. Nowadays it exudes the aura of an aging industrial gloom, but that seems to fade next to its gracefully down-at-the-heels Victorian monuments and glorious remnants from the time of its powerful prince-bishops. Liège has always had an independent spirit. Its 12th-century charter decreed that the *"pauvre homme en sa maison est roi"* (the poor man in his home is king), a proclamation the citizens were not about to forget—it's an attitude that is still vividly alive in Liège today.

Liège's nickname is "La Citéé Ardente" (the Hot-Blooded City). The prince-bishops of Liège, who held sway over both secular and religious matters from the 10th through the 18th centuries, rebelled frequently and vigorously against foreign would-be rulers. In fact, they so angered Charles the Bold of Burgundy in 1468 that he ordered the complete destruction of the city, a task that continued for several weeks as one of history's most awesome feats of utter devastation and left only the churches intact.

The prince-bishopric was finally abolished with the help of the French revolutionary army in 1795. When Napoléon took over in

Liège

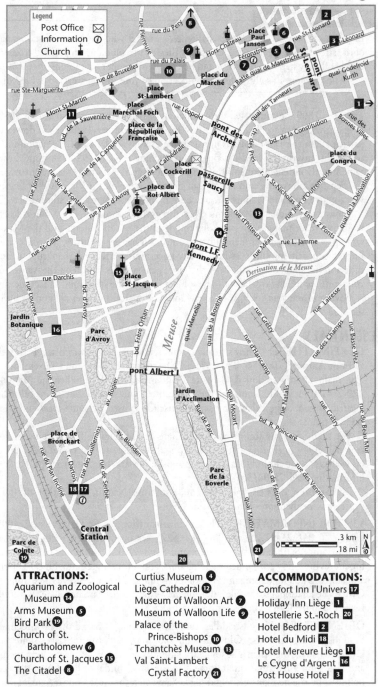

Legend
Post Office ✉
Information ⓘ
Church ✝

ATTRACTIONS:
Aquarium and Zoological Museum ⓮
Arms Museum ❺
Bird Park ⓳
Church of St. Bartholomew ❻
Church of St. Jacques ⓯
The Citadel ❽
Curtius Museum ❹
Liège Cathedral ⓬
Museum of Walloon Art ❼
Museum of Walloon Life ❾
Palace of the Prince-Bishops ❿
Tchantchès Museum ⓭
Val Saint-Lambert Crystal Factory ㉑

ACCOMMODATIONS:
Comfort Inn l'Univers ⓱
Holiday Inn Liège ❶
Hostellerie St.-Roch ⓴
Hotel Bedford ❷
Hotel du Midi ⓲
Hotel Mereure Liège ⓫
Le Cygne d'Argent ⓰
Post House Hotel ❸

185

The Town Mascot

Liège's most beloved symbol is Tchantchès, a puppet who has been the spokesman of the streets since the 1850s. He's usually dressed in a blue smock, patched trousers, tasseled floppy hat, and red scarf, and he's constantly either grumbling or espousing every noble cause in sight—the personification of your average, everyday Liègeois.

France in 1800, he completed the occupation of Belgium. After his defeat in 1815, Belgium was given to Holland—but not for long; volunteers left Liège in droves to participate in the 1830 Brussels uprising that established Belgium as a nation in its own right. Invading German troops, upon reaching Liège in 1914, confronted that same fiercely independent spirit. But throughout all the conflict, the city managed to keep traditions alive and nurture an impressive list of musicians: César Franck was a native son, and violinists Ysaye, Beriot, and Vieuxtemps also studied here.

Today Liège is one of Belgium's most important crossroads, with a railroad network and three major expressways linking it to the rest of Europe, and the Meuse serving as a principal commercial trade route, as it has for centuries. In recent years Liège has had its problems, with the city government effectively bankrupt at one time and the smokestack industries that once generated its wealth on the wane. But you won't see much evidence of these somber facts on the street, and in fact the city is moving to reinvent itself, with a new focus on its tourist potential and its lively social scene.

ESSENTIALS

GETTING THERE   There's frequent train service to Liège from Brussels, as well as from Antwerp, Tournai, Mons, Paris, Maastricht, Cologne, and Luxembourg. The main railway station is **Gare de Guillemins,** rue des Guillemins (☎ 04/229-26-10), 1.5-miles south of the city center. The smaller but more centrally located station Liège Palais, on rue de Bruxelles, is used by some local and connecting trains.

The main city **bus station** is outside Gare de Guillemins. Buses are useful for regional service, including destinations along the Meuse such as Namur and Dinant (as well as Maastricht in Holland), and points in the Ardennes, such as Spa. For bus information, call ☎ **04/361-94-44.**

By car from Brussels, take the E40 east; from Namur, take either the E42 expressway or the more-scenic riverside N90.

VISITOR INFORMATION   The city **tourist office** is at En Féronstrée 92, 4000 Liège (☎ **04/221-92-21;** fax 04/221-92-22). It's open Monday through Friday 9am to 5pm, Saturday 10am to 4pm, and Sunday 10am to 2pm. The office has brochures outlining self-guided walking tours, and during the summer it can supply a qualified guide to accompany you for a very modest fee. **Liège Province Tourist Office** (Fédération Provinciale du Tourisme) is at bd. de la Sauvenière 77, 4000 Liège (☎ **04/232-65-10;** fax 04/232-65-11).

ORIENTATION   Liège straddles the Meuse, with a backdrop of Ardennes foothills. You'll find the **Old City** on the west bank of the river, and the **Outremeuse** on the other. The Old City has most of Liège's sightseeing attractions, and also some nighttime entertainment in the small student-filled **Carré** district, bounded by rue de l'Université, bd. de la Sauvenière, and rue Pont-d'Avroy. However, the Outremeuse has a wider selection of lively bars, discothèques, and cabarets. You'll find good shopping in the several small pedestrian-only streets off of place

St-Lambert in the Old City. Along the river banks there are tree-lined walkways. For the best views of the city, stroll up one of the three hills on the periphery.

GETTING AROUND   Sightseeing highlights in the Old City are close together, so central Liège makes for easy walking. The downside for pedestrians is that traffic in the busy city center is frantic, and for some years ahead the main square, place St-Lambert, will be reduced to a huge building site as a massive redevelopment scheme is implemented. The other problem is that outside the Old City there are lots of uninteresting offices, generic buildings, and parking lots between the sightseeing attractions. Buses are useful for these sights.

City buses charge 40 BF ($1.10). Discounted eight-ride and 24-hour tickets can be purchased at ticket booths at major route stops, the railway station, and from drivers. For bus information, call ☎ **04/361-94-44.** The bus system here is excellent and not too hard to figure out.

EXPLORING LIÈGE

Most of the places you'll want to see lie along a 2-mile route, easily covered on foot. From May through September, there are **boat cruises** on the Meuse (sailing schedules and points of departure are available from the tourist office).

Place St-Lambert and neighboring **place du Marché** are the hub of Liège's throbbing daily life. This is where you'll find the 1698 **Perron Fountain,** the symbol of freedom to these liberty-loving people, and the 18th-century **Town Hall** (Hôtel de Ville), which features sculptures by Delcour in its lobby. French troops destroyed the sumptuous St-Lambert's Cathedral in 1794, leaving only its outline preserved in modern paving on place St-Lambert.

CHURCHES

Church of St-Bartholomew (Église St-Barthélemy). place St-Barthélemy. ☎ **04/ 221-89-44.** Admission 80 BF ($2.20) adults, 50 BF ($1.40) children. Mon–Sat 10am–noon and 2–5pm, Sun 2–5pm.

This twin-towered Romanesque church in the city center dates back to 1108. Its Baptismal Font (Fonts Baptismaux) is counted among "Belgium's Magnificent Seven," the country's most important historical treasures. The huge copper-and-brass font rests on the backs of 10 small oxen and is surrounded by five beautifully sculpted biblical scenes—it's truly magnificent. The object was cast in the early 1100s by master metalsmith Renier de Huy.

✪ **Church of St-Jacques (Église St-Jacques).** place St-Jacques 8 (south of the Cathedral of St-Paul). ☎ **04/222-14-41.** Free admission. Mid-Sept to mid-June (except Easter vacation) Mon–Sat 8am–noon, Sun 10am–noon; Easter vacation and mid-June to mid-Sept Sun–Fri 10am–noon and 2–6pm, Sat 10am–noon and 2–4:15pm.

This church is a happy mixture of architectural styles: the exterior is Gothic Flamboyant, the narthex Romanesque, and the porch Renaissance. But it is the intricately designed vaulted ceiling inside that makes this one of the most beautiful interiors in Liège. Call for guided-tour information.

✪ **Liège Cathedral (Cathédral de Liège).** rue Bonne Fortune 6. ☎ **04/232-61-32.** Free admission to Cathedral; Treasury, 100 BF ($2.80) adults, 50 BF ($1.40) children 6–18, free under 6. Daily 2–5pm.

Except during church services, you can ask the sacristan to show you the cathedral's priceless treasures (not to worry, you'll be expected). This a sight not to be missed, if only because of the white-marble-and-oak pulpit and the 13th-century polychrome *Madonna and Child* by the high altar. The treasury in the cloisters holds a small but exquisite collection that includes the gold reliquary that was Charles the Bold's gift of penance after he wiped out the city and every able-bodied man in it in 1468. This small masterpiece, the work of Charles's personal court jeweler, shows a repentant Charles kneeling as St-George looks on. Nearby, a bas-relief depicting the Crucifixion is said to contain a piece of the True Cross. Also impressive is the bust reliquary of St-Lambert, which dates from the early 1500s and holds the saint's skull.

MUSEUMS

Arms Museum (Musée d'Armes). quai de Maestricht 8 (on the riverfront, north of place St-Lambert). ☎ **04/221-94-00.** Admission 50 BF ($1.40) adults, 20 BF (55¢) children. Mon, Wed, and Thurs–Sat 10am–1pm and 2–5pm; Sun 10am–1pm.

The manufacture of weapons for sale around the world was a major industry in Liège for centuries. This museum displays more than 3,000 prime historic examples, including a prehistoric stone ax and muzzle-loaded firearms of the 15th century. The exhibits are housed in a private mansion that hosted Napoléon when he visited in 1803.

Curtius Museum (Musée Curtius). quai de Maestricht (on the riverfront north of place St-Lambert). ☎ **04/221-94-04.** Admission 50 BF ($1.40) adults, 20 BF (55¢) children. Mon, Wed, and Thurs–Sat 10am–1pm and 2–5pm; Sun 10am–1pm.

This turreted redbrick mansion in the city center is one of Liège's most beautiful houses and Belgium's most important museums. It was built in the early 1600s by local arms manufacturer Jean Curtius. Its archaeological and crafts collections trace the history of the Meuse region from the Gallo-Roman and Frankish eras through the medieval period and on into the 18th century. Coins, jewelry, swords, and hundreds of other artifacts tell the continuing story. One room holds the relics of Bishop Notger of the 900s, whose "Evangeliary" (prayer book) is covered with exquisitely carved ivory. There are also portraits of the prince-bishops, and even some of their richly embroidered vestments. Furniture and works of art from homes of wealthy Liègeois are on display as well.

Also housed here is the **Glass Museum** (Musée de Verre), with fine examples of Venetian, Phoenician, Roman, Chinese, and—of course!—Belgian glassware. This museum presents a remarkable glimpse of the breathtaking riches of this city's past.

Museum of Walloon Art (Musée de l'Art Wallon). En Féronstrée 86 (by the river in the city center). ☎ **04/221-92-31.** Admission 50 BF ($1.40) adults, 20 BF (55¢) children. Tues–Sat 1–6pm, Sun 11am–4:30pm.

This small but impressive collection of the works of Walloon (French-speaking Belgian) artists and sculptors extends from the 16th century to the present. Paul Delvaux's *L'Homme de la Rue* is one of the premier works on display, but many other well-known, and not-so-well-known, Walloon artists from the 16th to the 20th centuries are represented, including Constant Meunier, Antoine Wiertz, Félicien Rops, René Magritte, Roger Somville, and Pierre Alechinsky.

✪ **Museum of Walloon Life (Musée de la Vie Wallonne).** Cour des Mineurs (in the city center, north of place St-Lambert). ☎ **04/223-60-94.** Admission 80 BF ($2.20) adults, 40 BF ($1.10) children 6–18, under 6 free. Tues–Sat 10am–5pm, Sun 10am–4pm.

This 17th-century Franciscan convent is home to an incredible array of exhibits that bring vividly to life the days of 19th-century Liègeois and their rich contemporary Walloon traditions and customs. The collection affords the unusual opportunity of viewing in one place examples of popular art, crafts, recreation, and even the workings of a coal mine, which is reproduced in the building's basement. Here, too, is a marvelous puppet collection, which includes the beloved Tchantchès (his main "home" is the Museum Tchantchès, but he is also represented here), and a representation of another local hero, if not perhaps quite so beloved, the Emperor Charlemagne.

✪ **Tchantchès Museum (Musée Tchantchès).** rue Surlet 56, Outremeuse. ☎ **04/ 342-75-75.** Admission 50 BF ($1.40), adults 30 BF (85¢) children. Tues, Thurs 2–4pm. Closed July.

If you (or your children) have fallen under the spell of Liège's favorite puppet, come here to find a marvelous collection of his cohorts and their costumes. From mid-September through Easter, there are frequent marionette performances; call ahead for schedules.

OTHER SIGHTS

Aquarium and Zoological Museum (Aquarium et Musée de Zoologie). quai van Beneden 22. ☎ **04/366 50-21.** Admission 150 BF ($4.15) adults, 100 BF ($2.80) children 6–12, free for children under 6. Mon–Fri 10am–12:30pm and 1:30–5pm, Sat–Sun 10:30am–12:30pm and 2–6pm.

Although owned by Liège University, the Aquarium is much more than an academic institution. Its attractively presented displays of the underwater world bring together some 2,500 examples from 250 marine species. The exhibits cover a lot of ground—or water—in their 42 display tanks. Pride of place, for younger visitors at any rate, goes to the 4,420-gallon shark tank. The Coral Room (Salle des Coraux) contains beautiful specimens collected from Australia's Great Barrier Reef by a university expedition in 1966–67.

The **Zoological Museum** is on the same premises. It has some 20,000 exhibits, including the skeleton of a 19-meter (62-foot) whale. Also here you can see the mural *Genesis* (1960) by the celebrated Belgian artist Paul Delvaux.

Palace of the Prince-Bishops (Palais des Prince-Evêques). place St-Lambert. Free admission (to courtyards only; contact the tourist office for information on guided tours). Mon–Fri 10am–5pm.

The palace of the prince-bishops of Liège, who ruled the city and the surrounding territory from 980 to 1794, is the largest secular Gothic structure in the world. Of primary interest are the two inner courtyards, one lined with 60 carved columns depicting the follies of human nature, and the other housing an ornamental garden. The council chambers of the palace, which are hung with gorgeous Brussels tapestries, are not normally open to visitors, but it's sometimes possible to arrange a guided tour through the tourist office. Today this historic building is Liège's Palace of Justice, housing courtrooms and administrative offices.

✪ **Val Saint-Lambert Crystal Factory.** rue de Val 245, Seraing (southwest of Liège, on the N90 beside the River Meuse). ☎ **04/337-39-60.** Admission 200 BF ($5.55) adults, 125 BF ($3.45) children 5–16, free for children under 5. Daily 9am–5pm.

This place would be interesting enough even if only to watch the company's craftsmen at work making the renowned, hand-blown crystal that bears the Val Saint-Lambert label. But the factory also occupies a fascinating location that contains the remains of a 13th-century Cistercian abbey, a 16th-century Mosan Renaissance-style house, and examples of industrial archaeology from the 18th and 19th centuries. There is also, of course, an on-site shop where you can buy recently made pieces (the sales pitch is low-key), including slightly flawed examples at a considerable price reduction. You can also visit the **Crystal Museum** (Musée du Cristal) and wander around the site.

STROLLING THROUGH THE CITY

For a feel of **Old Liège,** stroll through the narrow, twisting streets and stairways on Mont St-Martin, which are all lined with fine old houses.

For superb views of the city and the broad, curving Meuse, climb the 353 steps of the **Montagne de Beuren** off rue Hors-Château. At the top is the hill of **Ste-Walburge,** which has been the setting for more than its share of the bloodier side of Liège's history. It was here in 1468, for instance, that 600 citizens made an unwise attempt to assassinate Duke Charles the Bold, who was encamped with his Burgundian troops. They failed and were massacred to the man. In 1830 a decisive battle in Belgium's fight for independence took place here; in 1914 locals held German forces at bay here long enough for the French to regroup and go on to the vitally important Battle of the Marne; and in 1940 it was here that invading German troops met with typically stubborn resistance from the city's defenders.

On the hill of Cointe, the wooded **Bird Park** (Parc des Oiseaux) is a pleasant, relaxing vantage point for panoramic views of the city. The third hill overlooking Liège is Robermont, where 50 local patriots were executed en masse in 1914.

WHERE TO STAY
EXPENSIVE

Holiday Inn Liège. Esplanade de l'Europe 2 (alongside the Meuse, on the Outremeuse side), 4000 Liège. ☎ **04/342-60-20.** Fax 04/343-48-10. 219 units. A/C TV TEL. 6,990 BF ($194.15) double; 12,500 BF ($347.20) suite. Rates include buffet breakfast. AE, DC, MC, V. Parking 250 BF ($6.95).

This giant modern hotel offers all you'd expect from this international chain. The exceptionally large, nicely decorated rooms have queen-size beds in addition to all the usual amenities. There's also a pool. All rooms have hair dryers.

Dining/Diversions: The hotel has a good restaurant and a pleasant bar, popular with locals as well as guests.

Amenities: Laundry and dry cleaning service, express checkout, heated indoor pool, bicycle rental, health club, Jacuzzi, sauna, conference rooms.

✪ **Hotel Bedford.** quai St-Léonard 36, 4000 Liège. ☎ **04/228-81-11.** Fax 04/227-45-75. 149 units. A/C MINIBAR TV TEL. 8,450 BF ($234.70) double. Rates include buffet breakfast. AE, DC, MC, V. Free parking.

This is a fairly new hotel with a good location beside the Meuse and with front-room windows overlooking the river. The city center is only a 10-minute walk away. The hotel is fully equipped to modern business standards. Rooms have comfortable armchairs along with firm beds and hair dryers.

Dining/Diversions: La Taverne restaurant specializes in Belgian cuisine; main courses range from 890 to 1,090 BF ($24.70 to $30.30). There's also a bar.

Amenities: Concierge, room service, laundry service, newspaper delivery, baby-sitting, secretarial services.

Hôtel Mercure Liège. bd. de la Sauvenière 100 (on the edge of the Old City), 4000 Liège. ☎ **04/221-77-11.** Fax 04/221-77-01. 106 units. A/C MINIBAR TV TEL. 3,500–5,500 BF ($97.20–$152.80) double; 6,500 BF ($180.55) suite. Rates include buffet breakfast. AE, DC, MC, V. Parking garage.

The wonderfully located Mercure is thoroughly modern. The recently refurbished, attractive guest rooms have modern decor and furnishings. This hotel is a favorite with European business visitors, as well as with leisure travelers.

Dining/Diversions: The hotel's Rôtisserie de la Sauvenière restaurant is highly recommended. In addition, there is the Cercle de la Sauvenière bar.

MODERATE

✪ **Le Cygne d'Argent.** rue Beeckman 49 (near the train station and Liège's commercial center), 4000 Liège. ☎ **04/223-70-01.** Fax 04/222-49-66. 23 units. MINIBAR TV TEL. 2,500 BF ($69.45) double. AE, DC, MC, V.

There's a nice homey atmosphere at this small hotel. The guest rooms vary in size and feature furnishings in traditional style. The hotel can provide photocopying services for guests, as well as limousine service and car rental.

Post House Hotel. rue Hurbise 160 (7 miles outside Liège, off the E40 expressway), 4400 Herstal. ☎ **04/264-64-00.** Fax 04/248-06-90. 96 units. TV TEL. 5,370 BF ($149.15) double. Rates include breakfast. AE, DC, MC, V.

If it's comfortable accommodations you're after, this deluxe modern hotel is the place to stay. The guest rooms are all nicely furnished and decorated. There's a pool as well. The hotel restaurant, La Diligence, is highly recommended (see "Where to Dine," below).

INEXPENSIVE

Some of the least expensive accommodations in Liège are in the vicinity of the main railway station. Most are small establishments, clean and comfortable, that offer the money-saving option of forgoing a private bathroom. Rates range from 1,000 to 1,400 BF ($27.80 to $38.90) for a double without bathroom; 1,400 to 1,900 BF ($38.90 to $52.80) for a double with bathroom. You can shop around for the best deals, but I especially recommend the following inexpensive choices.

Comfort Inn l'Univers. rue des Guillemins 116 (near the railway station), 4000 Liège. ☎ **04/254-55-55.** Fax 04/254-55-00. 47 units. TV TEL. 2,700 BF ($75) double. AE, DC, MC, V. Parking 80 BF ($2.20).

There's good value for the dollar in this medium-size hotel, where the guest rooms are modest in decor but quite comfortable. There's no restaurant on the premises, but several are within walking distance. A major renovation program, including all-new bathrooms, has recently been completed. All rooms have hair dryers.

✪ **Hôtel du Midi.** place des Guillemins 1 (near the main railway station), 4000 Liège. ☎ **04/252-20-04.** Fax 04/252-16-13. 24 units. TEL. 1,400 BF ($38.90) double (with shower). Rates include breakfast. MC, V.

This hotel is a small but friendly, a clean and comfortable place. It makes up for its relative lack of facilities with reasonable prices.

A NEARBY INN

✪ **Hostellerie Saint-Roch.** rue du Parc 1, 4180 Comblain-la-Tour (south of Liège on the Durbuy road). ☎ **04/369-13-33.** Fax 04/369-31-31. 16 units. MINIBAR TV TEL. 4,900 BF ($136.10) double; 7,300 BF ($202.80) suite. Rates include full breakfast. AE, DC, MC, V. Free parking.

Although it entails an 18-mile drive to and from the city, this country inn is loaded with charm. It makes an ideal base for Ardennes day trips, and its gourmet restaurant makes the drive worthwhile for a meal, even if you elect to stay elsewhere. The elegant dining room looks out onto well-tended lawns and gardens dotted with comfortable seating, and there's a riverside terrace for drinks on a summer evening. Each of the luxurious guest rooms is done up in a refined country style. I suspect that it's the warm friendliness of owners Frances and Nicole Dernouchamps that prompts so many Americans to extend an overnight stay into several days. The hotel is usually fully booked for summer weekends, but weekdays are often pretty quiet, though advance reservations are always recommended.

WHERE TO DINE

Liège is the center of Walloon cuisine. The city supports a network of restaurants specializing in this traditional style, whose popularity has waned in recent decades in favor of more "exotic" tastes, but which is now making a strong comeback. The Liègeois are especially proud of their local white sausage (*boudin blanc de Liège*), and are also fond of thrushes (*grives*) and goose.

EXPENSIVE

✪ **Au Vieux Liège.** quai de la Goffe 41. ☎ **04/223-77-48.** Reservations required. Main courses 590–890 BF ($16.40–$24.70); menu du saison 1,250 BF ($34.70); lobster menu 2,650 BF ($73.60) at dinner. AE, DC, MC, V. Mon–Sat noon–2:45pm and 6:30–9:45pm. Closed mid-July to mid-Aug. SEAFOOD/CONTINENTAL.

This marvelous restaurant is located in the city center in a four-story 16th-century town house furnished with antiques of that era. Dinner is by candlelight and the waiters wear formal attire; but the food outshines even the excellent setting. Almost any fish dish is a good choice, but there's also more experimental fare including rare-cooked *escargots niçoises* (snails) and lobster ravioli. More conventional diners can stick with Irish steak with bacon or grilled salmon.

Déjeuner Sur l'Herbe. rue des Bégards 2 (at the foot of Mont St-Martin on the edge of the Old City). ☎ **04/222-92-34.** Main courses 480–840 BF ($13.35–$23.35); fixed-price menus 1,000–2,000 BF ($27.80–$55.55). AE, DC, MC, V. Tues–Fri noon–2pm; daily 6–10pm. FRENCH.

At Déjeuner Sur l'Herbe you dine in an intimate, 16th-century open-air setting amid a magnificent garden. The menu is extensive. I am especially partial to the way they prepare duck. You might also try the pork chop with duck-liver pâté or the poached fillet of trout with spinach. The squeamish should probably avoid the *riz de veau* (calf's brains).

La Diligence. In the Post House (on the outskirts of Liège off of E40), rue Hurbise 160, Herstal. ☎ **04/264-64-00.** Main courses 580–760 BF ($16.10–$21.10); fixed-price menus 750–1,200 BF ($20.85–$33.35). AE, DC, MC, V. Daily noon–2pm and 6:30–10pm. FRENCH.

This fine restaurant in the large, modern Post House Hotel (see "Where to Stay," above) is well worth the drive. Prominent on the menu are several traditional Ardennes dishes, as well as steak, roast beef, and veal—the veal tagliatelle with tomato sauce is especially delectable.

MODERATE

✪ **Brasserie as Ouhès.** place du Marché 21 (across from Town Hall) ☎ **04/223-32-25.** Main courses 380–760 BF ($10.55–$21.10). AE, MC, V. Mon–Fri noon–2:30pm; Mon–Sat 6pm–midnight. BELGIAN.

Liège specialties are served with a flair in this tastefully decorated, rather large restaurant set on a narrow oblong public plaza that also holds a number of other quite adequate, moderately priced eateries. Ouhès, however, is the best in its price range, and its menu is large enough to suit everyone's taste. Duck appears in more than one guise. I prefer the *homard grillé* (grilled lobster) with béarnaise sauce. The restaurant is extremely popular with local businesspeople at lunch, so go early or late.

Brasserie du Midi. In the Hôtel du Midi, place des Guillemins 1 (in front of the Gare des Guillemins train station). ☎ **04/252-20-04.** Main courses 300–450 BF ($8.35–$12.50); plat du jour 350 BF ($9.70); fixed-price menu 900 BF ($25). MC, V. Daily 6am–2am. BELGIAN/FRENCH.

This conveniently located restaurant serves straightforward but trustworthy Belgian favorites. Dominating the menu are such items as *steak-frites* (steak with french fries), *stoemp* (mashed potatoes and vegetables) with sausage, and mussels.

✪ **Mamé Vî Cou.** rue de la Wache 9. ☎ **04/223-71-81.** Main courses 375–575 BF ($10.40–$15.95). AE, DC, MC, V. Daily noon–2:30pm and 6:30–11:30pm. WALLOON.

"Mamé Vî Cou" is Walloon dialect for "A Nice Old Lady," and though I would never call Madame Dupagne old, her welcome is certainly nice enough. Her character-filled, oak-beamed restaurant is a Liège institution, serving traditional Walloon specialties such as pig's kidneys flamed in Pekèt (Belgian gin), chicken in beer, and hot black pudding with acid cherries.

Rôtisserie de la Sauvenière. In the Hôtel Mercure Liège, bd. de la Sauvenière 100 (on the edge of the Old City). ☎ **04/221-77-11.** Main courses 320–680 BF ($8.90–$18.90); fixed-price menus 800–1,500 BF ($22.20–$41.65). AE, DC, MC, V. Mon–Fri noon–2:30pm and 7–10:30pm, Sat noon–2:30pm, Sun 7–10:30pm. FRENCH.

Classic French cuisine is featured at this hotel restaurant. The set menus offer a host of mouth-watering specialties. Fillet of deer, fresh from the nearby Ardennes, is a popular starter here, and other good choices include Argentinian steak with *frites*; grilled sole with potatoes; and grilled swordfish with mushrooms, onions, and cream curry sauce. And don't miss out on the succulent leg of lamb.

MORE DINING OPTIONS

A concentration of quite good, inexpensive restaurants (along with a few costlier eateries that have moved across the river) can be found along rue Roture in Outremeuse, which can be reached from the Old City via a convenient footbridge. Meals in most of these restaurants can be selected from a la carte menus, with main courses at about 300 BF ($8.35). Don't be fooled by outward appearances, though, for along with the plain, almost shabby, exteriors (and interiors, as well) comes very good food, with pleasant service and the company of locals who know good value when they see it. Good choices include **Comme Chez Nous,** rue Roture 84 (☎ **04/343-19-85**), which serves Liègeois cuisine; **La Doudeunette,** rue Roture 22 (☎ **04/341-39-16**), for classic French fare; and **Calabaza,** rue Roture 13 (☎ **04/342-27-09**), for Latin American food.

A NEARBY RESTAURANT

✪ **Hostellerie Saint-Roch.** rue du Parc 1, Comblain-la-Tour (18 miles from Liège). ☎ **04/369-13-33.** Reservations required. Fixed-price meals 1,600–2,600 BF ($44.45–$72.20). AE, DC, MC, V. Sept–June, Wed–Sun noon–2pm and 7–9:30pm; July–Aug, Wed–Mon noon–2pm and 7–9:30pm. BELGIAN/CONTINENTAL.

Meals in this delightful inn (see "Where to Stay," above) deserve the designation "gourmet." The setting alone is worth the trip out of town—but when pike or trout fresh from the river arrives at your table accompanied by vegetables from the inn's own garden, well, everything else fades into insignificance. In season, venison from the Ardennes region also makes an appearance.

SHOPPING

Liège has made shopping a joy by taking the simple measure of closing principal streets to all but pedestrian traffic. The best shopping streets, with some 5,000 shops and boutiques, are rue du Pont-d'Avroy, Vinave d'Ile, rue des Dominicains, rue St-Paul, bd. d'Avroy, bd. de la Sauvenière, rue de la Cathédrale, rue Charles-Magnette, rue de la Régence, rue de l'Université, place du Marché, Neuvice et Féronstrée, rue Puits-en-Sock, and rue Jean-d'Outremeuse.

LA BATTE MARKET   On Sunday mornings, what is said to be the oldest ✪ **street market** in Europe—and surely one of the most colorful—is strung out for about a mile along the quai de la Batte on the city side of the Meuse. You'll find brass, clothes, flowers, foodstuffs, jewelry, birds, animals, books, radios, and . . . the list is simply endless. Shoppers from as far away as Holland and Germany join sightseers from overseas, as well as what seems to be at least half the population of Liège. If you're anywhere near Liège on a Sunday, plan to check out this marvelous shopping hodgepodge, even if only for the people-watching.

LIÈGE AFTER DARK
The Performing Arts

The **Opéra Royal de Wallonie** performs at the Théâtre Royal de Liège, rue des Dominicains 1 (☎ **04/223-59-10**). The Théâtre Royal de LAC, near the Church of St-Jacques, presents concerts by the city's excellent philharmonic orchestra, as well as operas, operettas, and ballets. Concerts are also performed at the Conservatory of Music. For schedules and prices of current performances, contact **Infor-Spectacles,** En Feronstrée 92 (☎ **04/222-11-11**), between 11am and 6pm Monday through Friday.

Theaters staging puppet shows performed by the ✪ **Théâtre des Marionettes** (in dialect, but easy to follow) are in the Museum of Walloon Life (see above), the Tchantchès Museum (see above), and the Al Botroûle Museum, rue Hocheporte 3 (☎ **04/223-05-76**). Liègeois wit is especially apparent in the puppets' appearance; each puppet is sized according to its historical importance—for example, a huge Charles the Bold is attended by lilliputian archers (although just how important Charles would have been without those archers is debatable!).

Cafes, Taverns & Other Nightspots

When the sun goes down (and even when it's up), the native Liègeois head for their pick of the city's hundreds of **cafes** and **taverns** to quaff Belgium's famous beers and engage in their favorite entertainment—good conversation. If a quiet evening of the same appeals to you, you'll have no problem finding a locale. Two of the best are the **British Pub,** rue Tête-de-Boeuf 14 (☎ **04/343-39-31**), and **Tchantchès,** En Grande-Bêche 35 (☎ **04/221-05-70**) in Outremeuse.

For livelier nighttime fun, there are numerous nightspots in the Old City's "carré" (bounded by rue du Pot-d'Or, rue St-Jean, and rue Tête-de-Boeuf) and along rue Roture in Outremeuse. Some good examples include **La Chapelle,** place St-Denis (☎ **04/223-26-85**); **Palace Club,** place St-Paul 8 (☎ **04/223-40-53**); **Le Premier,** rue du Pot d'Or (☎ **04/222-28-46**); **Les Trois Frères,** rue d'Amay 3 (☎ **04/223-07-44**); and, in Outremouse, **Le Lion s'Envole,** rue Roture 13 (☎ **04/341-0241**).

A SIDE TRIP FROM LIÈGE
Jehay-Bodegnée

The small village of Jehay-Bodegnée is an interesting diversion for travelers driving from Liège. This is the site of one of the most beautiful castles in the Meuse Valley, the **Château de Jehay.** To get there, take a short detour off of the Liège–Huy road (N17) about halfway between Huy and Liège—look for the turnoff to Amay, then turn left at Amay toward Tongeren (Tongres in French).

✪ **Château de Jehay.** 4540 Jehay. ☎ **085/31-17-16.** Admission 200 BF ($5.55) adults, 80 BF ($2.20) children 6–18, under 6 free. Open Sat, Sun, and public holidays in July and Aug 2–6pm.

No visitor should miss this estate, which contains not only a wondrous moated castle but also a museum containing a remarkable private collection of artifacts of humankind's past in the Meuse Valley. The Château is now presided over by the talented and charming Comte Guy van den Steen de Jehay, whose personal history is as fascinating as that of his home. Artist, sculptor, and ironwright, with a keen interest in archaeology, the count is often on hand as visitors roam through the castle that has belonged to his family since the late 1600s. Moats reflect the castle's striking construction of light and dark stone arranged in a checkerboard pattern, with round towers at each end of a central rectangular block. Inside, the rooms are filled with paintings, tapestries, lace from the private collections of the prince-bishops of Liège, silver and gold pieces, jewels, porcelain and glass, antique furniture, and family heirlooms.

Not the least of the castle's treasures, however, are the works of the present count. Be sure to look especially for the bronze *Pythagoras* and the stunning *Marsyas Tortured by the Nymph,* a three-dimensional progressive relief that was made with the count's own innovative technique. The magnificent ironwork you see in the gates and railings is his work as well. The count has also restored and redesigned his lawns and gardens, which are beautified with many sculptures and Italian fountains.

But anyone with even a smidgen of historical curiosity will want to inspect the Celtic foundations that have been unearthed by the present owner. His archaeological findings on the estate have revealed clear evidence that this site was inhabited more than 30,000 years ago. There's a fascinating museum in the vaulted cellars where you can view the leavings of the Mesolithic age, as well as those of Romans, Gauls, Carolingian Franks, and their medieval successors. Nor should you miss the castle's chapel on a small islet, which has always served as the parish church, as it does today.

2 Huy

34km (21 miles) SW of Liège

The drive from Liège to Namur follows the River Meuse. Once you move beyond the industrial outskirts of Liège, the scenery along the river evolves into a picturesque landscape with small towns every few miles and one of the many castles of the Meuse Valley never far away.

The charming little town of Huy on the Meuse began as a thriving center for tin, copper, and wine merchants (its charter was granted in 1066), and has a long tradition of local metalwork. Its most famous native son, Renier de Huy, was the 12th-century goldsmith who designed the baptismal font in Liège's Church of St-Barthólémey. Today, pewter is the alloy of choice, and Huy's shops are filled with lovely pewter bowls, goblets, pitchers, and other items. The town has several notable examples of the 16th- and 17th-century architectural style known as Mosan Renaissance.

ESSENTIALS

GETTING THERE   There is frequent train service from Liège to Huy's **Gare du Nord,** at place Zenobe Gramme (☎ **085/21-36-55**). Across the square is the **bus station.** For bus information, call ☎ **081/72-08-40.**

By car from Liège, take the N90 southwest.

VISITOR INFORMATION   The **Tourist Office** is at quai de Namur 1, 4500 Huy (☎ **085/21-29-15;** fax 085/23-29-44). It's open from Easter through June and September through mid-October Monday to Friday 8am to noon and 1:30 to 5pm, Saturday and Sunday 10am to noon and 2 to 5pm; July and August Monday to Friday 8am to 12:30pm and 1:30 to 6pm, Saturday and Sunday 10am to 1pm and 2 to 6pm; mid-October to the week before Easter, Monday to Friday 8am to noon and 1:30 to 5pm.

EXPLORING HUY

Like many Mosan towns, Huy is dominated by its hilltop Citadel, the **Fort de Huy,** chaussée Napoléon (☎ **085/21-53-34**), which affords a marvelous view of the town, the river below, and the King Baudouin (*Roi Baudouin*) suspension bridge. The Fort was built in 1818 on the site of earlier castles and forts that date back to the Gallo-Roman period at the very least. In World War II the Nazis used the Fort as a concentration camp, and a museum on the site tells that tale as well as that of the Belgian Resistance fighters. The Fort can be reached on foot or by cable-car (☎ **085/21-18-82**) from the riverside at the corner of rue d'Amérique and rue d'Arsin. Cable-car fare is 125 BF ($3.45) for a one-way ticket and 175 BF ($4.85) round-trip for adults, 80 BF ($2.20) one-way and 100 BF ($2.80) round-trip for children. The fort is open in July and August daily from 10am to 8pm; from April through June and in September it's open Monday to Friday from 10am to 6pm and weekends 10am to 7pm. Admission is 120 BF ($3.35) for adults, 100 BF ($2.80) for children.

The **Town Museum** (Musée Communal), at rue Vankeerberghen 20 (☎ **085/23-24-35**), located in a 17th-century former monastery of the Friars Minor, displays local metalwork as well as glass objects. Its finest single piece is the wooden crucifix known as the "Good Lord of Huy" (*Beau Dieu de Huy*), dating from 1240. The museum is open from April through September daily from 2 to 6pm. Admission is 100 BF ($2.80) for adults, 30 BF (85¢) for children.

In the Grand-Place, the beautiful 18th-century copper fountain known as **Li Bassinia** stands in front of the elegant neo-classical **Town Hall** (Hôtel de Ville) from the same period—with any luck you'll be on hand when its carillon rings out *Brave Liègeois,* as it does every hour.

The vast 14th-century Gothic ✪ **Notre-Dame Collegiate Church** (Collégiale Notre-Dame), parvis Théoduin de Bavière (☎ **085/21-20-05**), is famed for its magnificent stained-glass windows, including Li Rondia, a beautiful Gothic rose window, as well as other stained windows in the choir. Its **Treasury** (Trésor) contains the Romanesque reliquaries of St-Domitien and St-Mengold, and many items in chiseled copper. The Treasury is open Saturday through Thursday from 9am to noon and 2pm to 5pm (except during services). Admission to the church is free; visiting the Treasury costs 50 BF ($1.40) for adults, free for children. Take note, too, of the stone bas-reliefs along tiny arcaded rue des Cloîtres that runs along the side of the church.

Huy's quaint, enchanting little streets are great for walking. For a stroll through history, start in Grand-Place and walk down rue des Rôtisseurs, rue des Augustins,

Great for Kids

A welcome break for children can be had at the **Mont Mosan Leisure Park,** plaine de la Sarte (☎ **085/23-29-96**), in the eastern suburbs, reachable by road and by the cable-car to the Fort de Huy, referred to above. The park has sea lions, rides, and games, and a resident clown. It's open from Easter through the end of October daily from 10am to 8pm. Admission is 130 BF ($3.60) per person.

and rue Vierset-Godin. For a more mobile excursion, take a **river cruise** on the boat Val Mosan (☎ **085/21-29-15**), which sails from quai de Namur in front of the Tourist Office. Departures in May, June, and September are daily at 2, 3, and 4:30pm; in July and August Monday through Sunday at 2, 3, and 4:30pm, and on Sunday also at 5:30pm. Tickets are 120 BF ($3.35) for adults, 100 BF ($2.80) for children.

3 Namur

29km (18 miles) SW of Huy

This handsome riverside town of some 40,000 inhabitants is the capital of Wallonia. It's a pleasant yet bustling place, boasting fine museums and churches, a casino, and an elegant abundance of good cafes and restaurants, particularly along the narrow and atmospheric side streets of its old quarter. The whole town is dominated by its vast hilltop Citadel.

Namur is considered to be the true "Gateway to the Ardennes," and many choose to make this their touring base. Accommodations are limited, however, and you may want to seek lodging a little farther into the Ardennes, where several excellent hostelries await (see chapter 10).

ESSENTIALS

GETTING THERE   There are on average two trains an hour from Huy and Liège. The **train station** is at square Léopold (☎ **081/25-22-22**), with the **bus station** just in front (☎ **081/25-35-55**).

From Huy by car, take the N90 southwest.

VISITOR INFORMATION   The main **Tourist Office** is in the Town Hall (Hôtel de Ville), rue de Fer 42, 5000 Namur (☎ **081/24-64-44;** fax 081/24-65-54). Open Monday through Saturday from 9am to 12:30pm and 1:30 to 6pm. There are also two smaller **Tourist Information Centers,** one adjacent to the train station in square Léopold (☎ **081/24-64-49**) and one at the confluence of the rivers Meuse and Sambre, at place du Grognon (☎ **081/24-64-48**).

A tourist office serving the entire **Province of Namur** is located in the nearby village of Naninne, at rue Pieds d'Alouette 18, 5100 Naninne (☎ **081/40-80-10;** fax 081/40-80-20).

EXPLORING NAMUR

The presence of the great, brooding Citadel is evidence of the strategic importance attached to Namur in centuries past. Today, however, you will find this a quiet, peaceful town, with interesting churches and rows of 17th-century brick homes.

✪ **Citadel (Citadelle).** route Merveilleuse 8. ☎ **081/22-68-29.** Admission to Citadel and museums (includes a 20-minute film), 210 BF ($5.60) adults, 100 BF ($2.80) each for the first 2 children, thereafter 80 BF ($2.20) per child from the same family. June–Sept daily 11am–5pm; Easter–May Sat, Sun, and public holidays 11am–5pm.

The hilltop Citadel is a sightseeing must. To reach it, you can take either a cable car that departs from rue Notre-Dame—it costs 180 BF ($5) for adults, 90 BF ($2.50) for children—or one of two scenic drives that wind up the steep cliff side.

There has been a fortification atop this bluff since Celtic times, but the Dutch are responsible for the Citadel's present shape. Today the structure is part of a 16-acre wooded estate that includes museums, children's play parks, restaurants, cafes, and craft shops. Visitors are shown a film on the history of the Citadel and given a tour of the fortifications. The intriguing underground caverns can be explored (by torchlight) with a guide on a 45-minute tour. There's also an interesting museum of the forest. A small excursion train runs through the extensive grounds on a 30-minute round-trip.

Cathedral of St-Aubain (Cathédral de St-Aubain). place St-Aubain. ☎ **081/22-03-20.** Free admission to church; admission to Diocesan Museum 50 BF ($1.40) adults, 30 BF (85¢) children. Museum open Easter Tuesday–Oct Tues–Sat 10am–noon and 2:30–6pm, Sun 2:30–6pm; Nov–Easter Sunday Tues–Sun 2:30–4:30pm.

The domed Cathedral of St-Aubain dates from 1751. Its Italian architect designed it in the light, ethereal, Renaissance style of his native land, with columns, pilasters, cornices, vessels, and balustrades. The cathedral was built on the site of a 1047 collegiate church of the same name that became the cathedral of the diocese of Namur in 1559—the old church's belfry still survives in the existing structure. In the **Diocesan Museum** (Musée Diocesain), place du Chapitre 1 (☎ 081/22-21-64), on the left as you leave the cathedral, is a small but impressive collection of ecclesiastical relics, gold plate, and sculptures.

Convent of the Sisters of Notre-Dame. rue Julie-Billiart 17. ☎ **081/23-04-49.** Admission 50 BF ($1.40). Tues–Sat 10am–noon and 2–5pm, Sun 2–5pm. Closed Dec 11–27.

The convent in the center of town holds Namur's richest prize, the treasures of the Oignies Priory. These feature the work of 13th-century master goldsmith Brother Hugo of Oignies. The jewel-studded crosses and reliquaries he created are decorated with forest motifs and hunting scenes.

Archaeological Museum (Musée Archéologique). rue du Pont. ☎ **081/23-16-31.** Admission 80 BF ($2.20) adults, 40 BF ($1.10) children (under 6 free). Tues–Fri 10am–5pm, Sat–Sun 10:40am–5pm.

This Renaissance-style museum, which dates from the 15th century, is located in the former meat market on the banks of the River Sambre. It displays important remains of the life and times of the Meuse Valley, from prehistoric times through the Celtic, Roman, and Frank periods into the Middle Ages. The collection includes glassware and pottery from the Roman period, old jewelry and coins, and a relief map of the city dating from 1750.

Félicien Rops Museum. rue Fumal 12. ☎ **081/22-01-10.** Admission 100 BF ($2.80) adults, 50 BF ($1.40) children. July–Aug daily 10am–6pm; Sept–June Tues–Sun 10am–5pm.

Namur sometimes seems unsure of what to make of one of its best-known sons, the bizarre and erotic 19th-century painter and engraver Félicien Rops. His museum is tucked away in a narrow side street, near the artist's birthplace in the old quarter of town—but inside, exposure is the name of the game. The perfection of Rops's soft-ground etchings and drypoint work is internationally recognized, and he is indisputably one of the most outstanding engravers of the late 19th century. Some important examples of Rops's work on display are *Pornokrates, Mors Syphilitica,* and *The Beach at Heist.*

SIGHTSEEING TOURS

From May through October, the Namur Tourist Office organizes a program of **guided tours** of the old town, the Citadel, and the riverside. These 1½-hour tours leave from the Tourist Information Center at place du Grognon (see "Visitor Information," above) at 11:15am and 2:15pm. The cost is 140 BF ($1.10) for adults, and 60 BF ($1.65) for children 14 and under.

A variety of **river cruise** options is available from Namur, including trips to Dinant and Wépion, other tours of the Meuse and Sambre rivers, and a cruise called "Namur by Night." All of them leave from the junction of the Meuse and

Sambre rivers, beside bd. Baron Louis Huart. The cruise company is based in nearby Dinant (see below); call ☎ **082/22-23-15** for information.

NAMUR AFTER DARK

Gamble the night away over the roulette and blackjack tables of the ✪ **Casino de Namur,** av. Baron de Moreau 1 (☎ **081/22-30-21**). There's also a fine French-style restaurant here, called the Casino Club, with fixed-price menus from 395 to 595 BF ($10.95 to $16.55). A jacket and tie are required for men. The casino is open daily from 2pm to dawn.

NEARBY PLACES OF INTEREST

Ten miles south of Namur, a short way inland on the N932, you'll come to ✪ **Les Jardins d'Annevoie,** route des Jardins, Annevoie-Rouillon (☎ **082/61-15-55**), which should top every regional sightseeing list. Annevoie's ornamental gardens and fountains, and the manor house they surround, make a splendid display. The present owner, Jean de Montpellier, lives here with his family.

The estate is sometimes called the "Versailles of Belgium," and while these gardens indeed share similarities with their French cousins, they are also reminiscent of Italian and English gardens, yet still possess their own unique qualities. The delightful fountains, waterfalls, lagoons, and peaceful canals here are all engineered without the use of any artificial power. No throbbing pump or other machinery intrudes on their tranquillity and exquisite beauty. The grounds were originally laid out in the mid-1700s by a member of the de Montpellier family and have been carefully tended and added to by successive generations.

The 18th-century **château** and its outbuildings are laid out in a harmonious design, which is reflected in the neighboring lagoon. Inside there are fine architectural details in the woodwork, stuccos, fireplaces, and family chapel.

The gardens are open April through October daily from 9:30am to 6:30pm; the château is open July and August daily from 9:30am to 1pm and 1:30 to 6:30pm, and from April through June and in September on Saturdays, Sundays, and public holidays only. Admission to both the gardens and château is 210 BF ($5.85) for adults, 145 BF ($4.05) for children; for gardens only, 180 BF ($5) for adults, 125 BF ($3.45) for children; for the château only, 100 BF ($2.80) adults, 70 ($1.95) for children. In addition to a gift shop, there's a a full-service restaurant and a rustic cafe, decorated with ancient farming implements, that serves snacks.

Continue away from the river on the N932 for 3 miles before turning left on the N971 to get to **Maredsous Abbey**, near Denée (☎ **082/69-82-11**). The neo-Gothic Benedictine abbey's twin towers stand out clearly above the rugged, forested countryside. The abbey is famed for its beer, cheese, and bread, all of which can be consumed in a giant cafe on the grounds—and all of which are consumed in giant quantities at peak times. The abbey is open daily from 9am to 6pm. Admission is free.

WHERE TO STAY

Accommodations are a bit limited in Namur. The tourist office can help, and there's also the option of staying in a nearby town.

Hôtel Excelsior. av. de la Gare 4, 5000 Namur. ☎ **081/23-18-13.** Fax 081/23-09-29. 14 units. TV TEL. 2,000 BF ($55.55) double. AE, DC, MC, V. Limited parking available on street.

This comfortable small hotel with wheelchair access is conveniently located in the town center. The room style is modern, with white furnishings, halogen lamps, and curtains and carpets in red or blue. There's a bar and restaurant on the premises.

✪ **Hôtel Les Tanneurs.** rue des Tanneries 13, 5000 Namur. ☎ **081/23-19-99.** Fax 081/26-14-32. 22 units. www.promin.be/tanneurs.htm. MINIBAR TV TEL. 1,750–8,500 BF ($48.60–$236.10) double. AE, DC, MC, V. Limited parking available on street.

Les Tanneurs is a luxuriously appointed hotel occupying a refurbished, character-filled old building close to the confluence of the rivers Meuse and Sambre. The buildings in this area were almost falling down from neglect a few years ago, but an imaginative restoration program has re-created an old-world atmosphere. The rooms are individually decorated, all with an effective mix of antiques and modern fittings. Several have recently been fully renovated. There's a fine restaurant, L'Espièglerie, and a steakhouse, Le Grill des Tanneurs, in the hotel, but these tend to specialize in groups and parties, and can get busy.

Novotel Namur. chaussée de Dinant 1149 (less than 3 miles from Namur), 5100 Wépion. ☎ **800/NOVOTEL** or 081/46-08-11. Fax 081/46-19-90. www.hotelweb.fr. 110 units. TV TEL. 3,700 BF ($102.80) double. AE, DC, MC, V. Free parking. Take the E411 Brussels–Luxembourg expressway to Exit 14.

This is an excellent hotel in a garden setting, located in the village known as Belgium's "strawberry capital." The airy guest rooms are furnished in modern style with bright colors, and most of them have been fully refurbished in recent years (those rooms all have a mini-bar and hair dryer). Hotel facilities include a children's playground, ping-pong table, and both an outdoor and an indoor swimming pool. Golf, tennis, and squash facilities are close by. There's also a cozy bar and good restaurant (see "Where to Dine," below).

Queen Victoria. av. de la Gare 12, 5000 Namur. ☎ **081/22-29-71.** Fax 081/24-11-00. 12 units. TV TEL. 1,750 BF ($48.60) double. Rates include breakfast. AE, DC, MC, V.

Although small, this is one of the best hotels in town. Guest rooms are comfortable and nicely furnished. There's a bar as well.

WHERE TO DINE

Some of the best meals in and near Namur are in the hotel restaurants listed below and in the small, moderately priced bistros (many with sidewalk cafe service in good weather) around place Marché-aux-Legumes, rue des Frippiers, and rue de la Croix. For inexpensive meals, look to the cluster of restaurants near the Citadel.

✪ **Brasserie Henry.** place St-Aubin 3 (just outside the Cathedral of St-Aubin). ☎ **081/22-02-04.** Main courses 300–480 BF ($8.35–$13.35); fixed-price menus 490–980 BF ($13.60–$27.20). AE, DC, MC, V. Daily 8am–1am. BELGIAN.

This restaurant in one of Namur's nicest squares is a good place to get a feel for the new Namurois style (the restaurant is a haven for the trendy). It's a pretty informal place, yet things are still done with a touch of class, and the food is very good. In addition to the long and elegant main dining room, there's also a plant-bedecked outdoor terrace at the back.

Château de Namur. av. de l'Ermitage 1. ☎ **081/74-26-30.** Main courses 420–720 BF ($11.65–$20); fixed-price menus 900–1,600 BF ($25–$44.45). AE, DC, MC, V. Daily noon–2:30pm and 7–9:30pm.

In this area, there's no more refined place to dine than the magnificent Château de Namur, a restaurant whose location up in the Citadel Park overlooking the town has made it especially popular. You'll eat in an arched dining room with lots of light. Try their *truite au bleu* (oven-baked trout), a moderately priced specialty.

Grand Cafe des Galeries St-Loup. rue du College 25–27. ☎ **081/22-71-46.** Main courses 250–450 BF ($6.95–$12.50). AE, DC, MC, V. Mon–Fri 9am–1am, Sat–Sun 9am–2am. BELGIAN/FRENCH.

This superb brasserie-style grand cafe has tables on two levels (the upper level is a wrought-iron bordered balcony) as well as a long, long L-shaped bar. The kitchen specializes in regional cuisine—try the *magret de canard* (fillet of duck) with honey and orange.

Novotel Namur. chaussée de Dinant 1149, Wépion (3 miles from Namur). ☎ **081/ 46-08-11.** Main courses 450–750 BF ($12.50–$20.85). AE, DC, MC, V. Daily 8am–10pm. Take the E411 Brussels–Luxembourg expressway to Exit 14. BELGIAN.

This quietly elegant hotel restaurant specializes in dishes based on local ingredients prepared with traditional regional techniques. Look for fresh trout, Ardennes ham, and lamb.

✪ **La Petite Fugue.** place Chanoine Descamps 5. ☎ **081/23-13-20.** Main courses 280–520 BF ($7.80–$14.45). MC, V. Tues–Fri noon–1:30pm and 7–9:30pm; Sat 7–9:30pm; Sun noon–2:30pm. FRENCH.

This intimately atmospheric little place in the heart of old Namur is located in a converted 18th-century presbytery. Its interior is typical of bourgeois Namur houses of the time, with a wooden staircase and all-wood fixtures and fittings. Try the salmon fillet with cabbage, potatoes, and mushrooms, or the lobster in a Chablis butter sauce. Prices are reasonable considering the superb food and service, and the restaurant's 20 or so places fill up fast during its short open hours. There's also a good wine selection and some good advice to go with it.

4 Dinant

20km (12.5 miles) S of Namur

Like other towns in the Meuse Valley, Dinant has suffered from the turmoil of history. In the 1400s, the Duke of Burgundy demolished the town completely and drowned more than 800 of its residents in the Meuse. And in World War I the Germans—in a chilling replay of that 15th-century tragedy—executed nearly 700 citizens for their stubborn resistance. A reminder of Dinant's military past is never far from view, for the 1530 Citadel that crowns a 100-meter bluff dominates the skyline.

Despite all the bloodshed, the town developed such skill in working hammered copper that its engravings were widely sought after as early as the 13th century. Charles the Bold put a stop to such artistry when he razed the town, but in recent years the skill has once more come back to life, and you will see fine examples of engravings in town shops.

And the town has still another claim to fame: Adolphe Sax, inventor of the saxophone, was born here in 1814 (see box below).

ESSENTIALS

GETTING THERE   There are on average two trains an hour to Dinant from Namur, as well as regular bus service. The **train and bus stations** are at rue de la Station on the west bank of the Meuse.

By car from Namur, take the N92 south.

VISITOR INFORMATION   The **Tourist Office** at rue Grande 37 (☎ **082/ 22-28-70;** fax 082/22-77-88), is open April through November, Monday to Friday from 9am to 7pm.

EXPLORING DINANT

✪ **Citadel (La Citadelle).** chemin du Fort. ☎ **082/22-36-70.** Admission 200 BF ($5.55) adults, 150 BF ($4.15) children (includes the cable-car fare). Apr–Sept daily 10am–6pm; Oct–Dec and Feb–Mar Sat–Thurs 10am–5:30pm; Jan Sat–Sun 10am–5:30pm.

Sax Appeal

Most people would call New Orleans the spiritual home of jazz. But the town of Dinant can lay claim to at least part of that heritage, for it was here in 1814 that Adolphe Sax, inventor of the saxophone, was born.

Sax was a prolific instrument maker and designer. In 1838, he developed the bass clarinet, which was based on some of the same principles he later used for the saxophone. The first saxophone was probably made in 1841–42, and the first recorded reference to it was in a newspaper article by the composer Hector Berlioz, a close friend of Sax's. Sax patented his new instrument in 1846.

The saxophone was a controversial instrument from the start, never gaining wide acceptance in the orchestra, despite the support of Berlioz and a few other composers such as Saint-Saens and Massenet. Sax's saxophone class at the Paris Conservatory was closed in the 1870s, and Sax himself went bankrupt, and finally died a saddened man in 1894.

Salvation for the instrument came in the 1920s and 30s, as the saxophone became increasingly popular in jazz, big band, and even military music. The composer must have felt vindicated, watching from the big saxophone concert in the sky, when his brainchild celebrated its 150th anniversary in 1996. His home town, Dinant, was a throbbing, foot-tapping center of the festivities.

The 16-century Citadel, perched on a cliff high above the town and river, can be reached by car or cable car. Alternatively, if you're feeling particularly energetic or can't turn down the challenge, you can climb the 400 steep steps leading to the bluff top and its spectacular view. The **Weapons Museum** (Musée d'Armes) and **War Museum** (Musée de Guerre) inside are interesting, and there's an audiovisual historical presentation in three languages (including English). But when all is said and done, it's the view that takes your breath away.

Church of Our Lady (Collégiale Notre-Dame). place Astrid. ☎ **082/22-28-70.** Free admission. Open daily.

This riverside collegiate church looks impressively old, but in fact it was rebuilt twice within the last 80 years, after both World War I and World War II. Nevertheless, the church is notable enough. Its big bulbous spire, which originally dates from 1697, is a majestic sight beneath the looming presence of the Citadel.

SIGHTSEEING TOURS

Dinant is the best place on the Meuse for cruising. A variety of **river cruise** options are on offer from Easter through October, ranging from 45 minutes to 3½ hours, with several different companies plying the river. Boats leave from either side of the road bridge in the center of town. For schedule information, call ☎ **082/22-23-15.**

WHERE TO STAY

✪ **Hôtel de la Couronne.** rue Adolphe-Sax 1, 5500 Dinant. ☎ **082/22-24-41.** Fax 082/22-70-31. 25 units. TV TEL. 2,200 BF ($61.10) double; 3,000 BF ($83.35) suite. Rates include continental breakfast. AE, MC, V. Limited parking available on street.

This is a pleasant classic-style family hotel, built after the war. It's located right in the center of town and features comfortable and attractive rooms and a good, moderately priced restaurant and tavern. The traditional decor and furnishings lend a homey feeling to the place.

L'Auberge de Bouvignes. rue Fétis 112, route de Namur (2 miles from Dinant center), 5500 Dinant. ☎ **082/61-16-00.** 6 units. TV TEL. 3,000 BF ($83.35) double. Rates include breakfast. AE, DC, MC, V. Limited parking available on street.

This is a lovely, rustic, country-style inn, right on the banks of the Meuse. The six charming guest rooms are decorated in blue or pink and brightened with lots of flowers and photogravures (etched images from photographic negatives) of scenes along the river. Rooms at the front have a fine view of the Meuse. The kitchen is also excellent. Try to book well in advance.

WHERE TO DINE

Restaurant Thermidor. rue de la Station 3. ☎ **082/22-31-35.** Main courses 400–680 BF ($11.10–$18.90). AE, MC, V. Wed–Mon noon–2:30pm; Wed–Sun 6–10pm. FRENCH.

This old-fashioned, family-run place in the town center is widely considered the best restaurant in Dinant. Specialties include *truite au bleu* (oven-baked trout) and a terrific country-style *pâté de canard* (duck pâté). You should also try the grilled kidneys with mustard sauce, a local favorite.

10 The Ardennes

The Ardennes is Belgium's wildest, most heavily forested region, and its least populated. The country's landscape slides easily from Flanders's flatness into the rolling hills along the Meuse Valley, then almost abruptly begins to climb into the dense greenery of the low but rugged Eifel Massif mountain range, which stretches from Germany across Luxembourg and this part of Belgium, then on into France.

As you approach the Ardennes, villages become farther apart and take on a more uniformly antique look, although some were rebuilt after the destruction of the Battle of the Ardennes in the winter of 1944–1945. To the northeast, in the area called the Ostkantone (East Cantons), you'll most often hear German spoken, a residue from the years before 1919 when this part of the Ardennes belonged to Germany. French is the most common language to the south and west.

For Belgians, the Ardennes vies with the coast for the title of the nation's top vacation spot (the Walloons's desire to see the sea and the Flemings's love of the Ardennes keep the roads and railways busy in summer). The foreign visitor will find the region a scenic and gastronomic delight, and a welcome respite from sightseeing centered around ceaseless museum hopping. That's not to say that the Ardennes is without worthwhile museums—only that with the change in landscape comes a shift in emphasis, away from treasures hoarded indoors and toward the outdoor riches of bracing air, scenic winding mountain roads, sparkling streams, and tranquil lakes. Add a sprinkling of pretty resort towns, mostly nestled in steep, winding river valleys, and old country inns that provide the ultimate in comfort without losing one whit of their unique character, and you pretty much have the essence of a tour through the Ardennes.

For the sports lover, the Ardennes offers a cornucopia of possibilities: canoeing, fishing, hunting, golf, tennis, horseback riding, and swimming. Tourist offices can point the way to any necessary rental equipment, and there will always be contingents of local enthusiasts to share the fun.

Food lovers should know that this region is the home of that delicately smoked Ardennes ham (*jambon d'Ardenne*) so proudly served all over Belgium, and also of other regional specialties, including game and fresh trout and pike. The Ardennes is famed for its wealth

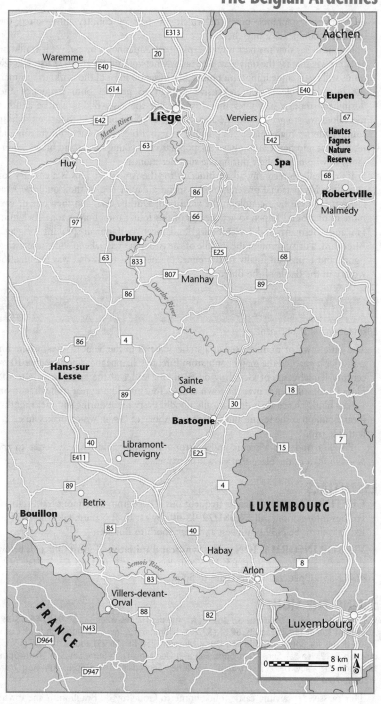

of gourmet restaurants, many of which are part of country inns—often the innkeeper doubles as a fine chef.

It's fair to say that the best way to explore the Ardennes is by car, yet it would be unfair to say that it's the only way. The railway network in this area is sparse, though trains still reach some important points, but buses do most of the work. In summer, the bus timetable is comprehensive enough to provide both frequency and flexibility—though in winter that's usually not the case. Biking can be another marvelous way to get around the area, as long as you're prepared to tackle the hilly countryside. In many places it's possible to rent a bicycle at one train station and return it at another. Camping is very popular with young hikers and bikers, thousands of whom flock here during the summer months.

It's difficult to recommend an itinerary for the Ardennes: This is a country for rambling. My personal preference is to spend a day or two in the Bouillon-Orval district, followed by a couple in the vicinity of Durbuy-Spa, and then one or two more in or around Eupen to get the feel of this four-nation border zone (Belgium, Holland, Germany, and Luxembourg) and meet the German-speaking Belgians. Afterward, a drive through the middle of the Ardennes will take in some interesting sights, and bring you finally to Bastogne, the besieged town that was the anvil of victory in the Battle of the Bulge.

1 Bouillon

60km (38 miles) SE of Dinant

The little town of Bouillon sits at a strategic bend in the Semois River, where for centuries it guarded the major route from Eifel to Champagne. The awesome 10th-century feudal castle of Godefroy de Bouillon, leader of the First Crusade to the Holy Land, still stands over the town today, crouching like a great stone dragon on a steep bluff. The castle is dramatically floodlit every night during summer months. Near Bouillon is the serene and fascinating Abbey of Orval, which makes an excellent side trip.

Bouillon today is a scenic and gastronomic stronghold—where better to try *bouillon* than in the place that gave it its name?

ESSENTIALS

GETTING THERE There is frequent bus service from Libramont train station. For bus information, call ☎ **081/72-08-40.** By car from Namur, take the E411 to Exit 25, then the N89 southwest and then south to Bouillon.

VISITOR INFORMATION The **Syndicat d'Initiative** (Tourist Office) is below the castle at Château Fort, BP 13, 6830 Bouillon (☎ **061/46-62-57;** fax 061/46-82-85). Open daily from 10am to 5pm.

SEEING THE SIGHTS

✪ **Bouillon Castle (Château de Bouillon).** rue des Hautes-Voies 33. ☎ **061/46-68-39.** Admission 150 BF ($4.15) adults, 80 BF ($2.20) children 6–12, free for children under 6. Combined tickets for Bouillon Castle and Ducal Museum 250 BF ($6.95) adults, 120 BF ($3.35) children 6–12. Jan Sat–Sun 10am–5pm; Feb and Dec Mon–Fri 1–5pm, Sat–Sun 10am–5pm; Mar and Oct–Nov daily 10am–5pm; Apr–June, Sept daily 10am–6pm; July–Aug daily 9:30am–7pm.

This massive, sprawling castle, once home to Godefroy de Bouillon, is the town's highly visible and dramatic centerpiece. The worthy de Bouillon actually put the castle in hock in order to raise funds for his great venture, the First Crusade—sadly, he died in 1096 in a foreign land, far from his impressive home. The mortgaged castle passed by default into the hands of the prince-bishops of Liège, who continued to hold it for 6 centuries. After the 15th century, it was conquered and reconquered several times, as local rulers and invading forces fought over this strategic spot. Life within the castle's thick walls during its turbulent history will come to life as you walk through the ruins and visit the old prisons and gallows and the so-called Hall of Justice.

Ducal Museum (Musée Ducal). rue du Petit 1. ☎ **061/46-68-39.** Admission 150 BF ($4.15) adults, 80 BF ($2.20) children 6–12, free for children under 6. Combined tickets for Bouillon Castle and Ducal Museum 250 BF ($6.95) adults, 120 BF ($3.35) children 6–12. July–Aug daily 9:30am–7pm; Sept–Oct, Apr–June daily 10am–6pm; Nov–Dec, mid-Jan to Mar Sat–Sun noon–5pm.

This museum, located in an 18th-century house, contains exhibits on the region's archaeology, iron industry, and folklore. It also includes the Godfrey of Bouillon Museum, which holds souvenirs of the Crusades and of gallant Godfrey, including a model of Godfrey's tomb in Jerusalem and armor, weapons, and religious objects of the period.

WHERE TO STAY

✪ **Auberge du Moulin Hideux.** route de Dohan 1, 6831 Noirefontaine (2.5 miles from Bouillon). ☎ **061/46-70-15.** Fax 061/46-72-81. 12 units. MINIBAR TV TEL. 7,000 BF ($194.45) double; 8,500 BF ($236.10) suite. Rates include full breakfast. AE, DC, MC, V. Free parking.

This country inn set beside an old water mill, with wooded hills almost at its doorstep, is one of Belgium's prettiest. Inside there's a warm, subdued sophistication to the décor. A focal point for guests is the crackling log fire, which is surrounded by luxurious leather furniture and touches of brass to complete the lounge scene. The glassed-in bar is decorated with plants. The dining room gets top rating (see "Where to Dine," below). The 12 guest rooms are appointed with the same sense of style. Extras include tennis and fishing on the grounds, a heated indoor swimming pool, and beautiful forest walks and horse riding trails nearby.

Aux Armes de Bouillon. rue de la Station 9–15, 6830 Bouillon. ☎ **061/46-60-79.** Fax 061/46-60-84. 60 units. MINIBAR TV TEL. 2,100–4,000 BF ($58.35–$111.10) double. Rates include buffet breakfast. AE, DC, MC, V. Limited parking available on street.

This large hotel in the town center has nicely appointed guest rooms. It also offers an indoor heated swimming pool, as well as a private garden, sauna, whirlpool, Jacuzzi, and sunlamp. There's also a bar and a moderately priced restaurant on the premises.

✪ **Hostellerie du Prieuré des Conques.** rue de Conques 179, 6820 Ste-Cécile (Florenville). ☎ **061/41-14-17.** Fax 061/41-27-03. 18 units. MINIBAR TV TEL. 4,200–5,700 BF ($116.65–$158.35) double. Rates include full breakfast. AE, DC, MC, V. Free parking. Take N884 about 14 miles from Bouillon.

This is a great spot to enjoy perfect tranquillity on the edge of an Ardennes forest. This hotel is set in what was once a 7th-century convent (although the oldest surviving remains only go back as far as the 12th century). It overlooks green lawns, rose gardens, and the Semois River. The charming guest rooms all have individual shapes and character—some have alcoves, some are just peeking from under the eaves—and their comfort rates just as high as their charm. The vaulted main dining room is warmed by an open fire, and any overflow of diners spills into a bevy of smaller rooms, also vaulted. Two rooms are air-conditioned and all have hair dryers and easy chairs.

The Battle of the Bulge

Hitler aimed his last great offensive squarely at the Americans, because he believed that if he hit them hard enough, their easygoing, multi-ethnic, citizen army would break apart and run. By mid-December 1944 he had assembled his last reserves of men, tanks, and guns, including the elite SS Panzer divisions, in the hilly, misty Eifel region of Germany, opposite the thinly held American lines in the Ardennes.

On the morning of December 16, the German forces came charging out of the forests. Their aim was far-reaching: to smash straight through the American line, cross the River Meuse before Allied reinforcements had time to react, capture Brussels and the vital port of Antwerp, split the Americans from the British and Canadians, and break the Allied coalition.

Hitler's ambition outstripped his means, but in the Ardennes he had overwhelming strength for the attack. A few of the hard-hit American defenders did flee, but most held their ground until forced back or overrun. Savage struggles all across the Ardennes in Belgium and Luxembourg put the names of obscure towns, villages, and places into the history books: Rocherath-Krinkelt, the Elsenborn Ridge, Malmédy, Stavelot, Trois Ponts, Sankt-Vith, Clervaux, Wiltz, and, of course, Bastogne. The action came to be called the Battle of the Bulge, after the shape the front took as German forces pushed through the middle of the Ardennes.

The lightly equipped U.S. 82nd and 101st Airborne Divisions were rushed in to stem the German-armored tide until heavier reinforcements could be moved into position. While the 82nd fought no-quarter battles with SS troops who had massacred American prisoners, the 101st found itself cut off in Bastogne, holding the vital road junction there.

By December 26, however, the enemy spearhead was finally destroyed a few miles short of the Meuse, and General George Patton's Third Army could counterattack from the south. Bastogne was relieved. Further weeks of heavy fighting pushed the German army back to its start line. Hitler's great gamble had failed. The victors were the ordinary GIs who, in the depths of winter, outnumbered, and faced with a surprise offensive from a still powerful foe, had refuted Hitler's contemptuous opinion of them in the only way that mattered. The price paid for the victory was some 80,000 American casualties.

Memorials all over the Ardennes testify to their courage and sacrifice.

WHERE TO DINE

✪ **Auberge du Moulin Hideux.** In a country inn 2.5 miles (4km) from Bouillon, on route de Dohan 1, Noirefontaine. ☎ **061/46-70-15.** Reservations required. Main courses 950–1,350 BF ($26.40–$37.50). AE, DC, MC, V. Mid-Mar to July Fri–Tues noon–2pm; daily 7:30–9pm; Aug–Nov daily noon–2pm and 7:30–9pm. Closed Dec to mid-Mar. CONTINENTAL.

This place is one of Belgium's top restaurants. It serves gourmet meals featuring lamb, saddle of pork, game, and fish delicacies such as baby lobsters (which are kept in a tank out in the garden). Everything is cooked to order, so be prepared to wait a bit for your fine dinner—your patience will be well rewarded. The wine list here is excellent, and you really should indulge in a good selection to do the food justice.

Hostellerie du Prieuré des Conques. 14 miles (22.5km) from Bouillon, rue de Conques 179, Ste-Cécile (Florenville). ☎ **061/41-14-17.** Main courses 580–780 BF ($16.10–$21.65); fixed-price menus 1,400–2,200 BF ($38.90–$61.10). AE, DC, MC, V. Thurs–Mon 12:45–2pm; Wed–Mon 7:30–9pm. Closed Dec 26 to mid-Mar. CONTINENTAL.

Try to have at least one meal in this atmospheric inn on the banks of the Semois, where fresh produce, fish, and meats are presented in simple but elegant combinations. Rack of lamb, a favorite with patrons, comes with potatoes and a fluffy turnip purée. There's also a very good and moderately priced wine list.

A SIDE TRIP TO ORVAL
27km (17 miles) SE of Bouillon

GETTING THERE   There is infrequent bus service to Orval from Bastogne, via Neufchâteau. For bus information, call ☎ **081/72-08-40.** By car from Bouillon, take the country road southeast through Florenville.

VISITOR INFORMATION   There is no tourist office at Orval, but the Bouillon office has information about the area.

○ **Orval Abbey (Abbaye d'Orval).** Villers-devant-Orval. ☎ **061/31-10-60.** 100 BF ($2.80) adults, 60 BF ($1.65) children 7–14, free for children under 7. Mar–May and Oct daily 9:30am–12:30pm and 1:30–5:30pm; June–Sept daily 9:30am–12:30pm and 1:30–6:30pm; Nov–Feb daily 10:30am–12:30pm and 1:30–5:30pm.

A handful of monks administer this impressive complex of religious buildings, set in the forest. The abbey dates back to the coming of the first Cistercians in 1110, though much was left in ruins after a destructive visit from the French in 1793. Today the complex includes the old ruins as well as a church, its gardens, and a brewery that produces one of Belgium's finest beers.

A visit to the abbey is an exercise in serenity these days, since there is now little to suggest the enormous power its Cistercian monks wielded in past centuries. The old ruins are fascinating. Legend has it that somewhere in the web of underground passages that connected the abbey to seven nearby lakes, a vast treasure lies hidden.

2 Bastogne & Han-sur-Lesse

These two towns offer dramatically different experiences, while sharing the scenic beauty and fresh air that are the Ardennes's strongest suit.

BASTOGNE
158km (99 miles) SE of Brussels; 70km (44 miles) S of Liège

For most Americans, Bastogne is a place of pilgrimage. It was here, during the fierce Battle of the Bulge in the bitter winter of 1944–45, that the American 101st Airborne Division held overwhelmingly superior numbers of German troops at bay until weather conditions improved and Allied reinforcements could be brought in. Without the valiance of the 101st and its heroic leader, Brigadier General Anthony MacAuliffe, Hitler might have turned the tide of World War II. Outnumbered and cut off from any support, MacAuliffe answered German demands for surrender with a single word that has become legend: "Nuts!"

Since the end of the war, Bastogne has been the appointed keeper of memorials to that near-disaster and the men who prevented it.

ESSENTIALS

GETTING THERE Bastogne is a good day trip from almost any point in the Ardennes, but is a little out of the way to use as a base for exploring. There are regular buses to Bastogne from Liège and Luxembourg City—take the Liège–Athus line from Libramont train station, and the Luxembourg–Arlon–Bastogne line from Luxembourg City. By car from Liège, take Exit 53 or 54 off of the E25 Liège–Luxembourg expressway.

VISITOR INFORMATION The **Syndicat d'Initiative** (Tourist Office) is at place MacAuliffe, 6600 Bastogne (☎ **061/21-27-11**).

EXPLORING BASTOGNE

✪ **American Memorial & Bastogne Historical Center.** Colline du Mardasson (1 mile outside Bastogne). ☎ **061/21-14-13.** Admission 295 BF ($8.20) adults, 195 BF ($5.40) children. July–Aug daily 9am–6pm; June, Sept daily 9:30am–5pm; Mar–Apr and Oct to mid-Nov daily 10am–4pm. Closed mid-Nov to Feb.

A visit to the Historical Center will lay the groundwork for a better appreciation of the great battle fought here in December 1944. General MacAuliffe of the 101st Airborne Division and his opponent, General Hasso von Manteuffel of the Fifth Panzer Army, both gave advice in putting together the film, dioramas, and commentary that tell the story of the siege of Bastogne. Afterward, visitors can climb up to the gigantic star-shaped memorial. Key points of the battlefield are clearly posted for those interested in retracing the course of the fighting.

HAN-SUR-LESSE

150km (94 miles) SE of Brussels; 62.5km (39 miles) SW of Liège

This is a particularly good stop for those traveling with children, though the two places described below are very interesting for adults as well.

ESSENTIALS

GETTING THERE Trains from Namur and Liège stop at nearby Jemelle, from where a bus service connects with Han-sur-Lesse. By car, take the E411 south from Namur to Exit 23, then go north on the N86.

VISITOR INFORMATION The **tourist office** (open in summer only) is at place Théo Lannoy, 5580 Han-sur-Lesse (☎ **084/37-75-96**).

EXPLORING HAN-SUR-LESSE

✪ **Caves of Han (Grottes de Han).** rue des Grottes 46. ☎ **084/37-72-12.** Admission (guided tours only) 350 BF ($9.70) adults, 220 BF ($6.10) children 3–12, free for children under 3. Mar and Nov Sat–Sun 11:30am, 1, 2:30, and 4:30pm; Apr and Sept–Oct daily 10am–noon and 1:30–4:30pm; May–June daily 9:30–11:30am and 1–4:30pm (to 5pm weekends in May, to 5:30pm weekends in June); July–Aug daily 9:30–11:30am and 1–6pm.

Of the several cave complexes in the Ardennes, this one is probably the most spectacular and worth visiting. Only about one-fifth of the cave is open to the general public, though other parts are accessible to experienced speleologists. Guides take visitors on an hour-long tour to see the stalagmites and stalactites, marvel at the sometimes bizarre and sometimes graceful shapes taken on by the limestone rock of the caves, and listen to the echo in the great subterranean chambers carved out by the River Lesse. The highlight is a boat trip on the underground river.

Wildlife Reserve (Réserve d'Animaux Sauvages). Departures from rue Joseph Lamotte 2, Han-sur-Lesse. ☎ **084/37-72-12.** Admission (guided tours only) 350 BF ($9.70) adults, 220 BF ($6.10) children 3–12, free for children under 3. Mar and Nov Sat–Sun 11:30am, 1, 2:30, and 4:30pm; Apr and Sept–Oct daily 10am–noon and 1:30–4:30pm; May–June daily 9:30–11:30am and 1–4:30pm (5pm weekends in May, 5:30pm weekends in June); July–Aug daily 9:30–11:30am and 1–6pm.

The Wildlife Reserve, which is part of the same tourist complex as the Grottes, gives a breath of fresh air after the damp and chilly caves. You can take a guided tour by road train through the scenic Massif du Boine estate, where you may see wild boars, wild horses, stags, fallow deer, wolves, bison, ibex, chamois, tarpans, lynx, brown bears, and others—many of the animals are native to the area, but some have been imported.

3 Durbuy

118.5km (74 miles) SE of Brussels; 31km (19.5 miles) S of Liège

Durbuy makes an ideal touring base. It's a tiny, quaint medieval town on a bend in the river, with narrow, twisting streets lined with pretty, flower-trimmed stone houses. There's even an 11th-century castle to complete the scene.

ESSENTIALS

GETTING THERE　In July and August only, there is one bus to Durbuy a day from Barvaux train station. By car from Liège, take Exit 48 west from the E25.

VISITOR INFORMATION　The **tourist office** is in the Vieille Halle aux Blés, rue du Comte Théodule d'Ursel, 6940 Durbuy (☎ **086/21-24-28;** fax 086/21-36-80). For 50 BF ($1.40), the staff will sell you the **Walk Through the Past of Durbuy** booklet, which discusses the history of virtually every building in town.

EXPLORING DURBUY

Durbuy is pretty without having any particularly outstanding sights. Wander about the town to see the medieval stone-built houses, many of which house artists and craftsmen; or take a walk by the plunging valley of the River Ourthe or into the nearby forests. There also are several scenic overlooks that provide excellent views of the town.

WHERE TO STAY

✪ **Le Clos des Récollets.** rue de la Prévoté, 6940 Durbuy. ☎ **086/21-12-71.** Fax 086/21-36-85. 10 units. TV TEL. 2,700 BF ($75) double. Rates include full breakfast. AE, DC, MC, V. Free parking.

This hotel is situated in the heart of the old village, in a pedestrian zone fronted by 17th-century buildings. The structure dates from the 17th century, but has 18th-century modifications. The interior conserves the style of the period, with oak doors, oil paintings, and wooden furnishings. Illumination is provided by candle, as much as possible. The guest rooms are rather plainly furnished, but quite comfortable. On the premises is a good moderately priced restaurant, with umbrella tables on a terrace for outdoor dining. Menu items include game in season, such as pheasant, and lobster stew with vegetables.

✪ **Hostellerie le Sanglier des Ardennes.** rue Comte d'Ursel 14, 6940 Durbuy. ☎ **086/21-32-62.** Fax 086/21-24-65. 70 units. MINIBAR TV TEL. 4,200–8,500 BF ($116.65–$236.10) double. 1- to 3-day package rates (including some meals) available. AE, DC, MC, V. Free parking.

Skiing the Ardennes

It may not be the Alps, and it's certainly not the Rockies, but Belgium's Ardennes region can be something of a skier's paradise—so long as the snow shows up, of course.

Therein lies the problem. In the low Ardennes hills—the highest point is a mere 2,256 feet above sea level—snow's appearances are often brief and unpredictable. Some years it stays away altogether. Still, when the thermometer starts dropping, ski aficionados in Belgium take serious notice. Skiing in Belgium is particularly popular on weekends.

While there are some downhill slopes, cross-country is more popular. Traversing the gentle wooded hills or the high plateau of the Hautes Fagnes Nature Reserve can be a memorable experience.

The main ski zones lie in the north of the Ardennes, around Botrange, Robertville, Bütgenbach, Spa, Stavelot, Vielsalm, La Roche-en-Ardenne, and Bastogne. Parts of Luxembourg and the neighboring Eifel district of Germany also offer good facilities.

For further information, contact **Ardennes et Meuse Tourisme,** rue de l'Eglise 15, 6980 La Roche-en-Ardenne (☎ **084/41-19-81**).

This stellar, centrally located hotel offers comfortable rooms replete with old-fashioned charm. Those in the back overlook the River Ourthe; those in the front have a postcard-pretty view of the old town, with mountains in the background. All rooms have hair dryers. The restaurant on the ground floor is internationally known (see below).

Hôtel Château Cardinal. rue des Récollectines 1, 6940 Durbuy. ☎ **086/21-32-62.** Fax 086/21-24-65. 6 units. MINIBAR TV TEL. 5,000–8,500 BF ($138.90–$236.10) suite. AE, DC, MC, V. Free parking.

The Cardinal could get a top recommendation for either its accommodations or its setting—the combination is irresistible! The owner, Maurice Caerdinael (the award-winning chef of Le Sanglier des Ardennes, listed below), has created six pretty suites in a stone building that once was part of an ancient convent. The house, which has a square tower at one side, is set at the end of a street in the old town, behind 14th-century walls that enclose a small and peaceful garden shaded by fine old trees. Inside, the apartments are beautifully furnished. Even the towels and soap in the private bathrooms have been selected with care to provide the very best. Each refrigerator holds a supply of gourmet goodies—pâté, cheese, beverages, and more—that reinforces the notion that this is truly your "home away from home." All rooms have hair dryers.

Hôtel la Falize. rue A. Eloi 1, 6940 Durbuy. ☎ **086/21-26-66.** 14 units. MINIBAR TV. 1,800 BF ($50) double. Rates include breakfast. AE, DC, MC, V. Free parking.

Old-fashioned, comfortable, cozy—all these apply to this small hotel on a quiet, narrow street in the old town. Its parlor, with a cast-iron stove in one corner, is reminiscent of those homey living rooms of several generations back, as is the warm friendliness of the owners. The rooms are simply furnished. Colorful potted plants flank the doorway.

Le Vieux Durbuy. rue Jean-de-Bohème, 6940 Durbuy. ☎ **086/21-32-62.** 12 units. MINIBAR TV TEL. 4,200 BF ($116.65) double. AE, DC, MC, V. Free parking.

This is another fine old building, once a private home, on a narrow street in the heart of the old town. Its rooms are outfitted with period pieces quite in keeping with their setting, and the same loving care has been taken in supplying baths with luxurious supplies. Breakfast is served in the superb restaurant Le Sanglier des Ardennes, just a short walk away. All rooms have hair dryers.

WHERE TO DINE

✪ **Le Sanglier des Ardennes.** Grand' rue 99. ☎ **086/21-32-62.** Main courses 795–950 BF ($22.10–$26.40); fixed-price menus 1,550 BF–2,500 ($43.05–$69.45). AE, DC, MC, V. Fri–Wed noon–2pm and 7–9pm. Closed Jan. CONTINENTAL.

In this cozy spot overlooking the River Ourthe on the main street in the town center, master chef Maurice Caerdinael creates internationally acclaimed classic dishes. Fish straight from the river outside come to the table full flavored, with subtle sauces or seasonings that add to their delicacy. Regional specialties such as game, the famed smoked jambon (ham), and others take on new dimensions after passing through this extraordinary kitchen. The superb wine cellar also reflects the chef's expertise; the more than 500 bottles are all stored with care and sold at surprisingly moderate prices. There's a covered terrace for outdoor dining.

4 Spa

110km (67 miles) SE of Brussels; 27.5km (17 miles) SE of Liège

To uncover the origin of mineral springs you should go straight to the source. Where better to begin than a town called Spa? Spa is virtually floating on some of the healthiest H_2O ever to bubble up to the surface. The place has been a bustling resort ever since a medieval blacksmith from other parts bought up the land holding these wondrous springs. The town that grew up around them has catered to the likes of Charles II of England, Montaigne, the queen of Sweden, and Tsar Peter the Great of Russia. So universally was its name equated with the miracles of thermal springs and mineral waters that the word "spa" is now applied to health and fitness centers of every description.

ESSENTIALS

GETTING THERE   There's frequent train service to Spa from Liège, but you'll have to change trains at Verviers. For train information, call ☎ **087/77-10-36.** Buses leave regularly from in front of Verviers train station. For bus information, call ☎ **04/361-9444.** By car from Liège, take the E25 southeast to Exit 46, then follow the signs for Remouchamps, and from there take the N697 east.

VISITOR INFORMATION   The **Spa Tourist Office** is at place Royale 41, 4900 Spa (☎ **087/79-53-53;** fax 087/79-53-54).

EXPLORING SPA

Belgians and tourists alike continue to gather in Spa both for the healing treatments and for its lively casino action. The turn-of-the-century **Grand Casino** is at rue Royale 4 (☎ **087/77-20-52**), in the center of town. If you're here for the "cures," head for the ornate mineral baths, the ✪ **Thermes de Spa,** place Royale 2 (☎ **087/77-25-60**). There, they can tell you everything you'll need to know about thermal cures, walking cures, drinking cures (not the alcoholic kind!), and more. The baths are open Monday through Friday from 8:30am to noon and 1:30 to 4:30pm, Saturday from 8:30am to noon.

Another attraction in town is the **Peter the Great Spring** (Pouhon Pierre le Grand), place Pierre le Grand (☎ **087/77-29-13**), located in what was formerly a winter garden and is now a small art gallery. The pavilion was built in the elegant belle époque style, with lots of wrought iron and windows combining to give it a light and airy feel. The place usually hosts small exhibitions. The spring is open from April through October daily 10am to noon and 1:30 to 5pm; November through March Monday to Friday 1:30 to 5pm, Saturday and Sunday 10am to noon and 1:30 to 5pm.

There are numerous springs in the countryside around Spa, and at some of them you can draw as much water as you like for free (bring your own container). The water is said to be very healthy and full of iron, but most of it smells remarkably bad. To visit these springs, get a free route description of the "route des Fontaines" from the tourist office.

WHERE TO STAY

Dorint Hotel Spa-Balmoral. route de Balmoral 33, 4900 Spa. ☎ **087/77-25-81.** Fax 087/77-41-74. www.dorint.be. E-mail: dorintspa@dorintspa.be. 98 units. MINIBAR TV TEL. 4,500–6,700 BF ($125–$186.10) double. Rates include breakfast. AE, DC, MC, V. Free parking.

This hotel on the outskirts of town overlooking the little Warfaaz Lake (Lac de Warfaaz) is a study in modernity. Its gleaming glass front stands out among the pine forests that surround it. All the guest rooms are spacious and sunny, and all have balconies as well as luxury touches. All rooms have hair dryers. Other amenities include an indoor swimming pool and sauna, a solarium, Ping-Pong tables, bars (with periodic entertainment), and the fine Rendez-vous de l'Europe restaurant.

✪ **Hôtel la Heid des Pairs.** av. Professor-Henrijean 143, 4900 Spa. ☎ **087/77-43-46.** Fax 087/77-06-44. E-mail: christian.depreter@ping.be. 11 units. TV TEL. 2,900–5,200 BF ($80.55–$144.45) double. Rates include full breakfast. AE, MC, V. Free parking.

This villa outside the center of town is surrounded by lawns dotted with ancient trees. It was built for Baron Nagelmackers, whose family founded the Orient Express. The ambiance is still that of a private home. The comfortable drawing room and homey guest rooms furnished with a mixture of period and functional pieces give the inn a welcoming, "at home" feel. These touches begin with fruit and sweets in your room on arrival. Three of the rooms have private balconies; you can elect to have your breakfast served there or on the terrace downstairs. There's an outdoor swimming pool. All rooms have hair dryers.

✪ **L'Auberge de Spa.** place du Monument 4, 4900 Spa. ☎ **087/77-44-10.** Fax 087/77-21-79. 32 units. 4,200 BF ($116.65) double; 6,950 BF ($193.05) suite. Rates include breakfast. AE, DC, MC, V.

This attractive hotel in the town center opens onto a small square. Older rooms are comfortable and homey and look out through casement windows to the town outside. There are also tastefully furnished luxury suites, with bedroom, large living room, fully equipped kitchen, and bath. Each can accommodate up to four people. The hotel's ground floor houses a good restaurant.

WHERE TO DINE

Your best meals will probably be taken in the hotels recommended above. There are also a number of other good restaurants in or near Spa.

✪ **A la Retraite de l'Empereur.** About 8km (5 miles) from Spa, Basse Desnié 842, La Reid. ☎ **087/37-62-15.** Reservations required. Main courses 595–995 BF ($16.50–$27.65); à la carte meals 995–2,350 BF ($27.65–$65.30). AE, DC, MC, V. Thurs–Mon noon–2pm and 7–9pm. Closed last 3 weeks in July, and 3 weeks in Dec–Jan. FRENCH.

This beautifully rustic restaurant, in a long stone building set right on the main street of a tiny village, has won several prestigious awards for its classical French cuisine. Specialties include game (in season) and lobster, as well as other good seafood selections, including a mixed seafood dish of cod, salmon, mussels, scampi, and clams. The chef's specialty is corn-fed chicken in Bourgogne vinegar. House wines are inexpensive. The drive out through tranquil, rolling countryside is a delight.

Eurotaverne. place Royale 4. ☎ **087/77-39-26.** Main courses 150–550 BF ($4.15–$15.30). MC, V. Thurs–Tues 10am–10pm. REGIONAL.

This modestly priced local restaurant fills a gap in Spa. The fish soup, mussels, and breast of chicken in green pepper sauce are good options. This place offers outstanding value and fun.

La Brasserie du Grand Maur. rue Xhrouet 41. ☎ **087/77-36-16.** Fixed-price meal 1,500 BF ($41.65). AE, DC, MC, V. Wed–Sun noon–2pm and 7–9pm. Closed Jan. FRENCH/BELGIAN.

This elegant restaurant in the town center, set in a 200-year-old building, specializes in regional gourmet dishes prepared with the very best of local produce. The *pâté de foie gras* (duck liver pâté) is excellent, as is the side of lamb in mustard sauce.

MORE DINING OPTIONS

If you walk the 6-mile route des Fontaines that links the mineral springs in the countryside around Spa, you'll find rustic little restaurants conveniently located about ten steps from each spring—you'd almost think it had been planned that way. The first spring on the route, the Fontaine de Barisart, has the least interesting eatery, a blocky, cafeteria-style place with all the charm of a missile silo. After that, however, things pick up. **La Géronstère** (☎ 087/77-03-72), is a stone-built farmhouse-style building that stocks good snacks, beside the Fontaine de la Géronstère; **La Sauvenière** (☎ 087/77-51-68), also stone-built and in a farmhouse style, is beside the Fontaine de la Sauvenière and the adjacent Fontaine de Groesbeeck; and the Italian ✪ **La Fontaine du Tonnelet** (☎ 087/77-26-03), in a red-and-white pavilion, its interior decorated in the style of a Tuscan villa, is beside the Fontaine du Tonnelet. Back in Spa, if you're in a hurry, the **Chalet du Parc** (☎ 087/77-22-84) in the Parc de Sept Heures behind the tourist office, is a good place for a snack—in the open air if the weather is fine.

5 The East Cantons

The East Cantons (*Ostkantone;* or *Cantons de l'Est*) district in the east of Belgium has a population of about 100,000, some two-thirds of whom speak German and the remainder French. The whole area is sparsely populated and wonderfully scenic, with no end in sight of hills, forests, and streams. Outdoor pursuits are a way of life here. The district shares borders with Germany, Holland, and Luxembourg.

EUPEN

This character-filled little town (pop. 17,000) is the capital of the East Cantons. It has a local parliament, a prime minister, and German-language radio and television stations.

ESSENTIALS

GETTING THERE   There are hourly trains to Eupen from Brussels and Liège, some direct and some involving a change at Verviers. Buses leave every 30 minutes from outside Verviers train station.

By car from Brussels and Liège, take Exit 38 off of the E40.

VISITOR INFORMATION   The Eupen **Tourist Office** (Verkehrsamt) is at Marktplatz 7, 4700 Eupen (☎ **087/55-45-45;** fax 087/55-34-50). For more information about the East Cantons in general, contact the **East Cantons Tourist Office** (Verkehrsamt der Ostkantone), Mühlenbachstrasse 2, 4780 Sankt-Vith (☎ **050/38-02-96;** fax 087/22-65-39).

WHAT TO SEE & DO

Eupen's **Parliament** (Exekutive) building, Klötzerban 32 (☎ **087/55-34-50**), is a handsome patrician house dating from 1761. Guided tours are free but can only be made by prior arrangement. The **Church of St Nicholas** (Sankt-Nikolaus Pfarrkirche) on the Marktplatz dates from the 1720s. Its two bulbous spires are a symbol of the town. The church is open daily, and admission is free.

Eupen's main role touristically—apart from its hotels, restaurants, cafes, and shops—is as a gateway to the wide green yonder. Outside the town lies the Hertogenwald Forest, with its many marked walking and riding trails. Beyond the forest, in the direction of Malmédy, is Belgium's biggest national park, the **Hautes Fagnes Nature Reserve,** a high and boggy moorland plateau with a unique sub-alpine flora, fauna, and microclimate. You can access the reserve through Baraque-Michel and Mont-Rigi, although it's closed for some weeks in spring because of the breeding season (for birds, foxes, and other mammals), and may be closed in summer due to the increased fire risk. At all other times you must stick to the boardwalks and signposted paths. For the complete lowdown on the Hautes Fagnes, visit the **Botrange Nature Center** (☎ **080/44-03-00**), signposted off the road to Sourbrodt, which documents the history and ecology of the reserve. The center is open daily from 10am to 6pm; admission is 100 BF ($2.80) for adults, 50 BF ($1.40) for children 6 to 18, free for children under 6. Close by is the **Signal de Botrange,** a tower that marks the less-than-dizzying highest point in Belgium, 694m (2,290 ft.) above sea level.

WHERE TO STAY

The entire German-speaking East Cantons district, of which Eupen is the capital, is a popular vacation zone and has a wide array of hotels, guest houses, and camping sites. Many people prefer to stay in the countryside, but for those who like the amenities of a small town, Eupen has some good lodging possibilities.

Ambassador Hotel Bosten. Haasstrasse 77–81, 4700 Eupen. ☎ **087/74-08-00.** Fax 087/74-48-41. 30 units. MINIBAR TV TEL. 3,500–3,900 double; 5,500 BF ($97.20–$108.35) suite. Rates include buffet breakfast. AE, DC, MC, V. Parking 300 BF ($8.35).

This hotel occupies a good location on the eastern edge of town, beside the road that leads out to the Hertogenwald Forest and the Hautes Fagnes National Park. Nearby is a park with a fountain. The modern rooms are comfortable and well equipped, with a balcony. The decor is warm, with peach-colored walls and lush floral patterns on the curtains and bedcovers. Eight of the units are newly added deluxe rooms. All rooms have hair dryers. The hotel's classic French-style Le Gourmet restaurant is one of the most highly regarded in the East Cantons.

Rathaus Hotel. Rathausplatz 13, 4700 Eupen. ☎ **087/74-28-12.** Fax 087/74-46-64. 18 units. MINIBAR TV TEL. 2,850 BF ($79.15). Rates include buffet breakfast. AE, DC, MC, V. Free parking.

Don't be put off by the name, which sounds just like Rat House in English. In German "Rathaus" means City Hall (come to think of it, the expression in English might sometimes have a certain validity). This is a fine hotel facing the flower-bedecked Town Hall, with a friendly welcome that begins in the white-marble reception area. The rooms all have a private bathroom and hair dryer, and some have a balcony. The decor and furnishings are simple but bright and clean, with pine beds covered by colorful quilts, pine furnishings, gray carpeting, and walls adorned with floral paintings. The bistro-style bar serves snacks. The in-house restaurant is well up to the standard expected in this gastronomy-fixated part of Belgium.

WHERE TO DINE

✪ **Brasserie-Restaurant Le Mont-Rigi.** route de Botrange 135, Mont-Rigi (beside the Hautes Fagnes Nature Reserve). ☎ **080/44-48-44.** Tues–Sun 10am–8pm or 9pm (depending on custom). Main courses 250–450 BF ($6.95–$12.50); menus du jour 395–595 BF ($10.95–$16.50). MC, V. BRASSERIE.

This stone-built brasserie-restaurant a few miles out of Eupen is blessed with one of the finest outdoor terraces imaginable—it looks out southward over the high, wide moorland bordered by forests of the Fagne de la Poleûr. The place gets busy with day-trippers, especially on weekends, but at other times can be very quiet. Meals range from simple snacks, through the ubiquitous Belgian *steak-frites*, to game dishes in season.

ROBERTVILLE

131.5km (82 miles) SE of Brussels; 44km (27 miles) SE of Liège

Beyond the Hautes Fagnes, in the direction of the German border, is the **Lac de Robertville,** a 153-acre lake that's a popular area for swimming and water sports in summer.

✪ **Burg Reinhardstein (Castle Reinhardstein).** Ovifat-Robertville (signposted from the village). ☎ **080/44-68-68.** Admission (guided tours only) 200 BF ($5.55) adults, 80 BF ($2.20) children 6–14, free for children under 6. Mid-June to mid-Sept Sun 2:15–5:15pm; July–Aug Tues, Thurs, Sat 3:30pm.

This is the very image of a fairy-tale castle, though it's perhaps a little more homey than formidable in appearance. Nevertheless, its battlemented towers stand on a rugged rocky outcrop overlooking a forest and a plunging stream. The castle used to belong to the Metternich family. After having tumbled into near ruin, it was saved from total destruction by a Belgian castle enthusiast, the late Professor Jean Overloop, and fully restored. Now you can tour its towers and chambers in the company of guides who have inherited Overloop's love for the place.

WHERE TO STAY & DINE

✪ **Hôtel des Bains.** Lac de Robertville, Waimes. ☎ **080/67-95-71.** Fax 080/67-81-43. 14 units. MINIBAR TV TEL. 3,600–4,500 BF ($100–$125). Rates include buffet breakfast. AE, CB, V. Free parking. A short way from Spa on the E5 highway to Exit A27, signposted Malmédy-Waimes.

This fine hotel sits on the shores of the Lac de Robertville , near the Hautes Fagnes Nature Reserve. Its rooms are stylish yet cozy, with twin beds and an all-round sense of good taste. The hotel restaurant's classic French cuisine is served with a light, delicate touch. Pike from the lake comes poached and served on lettuce with a white butter sauce—*the* choice when it's available. Main courses run from 720 to 990 BF ($20 to $27.50), and set menus from 1,300 to 2,700 BF ($36.10 to $75). The restaurant is open Thursday to Tuesday from noon to 3pm and 7 to 10pm.

11 Hainaut: The Green Province

Hainaut, the large Walloon province that stretches across most of the Belgian/French border, was the setting for countless conflicts between French nobility who coveted the rich Low Countries and fractious Flemish determined to resist them. Each side enlisted allies, annexed territory through political marriages, engaged in pitched battles, and struggled to keep the local populations properly subdued—even the Flemish lords faced fairly constant rebellions from their own people whenever the lower classes felt the blue-bloods were trampling too heavily on their rights.

Later on, as coal mining grew in importance, Hainault gave way to industrialization. Charleroi, the largest city in the province, sits in the central coal basin; and even today, though there's no longer much coal mining in Belgium, great slag heaps dot the Borinage countryside around Mons. But nowadays industrialization mainly takes the form of engineering and manufacturing, and peaceful farmlands still exist as they have for centuries. Much of the landscape in lush and verdant. As you drive through, it's difficult to picture the days when this was dubbed Belgium's "black country."

The province has a rich, colorful history and is the repository of great art treasures from the past. Charleroi is of little interest to visitors outside the engineering field. But Tournai, undisputed art center of Hainaut, and Mons, the site of many antiquities and museums, draw visitors like powerful magnets, as do the region's lovely lakes.

1 Tournai

80km (49 miles) SW of Brussels; 44km (27 miles) NW of Mons

When you talk about Tournai, you must speak of survival. This city, the second-oldest in Belgium (Tongeren is the oldest), has survived a multitude of devastating political, military, and economic disasters.

During medieval and Renaissance times, Tournai maintained a position of prominence in Europe as an ecclesiastical center. Its importance in even more ancient centuries was forgotten, however, until 1653, when a workman, quite by chance, opened the tomb of Childeric, King of the Franks—whose son, Clovis, founded the Merovingian dynasty that ruled for nearly 3 centuries. This led to the discovery that Tournai's predecessor at this major crossroads on

Tournai

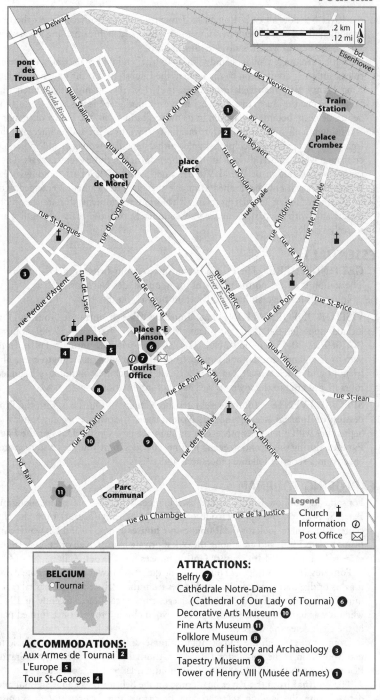

Legend
Church †
Information ⓘ
Post Office ✉

BELGIUM
○ Tournai

ACCOMMODATIONS:
Aux Armes de Tournai **2**
L'Europe **5**
Tour St-Georges **4**

ATTRACTIONS:
Belfry **7**
Cathédrale Notre-Dame
  (Cathedral of Our Lady of Tournai) **6**
Decorative Arts Museum **10**
Fine Arts Museum **11**
Folklore Museum **8**
Museum of History and Archaeology **3**
Tapestry Museum **9**
Tower of Henry VIII (Musée d'Armes) **1**

the River Scheldt, an early Roman settlement known as Tornacum, was the first capital of the Frankish empire. The tomb also yielded breathtaking royal treasures—the best of which, sadly, are now in Paris.

In the years since Childeric and Clovis, Tournai endured a succession of foreign rulers, suffering domination by the French, the English (it was the only Belgian city King Henry VIII managed to conquer, in 1513), the Spanish, the Dutch, the French again, the Austrians, French Empire revolutionary forces, and, for a time before Belgium became a kingdom in its own right in 1830, the Dutch once more.

Through it all Tournai retained its magnificent works of art and architecture, the legacy of its painters, sculptors, goldsmiths, tapestry weavers, and porcelain craftsmen who persistently kept at their labors during all those eventful years. Then came the devastation of World War II, when a full 60% of its buildings were destroyed. It can only be deemed a miracle that the great cathedral emerged with little damage. Today, Tournai greets us with glorious monuments that are once more intact, and with its past recaptured so completely that the scars of conflict are scarcely visible.

ESSENTIALS
GETTING THERE   There's good train service from Brussels, a 1½-hour ride. The station is on the northern edge of town, on bd. des Nerviens.

Tournai is less than an hour's drive from Brussels on the A8.

VISITOR INFORMATION   The **Tourist Office (Centre de Tourisme)** is located opposite the Belfry at Vieux Marché aux Poteries 14, 7500 Tournai (☎ **069/22-20-45;** fax 069/21-62-21). It's open Monday through Friday from 9am to 7pm, and Saturday and Sunday from 10am to noon and 2pm to 6pm. The friendly and efficient staff can supply excellent brochures outlining self-guided tours in and around the town, as well as other information.

SPECIAL EVENTS   Tournai celebrates the Nativity of Our Lady with the **Procession of Tournai** (see "Cathédrale Notre-Dame," below) the second Sunday in September with a religious procession through the city. On the **Days of the Four Parades,** during the second weekend in June, episodes from Tournai's history are reenacted in a series of folklore processions and events.

EXPLORING TOURNAI
For some idea of how Tournai looked back in medieval times, take a stroll along rue Barre St-Brice on the opposite side of the River Scheldt (Escaut) from the city center. Once there, look for the **Romanesque houses** at nos. 10 and 12, which date from the late 1100s and are among the oldest private houses in all of Europe. In the same neighborhood, 13th-century **Gothic houses** line rue des Jésuites.

Pont des Trous ("Bridge of Holes") on the quai Sakharov is an appropriate name for this bridge over the Scheldt, which dates from the 13th century. It has taken its lumps from any number of battles and sieges since then—most recently in 1944, when it was blown up. The bridge and its two anchoring towers once formed part of the city's defensive walls.

From April through the end of August, **horse-drawn carriages** are available to take you through the cobblestone streets of Tournai. They leave from the Grand-Place and cost 500 BF ($13.90) for a 30-minute ride for 1 to 5 people.

The **Tournai from the River** boat cruise on the Scheldt lasts about an hour and departs from the landing stage at Pont des Trous from May through August, Tuesday to Sunday at 11am, 2:30pm, and 4:15pm. Fares are 100 BF ($2.80) adults, 90 BF ($2.50) seniors and students, and 50 BF ($1.40) children 6 and under.

Belfry (Beffroi). Grand-Place. Admission 80 BF ($2.20). Wed–Mon 10am–noon and 2–5:30pm.

The Belfry of Tournai dates from the late 1100s, making it the oldest in Belgium. If you're up to it, you can climb the 265 steps to the top of this 72m-high (236 ft.) tower for a glorious view of the town and surrounding countryside. The Belfy's 44-bell carillon plays Saturday-morning concerts.

✪ **Cathédrale Notre-Dame (Cathedral of Our Lady).** place de l'Evêché (just off the Grand-Place). ☎ **069/22-31-91.** Free admission to Cathedral; Treasury (Trésor) 30 BF (85¢). Cathedral: Apr–Oct daily 9am–noon and 2–6pm; Nov–Mar daily 9am–noon and 2–6pm. Treasury: Apr–Oct Mon–Sat 10:15–11:45am and 2–5:45pm, Sun 2–4:45pm; Nov–Mar Mon–Sat 10:15–11:45am and 2–3:45pm, Sun 2–3:45pm.

This magnificent five-towered cathedral in the city center was completed in the late 1100s, but it's not the first place of worship to stand on this spot. There was a church here as early as A.D. 761, and it's thought that there was a pagan temple on this site before that. The 8th-century church was replaced by another in 850, which was burned to the ground by invading Norsemen in 881, only to be quickly rebuilt. After fire once again destroyed the church in 1060, it was rebuilt by 1089 and became a place of refuge for a plague-stricken population. On September 14, 1090, after the dreaded disease had finally abated, a grateful bishop led a great procession through the cathedral to honor Our Lady, who was credited with several miraculous cures after hordes of the stricken had poured into the cathedral to pray before her statue. In the years since, the **Procession of Tournai** has taken place every year, except in 1559 when Calvinists broke into the cathedral in a destructive orgy. Anyone planning a September visit to Europe should reserve the second Sunday of that month for Tournai in order to view its splendid pageantry.

The present cathedral is one of the most striking examples of Romanesque architecture in Europe. Its classical Romanesque style was, however, in the eyes of a 13th-century bishop, hopelessly old-fashioned compared to the Gothic buildings that were then appearing all over Europe. He therefore ordered stained-glass windows and had the Romanesque choir replaced by a Gothic one. Before the money ran out entirely, he had managed to create a soaring, graceful choir adjoining the long, low Romanesque nave, which never did get its Gothic facelift. Amazingly, when you visit this schizophrenic building today, there is no sense of disharmony, but rather a strange sort of compatible marriage of the two styles.

The cathedral itself holds such treasures as paintings by Rubens and Jordaens, 700-year-old murals, a Renaissance pulpit, and a "rose window" of stained glass. But even these wonders pale before the display in the cathedral's Treasury, which houses a vast collection of priceless religious relics and antiquities. The centerpiece is the reliquary casque known as *La Chasse de Notre-Dame,* with its astonishingly beautiful gold-sculpted covering created by Nicholas of Verdun in 1205; this object always takes the place of honor in the Procession of Tournai each September. Other treasures include 15th-century tapestries (one is a full 72 feet long!), a jewel-encrusted 10th-century Byzantine cross, and a 14th-century ivory statue of the Virgin.

MUSEUMS

Decorative Arts Museum (Musée des Arts Décoratifs). rue St-Martin 50. ☎ **069/22-40-69.** Admission 80 BF ($2.20) adults, 30 BF (85¢) students. Wed–Sun 10am–noon and 2–5:30pm.

This museum features examples of the exquisite porcelain and china made in Tournai in the 18th century, including the dinner service for the Duc d'Orléans, as well as displays of fine silverware and historical coins.

✪ **Fine Arts Museum (Musée des Beaux-Arts).** enclos St-Martin (off rue St-Martin).
☎ **069/22-20-43.** Admission 120 BF ($3.35) adults (price includes an audio guide), 40 BF
($1.10) students. Wed–Mon 10am–noon and 2–5:30pm.

It's hard to say which is more impressive: this museum's 700 works of art, or the
building dating from 1928 that houses them. The marvelous, star-shaped white
stone structure was designed by noted art nouveau architect Victor Horta. Its interior is illuminated by natural light. The art collection contains such outstanding
works as *Virgin and Child* by 15th-century native son Roger de La Pasture, better-
known as Roger van der Weyden, and Edouard Manet's *Argenteuil* and *At Father
Lathuille's*. Other artists represented include Brueghel the Younger, James Ensor,
Henri de Braekeleer, and Sir Anthony Van Dyck.

Folklore Museum (Musée de Folklore). réduit des Sions. ☎ **069/22-40-69.** Admission
100 BF ($2.80) adults, 40 BF ($1.10) students. Wed–Mon 10am–noon and 2–5:30pm.

This museum preserves the atmosphere of Tournai in times gone by. Two marvelous
17th-century buildings in the city center, complete with gables and mullioned windows, provide just the right setting for a series of authentically re-created rooms that
represent an ancient farmhouse, a tavern, a weaver's workroom, a blacksmith's forge,
and many other old buildings. One "fast-food stall" shows how french fries were
dispensed at the turn of the century.

Museum of History and Archaeology (Musée d'Histoire et d'Archéologie). rue des
Carmes 8. ☎ **069/22-16-72.** Admission 80 BF ($2.20) adults, 30 BF (85¢) students.
Wed–Sun 10am–noon and 2–5:30pm.

This museum, located in a 17th-century pawnshop in the city center, features a collection of Tournai relics covering virtually every period in its history. The Merovingian section features items recovered from in and around the tomb of Childeric,
including the skeletons of horses that were sacrificed during the 5th-century
Frankish king's funeral. There's also a fine collection of glassware from the Gallo-
Roman period of the 1st to the 4th centuries.

Tapestry Museum (Musée de la Tapisserie). place Reine Astrid 9. ☎ **069/23-42-85.**
Admission 80 BF ($2.20) adults, 40 BF ($1.10) students. Wed–Sun 10am–noon and
2–5:30pm.

In the late Middle Ages, Tournai was one of the great European centers of tapestry
making, and this museum reflects that heritage. Several historical tapestries are on
display, but, interestingly, the museum focuses more on contemporary works,
including pieces by top modern Belgian artists like Roger Somville.

Tower of Henry VIII. rue du Rempart. ☎ **069/22-38-78.** Admission 80 BF ($2.20) adults,
30 BF (85¢) students. Wed–Mon 10am–noon and 2–5:30pm.

England's King Henry VIII (of the six wives fame) occupied Tournai from 1512 to
1518, and left in his wake this 80-foot tower in the city center. It now houses an
impressive **Museum of Arms and Military History** (Musée d'Armes et d'Histoire
Militaire), which has a collection of small arms and uniforms and also a fascinating
exhibit on the Belgian Resistance in World War II.

WHERE TO STAY

Tournai and Mons both make an easy day trip from Brussels. Those who elect to
stay overnight in the area will find the hotel selection in Tournai rather limited. A
wider assortment is available in Mons.

IN TOURNAI

Aux Armes de Tournai. place de Lille 24, 7500 Tournai. ☎ **069/22-67-23.** 15 units. TEL. 1,225–1,600 BF ($34–$44.45) double. Rates include breakfast. AE, DC, MC, V. Free parking.

This small hotel is conveniently located in the center of town. It offers comfortable rooms with attractive decor and furnishings. There's a good restaurant in the same building.

L'Europe. Grand-Place 36, 7500 Tournai. ☎ **069/22-40-67.** Fax 069/23-52-38. 8 units. TV TEL. 2,300 BF ($63.90) double. Rates include breakfast. AE, DC, MC, V. Limited parking available on street.

This hotel right in the central square follows the rustic style common in Tournai, with antique paintings and lots of flowers in the public spaces. The rooms, plain but comfortable, are more modern in their furnishings, and some of them look out over the Grand-Place. On the ground floor is a pleasant, moderately priced restaurant.

Tour St-Georges. rue St-Georges 2, 7500 Tournai. ☎ **069/22-53-00** or 069/22-50-35. 10 units. TV TEL. 1,100–1,580 BF ($30.55–$43.90) single or double. Rates include continental breakfast. No credit cards. Free parking.

This quiet, conveniently located hotel in the city center has comfortable and attractive rooms. There's a good restaurant and bar on the premises with moderate prices.

EN ROUTE TO MONS

✪ **Hostellerie le Vert Gazon.** 7980 Stambruges-Grandglise (just off Highway A16 between Tournai and Mons). ☎ **069/57-59-84.** 6 units. TV TEL. 2,400–3,600 BF ($66.65–$100) double. Rates include buffet breakfast. AE, DC, MC, V. Free parking.

This restful place is an ideal base for sightseeing forays into both Mons and Tournai. The turreted château, set amid green, flower-bordered lawns, is a short distance from a charming little village. Guest rooms are beautifully furnished, as are the reception rooms and the dining room, where excellent meals are served for about 1,900 BF ($52.80). Be sure to reserve as far in advance as possible.

WHERE TO DINE

Almost any of the sidewalk cafes lining the Grand-Place will provide good meals at moderate prices, but the restaurants listed below are exceptionally good. For inexpensive meals averaging less than 800 BF ($22.20), try the restaurants on place Crombez in front of the railway station.

✪ **Charles Quint.** Grand-Place 3. ☎ **069/22-14-41.** Main courses 550–850 BF ($15.30–$23.60). AE, DC, MC, V. Fri–Wed noon–2:30pm; Fri–Tues 7–10:30pm. BELGIAN.

This popular, graceful restaurant is nearly always crowded at lunch, and deservedly so. Its kitchen produces excellent fish, fowl, and meat dishes. Try the *foie de canard au chicon* (duck liver with chicory) or the exceptional beef filet with onions and bacon. The restaurant is in art deco style, with mixed brown and orange colors, and is located in the city center overlooking the Belfry.

Le Pressoir. Marché aux Poteries 2. ☎ **069/22-35-13.** Main courses 400–750 BF ($11.10–$20.85); fixed-price menu 995 BF ($27.65). AE, DC, MC, V. Sun–Thurs noon–2:30pm; Fri–Sat noon–2:30pm and 6:30–9:30pm. CONTINENTAL.

This elegant restaurant is located in the 17th-century former wine-press of Tournai Cathedral. It retains as much of its antique ambiance as possible in its interior fittings and silver tableware. The setting is subdued and sophisticated, and the fare is mouthwatering. Look out for the duck and fish specialties, as well as such dishes as grilled lobster with fresh herbs, oven-baked turbot with fried shallots, and kidney with orange sauce and herbs.

2 Mons

55km (34 miles) SW of Brussels; 44km (27 miles) SE of Tournai

Mons, the administrative capital of Hainaut Province, began life as a fortified Roman camp, and today is home to SHAPE (Supreme Headquarters Allied Powers Europe). In between those military bookends of history, it has had a rich and eventful past.

The Roman camp, set in this landscape of rolling hills (*Mons,* in fact, means "mount" in Latin), later became a town when Ste-Waudru, daughter of a local nobleman, founded a convent here in the 600s. Mons was fortified by Baldwin of Mons in the 12th century, and again by the Dutch in the early 1800s. Mons's present character reflects its more recent history as a center of industrialization and coal mining, but its Grand-Place (Main Square) still remains all but unchanged, surrounded by fine buildings of the past.

ESSENTIALS

GETTING THERE   There is frequent train service to Mons from Brussels and via Brussels–Paris express trains. The railway station is on place Léopold, a short walk west from the town center.

To get to Mons by car from Brussels, take the E19; from Tournai, take E42.

VISITOR INFORMATION   The excellent **tourist office** is at Grand-Place 22, 7000 Mons (☎ **065/33-55-80;** fax 065/35-63-36), and is open Monday through Saturday from 9am to 6pm (5:30pm in winter), and from 10am to 6pm on Sundays (5:30pm in winter). The staff is friendly, efficient, and enthusiastic.

SPECIAL EVENTS   Each spring on Trinity Sunday (the eighth Sunday after Easter) Mons erupts in a burst of vivid color, mock drama, and general revelry, when it celebrates the ✪ **Ducasse de la Trinité Festival.** It begins with the Procession of the Golden Chariot, when that gorgeous vehicle is drawn through the streets by a team of white horses, followed by richly dressed girls and clerics bearing the gilded copper reliquary that holds the skull of Ste Waudru. When the procession has returned to the church, there follows a mock battle between St George and the Dragon (known here as the "Lumeçon"), enthusiastically enjoyed by the throngs who continue to celebrate until the evening performance of the Pageant of Mons by some 2,000 musicians, singers, and actors brings the day to a close.

EXPLORING MONS

Mons is a sightseer's dream: Almost everything you'll want to see is either in, or no more than a short walk from, the Grand-Place.

THE GRAND-PLACE

The first thing you're likely to notice about Mons is its **Belfry Tower,** which sits at the highest point in the town. Don't worry if you feel an irresistible urge to giggle at your first sight—its appearance is a bit comical, and as Victor Hugo remarked, it does look somewhat like "an enormous coffee pot, flanked below the belly-level by four medium-sized teapots." And don't be perplexed if you hear the tower referred to as "le château"—it sits near the site of an old castle of the counts of Hainaut, and

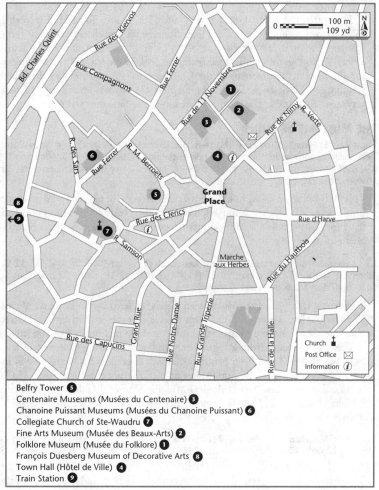

0 ⊢━━━━⊣ 100 m
          109 yd

Grand Place

Rue des Capucins

Marche aux Herbes

Rue d'Harve

Church ✝
Post Office ✉
Information ⓘ

Belfry Tower ➎
Centenaire Museums (Musées du Centenaire) ➌
Chanoine Puissant Museums (Musées du Chanoine Puissant) ➏
Collegiate Church of Ste-Waudru ➐
Fine Arts Museum (Musée des Beaux-Arts) ➋
Folklore Museum (Musée du Folklore) ➊
François Duesberg Museum of Decorative Arts ➑
Town Hall (Hôtel de Ville) ➍
Train Station ➒

even though the castle was demolished in 1866, people hereabouts have never broken the habit of using the old designation. Nothing is left of the old castle except interesting subterranean passages.

Just a short distance from the Belfry Tower is the **Chapel of St-Calixte** (☎ **065/35-12-08**), the oldest structure in Mons, dating from 1051. The chapel now holds the **Museum of the Counts' Castle** (Musée du Château des Comtes), with relics, models, and archaeological finds. It's open from May through October, Tuesday to Sunday noon to 6pm. Admission is 100 BF ($2.80) for adults, 50 BF ($1.40) for students, free for children 12 and under.

The remarkable Gothic ✪ **Collegiate Church of Ste-Waudru** (1450) honors the daughter of the count of Hainaut whose 7th-century convent marked the beginning of Mons. The church stands below the Belfry-Tower Hill, a little to the west. Inside its vast, vaulted room are sculptures and wall carvings by Mons-born Jacques du Broeck that date from the 16th century. Around the choir, a series of 16th-century stained-glass windows depict biblical scenes. At the entrance of the church, the **Golden Chariot** (Car d'Or) waits for its annual spring outing (see "Special Events," above).

The centerpiece of the Grand-Place is the 15th-century **Town Hall (Hôtel de Ville)**. Access is only by free guided tours from the tourist office, given daily during July and August at 2:30pm (at other times by prior arrangement with the tourist office). As you go through its main entrance, look to the left and perhaps stop to rub the head of "the monkey of the Grand-Garde," an iron monkey that's been granting good luck since the 15th century. Needless to say, by this time he has a very shiny pate. Inside the Town Hall are interesting tapestries and paintings.

THE MUSEUMS OF MONS

Chanoine Puissant Museums (Musées du Chanoine Puissant). rue Notre-Dame-Debonnaire 22 and rue des Sars (near the railway station). ☎ **065/33-66-70.** Admission 100 BF ($2.80) adults, 50 BF ($1.40) children 12–18, under 12 free. Tues–Sat noon–6pm, Sun 10am–noon and 2–6pm.

This 16th-century lodging house holds a rich collection of Gothic and Renaissance furnishings collected by Canon Edmond Puissant. Nearby, viewed as part of the same tour, is the restored 13th-century Chapel of St. Margaret, with its beautiful examples of religious art.

✪ Centenairé Museums (Musées du Centenaire). Grand-Place. ☎ **065/33-52-13.** Admission 100 BF ($2.80) adults, 50 BF ($1.40) children 12–18, under 12 free. Tues–Sat noon–6pm, Sun 10am–noon and 2–6pm.

The main quadrangle of the Mons Town Hall is bordered by the Jardin du Mayeur (Mayor's Garden), a courtyard that leads to a cluster of three museums, collectively known as the Centenaire Museums. Outside, there's a prehistoric standing stone.

The **War Museum** (Musée de Guerre) displays its sobering collection of relics from World Wars I and II on two floors, as well as exhibits on Mons's role in the wars. The **Numismatic Museum** (Musée de Numismatique) has more than 13,000 coins and medals. The **Archaeological Museum** (Musée d'Archéologie), contains exhibits that are based on local prehistory of the Gallo-Roman and Frankish periods.

Fine Arts Museum (Musée des Beaux-Arts). rue Neuve 8 (bordering the Jardin du Mayeur). ☎ **065/40-53-06.** Admission 100 BF ($2.80) adults, 50 BF ($1.40) children 12–18, under 12 free. Tues–Sat noon–6pm, Sun 10am–noon and 2–6pm.

This museum emphasizes 19th- and 20th-century paintings and sculpture, but also displays older, 15th- and 16th-century works such as the *Ecce Homo* by Dirck Bouts and *La Mort* by Jan Provost.

Folklore Museum (Musée du Folklore). rue Neuve, in the Maison Jean Lescarts. ☎ **065/31-43-57.** Admission 100 BF ($2.80) adults, 50 BF ($1.40) children 12–18, under 12 free. Tues–Sat noon–6pm, Sun 10am–noon and 2–6pm.

This 17th-century former convent hospital in the town center houses interesting collections of antique furniture, as well as folk and craft objects. The displays are organized according to themes, such as public welfare among the poor, religious observances, weights and measures, and Mons's Procession of the Golden Coach (see "Special Events," above).

François Duesberg Museum of Decorative Arts. Square Franklin Roosevelt 12 (entrance rue de la Houssière 2). ☎ **065/36-31-64.** Admission 150 BF ($4.15) adults, 100 BF ($2.80) children 12–18, under 12 free. Tues, Thurs, Sat, Sun 2–7pm.

This museum, which is housed in the 19th-century former National Bank of Belgium building, has a fine collection of objects from the period of 1775–1825, including exotic clocks, gilded bronzes, porcelain, crockery, gold, silverwork, and other objects. In addition, it also displays the contents of the old Ceramic Museum—more than 3,000 fine pieces of porcelain from the 17th to the 19th centuries.

NEARBY PLACES OF INTEREST

✪ **Grand-Hornu.** rue Ste-Louise 82, Hornu (8 miles southwest of Mons). ☎ **065/ 77-07-12.** Admission 100 BF ($2.80) adults, 70 BF ($1.95) students, children under 6 free. Mar–Sept Tues–Sun 10am–6pm; Oct–Feb Tues–Sun 10am–6pm.

This monument of industrial archaeology is also a memorial to an idealistic—or paternalistic—employer. Mine-owner Henri de Gorge (1774–1832) built the complex between 1810 and 1830 in neoclassical style, and attached to it some 450 well-designed and well-equipped houses for his workers. Having fallen into disuse and dereliction, Le Grand-Hornu was bought in the 1970s by a local architect and restored. It is a fascinating place, an unlikely mixture of antiquarian sensibility and gritty industrial reality that showcases the Victorian entrepreneurial tradition at its best.

Van Gogh House (Maison Van Gogh). rue du Pavillon 3, Cuesmes (2 miles south of Mons). ☎ **065/35-56-11.** Admission 50 BF ($1.40). Tues–Sun 10am–6pm.

During his missionary days, the Dutch painter Vincent van Gogh lived in this miner's house, preaching the gospel to the mining families of the Borinage and painting and drawing them and the countryside at the same time. The house has been restored as a monument, with documents and an audio-visual presentation.

NEARBY CASTLES

If you're a romantic, the Province of Hainaut has castles to suit your every fancy, three of them within easy reach of Mons. The one you really shouldn't miss is Beloeil.

✪ **Beloeil Castle (Château de Beloeil).** Beloeil village (13.5 miles northwest of Mons). ☎ **069/68-94-26.** Admission 300 BF ($8.35) adults, 160 BF ($1.65) children. Easter–May, Sat–Sun 10am–6pm; June–Sept daily 10am–6pm.

Beloeil Castle, the ancestral home of the Prince de Ligne, has been called, with some justification, the "Versailles of Belgium." It is, quite simply, magnificent. The castle sits amid French-style gardens in its own park, on the shores of a huge ornamental lake. For more than a thousand years, the de Ligne family has been intimately involved with the history of Europe. And for all that time, they have lived in the grand style that pervades these vast rooms, filled with priceless antiques, paintings by the masters, historical mementos (there's even a lock of Marie Antoinette's hair), and more than 20,000 books, many of them rare editions.

If you can get together a party of 20 or more, you can arrange a private candle-light dinner in the palatial dining room, attended by liveried servants—a once in a lifetime experience for most of us!

Mariemont Castle (Château de Mariemont). Chaussée de Mariemont 100 (16 miles from Mons), 7140 Morlanweltz-Mariemont. ☎ **064/21-21-93.** Free admission. Tues–Sun 10am–6pm.

Mariemont Castle is primarily of interest for its superb park grounds and its museum of antiques, jade, and porcelain.

WHERE TO STAY

The best hotels lie outside the city center, but within easy driving distance. Those in the city are small and moderately priced.

Casteau Resort Hotel. chaussée de Bruxelles 38, 7061 Casteau (4 miles northeast of Mons). ☎ **065/32-04-00.** Fax 065/72-87-44. 71 units. MINIBAR TV TEL. 3,650 BF ($101.40) double. Rates include breakfast. AE, DC, MC, V. Free parking.

This large hotel is now under new ownership. The renovated guest rooms are well furnished and attractive. A fine restaurant, the Ry du Vivier, serves classic French cuisine at moderate prices—750 BF ($20.85) for the menu du jour—and there are tennis courts on the grounds.

Hôtel la Forêt. chaussée Brunehault 3, 7000 Masnuy-St-Jean (off Highway 56). ☎ **065/72-36-85.** Fax 065/72-41-44. 52 units. TV TEL. 3,900 BF ($108.35) double; 6,200 ($172.20) suite. AE, DC, MC, V. Free parking.

This is one of the city's larger hotels, a little way out of town in quiet, rural surroundings. The guest rooms are nicely appointed, with peaceful views of woodlands and fields. The lobby and other public spaces have a warm, inviting look. There's also a nice bar, a good restaurant with moderate prices, and an outdoor swimming pool.

Hôtel Saint-Georges. rue des Clercs 15, 7000 Mons. ☎ **065/31-16-29.** Fax 065/31-86-71. 9 units. TV TEL. 1,340–2,400 BF ($37.20–$66.65) double. AE, CB, DC, MC, V. Limited parking available on street.

This small, centrally located, well-run hotel is good value for the money. The comfortable rooms have antique wood furniture and no carpets—only a plain beige vinyl floor covering. Six rooms have kitchenettes and two have balconies.

✪ **Infotel.** rue d'Havré 32, 7000 Mons. ☎ **065/40-18-30.** Fax 065/35-62-24. E-mail: syc@infonie.be. 25 units. TV TEL. 3,100 BF ($86.10) double; 4,100 BF ($113.90) suite. Rates include continental breakfast. AE, DC, MC, V. Free parking.

The new, centrally located Infotel is a welcome addition to Mons's hotel scene. Its pretty guest rooms come with little extra-comfort touches—wooden furnishings offset by sky-blue curtains and salmon-pink walls, for example. The hotel offers a concierge, daytime room service, and laundry and dry-cleaning service.

WHERE TO DINE

Alter Ego. rue de Nimy 6. ☎ **065/35-52-60.** Main courses 380–520 BF ($10.55–$14.45); fixed-price menu 880 BF ($24.45). AE, DC, MC, V. Wed–Mon noon–2pm; Wed–Sat 7–10pm. BELGIAN.

This centrally located restaurant is the place to sample that Belgian favorite, rabbit hotpot. For a seafood dish, try the salmon.

✪ **Devos.** rue de la Coupe 7. ☎ **065/35-13-35.** Main courses 480–760 BF ($13.35–$21.10); 5-course fixed-price menu 1,900 BF ($52.80). AE, DC, MC, V. Daily noon–2pm; Mon–Tues and Thurs–Sat 7–9:30pm. Closed 1 week in Feb, 3 weeks from mid-July. BELGIAN.

This place in the center of town is one of Mons's best restaurants. Seafood dishes are a specialty, and beef and veal are good backups. The chef will also prepare a delicious roast duckling with black cherries if you request it when booking. Try some of the menu items cooked *à la bière* (in beer).

3 The Lakes of Hainaut

The "Green Province" is dotted with lakes and nature reserves. The biggest complex of lakes is ✪ **L'Eau d'Heure** at Boussu-lez-Walcourt in the Botte de Hainaut (Boot of Hainaut) south of Charleroi, beside the N798. These artificial lakes are maintained by two major dams and three smaller ones; one of these lakes, the **Plate Taille,** is the biggest in Belgium, covering 867 acres. The entire area has been developed as a water-sports center, with designated zones for windsurfing, jet-skiing, scuba diving, yachting, and waterskiing. For information on the ecology of the area, go to the **Visitor Center** (☎ **071/63-35-34**) beside the Plate Taille Dam, which is open from Easter through October Monday to Friday 10am to 6pm (to 7pm in July and August), Saturday and Sunday 10am to 7pm. Admission is 180 BF ($2.20) for adults, 160 BF ($1.65) for seniors and children 6 to 12, free for children under 6.

Farther south, near Chimay, is the **Lakes of Virelles** (Etangs de Virelles) nature reserve, 247 acres of natural lakes, wetlands, and forest. There are guided walking tours of the reserve, and observation points for watching the birdlife. The **Visitor Center,** rue du Lac, Virelles-lez-Chimay (☎ **060/21-13-36**) has an exhibition and audio-visual presentation and is open May through September daily from 10am to 6pm; admission is 100 BF ($2.80) for adults, 60 BF ($1.65) for children 6 to 12, free for children under 6.

12 Getting to Know Holland

Like an Atlantis in reverse, Holland emerged, dripping, from the sea. Look at old maps. The country was once mainly a crazy pattern of islands, precariously separated from the North Sea by dikes and dunes. As the centuries rolled past, these islands were patiently stitched together with characteristic Dutch ingenuity and much hard work. The feat of engineering required to reclaim all that land from the sea was simply amazing. The result is a canvas-flat, green-and-silver Mondrian-canvas of a country, with half its territory and two-thirds of its 15 million people lying below the waterline.

Perhaps no other country has had such an intimate relationship with the sea. After two thousand years of living in its wake and raising walls against its permanent threat, the Dutch have had the sea driven into their national consciousness. Holland without water is as unimaginable as Saudi Arabia without sand.

1 The Physical Landscape

While visiting Holland in 1859, Matthew Arnold was so incredulous at what he saw that he wrote home, "The country has no business to be there at all." Well, maybe so—about 50% of the country's land is, after all, below sea level, and was surely meant by the Almighty to stay that way. But the Dutch have a ready answer: "God made the earth," they'll tell you, "and the Dutch made Holland." That they did, by reclaiming land from the sea and protecting it with an ingenious system of dams, dikes, and canals. Approximately 40% of Holland actually lies *below* sea level. The project began all the way back in the 8th century, and the Dutch are still at it today, working away at Zeeland's huge Delta Project to wrest even more land from the sea with the same dogged determination and patience.

Even far inland, the Dutch are closely tied to water and the sea. There are 1,100 square miles of water within the Netherlands's boundaries, much of it channeled to create canals, rerouted rivers, and lakes where once there was open sea. Indeed it is the rivers that have given Holland its historically strategic position in world shipping and trading, for this is where three of Europe's important waterways empty into the sea. From earliest recorded history, the Rhine, the Maas (it's the Meuse until it crosses Holland's border from Belgium), and the Waal have brought the products of Europe to this point on the North Sea for shipment to markets around the world.

Hole Land?

First of all, there is the matter of its name: Holland or the Netherlands? Actually, it's both, and before either of those it was called Batavia. Why all the changes? Read Thomas Coryate, writing in 1611: "The name of Batavia was commonly in use til the yeare of our Lord 860, at what time there hapend such an exceeding inundation as overflowed a great part of the country, and did so scowre and wash the very bowels of the earth that it hath bene ever since . . . hollow and spungie. For which cause the old name of Batavia was afterward changed to Holland, . . . or Hol-land . . . for hol in the Flemish tongue doth signifie as much as our word hole."

Technically, in modern times that name applies only to the two western provinces of North and South Holland. The country itself is called the Netherlands (Nederland), meaning "low lands," a designation that included Belgium from medieval times until 1830. However, most foreigners continue to refer to the whole country as "Holland."

The rivers also draw natural divisions across the terrain. To the north, above the rivers, the land is lowest; below the rivers, in the south, are higher elevations. Not much higher, however—-Holland's highest mountain is only 1,093 feet. That modest peak is in the south-east province of Limburg. Except for the forests in the central provinces of Gelderland and Utrecht, most of Holland's countryside consists of flat green fields dotted with farmhouses, as often depicted on the canvases of Dutch masters.

Those natural geographical divisions also mark religious boundaries. To the north the population is primarily Calvinist, while below the rivers the southern population is traditionally Catholic.

2 History 101

BEFORE THE 16TH CENTURY The all-important dikes, which hold back the sea, began to evolve as far back as the first century A.D., when the country's earliest inhabitants settled on unprotected marshlands in the northern regions of Friesland and Groningen. These settlers first attempted to defend their land by building huge earthen mounds (*terpen*) on which they built their homes during recurring floods. Around the 8th and 9th centuries, they were building proper dikes; and by the end of the 13th century, entire coastal regions were enclosed by dikes that held back unruly rivers as well as the sea.

Incidentally, if you think a dike is a high wall, you'll be surprised to see that actually many of them are still great mounds of earth and stone that extend for miles—like a huge rope with a flattened top. Indeed many of the roads you'll travel on are built along the tops of dikes.

Dateline

- **A.D. 1st century** The area's first inhabitants, the Frisians, settle Friesland and Groningen.
- **A.D. 4th century** Saxons settle in the east and Franks in the south.
- **814** Charlemagne, king of the Franks, dies, and Holland is divided among his sons.
- **Early 1500s** Holland falls under the rule of Charles V of Spain.
- **1555** Philip II of Spain sends the Duke of Alba to the Low Countries to begin the Inquisition.

continues

Holland

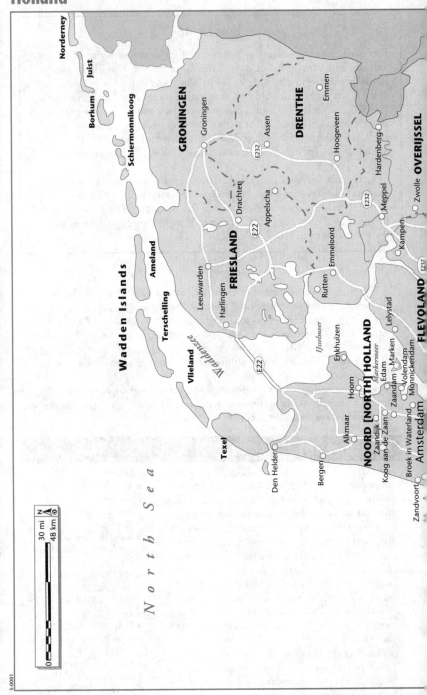

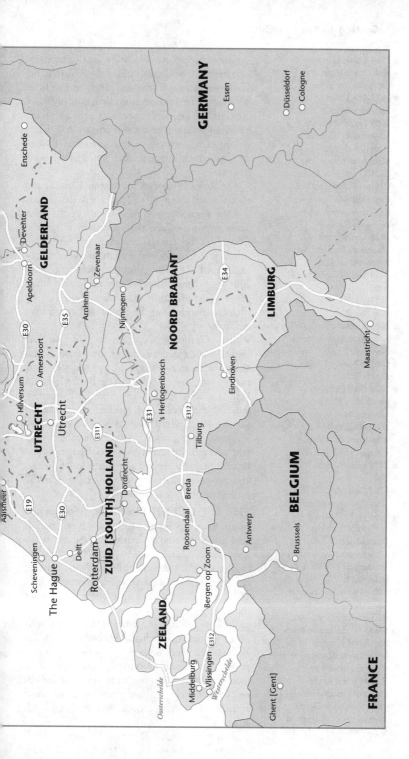

- **1568** Dutch rally against Spain in the beginning of the Eighty Years' War.
- **1579** The Union of Utrecht unites provinces of Holland.
- **1609** Beginning of the 12-year truce with Spain; Henry Hudson discovers Manhattan island.
- **1621** Dutch West India Company chartered, beginning Holland's "Golden Age" of discovery, exploration, and trade.
- **1626** Dutch purchase Manhattan from the Native Americans for $24.
- **1648** End of Eighty Years' War.
- **1652–54** First Anglo-Dutch War.
- **1664** English capture New Amsterdam and rename it New York.
- **1665–67** Second Anglo-Dutch War.
- **1672–74** Third Anglo-Dutch War; Dutch recapture New York.
- **1689** William III and his wife, Mary, become king and queen of England.
- **1780** Fourth Anglo-Dutch War.
- **1782** Dutch become first to officially recognize nationhood of the United States, and first to float loans to the United States.
- **1795** French forces occupy Amsterdam; William V flees to England.
- **1806–10** Holland ruled by Louis Bonaparte as part of the French Empire.
- **1814–31** Holland becomes the United Kingdom of the Netherlands, a constitutional monarchy headed by Willem I, first of the House of Orange-Nassau.
- **1917** Holland maintains strict neutrality throughout World War I.

continues

Historians believe Holland's first inhabitants were members of German tribes: the Frisians in the north, the Saxons in the east, and the Franks in the south. The Frisians probably appeared before the Christian era, while the others arrived with the barbarian invasions of the 4th century A.D. Excavations of ancient *terpen* have uncovered Roman artifacts which suggests that the Frisians were traders.

The Romans invaded the area in 12 B.C., and stayed until about A.D. 300, when the Saxons and the Franks poured in. Through it all, those hardy *terpen* dwellers, the Frisians in the north, refused to be conquered, even by religion—although the Franks in the south embraced Christianity in the late 5th century, it would be another 200 years before the Frisians abandoned their pagan gods, and then only when compelled by Charlemagne, king of the Franks and emperor of the West.

After Charlemagne's death in 814, his vast empire was divided among his sons. Soon Dutch history began to take shape through alliances, marriages, feuds, and outright warfare. By the 13th and 14th centuries the nobility were busy building most of the castles and fortified manor houses throughout Holland that now attract tourists. Meanwhile, the Catholic hierarchy grew both powerful and wealthy; the bishoprics of Maastricht and Utrecht played a key role in the politics of the era, and preserved their legacy by erecting splendid cathedrals, abbeys, and monasteries.

THE 16TH CENTURY As the 16th century began, foreign political maneuvering brought Holland under the rule of Charles V of Spain. At the same time, Dutch citizens were beginning to embrace the Protestant church. When Charles relinquished the Spanish throne to his son Philip in 1555, things took a nasty turn for the Dutch since the new king dispatched the infamous duke of Alba to the Low Countries to carry out the Inquisition's "death to heretics" edict. The Dutch statesman William the Silent declared: "I cannot approve of princes attempting to control the conscience of their subjects and wanting to rob them of the liberty of faith." Nor, as history has proved time and again in the years since, could the rest of the Dutch citizenry!

Rallying behind William the Silent, the Dutch mounted a fierce resistance even though city after city fell into Spanish hands. The turning point came at Leiden. In a desperate and brilliantly successful move, William flooded the province and sailed his ships to the very walls of the city, catching the Spanish troops at their dinner. The result was a rout—and a new national dish for the Dutch as well. The stew pot (*hutspot*) left bubbling by the fleeing enemy became a cherished symbol of the triumph of freedom.

With the Union of Utrecht, signed in 1579, the seven provinces of Holland united against their covetous neighbors: France, Spain, and England. However, the struggle with Spain was to continue until 1648—the conflict became known as the Eighty Years' War. By the early 1600s, however, William's son, Prince Maurice, headed a States-General governing body for the seven Dutch provinces, initiating a new era.

THE 17TH TO THE 19TH CENTURY   The 17th century, sometimes called Holland's "Golden Age," heralded an era of Dutch exploration and prosperity. The newly organized Dutch East India and Dutch West India companies were profiting from the spice trade; Dutch explorers were establishing the infant Nieuw Amsterdam (later to be called New York); Abel Tasman was sailing around the South Pacific, discovering New Zealand, the Fiji Islands, Tonga, and Tasmania; and the Dutch Indonesian colonies were established. At home, the merchants who financed all those voyages grew richer, built gabled houses, dug canal after canal, and applauded as the young William III married into the English royal family and shared the English throne with his wife.

Holland was also becoming a refuge for persecuted groups. The Pilgrims stopped here for a dozen years before embarking for America, Jews fled the oppressive Spanish and welcomed the tolerance of the Dutch, and refugees straggled in from France and Portugal. William the Silent had helped to create a climate of tolerance in Holland, which attracted talented newcomers who contributed to the expanding economic, social, artistic, and intellectual climate of the country.

Conflict arose, however, between Holland and England—in part because of their lively competition on the seas. Needless to say, Dutch support for the new United States of America (Holland was the first to recognize the fledgling country's nationhood and even extended three substantial loans to the new government) did little to heal the breach with the British. By the time William V—with his

- **1932** The Enclosing Dike is completed, turning the Zuiderzee into the freshwater lake IJsselmeer.
- **1940** Holland occupied by Nazi forces; Queen Wilhelmina enters exile in London.
- **1942** Dutch East Indies occupied by Japan.
- **1944–45** Holland liberated by Allied forces.
- **1948** Queen Wilhelmina abdicates in favor of her daughter, Juliana.
- **1949** Holland joins NATO; grants independence to Indonesia.
- **1953** Devastating North Sea storms produce significant coastal flooding. Dutch embark on long-range Delta Project to seal off river estuaries in the south-west.
- **1962** Dutch relinquish control over western part of New Guinea.
- **1975** Holland grants independence to Surinam.
- **1980** Queen Juliana abdicates, and her eldest daughter Beatrix accedes to the throne.
- **1981** Dutch vigorously oppose any U.S. missiles on their soil.
- **1990** Holland celebrates the centenary of Vincent van Gogh's death. Millions visit the special exhibition at the Vincent van Gogh Museum in Amsterdam.
- **1995** Wim Kok becomes Prime Minister, replacing Ruud Lubbers at the head of the coalition government.
- **1997** Holland is one of the few European Union nations to meet the strict financial criteria set by the Treaty of Maastricht for the European Monetary Union (EMU). The Treaty of Amsterdam is ratified during the "Eurotop" summit.

continues

- **1998** Wim Kok enters his second term as prime minister, at the head of "Paars-II," the 2nd "purple" coalition government.
- **1999** Holland joins ten other European Union countries in launching the new European currency, the euro.

mixed Dutch-Anglo background—ascended the Dutch throne, anti-British sentiment was so strong that in 1795 he was exiled to England and a new Batavian Republic was set up, aligning itself with France.

In 1808 Napoléon declared his brother, Louis Bonaparte, King of the Netherlands, and installed him in a palace that had been Amsterdam's Town Hall. In 1810 Napoléon was back in Holland, drawn by the threat of a British landing in Zeeland.

Then came Waterloo in 1815. With Napoléon finally defeated once and for all, the Dutch recalled the House of Orange and installed yet another William as king—this time as head of a constitutional monarchy. To mark the beginning of their new republic, the Dutch decided that *this* Willem (their native spelling) should become Willem I. Thus began the House of Orange-Nassau, which still reigns today.

THE 20TH CENTURY Holland escaped the ravages of World War I by maintaining a strict neutrality. It was a different story in World War II, however, as Nazi troops invaded in 1940. The occupation was complete and devastating: An estimated 104,000 of Holland's 112,000 Jews were murdered, Rotterdam sustained heavy bombings, and the rest of the country also suffered terribly at the hands of its invaders. During the war the Dutch operated one of the most effective underground movements in Europe, which became an important factor in the liberation of Holland in 1945.

That liberation began with Operation Market Garden in September 1944, the largest airborne operation in history. The U.S. 82nd and 101st Airborne Divisions, the British 1st Airborne Division, and the Polish 1st Parachute Brigade—a total of 35,000 paratroops and gliderborne infantry—landed at key points along the road from Eindhoven through Nijmegen to Arnhem, to capture the bridges over the rivers Maas, Waal, and Rhine for the ground forces to break through into Hitler's Germany. Amid grim fighting, the operation was a partial success, but the critical bridge over the River Rhine at Arnhem remained in German hands. The unliberated parts of Holland were plunged into the terrible Hunger Winter, as Allied troops fought their way slowly forward through mud and flooded polderland. The Canadians reached Amsterdam first in May 1945, but only after Germany's unconditional surrender.

During World War II the Dutch colonies in the Far East were captured by the Japanese. At war's end the Indonesian colonists took up a determined fight for their independence, which they finally achieved in 1949. In 1963 Holland relinquished control over the western half of New Guinea, which became part of Indonesia, and in 1975 it granted independence to Surinam.

Impressions

My love for plane geometry prepared me to feel a special affection for Holland. For the Dutch landscape has all the qualities that make geometry so delightful. A tour in Holland is a tour through the first book of Euclid. Over a country that is the ideal plane surface of the geometry books, the roads and the canals trace out the shortest distances between point and point.

—Aldous Huxley, *Along the Road* (1925)

In 1953, devastating North Sea storms broke through the dikes in many places along Holland's southwest coast, flooding significant areas. There was a substantial loss of life and property. In order to assure greater protection along its coastal areas, Holland embarked upon a long-range Delta Project to seal off the river estuaries in the south-west of the country.

HOLLAND TODAY   In recent decades, more land has been reclaimed from the sea; a large part of the new "*polder*," Flevoland, was pumped dry in 1957, followed by another dammed-in area in 1968. Some 100,000 Dutch citizens now live and work on land that used to be under an arm of the North Sea called the Zuiderzee.

Since Holland's population has tripled during this century, the Dutch are at work reclaiming more land. In 1997 Holland's population exceeded 16 million—due in part to immigration from the former Indonesian colonies—and the country is now one of the most densely populated countries in the world, with 960 people per square mile. The crowding is most noticeable in the western *Randstad* (Rim City), the heavily populated area that includes the cities of Amsterdam, Rotterdam, The Hague, Leiden, Haarlem, Utrecht, and Delft. Elsewhere, the land is much more sparsely populated.

With a scarcity of raw materials and the loss of Indonesia, Holland is making a concerted—and thus far successful—effort to develop high-technology industries. Many multinational conglomerates have established their headquarters, branch operations, or plants here. Despite this influx of new industry and the EU as a market for a significant proportion of its exports, Holland's unemployment is close to 10%, a number that only remains tolerable because of generous social benefits, which put a strain on the nation's finances and lead to high taxation.

For the visitor, Holland today presents much the same face it has over the centuries—a serenely scenic landscape and an industrious population who treasure their age-old tradition of tolerance and who welcome people of all political, religious, and ideological persuasions.

THE DUTCH POLITICAL SCENE

Holland is a constitutional monarchy headed by Queen Beatrix and her consort Prince Claus. The heir-apparent is their oldest son, Willem-Alexander (born 1967). Parliament consists of two houses—an Upper Chamber and a Lower Chamber. The three major political parties are the Christian Democrats, the Labor party, and the Liberal party.

In 1981 Prime Minister Van Agt supported the deployment of U.S. cruise missiles in Holland; public opposition to this (as well as his controversial economic policy) led to his defeat in the 1982 elections. He was followed by Ruud Lubbers, who in 1995 was replaced as Prime Minister by Wim Kok.

3 Art & Architecture

ART

The 17th century was the undisputed Golden Age of Dutch art. During this busy time, artists were blessed with wealthy patrons whose support allowed them to give free reign to their talents. Art held a cherished place in the hearts of average Dutch citizens too, as Peter Mundy, who traveled to Amsterdam in 1640, observed: "Many times blacksmiths and cobblers will have some picture or other by their forge and in their stall. Such is the general notion, inclination, and delight that these county natives have to paintings." The Dutch were particularly fond of pictures that depicted their world: landscapes, seascapes, domestic scenes, portraits, and still lifes. The art of this period remains some of the greatest ever created in Holland.

One of the finest landscape painters of all time was **Jacob van Ruysdael** (1628–1682), who depicted cornfields, windmills, and forest scenes, along with his famous views of Haarlem. In some of his works the human figure is very small, and in others it does not appear at all; instead the artist typically devoted two-thirds of the canvas to the vast skies filled with the moody clouds that float over the flat terrain of Holland.

Frans Hals (1581–1666), the undisputed leader of the Haarlem school, specialized in portraiture. The relaxed relationship between the artist and his subject in his paintings was a great departure from the formal masks of Renaissance portraits. With the lightness of his brushstrokes, Hals was able to convey an immediacy and intimacy. He not only produced perceptive psychological portraits, but also had a genius for comic characters—he showed men and women as they are and as a little less than they are in such works as *Malle Babbe* (1650). Hals also excelled in producing group portraits, such as *The Archers of St Aidan*. He carefully planned and balanced the directions of pose, gesture, and glance, but his *alla prima* brushwork (direct laying-down of a pigment) makes these public images appear as spontaneous reportage. It's worth visiting the Frans Hals Museum in Haarlem to see his techniques in action.

One of the geniuses of Western art was **Rembrandt van Rijn** (1606–69). This highly prolific and influential artist had a dramatic life filled with success and personal tragedy. Rembrandt was a master at showing the soul and inner life of man, in both his portraits and illustrations of biblical stories. His most famous work, the group portrait known as *The Night Watch* (1642), is on view in the Rijksmuseum in Amsterdam.

Rembrandt's use of lights and darks was influenced by Caravaggio, like Hals and Van Honthorst before him, but was much more refined. For him, the values of light and dark gradually and softly blended together; although his paintings probably lose some of the drama of chiaroscuro, they achieve a more truthful appearance. The light that falls upon a face in a Rembrandt portrait is mysterious yet revealing of character.

Rembrandt's series of religious paintings and prints are highly personal and human in spirit. The overall stillness of his religious work reflects an inner contemplation. He depicted Christ as a humble and gentle Nazarene, with a loving and melancholy expression. Rembrandt's religious prints (etchings) were a major source of income during his lifetime.

A spirituality reigns over his self-portraits as well; Rembrandt did about 60 of these during his lifetime. The *Self-Portrait with Saskia* shows the artist with his wife during prosperous times, when he was often commissioned by wealthy merchants to do portraits. But later self-portraits show his transition from an optimistic to an old man worn down by care and anxiety. At the Rembrandt House in Amsterdam—which has been restored to much the way it was when the artist lived and worked there—you can see the above self-portrait along with some 250 etchings.

In his later years, while at the height of his artistic powers, Rembrandt's work was judged too personal and eccentric by his contemporaries. Many considered him to be a tasteless painter obsessed with the ugly and ignorant of color; this was the prevailing opinion until the 19th century, when Rembrandt's genius was reevaluated.

Jan Vermeer (1632–75) of Delft is perhaps the best known of the "little Dutch masters." These painters restricted themselves to one type of painting, such as

Impressions

As for Holland: In the first place the cows wear coats; then the cyclists go in flocks like starlings, gathering together, skimming in and out. Driving is dangerous.
—Virginia Woolf (1935)

portraiture. Although the scope of their work was narrow, they rendered their subjects with an exquisite care and faithfulness to actual appearances.

The main subjects of Vermeer's work are the activities and pleasures of simple home life. Vermeer placed the figure(s) at the center of his paintings, and typically used the background space to convey a feeling of stability and serenity. Vermeer excelled at reproducing the lighting of his interior scenes. Art historians know that Vermeer made use of mirrors and the *camera obscura,* an early camera, as compositional aids. His paintings give a wonderful illusion of three-dimensionality: As light—usually afternoon sunshine pouring in through an open window—moves across the picture plane, it caresses and modifies all the colors.

If **Vincent van Gogh** (1853–90) had not failed as a missionary in the mining region of Belgium, he might not have turned to painting and become the greatest Dutch artist of the 19th century. *The Potato Eaters* (1885) was Van Gogh's first masterpiece. This rough, crudely painted work shows a group of peasants gathered around the table for their evening meal after a long day of manual labor—gone is the traditional beauty and serenity of earlier Dutch genre painting.

After the death of his father, Van Gogh traveled first to Antwerp and then to Paris to join his favorite brother, Theo. In Paris Van Gogh discovered and adopted the rich, brilliant color palette of the Impressionists. Through Theo, an art dealer, Van Gogh met Paul Gauguin, and the two had many conversations on the expressive power of pure color. Van Gogh developed a thick brushwork—with a textile-like texture—that complemented his intense color schemes.

In 1888, Van Gogh traveled to Arles in Provence, where he was dazzled by the Mediterranean sun. His favorite color, yellow, which signified love to him, dominated landscapes such as *Wheatfield with a Reaper* (1889). For the next 2 years until his death, Van Gogh remained in the south of France; here he painted at a frenetic pace in between bouts of madness. In *The Night Café* (1888), Van Gogh plays up the complementary colors of red walls and green ceiling to give an oppressive air to this billiard-hall scene. (With red and green, Vincent wrote, he tried to represent "those terrible things, men's passions.") We see the halos around the lights swirl as if we, like some of the patrons slumped over at their tables, have had too much to drink. Perhaps Van Gogh's best-known nightscape is *The Starry Night* (1889); with its whirling starlight, Vincent's turbulent universe is filled with personal anxiety and fear.

The Vincent van Gogh Museum in Amsterdam has more than 200 of his paintings—including all those named above —presented to Holland by Theo's wife and son with the provision that they not leave Vincent's native land.

Did you know that before **Piet Mondrian** (1872–1944) became a master/originator of De Stijl (also called neoplasticism) he painted windmills, cows, and prairies? One of his expressionistic masterpieces, *The Red Tree*—which looks as though it's exploding on fire against a background of blue—marked a turning point in his career as a contemporary painter. The artist had always said he would drop one of the two a's in his last name (it was originally spelled Mondriaan) when he had found his true personality; this canvas, which he completed at 41, he signed as Mondrian.

With his friend, Theo van Doesburg, Mondrian began a magazine in 1917 entitled *De Stijl* (The Style) in which he expounded the principles of neoplasticism: a simplification of forms, or in other words, a purified abstraction. In large part, this movement was an outgrowth of and reaction against the cubist work of Picasso and Braque, which Mondrian had seen while he lived in Paris from 1912 to 1914.

To Mondrian and the poets, sculptors, and architects associated with De Stijl, abstraction was a moral necessity. They believed that simplifying vision would simplify life, and that a universal plastic language would bring about a better world. The geometric painters of the De Stijl school attempted a "controllable precision." Their basic form was the rectangle—with horizontal and vertical accents at right angles. Their basic colors were the primaries—red, blue, and yellow—along with black and white. In works like *Composition in Blue, Yellow, and Black* (1936) (Haags Gemeentemuseum, The Hague), no part of the picture plane is more important than any other; with its design, Mondrian achieves an equilibrium but does not succumb to a mechanical uniformity.

Mondrian suppressed the use of curves and the color green in his later work because, he said, these reminded him of nature. But it's ironic to note that to support himself Mondrian had to paint flowers on porcelain for much of his life. In 1940 Mondrian moved to New York, which he loved, to escape the war in Europe. In the evenings he would take walks around the art deco Rockefeller Center; the geometry of the lighted windows reminded him of his paintings. Mondrian's last paintings were lively abstract representations of New York. One of those, *Victory Boogie Woogie,* was just purchased with a loan from the Dutch National Bank for a sweet $40 million! It's now on display in the Haags Gemeentemuseum in The Hague.

ARCHITECTURE

Few examples of early Dutch architecture remain. Chief among the Romanesque structures are the Basilica of Our Lady and the St. Servaasbasiliek, both in Maastricht. In the medieval period Holland was influenced by Germany and the Baltic countries, rather than by the more ornate Gothic architecture of France and Belgium. Utrecht and Haarlem Cathedrals are two examples of Dutch-style Gothic, along with the church of St. Peter in Leiden.

In the 16th and 17th centuries **Hendrick de Keyser** (1565–1621) developed the Renaissance-style house. Today the Herengracht, Keizersgracht, and Prinsengracht canals of Amsterdam are lined with these terraced homes. In his work, the medieval stepped gable gave way to a more ornate one with scrolled sides, decorative finials, and other features. De Keyser also built the city's Zuiderkerk, the Westerkerk, the Noorderkerk, and the landmark Mint Tower.

Later in the 17th century, Dutch Palladianism developed in The Hague. The most famous example is the city's Mauritshuis, which was designed by Pieter Post and Jacob van Campen. The Renaissance and Palladian styles of architecture remained popular until the advent of neoclassicism and the design of such Second Empire Renaissance buildings as Amsterdam's Amstel Hotel, by Cornelis Outshoorn. The best-known practitioner of neo-Gothic, though, is **P. J. Cuypers,** who designed both the Rijksmuseum and the Centraal Station in Amsterdam, with their gables, steep roofs, and dormers. He also designed the Vondelkerk and the Maria Magdalenkerk, both of brick with polychrome decoration and a wealth of turrets, spires, and arches.

At the end of the century this heavily ornamented look was simplified by, among others, Willem Kromhout, who designed the American Hotel in Amsterdam, which is worth visiting. Hendrik Berlage followed; his Amsterdam Stock Exchange and the

Diamond Workers' Trade Union building are two examples of a more austere Dutch style.

Holland showed little inclination to dabble in art nouveau, although J. M. van der Meij approached it with his Scheepvaarthuis (Shipping Offices) on the Prins Hendrikkade in Amsterdam. Among the more modern functionalists, J. P. Oud and Willem Dudok are the best known.

4 Sports & Recreation

Water sports, as you might expect, predominate in Holland. Sailing, yachting, windsurfing, and waterskiing are all popular, and you'll find the Dutch eager to assist any water-sports enthusiast. The VVV tourist offices can tell you where equipment can be rented. Holland's beaches can afford good swimming but the currents are often strong and treacherous—it's best to stick to resort areas where waters are safe and lifeguards present. There are also many public swimming pools, both indoor and outdoor.

Fishing is another favorite in Holland. The VVV can guide you to rental equipment for trying your luck on inland lakes and rivers as well as to charter boats for deep-sea fishing. No license is needed for fishing either out at sea or on the shore, and there are no seasonal restrictions. You must, however, have a license for inland fishing, available at any post office. Consult the tourist board pamphlet "Fishing" for complete details on regulations and a guide to good fishing locations.

Tennis and **golf** facilities are spotty in Holland, although local VVV offices can usually point you to tennis clubs and private golf clubs, many of which welcome visitors. Only five public golf courses exist in the country: at Rotterdam, Rhoon, Oostvoorne, Velsen/IJmuiden, and Wowse Plantage.

Equestrians will want to pick up a copy of the tourist board's "Horseriding" publication. It gives the addresses of stables, horseback-riding schools, and pony camps for children.

5 A Taste of Holland

FOOD

Dutch national dishes tend to be of the ungarnished, hearty, wholesome variety—solid, stick-to-your-ribs stuff. A perfect example is *erwtensoep*, a thick pea soup cooked with ham or sausage that provides inner warmth against cold Dutch winters and is filling enough to be a meal by itself. Similarly, *hutspot*, a potato-based "hotchpotch," or stew, is no-nonsense nourishment to which *klapstuk* (lean beef) is sometimes added. *Hutspot* also has an interesting intangible ingredient—see "History 101," for the story of its origin.

Seafood, as you might imagine in this traditionally seafaring country, is always fresh and well prepared. Fried sole, oysters from Zeeland, mussels, and herring (fresh in May, pickled other months) are most common. In fact, if you happen to be in Holland for the beginning of the herring season, it's an absolute obligation—at least once—to interrupt your sidewalk strolls to buy a "green" herring from a pushcart; prices run the gamut from dirt cheap to astronomical. The Dutch are also uncommonly fond of oily, freshwater eel.

At **lunchtime,** you're likely to find yourself munching on *broodjes*, small buttered rolls usually filled with ham and cheese or beef, although a *broodje gezond* (healthy sandwich) with cheese and vegetables is a good choice for vegetarians. Not to be missed are the delicious, filling pancakes called *pannekoeken,* often eaten as a savory dish with bacon and cheese. *Poffertjes* are a sweet, lighter, penny-sized version that are especially good topped with apples, jam, or syrup. **Desserts** at any meal lean toward dairy products, fruit with lots of fresh cream, ice cream, or *appelgebak,* a lovely and light apple pastry. Dutch *gebak* (pastries) are fresh, varied, and inexpensive; and you will notice the Dutch sitting down for a *koffee* and one of these delicious *hapjes* (small snacks, or literally, "bites") throughout the day—why not join them?

That, briefly, is the Dutch cuisine—which is not to say that it's the only cuisine available in Holland. Far from it! The popular Indonesian *rijsttafel* (rice table), a feast of 15 to 30 small portions of different dishes eaten with plain rice, has been a national favorite ever since it arrived in the 17th century. If you've never experienced this mini-feast, it should definitely be on your "must-eat" list for Holland—the basic idea behind the *rijsttafel* is to sample a wide variety of complementary flavors, textures, and temperatures: savory and sweet, spicy and mild. You'll also find the cuisines of France, China, Italy, Greece, Turkey, Yugoslavia, and several other nationalities well represented.

THE RESTAURANTS

At the top of the restaurant scale are those posh dining rooms affiliated with the prestigious Alliance Gastronomique Néerlandaise or the Relais du Centre. They're likely to be elegant and sophisticated or atmospherically Old World and quaint. They will certainly be expensive. Many restaurants are not open for lunch. Dinner is generally served from 6 to 10 or 11pm, 6 or 7 days a week.

For authentic Dutch dishes, look for the **neerlands dis** sign, which identifies restaurants specializing in the native cuisine. Tourist offices in the United States as well as Holland can supply a leaflet with the addresses of many of these places.

Then there are the numerous moderately priced restaurants and the brown cafes, which are cozy social centers with simple but tasty food, sometimes served outside on sidewalk tables in good weather. Sidewalk vendors, with fresh herring and the ubiquitous *broodjes* (sandwiches) or other light specialties, are popular as well.

Two things you should know about all restaurants: Dutch menus list appetizers, *not main courses,* under "entree"; and a 15% service charge plus VAT is included in almost all prices.

A GLOSSARY OF DUTCH CUISINE

Bitterballen   Fried potato balls, or croquettes, generally quite spicy. Often served at bars.

Broodjes   Sandwiches made of small rolls filled with beef, ham, cheese, or other stuffings.

Croquetten   Delicious fried croquettes with soft innards made from a variety of meats and served with mustard. Eaten "straight," or spread on bread as a warm *broodje.*

Erwtensoep   A thick pea soup (usually available only in winter) frequently served with sausage and brown bread—traditionally, it should be thick enough to hold a spoon upright!

Hutspot   The thick stew of potatoes, carrots, onions, and lean meat—hutspot was said to have been left behind by Spanish soldiers as they fled the Dutch attack on Leiden in 1574.

Nieuwe Haring   Fresh-caught herring, eaten raw in summer months only, with or without onions; pickled herring is eaten year-round.

Pannekoeken   Plate-size pancakes served with a choice of savory or sweet toppings ranging from savoury chicken ragout or ham and cheese to sweet cooked apples, with the sweet toppings usually drowned in lashings of pure cane syrup.

Poffertjes   Small pancake "puffs" sprinkled with confectioner's sugar.

Rijsttafel   An Indonesian "rice table," with as many as two or three dozen different small dishes served, along with plenty of rice to buffer the spicy vegetables and fruits. Among the customary dishes of a *rijsttafel* are *loempia* (classic Chinese-style egg rolls), *satay* or *sateh* (small kebabs of beef, chicken, or pork, grilled and served with a spicy peanut sauce), *perkedel* (meatballs), *gado-gado* (vegetables in peanut sauce), *daging smoor* (beef in soy sauce), *babi ketjap* (pork in soy sauce), *kroepoek* (crunchy, puffy shrimp toast), *serundeng* (fried coconut), *roedjak manis* (fruit in sweet sauce), and *pisang goreng* (fried banana). A *rijsttafel* is best accompanied by beer, mineral water, or a similar cold drink—not with milk or wine.

Saucijzenbroodje   A spicy Dutch sausage wrapped in flaky pastry, much like the British sausage roll.

Tosti's   Grilled cheese-and-ham sandwiches.

Uitsmijter   An open-face sandwich consisting of a slice of bread (or two), buttered and topped with cold slices of ham or roast beef and one or two fried eggs. (The name, incidentally, also means "bouncer," as in the burly doorman at a club.)

Vlammetjes (little flames)   These diminutive spring rolls belong to the same general family of *borrelhapjes* (drinking snacks) as *bitterballen*. As the name suggests, they (like Napoléon) make up in fiery aggression for what they lack in size.

DRINK

What to drink? **Beer,** for one thing. As you make the rounds of the brown cafes (the traditional Dutch watering holes) you can get the regular brands such as Heineken, Grolsch, or Amstel, or you could try something different. I happen to like the *witte* (white) beer, which is sweeter than *pils,* the regular beer. Or, on the opposite end of the spectrum, you can have a Belgian dark beer, like De Koninck or Duvel. (Belgian beers are very popular in Holland and are, in general, better made, more "artisanal," than the local brews.)

Then there is the marvelous—and potent!—native gin known as *jenever,* a fiery, colorless liquid served ice cold and drunk "neat"—without any mixer, or even ice. *Jonge* (young) jenever is less sweet and creamy than the *oude* (old) variety, but both are known for their delayed-action effectiveness. There are also very good Dutch liqueurs, such as Curaçao and Triple Sec. Wines from all over the world are available as well.

13

Planning a Trip to Holland

This chapter deals with the practicalities of a visit to Holland—and above all else, Holland is a practical country. Rail and bus connections to other European destinations are excellent. And whether you choose to drive or use the excellent Dutch public transportation system, getting around within the country is a simple matter.

1 Visitor Information & Money

VISITOR INFORMATION

International addresses for the Netherlands Board of Tourism are given in "Visitor Information" in chapter 2.

In Holland, you'll find one of the most efficient, best-organized tourist organizations you're likely to meet up with anywhere. The **Vereniging voor Vreemdelingenverkeer** (Association for Tourist Traffic), known simply as the **VVV,** operates more than 400 offices in cities, towns, and villages around the country. VVV offices can book accommodations for you, help with travel arrangements, tell you what's going on where, and . . . well, if there's anything they can't do, I have yet to discover it! Look for a blue-and-white sign (often triangular in shape) bearing the letters "VVV." The umbrella organization for the VVV offices is the **Netherlands Board of Tourism (NBT),** Vlietweg 15, Postbus 458, 2260 MG Leidschendam (☎ 070/371-5705; fax 070/320-1654).

MONEY

Holland's basic monetary unit is the guilder (abbreviated NLG), but it's often referred to as the Dutch florin (abbreviated f, fl, or Dfl, which is the form used in this book). There are 100 Dutch cents to a guilder, and prices are expressed in the familiar decimal system.

There are six Dutch **coins** currently in circulation: Dfl .05 (called a *stuivertje*), Dfl .10 (*dubbeltje*), Dfl .25 (*kwartje*), Dfl 1 (*gulden*), Dfl 2.50 (*rijksdaalder*), and Dfl 5 (*beatrix*). The six Dutch **banknotes** come in different colors: Dfl 10 (blue), Dfl 25 (red), Dfl 50 (orange/yellow), Dfl 100 (brown), Dfl 250 (purple), and Dfl 1,000 (green). Each note has a little rough patch in one corner indicating its value in braille.

CURRENCY EXCHANGE Banks usually offer the best exchange rates. It's possible to change your traveler's checks or

The Dutch Guilder

At this writing $1 = approximately Dfl 2 (or Dfl 1 = 50¢) and £1 = approximately Dfl 3.20 (or Dfl 1 = 31 pence); these were the rates of exchange used to calculate the dollar and pound values given in this book and the table below (rounded off).

Dfl	U.S. $	U.K. £	Dfl	U.S. $	U.K. £
.25	.13	.05	30	15.00	10.70
.50	.25	.20	35	17.50	12.50
.75	.37	.25	40	20.00	14.30
1.00	.50	.36	45	22.50	16.05
2.00	1.00	.70	50	25.00	17.85
3.00	1.50	1.05	60	30.00	21.45
4.00	2.00	1.45	70	35.00	25.00
5.00	2.50	1.80	80	40.00	28.55
6.00	3.00	2.15	90	45.00	32.15
7.00	3.50	2.50	100	50.00	35.70
8.00	4.00	2.85	125	62.50	44.65
9.00	4.50	3.20	150	75.00	53.55
10.00	5.00	3.55	175	87.50	62.50
15.00	7.50	5.35	200	100.00	71.40
20.00	10.00	7.15	250	125.00	89.30
25.00	12.50	8.90	300	150.00	107.15

foreign currency outside banking hours at some 65 GWK Bureau de Change offices: 30 of them are in railway stations and others are at border checkpoints. These places have extended evening and weekend hours; the offices at Amsterdam Centraal Station and at Schiphol Airport are open 24 hours daily. The GWK can also provide cash advances for holders of American Express, Diners Club, Master-Card, and Visa credit and charge cards, and handles money transfers via Western Union as well. It charges a small commission fee, to a maximum of Dfl 5 ($2.50), for each cash, traveler's check, or credit/charge-card cash-advance transaction.

Many tourist offices in coastal resorts also provide currency exchange, as do American Express offices, and numerous other commercial bureau de change companies, which invariably charge higher fees.

Luxembourg is one of the first wave of 11 countries that are establishing the new European currency called the euro (see the box in chapter 4).

2 When to Go

"In-season" in Holland means mid-April through mid-October. The peak of the tourist season is July and August, when the weather is at its finest. Weather, however, is never really extreme at any time of year; and if you're one of the growing numbers who favor shoulder- or off-season travel, you'll find Holland every bit as attractive during those months. Not only are airlines, hotels, and restaurants cheaper and less crowded during this time (with more relaxed and personalized service), but there are also some very appealing events going on. Holland's bulb fields

What Things Cost in Amsterdam	U.S. $
Taxi from the airport to the city center	30.00
Metro from Centraal Station to Waterlooplein	1.50
Local telephone call	.15
Double room at the Grand Hotel (very expensive)	410.00
Double room at the American Hotel (expensive)	275.00
Double room at the Ambassade Hotel (moderate)	162.50
Double room at Hotel Seven Bridges (inexpensive)	90.00
Lunch for one at Café de Jaren (moderate)	15.00
Lunch for one at Maoz Falafel (inexpensive)	4.00
Dinner for one, without wine, at De Goudsbloem (very expensive)	70.00
Dinner for one, without wine, at Bodega Keyzer (moderate)	30.00
Dinner for one, without wine, at 't Gasthuys (inexpensive)	12.00
Glass of beer	2.00
Coca-Cola	1.50
Cup of coffee	1.75
Roll of ASA 100 color film, 36 exposures	7.50
Admission to the Vincent van Gogh Museum	6.00
Movie ticket	7.50
Concert ticket for the Concertgebouw	17.50–62.50

are bursting with color from mid-April to mid-May; September usually has a few weeks of late summery weather; and there are even sunny spells in winter, when brilliant and crisp weather often alternates with dramatic clouded skies.

CLIMATE   Holland has a maritime climate, which means that there are few extremes in temperature in summer or winter. Summer temperatures average about 67°F (19°C); the winter average is 35°F (2°C). Expect more than a little rain, however (it's driest from February through May).

HOLIDAYS   Public holidays in Holland are January 1 (New Year's Day), Good Friday, Easter Sunday and Monday, April 30 (Queen's Day), Ascension Day, Whitsunday and Whit Monday (the 7th Sunday after Easter and the following day), December 25 (Christmas), and December 26 (Boxing Day).

In addition, there are two "Remembrance Days" related to World War II, neither of which is an official holiday, although you may find some shops closed: May 4 honors all those who died in the war, and May 5 celebrates Liberation Day.

HOLLAND CALENDAR OF EVENTS

One of the biggest and most eagerly awaited events in Holland is the **Elfstedentocht,** the 11-town race in which skaters compete over a 125-mile course through the Friesland province north of Amsterdam. The first race was run in 1909, and it has been run only 13 times since. Perhaps the weather and ice conditions will allow the race to be held when you are visiting. If so, it's well worth going out of your way to see—or even to take part in. Contact **Provincial VVV Friesland** (☎ **0900/ 202-4060**).

January
- **Rotterdam International Film Festival.** Contact Stichting Film Festival Rotterdam, Postbus 21696, 3001 AR Rotterdam (☎ **010/411-8080;** fax 010/413-5132). End of January and first week of February.

February
- **Carnival,** Maastricht, Den Bosch, and other southern towns and cities. Contact the provincial VVV offices in Limburg (☎ **043/601-3364;** fax 043/601-6725) and Noord-Brabant (☎ **0900/112-2334;** fax 073/612-8930). Dates vary; usually 7 weeks before Easter.
- **West Frisian Flora,** Bovenkarspel, North Holland. Bulb and household furnishings trade show. Contact Westfriese Flora, Postbus 23, 1610 AA Bovenkarspel (☎ **0228/511-644;** fax 0228/516-130). Throughout February.

March
- **Windmill Days,** Zandam. All windmills in the Zaanse Schans are open to the public. Contact VVV Zaandam (☎ **075/616-2221;** fax 075/670-5381). March through October.
- **European Fine Art Fair.** An international art and antiques fair at the Maastricht Exhibition and Congress Center, with art dealers from around the world presenting their finest objects. Contact TEFAF Maastricht, Postbus 1035, 5200 BA, Den Bosch (☎ **073/614-5165;** fax 073/614-7360). Second week in March.
- **Opening of Keukenhof Flower Gardens,** Lisse. Spectacular showing of hyacinths, narcissi, and tulips. Contact Keukenhof (☎ **0252/465-555**). Late March through May.

April
- **Flower Parade.** Floats keyed to a different theme each year parade from Noordwijk to Haarlem. Contact Corsosecretariat, Postbus 115, 2160 AC, Lisse (☎ **0252/434-710;** fax 0252/218-525). Late April.
- **Antique Fair,** Breda. Contact Nederlandse Kunst- en Antiekbeurs Breda, Postbus 1136, 4801 BC, Breda (☎ **076/514-8760**). Late April.
- **Queen's Day.** Countrywide celebration honoring the House of Orange, with parades, street fairs, and street entertainment. Throughout Holland, but best in Amsterdam. April 30.

May
- **World War II Memorial Day.** Countrywide observance, principally marked by 2 minutes of silence at 8pm. Throughout Holland. Just be on the streets in any town or village in Holland at 8pm. May 4.
- **Liberation Day.** Commemorates the end of World War II and Holland's liberation from Nazi occupation. Throughout Holland, but best in Amsterdam. Contact VVV Amsterdam (☎ **0900/400-4040**). May 5.
- **Weekly Antiques and Book Market in The Hague,** Lange Voorhout. Contact Dienst Marktwezen Den Haag (☎ **070/353-6249**). Thursdays and Sundays from May through September.
- **National Cycling and Windmill Day.** Working windmills around the country are open to the public, and special cycling tours are organized. Throughout Holland. Contact Nationale Molendag, Vereniging de Hollandsche Molen, Sarphatistraat 634, 1018 AV, Amsterdam (☎ **020/623-8703;** fax 020/638-3319). Second Saturday in May.
- **Flag Day (Vlaggetjesdag).** Fishing ports open the herring season, with a highly competitive race to bring the first herring back for Queen Beatrix. Scheveningen,

IJmuiden, and Vlaardingen. Contact VVV Scheveningen (☎ 0900/ 3403-5051), IJmuiden (☎ 0255/515-611), and Vlaardingen (☎ 010/ 434-6666). End of May.
- **Frisian Eleven Cities Tourist Cycle Race,** Bolsward, Friesland. Contact Provincial VVV Friesland (☎ 0900/202-4060). End of May.

June

- **Poetry International,** Rotterdam. Worldwide poetry competition, which attracts top talent. Contact Stichting Poetry International, Kruisstraat 2, 3012 CT, Rotterdam (☎ 010/413-4300; fax 010/433-4211). Mid-June.
- **Oerol Festival.** Open-air performances by international theater companies on Terschelling island. Contact VVV Terschelling-West (☎ 0562/443-000). Mid-June.

July

- **Tourist Market,** Hoorn. Colorful crafts collections. Contact VVV Westfriesland (☎ 0900/403-1055). Every Wednesday from July through mid-August.
- **North Sea Jazz Festival.** The Hague hosts one of the world's leading gatherings of top international jazz musicians. Contact North Sea Jazz, Postbus 3325, 2601 DH, Delft (☎ 015/214-8900; fax 015/214-8393). July 9 to 11, 1999; dates for 2000 similar but not announced at press time.
- **Skûtsjeseilen.** Sailing races with traditional barges on the Frisian Lakes. Contact VVV Friesland (☎ 0900/202-4060). Mid-July.
- **International Rose Exhibition and Competition,** Westbroek Park, The Hague. Contact Dienst Stadsbeheer (☎ 070/353-6300). Mid-July.
- **Summer Fireworks Displays.** Scheveningen Pier. Contact VVV Scheveningen (☎ 0900/3403-5051). Every Friday at 11pm, from mid-July through mid-August.

August

- **Flower Parade.** Rijnsburg-Leiden-Noordwijk. Contact Stichting Rijnsburgs Bloemencorso, Postbus 10, 2230 AA Rijnsburg (☎ 071/409-4444). First Saturday in August.
- **Equestrian Show,** The Hague. Annual show with international competitors. Contact Stichting Concours Hippique Den Haag, Populierendreef 11, 2272 RA, Voorburg (☎ 070/386-7707). Early August.
- **Holland Festival of Early Music,** Utrecht. Marvelous concerts of music from the Middle Ages through the Romantic era, in Utrecht. Contact Organisatie Oude Muziek, Postbus 734, 3500 AS, Utrecht (☎ 030/236-2236). August 27 to September 5, 1999; August 25 to September 3, 2000.
- **International Fireworks Festival.** On the pier and boulevard of Scheveningen. Call ☎ 0900/3403-5051. Late August.
- **Windmill Day,** Zandam. All mills at Zaanse Schans are open to the public. Contact VVV Zaandam (☎ 075/616-2221; fax 075/670-5381). Throughout the month.
- **Uitmarkt,** Dam Square and other venues. Amsterdam previews the soon-to-open cultural season with this great open market of information on Dam Square and free performances at impromptu outdoor venues as well as theaters and concert halls. Both professional and amateur groups take part in the shows, which run the gamut of music, opera, dance, theater, and cabaret. Contact **Amsterdam Uitmarkt** (☎ 020/626-2656). August 27 to 29, 1999; dates for 2000 not known at press time.

September

- **Flower Processions,** Aalsmeer. Contact KMPT, Afdeling Aalsmeer, Postbus 1454, 1430 BL, Aalsmeer (☎ **0297/344-033;** fax 0297/326-850). First 2 weeks of September.
- **Bloemencorso,** Aalsmeer to Amsterdam. Every year for nearly half a century, Amsterdam has been the final destination for the Flower Parade that originates in Aalsmeer. The parade features a large number of floats that carry a variety of in-season flowers (so don't expect to see tulips). The parade follows an established route and ends at Dam Square. Contact Stichting Bloemencorso (☎ **0297/ 939-393**). First Saturday in September.
- **Crossing Border Festival,** The Hague. Literature, pop music, and cinema are combined in this international festival in The Hague. Call ☎ **070/346-2127.** Mid-September.
- **Open Monumentendag.** A chance to see historical buildings not usually open to the public. All over the country. Contact Vereniging Open Monumentendag, Ruysdaelkade 4, 1072 AG, Amsterdam (☎ **020/470-1170;** fax 020/470-3370). Second Saturday in September.
- **Opening of Parliament,** The Hague. Queen Beatrix rides in a splendid gold coach to the Knights' Hall in The Hague to open the legislative session. Contact VVV Den Haag (☎ **0900/3403-5051**). Third Tuesday in September.
- **World Port Days.** Events and festivities around Rotterdam's harbor. Contact VVV Rotterdam (☎ **0900/403-4065**). Early September.

October

- **Herfstflora,** Naarden. Splendid display of autumn flowers. Contact VVV Gooi en Vechtstreek (☎ **035/694-2836**). Early October.

November

- **International Flower Show,** Aalsmeer. Largest exhibit of autumn-blooming flowers. Contact KMPT, Afdeling Aalsmeer, Postbus 1454, 1430 BL, Aalsmeer (☎ **0297/344-033;** fax 0297/326-850). Early November.

December

- **Saint Nicholas's Eve.** Traditional day in Holland for exchanging Christmas gifts. Join some Dutch friends or a Dutch family. December 5.
- **Gouda bij Kaarslicht,** Gouda. The Markt in Gouda is lit by thousands of candles. Contact VVV Gouda (☎ **0182/513-666**). Tuesday evening before Christmas.

3 Getting Around

Like Belgium, Holland is so compact it makes for easy sightseeing. Roads and expressways are excellent, and the railway system is one of Europe's best. For public transport information, call ☎ **0900/9292.**

BY PLANE

Because Holland is so small, you'll only need to fly from one city to another if you're extremely pressed for time. If that's the case, the KLM subsidiary, **KLM City-hopper,** can fly you from Schiphol Airport to Rotterdam, Eindhoven, and Maastricht. (It also flies to London, Birmingham, Belfast, the Channel Islands, Antwerp, Brussels, Stuttgart, Bremen, Hamburg, and Dusseldorf.) If you're only going for the day, ask about the attractive discounts on 1-day round-trip tickets, as well as weekend discounts. Call local KLM reservations offices for schedules and fares. Cityhopper timetables are also on display at most KLM ticket counters.

BY TRAIN

All major tourist destinations in Holland are within 2 to 2½ hours of Amsterdam via **Nederlandse Spoorwegen (NS),** Holland's national rail system. Spotlessly clean and always on time, these trains are a delightful way to travel with the Dutch, who use them even for short journeys to the next town up the line. The trains run so often that you can usually just go to the station and wait for the next train—your wait will be short. At even the smallest stations, there is half-hour service in both directions, and major destination points have between four and eight trains an hour in both directions. Service begins as early as 5am (slightly later on Sundays and holidays), and runs until around 1am. A special Night Train runs between Utrecht and Rotterdam, via Amsterdam, Schiphol, Leiden, and The Hague. A complete rail timetable (*spoorboekje*) is available at railway stations for a small charge, as well as a free intercity timetable (sufficient for most tourist needs).

If all or most of your travel will be by rail, consider investing in one of the NS special programs, such as Domino Holland, Summer Tour, Benelux Tourrail, and Multi Rover. For example, Summer Tour—valid only in June, July, and August—entitles you to 3 days of travel in Holland within 10 consecutive days and costs Dfl 99 ($50) in second class, Dfl 155 ($77.50) in first class, with a supplement of only Dfl 30 ($15) for a second person in second class and Dfl 40 ($20) for a second person in first class. For more details, contact the Netherlands Board of Tourism (see "Visitor Information" in chapter 2) or call the public transport information number in Holland (☎ **0900/9292**).

There are also hundreds of bargain day and weekend fares called "RailIdee," for trips to specific destinations, including picturesque walking and biking routes. These handy combination tickets include admission to attractions, maps, reduced hotel rates (if so desired), lunch packs, and bicycle hire. The family excursion fares are especially attractive. For information, pick up the "EropUit!" booklet, published by NS and available at tourist offices or major railway stations.

If you're going to travel in all three Benelux countries, the 3-day **Benelux Tourrail Ticket** is a good buy (see "Getting There" in chapter 2).

BY BUS

Most towns that don't have a train station are serviced by bus—the only problem is that intercity buses are usually slow because they stop at so many places en route, and you may have to change at an intermediate town or city on the way. A *strippenkaart* is a combined multi-journey public transport ticket costing Dfl 11.50 ($6.75) for 15 strips and Dfl 33.75($16.90) for 45 strips; fares are based on a zone system, and you stamp the number of zones plus one extra. This confuses everybody, so listen up. The country is divided up into a series of fare zones. You always have to cancel one strip more than the number of zones, so if you travel within one zone, you cancel two strips; if you travel between two zones, you cancel three strips; if you travel between five zones you cancel six strips; and so forth. You use the punch machine on board the bus to cancel the strips (or you can ask the driver to cancel them). Inspectors may check your ticket, so be sure to do it right.

For long-distance bus travel, an easier and cheaper solution is a *dagkaart* (day-ticket) for Dfl 24 ($12), offering travel-anywhere ease throughout the country. These tickets can be bought at the station, the Post Office, or tobacconists. They are valid on all public transport in Holland except the train. Traveling by train is definitely faster, but it is possible (and cheap) to travel longer distances using the bus. The railway timetable (*spoorboekje*), mentioned above and available at railway stations, includes a bus timetable for the towns not serviced by train. For schedules of the several regional bus companies, contact **VSN Groep,** Postbus 19222, 3501 DE Utrecht, or check with local bus stations, which are usually adjacent to or very near railway stations.

BY TAXI

To get a taxi in Holland, you must either wait at the numerous taxi stands found at hotels, railway stations, and shopping areas, or call by telephone. It's generally not allowed to hail one on the street, though nowadays they will sometimes stop for you. Tip and taxes are included in the meter price, and you need not add an extra tip unless there has been exceptional service (help with heavy luggage, for example).

BY CAR

Driving is easy in Holland except, as in most countries, in the larger cities where traffic congestion can be positively ulcer inducing. Outside the cities, however, both major expressways and local roads are excellent; they're well planned (as you'd expect from the efficient Dutch), well maintained, well signposted, and often well lit at night.

Surprisingly enough, the biggest problem on the roads is the other drivers: Many Dutch people cast off their usual social skills and conscience when they get behind the wheel and become as bad-tempered, erratic, and downright dangerous as, well, Belgians, whose roadway recklessness is infamous. This is most visible in their life-threatening practice of roaring up behind you in the fast passing lane of an expressway, and sitting millimeters from your tail, occasionally further enlivening the experience by flashing their headlights until they all but push you out of the way. Some victims of this practice flip on their own lights so that the aggressors think they are actually braking—but doing this can have unpredictable consequences. The best thing is to ignore the menace as much as you can, complete your own passing maneuver in your own time, signal, and move over smoothly to an inside lane.

RENTALS   Rental cars with U.S. specifications (automatic transmission and power steering) are available from rental desks at Schiphol Airport and the following Amsterdam addresses (airport pickup and drop-off is also available in most cases): **Hertz,** Overtoom 333 (☎ **020/612-2441**); **Avis,** Nassaukade 380 (☎ **020/683-6061**); and **Europcar,** Overtoom 51–53 (☎ **020/683-2123**). Expect to pay Dfl 70 to 160 ($35 to $80) per day, depending on the type of car (stick shift or automatic) and model you choose. You'll also pay an additional daily per-kilometer charge, plus insurance, and a 20% tax. Weekly rates, with unlimited mileage, represent a much better buy at Dfl 550 to 3,400 ($225 to $1,700), the latter rate for a luxury Mercedes.

GASOLINE   As we go to press, Dutch gas prices are between Dfl 2.20 and 2.30 ($1.10 and $1.15) per liter (0.26 gal.), but remember that these prices are among the most likely to fluctuate.

DRIVING RULES   To drive in Holland, U.S. citizens need only a valid passport, a U.S. driver's license, and a registration for the car you drive. The minimum age for drivers is 18. The speed limit is 120kmph (75 m.p.h.) on expressways; 100kmph (60 m.p.h.) on some marked stretches near cities; 50kmph (30 m.p.h.) in all cities and urban areas; and 80kmph (48 m.p.h.) in the outskirts of towns and cities.

Traffic approaching from the right has the right of way, unless the road you are on is posted with roadside orange diamond signs. Pedestrians on the crosswalks always have the right of way. Watch out for cyclists, who are vulnerable road users but don't always act as if they are.

ROAD MAPS   Perfectly adequate road maps for Holland, as well as street maps for major cities, are available from local VVV offices or in advance from Netherlands Board of Tourism offices. Road maps are also published by the **ANWB** or **KNAC** motoring organizations and are available from bookshops and some news vendors.

BREAKDOWNS/ASSISTANCE   If you're a member of a national automobile club, such as the American Automobile Association, you are automatically entitled to the services of **ANWB Royal Dutch Touring Club.** This organization sponsors the fleet of yellow Wegenwacht vans, a sort of repair shop on wheels that you'll see patrolling the highways. There are special yellow call boxes on all major roads to bring them to your assistance. Emergency call boxes marked *Politie* will bring the police on the double.

HITCHHIKING

Hitchhiking is illegal on major expressways (which lead to just about every sight-seeing destination). You can, however, hitch on entrance and exit roadways, and the Dutch are generally quite amenable to providing lifts.

SUGGESTED ITINERARIES

If you only have a short time in Holland, I strongly recommend that you base yourself in Amsterdam and make day trips to nearby cities and towns—many outstanding destinations are less than an hour away—or join one of the excellent narrated coach tours that fan out from Amsterdam each day covering important nearby destinations in half-day excursions. By returning each evening to Amsterdam, you'll not only develop a real feeling for that intriguing and fascinating city, but also save a lot of the wear and tear that comes with shifting accommodations every day or so. Of course, should one of those day trips trigger an instant love affair with a special spot, that's the place to plant yourself—you can always let Amsterdam be the day trip.

Amsterdam & Environs in 7 Days

This tour restricts itself to the city's myriad sights and to excursions into the bucolic greenery and history of neighboring towns and villages. For those in search of more cosmopolitan pleasures you can interchange the day trips here with the trips mentioned in "The Western Cities in 5 days" below. All those destinations are within an hour's train travel from Amsterdam.

Days 1 and 2   You'll need at least the first 2 days to explore Amsterdam and see the highlights of its outstanding cultural attractions, perhaps including the 3-hour sightseeing tour that makes stops at an important museum and a diamond-cutting exhibition.

Day 3   Take a 4-hour morning tour to Marken beside the IJsselmeer, visiting a wooden-shoe workshop en route; use the afternoon to visit another of Amsterdam's museums; save this evening for a candlelight cruise of Amsterdam's canals.

Day 4   If your visit falls between March and May when the tulips are at their peak, spend this day visiting the famous flower auction at Aalsmeer, then drive to the beautiful Keukenhof Gardens, passing through the acres of bulb fields between Haarlem and Leiden. The gardens are also lovely at other times of the year, since different species bloom in different months. If flowers don't appeal to you, the Haarlem-Leiden drive is worthwhile just for sightseeing. Nondrivers can take a sightseeing coach tour. Return to Amsterdam for the evening, perhaps to spend it at one of the city's jazz clubs.

Day 5   If this is a Friday, be sure to visit Alkmaar and its colorful morning cheese market, where giant wheels of cheese are auctioned in the town square (there's a coach tour every week), returning to Amsterdam by a circular route through windmill-studded countryside, stopping in Edam and Volendam. Nondrivers can join an afternoon tour from Amsterdam to Edam and Volendam. Spend the evening in Amsterdam.

Day 6   Use most of the day to travel up to the great Enclosing Dike that turned the salty, tidal Zuiderzee into a freshwater lake, the IJsselmeer; return to Amsterdam by way of a dam over the IJsselmeer and the new town of Lelystad in the newest polder, Flevoland. This trip will solidify your respect for all the Dutch have accomplished in taming the sea.

Day 7   Save this day for your last bit of Amsterdam sightseeing (have you been to the Anne Frank House yet?) or following up other tips you've picked up from fellow travelers. Remember the country is small, so you can reach almost any part of it by train within a mere 3 hours.

The Western Cities in 5 Days

The "Randstad" is the Dutch word for the conglomeration of cities in the western part of the Netherlands spreading from Amsterdam southward to Rotterdam. This is the most highly populated part of the Netherlands, but that doesn't mean there isn't plenty of history and character here. In between the bigger cities—The Hague and Rotterdam—there are plenty of smaller towns packed with museums and interesting sights, as well as the seaside for a breath of fresh air. A car is not essential for touring the Randstad, since every destination is easily reached by train or bus.

This itinerary will keep you hopping, so you may wish to extend your stays in each place mentioned, or be selective and save parts of it for your next visit. You may also want to juggle the suggested order, but bear in mind that travel will be easier if you save Zeeland for last if you're flying out of Amsterdam, or Maastricht if you're traveling on in Europe.

Day 1   Spend a day visiting The Hague—home of Dutch royalty, and the seat of Holland's government.

Day 2   The coastal resort of Scheveningen is just a short tram ride from The Hague, as is the historic city of Delft, famous for its blue porcelain.

Days 3 and 4   Gouda and Leiden are two other smallish but important cities, with rich histories and interesting museums that could keep you intrigued for at least a day each. A third alternative is the university city of Utrecht, less than an hour's train ride away.

Day 5   Rotterdam is a city of the 21st century, reconstructed from scratch after World War II. Town planning has some advantages, not the least of which are the culture and museums that are to be found amidst the impressively tall buildings and wide boulevards.

Getting Away from It All Up North

A drive along minor roads is one of the best ways to appreciate the lowlands of the provinces of Noord-Holland, Friesland, Groningen, and Drenthe. Many of the roads are signposted scenic routes that run along the tops of the dikes and offer wonderful views. One of the unique features of this region is the chain of the Wadden Islands, which stretch in an arc around the northwestern corner of the Netherlands. These islands are treasured by the Dutch as places of peaceful refuge from thronging crowds and rushing traffic. Nondrivers can make use of good rail services and local bus services in the more rural areas. Better still, do as the Dutch do, and get on your bike.

Days 1 and 2   Drive from Amsterdam north through the former fishing ports surrounding the IJsselmeer. If you haven't yet visited Edam and Volendam on trips from Amsterdam, take these in too. Hoorn was the capital of the former province of Westfriesland, and Enkhuizen has a museum that brings yesteryear's fishing villages back to life. The island of Texel, reached from the port of Den Helder, a naval base for centuries, is a tranquil overnight stop, and its unspoiled nature can be toured by bike in a day.

Day 3   Drive across the Enclosing Dike to Friesland proper. Now you can decide whether to spend a few days in Leeuwarden, capital of the province of Friesland, or head directly on to Groningen, capital of Groningen province and a slightly larger, more sophisticated city.

Day 4 and 5   From a base in Leeuwarden you can easily visit the tile-and-ceramic factory at Makkum, the pottery town of Workum, and the furniture painters of Hindeloopen, or simply explore the countryside. The more daring nature lover may want to take a ferry from Harlingen to the islands of Terschelling, Ameland, or Vlieland, and spend a night or two amidst nature reserves, windswept beaches, and rolling sand dunes.

Day 6 and 7   Head to Groningen. If you're driving, remember that the whole of the center of Groningen is pedestrianized, so follow signs to parking lots on the perimeter. Spend the day exploring the blissful sensation of no traffic and the many historical buildings. There are plenty of attractions and smaller towns within easy driving distance of this city. An excellent side trip from Groningen is to the Wadden Island called Schiermonikoog, which has less than 1,000 residents and is a protected nature reserve—rest is assured.

The Central & Southern Netherlands

This itinerary covers a large area, but is still manageable using trains and public transport. Instead of heading northeast from Amsterdam on the first leg, you may want to start with Apeldoorn.

Day 1   Drive along the series of former Hanse towns between Zwolle and Deventer.

Days 2   Make your base in Apeldoorn and take a tour of the former royal palace, then head for the wooded Hoge Veluwe National Park. Put on your walking or cycling shoes (free bicycles are supplied at the perimeter car parks) and be surprised by the museum of modern art in this idyllic setting. Rest and relax.

Day 3   Head on to Arnhem and Nijmegen for a reverent visit to one of the many memorials of the wars that have been fought on this border territory, and then carry on southward to Maastricht, the historic and sophisticated capital of the province of Limburg. Spend the afternoon visiting the awesome Caves of St. Pietersberg, and in the evening relax in one of the city's excellent gourmet restaurants and then check out a few of its interesting drinking spots. Stay overnight in Maastricht.

Day 4   Explore the hilliest and highest landscape in the country on foot or bike, or partake in the pleasures of a whole day at the spa.

Sightseeing Tips

WINDMILLS   No, they haven't disappeared from Holland's landscape, but their numbers have decreased from some 10,000 to a mere 1,000—only about 200 of which are in use these days. The VVV (or the Netherlands Board of Tourism) can furnish a list of those windmills officially open to the public, but you should know that the hospitable Dutch millers welcome visitors to private mills any time they hoist a flag outside to signify that they're inside and the mill is working.

FLOWERS   Of course you want to see Holland's famous tulip bulb fields! And you will if you visit between late March and mid-May. If you don't make it then, not to worry—there are gorgeous flowers in bloom right up to September, but not tulips. After May what you'll see are hyacinths, daffodils, roses, carnations, freesias, rhododendrons, hydrangeas, and even (in nurseries) Dutch orchids. The bulb fields are concentrated in the Leiden-Haarlem-Den Helder area and around Enkhuizen. To see the most lavish display of Dutch spring blooms, visit Keukenhof, the world's largest flower garden, near Lisse. For cut flowers, don't miss the floating flower market on Amsterdam's Singel Canal and the Aalsmeer flower auction just outside the city.

One look at Amsterdam's floating flower market and something in your soul is likely to prod you to buy one of the nicest of all souvenirs. If you're worried about failure rates or bug-ridden bulbs, don't! The Dutch have been perfecting their growing methods and strengthening their stock for more than 400 years. Check before buying, however, as not all bulbs are certified for entry into the U.S. Packages must have a numbered phytosanitary certificate attached to the label, allowing you to import the bulbs.

Day 5   Head back north via the finger of land squeezed in between Belgium and Germany, and visit 's Hertogenbosch, the provincial capital of Brabant.
Day 6   Drive across the country to Middelburg, in the province of Zeeland. Use the afternoon to explore this quaint city. Stay overnight in Middelburg.
Day 7   Make an early-morning visit to the massive Delta Project, another controlling "gate" to the sea, before driving back to Amsterdam.

FAST FACTS: Holland

American Express   See "Fast Facts: Amsterdam" in chapter 14.

Business Hours   Banks are open Monday through Friday from 9am to 4pm (some stay open until 5pm). Some banks also open on late-hour shopping nights and Saturdays. Shops generally stay open weekdays from 8:30 or 9am to 5 or 6pm, and Saturday until 4 or 5pm. Some shops close for lunch, and nearly all have one full closing day or one morning or afternoon when they're closed—signs are prominently posted announcing closing times. Many shops, especially in the larger towns, have late hours on Thursday and/or Friday evening, and in Amsterdam shops along the main streets are open on Sundays.

Drug Laws   Holland allows possession of up to 5 grams (0.2 oz.) of cannabis for your own consumption. You should, however, exercise a wide degree of discretion when actually smoking it in all parts of the country except Amsterdam, which is one of the world's most liberal-minded cities when it comes to drug use. Needless to say, you should not be caught actually peddling drugs to others.

Electricity   Holland runs on 220 volts, so if you plan to bring a hair dryer, radio (unless it's battery-operated), travel iron, or any other small appliance, pack a European-style adapter plug and a transformer.

Embassies/Consulates   Most countries have embassies in The Hague, and a few also have consulates in Amsterdam. The Embassy of the **United States** is at Lange Voorhout 102, 2514 AG The Hague (☎ **070/310-9209**), and there's a consulate in Amsterdam at Museumplein 19 (☎ **020/575-5309**). The Embassy of the **United Kingdom** is located at Lange Voorhout 10, 2514 ED The Hague (☎ **070/364-5800**), and there's a consulate in Amsterdam at Koningslaan 44 (☎ **020/676-4343**). The Embassy of **Australia** is located at Carnegielaan 4, 2517 KH The Hague (☎ **070/310-8200**); the Embassy of **Canada** is at Sophialaan 7, 2514 JP The Hague (☎ **070/311-1600**); the Embassy of the **Republic of Ireland** is located at Dr Kuyperstraat 9, 2514 BA The Hague (☎ **070/363-0993**); and the Embassy of **New Zealand** is at Carnegielaan 10, 2517 KH The Hague (☎ **070/346-9324**). The Embassy of **South Africa** is at Wassenaarseweg 40, The Hague (☎ **070/392-4501**).

Emergencies   Call ☎ **112** for police (*politie*), fire department, and ambulance assistance.

Fax   Main post offices in major cities can provide telex and fax services.

Safety   Whenever you're traveling in an unfamiliar city or country, stay alert. Be aware of your immediate surroundings. Wear a money belt and keep a close eye on your possessions. Be particularly careful with cameras, purses, and wallets—all favorite targets of thieves and pickpockets. Every society has its criminals. It's your responsibility to be aware and alert even in the most heavily touristed areas. Women especially should be cautious at night in Holland's larger cities, particularly Amsterdam.

Telephone   The country code for Holland is **31.** When calling Holland from abroad, you do not use the initial **0** in the area code. If, for example, you are phoning an Amsterdam number (area code **020**) from another country, you first dial the international access code (**011** in the U.S.), then **31,** and then **20** (for the area code), followed by the subscriber number. You only dial **020** for the area code when calling long distance within Holland.

Almost all public telephones are now operated using a phone card instead of coins. You can buy plastic phone cards at post offices, railway stations, and many tobacconists and news vendors for Dfl 10 ($5), Dfl 25 ($12.50), and Dfl 50 ($25). Public phones are a good option for long distance and especially international calls.

To operate one of the few remaining coin-paid Dutch public telephones you need a Dfl 0.25 (15¢) coin, called a *kwartje*, or a Dfl 1 (50¢) coin. You will no longer find coin-paid phones on the street, just in bars and restaurants, where you can expect to pay a very high rate.

For directory information inside Holland, call ☎ **0900/8008;** for international information, call ☎ **0900/8418;** for international collect calls, call ☎ **0900/0410.**

The USADirect number from any phone in Holland is ☎ **0800/022-9111.** Similar services are offered by MCI CallUSA, ☎ **0800/022-9122;** PhoneUSA,

☎ **0800/022-0224;** Sprint Express, ☎ **0800/022-9119;** Canada Direct, ☎ **0800/022-9116;** and British Telecom, ☎ **0800/022-9944.**

There are two main formats for Dutch telephone numbers: a three-digit area code followed by a seven-digit subscriber number, used mostly for cities; and a four-digit area code followed by a six-digit subscriber number, used for smaller towns and in the countryside. The exceptions are the free **0800** numbers (though you will still need to introduce a card to call these from public phone booths), and toll-paid **0900** special information numbers, which usually access taped information in Dutch and English, and follow a variety of styles, with from four to eight digits following the 0800 or 0900 prefix.

Time   Holland is in the central European time zone, 6 hours ahead of eastern standard time in the United States (9am in New York is 3pm in Holland). Clocks are moved ahead 1 hour each year at the end of March and back 1 hour at the end of September.

Tipping   The Dutch government requires that all taxes and service charges be included in the published prices of hotels, restaurants, cafes, discos, nightclubs, beauty/barbershops, and sightseeing companies. Even taxi fare includes taxes and a standard 15% tip. To be absolutely sure in a restaurant that tax and service are included, look for the words "inclusief BTW en service" (BTW is the abbreviation for the Dutch words that mean value-added tax)—or just ask. However, Dutch waitstaff always appreciate additional tips. To tip as the Dutch do, leave any small change up to the next guilder in a cafe or snack bar, and in a restaurant, up to the next 5 or 10 guilders. Of course, if you've had exceptional service and want to add a little more, that's perfectly acceptable.

14 Amsterdam

Live-and-let-live, easygoing, liberal, and tolerant are just some of the tags that Amsterdam is most often labeled with—and with good reason. For centuries Amsterdam has been a magnet for the oppressed and persecuted, particularly in the 17th century, when it became a haven for Jews and Huguenots being driven from France and other Catholic countries. That tradition of tolerance has continued into the 20th century. In the 1960s the city became the hippie capital of Europe, and in the 1990s Amsterdam and Holland have taken leading roles in liberalizing laws against homosexuality, even sanctioning gay marriages. Similar pragmatic liberal attitudes help explain the existence of Amsterdam's Red Light District, which is as much a popular city attraction as the Rijksmuseum, the Stedelijk museum, and the Anne Frankhuis.

It is surprising, however, how many people today still think of Amsterdam as caught in some rose-tinted time warp of free love, free drugs, free everything. The heady heyday of the 1960s and 1970s—if it ever really existed to the extent that legend and the soft-focus afterglow of memory would have us believe—has given way to 1990s realities. A tour of the burgeoning suburban business zones, whose award-winning modern architecture is light years away from the Golden Age gables of Old Amsterdam, is evidence enough of the city's new priorities. The city government has worked assiduously to transform Amsterdam from being a hippie haven to a cosmopolitan international business center, and there seems little doubt that it is succeeding.

Fortunately, it is not succeeding all the way. Amsterdam is still "different." Its citizens, bubbling along happily in their multiracial melting pot, are not so easily poured into the restrictive molds dictated by trade and industry. Not only do free thinking and free living still have their places, they are the watchwords by which Amsterdam lives its collective life. Don't kid yourself, though. Holland's standard of living is among the highest in the world, and Amsterdam is the national capital. The free living is fueled not so much by clouds of hashish smoke as by the wealth generated by a successful economy.

Despite all this modern prosperity, however, the magic of Old Amsterdam still remains. The city will soon capture you in its spell—especially at night, when the more than 1,200 bridges spanning the nearly 200 canals are lit with a zillion tiny lights that give them a fairy-tale appearance, or in the morning, when the landscape slowly unfolds through a mysterious fog or mist to reveal its treasures.

1 Frommer's Favorite Amsterdam Experiences

- **Cruising the Canals.** Hop aboard a glass-topped canal boat for a cruise through Amsterdam's beautiful canals and the best possible view of all those gabled Golden Age merchants' houses.
- **Seeing the Masters.** Stand in awe in front of Rembrandt's *The Night Watch* at the Rijksmuseum, where 200-plus rooms display works by Dutch and other European masters.
- **Viewing Vincent.** Visit the outstanding Vincent van Gogh Museum, where you can trace the artistic and psychological development of this modern master. Then head next door to the always challenging Stedelijk Museum of Modern Art.
- **Spending an Afternoon with Anne Frank.** Take some time to reflect on the tragic life of Anne Frank amid the surroundings of her World War II hideaway, now the Anne Frankhuis, where she wrote her famous diary.
- **Tiptoeing Through the Tulips.** Pick up a bunch of tulips at the floating Flower Market on the Singel, even if they're just to brighten up your hotel room.
- **Cycling the City.** Rent a bicycle and join the flow of cyclists for one of the classic Amsterdam experiences—but go carefully.
- **Enjoying an Evening Concert.** Take in a classical music concert at the Concertgebouw, one of the most acoustically perfect halls in the world.
- **Taking a Walk on the Wild Side.** Stroll through the Red Light District, to examine the quaint gabled architecture along its narrow canals—oh, yes, and you might also notice certain ladies watching the world go by through their red-fringed windows.
- **Shopping for a Steal.** Pick up bargains at the Waterlooplein Flea Market and the Albert Cuyp Market.
- **Relaxing in a Brown Cafe.** Spend a leisurely evening in a brown cafe, the traditional Amsterdam watering hole.

2 Orientation

ARRIVING

BY PLANE   For details on air travel to Holland, see chapter 2. The Netherlands has only one major airport that handles international arrivals and departures—Amsterdam's **Schiphol Airport.** For general and flight information call Helloport (☎ **0900/0141**). Schiphol is one of the easiest airports in the world to figure out. After you deplane, moving sidewalks will take you to the main terminal building, where you pass through Customs.

Getting to & from the Airport   The **KLM Hotel Shuttle** bus operates between the airport and the city center on a circular route serving 16 top hotels directly. The fare is Dfl 17.50 ($8.75) one-way. Check at the KLM Hotel Desk for information—their clerks can tell you which KLM Hotel Shuttle stop is closest to your lodgings.

Trains leave from Schiphol Station, downstairs from Schiphol Plaza, for Amsterdam's Centraal Station. Departures range from one per hour at night to six per hour at peak times. The single fare is Dfl 6.25 ($3.15), and the trip takes about 15 minutes.

Taxis operating from the airport are all metered and charge about Dfl 60 ($30) to the city center.

BY TRAIN & TRAM   Trains arrive at **Centraal Station,** built on an artificial island along the river IJ. Centraal Station is the point of origin for most of the city's trams and a departure point for canal-boat tours, bicycle ferries across the IJ waterway, taxis, water taxis, and the Museum Boat. It also houses an office of the VVV Amsterdam tourist organization and the GWK Bureau de Change. Schedule and fare information on travel in Holland is available from the large information office inside the station; recorded information is also available by dialing (☎ **0900/9292**) for national destinations, and (☎ **0900/9296**) for international travel. Both services cost around Dfl 1 (50¢)/minute.

Luggage deposit costs from Dfl 6.50 ($3.25) for a large locker and Dfl 4.50 ($2.25) per day for a standard locker.

The **tram** stops are on either side of the main station exit. Or you can head for the **taxi stand** in front of the station. (For details on transportation within the city, see "Getting Around," below.)

BY BUS   International coaches arrive at the main bus terminal opposite Centraal Station or at the Amstel Bus Station, which is outside Amstel train station. From the Amstel Bus Station, there are direct metro connections to Centraal Station; for the Leidseplein area, take the metro towards Centraal Station, but get out at the Weesperplein station, then go above ground to take tram numbers 6, 7, or 10.

BY CAR   European expressways (E19, E35, E231, and E22) reach Amsterdam from Belgium and/or Germany.

VISITOR INFORMATION

Holland Tourist Information has an office in Schiphol Plaza at Schiphol Airport. Amsterdam's tourist information organization, **VVV Amsterdam** (where you can also reserve hotel rooms), has offices inside Centraal Station on Platform 2, and opposite the station at Stationsplein 10, Leidseplein 1, and in the south of town at the corner of Stadionplein and Van Tuyll van Serooskerkenweg. For telephone information, call ☎ **0900/400-4040** Monday through Friday from 9am to 5pm (handle this number with caution, as it costs a steep Dfl 1 (50¢) a minute). VVV Amsterdam will help you with almost any question about the city and can provide brochures, maps, and the like. There are also separate desks for reserving hotel rooms. The offices are open from 9am to 5pm outside the peak season and on a varying longer schedule as the season proceeds, including Sundays and late evening.

CITY LAYOUT

Amsterdam's center is small enough that its residents think of it as a village. Finding your way around can be confusing, however, until you get the hang of it. The concentric rings of major canals are the city center's defining characteristic, along with several important squares that act as focal points.

A map is essential. All you need to know is that in Dutch -*straat* means street, -*gracht* means canal, -*plein* means square, and -*laan* means boulevard, all of which are used as suffixes attached directly to the name of the thoroughfare (for example, Princes' Canal becomes *Prinsengracht*, one word).

STREET MAPS   Surrland/N.V. Falkplan's Amsterdam Tourist Map is among the handiest and is available from news vendors. It sells for Dfl 7.95 ($4). VVV offices have several other maps available, including the small but detailed VVV Amsterdam map, which costs Dfl 3.50 ($1.75).

NEIGHBORHOODS IN BRIEF

For touring purposes, the city of Amsterdam can be divided into six major neighborhoods (see the map on pages 268-269).

The Center   This is the oldest part of the city, around Dam Square and the Centraal Railway Station. It includes the major downtown shopping areas and such attractions as the Royal Palace, the Amsterdam Historical Museum, and the canal-boat piers.

The Canal Area   The semicircular, multistrand "necklace" of waterways built around the old part of the city during the 17th century includes elegant gabled houses, many restaurants, antiques shops, and small hotels, plus such sightseeing attractions as the Anne Frankhuis and the canal-house museums.

The Jordaan   This nest of small streets and canals lies west of the Center, beyond the major canals. Once a working-class neighborhood, it's now fast becoming a fashionable residential area—like New York City's SoHo—with a growing number of upscale boutiques and restaurants. Still, its "indigenous" residents are alive and well and show no sign of succumbing to the temptations of the gentrification going on around them.

The Museumplein Area   A gracious residential area surrounds the three major museums of art: the Rijksmuseum, the Vincent van Gogh Museum, and the Stedelijk Museum of Modern Art. The area includes Vondelpark, the Concertgebouw concert hall, many restaurants and small hotels, and Amsterdam's most elegant shopping streets, P. C. Hooftstraat and Van Baerlestraat.

Amsterdam South   The most prestigious modern residential area of Amsterdam is the site of a number of hotels, particularly along the Apollolaan, a wide boulevard that the locals have nicknamed the Gold Coast for its wealthy inhabitants and stately mansions.

Amsterdam East   This is another residential area on the far bank of the Amstel River, the location of such sightseeing attractions as the maritime and tropical museums, and Artis, the local zoo.

3 Getting Around

BY PUBLIC TRANSPORTATION

FARE INFORMATION & DISCOUNT PASSES   There are 11 public transport fare zones in greater Amsterdam, although tourists rarely travel beyond the city center, zone 5700 (Centrum). Most tickets are valid on buses, trams, the metro, and light rail. A **day ticket** (*dagkaart*) is valid for the entire day of purchase and also the following night, and can be bought from any bus or tram driver, conductor, or ticket dispenser for Dfl 12 ($6). **Two-** to **eight-day** tickets are also available, ranging in price from Dfl 16 to Dfl 38.50 ($8 to $19.25); these must be purchased at the **GVB** (Amsterdam Municipal Transport) ticket booths (on Stationsplein in front of Centraal Station).

A single journey ticket (an *enkeltje*) costs from Dfl 3 to Dfl 7.50 ($1.50 to $3.75) depending on how many zones you travel through. For multiple journeys buy a **strip card** (*strippenkaart*) from the driver. Discount strip cards are available at train and metro station ticket counters, the GVB ticket office in front of Centraal Station, post offices, and many news vendors, where you pay Dfl 11.25 ($5.65) for a card with 15 strips, or Dfl 33 ($16.50) for 45 strips. You are responsible for stamping the required number of strips for your journey, but feel free to ask the bus or tram conductor to help you.

Ticket Validation   Bus and tram tickets in Amsterdam must be validated when you board. Be sure to use the ticket-validating machines located in the middle and rear of the tram, or visit the conductor at the back, and be sure to keep your ticket with you until it's no longer valid. To use the machine, just fold at the line and punch in; you don't need to punch in each individual strip—just count down the number of strips you need and punch in the last one. Most Amsterdam trams operate on the honor system, but a team of inspectors—in uniform or plain clothes—occasionally hit a tram like gangbusters; in the aftermath of the stampede to reach ticket machines that—ah, too late!—have just been turned off, they will ask to see your ticket. You also must have a cancelled ticket to enter the metro platforms. The fine for riding without a ticket or not having it properly stamped, is Dfl 60 ($30), plus Dfl 4.50 ($2.25) for a ticket. And don't think that being foreign and not speaking Dutch, saying you don't have money on you, or giving Mickey Mouse at 22 Yellow Brick Road as your name and address, will help much. The inspectors speak excellent English, and they know where Mickey Mouse lives, having accompanied him to the nearest police station often enough.

BY METRO & LIGHT RAIL   Amsterdam's metro isn't much compared to the labyrinthine systems of Paris, London, and New York, but there are two subway lines and three light rail (*sneltram*) lines that bring people in from the suburbs.

BY BUS & TRAM   An extensive bus network complements 16 tram routes, 10 of which begin and end at Centraal Station. Most bus/tram shelters have maps that show the entire system. A detailed tram map is available from the VVV or at the offices of GVB/Amsterdam Municipal Transport, Stationsplein, or you can call the transportation information number (☎ **0900/9292**) for assistance. Line 20 is the **Circle Tram,** which has trams every 10 minutes at peak times. This route is especially designed to get you to many of the city's main attractions, and there is a hop-on, hop-off ticket especially for tourists.

BY TAXI

Officially, you can't hail a cab from the street, but more and more often taxis will stop anyway if you do so. Otherwise, find one of the strategically placed taxi stands sprinkled around the city, marked by their distinctive yellow phone boxes. Alternatively, you can call the **Taxi Centrale** (☎ **020/677-7777**). Taxis are metered, and fares—which include the tip—begin at Dfl 5.80 ($2.90) when you get in and run up at the rate of Dfl 2.85 ($1.45) per kilometer.

BY WATER

With all the water in Amsterdam, it makes sense to use it for transportation, and although the options are minimal (with the exception of cruise and excursion traffic), they do exist, and as an additional benefit they offer the unique view of the city from the water.

BY CANAL BUS   Two services bring you to many of the city's top museums and other attractions. The **Canal Bus** company (☎ **020/623-9886**) operates two routes—the Green Line and the Red Line—with a total of six stops. A day ticket costs Dfl 22 ($11), and allows you to hop on and off as many times as you like until noon the next day. The **Museumboot** (Museum Boat) (☎ **020/622-2181**)— *"boot"* is pronounced just like "boat"—operates a scheduled service every 30–45 minutes from Centraal Station to Prinsengracht, Leidseplein, Museumplein, Herengracht, Muziektheater, and the Eastern Dock area. A day ticket costs Dfl 25 ($12.50) for adults, and includes discounts on museum/attraction entry prices. Canal buses are a wonderful way to get your bearings when you first arrive in Amsterdam, and are also a pleasant way to rest your feet during a long day of sightseeing.

BY MOTORBOAT   Be your own captain aboard an environmentally friendly, silent electric motorboat. **Canal Motorboats** (☎ **020/422-7007**) operates two landing stages, one close to Centraal Station on the Oosterdokskade (next to the floating Sea Palace Chinese restaurant), the other where the Kloveniersburgwal meets the Amstel river (opposite the Hôtel de l'Europe). Each boat takes up to six people, and costs Dfl 65 ($32.50) for 1 hour and Dfl 150 ($75) for 3 hours. You will need to leave some ID plus Dfl 300 ($150) or a credit card as a deposit.

BY WATER TAXI   Water taxis do more or less the same thing as landlubber taxis, except that they do it on the water. To order one, call **Watertaxi** (☎ **020/ 622-2181**), or pick one up at the landing stage outside Centraal Station (to the left of the VVV office). Water taxis hold up to eight people and cost Dfl 90 ($45) for the first 30 minutes, or part thereof, then Dfl 30 ($15) for each 15 minutes thereafter.

BY FERRY   They don't have quite the same cachet as the Staten Island ferry, but the **IJ ferries** make the 5-minute crossing of the IJ channel to north Amsterdam around the clock—and they're free. Ferries leave from De Ruyterkade, behind Centraal Station.

BY CAR

Don't rent a car to get around Amsterdam. You will regret both the expense and the hassle. The city is a jumble of one-way streets, narrow bridges, and no-parking zones. Parking fees are expensive, and street parking is hard to come by. If you are driving and want to avoid parking headaches, leave your car at the free Park & Ride car parks at some of the outer metro and railway stations (directions are indicated with blue-and-white P&R signs on the way). The **Dienst Parkeerbeheer** (Parking Management Service) (☎ **020/553-0300**), with various offices around the city, is responsible for the clamping and/or towing of illegally parked cars. The service's staff is efficient, hard working, and enthusiastic.

Outside of the city, driving is another story. You may well want to rent a car for a foray into the Dutch countryside. The principal rental offices are: **Avis** at Nassaukade 380 (☎ **020/683-6061**), **Budget** at Overtoom 121 (☎ **020/612-6066**), and **Hertz**, at Overtoom 333 (☎ **020/612-2441**).

BY BICYCLE

Instead of renting a car, follow the Dutch example and rent a bicycle—there are more than 550,000 on the streets of Amsterdam to keep you company. Bike-rental rates average Dfl 10 to 12 ($5 to $6) per day or Dfl 50 to 60 ($25 to $30) per week, plus a deposit in the form of cash or an ID card. You can rent bikes at Centraal Station when you arrive, or at the following shops, all of which have similar rates. **MacBike** rents a range of bicycles, including tandems and six-speed touring bikes;

it has branches at Mr. Visserplein 2 (☎ 020/620-0985), conveniently close to the Muziektheater, and Marnixstraat 220 (☎ 020/626-6964), a 5-minute walk from Leidseplein. **Damstraat Rent-a-Bike** is located in the cellars of the Beurs van Berlage (Berlage's Stock Exchange) near Dam Square, at Damstraat 22–24 (☎ 020/625-5029).

BY WATER BICYCLE

A canal bike is a boat that you peddle with your feet. These vehicles seat two or four and cost Dfl 19.50 ($9.75) for a 1-hour jaunt for two, and Dfl 29.50 ($14.75) for four. These boats can be rented daily from 10am to 7pm (to 11pm in summer) from **Canal Bike** (☎ 020/626-5574). There are four moorings: Leidseplein; Westerkerk near the Anne Frankhuis; Stadhouderskade, beside the Rijksmuseum; and at Toronto Bridge on the Keizersgracht, near Leidsestraat.

ON FOOT

This is almost always the best way to see Amsterdam. Amsterdam's center is small enough to see on foot, although not all at once. Be sure to wear good walking shoes, as those charming cobbles get under your soles and on your nerves after a while. When crossing the street, watch out for trams and also bicycles, particularly when walking across the bicycle lanes, which are usually marked in red tarmac.

4 Special-Interest Networks & Resources

FOR STUDENTS   The VVV can supply information on student organizations, and the monthly publication *Agenda,* which lists current events and information on various services available to students, is generally geared toward student-age readers. If you're interested in cultural events and are under age 26, go by the **Amsterdam Uit Buro** (AUB), at the corner of Leidseplein and Marnixstraat (☎ 020/621-1211), and pick up a **CJP** (Cultural Youth Pass) for Dfl 20 ($10). This pass will grant you free admission to most museums and discounts on most cultural events. The AUB is open Monday through Saturday from 10am to 6pm.

FOR GAYS & LESBIANS   Information and assistance for gays and lesbians is available through **COC**, Rozenstraat 14 (☎ 020/626-3087), a local organization addressing gay issues, or from the **Gay and Lesbian Switchboard** (☎ 020/623-6565). *Frommer's Gay & Lesbian Guide to Europe* devotes a chapter to Amsterdam.

You'll find most of Amsterdam's gay and lesbian bars in the Kerkstraat, Reguliersdwarsstraat, Amstel, Amstelstraat, and Warmoesstraat areas.

FOR WOMEN   For a central information and organizing center for women's cultural events, as well as other social events, head to the **Vrouwenhuis** (Women's Center) at Nieuwe Herengracht 95 (☎ 020/625-2066). Its cafe is open on Wednesdays from noon to 5pm and Thursdays from noon to 9pm.

FOR SENIORS   The VVV office can furnish addresses and telephone numbers for church and social organizations whose activities are slanted toward the upper age brackets. It can also advise you of municipal social agencies for help with specific problems.

FAST FACTS: Amsterdam

American Express   Amex offices in Amsterdam are located at Damrak 66 (☎ 020/520-7777) and Van Baerlestraat 39 (☎ 020/671-4141).

Area Code   The country code for Holland is **31.** The area code for Amsterdam is **020.** If you're phoning an Amsterdam number from the United States, or from any other country, don't dial the first **0** of the area code; dial only **31-20** followed by the subscriber number. And don't dial the area code at all if you're phoning an Amsterdam number from within the city; the subscriber number alone is enough. You only dial the full area code if you're phoning an Amsterdam number from elsewhere in Holland.

Business Hours   Banks are open Monday through Friday 9am to 5pm; some stay open to 7pm on Thursday. Government offices are open Monday through Friday 8:30am to 4pm. Shops are generally open Tuesday through Saturday from 9am to 6pm (some stay open to 9pm for late-night shopping on Thursdays), while on Monday it's hard to find anything open before 1pm. Department stores and bigger shops are the only stores often open on Sunday, from noon to 5pm. Most supermarkets are open Monday through Friday 8am to 8pm, and 8am to 6pm on Saturday. There are also some evening shops that open at around 3 to 5pm and stay open until midnight or later, but Amsterdam is in no way a 24-hour city in this respect.

Bookstores   The American Book Center, Kalverstraat 185 (☎ **020/625-5537**) and Waterstone's, Kalverstraat 152 (☎ **020/638-3821**), have the best and most comprehensive selection of English-language books.

Currency Exchange   You can change your money at the VVV tourist office, at a bank, or at American Express, Damrak 66 (☎ **020/520-7777;** open Monday through Friday from 9am to 5pm). Other decent options are the **Grenswisselkantoor (GWK)** offices, which also handle money transfers via Western Union and operate a free infoline (☎ **0800/0566**). There are 24-hour GWK exchanges at Schiphol Airport (☎ **020/653-5121**) and Centraal Station (☎ **020/627-2731**). GWK's commission charges for buying foreign currencies such as U.S. dollars are very reasonable compared with most, and perhaps all, private bureaus. See "Money" in chapter 13 for more details.

Dentist/Doctor   In addition to looking up the regular listings of all doctors and dentists in the Amsterdam telephone directory, the Central Medical Service can be reached by calling ☎ **0900/503-2042.**

Directory Assistance   For telephone numbers throughout Holland, call ☎ **0900/8008;** for international directory assistance, call ☎ **0900/8418.** The operators are fluent in English.

Drugstores   In Holland there are two different kinds of drugstores: one for prescriptions (*apotheek*) and another for such items as toothpaste, deodorant, and razor blades (*drogist*). Your hotel can give you the addresses of those close by.

Embassies/Consulates   See "Fast Facts: Holland" in chapter 13.

Emergencies   Amsterdam's equivalent to the American 911 is ☎ **112.** Of course, like 911, you should use this number only in an emergency to call the police, fire department, or ambulance.

Hospitals   Most hospitals in the Amsterdam area are outside the city center; the most convenient emergency department is at **Onze Lieve Vrouwe Gasthuis,** Eerste Oosterparkstraat 179 (☎ **020/599-9111**). By public transport take tram 3, or the metro to Wibautstraat station.

Laundry/Dry Cleaning   Clean Brothers Launderettes have several locations throughout Amsterdam, among them Kerkstraat 56 (☎ **020/622-0273**) and Westerstraat 26 (☎ **020/627-7376**). **Cleancenter,** Ferdinand Bolstraat 7–9

(☎ 020/662-7167) and **Wassalon Java,** Javastraat 23 (☎ 020/668-2483), are two others. For dry cleaning, try **Weerd van Der** at Vaartstraat 64–68 (☎ 020/662-5616).

Lost Property To recover lost items, try calling ☎ 020/551-4911 for tram, bus, and metro; ☎ 020/557-8544 for trains and stations; ☎ 020/649-1433 for Schiphol Airport; and ☎ 020/599-8005 for others—but don't be too optimistic about your chances. There are plenty of honest Amsterdammers, of course, but it seems that they're are all out of town when you happen to lose something.

Photographic Needs For 1-hour photograph developing, you'll find conveniently located drop-off stations on the Rokin, near Centraal Station, and on Kalverstraat. **Swank Shot Studios** is a good bet; it's located at Spui 4 (☎ 020/623-6926) and Rokin 22 (☎ 020/624-4000).

Police See "Emergencies," above. For less urgent business, contact police headquarters at Elandsgracht 117 (☎ 020/559-9111).

Post Office The main post office is at Singel 250, behind the Royal Palace at Dam Square, at the corner of Raadhuisstraat (☎ 020/556-3311), open Monday through Friday from 9am to 6pm and on Saturday from 9am to 3pm. To mail a large package, go to the post office at Oosterdokskade 3, a large modern building to the right as you face Centraal Station. Hotels and retail outlets in Amsterdam generally keep a supply of stamps on hand to sell to guests.

Radio BBC World News is broadcast on medium- and short-wave radio several times a day, with varying wavelengths and times of broadcast—inquire at your hotel or consult local newspaper listings.

Safety In Amsterdam, if something isn't bolted to the floor, somebody will try to steal it. Be wary of pickpockets on public transport and in train stations (there are constant public announcements at Centraal Station to this effect, and signs on the trams saying ATTENTION: PICKPOCKETS). Watch out in the Red Light District and in transit areas such as train stations and the airport. Amsterdam is not a violent city, although violence is not unknown, but it is a drugs mecca, and drug-related, mostly petty crime is prevalent.

Television If the hotel you're staying in has cable television, you'll be able to watch both BBC 1 and BBC 2, as well as the local stations. CNN is also broadcast 24 hours a day, but is currently in dispute with the cable provider, and may be replaced by BBC World 24.

Transit Information For information regarding the Amsterdam tram, bus, and metro, call ☎ 0900/9292 Monday through Saturday from 6am to midnight, and Sunday from 7am to midnight.

5 Accommodations

Is your preference old-world charm combined with luxurious quarters? Glitzy modernity with every conceivable amenity? Small family-run hotels where guests become a part of the family circle? A bare-bones room in a dormitory, which frees up scarce dollars for other purposes? Amsterdam has all of these types of rooms, and many others.

There are almost 30,000 hotel and hostel beds available in Amsterdam (the majority in expensive and moderately priced hotels). If a particular hotel strikes your fancy but is out of your price range, it might pay to inquire if special off-season, weekend, or other offers will bring prices down to your level.

Note: Unless otherwise indicated, all the accommodations recommended below come with a private bathroom. Five-star hotels have to add an extra 5% city tax to their rates. Single rates are also available in many hotels, usually, though not always, for a significant reduction over double occupancy.

RESERVATIONS   You may, of course, make reservations directly with any of the hotels below (they will often ask you to confirm by fax, and/or give your credit card number), but be sure you provide ample time for them to reply before you leave home. Especially during summer months and the tulip season (early April through mid-May), it's advisable to make your reservations either through a travel agent; through the **Netherlands Reservations Center,** P.O. Box 404, 2360 AK Leidschendam (☎ **070/419-5500;** fax 070/419-5519), which can also book apartments and theater tickets; or, if you're booking from within Holland, through a VVV office.

Some Amsterdam hotels, in all price categories, offer significant rate reductions between November 1 and March 31, with the exception of the Christmas and New Year period. Amsterdam has many charms in the off-season, when the calendar is full of cultural events; many traditional Dutch dishes are offered that aren't available in warm weather; and the streets, cafes, restaurants, and museums are filled more with locals than visitors.

Should you arrive in Amsterdam without an advance reservation, head to the **VVV Amsterdam Tourist Office,** which has locations at Schiphol Airport, on Spoor 2 (platform 2) in Centraal Station, just opposite the railway station at Stationsplein 10 and at Leidseplein 1, and in the south of town at the corner of Stadionplein and Van Tuyll van Serooskerkenweg. For telephone information, call ☎ **0900/400-4040** Monday through Friday from 9am to 5pm. For the moderate charge of Dfl 5 ($2.50), plus a refundable room deposit, the VVV will help you find a room, though at the busiest times it may not be your ideal choice.

OVERLOOKING THE AMSTEL RIVER
VERY EXPENSIVE

Amstel Inter-Continental Amsterdam. Prof. Tulpplein 1 (beside the Torontobrug over the River Amstel), 1018 GX Amsterdam. ☎ **800/327-1177** in the U.S. and Canada, or 020/622-6060. Fax 020/622-5808. www.interconti.com/pages/a/amsica. E-mail: amstel@interconti.com. 79 units. A/C MINIBAR TV TEL. Dfl 825–925 ($412.50–$462.50) double; suites from Dfl 1,100 ($550) and way up; add 5% city tax. AE, DC, MC, V. Valet parking available. Tram: 6, 7, 10, or 20 to Sarphatistraat.

One of the best night views in Amsterdam is across the River Amstel to the Amstel Hotel—and the view from inside the hotel isn't bad either. The stately Amstel, dating from 1867, offers the ultimate in luxury. This is a place where visiting royalty sleeps and where a superstar can hide from eager fans.

An extensive renovation effort has restored the Amstel to its original glorious condition, with all modern conveniences thrown in for good measure. The hotel sports a mansard roof and wrought-iron window guards, a graceful Grand Hall, and rooms that boast all the elegance of a country manor, complete with antiques and genuine Delft blue porcelain. Each of the large rooms has a fax machine, personal answering machine, VCR, stereo sound system, and CD player complete with guests' favorite CDs. The Italian marble bathrooms have separate toilets and showers. Staff members note each guest's personal preferences for the next visit.

Dining/Diversions: The French La Rive restaurant has a Michelin star and is one of the hallowed temples of Amsterdam cuisine (see section 6, "Dining," for full details). The Amstel Lounge, Amstel Bar & Brasserie, and the terraces overlooking the river are less formal.

Accommodations in Central Amsterdam

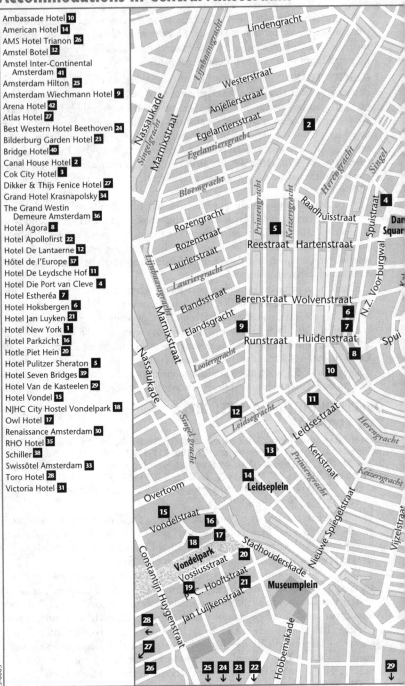

Ambassade Hotel 10
American Hotel 14
AMS Hotel Trianon 26
Amstel Botel 32
Amstel Inter-Continental
  Amsterdam 41
Amsterdam Hilton 25
Amsterdam Wiechmann Hotel 9
Arena Hotel 42
Atlas Hotel 27
Best Western Hotel Beethoven 24
Bilderburg Garden Hotel 23
Bridge Hotel 40
Canal House Hotel 2
Cok City Hotel 3
Dikker & Thijs Fenice Hotel 27
Grand Hotel Krasnapolsky 34
The Grand Westin
  Demeure Amsterdam 36
Hotel Agora 8
Hotel Apollofirst 22
Hotel De Lantaerne 12
Hôtel de l'Europe 37
Hotel De Leydsche Hof 11
Hotel Die Port van Cleve 4
Hotel Estheréa 7
Hotel Hoksbergen 6
Hotel Jan Luyken 21
Hotel New York 1
Hotel Parkzicht 16
Hotle Piet Hein 20
Hotel Pulitzer Sheraton 5
Hotel Seven Bridges 39
Hotel Van de Kasteelen 29
Hotel Vondel 15
NJHC City Hostel Vondelpark 18
Owl Hotel 17
Renaissance Amsterdam 30
RHO Hotel 35
Schiller 38
Swissôtel Amsterdam 33
Toro Hotel 28
Victoria Hotel 31

268

3-0003

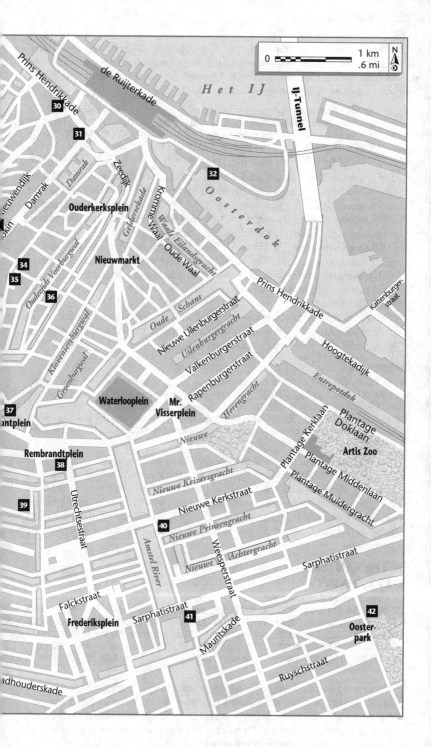

de Ruijterkade

Prins Hendrikkade

30

31

Het IJ

Oosterdok

IJ-Tunnel

0   1 km
          .6 mi

N

Zeedijk

Nieuwendijk

Damrak

Damrak

Geldersekade

Kromme Waal

Waal

Eilandsgracht

Skin

32

Ouderkerksplein

Oudezijds Voorburgwal

34

35

36

Nieuwmarkt

Oude Waal

Prins Hendrikkade

Kattenburger-
straat

Oude   Schans

Nieuwe Uilenburgerstraat

Uilenburgergracht

Hoogtekadijk

Kloveniersburgwal

Groenburgwal

Valkenburgerstraat

Rapenburgerstraat

Entrepotdok

Herengracht

37

ntplein

Waterlooplein

**Mr.
Visserplein**

Nieuwe

Plantage
Doklaan

Artis Zoo

Rembrandtplein

38

Plantage Kerklaan

Plantage Middenlaan

Plantage Muidergracht

Nieuwe Keizersgracht

Utrechtsestraat

39

Nieuwe Kerkstraat

40

Nieuwe Prinsengracht

Amstel River

Nieuwe Weespterstraat

Nieuwe Achtergracht

Sarphatistraat

Falckstraat

Frederiksplein

Sarphatistraat

41

Mauritskade

42

**Ooster-
park**

adhouderskade

Ruyschstraat

269

Amenities: Health club with heated indoor pool, Jacuzzi, sauna, solarium, weight room, Turkish bath, professional masseurs and trainers, beauty specialists, 24-hour room service, dry cleaning and laundry, limousine service, antique motor-launch, banquet and conference suites.

✪ Hôtel de l'Europe. Nieuwe Doelenstraat 2–8 (facing Muntplein), 1012 CP Amsterdam. ☎ **0800/223-6800** in the U.S. and Canada, or 020/531-1777. Fax 020/531-1778. www.leurope.nl. E-mail: hotel@leurope.nl. 100 units. A/C MINIBAR TV TEL. Dfl 580–680 ($290–$340) double; suites from Dfl 820 ($410) and up; add 5% city tax. AE, DC, MC, V. Valet parking and self-parking Dfl 50 ($25). Tram: 4, 9, 16, 20, 24, or 25 to De Munt.

The elegant, old, and prestigious Hôtel de l'Europe occupies a prime central location on the banks of the River Amstel facing Muntplein. This hotel has a grand style and a sense of ease. It was originally built in 1896 and extensively renovated in 1995. Rooms are spacious, bright, and furnished with classic good taste. Some have mini-balconies overlooking the river, and all boast marble baths.

Dining/Diversions: The Hôtel de l'Europe's formal dining room is the Restaurant Excelsior (see section 6 "Dining" for full details), which serves breakfast, lunch, and dinner daily. Restaurant Le Relais offers less formal surroundings for light lunches or dinners. Le Bar and La Terrasse serve drinks and hors d'oeuvres (summer only) daily from 11am to 1am.

Amenities: Concierge, 24-hour room service, dry cleaning and laundry, twice-daily maid service, baby-sitting, business center, secretarial services, heated indoor pool, health club with sauna and massage, gift shop.

MODERATE

Bridge Hotel. Amstel 107–111 (near the Magere Brug), 1018 EM Amsterdam. ☎ **020/623-7068.** Fax 020/624-1565. www.thebridgehotel.demon.nl. E-mail: postbus@thebridgehotel.demon.nl. 28 units. TV TEL. Summer Dfl 160–250 ($80–$125) double, winter Dfl 125–175 ($62.50–$87.50); Dfl 330 ($165) apartment. Children under 4 stay free in their parents' room. Rates include continental breakfast. Parking Dfl 30 ($15). AE, DC, MC, V. Tram: 6, 7, 10, or 20 to Sarphatistraat.

The bridge in question is the famous Magere Brug (Skinny Bridge) over the River Amstel, which the Bridge Hotel overlooks. This small and tastefully decorated hotel probably offers its guests more space per guilder than any other hotel in town. Its pine-furnished rooms seem like studio apartments, with couches, coffee tables, and easy chairs arranged in lounge areas in such a way that there's plenty of room left between them and the beds for you to do your morning exercises. Renovations are planned for 1999.

IN THE CENTER
VERY EXPENSIVE

✪ Grand Hotel Krasnapolsky. Dam 9 (facing the Royal Palace), 1012 JS Amsterdam. ☎ **020/554-9111.** Fax 020/622-8607. 539 units. www.krasnapolsky.nl. E-mail: book@krasnapolsky.nl. A/C MINIBAR TV TEL. Dfl 455–625 ($227.50–$312.50) double; Dfl 1,050–1,300 ($525–$650) suite; add 5% city tax. Children under 5 stay free in their parents' room; children 6–12 are charged half-price. AE, CB, DC, MC, V. Valet parking and self-parking Dfl 40 ($20). KLM Hotel Shuttle service from Schiphol Airport. Tram: 4, 9, 16, 20, 24, or 25 to Dam.

The Grand Hotel Krasnapolsky is one of Amsterdam's landmark hotels. It began life as the Wintertuin ("Winter Garden") restaurant, where Victorian ladies and gentlemen sipped wine and nibbled pancakes beneath the lofty skylight ceiling and hanging plants—and today the restaurant still dominates the hotel's ground floor. Over the past century the hotel has spread over a whole complex of buildings. The sizes and shapes of the rooms vary, with some tastefully converted into individually decorated mini-apartments. All rooms have hair dryers and coffeemakers. Recent renovations have added a new wing featuring a Japanese garden and a Dutch roof garden.

Dining: There are several great dining possibilities here. The Winter Garden is the most elegant place in Amsterdam for a buffet lunch. Brasserie Reflet specializes in French cuisine. There are also two fine Japanese restaurants: Edo and Kyo. But the most novel option is the Bedouin banquet dinner at the Shibli from Friday through Sunday, costing Dfl 115 to 127.50 ($57.50 to $63.75).

Amenities: Concierge, 24-hour room service, dry cleaning and laundry, baby-sitting, secretarial services, express checkout, health club, business center, conference rooms, tour desk, beauty salon, boutiques, wheelchair access.

✪ **The Grand Westin Demeure Amsterdam.** Oudezijds Voorburgwal 197 (3 blocks east of Dam), 1012 EX Amsterdam. ☎ **800/228-3000** in the U.S. and Canada, or 020/555-3111. Fax 020/555-3222. 182 units. A/C MINIBAR TV TEL. Dfl 820 ($410) double; suites from Dfl 930 ($465) and up; add 5% city tax. AE, CB, DC, JCB, MC, V. Parking Dfl 50 ($25). Tram: 4, 9, 16, 20, 24, or 25 to Dam.

The Grand Amsterdam is indeed one of the grandest hotels in Amsterdam. It's in a building that was once a convent, a royal "guest house," headquarters of the Dutch Admiralty, and the City Hall. To reach the lobby, you'll walk through a fountained courtyard, then through the brass-and-wood revolving door. There are fresh flower arrangements on all the tables in the lobby and lounge area, where tea is served in the afternoon. The black-and-white marble floors are covered with Oriental rugs.

The individually styled and furnished guest rooms are designed to reflect the different phases of the building's illustrious past. They're about the last word in plushness (although some put a refreshingly simple slant on this). Most rooms have space enough for couches and armchairs; all have a personal safe, fax machine, voice mail, and charming views. All bathrooms are equipped with hair dryers.

Dining: The hotel restaurant, done in deep red with plaid upholstery and wood furnishings, has a full bar and serves an elegant lunch and dinner. You can also have lunch or dinner at the stylish and bright Café Roux, which has an original Karel Appel mural.

Amenities: Indoor pool, health club with Jacuzzi, sauna, Turkish bath, massage, and solarium, concierge, 24-hour room service, twice-daily maid service, dry cleaning and laundry, newspaper delivery, in-room massage, baby-sitting, conference facilities, secretarial services, express checkout, courtesy car.

Renaissance Amsterdam. Kattengat 1 (between Prins Hendrikkade and the Singel), 1012 SZ Amsterdam. ☎ **800/HOTELS1** in the U.S. and Canada, or 020/621-2223. Fax 020/627-5245. 405 units. www.renaissancehotels.com. A/C MINIBAR TV TEL. Dfl 455–535 ($227.50–$267.50) double; Dfl 850 ($425) suite; add 5% city tax. Children under 18 stay free in their parents' room. Extra person Dfl 60 ($30). Continental breakfast included in Clubfloor rooms. AE, DC, JCB, MC, V. Parking Dfl 60 ($30). Tram: 1, 2, 5, 13, 17, or 20 to Nieuwezijds Voorburgwal.

The six-story Renaissance blends with the gabled facades nearby. The influence of antiquity stops at the front door, however: The Renaissance is supermodern, offering big beds and color TVs. You'll also find electronic security and message-retrieval systems. And there's a hair dryer in each room. Whether or not you like the Renaissance's use of the adjacent Lutheran Domed Koepelkerk—dating from 1671 and painted by Van Gogh in 1885—as an "ultramodern conference center" will be a matter of taste. The restored and strikingly beautiful old church looks more atmospheric when it's in use as a dining chamber.

Dining/Diversions: The Brasserie Noblesse serves French and international cuisine in the evenings. The Koepel café serves local dishes all day, and the Patio

Lounge serves coffee, drinks, and snacks. Later on, let your hair down at the Boston Club disco.

Amenities: Health club with Jacuzzi and sauna, business center, conference rooms, secretarial services, car-rental desk, tour desk, beauty salon, boutiques, concierge, 24-hour room service, dry cleaning and laundry, baby-sitting, express checkout, video rentals.

EXPENSIVE

Swissôtel Amsterdam. Damrak 96 (beside Dam Square), 1012 LP Amsterdam. ☎ **020/ 626-0066.** Fax 020/627-0982. www.swissotel.com. 112 units. A/C MINIBAR TV TEL. Dfl 325–450 ($162.50–$225) double; Dfl 600 ($300) suite. Children under 12 stay free in their parents' room. Extra person Dfl 75 ($37.50). AE, CB, DC, MC, V. Paid street parking only. KLM Hotel Shuttle service from Schiphol Airport stops at Dam Square. Tram: 4, 9, 16, 20, 24, or 25 to Dam Square.

If you like to stay at small, elegant hotels, you'll be pleased by the Swissôtel Amsterdam Ascot. Like so many in Amsterdam, this hotel was built within the walls of a group of traditional canal-house buildings. The location is superb, just footsteps off of Dam Square and directly across from De Bijenkorf department store. The service is personal and thoughtful. Guest rooms are large and quiet, thanks to double-glazed windows, and all have hair dryers and coffeemakers. Bathrooms are fully tiled in marble.

Dining: Le Bistro serves excellent French cuisine and casual meals at modest prices.

Amenities: Concierge, 24-hour room service, dry cleaning and laundry, newspaper delivery, in-room massage, baby-sitting, secretarial services, express checkout, gift shop.

Victoria Hotel. Damrak 1–5 (facing Centraal Station), 1012 LG Amsterdam. ☎ **800/ 670-PARK** in the U.S. and Canada, or 020/623-4255. Fax 020/625-2997. www.parkhotel. com. E-mail: victoria@euronet.nl. 305 units (10 with shower only). MINIBAR TV TEL. Dfl 510–560 ($255–$280) double; suites from Dfl 650 ($325). Extra person Dfl 60 ($30). AE, CB, DC, MC, V. Parking opposite the hotel Dfl 36 ($18). Tram: Any tram to Centraal Station. Free 1st-class train ticket to and from Schiphol Airport.

This is as close as you can be to Centraal Station, the hub of local transportation. For years the Victoria has been a turreted landmark at the head of the Damrak, overlooking the canal-boat piers and the gaggle of bicycles usually parked in the square. There's a neon-lit mood to the Damrak beyond the hotel, but the Victoria maintains its inherent elegance. Its spacious rooms were recently redecorated and refurnished, and the windows have been replaced with double-glazed panes. All the rooms have trouser presses, Internet connections, and hair dryers. The idea of its new owners is to give you a five-star hotel at four-star rates.

Dining/Diversions: The Seasons Garden Restaurant has a Swedish atmosphere. The Tasman Bar is a nice place to have a cocktail. Brasserie Vic's serves tea and lunch and offers a great fly-on-the-wall view of the bustling Damrak from its glassed-in terrace.

Amenities: Heated indoor pool, health club, solarium, business center with secretarial services, concierge, limited-hours room service, dry cleaning and laundry, newspaper delivery, in-room massage, baby-sitting, express checkout, valet parking on request.

MODERATE

✪ **Cok City Hotel.** Nieuwezijds Voorburgwal 50 (between Centraal Station and Dam Square), 1012 SC Amsterdam. ☎ **800/44-UTELL** in the U.S. and Canada, or 020/ 422-0011. Fax 020/420-0357. 106 units. TV TEL. Dfl 280 ($140) double. Extra person Dfl 55

($27.50). Rates include Dutch buffet breakfast. AE, DC, MC, V. Tram: 1, 2, 5, 13, 17, or 20 to Nieuwezijds Voorburgwal.

This six-floor hotel is only 5 minutes' walk from Centraal Station and Dam Square. It's one of Amsterdam's last family-owned hotels, and the personal service offered is excellent. The comfortable, modern rooms are brightly decorated in different colors and come equipped with trouser presses, hair dryers, and safes. Added conveniences include food, beverage, and ice dispensers on every floor. This hotel is altogether a good value for the money.

✪ **Hotel Die Port van Cleve.** Nieuwezijds Voorburgwal 176–180 (behind the Royal Palace), 1012 SJ Amsterdam. ☎ **020/624-4860.** Fax 020/622-0240. E-mail: dieportvancleve.amsterdam@wxs.nl. 120 units. TV TEL. Dfl 340–415 ($170–$207.50) double; Dfl 625 ($312.50) suite. Extra person Dfl 95 ($47.50). Rates include breakfast. KLM Hotel Shuttle service from Schiphol Airport. AE, CB, DC, MC, V. Nearby parking lot Dfl 40 ($20) per day. Tram: 1, 2, 5, 13, 17, or 20 to Magna Plaza.

The Port van Cleve is one of the city's oldest hotels; it has been harboring notable Amsterdam visitors for the last hundred years. The ornamental facade, complete with turrets and alcoves, is original, but the interior was completely gutted, rebuilt, and modernized in 1997. The rooms are furnished in a modern but cozy style. All have hair dryers, and some have minibars. Limited-hours room service, dry cleaning and laundry, and baby-sitting are all provided. Meals are available downstairs in the traditional Dutch setting of the Brasserie de Poort, and you can drink in the Bodega de Blauwe Parade, surrounded by Delft Blue tiles.

RHO Hotel. Nes 5–23 (beside Dam Square), 1012 KC Amsterdam. ☎ **020/620-7371.** Fax 020/620-7826. 170 units. MINIBAR TV TEL. Dfl 175–225 ($87.50–$112.50) double. Rates include continental breakfast. AE, MC, V. Parking Dfl 40 ($20). Trams: All Centraal Station trams to Dam/Royal Palace.

Once you find it, you'll bless the easy convenience of the RHO Hotel. It's located just off of Dam Square in a building that was once the offices of a gold company, and before that housed a theater in the space that now holds the reception desk and breakfast area. Rooms have been recently renovated, the location is excellent, and the price is right.

INEXPENSIVE

Amstel Botel. Oosterdokskade 2–4 (beside Centraal Station), 1011 AE Amsterdam. ☎ **020/626-4247.** Fax 020/639-1952. 176 units. TV TEL. Dfl 147 ($73.50) double. AE, DC, JCB, MC, V. Public parking available on quayside. Tram: Any tram to Centraal Station. Turn left out of Centraal Station, pass the bike rental, and you'll see it floating in front of you.

This is a boat-hotel moored 250 yards from Centraal Station. Once aboard, you'll find 176 cabins spread out over four decks connected by elevator. The rooms are quite small, in keeping with the nautical feel, but all have large windows and comfortable beds. This offbeat hotel has become very popular since it opened because of its central location, adventurous quality, and comfort at reasonable rates. Rooms on the land-side offer a view of a post office designed by Le Corbusier, but the waterside rooms have a more inspiring view of the harbor.

AROUND LEIDSEPLEIN
VERY EXPENSIVE

✪ **American Hotel.** Leidsekade 97 (facing Leidseplein), 1017 PN Amsterdam. ☎ **020/624-5322.** Fax 020/625-3236. www.interconti.com/pages/a/amsamea. E-mail: american@interconti.com. 188 units. A/C MINIBAR TV TEL. Dfl 550 ($225) double; Dfl 750 ($375) suite. AE, CB, DC, JCB, MC, V. Parking at nearby lot Dfl 60 ($30). KLM Hotel Shuttle service from Schiphol Airport stops nearby. Tram: 1, 2, 5, or 20 to Leidseplein.

This marvelous century-old hotel is as European as its name suggests it isn't. It has a turreted exterior and an art nouveau cafe that's been declared a national monument. Some of the guest rooms have balconies overlooking a canal, and all have modern furnishings and decor. The American has become a traditional meeting place for Amsterdammers when they're in the Leidseplein area. Every tourist should take at least one look inside the splendid old building, now restored to its original glory.

Dining/Diversions: The famous Café Américain, an art deco marvel, is a mecca for writers and artists. It's more casual than the rather formal dining room. There's also the Brasserie, and the Nightwatch Bar, which has a closed-in terrace looking out onto Leidseplein.

Amenities: 24-hour room service, concierge, health club with sauna, laundry and dry cleaning, business and secretarial services, gift shop.

INEXPENSIVE

Hotel De Lantaerne. Leidsegracht 111 (near Leidseplein), 1017 ND Amsterdam. ☎ **020/ 623-2221.** Fax 020/623-2683. 24 units (17 with bathroom). TV TEL. Dfl 130–140 ($65–$70) double with bathroom, Dfl 100–110 ($50–$55) double without bathroom. Rates include buffet breakfast. AE, MC, V. Limited parking available on street. Tram: 1, 2, or 5 to Leidsestraat.

The Hotel de Lantaerne is small and inexpensive, perfect for long stays because it feels like home—for a couple of reasons. For one, not only are the standard rooms perfectly comfortable, but there are four studios that have kitchenettes, color TVs, and minirefrigerators—perfect if you're doing Amsterdam on a budget and would like to cook some of your own meals. The other thing that makes this place homey is the breakfast room. It's bright and airy, with an exposed beam ceiling, large windows, and red- and white-checked tablecloths. All rooms have hair dryers.

ALONG THE CANAL BELT
VERY EXPENSIVE

✪ **Hotel Pulitzer Sheraton.** Prinsengracht 315–331 (near Westermarkt), 1016 GZ Amsterdam. ☎ **800/325-3535** or 020/523-5235. Fax 020/627-6753. www.sheraton.com. 224 units. MINIBAR TV TEL. Dfl 495–585 ($247.50–$292.50) double; Dfl 1,495 ($747.50) suite; add 5% city tax. Extra person Dfl 90 ($45). AE, CB, DC, MC, V. Valet parking and self-parking Dfl 50 ($25). KLM Hotel Shuttle service from Schiphol Airport. Tram: 13, 14, 17, or 20 to Westermarkt.

Before this hotel opened near Westermarkt, the only way a tourist could stay overnight in a gabled canal house was to forgo the style of first-class accommodations. The Pulitzer, however, is an all-new, top-service hotel that was built within the historic walls of a block of 24 different canal houses. The houses, most of which are between 200 and 400 years old, adjoin one another, side by side and garden to garden, in a U-shape that faces two canals and one small side street. From the outside, the Pulitzer blends inconspicuously with its neighborhood. You walk between two houses to enter the lobby or climb the steps of a former merchant's house to enter the ever-crowded and cheerful bar. If you stay in a deluxe duplex room, you may even get a key to your own canal-side front door. Rooms are modern, spacious, and decorated with warm color schemes. The lobby/reception area and about 80 rooms have just been upgraded to offer air-conditioning, video-on-demand, and telephones with voice mail and data facilities. The second phase will upgrade another hundred rooms and the dining and bar areas. All rooms have hair dryers.

Dining/Diversions: The handsome lounge bar is a favorite gathering place for locals as well as guests; during the summer, it spills out into the peaceful inner courtyard. The stylish but intimate new restaurant, designed by Yves Rochon, serves gourmet French cuisine.

Amenities: Concierge, 24-hour room service, laundry and dry cleaning, newspaper delivery, in-room massage, baby-sitting, secretarial services, valet parking, conference rooms, tour desk.

EXPENSIVE

✪ **Dikker & Thijs Fenice Hotel.** Prinsengracht 444 (corner with Leidsestraat), 1017 KE Amsterdam. ☎ **020/626-7721.** Fax 020/625-8986. 26 units. MINIBAR TV TEL. Dfl 315–450 ($157.50–$225) double. Children 12 and under stay free in their parents' room. Rates include continental breakfast. AE, DC, JCB, MC, V. Parking at nearby lot Dfl 40 ($20). Tram: 1, 2, 5, or 20 to Leidsestraat.

This small hotel is situated on one of Amsterdam's most famous canals, and just 2 blocks away from the Leidseplein. Upstairs, the spacious and tastefully styled rooms are clustered in groups of two or four around small lobbies, which makes the Dikker & Thijs feel more like an apartment building than a hotel. Welcoming touches are flowers in the rooms, a subtle but elegantly modern art deco decor, and double-glazed windows to eliminate the noise rising up from lively Leidsestraat at all hours of the day and night. All rooms were renovated during 1997 and 1998. Those at the front have a super view of the classy Prinsengracht.

Dining: The Prinsenkelder ("Prince's Cellar") restaurant, just next door, serves fine French and Italian food for dinner in an atmospheric setting.

Amenities: Concierge, room service, dry cleaning and laundry, in-room massage, baby-sitting, secretarial services, bicycle rental, tour desk.

MODERATE

✪ **Ambassade Hotel.** Herengracht 335–353 (near Spui), 1016 AZ Amsterdam. ☎ **020/626-2333.** Fax 020/624-5321. www.ambassade-hotel.nl. E-mail: info@ ambassade-hotel.nl. 52 units. TV TEL. Dfl 325 ($162.50) double; suite from Dfl 425 ($212.50). Extra person Dfl 60 ($30). Rates include full breakfast. AE, DC, MC, V. Parking in nearby lot Dfl 40 ($20). Tram: 1, 2, or 5 to Spui.

The elegant Ambassade occupies ten neighboring canal-houses in the "Golden Bend"—for centuries the city's most fashionable address. Most of the hotel's individually styled and spacious rooms have large, multipane windows overlooking the canal, and most are accessible by elevator (a couple still require a trip up a steep, winding staircase). Everyone who stays at the Ambassade enjoys the view each morning at breakfast in the split-level chandeliered breakfast room. There are also two classically furnished parlors overlooking the canal, with Persian rugs, comfy armchairs for reading, and stately grandfather clocks ticking away. When you look through the floor-to-ceiling windows at the Ambassade's elegant neighbors across the canal, you really feel that you're in the home of a rich 17th-century merchant. The Ambassade is growing in popularity, and with good reason, so be sure to make your reservations months in advance.

Amsterdam Wiechmann Hotel. Prinsengracht 328–330 (at Looiersgracht), 1016 HX Amsterdam. ☎ **020/626-3321.** Fax 020/626-8962. 38 units. TV TEL. Dfl 195–250 ($97.50–$225) double. Rates include breakfast. No credit cards. Limited parking available on street. Tram: 10, 17, or 20 to Marnixstraat.

It takes only a moment to feel at home in the antique-adorned lobby of the Amsterdam Wiechmann, owned by American T. Boddy and his Dutch wife, Nicky. The Wiechmann is a comfortable, casual sort of place. Besides that, the location is one of the best you'll find in this or any price range: 5 minutes in one direction is the Kalverstraat shopping street; 5 minutes in the other, the Leidseplein. The hotel occupies three restored canal houses. Oriental rugs grace many of the floors in the public spaces. The higher-priced doubles have antique furnishings, and many have a view of the two canals. The breakfast room has hardwood floors and lots of greenery, for a bright and breezy start to your day. There's also a lounge and bar.

Canal House Hotel. Keizersgracht 148 (near Leliegracht, just north of the Raadhuisstraat), 1015 CX Amsterdam. ☎ **020/622-5182.** Fax 020/624-1317. E-mail: canalhousehotel@ compuserve.com. 26 units. TEL. Dfl 245–290 ($122.50–$145) double. Rates include continental breakfast. AE, DC, MC, V. Limited parking available on street. Tram: 13, 14, 17, or 20 to Westerkerk.

This small hotel's American owner has taken a traditionalist approach to reestablishing elegant canal-house atmosphere. The hotel occupies two adjoining houses that date from 1640; they were gutted and rebuilt to provide private bathrooms and are filled with antiques, quilts, and Chinese rugs. Fortunately, the hotel is blessed with an elevator, plus a manageable staircase (which still has its beautifully carved old balustrade), and, overlooking the back garden (which is illuminated at night), a magnificently elegant breakfast room that seems to have been untouched since the 17th century. On the parlor floor, the owner has created a cozy Victorian-era saloon. This is a welcoming home away from home. Families should take note that children under the age of 12 are not encouraged.

Hotel Estheréa. Singel 303–309 (near Spui), 1012 WJ Amsterdam. ☎ **020/624-5146.** Fax 020/623-9001. 75 units. MINIBAR TV TEL. Dfl 340–390 ($170–$195) double. Children 12 and under stay free in parents' room. Extra person Dfl 50 ($25). Rates include breakfast. AE, DC, JCB, MC, V. Parking nearby Dfl 40 ($20) per day. Tram: 1, 2, 5, or 20 to Spui.

The Estheréa, which has been owned by the Esselaar family since its beginnings, is built within the walls of neighboring 17th-century canal houses. It offers the blessed advantage of an elevator, a rarity in these old Amsterdam homes. In the 1930s the owners spent a lot of money on wood paneling and fixtures, which are still in place. While the hotel will look dated to some, most agree that the wooden bedsteads and dresser-desks lend warmth to the recently renovated and upgraded rooms. The room sizes vary according to their location in the canal houses. Most of the rooms are doubles, but there are a few larger rooms that are ideal for families. All have hair dryers. Extras include room-service meals from the excellent Greek traîterie next door, a concierge, limited-hours room service, dry cleaning and laundry, in-room massage, baby-sitting, secretarial services, bicycle rental, tour desk, and free coffee in the lobby.

Hotel New York. Herengracht 13 (10 minutes' walk from Centraal Station), 1015 BA Amsterdam. ☎ **020/624-3066.** Fax 020/620-3230. 18 units. TV TEL. Dfl 200–250 ($100–$125) double. Rates include breakfast. AE, DC, MC, V. Limited private parking Dfl 35 ($17.50). Tram: All trams to Centraal Station.

This charming hotel is on one of the city's most picturesque canals, overlooking the famous Milkmaid's Bridge. It's composed of three historic 17th-century buildings which were joined together. The guest rooms are spacious and furnished in a modern style. Additional facilities and services include a cocktail lounge and same-day laundry service. Note that there's no elevator. The Hotel New York welcomes gay visitors (though it's not exclusively gay).

INEXPENSIVE

Hotel Agora. Singel 462 (adjacent to Koningsplein), 1017 AW Amsterdam. ☎ **020/ 627-2200.** Fax 020/627-2202. home.worldonline.nl/~agora. E-mail: agora@worldonline.nl. 16 units (13 with bathroom). TV TEL. Dfl 170–210 ($85–$105) double with bathroom, Dfl 115–145 ($57.50–$72.50) double without bathroom. Children 6 and under are charged

Dfl 25 ($12.50). Extra person Dfl 40 ($20). Rates include breakfast. AE, DC, JCB, MC, V. Parking Dfl 30 ($15). Tram: 1, 2, or 5 to Koningsplein.

Up-to-date chic and old-fashioned friendliness are the keynotes of the Agora, which also enjoys one of the most convenient locations in town: 1 block from the Flower Market in one direction, 1 block from Spui in the other. Although housed in a canal house built in 1735, the Agora has a style that's distinctively eclectic. Furniture from the 1930s and 1940s mixes with fine mahogany antiques. Also, bursting bouquets greet you as you enter, and a distinctive color scheme creates an effect that is both peaceful and dramatic at the same time. Owners Yvo and Els also managed to find an abundance of overstuffed furniture; nearly every room has a puffy armchair you can sink into after a wearying day of sightseeing. All rooms have hair dryers.

Hotel De Leydsche Hof. Leidsegracht 14 (off Herengracht), 1016 CR Amsterdam. ☎ **020/623-2148.** 10 units (4 with bathroom). Dfl 85–95 ($42.50–$47.50) double. No credit cards. Limited parking available on street. Tram: 1, 2, 5, or 20 to Leidsestraat.

This hotel's greatest advantage is its location, just off of the Herengracht and along the Leidsegracht canal. The accommodations are basic but well cared for and clean. The owners no longer serve breakfast, but there are many cafes in the immediate area.

Hotel Hoksbergen. Singel 301 (near Spui), 1012 WA Amsterdam. ☎ **020/626-6043.** Fax 020/638-3479. E-mail: hotel hoksbergen@wxs.nl. 14 units. TV TEL. Dfl 150–180 ($75–$90) double. Children 4 and under stay free in their parents' room. Extra person Dfl 25 ($12.50). Rates include breakfast. AE, DC, JCB, MC, V. Parking at nearby lot Dfl 35 ($17.50). Tram: 1, 2, 5, or 20 to Spui.

This inexpensive hotel in a 300-year-old canal house isn't flashy or elegant, but it's bright and fresh (a complete renovation was finished early in 1998), which makes it a good deal for budget-conscious travelers who don't want to swap creature comforts for guilders. Its central location at a tranquil point on elegant Singel canal makes it easy to get to all the surrounding sights and attractions. All rooms have fans, and hair dryers are available at reception.

AROUND REMBRANDTPLEIN
EXPENSIVE

✪ **Schiller.** Rembrandtplein 26–36, 1017 CV Amsterdam. ☎ **020/554-0700.** Fax 020/624-0098. www.krasnapolsky.nl. 92 units. TV TEL. Dfl 385–495 ($192.50–$247.50) double; suite from Dfl 525 ($262.50). AE, DC, MC, V. Limited parking available on street. Tram: 4, 9, or 20 to Rembrandtplein.

The Schiller is a true Amsterdam gem, a stylish blend of jugendstil and art deco in its public spaces and tasteful decor and furnishings in the rooms. Its sculpted facade, wrought-iron balconies, and stained-glass windows stand out on the often brash Rembrandtplein. The Schiller Café, next door to the hotel, is one of the trendiest watering holes in town. The hotel gets its name from the painter Frits Schiller, who built it in 1912. His outpourings of artistic expression, in the form of 600 portraits, landscapes, and still lifes, are displayed in the halls, rooms, stairwells, and public areas, and their presence fills this hotel with a unique sense of vitality, creativity, and personality. One in three rooms has a minibar, and all have a coffeemaker and hair dryer. All things considered, the Schiller is good value for money.

Dining: Experience jugendstil design along with some good Dutch food and the hotel's own beer, Frisse Frits, in the Brasserie Schiller, or join the in crowd for a drink amid the art deco splendor of the Café Schiller.

Amenities: 24-hour room service, laundry and dry cleaning, baby-sitting, health club, conference rooms.

MODERATE

✪ **Hotel Seven Bridges.** Reguliersgracht 31 (at Keizersgracht), 1017 LK Amsterdam. ☎ **020/623-1329.** 11 units (6 with bathroom). TV. Dfl 150–300 ($75–$150) double. Rates include full breakfast. AE, MC, V. Limited parking available on street. Tram: 4, 9, or 14 to Rembrandtplein.

The Seven Bridges is another of Amsterdam's true gems. Each room is individually decorated with antique furnishings and posters of Impressionist art on the walls. The biggest room, which is enormous and can accommodate up to four, is on the first landing, and has a huge bathroom with wood paneling, double sinks, a fair-sized shower, and a separate area for the lavatory. There are also some attic rooms with sloped ceilings and exposed wood beams, and some big, bright basement rooms done almost entirely in white. The attic and basement rooms have shared baths. The latest upgrade added handmade Italian drapes, hand-painted tiles, and wood-tiled floors.

AROUND MUSEUMPLEIN & THE VONDELPARK
EXPENSIVE

✪ **Hotel Jan Luyken.** Jan Luykenstraat 54–58 (near Rijksmuseum), 1071 CS Amsterdam. ☎ **020/573-0730.** Fax 020/676-3841. www.janluyken.nl. E-mail: info@janluyken.nl. 63 units. MINIBAR TV TEL. Dfl 330–435 ($165–$217.50) double. Children 4–12 are charged half price; children under 4 stay free in their parents' room. Extra person Dfl 85 ($42.50). Rates include Dutch buffet breakfast. AE, DC, MC, V. Limited parking available on street. Tram: 2, 3, 5, or 10 to Paulus Potterstraat.

The Jan Luyken is just 1 block from both the Vincent van Gogh Museum and the elegant P. C. Hooftstraat shopping street. The hotel maintains a balance between its sophisticated lineup of facilities and its intimate and personalized approach, appropriate to this residential neighborhood. The owners are proud of the atmosphere they've created, and they're constantly improving the look of the hotel.

MODERATE

Atlas Hotel. Van Eeghenstraat 64 (near Vondelpark), 1071 GK Amsterdam. ☎ **020/676-6336.** Fax 020/671-7633. 23 units. TV TEL. Dfl 200 ($100) double. Extra person Dfl 40 ($20). Rates include breakfast. AE, DC, JCB, MC, V. Limited parking available on street. Tram: 2 to Jacob Obrechtstraat.

The Atlas is a converted mansion, convenient for chic shoppers, concertgoers, and museum lovers. Staff back up the homey feel with attentive service. The guest rooms are small but tidy, decorated attractively in gray with blue comforters on the beds and a welcoming basket of fruit on the desk. Leather chairs fill the front lounge, which has a ticking grandfather clock in the corner. A small bar/restaurant provides 24-hour room service. Laundry and dry-cleaning service is available during the week. A hair dryer is available at the reception desk.

Hotel Vondel. Vondelstraat 28–30 (near Marriott Hotel), 1054 GE Amsterdam. ☎ **020/612-0120.** Fax 020/685-4321. 72 units. MINIBAR TV TEL. Dfl 345 ($172.50) double; Dfl 495 ($247.50) triple. Rates include breakfast. AE, DC, MC, V. Limited parking available on street. Tram: 1 to Overtoom; 20 to Eerste Constantijn Huygensstraat.

This five-floor hotel, named after the famous 17th-century Dutch poet Joost Van den Vondel, has become one of the leading three-star hotels in Amsterdam. Each room is named after one of Vondel's poems. The furniture is solid, rooms are spacious, and the service is good. This is a comfortable place, conveniently located near the museum area and Leidseplein.

Toro Hotel. Koningslaan 64 (off Oranje Nassaulaan), 1075 AG Amsterdam. ☎ **020/673-7223.** Fax 020/675-0031. 22 units. MINIBAR TV TEL. Dfl 250 ($125) double with bathroom, Dfl 300 ($150) triple with bathroom. Rates include buffet breakfast. AE, DC, MC, V. Parking Dfl 16.50 ($8.25), except Sunday. Tram: 2 to Valeriusplein.

This beautiful hotel is nestled amidst some of the city's most exclusive turn-of-the-century, villa-style residences, on the fringes of Vondelpark. It maintains the atmosphere of a country-style mansion. The tasteful decor combines Louis XIV and Liberty styles and features stained-glass windows and Murano chandeliers. Guests can enjoy the private garden and terrace, and there's a dry cleaning and laundry service. All rooms have hair dryers. Leidseplein is a 10-minute walk away through Vondelpark.

INEXPENSIVE

✪ **AMS Hotel Trianon.** J.W. Brouwersstraat 3–7 (behind the Concertgebouw), 1071 LH Amsterdam. ☎ **020/673-2073.** Fax 020/673-8868. www.hospitality.nl/ams. E-mail: info@ams.nl. 52 units. TV TEL. Dfl 140–200 ($70–$100) double. Extra person Dfl 45 ($22.50). Rates include breakfast. AE, DC, JCB, MC, V. Limited parking available on street. Tram: 5 to Concertgebouw.

The showpiece of the AMS Hotel group is the Trianon, located in a quiet residential neighborhood directly behind the Concertgebouw concert hall. The hotel has recently undergone a top-to-bottom renovation, redecoration, and redirection that took it from serviceable to sophisticated. Rooms are fitted with old-style, dark-wood furnishings; all have hair dryers. There's a laundry service, baby-sitting service, and airport shuttle, as well as an Italian restaurant.

✪ **Owl Hotel.** Roemer Visscherstraat 1 (off Eerste Constantijn Huygensstraat), 1054 EV Amsterdam. ☎ **020/618-9484.** Fax 020/618-9441. E-mail: manager@owl-hotel. demon.nl. 34 units. TV TEL. Dfl 160–205 ($80–$102.50) double. Rates include continental breakfast. AE, DC, JCB, MC, V. Limited parking available on street, or at nearby parking lot for Dfl 20 ($10). Tram: 1, 2, 5, 6, 10, or 20 to Leidseplein; 3 or 16 to Eerste Constantijn Huygensstraat.

If "small but chic, and reasonably priced" describes the sort of hotel you prefer, you'll be pleased to learn about the Owl, located in the central but pleasantly quiet residential area around Vondelpark. One of Amsterdam's best buys, the Owl Hotel is bright, tidy, and well kept. Rooms aren't very big but they're not cramped either, and the bathrooms, all of which were renovated in 1997, are tiled floor to ceiling. There's also a pleasant lounge/bar overlooking a small garden. Amenities include a concierge, limited-hours room service, dry cleaning and laundry, baby-sitting, and secretarial services. All rooms have hair dryers.

Hotel Parkzicht. Roemer Visscherstraat 33 (off Eerste Constantijn Huygensstraat), 1054 EW Amsterdam. ☎ **020/618-1954.** Fax 020/618-0897. 14 units (11 with bathroom). TV TEL. Dfl 140–160 ($70–$80) double with bathroom. Rates include breakfast. AE, MC, V. Limited parking available on street. Tram: 1, 2, or 5 to Leidseplein.

This hotel features large rooms with brass beds, old Dutch furniture, occasional fireplaces, and baths as large as the bedrooms. Many of the guests who stay here are English-speaking tourists. Try to book one of the large apartmentlike doubles on the second floor (no. 5 or 6), overlooking Vondelpark.

Hotel Piet Hein. Vossiusstraat 52–53 (off Eerste Constantijn Huygensstraat), 1071 AK Amsterdam. ☎ **020/662-7205.** Fax 020/662-1526. www.hotelpiethein.com. E-mail: info@hotelpiethein.nl. 36 units. TV TEL. Dfl 125–195 ($62.50–$97.50) double. Rates include continental breakfast. AE, DC, JCB, MC, V. Parking at nearby lot Dfl 20 ($10). Tram: 1, 2, 5, or 20 to Leidseplein.

The appealing Hotel Piet Hein is one of the best-kept establishments in town. It's located in a dream villa facing Vondelpark, and is named after a Dutch folk hero, a 17th-century admiral who captured a Spanish silver shipment. The rooms are spacious and well furnished, and the staff is charming and professional. Half the rooms overlook the park, and two second-floor double rooms feature semicircular balconies. The lower-priced rooms are in the annex behind the hotel. Hair dryers are available on request. The Piet Hein also provides concierge, room service for drinks, dry cleaning and laundry, and baby-sitting.

✪ Hotel Van de Kasteelen. Frans van Mierisstraat 34 (off Van Baerlestraat), 1071 RT Amsterdam. ☎ **020/679-8995.** Fax 020/679-8995. 13 units (none with bathroom). Dfl 90–100 ($45–$50) double. No credit cards. Limited parking available on street. Tram: 3, 5, or 20 to Van Baerlestraat.

This hotel is on a relatively quiet side street just off of Van Baerlestraat and not far from the Concertgebouw. It's run by an elderly Indonesian couple who give a gracious welcome to their guests. Rooms are spartan but clean and the price ensures that there's no lack of demand. A simple breakfast is served in the lounge, where there's also a television that guests can watch in the evening.

IN AMSTERDAM SOUTH
VERY EXPENSIVE

Amsterdam Hilton. Apollolaan 138–140 (at Minervalaan), 1077 BG Amsterdam. ☎ **800/ HILTONS** or 020/678-0780. Fax 020/662-6688. www.hilton.com. E-mail: amsterdam@ hilton.com. 271 units. A/C MINIBAR TV TEL. Dfl 390–615 ($195–$307.50) double; add 5% city tax. Children stay free in their parents' room. AE, DC, MC, V. Limited parking available on street. KLM Hotel Shuttle service from Schiphol Airport. Tram: 16 to De Lairessestraat.

The Amsterdam Hilton was the first American chain hotel to open in Amsterdam, and it's still among the most gracious and well-appointed hotels in town. There's an expanse of green lawn in front of the wide front porch, and a view from both the lobby and the dining room over the Noorder Amstelkanaal (Northern Amstel Canal) to some of the expensive homes that give the neighborhood its local nickname, the "Gold Coast." All the big, well-equipped rooms are done in a modern, restrained style and have a coffeemaker and hair dryer. This is where John Lennon and Yoko Ono staged their 1969 "bed-in for peace," and if you're willing to shell out an extra Dfl 100 ($50) per night you can stay in the suite that's decorated with their memorabilia. An added bonus is the Hilton's Marina and Yacht Club, where you can rent classic wooden motorboats.

Dining/Diversions: Roberto's is a Mediterranean-style restaurant that adds a touch of sunshine to the gloomiest day. The Half Moon Lounge and Yacht Club cafe serve drinks and light snacks. Laugh to stand-up comedy in English at Toomlers.

Amenities: Concierge, 24-hour room service, laundry and dry cleaning, newspaper delivery, twice-daily maid service, baby-sitting, secretarial services, express checkout, bicycle rental, health club, sauna, business center, conference rooms, hairdresser, souvenir shop, and gift shop.

EXPENSIVE

Bilderberg Garden Hotel. Dijsselhofplantsoen 7 (off Apollolaan), 1077 BJ Amsterdam. ☎ **0800/641-0300** (U.S. only), or 020/664-2121. Fax 020/679-9356. www.bilderberg.nl. E-mail: garden@bilderberg.nl. 98 units. A/C MINIBAR TV TEL. Dfl 275–495 ($137.50– $247.50) double; add 5% city tax. Extra person Dfl 75 ($37.50). AE, DC, JCB, MC, V. Limited parking available on street. KLM Hotel Shuttle service from Schiphol Airport stops nearby. Tram: 16 to De Lairessestraat.

Because of its excellent Mangerie De Kersentuin restaurant (see below), the Garden considers itself a "culinary hotel," an idea that extends to the rooms, whose color schemes are salad-green, salmon-pink, *parfait d'amour* lilac, and grape-blue. The rooms are furnished and equipped with refined taste to the highest standards. The bathrooms, all in marble, are equipped with Jacuzzi tubs and hair dryers. The Garden's spectacular lobby has a wall-to-wall fireplace with a copper-sheathed chimney.

Dining/Diversions: The Mangerie De Kersentuin (Cherry Orchard) restaurant, a member of Les Etappes du Bon Goût, has an international reputation (see section 6, "Dining") and moderate prices. The Kersepit (Cherry Pip) is a cozy bar with an open fireplace.

Amenities: Conference room, 24-hour room service, dry cleaning and laundry, newspaper delivery, baby-sitting, secretarial services, health club across the street, conference rooms, car rental, and tour desk.

MODERATE

Best Western AMS Hotel Beethoven. Beethovenstraat 43 (near Apollolaan), 1077 HN Amsterdam. ☎ **0800/0221-455** or 020/664-4816. Fax 020/662-1240. www.hospitality.nl/ams. E-mail: ams@hospitality.nl. 62 units. 52 units. MINIBAR TV TEL. Dfl 220–310 ($110–$155) double. Extra person Dfl 65 ($32.50). AE, DC, JCB, MC, V. Limited parking available on street. Tram: 5 or 24 to Beethovenstraat.

If you like to experience neighborhood atmosphere wherever you travel, make note of the AMS Hotel Beethoven. It's located in the heart of one of Amsterdam's most desirable areas, on one of its most beautiful shopping streets. The Beethoven has been treated to a top-to-bottom redecoration that includes the addition of personal safes in all the rooms. Plus, to the delight of locals as well as hotel guests, the Beethoven also gained an attractive restaurant, Brasserie Beethoven, that has a year-round sidewalk cafe (which closes at 7:30pm).

Hotel Apollofirst. Apollolaan 123 (off Minervalaan), 1077 AP Amsterdam. ☎ **020/673-0333.** Fax 020/675-0348. E-mail: apolfi@xs4all.nl. 40 units. TV TEL. Dfl 250–285 ($125–$142.50) double; Dfl 485 ($242.50) suite. Rates include breakfast. AE, DC, MC, V. Limited parking available on street. Tram: 5 or 24 to Beethovenstraat.

The small and very elegant Apollofirst, a family-owned hotel set amid the Amsterdam School architecture of Apollolaan, advertises itself as the "best quarters in town in the town's best quarter." The boast may be debatable, but all the rooms in this intimate hotel are quiet, spacious, and grandly furnished. Baths are fully tiled, and rooms at the back of the hotel overlook the well-kept gardens. Guests can have a snack or a cocktail on the summer terrace. Room service and a laundry and dry-cleaning service are available. The hotel's elegant French-style Restaurant Chambertin offers an international menu.

DORMS, HOSTELS, AND BED & BREAKFASTS

Arena Hotel. 's-Gravesandestraat 51 (at Oosterpark), 1092 AA Amsterdam. ☎ **020/694-7444.** Fax 020/663-2649. www.hotelarena.nl. E-mail: info@hotelarena.nl. 116 unit, 464 beds. Dfl 100–125 ($50–$62.50) double with bathroom; Dfl 35–40 ($17.50–$20) per person in 4-, 6-, and 8-bed rooms with bathroom; Dfl 25–30 ($12.50–$15) for a dorm bed. Breakfast Dfl 12.50 ($6.25). AE, MC, V. Limited parking available on street. Tram: 7 or 10 from Centraal Station to Korte 's-Gravesandestraat; 9 or 14 to Tropenmuseum/Mauritskade; 3 to Oosterpark.

During 1999, the Arena will be undergoing an upgrade from a budget hotel to a low-cost two-star hotel. There will still be three dorms with 24 beds each, but most dormitory space is being converted into four-, six-, and eight-person rooms with private shower and toilet. Most of those rooms will offer split-level sleeping space and therefore more privacy. The hotel is in a huge redbrick hospital built in 1890, and also serves as a lively cultural center. There's an information counter, a concert/dance hall, a TV video lounge, a restaurant, and a garden.

ⓘ Family-Friendly Hotels

Hotel Estheréa *(see p. 276)*   Though most of the rooms in this canal house hotel are rather small, all are tastefully furnished, and a few, ideal for families, are equipped with bunk beds.

Hotel Hoksbergen *(see p. 277)*   Children under 4 years of age stay for free at this centrally located hotel. The simple but comfortable atmosphere is ideal for allowing the kids some informal holiday freedom.

NJHC City Hostel Vondelpark *(see p. 282)*   This is an ideal choice for families traveling on a limited budget. The hostel offers a good blend of facilities, space, easygoing atmosphere, and security, in addition to a green location in the city's famous Vondelpark.

Amstel Botel *(see p. 273)*   Although it's more common to find youthful spirits traveling alone or in small groups here, there's no reason why the Amstel Botel wouldn't work for families, and there's the added interest for the kids of being on a ship, even if it isn't going anywhere.

✪ **NJHC City Hostel Vondelpark.** Zandpad 5 (in Vondelpark), 1054 GA Amsterdam. ☎ **020/589-8999.** Fax 020/589-8955. 101 units (475 beds). Dfl 32.50 ($16.25) dormitory; Dfl 67 ($33.50) single; Dfl 80 ($40) double; Dfl 148 ($74) 4-bed room; Dfl 195 ($97.50) 6-bed room. Dfl 5 ($2.50) supplement for nonmembers of IYHF. Rates include breakfast. AE, MC, V. No parking. Tram: 1, 2, 5, or 20 to Leidseplein.

"The new generation of city hostel" is how the Dutch youth hostel organization describes this place, and that seems a fair description. This is a marvelous and great-value place to stay. Its location, inside but on the edge of Vondelpark and facing Leidseplein, could hardly be bettered. The core of the hostel is a former Girl's Housekeeping School, a protected monument, in and around which the newly built complex opened in 1998. All rooms are simply but modernly and brightly furnished, and all have an en suite bathroom. The four- and six-bed rooms make ideal locations for families traveling on a limited budget as well as for groups of friends. Some rooms are adapted for disabled people. Although the hostel is open 24 hours a day, security is taken seriously, and all guests have key cards that are automatically invalidated on checking out. There are even coin-operated Internet stations for those who have to surf. The Backpacker's Lounge is a pleasant place to meet fellow travelers.

Bed & Breakfast. Vossiusstraat 24 (at Vondelpark), 1017 AE Amsterdam. ☎ **020/676-2856.** Dfl 125 ($62.50) double. Extra adult Dfl 35 ($17.50), extra child Dfl 25 ($12.50). Limited parking available on street. Tram: 20 to Van Baerlestraat; 2, 5, or 10 to Paulus Potterstraat.

This delightful place is beside the Vondelpark, near Museumplein. Your host is Mrs. Elisabeth Kühling, who speaks English fluently and is warm and friendly to guests. Her knowledge of the country and her library of books, maps, and transportation information are very helpful to visitors. She provides a large room decorated gracefully with all modern accommodations and two big windows overlooking Vondelpark. There's access to a private bathroom, and a big breakfast is served in her warm and cheerful kitchen.

6 Dining

If cities get the cuisine they deserve, Amsterdam's ought to be liberal, multiethnic, and adventurous, though still satisfying the sound Dutch insistence on value for each guilder spent. Guess what? It is. As a trading city with a true melting-pot character, Amsterdam has absorbed culinary influences from far and wide and rustled them all up to its own collective satisfaction.

Just about any international cuisine type can be found on the city's restaurant roster—in Amsterdam, they say, you can eat in any language. From elegant 17th-century dining rooms, to cozy canal side bistros, to exuberant taverns with equally exuberant Greek attendants, to exotic Indonesian rooms attended by turbaned waiters, to the *bruine kroegjes* (brown cafes) with their smoke-stained walls and friendly table conversations, the eateries of Amsterdam confront the tourist with the exquisite agony of being able to choose only one or two from their vast number each day.

A relatively recent and highly popular trend in Amsterdam that combines eating and drinking is the emerging **grand cafe** scene. These are cafes in the, well, grand tradition of Paris, Vienna, and Rome, cafes with balconies or terraces and lots of style and ambiance—see and be seen kind of places. They're distinguished by their emphasis on food, architecture, production values, and style. The grand cafes listed below are definitely grand, yet you should be aware that there are others that use the name even though they may not be particularly impressive—the definition is an elusive one, merging into restaurants with terraces at one end and ordinary cafes at the other.

There are a few distinctively **Dutch foods** whose availability is determined by when you visit. Among them: asparagus, beautifully white and tender, in May; "new" herring, fresh from the North Sea and eaten raw, in May or early June (great excitement surrounds the first catch of the season, part of which goes to the queen and the rest to restaurateurs amid spirited competition); and Zeeland oysters and mussels (*Zeeuwse oesters* and *Zeeuwse mosselen*), from September to March.

RESTAURANT ORIENTATION

Keep in mind that Dutch menus list appetizers, not main courses, under "entrée," and that a 15% service charge plus value-added tax (BTW) and any local taxes are included in all prices.

HOURS   Most restaurants are open from noon to 2:30pm for lunch, and from 6 or 7 to 10 or 11pm for dinner 6 or 7 days a week. Although more restaurants are staying open later, the Dutch in general dine early; in many cases last orders are taken no later than 10pm.

TIPPING   Since a 15% service charge is already included in the prices shown on the menus, you needn't leave an extra tip; but if you want to do as the Dutch do, round up to the next guilder or two, or in the case of a large check, up to the next 5 or 10 guilders.

RESERVATIONS   Unless you eat especially early or late, reservations are generally recommended at top restaurants and at those on the high end of the moderate price range. Restaurants are often small and may be crowded with neighborhood devotees. Terraces are always in big demand on pleasant summer evenings.

Dining in Central Amsterdam

3-0005

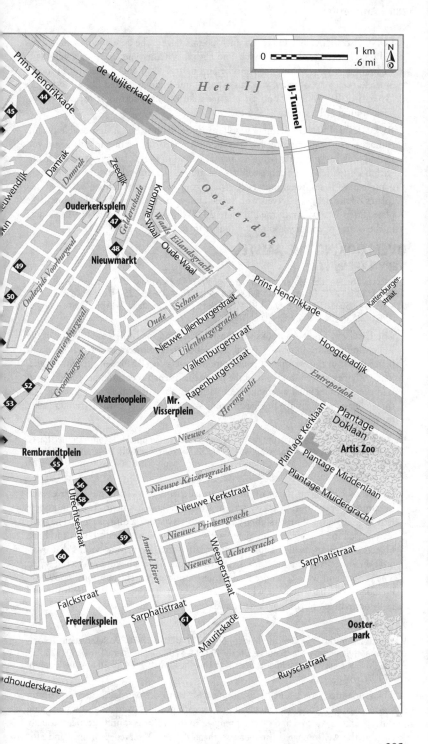

0   1 km
    .6 mi
N

Prins Hendrikkade

de Ruijterkade

Het IJ

IJ-Tunnel

45

44

Damrak

Damrak

Zeedijk

Geldersekade

Kromme Waal

Waals Eilandsgracht

Oosterdok

Ouderkerksplein

47

Nieuwmarkt

48

Oude Waal

Oudezijds Voorburgwal

49

Nieuwendijk

Kattenburgerstraat

50

Prins Hendrikkade

Oude Schans

Hoogtekadijk

Nieuwe Uilenburgerstraat

Kloveniersburgwal

Uilenburgergracht

Valkenburgerstraat

Groenburgwal

Rapenburgerstraat

Entrepotdok

52

Herengracht

53

Waterlooplein

Mr.
Visserplein

Plantage Kerklaan

Plantage
Doklaan

Nieuwe

Artis Zoo

Rembrandtplein

55

Plantage Middenlaan

56

57

Nieuwe Keizersgracht

Plantage Muidergracht

58

Utrechtsestraat

Nieuwe Kerkstraat

60

59

Nieuwe Prinsengracht

Amstel River

Achtergracht

Nieuwe Weesperstraat

Sarphatistraat

Falckstraat

Sarphatistraat

Frederiksplein

61

Mauritskade

Ooster-
park

dhouderskade

Ruyschstraat

LUNCH & SNACK COSTS   Lunch doesn't have to be an elaborate affair. Typical Dutch lunches are light, quick, and cheap. Whether you have two small sandwiches and a glass of milk, a pancake and coffee, soup and French bread, or an omelet and a glass of wine, you can expect a quick lunch to cost Dfl 10 to Dfl 25 ($5 to $12.50). An afternoon pit stop for cake and cappuccino or tea will set you back around Dfl 8 to Dfl 12 ($4 to $6).

BUDGET DINING   Eating cheaply in Amsterdam is not an impossible dream. Almost every neighborhood has its modestly priced restaurant. In this genre you should look out particularly for *eetcafés*. The food in these places is generally mainstream Dutch (although some eetcafés are more adventurous), and it usually comes complete with unpretentious taste. Main courses, often described as *dagschotels* (plates of the day), are served with vegetables, french fries, and salad on one large plate. They usually cost in the Dfl 15 to 20 ($7.50 to $10) range. Many restaurants in the center of the city also offer a tourist menu.

OVERLOOKING THE AMSTEL
VERY EXPENSIVE

✪ **Excelsior.** In the Hôtel de l'Europe, Nieuwe Doelenstraat 2–8 (facing Muntplein). ☎ **020/531-1777.** Main courses Dfl 48.50–78.50 ($24.25–$37.25); fixed-price menus Dfl 95–165 ($47.50–$82.50). AE, DC, MC, V. Sun–Fri 12:30–2pm, daily 7–11pm. Tram: 4, 9, 16, 20, 24, or 25 to the Munt. CONTINENTAL.

The Excelsior, which overlooks the Amstel River and the Mint Tower, is one of the finest dining rooms in town. Crystal chandeliers, fresh flowers, candlelight, and soft piano music in the evening all contribute to the classic elegance of the atmosphere. Veal with leek sauce is only one of the many fine French specialties here, and Dutch traditional dishes such as smoked eel with dill also turn up fairly regularly. The three-course menus make fine gastronomy more affordable. Formal attire (a jacket for men) is required.

La Rive. In the Amstel Intercontinental Hotel, Professor Tulpplein 1 (off Weesperstraat). ☎ **020/622-6060.** Main course Dfl 45–130 ($22.50–$65); fixed-price menus Dfl 135–195 ($67.50–$97.50). AE, DC, MC, V. Mon–Fri noon–2pm, Mon–Sat 6:30–10:30pm. Tram: 6, 7, 10, or 20 to Sarphatistraat. FRENCH.

La Rive, which sports a pair of prestigious Michelin stars, overlooks the river, and in summer opens onto a grassy terrace along the embankment. The atmosphere here suggests a small private library called into service for a dinner party. The walls are paneled in cherry and punctuated with tall cabinets filled with books and brass objects. Along one wall is a row of particularly romantic private booths that overlook the other tables and provide a view through tall French windows to the water. The service and wine cellar are in the finest modern French traditions. Specialties include grilled baby abalone with citrus-pickled onion purée and garlic juice, and grill-roasted rack of lamb with dates and Zaanse mustard.

MODERATE

Koriander. Amstel 212 (near the Magere Brug). ☎ **020/627-7879.** Reservations recommended at theater time. Main courses Dfl 28–40 ($14–$20); theater menu Dfl 47.50 ($23.75). AE, CB, MC, V. Daily 5pm–midnight. Tram: 4 to Utrechtsestraat; 9, 14, or 20 to Waterlooplein. FRENCH.

The Koriander, just a quick last-minute dash from the Muziektheater or Theater Carré, has grown skilled at getting slow-eating, clock-watching, theater-going diners fed and watered and off the premises in time. If this sounds hectic, it usually isn't, as the well-prepared three-course theater menu is served promptly and efficiently, and the cool setting beside the river, with lots of light, lots of plants, and a restrained use of Delft blue tiles, makes for a pleasant and relaxed atmosphere. You'll do better, though, if you give them a chance by getting there in time. Try the terrine of smoked fish as an appetizer, and the fillet of catfish with lobster sauce as a main course.

INEXPENSIVE

Café de Jaren. Nieuwe Doelenstraat 20–22 (near Muntplein). ☎ **020/625-5771.** Main courses Dfl 16–30 ($8–$15). No credit cards. Daily 10am–1am (Fri, Sat 2am). Tram: 4, 9, 16, 20, 24, or 25 to the Munt. GRAND CAFE.

Café de Jaren, one of the largest cafes in the city, has 300 seats inside and can seat more out on the terrace beside the River Amstel—a marvelous place to soak up the sun. Many students sick of cafeteria food eat lunch here, and it's also popular with the media crowd. You can enjoy everything from a cup of coffee or a glass of *jenever* (gin) to spaghetti bolognese and rib-eye steak. The building originally served as a bank; it's spacious and has unusually high ceilings.

IN THE CENTER
EXPENSIVE

Christophe. Leliegracht 46 (between Prinsengracht and Keizersgracht). ☎ **020/625-0807.** Main courses Dfl 55–60 ($27.50–$30); fixed-price menus Dfl 85–105 ($42.50–$52.50). AE, DC, MC, V. Tues–Sat 6:30–10:30pm. Tram: 13, 14, 17, or 20 to Westermarkt. FRENCH.

Owner and chef Jean Christophe is the star of this show—and it's a one Michelin star turn, in fact. He combines influences from his childhood in Algeria and southwest France with his experience at top restaurants in New York, Baltimore, and Massachusetts, to create an updated version of classic French cuisine. Christophe serves sensuous and sophisticated food in an elegant setting featuring dark cherry-wood paneling, thick carpets, rice paper lampshades, stately cacti by the windows, and floral paintings by contemporary Dutch artist Martin van Vreden. The food is similarly refined, using traditional Mediterranean ingredients—figs, truffles, olives, and saffron—in exciting new ways. Try the roasted milkfed Pyreneean lamb, or roasted turbot in a light curry sauce, and finish with a light tart of prunes with Armagnac.

✪ **De Silveren Spiegel.** Kattengat 4–6 (off Singel). ☎ **020/624-6589.** Main courses Dfl 47.50–55 ($23.75–$27.50); fixed-price menus Dfl 75–85 ($37.50–$42.50). AE, MC, V. Daily 6–11pm (open for lunch by reservation). Tram: 1, 2, 5, 13, 17, or 20 to Nieuwendijk. DUTCH/FRENCH.

The new owner of this traditional old restaurant, one of the best known in Amsterdam, has introduced a fresh approach. The two houses that form the premises were built in 1614 for a wealthy soap maker, Laurens Jansz Spieghel. It's typically Old Dutch inside, with the bar downstairs and more dining rooms where the bedrooms used to be. The whole place emanates a traditionally Dutch tidiness that's very welcoming. There's a garden in back. The menu has been updated, and now offers new finely prepared seafood and meat dishes, such as baked sole fillets with wild spinach, and trilogy of lamb with ratatouille—but just as in the old days, the lamb is still Holland's finest, from Texel, and the traditional Zaanse mustard is never far away.

Dynasty. Reguliersdwarsstraat 30 (behind the Flower Market). ☎ **020/626-8400.** Main courses Dfl 35–67 ($17.50–$33.50); fixed-price menus Dfl 70–98 ($35–$49). AE, DC, MC, V. Wed–Mon 5:30–11pm. Tram: 1, 2, or 5 to Koningsplein. CHINESE/ASIAN.

For summer dining in a formal Louis XV-style canal-house garden or winter dining in a cozy cavern of exotic colors and upturned Chinese umbrellas, try Dynasty, located between the Singel and Herengracht canals. It offers a selection of specialties from Chinese (Szechuan), Thai, Malay, and Filipino cuisine. Among the intriguing possibilities is the Promise of Spring, an appetizer of crisp pancakes filled with bamboo shoots and minced meat. Or perhaps you'd rather get together a group of six like-minded diners to share the magnificent 10-course Festive Meal, an extravaganza of flavors—among its delights are lobster, coquille St-Jacques, duck, lamb, pigeon, and Szechuan beef.

Lucius. Spuistraat 247 (near Spui). ☎ **020/624-1831.** Main courses Dfl 33–60 ($16.50–$30); fixed-price menu Dfl 50 ($25). AE, DC, MC, V. Mon–Sat 5pm–midnight. Tram: 1, 2, or 5 to Spui. SEAFOOD.

Lucius, which means "pike" in Latin, has earned a reputation for fine seafood at reasonable prices. Oysters and lobsters imported from Norway and Canada are the specialties here. The three-course fixed-price menu is also very popular. Among the half dozen or so choices featured on the chalkboard menu, you might find fish soup to start, followed by grilled plaice, Dover sole, bass, or John Dory. The spectacular seafood plate includes 6 oysters, 10 mussels, clams, shrimp, and half a lobster. The long, narrow dining room is cooled by ceiling fans and features an aquarium. In summer, chairs are placed out on the sidewalk.

✪ **Restaurant d'Vijff Vlieghen.** Spuistraat 294–302 (entrances on Singel and Spuistraat). ☎ **020/624-8369.** Main courses Dfl 44–55 ($22–$27.50); fixed-price menus Dfl 75–97.50 ($37.50–$48.75). AE, DC, MC, V. Daily 5:30pm–midnight. Tram: 1, 2, or 5 to Spui. DUTCH.

You know all those jokes that begin, "Waiter, there's a fly in my soup . . ."? Well, how about five flies? Restaurant d'Vijff Vlieghen ("The Five Flies") is one of the most famous restaurants in Amsterdam and occupies five canal houses (hence the name). The decor is vigorously Old Dutch, and there are interesting stories about each of the seven separate dining rooms, which include the Glass Room, with its collection of Golden Age handmade glass, and the Rembrandt Room, which has four original etchings by the artist. The chef is determined to convey the culinary excellence inherent in many traditional Dutch recipes, but in an updated "New Dutch" form. Main courses include stuffed fillet of rabbit wrapped in Brabant gammon.

MODERATE

✪ **Café-Restaurant Amsterdam.** Watertorenplein 6 (off Haarlemmerweg). ☎ **020/682-2666.** Reservations recommended on weekends. Main courses Dfl 16.50–40 ($8.25–$20). AE, DC, MC, V. Daily 11:30am–1am. Tram: 10 to Van Hallstraat. CONTINENTAL.

Think of it as *Amsterdam: the Restaurant*, because it's quite a performance. Café-Restaurant Amsterdam is based in a century-old water-pumping station, complete with diesel-powered engine. The owner has taken this monument of Victorian industrial good taste and made of it a model of contemporary good eats. You dine amidst a buzz of conviviality in the big, brightly lit former pumping hall, which had been so carefully tended by the water workers that some of its elegant decoration didn't even need repainting. Service is friendly and the food is good and moderately priced. The fried sweetbreads are popular. If you're feeling flush, spring for a double starter of half lobster with six Zeeland oysters. The Amsterdam is a little bit off the center, but easily worth the tram ride.

✪ **Café Luxembourg.** Spuistraat 24 (beside Spui). ☎ **020/620-6264.** Snacks Dfl 9.50–19.50 ($4.75–$9.75); main courses Dfl 18–27 ($9–$13.50). MC, V. Mon–Thurs 9am–1am, Fri–Sat 9am–2am. Tram: 1, 2, or 5 to Spui. GRAND CAFE.

"One of the world's great cafes," wrote the *New York Times* about this stylish place. Unlike other cafes in Amsterdam, which often draw a distinctive clientele, Café

Luxembourg attracts all kinds of people because it offers amazingly large portions of food at reasonable prices. Soups, sandwiches, and such dishes as meat loaf are available. A special attraction is that some of the dishes are specialties from other well-known Amsterdam restaurants—for example, the dim sum comes from the China Treasure and the chicken salad from Café Wildschut (the club sandwich is Luxembourg's own). This is a relaxing place where people are encouraged to linger and read one of the many international newspapers on hand. In summer there's sidewalk dining.

Café-Restaurant Blincker. St. Barberenstraat 7 (off Rokin). ☎ **020/627-1938.** Main courses Dfl 15–30 ($7.50–$15). AE, DC, MC, V. Mon–Sat 4pm–1am. Tram: 4, 9, 16, 20, 24, or 25 to Rokin. CONTINENTAL.

To find Café Blincker, turn into Ness from Dam Square (which runs parallel to Rokin), then turn left after the Frascati Theater. This intimate restaurant attracts actors, journalists, artists, and other assorted bohemians. At night the place is jammed with people clustered around the bar. The simple but tasty fare includes lamb chops with garlic, pancakes with cheese and mushrooms, homemade pasta, and cheese fondue.

Treasure. Nieuwezijds Voorburgwal 115–117 (near Dam Square). ☎ **020/626-0915.** Main courses Dfl 18–27 ($9–$13.50); fixed-price menus Dfl 25–75 ($12.50–$37.50). AE, DC, MC, V. Thurs–Tues noon–11pm. Tram: 1, 2, 5, 13, 17, or 20 to Nieuwezijds Voorburgwal. CHINESE.

In this city with a passion for Indonesian flavors, it can be difficult to find traditional Chinese cuisine, let alone good Chinese cuisine. But don't despair—make a beeline for China Treasure, which has become a legend in its own lunchtime (and dinnertime too). This place has been rated among the best restaurants in Amsterdam by *Avante Garde.* It offers classic Chinese culinary traditions and a wide array of choices with lovely Chinese ambiance. The decor is traditional Chinese, with lots of lanterns, watercolor paintings, and Chinese scripts. You can eat dishes from the four main styles of Chinese cooking—Beijing, Shanghai, Cantonese, and Szechuan. Look for specialties such as the vast range of dim sum items from the dedicated Dim Sum Bar, Beijing duck, and Szechuan-style prawns (very spicy).

Haesje Claes. Spuistraat 273–275 (beside Spui). ☎ **020/624-9998.** Main courses Dfl 22–35 ($11–$17.50). AE, DC, MC, V. Daily noon–midnight. Tram: 1, 2, or 5 to Spui. DUTCH.

If you're yearning for a cozy Old Dutch environment and hearty Dutch food at moderate prices, go to Haesje Claes. This inviting place has lots of nooks and crannies decorated with Delftware and wooden barrels. Brocaded benches and traditional Dutch hanging lamps with fringed covers give an intimate, comfortable feeling to the tables. The menu covers a lot of ground, ranging from canapés to caviar, but you'll have the most luck with Dutch stalwarts such as omelets, tournedos, *hutspot* (stew), *stampot* (mashed potatoes and cabbage), and various fish stews, including those with *IJsselmeer paling* (eel).

In de Waag. Nieuwmarkt 4. ☎ **020/422-7772.** Main courses Dfl 25–38 ($12.50–$19). AE, DC, MC, V. Daily 10am–1am. Metro: Nieuwmarkt. CONTINENTAL.

This cafe-restaurant is called In de Waag because it's in the Waag (see, you can speak Dutch). And what is the Waag? In medieval times it was the St. Antoniespoort Gate in the city walls, which by the time of Amsterdam's Golden Age had become a weigh house: De Waag. Nowadays, this castle-like structure holds one of Amsterdam's newest and most stylish cafe-restaurants. The indelibly romantic setting is a blaze of candlelight in the evening, with long banquet-style tables where you can mix easily with other diners. Starters, usually served in massive portions, are the kitchen's forte, while main courses such as breast of Barbary duck or braised vegetables and coriander-yogurt sauce are simply presented and not extraordinary.

✪ **Kantjil en de Tijger.** Spuistraat 291 (beside Spui). ☎ **020/620-0994.** Reservations recommended on weekends. Main courses Dfl 21.50–29.50 ($10.75–$14.75); *rijsttafels* Dfl 75–95 ($32.50–$47.50). AE, DC, MC, V. Daily 4:30–11pm. Tram: 1, 2, or 5 to Spui. JAVANESE/INDONESIAN.

Unlike Indonesian restaurants that wear their ethnic origins on their sleeve, Kantjil en de Tijger is chic, modern, and cool. The two best-sellers in this very popular restaurant are *nasi goreng Kantjil* (fried rice with pork kebabs, stewed beef, pickled cucumbers, and mixed vegetables) and the 20-item rijsttafel for two. Other choices include stewed chicken in soja sauce, tofu omelet, shrimp with coconut dressing, Indonesian pumpkin, and mixed steamed vegetables with peanut-butter sauce. Finish off your meal with the multi-layered cinnamon cake or (try this at least once) the coffee with ginger liqueur and whipped cream. The restaurant's name means "Antelope and the Tiger."

✪ **Oibibio.** Prins Hendrikkade 20–21 (facing Centraal Station). ☎ **020/553-9328.** Main courses Dfl 27.50–34.50 ($13.75–$17.25). AE, DC, V. Mon noon–6:30pm, Tues–Sun 10am–6:30pm. Tram: Any tram to Centraal Station. VEGETARIAN.

Oibibio, one of the more interesting of the new breed of Amsterdam eateries, is much more than a cafe-restaurant. This "New Age" complex boasts a grand cafe, minimalist tea garden, department store, healing center, sauna, and concert space. The complex's restaurant is a stylish affair, with a bar, wooden tables, terra-cotta floor, and glass roof. The decor and the ethereal music wafting through give the restaurant a light, airy feeling that transmits itself to the food. Wash the wide range of inventive vegetarian dishes down with biodynamic beetroot juice.

Purnama. Nieuwendijk 33 (near Centraal Station). ☎ **020/620-5325.** Main courses Dfl 18.50–25 ($9.25–$12.50); *rijsttafels* Dfl 28.50–49.50 ($14.25–$24.75);. AE, DC, MC, V. Daily noon–10pm. INDONESIAN.

This small restaurant is always crowded with locals enjoying the high-quality food. Among the favorite dishes are the mini-rijsttafel and the special rijsttafel. The first consists of 11 items, the second of 15 items; both combine sweet and sour tastes and other contrasting spices and flavors. If this is too much for you, try the nasi or bami goreng or choose one of the 8 meat and 10 fish dishes. For starters try the sot ayam, a spicy soup.

Rose's Cantina. Reguliersdwarsstraat 38–40 (1 block behind the Flower Market). ☎ **020/625-9797.** Main courses Dfl 19.50–42.50 ($9.75–$21.25). AE, DC, MC, V. Daily 5–11pm. Tram: 1, 2, or 5 to Koningsplein. MEXICAN.

Rose's Cantina attracts English-speaking guests with typical American favorites like hamburgers and meatballs, although the decor and most of the cuisine are Mexican inspired. A meal starting with tortilla chips and salsa, followed by a plato mixto or fried galinhas (roast chicken with fries and red peppers), and washed down with a Mexican beer will cost you less than Dfl 50 ($25). The tables are oak, the service is decent (though a bit slow), and the atmosphere is Latin American and buzzing with good cheer. Just be careful of long waiting times, during which you sit at the bar and, more likely than not, down one after another of Rose's excellent margaritas.

Sluizer. Utrechtsestraat 43–45 (between Herengracht and Keizersgracht). ☎ **020/626-3557.** Main courses Dfl 25–30 ($12.50–$15). AE, DC, MC, V. Mon–Fri noon–2:30pm and 5pm–1am, Sat–Sun 5pm–1am. SEAFOOD/CONTINENTAL.

This is a great place for seafood in an art deco atmosphere. There are at least 10 specials offered daily—from simple cod or eel to coquille St-Jacques (scallops), crab casserole, Dover sole, halibut, and octopus. A favorite specialty is the *waterzooï*, or fish stew. Meat dishes are also on the menu, such as beef stroganoff and chicken supreme.

Tempo Doeloe. Utrechtsestraat 75 (between Herengracht and Keizersgracht). ☎ **020/625-6718.** Main courses Dfl 25–35 ($12.50–$17.50); *rijsttafels* Dfl 55–80 ($27.50–$40). AE, DC, MC, V. Daily 6–11:30pm. Tram: 4 to Herengracht. INDONESIAN.

For authentic Indonesian cuisine this place is hard to beat, although its local reputation seems to go up and down with the tide. The attractive décor, fresh linen tablecloths, and fine china are unexpected pluses: You eat in an ambiance that is Indonesian, of course, but not to the extent of being kitsch. If anything, this restaurant errs on the side of elegance and restraint. Try the *rijsttafels*, the *nasi koening*, or any of the vegetarian dishes. Finish with the *spekkoek*, a layered spice cake. Beware that when a dish is described on the menu as *pedis*, or hot, that's exactly what it is.

INEXPENSIVE

Keuken van 1870. Spuistraat 4 (at Martelaarsgracht). ☎ **020/624-8965.** Reservations not accepted. Main courses Dfl 12.50–17.50 ($6.25–$8.75). AE, DC, MC, V. Mon–Fri 12:30–8pm, Sat–Sun 4–9pm. Tram: 1, 2, 5, 13, 17, or 20 to Nieuwendijk (1 short stop from Centraal Station). DUTCH.

Keuken van 1870 is one of the cheapest places to eat in Amsterdam. It was originally built in the year of its name as a public soup kitchen by a charitable foundation, and is still a nonprofit concern. It also must surely be the plainest place to eat: Meals are served cafeteria-style, tables are bare, décor is minimal, and dishes are plain—but the food is good. Pork chops, fish, and chicken—all accompanied by vegetables and potatoes—are some of the unremarkable but reliable main courses available on the menu. This place is typical Dutch, popular with Amsterdammers, and good for travelers on a tight budget.

Nam Kee. Zeedijk 111–113 at Nieuwmarkt. ☎ **020/624-3470.** Main courses Dfl 12–34.50 ($6–$17.25). AE, DC, MC, V. Daily 11:30am–midnight. Metro: Nieuwmarkt. CHINESE.

The area around Zeedijk and Nieuwmarkt, which in the bad old days (a few years back) was a shooting gallery for heroin addicts, has been cleaned up and is moving upmarket. The city's growing Chinatown is here, along with some genuine Chinese restaurants, of which Nam Kee is a good example. Nam Kee's long dining room has few obvious graces, but the food makes up for it. Among the mere 140 menu items, the steamed duck with plum sauce is to die for. Judging by the number of Chinese customers clicking chopsticks around, Nam Kee does all right when it comes to ethnic credibility.

't Gasthuys. Grimburgwal 7 (near the Spui). ☎ **020/624-8230.** Main courses Dfl 15–25 ($7.50–$12.50). No credit cards. Sun–Fri noon–1am, Sat noon–2am.

This *eetcafé*, popular with locals and students alike, is abuzz every night of the week. The place stretches back and back, eventually splitting off into three different levels. The food formula hits the spot: good-quality meat prepared à la minute, with simple sauces, a generous heap of salad, and probably the best fries in town.

ALONG THE CANAL BELT
EXPENSIVE

✪ **Les Quatre Canetons.** Prinsengracht 1111 (near the River Amstel). ☎ **020/624-6307.** Main courses Dfl 49–55 ($24.50–$27.50); menu surprise Dfl 65–105 ($32.50–$52.50); wine arrangement Dfl 35–55 ($17.50–$22.50). AE, CB, DISC, DC, MC, V. Mon–Fri noon–2:30pm and 6–11pm, Sat 6–11pm. Tram: 4 to Utrechtsestraat. INTERNATIONAL.

This is a long-standing favorite among Amsterdammers. The "Four Ducklings," situated in what used to be the garden of a 17th-century canal house, is one of Amsterdam's most stylish restaurants. The interior evokes the atmosphere of a garden behind the gables, bright and airy, with delicate countryside images on the walls. Yet the emphasis is more on food than fuss. Owners Ailko Faber and Jacques Roosenbred, who have been here since 1979, are credited, along with others, for elevating Amsterdam to the rank of European culinary capital. Seasonal specialties and imaginative choices, such as duck breasts with prunes, make this a delightful place to dine. The menu changes frequently and the *menu surprise* changes every day (otherwise it wouldn't be a surprise). In summer, the restaurant deploys a sidewalk terrace.

MODERATE

✪ **Bolhoed.** Prinsengracht 60–62 (near Noordermarkt). ☎ **020/626-1803.** Main courses Dfl 22–30 ($11–$15). No credit cards. Sun–Fri noon–11pm, Sat 11am–11pm. Bus: 18 or 22 to Haarlemmer Houttuinen. VEGETARIAN.

Forget the wholesome, dull, corn-sheaf-and-brown-rice image of vegetarian dining—Bolhoed adds a touch of spice to its health food formula with its Latin style, world music background, candlelight in the evenings, and fine view of the canal from its twin rooms beside the Prinsengracht. Service is zestful and friendly. Try such veggie delights as the *ragoût croissant* (pastry filled with leeks, tofu, seaweed, and curry sauce), or *zarzuela.* If you want to go whole hog, so to speak, and eat vegan, most of Bolhoed's dishes can be so prepared on request, and in any case most are made with organically grown produce.

Café van Puffelen. Prinsengracht 377 (facing Lauriergracht). ☎ **020/624-6270.** Main courses Dfl 25–35 ($12.50–$17.50); dish of the day Dfl 25–31 ($12.50–$15.50). AE, DC, MC, V. Mon–Fri 3pm–1am (Fri 2am), Sat noon–2am, Sun noon–1am. Tram: 13, 14, 17, or 20 to Westermarkt. DUTCH/CONTINENTAL.

At this large cafe-restaurant near the Westerkerk, the most popular feature is the three menus that change daily. Choices might include suckling pig, veal steak, grilled lamb chops, vegetable platters, and mozzarella with tomato. Save room for the house specialties—delicious handmade chocolates.

Casa di David. Singel 426 (at the Flower Market). ☎ **020/624-5093.** Main courses Dfl 20–40 ($10–$20). AE, DC, MC, V. Daily 5–midnight. Tram: 1, 2, 5, or 20 to Spui. ITALIAN.

A friend recommended Casa di David as the best Italian restaurant in Amsterdam, and she might just be right. The ambiance is very romantic and typically Italian—dark paneling, red-and-white-checked tablecloths, and wine casks—but mingled with the flavor of an old, wood-beamed Amsterdam canal house. There's a view of both the Singel and Herengracht canals from the restaurant's two floors. Casa di David is most famous for its freshly made in-house pasta and its pizzas-for-one.

✪ **De Belhamel.** Brouwersgracht 60 (at Herengracht). ☎ **020/622-1095.** Reservations recommended on weekends. Main courses Dfl 28–38 ($14–$19); specials Dfl 32.50 ($16.25). AE, MC, V. Daily 6pm–midnight. Bus: 18 or 22 to Haarlemmerstraat. CONTINENTAL.

Soft classical music complements the art nouveau style of this graceful, two-level restaurant overlooking the junction of the Herengracht and Brouwersgracht canals. Tables fill up quickly most evenings, so make reservations or go early. The menu changes seasonally but you can expect such dishes as puffed pastries layered with salmon, shellfish, crayfish tails, and *chervil beurre-blanc* for a starter, and beef tenderloin in Madeira sauce with zucchini *rösti* and puffed garlic for a main course. Vegetarian dishes are also served.

De Kelderhof. Prinsengracht 494 (near Leidsestraat). ☎ **020/622-0682.** Main courses Dfl 28.50–39.50 ($14.25–$19.75). AE, DC, MC, V. Daily 5:30–11pm. Tram: 1, 2, or 5, to Prinsengracht. CONTINENTAL.

Rattan chairs, wooden tables, lots of plants, and a cobbled floor give this cellar restaurant the atmosphere of a French village restaurant, and the French wine list adds to the feeling. The menu, though not extensive, has a good mix of soups, seafood, and grilled meat dishes, all prepared in the Mediterranean style. The fresh seasonal fish is close to the "heaven on earth" the place claims for it. The kitchen does a pretty mean Caesar salad as well.

Het Land van Walem. Keizersgracht 449 (beside Leidsestraat). ☎ **020/625-3544.** Reservations accepted. Main courses Dfl 20–40 ($10–$20). AE, DC, MC, V. Sun–Thurs 9am–1am, Fri–Sat 9am–2am. Tram: 1, 2, or 5 to Keizersgracht. GRAND CAFE.

Het Land van Walem, a clean-cut space originally designed by the noted Dutch architect Rietveld, has just undergone a revamp, and the furniture has turned post-modern—think Philippe Starck. But that's not all. The lunch menu has added some exotic and adventurous dishes, and the dinner menu has expanded to new culinary heights (and prices). It boasts two terraces, one outside beside the canal, and the other at the back in a garden patio. Menu items include pasta specialties, but also steak, chicken, and salads.

✪ **Kort.** Amstelveld 12 (at Prinsengracht). ☎ **020/626-1199.** Reservations required for outside terrace. Main courses Dfl 25–40 ($12.50–$20); fixed-price menu Dfl 49.50 ($24.75). AE, CB, DC, MC, V. Wed–Mon 11:30am–midnight. Tram: 4 to Prinsengracht. CONTINENTAL.

Kort is one of the few restaurants that accepts reservations for eating outdoors on a warm summer evening—a time when most terraces fill up almost instantly. The tree-shaded terrace is on the edge of a canal and a wide, open square, far enough from traffic to be unaffected by noise and fumes. Service is friendly, and the food is very good. Menu items include several excellent vegetarian dishes, such as grilled goat's cheese with spinach and salad, as well as Eastern spiced fish, a house specialty. Dining indoors is also recommended, in the atmospheric ambiance of the wooden 17th-century Amstelkerk, a restored church converted to a restaurant.

INEXPENSIVE

✪ **De Prins.** Prinsengracht 124 (at Leliegracht). ☎ **020/624-9382.** Reservations not accepted. Main courses Dfl 12–25 ($6–$12.50); dish of the day Dfl 19.50 ($8.75). AE, MC, V. Daily 10am–midnight. Tram: 13, 14, 17, or 20 to Westermarkt. DUTCH/FRENCH.

This companionable restaurant, housed in a 17th-century canal house, has a smoke-stained, brown-cafe style and food that could easily grace a much more expensive place. De Prins offers an unbeatable price-to-quality ratio for typically Dutch/French menu items, and long may it continue to do so. The youthful clientele is loyal and enthusiastic, so the relatively few tables fill up quickly. This is a quiet neighborhood place—nothing fancy or trendy, but quite appealing in a human way. There's a bar on a slightly lower level than the restaurant. From March through September De Prins spreads a terrace out onto the canal-side.

Espresso Corner Baton. Herengracht 82 (at Herenstraat). ☎ **020/624-8195.** Sandwiches Dfl 5–15 ($2.50–$7.50). No credit cards. Mon–Sat 8am–6pm, Sun 9am–6pm. Bus: 18 or 22 to Haarlemmer Houttuinen. LIGHT FARE.

This place deserves special mention. It looks small from the outside but actually seats more than 100 people: 40 inside on two levels and 60 out on the sidewalk terrace. Salads, quiches, a choice of 30 hot or cold sandwiches—plus pastries and such desserts as tiramisu—make up the menu. This is a relaxing spot to while away a couple of hours watching the excursion boats slowly drifting past on the canal.

Lunchcafé Singel 404. Singel 404 (near Spui). ☎ **020/428-0154.** Snacks Dfl 5–12 ($2.50–$6). No credit cards. Daily 10am–8pm. Tram: 1, 2, or 5 to Spui. LIGHT FARE.

If you find yourself growing weary of eating at local grand cafes, where they charge you an arm for ambiance and a leg for lunch, Singel 404 makes an acceptable alternative. It has the blessing of simplicity and the advantage of low cost. You won't have to pretend that you're cool, or smart, or hip; you can just eat. Service is friendly and the salads and sandwiches are very good.

The Pancake Bakery. Prinsengracht 191 (near Westermarkt). ☎ **020/625-1333.** Reservations required for large groups. Pancakes Dfl 8–20 ($4–$10). AE, MC, V. Daily noon–9:30pm. Tram: 13, 14, 17, or 20 to Westermarkt. PANCAKES.

This two-story canal-house restaurant serves almost nothing but pancakes—an appropriate choice for any meal. The satisfyingly large pancakes come adorned with all sorts of toppings, both sweet and spicy, including Cajun chicken (on the spicy end of the taste spectrum), ice cream and liqueur (on the sweet end), and curried turkey with pineapple and raisins (for a little bit of both). The decor is simple, with winding staircases and exposed beams contributing to the pleasant ambiance, and the windows provide a pretty view out over the Prinsengracht. In the summertime you can dine outside at long wooden tables, but beware: All the syrup, honey, and sugar being passed around tends to attract bees and hornets. Nonetheless, the Pancake Bakery remains a firm local favorite, especially among children.

✪ **Traiterie Grekas.** Singel 311 (near Spui). ☎ **020/620-3590.** Reservations not accepted. Main courses Dfl 15–25 ($7.50–$12.50). No credit cards. Tues–Fri and Sun 4–9:30pm, Sat 1–9:30pm. Tram: 1, 2, or 5 to Spui. GREEK.

With a maximum of seven tables and room for only 14 diners, Grekas would be more of a frustration than anything else, except that its main business is its takeout service. If you're staying at one of the hotels in this neighborhood (particularly the Estheréa, next door, to which Grekas provides room service), this place can even become your local diner. The food is fresh and authentic, and you can choose your meal like you would in Mykonos, by pointing to the dishes you want. If there are no free tables, you can always take your choices back to your room, or eat al fresco on the canal-side. Menu items are standard Greek but with a freshness and taste that are hard to beat. The *moussaka* and *pasticcio* are heavenly; the roast lamb with wine, herbs, olive oil, and bouillon is excellent; the kalamari in the kalamari salad seems to have come straight out of Homer's wine-dark sea; and there's a good Greek wine list, too. Take-out dishes cost a few guilders less.

AROUND LEIDSEPLEIN
EXPENSIVE

✪ **Café Américain.** In the American Hotel, Leidsekade 97 (at Leidseplein). ☎ **020/624-5322.** Main courses Dfl 35–52 ($17.50–$26). AE, DC, MC, V. Daily 10:30am–midnight (lunch noon–3pm; dinner 5–10:30pm). Tram: 1, 2, 5, 6, 7, 10, or 20 to Leidseplein. CONTINENTAL.

The lofty dining room here is a national monument of Dutch jugendstil. Since its opening in 1900 the place has been a hangout for Dutch and international artists, writers, dancers, and actors. Seductress/spy Mata Hari held her wedding reception here in her pre-espionage days. Leaded windows, newspaper-littered reading tables, bargello-patterned velvet upholstery, frosted-glass chandeliers from the 1920s, and tall carved columns are all part of the dusky sit-and-chat atmosphere. Seafood specialties include monkfish, perch, salmon, and king prawns; meat dishes include rack of Irish lamb and rosé breast of duck with creamed potatoes. Jazz lovers can stock up on good music and good food at the Sunday jazz brunch.

De Oesterbar. Leidseplein 10. ☎ **020/623-2988.** Main courses Dfl 38.50–85 ($19.25–$42.50). AE, DC, MC, V. Daily noon–1am. Tram: 1, 2, 5, 6, 7, 10, or 20 to Leidseplein. SEAFOOD.

De Oesterbar, which is more than 50 years old, is the best known and most popular fish restaurant in Amsterdam. Its seafood is delivered fresh twice daily. The decor is a delight: all white tiles with fish tanks bubbling at your elbows on the street level, and Victorian brocades and etched glass in the more formal dining room upstairs. The menu is a directory of Dutch seafood dishes, but also includes a few meat selections. Choices include *sole Danoise* with the tiny Dutch shrimp; *sole Véronique* with muscadet grapes; stewed eel in wine sauce; and the assorted fish plate of turbot, halibut, and fresh salmon.

't Swarte Schaep. Korte Leidsedwarsstraat 24 (at Leidseplein). ☎ **020/622-3021.** Main courses Dfl 45–52.50 ($22.50–$26.25); fixed-price menu Dfl 77.50 ($38.75). AE, DC, JCB, MC, V. Daily noon–11pm. Tram: 1, 2, 5, 6, 7, 10, or 20 to Leidseplein. DUTCH.

't Swarte Schaep is much better known by its English name, "The Black Sheep." It's located in a house that dates from 1687, and still seems like an old Dutch home. You climb a steep flight of tiled steps to reach the second-floor dining room, where the oak beams and ceiling panels are dark with age. This cozy, almost crowded place is made both fragrant and inviting by the fresh flowers that stand on every table and spill from the polished brass buckets hanging from the ceiling beams. The Black Sheep is well known for its wine list and its *crêpes suzette.* Menu choices might include *sole meunière* with asparagus or grilled salmon with fresh thyme.

MODERATE

Aphrodite. Lange Leidsedwarsstraat 91 (off Leidseplein). ☎ **020/622-7382.** Main courses Dfl 15–25 ($7.50–$12.50). No credit cards. Daily 5pm–midnight. Tram: 1, 2, 5, 6, 7, 10, or 20 to Leidseplein. GREEK.

In an area awash with Greek restaurants that wear their Greekness on their sleeves (who doesn't like a touch of island-taverna charm?), Aphrodite stands out for putting more emphasis on taste and less on dazzling Aegean colors, fishing nets, and the lords and ladies of Olympus. Its single room is modern, restrained in its decor, and softly lit. The specialties—*afelia* (cubes of lamb meat in a coriander-and-wine sauce), *moussaka, kleftiko* (oven-baked lamb), and others—are not much different in principle from those of other Greek restaurants in the area, but are generally better prepared and served—which, after all, is difference enough.

Bistro La Forge. Korte Leidsedwarsstraat 26 (off Leidseplein). ☎ **020/624-0095.** Main courses Dfl 22.50–39.50 ($11.25–$19.75); fixed-price menu Dfl 45 ($22.50). AE, DC, MC, V. Daily noon–2pm lunch (pancakes only), 5–11pm dinner. Tram: 1, 2, 5, 6, 7, 10, or 20 to Leidseplein. BISTRO.

Just off of the Leidseplein and right next to the famous and pricey Black Sheep (see above) is Bistro La Forge, which serves a fairly traditional French/continental menu of meats and fish (like halibut, steak, and rabbit) at moderate prices. The big attraction here is the open fireplace. Starters include escargots or frogs' legs. The à la carte menu has a variety of fish dishes, including salmon in puff pastry, as well as meat dishes, such as fillet of rabbit or filet of beef with sweet-pepper sauce. The dessert menu includes a cheese plate, sorbet, *crêpes,* and *cherries flambé* served with vanilla ice cream. There's also an extensive wine list.

De Blauwe Hollander. Leidsekruisstraat 28 (off Leidseplein). ☎ **020/623-3014.** Main courses Dfl 15–30 ($7.50–$15). No credit cards. Daily 5–11pm. Tram: 1, 2, 5, 6, 7, 10, or 20 to Leidseplein. DUTCH.

If you'd like a taste of sociable Dutch life, sitting shoulder to shoulder with the natives, the handful of big communal tables at this restaurant should fit the bill perfectly. De Blauwe Hollander can be considered either a best buy as a moderate restaurant or a step-up alternative in the budget category. There's a small sidewalk gallery here that gives you a good view of the passing parade in this busy area of town, but be warned that the menu has very little that's more imaginative than roast beef, spareribs, or chicken. Everything is served with fries and a salad or vegetable, and there's usually a *budget schotel* (budget plate).

AROUND REMBRANDTPLEIN
MODERATE

Brasserie Schiller. In the Hotel Schiller, Rembrandtplein 26–36. ☎ **020/554-0700.** Main courses Dfl29.50–35 ($14.75–$17.50); fixed-price menu Dfl 49.50 ($24.75). AE, DC, MC, V. Daily 7am–11pm. Tram: 4, 9, 14, or 20 to Rembrandtplein. CONTINENTAL.

Beamed and paneled in well-aged oak and graced with etched glass and stained-glass skylights, this 100-plus-year-old jugendstil landmark is a splendid sight (don't mistake it for the equally notable Café Schiller next door). Paintings by the artist who built the hotel, Frits Schiller, adorn the walls. Elderly former chefs have supplied the restaurant with the exact recipes and techniques used in the old days. On the classic menu you'll find everything from stewed eel and potato-and-cabbage casserole to T-bone steak, roast leg of lamb with mint sauce, and spaghetti bolognese.

INEXPENSIVE

✪ **Maoz Falafel.** Reguliersbreestraat 1 & 45. ☎ 020/624-9290. Snacks Dfl 6 ($3). No credit cards. Daily 10am–1am. ISRAELI.

This tiny gem of a restaurant really needs a category all to itself: "Almost Cost-Free" comes to mind. The specialty of the house will set you back a mere Dfl 5.50 ($2.75). It's falafel, but don't laugh—it's probably the best falafel this side of the River Jordan: mashed chickpeas mixed with herbs, rolled in a ball along with what must be some magic ingredient, fried, and served in pita bread with salad. The snack bar is capable of seating about eight people at a push, plus more at a few tables outside when the sun shines, and is tastefully decorated with an Israeli highway board and a poster for an exhibition on Hebraic script in Zürich that probably happened about 20 years ago.

IN THE JORDAAN
EXPENSIVE

Bordewijk. Noordermarkt 7 (at Prinsengracht). ☎ **020/624-3899.** Main courses Dfl 42.50–47.50 ($21.25–$23.75); fixed-price menu Dfl 63.50–84.50 ($31.75–$42.25). AE, MC, V. Tues–Sun 6:30–10pm. Bus: 18 or 22 to Haarlemmer Houttuinen. FRENCH.

This pleasantly located restaurant is often regarded as one of the best in the city. The decor is tasteful, with green potted plants offsetting the severity of the white walls and metallic black tables. Service is relaxed yet attentive, and on mild summer evenings you can't beat dining al fresco on the canal-side terrace. But the real treat is the food. An innovative kitchen staff uses Italian and Asian flourishes to accent French standards. The menu changes often, but might include salted rib roast with

Bordelaise sauce, *serrano* ham marinated in wine and vinegar and served with fresh pasta, pigeon cooked in the style of *Bresse*, or even Japanese-style raw fish. Dinner is followed by a fine selection of cheeses. The wine list is superb.

MODERATE

✪ **Spanjer & Van Twist.** Leliegracht 60 (off Keizersgracht). ☎ **020/639-0109.** Reservations not accepted. Main courses Dfl 20–30 ($10–$15). No credit cards. Daily 6pm–1am (only light snacks after 11pm). Tram: 13, 14, 17, or 20 to Westermarkt. DUTCH/INTERNATIONAL.

This place would almost be worth a visit for its name alone, so it's doubly gratifying that the food is so good too. The interior is in typical *eetcafé* style, with the day's specials chalked on a blackboard, a long table with newspapers at the front, and the kitchen visible in back. High standards of cooking, however, put this place above others of the kind. You'll find Thai fish curry with *pandan* rice on the menu as well as *saltimbocca* of trout in white wine sauce, alongside Dutch favorites such as steak with herb butter or spring onion sauce. In fine weather, you can eat on a terrace beside the canal.

Speciaal. Nieuwe Leliestraat 140–142 (off Prinsengracht). ☎ **020/624-9706.** Main courses Dfl 21.50–27.50 ($10.75–$13.75); *rijsttafel* Dfl 60 ($30). AE, MC, V. Daily 5:30–11pm. Tram: 13, 14, 17, or 20 to Westermarkt. INDONESIAN.

"Special" is the perfect word to describe Speciaal if you're a devoted fan of Amsterdam's finest rijsttafel restaurants. This cozy little place is owned and operated by a young Indonesian. Its walls are adorned with the mats that traditionally covered the spice crates that were sent to Speciaal from the East Indies. Equally true to the traditions of those islands is the cooking. The *saté*, or kebabs, of goat meat are charcoal roasted to perfection. The specialty of the house is the multilayered Indonesian cake called *spekkoek*.

Toscanini. Lindengracht 75 (off Brouwersgracht). ☎ **020/623-2813.** Reservations required. Main courses Dfl 24–38 ($12–$16). No credit cards. Daily 6–10:30pm. Bus: 18 or 22 to Haarlemmer Houttuinen. ITALIAN.

This small Jordaan restaurant has a warm and welcoming ambiance and excellent southern Italian food. It's popular with the artists and bohemians who inhabit this neighborhood. Toscanini has the type of unembellished country-style decor that speaks of authenticity, as does the fresh, homemade food. Service is congenial but can be slow, though that doesn't seem to deter the loyal regulars, who clamor for such specialties as the delicious veal lasagna and *fazzoletti,* green pasta stuffed with ricotta, mozarella, and mortadella.

INEXPENSIVE

Tapas Café Duende. Lindengracht 62 (off Prinsengracht). ☎ **020/420-6692.** Reservations not accepted. Tapas dishes Dfl 3.50–9.50 ($1.75–$4.75). No credit cards. Daily 5pm–1am. Bus: 18 or 20 to Haarlemmerstraat. SPANISH.

Dark, smoky, atmospheric, friendly—there's no better place than Duende to experience the varied palette of little dishes that are Spanish *tapas*. Take just one or two and you have a nice accompaniment to a few drinks; put five, six, or more together and you have a full-scale meal on your hands. Pick from dozens of choices, including *tortilla Española, champiñones al ajillo,* and *calabacín a la marmera* (aubergines with seafood). Wash them down with *sangría,* jump into the arena of friendly conversation, and you'll be clapping your hands and stamping your feet before long. Only bear in mind that although individually the *tapas* dishes are cheap, they soon add up.

AROUND MUSEUMPLEIN & VONDELPARK

EXPENSIVE

✪ Bodega Keyzer. Van Baerlestraat 96 (beside the Concertgebouw). ☎ **020/ 671-1441.** Main courses Dfl 39.50–68.50 ($19.75–$34.25); fixed-price menu Dfl 63 ($31.50). AE, DC, MC, V. Mon–Sat 9am–midnight, Sun 11am–midnight. Tram: 2 to Willemsparkweg; 3, 5, 12, or 20 to Van Baerlestraat; 16 to De Lairessestraat. DUTCH.

Whether or not you attend a concert at the Concertgebouw, you may want to visit its next-door neighbor, Bodega Keyzer. An Amsterdam landmark since 1903—old-timers say it hasn't changed a whit through the years—the Keyzer has enjoyed a colorful joint heritage with the world-famous concert hall. Among the many stories still told here is the one about the night a customer mistook a concert soloist for a waiter and tried to order some whiskey from him. The musician, not missing a beat, lifted his violin case and said graciously, "Would a little Paganini do?" The traditional dark-and-dusky decor and highly starched pink linens add elegance to the place. The menu leans heavily to fish from Dutch waters and, in season, to game specialties, such as hare and venison.

MODERATE

Brasserie van Baerle. Van Baerlestraat 158 (near the Concertgebouw). ☎ **020/679-1532.** Main courses Dfl 34–39.50 ($17–$19.75); fixed-price menus Dfl 55–69.50 ($27.50–$34.75). AE, MC, V. Mon–Fri noon–11pm, Sun 10am–11pm. Tram: 3, 12, or 20 to Van Baerlestraat; 2 or 5 to Paulus Potterstraat. FRENCH.

Filling the gap between budget fare and haute cuisine is the goal of this restaurant's young owners. They accomplish that aim with their exciting nouvelle cuisine—soups, salads, and other light dishes. In summer you can dine in the garden. This is a popular gathering place for the writers, photographers, and advertising people who live and work in the area.

Café-Restaurant Wildschut. Roelof Hartplein 1–3 (off Van Baerlestraat). ☎ **020/ 676-8220.** Main courses Dfl 16–27.50 ($8–$13.75); fixed-price menu Dfl 50 ($25). MC, V. Mon–Fri 9am–1am, Sat 10:30am–1am, Sun 9:30am–midnight. Tram: 3, 12, 20 or 24 to Roelof Hartstraat; 5 to Joh. M. Coenenstraat. BISTRO.

Wildschut is one of those places that keeps its chic reputation through thick and thin. It occupies a curved dining room at the junction of Van Baerlestraat and Roelof Hartstraat. Amsterdam's bold-and-beautiful like to see and be seen on the fine terrace in summer or amidst the smoke in the brasserie-style interior in winter. It gets crowded here on Friday and Saturday evenings so be prepared to join the standing throng while waiting for a table. The food is straightforward but good, ranging from BLTs, to vegetarian lasagna, to American rib eye with green pepper sauce. If at all possible try to wear something that gets you noticed—but not too much, if you get the idea.

De Knijp. Van Baerlestraat 134 (near the Concertgebouw). ☎ **020/671-4248.** Reservations required for lunch and for more than 5 people. Main courses Dfl 29.50–39.50 ($14.75–$19.75); fixed-price menus Dfl 47.50–67.50 ($23.75–$33.75). AE, DC, MC, V. Lunch Mon–Fri noon–3pm; dinner daily 5:30pm–1:30am. Tram: 3, 5, 12, 20, or 24 to Van Baerlestraat; 16 to De Lairessestraat. DUTCH/FRENCH.

One of the advantages of this fine restaurant is that it's open later than many others—its kitchen is still taking orders when chefs at many other Amsterdam restaurants are sound asleep back home. This would not count for much, of course, if the food were no good, but De Knijp is definitely worth staying up late for, or worth stopping by for after a performance at the nearby Concertgebouw. The menu is not wildly inventive, but you might try such specialties as carpaccio with pesto, poached salmon with tarragon sauce, and goose breast with pink pepper sauce. Look also for friendly, if sometimes a little worn-out, service (this is a hard-working place), and an intimate bistro ambiance, with lots of wood and tables on two levels.

De Orient. Van Baerlestraat 21 (near the Concertgebouw). ☎ **020/673-4958.** *Rijsttafel* Dfl 30–65 ($15–$32.50). AE, DC, MC, V. Daily 5–10:30pm. Tram: 2 to Willemsparkweg; 3, 5, 12, or 20 to Van Baerlestraat; 16 to De Lairessestraat. INDONESIAN.

De Orient specializes in *rijsttafels;* it offers three regular variations (12, 19, and 25 dishes), and three vegetarian ones. On Wednesday nights there's a *rijsttafel* buffet as well (be careful of the spicier items on the table if you're not used to them—Indonesian food can be very hot). The decor is traditional Indonesian. The place has been owned since 1948 by a friendly Indonesian couple who lived in California for a while.

EXPENSIVE

Mangerie de Kersentuin. In the Garden Hotel, Dijsselhofplantsoen 7 (off Apollolaan). ☎ **020/664-2121.** Reservations recommended on weekends. Main courses Dfl 42.50–49 ($21.75–$24.50); fixed-price menus Dfl 52.50–72.50 ($26.25–$36.25). AE, DC, MC, V. Mon–Fri noon–2pm, Mon–Sat 6–11pm. Tram: 16 to De Lairessestraat. INTERNATIONAL.

All cherry red and gleaming brass, the spectacular De Kersentuin ("Cherry Orchard") has floor-to-ceiling windows looking onto the residential street outside and semi-screened interior windows looking into the glimmering kitchen inside. Attention to detail has made this restaurant a mecca for visiting stars. You eat with Christofle silver-plate flatware and drink wine or champagne that was personally selected by the restaurateur and his chef. From nouvelle cuisine and a strictly French approach to cooking, this place has progressed to its own unique culinary concept, based on regional recipes from around the world, and using fresh ingredients from Dutch waters and farmlands. The menu changes every 2 months, but these samples give some idea of what to expect: lamb fillet prepared in goose fat with creamy salsifies and coriander-scented vanilla sauce; sea bass sautéed with peppers, garlic, sea salt, and sesame seeds, served on stir-fried *pak-choi* and tofu, with lemon-grass butter.

MODERATE

Umeno. Agamemnonstraat 27 (off Olympiaplein). ☎ **020/676-6089.** Main courses Dfl 28–49 ($14–$24.50). No credit cards. Tues–Sun noon–2pm and 6–11pm. Tram: 16 to Olympiaplein. JAPANESE.

This intimate Japanese eatery is slightly off the beaten track, near the Olympic Stadium, but the food and service make the trip worthwhile. It's relatively easy to get a seat but you should call ahead—the restaurant only seats 36. The sushi and sashimi are always fresh. Other traditional dishes include *shabu-shabu, sukiyaki, yakitori,* and *tonkatsu.*

INEXPENSIVE

Artist. Tweede Jan Steenstraat 1 (off Van Woustraat). ☎ **020/671-4264.** Main courses Dfl 9–19 ($4.50–$9.50); fixed-price menu (*meze*) Dfl 20 ($10). AE, DC, MC, V. Daily 5pm–11pm. Tram: 4 to Van Woustraat. LEBANESE.

Owners Ralfo and Simon have brought a little piece of the eastern Mediterranean to Amsterdam South and presented it in a simple, authentic way at low cost and with good taste guaranteed. Members of the city's Lebanese community are often seated at the tables here—always a good sign for an ethnic restaurant. Specialties

---

ⓘ Family-Friendly Restaurants

Café-Restaurant Amsterdam *(see p. 288)*   The spaciousness and the bar area with a pool table and benches mean that children can mingle with local youngsters without getting in the way, and have as fine a meal as the adults.

De Orient *(see p. 299)*   Kids will have fun sampling the different Indonesian foods of the *rijsttafels* (comprised of 12, 19, or 25 dishes) at De Orient. There are a couple of dishes especially for children who don't like spicy food.

Enfant Terrible   This cafe at De Genestetstraat 1 (☎ 020/612-2032) is in a quiet residential area, not far from the Leidseplein. You can take a break here and have a coffee on your own, or have lunch or dinner together with the children. The cafe has a large playroom and a playpen for the very young, and also offers a baby-sitting service (maximum 3 hours).

✪ KinderKookKafé   Children are the chefs and waiters in this small restaurant at Oudezijds Achterburgwal 193 (☎ 020/625-3527)—with the help of some adult cooks, they prepare dinner on Saturday and bake cookies and pies for high tea on Sunday. If your kids want to, they too can join the kitchen brigade; or you can all just relax and enjoy the meal. Kids must be at least 8 years old to help with the Saturday dinner, and 5 for the Sunday bake.

New York Pizza   When your kids are longing for a piece of pizza, head to New York Pizza, Amsterdam's answer to Pizza Hut. You can order three different kinds of pizza—traditional, deep pan, or "whole meal." There are branches at Damrak 59 (☎ 020/639-0494), Reguliersbreestraat 15–17 (☎ 020/420-5585), Damstraat 24 (☎ 020/422-2123), and Leidsestraat 23 (☎ 020/622-8689).

The Pancake Bakery *(see p. 294)*   I have yet to meet a kid who doesn't love pancakes, and this restaurant at Prinsengracht 191 (☎ 020/625-1333) is *the* best pancake source around. Pancakes here come with various inventive toppings, and the child-oriented meals and desserts come with suitably colorful ornaments like umbrellas and clowns.

---

include Lebanese meze and a selection of small dishes that add up to a big meal, including falafel, couscous, and even Lebanese pizza. Many of the dishes here are vegetarian.

Sal Meijer's Sandwich Shop. Scheldestraat 45 (off Ferdinand Bolstraat). ☎ 020/673-1313. Sandwiches Dfl 4.50–9.50 ($2.25–$4.75). No credit cards. Mon–Fri 10am–7:30pm. Tram: 25 to Churchilllaan. KOSHER.

If the shortage of good pastrami on rye in Amsterdam starts to get to you, take the no. 25 tram out from the center to this nostalgic sandwich shop, where members of the city's Jewish community gather each day. Both the sandwiches and the conversation are excellent. Sal also delivers, depending on where you are and how many sandwiches you want. To find his place, watch for the moment when the tram does a 90-degree left turn off of Ferdinand Bolstraat onto Churchilllaan, get off at the first stop, backtrack to the crossroad, and then go left for a block and a half.

LOCAL FAVORITES

You'll have no trouble finding *broodjes* (small sandwiches) on menus all over Amsterdam, but to eat a broodje in a real *broodjeswinkel* (sandwich shop), head to the ever-crowded **Eetsalon Van Dobben,** at Korte Reguliersdwarsstraat 5–9, just off of Rembrandtplein, or one of the two branches of **Broodje van Kootje,** conveniently located at Leidseplein and at Spui and easily identified by their bright-yellow broodje-shaped signs. A broodjeswinkel close to the Kalverstraat and Koningsplein shopping district is the **Tearoom Pott** annex at Voetboogstraat 22–24, near Heiligeweg.

LIGHT, CASUAL & FAST FOOD

BAKERIES & CROISSANTERIES   Croissanteries are popping up all along Amsterdam's shopping streets to offer the Dutch a crispy alternative to their traditional *broodje.* Three spots on Damrak where you can have a quick breakfast of croissant, coffee or tea, and orange juice are **Outmeyer, Bakkerij de Waal,** and **Delifrance.**

Lovers of fresh-baked goodies will appreciate **Lanskroon,** Singel 385 (☎ 020/ 623-7743), just down the Wijde Heisteeg alleyway from the Spui, a tearoom/bakery serving savories and sweets. The company is a supremo of the *vlaai,* the Dutch version of a fruit pie, filled with the ubiquitous apple, but also sometimes bilberries, gooseberries, and even rhubarb. Just as unique are their traditional Dutch waffles—a double crisp biscuit sandwiched around honey, hop-flavored syrup, or figs. The savory pastries also take some beating—and savoring.

If you thought Amsterdam was a bagel-free zone, think again. Some of the best bagels come from **Gary's Muffins** (they sell muffins too). There are four branches: Prinsengracht 454 (☎ 020/420-1452), Marnixstraat 121 (☎ 020/638-0186), Jodenbreestraat 15 (☎ 020/421-5930), and Reguliersdwarsstraat 53 (☎ 020/ 420-2406). The first three are open daily from between 8:30 and 10am to 6 or 7pm; the fourth is open daily from noon to 3am or 4am.

Among the other conveniently located cafes and tearooms are the previously mentioned **Tearoom Pott,** near the Kalverstraat at Voetboogstraat 22–24, near Heiligeweg; and the **Berkhoff Tearoom** at Leidsestraat 46. Opposite Centraal Station and overlooking the inner harbor is **Noord-Zuid Holland Coffee House,** Stationsplein 10, which was built to duplicate a turn-of-the-century Amsterdam landmark. This restaurant and tearoom has a waterside terrace in summer, a good place to watch the canal boats float by. **Greenwood's,** Singel 103 (☎ 020/ 623-7071) serves a great breakfast and homemade savory pies at lunchtime, and offers a quintessentially English ambiance to accompany its tea, homemade scones with jam and clotted cream, and lemon meringue pie.

7 Attractions

For sightseers in Amsterdam, the question is not simply what to see and do, but rather how much of this intriguing city's marvelous sights you'll be able to fit into the time you have!

There are miles and miles of canals to cruise, hundreds of narrow streets to wander, countless historic buildings to visit, more than 40 museums holding collections of everything from artistic wonders to obscure curiosities, not to mention all the diamond cutters and craftspeople to watch as they practice generations-old skills . . . the list is as long as every tourist's individual interests.

Your very first stop on any sightseeing excursion, of course, should be the **VVV** tourist office—the staff there has information on anything you might want to know and some things you might not even have known you wanted to know. One absolute must-do in Amsterdam is a **canal-boat cruise** (see "Organized Tours," below). The view of the elegant canal houses from the water is unforgettable.

One way to save money in Amsterdam is to purchase the **Amsterdam Culture Pass,** developed by the Amsterdam Tourist Office. The booklet contains about 30 coupons for free or discounted admission to the Rijksmuseum, the Stedelijk Museum, and the Van Gogh Museum, plus discounts on admission to other attractions, excursions, and restaurants, including reduced rates for the Museum Boat and the Canal Bus. The Culture Pass costs Dfl 36.75 ($18.40) and can be obtained through the VVV in Amsterdam. You can also buy a **Museumjaarkaart (Museum Year Pass)** costing Dfl 47.50 ($23.75) for ages 25 to 54, Dfl 37.50 ($18.75) for ages 55 and over, and Dfl 17.50 ($8.75) for ages 24 and under. The pass covers free admission to some 250 museums throughout the country (16 of which are in Amsterdam) and can be bought from the VVV, as well as most museums. This is a good investment if museums are high on your sightseeing agenda, even if Amsterdam is your only stop in Holland.

THE TOP ATTRACTIONS

✪ **Rijksmuseum.** Stadhouderskade 42 (behind Museumplein). ☎ **020/674-7000.** Admission Dfl 15 ($7.50) adults, Dfl 7.50 ($3.75) children age 6–18, free for children under 6. Daily 10am–5pm. Tram: 2, 5, or 20 to Hobbemastraat; 6, 7, or 10 to Speigelgracht.

The most significant and permanent outgrowth of Holland's 17th-century Golden Age was its magnificent body of art. Many of these works are now housed in the Rijksmuseum, which ranks with the Louvre, the Uffizzi, and the Hermitage among major museums of European painting and decorative arts. Architect P. J. H. Cuypers designed the core of the present museum; his monumental neo-Gothic building opened in 1885. Since then, many additions have been made to the collections and the building so that the museum now encompasses five departments: Painting, Print Room, Sculpture and Decorative Arts, Dutch History, and Asiatic Art.

The Rijksmuseum contains the world's largest collection of paintings by the Dutch masters, including the most famous of all, a single work that all but defines the Golden Age and has its own direction-indicator arrows inside the museum. Traffic on that route is busy—it leads to a rectangular gallery containing a painting flanked by a guard, two marble Corinthian columns, and three fire extinguishers. The painting is *The Shooting Company of Captain Frans Banning Cocq and Lieutenant Willem van Ruytenburch, 1642,* better known as *The Night Watch,* by Rembrandt. The scene it so dramatically depicts is surely alien to most of the people who flock to see it: gaily uniformed militiamen checking their weapons and

---

A New Museumplein

Amsterdam's flagship museums—the Rijksmuseum, Vincent van Gogh Museum, and Stedelijk Museum of Modern Art—are conveniently clustered around Museumplein, the big open square lying just south of the old city. Over the last few years, the square has been undergoing a transformation to turn it into an attractive focal point for visitors to the city. The new Museumplein will be an invitingly green, car-free public space, with avenues of lime trees, lawns, a pond with fountains, a group of modernistic pavilions housing a new cafe/restaurant, a large underground parking lot, and even sports facilities.

The extensive rebuilding work being carried out on the museums themselves is integral to the look of the new square. The *Zuidvleugel* (South Wing) of the Rijksmuseum has just reopened following renovation; the new extension to the Vincent van Gogh Museum will be completed in spring 1999. The Stedelijk Museum of Modern Art is also about to be renovated.

accoutrements before moving out on patrol. Captain Cocq, Lieutenant van Ruyten-burch, the troopers, and observers (including Rembrandt himself) gaze down at us through the corridor of time, and we are left to wonder what is going on under-neath the paint, inside their minds. This masterpiece was restored after having been slashed in 1975.

Rembrandt, van Ruysdael, van Heemskerck, Frans Hals, Paulus Potter, Jan Steen, Vermeer, de Hooch, Terborch, and Gerard Dou are also represented in this mag-nificent museum, as are Fra Angelico, Tiepolo, Goya, Rubens, Van Dyck, and later Dutch artists of the Hague school and the Amsterdam Impressionist movement. There are individual portraits and guild paintings, landscapes and seascapes, domestic scenes and medieval religious subjects, allegories, and the incredible (and nearly photographic) Dutch still lifes, plus prints and sculptures, furniture, a col-lection of 17th-century dollhouses, Asian and Islamic art, china and porcelain, trin-kets and glassware, armaments and ship models, costumes, screens, badges, and laces.

To get to the heart of the Golden Age, head for Rooms 207–236, where you will find many works by Rembrandt, such as *The Jewish Bride* and *The Syndics,* as well as a great many by other masters such as gerrit Dou, Jan Vermmer, Frans Hals, Jan Steen, Jacob van Ruisdael, Willem van de Velde, and others. The South Wing houses Asiatic Art and works by the 18th-century painters of The Hague school, such as Jozef Israëls and Anton Mauve. In Rooms 101–112, you'll find exhibits on Dutch history, including beautifully realized model ships, weaponry, paintings of sea battles, trophies of war, paintings of scenes from the Dutch colonies, and sim-ilar such items. The new ARIA interactive information center helps you manage this enormous museum—its touch-screens provide visual and text links to 700 of the museum's exhibits.

✪ **Vincent van Gogh Museum.** Paulus Potterstraat 7 (at Museumplein). ☎ **020/ 570-5200.** Admission Dfl 12.50 ($6.25) adults, Dfl 5 ($2.50) children age 6–18, free for children under 6. Daily 10am–5pm. Tram: 3, 5, 12, or 16 to Museumplein/Concertge-bouwplein.

After extensive renovations, including the addition of a new wing, this museum is scheduled to re-open in May, 1999. Anyone who has ever responded to van Gogh's vibrant colors and vivid landscapes will find walking through the rooms of this rather stark contemporary building a moving experience. The museum displays, in chronological order, more than 200 van Gogh paintings. As you move through the rooms, the canvases reflect the artist's changing environment and much of his inner life, so that gradually van Gogh himself becomes almost a tangible presence standing at your elbow. You'll see the early, brooding *The Potato Eaters* and *The Yellow House,* as well as the painting known around the world simply as *Sunflowers,* although van Gogh actually titled it *Still Life with Fourteen Sunflowers.* By the time you reach the vaguely threatening painting of a flock of black crows rising from a waving cornfield, you can almost feel the artist's mounting inner pain.

In addition to the paintings, there are nearly 600 drawings by van Gogh, which will be on permanent display in the museum's new wing. This free-standing, multi-story, half-oval structure, designed by the Japanese architect Kisho Kurokawa, is constructed in a bold combination of titanium and gray-brown stone, and is con-nected to the main building by a subterranean walkway. There are no guided tours of the museum, though audio tours are available for Dfl 7 ($3.50).

✪ **Stedelijk Museum of Modern Art.** Paulus Potterstraat 13 (at Museumplein). ☎ **020/573-2737.** Admission Dfl 9 ($4.50) adults, Dfl 4.50 ($2.25) children age 7–16, free

Attractions in Central Amsterdam

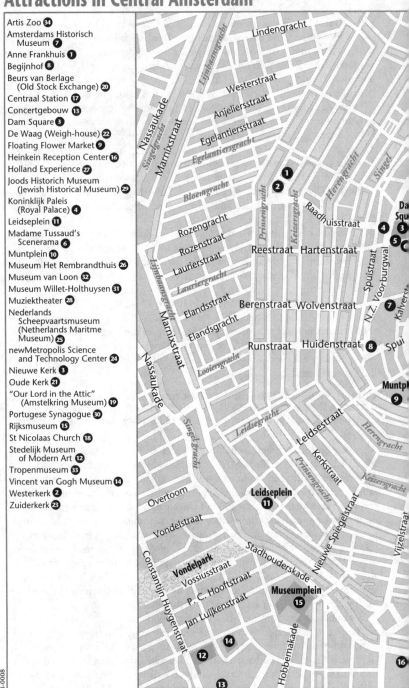

3-0008

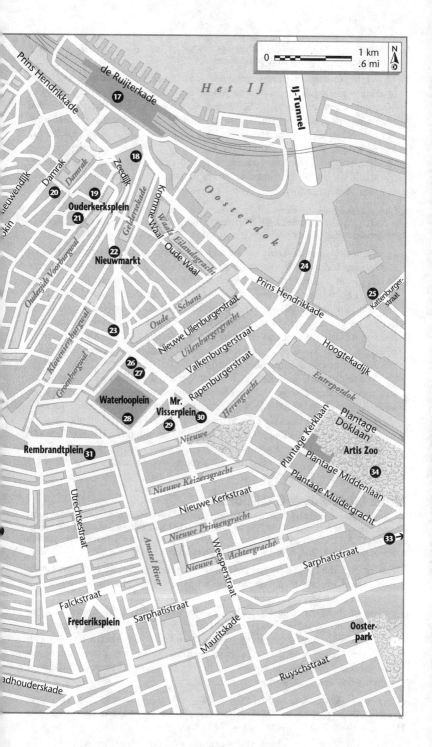

for children under 7. Apr–Oct daily 11am–5pm, Nov–Mar 10am–6pm. Tram: 2, 5, or 20 to Paulus Potterstraat; 3, 12, or 16 to Museumplein.

This is the contemporary art museum of Amsterdam. It's the place to see the works of such modern Dutch painters as Karel Appel, Willem de Kooning, and Piet Mondrian; there are also works by Chagall, Cézanne, Picasso, Renoir, Monet, and Manet, as well as those by American artists such as Calder, Oldenburg, Rosenquist, Warhol, Nauman, and Koons. The Stedelijk centers its collection around the following schools of modern art: De Stijl, Cobra, and post-Cobra painting, nouveau réalisme, pop art, color-field painting, zero and minimal art, and conceptual art. The building has been restored as closely as possible to its original 1895 neo-Renaissance appearance.

✪ **Anne Frankhuis.** Prinsengracht 263 (beside Westermarkt). ☎ **020/556-7100.** Admission Dfl 10 ($5) adults, Dfl 5 ($2.50) children age 10–17, free for children under 10. Apr–Aug daily 9am–9pm, Sept–Mar daily 9am–5pm. Tram: 13, 14, or 17 to Westermarkt.

In summer you may have to queue for an hour or more to get in, but no one should miss seeing and experiencing this house, where eight people from three separate families lived together in near total silence for more than 2 years during World War II. The hiding place Otto Frank found for his family and friends kept them safe until, tragically close to the end of the war, it was raided by Nazi forces, and its occupants were deported to the concentration camps. It was here that Anne wrote her famous diary as a way to deal with the boredom and her youthful jumble of thoughts, which had as much to do with personal relationships as with the war and the Nazi terror raging outside her hiding place.

The rooms of this building, which was an office and warehouse at that time, are still as bare as they were when Anne's father returned, the only survivor of the eight *onderduikers* (divers or hiders). Nothing has been changed, except that protective Plexiglas panels have been placed over the wall where Anne pinned up photos of her favorite actress, Deanna Durbin, and of the young English princesses Elizabeth and Margaret. As you tour the small building, it's easy to imagine Anne's experience, growing up in this place, awakening as a young woman, and writing down her secret thoughts in a diary.

MORE MUSEUMS & GALLERIES

✪ **Amsterdams Historisch Museum (Amsterdam Historical Museum).** Kalverstraat 92 and Nieuwezijds Voorburgwal 359. ☎ **020/523-1822.** Admission Dfl 9 ($4.50) adults, Dfl 4.50 ($2.25) children age 6–16, free for children under 6. Mon–Fri 10am–5pm, Sat–Sun 11am–5pm. Tram: 1, 2, 4, 5, 9, 16, 20, 24, or 25 to Spui.

Few cities in the world have gone to as much trouble and expense as Amsterdam to display and explain their history. This intriguing and informative museum is housed in the huge, beautifully restored 17th-century buildings of the former city orphanage. It has three courtyards and a civic-guard gallery (with large-scale 17th-century group portraits) linking it to the Begijnhof. The museum will give you a better understanding of everything you see when you go out to explore the city on your own. Gallery by gallery, century by century, you see how a small fishing village became a major world power; you also see the historical context of the great Dutch artists and their work.

CoBrA Museum of Modern Art. Sandbergplein 1–3, Amstelveen. ☎ **020/547-5050.** Admission Dfl 6 ($3) adults, Dfl 3 ($1.50) for children age 16 and under. Tues–Sun 11am–5pm. Tram: 5 to Binnenhof; light rail 51 to Beneluxbaan.

Out in the dormitory suburb of Amstelveen, to the south of Amsterdam, is one of the most exciting new museums in the country. This institute of modern art is dedicated to the post–World War II art of the CoBrA group, who took their name from the initials of the artists' home cities: Copenhagen, Brussels, and Amsterdam. The works of artists like Asger Jorn, Karl Appel, and Lucebert weren't instantly popular in their day, but their brashly colorful, almost childlike work is undoubtedly a substantial force in 20th-century art.

Joods Historisch Museum (Jewish Historical Museum). Jonas Daniël Meijerplein 2–4 (facing Waterlooplein). ☎ **020/626-9945.** Admission Dfl 8 ($4) adults, Dfl 4 ($2) children age 10–16, free for children under 10. Daily 11am–5pm. Tram: 9, 14, or 20 to Waterlooplein.

In 1987, this museum opened in the restored Ashkenazi Synagogue complex, a cluster of four former synagogues, in the heart of what was once Amsterdam's thriving Jewish Quarter. It's home to the collection of paintings, decorations, and ceremonial objects once held in the Amsterdam Historical Museum, then confiscated during World War II, and later patiently reestablished in the post-war period. The museum tells three intertwining stories through its objects, photographs, artworks, and interactive displays—the stories of Jewish identity, Jewish religion and culture, and Jewish history in the Netherlands. Leave time to appreciate the beauty and size of the buildings themselves, which include the oldest public synagogue in Europe. This is a museum for everyone—Jewish or otherwise—that presents the community through both good times and bad and provides insights into the Jewish way of life over the centuries. There are also frequent temporary exhibitions of international interest.

Museum Het Rembrandthuis. Jodenbreestraat 4–6 (at Waterlooplein). ☎ **020/520-0400.** Admission Dfl 7.50 ($3.75) adults, Dfl 5 ($2.65) children 10–15, free for children under 10. Mon–Sat 10am–5pm, Sun and holidays 1–5pm (main museum closed until Sept 1999; Saskia House remains open). Tram: 9, 14, or 20 to Waterlooplein.

Be advised that this museum (except for the new Saskia wing) will be closed for restoration until September 1999.

For the greatest of Rembrandt's masterpieces you must visit the Rijksmuseum, but here you'll find a more intimate sense of the artist himself. This house was bought by Rembrandt in 1639 when he was Amsterdam's most fashionable portrait painter. Here Rembrandt's son Titus was born and his wife Saskia died. The artist was bankrupt when he left the house in 1658, and it wasn't until 1906 that the building was rescued from a succession of subsequent owners and restored as a museum.

When the museum reopens, renovations will have been completed to return the house to the way it looked when Rembrandt lived and worked here. You'll be able to see Rembrandt's printing press, as well as about 120 of the master's etchings on the walls. These works include self-portraits, landscapes, and several that relate to the traditionally Jewish character of the neighborhood, such as the portrait of Rabbi Menassah ben Israel, who lived across the street. In 1998, a new wing opened in the adjacent former house of Rembrandt's wife Saskia; this section is used mainly for temporary exhibitions.

Museum van Loon. Keizersgracht 672 (near Vijzelstraat). ☎ **020/624-5255.** Admission Dfl 7.50 ($3.75) adults, Dfl 5 ($2.50) seniors 65 and over, children age 12 and under free. Fri–Mon 11am–5pm. Tram: 16, 24, or 25 to Keizersgracht.

The history of this magnificent house is a long saga of ne'er-do-well spouses and ailing orphans, of misguided inheritances and successive bankruptcies; yet the achievements of the people whose portraits now hang here are as illustrious as any you can imagine. The house's completely restored period rooms are filled with richly decorated paneling, stucco work, mirrors, fireplaces, and furnishings. On the walls of this elegant patrician home are more than 80 van Loon family portraits, including those of Willem van Loon, one of the founding fathers of the Dutch East India Company; Nicolaes Ruychaver, who liberated Amsterdam from the Spanish in 1578; and another, later, Willem van Loon, who became mayor of Amsterdam in 1686. There's also a formal landscaped garden.

Museum Willet-Holthuysen. Herengracht 605, near Amstel. ☎ **020/523-1870.** Admission Dfl 7.50 ($3.75) adults, Dfl 3.75 ($1.90) children age 16 and under. Mon–Fri 10am–5pm, Sat–Sun 11am–5pm. Tram: 4 to Utrechtsestraat.

This museum presents another rare opportunity to visit an elegant canal house. This particular house was built in 1687 and was renovated several times before its last inhabitant gave the house and its contents to the city of Amsterdam in 1889. Among the most interesting rooms are the Victorian-era bedroom on the second floor, a large reception room with tapestry wall panels, and the 18th-century basement kitchen that's still so completely furnished and functional you could swear the cook had merely stepped out to go shopping.

✪ **Nederlands Scheepvaartmuseum (Netherlands Maritime Museum).** Kattenburgerplein 1 (in the Eastern Dock). ☎ **020/523-2222.** Admission Dfl 12.50 ($6.25) adults, Dfl 8 ($4) children 17 and under. Tues–Sat 10am–5pm (also Mon, mid-June to mid-Sept), Sun noon–5pm. Bus: 22 or 32 to Kattenburgerplein.

What a bonanza for anyone who loves ships and the sea! The Netherlands Maritime Museum is housed in a former arsenal of the Amsterdam Admiralty dating from 1656, and overlooks the busy Amsterdam harbor. The inner courtyard is stunning. Surrounding it are 25 rooms with exhibits: ship models, charts, instruments, maps, prints, and paintings—a chronicle of Holland's abiding ties to the sea through commerce, fishing, yachting, navigational development, and even war. Brief texts explain each exhibit, and desks with more extensive information are found in every room.

A full-size replica of the *Amsterdam,* which foundered off of Hastings in 1749 on her maiden voyage to the fabled Spice Islands (Indonesia), is moored at the museum's wharf, as is a recently completed replica of the *Stad Amsterdam,* a three-masted iron clipper from 1854. Other ships that can be seen include a steam ice-breaker, a motor lifeboat, and a herring lugger. Environmentalists will want to board Greenpeace's *Rainbow Warrior,* a warrior of environmental protection on the high seas. You can reach this museum by taking a 20-minute walk along the historical waterfront, the *Nautisch Kwartier* (the Nautical Quarter).

✪ **Tropenmuseum (Tropical Museum).** Linnaeusstraat 2 (at Mauritskade). ☎ **020/568-8215.** Admission Dfl 12 ($6) adults, Dfl 8 ($4) children 18 and under. Mon–Fri 10am–5pm, Sat–Sun and holidays noon–5pm. Tram: 6, 9, 10, or 14 to Mauritskade; 20 to Sarphatistraat.

One of Amsterdam's more intriguing museums is run by the Royal Tropical Institute, a foundation devoted to the study of the cultures of tropical areas around the world. The Tropical Institute building complex alone is worth the trip to Amsterdam East and the *Oosterpark* (East Park); its heavily ornamented facade is an amalgam of Dutch architectural styles—turrets, stepped gables, arched windows, and delicate spires—and the monumental galleried interior court is one of the most impressive spots in town.

The most interesting exhibits are the walk-through model villages and city-street scenes that seem to capture a moment in the daily life of such places as India and Indonesia; as well as the exhibition on the tools and techniques used to produce *batik,* the distinctively dyed Indonesian fabrics; and the displays of the tools, instruments, and ornaments that clutter a tropical residence. There's also a new permanent exhibition on people and the environment in West Asia and North Africa. Part of the premises is given over to the children-only Kindermuseum—the Tropical Museum Junior—with its educational and interactive exhibits.

HISTORIC BUILDINGS & MONUMENTS

Beurs van Berlage (Old Stock Exchange). Damrak 277 (near Dam Square). ☎ **020/ 626-8936.** Admission Dfl 6 ($3) adults, Dfl 4 ($2) children age 5–16, free for children under 5. Mon–Fri 9am–5pm. Tram: 1, 2, 4, 5, 9, 13, 14, 16, 17, 20, 24, or 25 to Dam Square.

This building, designed by architect Hendrik Petrus Berlage and built between 1896 and 1903 as Amsterdam's Beurs (Stock Exchange), represented a revolutionary break with 19th-century architecture. It's no longer the stock exchange, but it's still well worth visiting as the prime example of Amsterdam School architecture, which was contemporaneous with the work of Frank Lloyd Wright in America. Note the gable relief of two fishermen with a dog in a boat, depicting a legend of Amsterdam's foundation. Today the building is used as a space for conferences, concerts, and exhibitions.

✪ **Koninklijk Paleis (Royal Palace).** Dam Square. ☎ **020/624-4060.** Admission Dfl 7 ($3.50) adults, Dfl 2.50 ($1.25) children age 5–12, free for children under 5. Easter and June–July daily 10am–6:30pm, Aug–Oct daily 12:30–5pm. Closed mid-Dec to mid-Feb; otherwise usually Tues–Thurs 12:30–5pm (opening days and hours are highly variable; check before going). Tram: 1, 2, 4, 5, 9, 13, 14, 16, 17, 20, 24, or 25 to Dam Square.

Dominating the Dam Square is the 17th-century, neoclassical facade of the Royal Palace. The building was originally designed by Jacob van Campen as a town hall, but in 1808, when Napoléon Bonaparte's younger brother Louis reigned as King of the Netherlands, it became a palace and was filled with Empire-style furniture. During the summer, you can visit the high-ceilinged Citizens' Hall, the Burgomasters' Chambers, and the Council Room. Since the return to the throne of the Dutch House of Orange, this has been the official palace of the reigning king or queen of the Netherlands. However, it's only used for occasional state receptions or official ceremonies (Queen Beatrix prefers living at Huis ten Bosch in The Hague).

De Waag. Nieuwmarkt. ☎ **020/557-9898.** Free admission (but some exhibitions charge admission). Sun–Thurs 10am–1am, Fri–Sat 10am–2am. Metro: Nieuwmarkt.

The 14th-century De Waag started its life as one of the city's fortified gates and later became a guild house. Among the guilds lodged here was the Surgeon's Guild, immortalized in Rembrandt's painting *The Anatomy Lesson* (1632), which depicts a dissection performed in the Theatrum Anatomicum on the upper floor. Today the Waag is used as a multimedia center for exhibitions, theater, and music performances. The reading table in its cafe not only features newspapers, as is common in Amsterdam, but also Internet access and a selection of CD-ROMs.

SIGHTS OF RELIGIOUS SIGNIFICANCE

Religion has always played an important part in Amsterdam's history. Most of the city's hundreds of churches can be visited during regular services; some also have open doors during weekdays so that visitors may have a look around.

✪ **Begijnhof.** Gedempte Begijnensloot (at Spui). No phone. Free admission. Daily until sunset. Tram: 1, 2, or 5 to Spui.

Too few tourists take the time to see this cluster of small, 16th- and 17th-century homes around a garden courtyard. This is one of the best places to appreciate the earliest history of the city, when Amsterdam was a destination for religious pilgrims and an important center of Catholic nunneries. The Begijnhof itself was not a convent (that was located next door, where the Amsterdams Historisch Museum now stands); it was an almshouse for pious lay women—*begijnen*—involved in religious and charitable work for the convent. It remained in operation even after the about-face changeover of the city from Catholicism to Protestantism in the late 16th century. The last of the *begijnen* died in 1971, but you can still pay homage to these pious women by pausing for a moment at the small flower-planted mound that lies just at the center garden's edge across from the English Reformed church. Opposite the front of the church is a secret Catholic chapel built in 1671 and still in use. You're welcome to visit the Begijnhof during daylight hours (the city's poor senior citizens now reside in the old homes, and their privacy is respected after sunset).

Nieuwe Kerk (New Church). Dam Square (facing the Royal Palace). ☎ **020/638-6990.** Admission Dfl 2.50 ($1.25) adults, Dfl 1 (50¢) children. Hours vary, but usually Mon–Sat 11am–4pm, Sun noon–2pm. Closed Jan–Feb, and for private events. During exhibitions, entrance fee is higher and opening hours are longer. Tram: 1, 2, 4, 5, 9, 13, 14, 16, 17, 20, 24, or 25 to Dam Square.

This beautiful church was built in the last years of the 14th century, when the Oude Kerk (see below) had become too small to accommodate its congregation. Many of the Nieuwe Kerk's priceless treasures were removed or painted over in 1578 when it passed into Protestant hands, but much of the church's original grandeur has since been recaptured. In 1814, the king first took the oath of office and was inaugurated here (Dutch royalty are not crowned). The church has a stately arched nave, an elaborately carved altar, a great pipe organ that dates from 1645, several noteworthy stained-glass windows, and sepulchral monuments for many of Holland's most revered poets and naval heroes.

Oude Kerk (Old Church). Oudekerksplein 1 (off Oudezijds Voorburgwal). ☎ **020/624-9183.** Free admission. Daily 11am–4pm. Tram: 1, 2, or 5.

This late-Gothic church was begun in the year 1250. On its southern porch, to the right of the sexton's house, you will see a coat of arms belonging to Maximilian of Austria, who, with his son Philip, contributed to the porch's construction. Rembrandt's wife Saskia is buried here. The church contains a magnificent organ from 1724 and is used regularly for organ recitals. Nowadays, the pretty little gabled almshouses around the Oude Kerk feature red-fringed windows through which the scantily dressed ladies of the Red Light District can be seen.

Portuguese Synagogue. Mr. Visserplein 3. ☎ **020/624-5351.** Admission Dfl 5 ($2.50) adults, Dfl 2.50 ($1.25) children. Apr–Oct Sun–Fri 10am–12:30pm and 1–4pm; Nov–Mar Mon–Thurs 10am–12:30pm and 1–4pm, Fri 10am–3pm, Sun 10am–noon. Tram: 9, 14, or 20 to Waterlooplein.

Sephardic Jews fleeing Spain and Portugal during the 16th and early 17th centuries established a neighborhood east of the center known as the Jewish Quarter. In 1665 they built an elegant Ionic-style synagogue within an existing courtyard facing what is now a busy traffic circle. The total cost of the magnificent building was 186,000 florins—a king's ransom in those days, but a small price to pay for the city's Jews, who for the first time in 200 years could worship openly. The building was restored in the 1950s. Today it looks essentially as it did 320 years ago, with its women's gallery supported by 12 stone columns to represent the Twelve Tribes of Israel, and the large, low-hanging brass chandeliers that together hold 1,000 candles, all of which are lighted for the private weekly services.

Westerkerk (West Church). Westermarkt. ☎ **020/624-7766.** Admission to church free; to tower Dfl 4 ($2) adults, Dfl 2 ($1) children. Church open Mon–Sat 11am–5pm, Sun 1–5pm; tower open June–Sept Wed–Sat 10am–4pm. Tram: 13, 14, 17, or 20 to Westermarkt.

The Renaissance-style Westerkerk holds the remains of Rembrandt and his son, Titus; this is also where Queen Beatrix said her marriage vows in 1966. The church was begun in 1620 and was designed by Hendrick de Keyser, who was succeeded, after his death, by his son Pieter. The church opened in 1631. Its light and spacious interior holds a fine organ. The 277-foot tower, the Westertoren, is the tallest in Amsterdam, providing a spectacular view of the city. The tower is surmounted by the blue, red, and gold crown of the Holy Roman Empire, a symbol bestowed on the city by the Austrian Emperor Maximilian.

OTHER SITES & ATTRACTIONS

✪ **Artis Zoo.** Plantage Kerklaan 38–40. ☎ **020/523-3400.** Admission Dfl 23.50 ($11.75) adults, Dfl 15.50 ($7.75) children age 4–11, free for children under 4. Daily 9am–5pm. Tram: 9 or 14 to Plantage Middenlaan.

If you're at a loss for what to do with the kids, the Artis Zoo is a safe bet. Not only does it house over 6,000 animals, but it also has much more besides, all included in the price of admission. The Aquarium, built in 1882 and recently renovated, is superbly presented, particularly the sections on the Amazon River, coral reefs, and Amsterdam's own canals, with their fish population and burden of urban detritus. In the children's farm, kids can help tend to the needs of resident sheep, goats, chickens, and cows. There's also the excellent Planetarium (closed Monday morning) and a Geological and Zoological Museum.

Heineken Reception Center. Stadhouderskade 78. ☎ **020/523-9666.** Admission Dfl 2 ($1) donated to charity. Guided tours Mon–Fri 9:30 and 11am; June to mid-Sept also 1 and 2:30pm; July–Aug also Sat 11am, 1, and 2:30pm. Tram: 25 to Stadhouderskade.

At this center, you can take a tour of the former Heineken brewing facilities, which date from 1868. Before the brewery stopped functioning in 1990, it was producing more than a million hectoliters annually. The fermentation tanks, each capable of holding a million glassfuls of Heineken, are still there for visitors to see. Guides explain the brewing process and show a film about the company's history on a multiscreen video wall; you'll go through 5,000 years of brewing history in 5 minutes flat. Heineken's hospitality extends to two complimentary glasses per person—enough to cast a warm glow of appreciation over the visit, and not enough to spoil it.

Holland Experience. Waterlooplein 17. ☎ **020/422-2233.** Admission Dfl 17.50 ($8.75) adults, Dfl 15 ($7.50) seniors and children age 12 and under. Daily 10am–10pm. Tram: 9, 14, or 20 to Waterlooplein.

This multidimensional film and theater show takes you through the landscapes and culture of Holland at different periods of its history as well as today. If you've ever nervously wondered what would happen to the city if all that sea water should ever break through the defensive dikes, Holland Experience will give you a taste; in its simulated dike collapse, 80,000 liters of water pour towards you. Other exhibitions include farming and fishing scenes. The toilets here are themselves of interest (I can only vouch for the men's); they're designed to look like the deck of a ship passing along the Dutch coast and come complete with marine sound effects and salt-air breeze.

Madame Tussaud's Scenerama. Dam Square 20. ☎ **020/622-9949.** Admission Dfl 18.50 ($9.25) adults, Dfl 15 ($7.50) seniors and children age 14 and under. July–Aug daily 9:30am–5:30pm, Sept–June daily 10am–5:30pm. Tram: 1, 2, 4, 5, 9, 13, 14, 16, 17, 20, 24, or 25 to Dam Square.

If you like your celebrities with a waxen stare, don't miss Madame Tussaud's. This is a uniquely Amsterdam version of the London attraction, with its own cast of

Dutch characters (such as Rembrandt, Queen Wilhelmina, Erasmus, and Mata Hari) among the ranks of international favorites (Churchill, Kennedy, Gandhi, and Pope John XXIII).

✪ **newMetropolis Science and Technology Center.** Oosterdok 2 (above the IJ tunnel in the eastern harbor). ☎ **0900/919-1100.** Admission Dfl 22.50 ($11.25) adults, Dfl 15 ($7.50) children age 4–16, free for children under 4. July–Aug daily 10am–9pm; Sept–June Mon–Thur 10am–6pm, Fri–Sun 10am–9pm. Bus: 22 to Kadijksplein.

The newMetropolis Science & Technology Center was designed by Renzo Piano, most famous for his Centre Pompidou in Paris. The building rises like a copper-green hull above the tunnel under the North Sea Canal in the eastern harbor. This place is a hands-on experience as much as a museum, with interactive exhibits, hands-on experiments, and Internet-linked computers. You'll learn how to steer a supertanker safely into port, boost your earnings on the floor of the New York Stock Exchange, and execute a complicated surgical procedure.

MARKETS

With more than 50 outdoor markets every week in Amsterdam, some of them permanent or semipermanent and others just passing through, there's certainly no lack of choice for open-air shopping. Here are three of the best.

The ✪ **Floating Flower Market** on Singel is a stunning mass of flowers strung along the canal on permanently moored barges. Awnings stretch to cover stall after stall of brightly colored blossoms, bulbs, and potted plants. A stroll down that fragrant line is surely one of Amsterdam's most heart-lifting experiences. Open Monday through Saturday 10am to 4pm. Looking for a bargain-basement souvenir is made easy at the ✪ **Waterlooplein Flea Market,** on Waterlooplein, naturally enough. You'll find all kinds of stuff here, not all of it junk, and a constant press of people with good buys on their mind. Open daily 9am to 5pm. The **Albert Cuyp Markt,** on Albert Cuypstraat, is more of an everyday market for food, clothes, and other things, but is almost as colorful as the other two. Open Monday through Saturday 10am to 4pm.

RED LIGHT DISTRICT (ROSSE BUURT OR DE WALLEN)

This warren of streets and old canals around Oudezijds Achterburgwal and Oudezijds Voorburgwal by the Oude Kerk is on most people's sightseeing agenda. However, a visit to this area is not for everyone, and if you're liable to be offended by the sex industry exposed in all its garish colors, don't go. If you do choose to go, you need to exercise some caution because the area is a center of crime, vice, and drugs. As always in Amsterdam, there's no need to exaggerate the risks; and, in fact, the nightclubs' own security helps keep the brightly lit areas quite safe. Plenty of tourists visit the Rosse Buurt and suffer nothing more serious than a come-on from one of the prostitutes.

At night especially, however, stick to the crowded streets and be wary of pickpockets at all times. There can be a sinister air to the clusters of often weird-looking men who gather on the bridges, and there is a sadder aura around the "heroin-whores" who wander the darker streets. And be warned that you should never take photographs of the women in the windows, many of whom don't want mom and dad to know how they earn a living. Hired men are always on the lookout, and they won't hesitate to throw your camera (and maybe your person) into the canal.

Still, it's extraordinary to view the prostitutes in leather and lace sitting in their storefronts with their radios and TVs blaring as they do their knitting or adjust their makeup, waiting patiently for customers. The district seems to reflect Dutch pragmatism; if you can't stop the oldest trade in the world, you can at least confine it to a particular area and impose health and other regulations on it. And the fact is that underneath its tacky glitter, the Red Light District contains some of Amsterdam's prettiest canals and loveliest old architecture, as well as some excellent bars and restaurants, secondhand bookshops, and other specialty shops (not all of which work the erogenous zones).

To get there, take tram 4, 9, 16, 20, 24, or 25 to Dam Square, then pass behind the Grand Hotel Krasnapolsky.

GREEN AMSTERDAM

Amsterdam is not a notably green city, particularly in the old center, where the canals are the most obvious and visible encroachment of the "natural" world. Still, the city as a whole has plenty of parks, including the famous ✪ **Vondelpark.** You'll find frisbee flipping, inline skating, soccer, open-air performances, smooching in the undergrowth, picnics, and, perhaps not-so-standard, topless sunbathing. Best of all, it's free, or, as the Dutch say, *gratis.* The Vondelpark lies southwest of Leidseplein, with the main entrance adjacent to the Leidseplein, on Stadhouderskade.

You can rent in-line skates from **Rent A Skate,** beside the Amstelveenseweg entrance (☎ 020/693-9574), and tour the park in style. Including protective gear, rentals cost Dfl 7.50 ($3.75) an hour for adults, or Dfl 15 ($7.50) for a half day and Dfl 25 ($12.50) for a full day; for children age 10 and under, rentals are Dfl 5 ($2.50) an hour, Dfl 10 ($5) for a half day, and Dfl 17.50 ($8.75) for a full day. Coaching is available.

To enjoy scenery and fresh air, you should head out to the giant **Amsterdamse Bos (Amsterdam Wood),** whose main entrance is on Amstelveenseweg, in the southern suburb of Amstelveen. This is nature on the city's doorstep. The park was laid out during the Depression years as a public works project. The **Bosmuseum** (☎ 020/643-1414), signposted from all entrances, traces the park's history and gives information about its wildlife. This free museum is open daily from 10am to 5pm. Nearby is a big pond called the **Grote Vijver,** where you can rent boats (☎ 020/647-7831). The **Openluchttheater** (Open-Air Theater) often has performances on summer evenings.

The best way to get to the **Amsterdamse Bos** from the center is to take tram 6, 16, or 24 to Stadionplein, then any bus, except the no. 23, along Amstelveenseweg to the entrance.

FREE AMSTERDAM

The words "free" and "Dutch" are generally thought to mix together about as well as oil and water. Perhaps rattled by accusations that Amsterdam has grown too expensive, and by stiff competition from Prague in the young-and-alternative market, the VVV tourist office has drawn up a list of free things to see and do in the city. Here are some highlights:

- Admire 15 enormous 17th-century paintings of the Amsterdam Civic Guards, in the **Schuttersgalerij,** a covered passageway between the Begijnhof and the Amsterdams Historisch Museum.
- Visit the **Begijnhof** itself (see "Sights of Religious Significance" earlier in this chapter).
- Judge horseflesh at the **Hollandsche Manège (Dutch Stables),** at Vondelstraat 140, built in 1882 and inspired by the Spanish Riding School in Vienna.
- Cross the bridge over Reguliersgracht at Herengracht, from which you can see no fewer than **15 bridges.**

- Breathe scented air in the **Rijksmuseum Garden,** and see fragments from ruined old buildings that are "stored" there.
- Find out where Amsterdam is going as a city at the permanent town planning exhibition in the **Zuiderkerk.**
- Test the level of the sea at the **Normaal Amsterdams Peil (Normal Amsterdam Level),** a bronze plaque in the passageway between the Muziektheater and the Stadhuis (Town Hall). Beside it are three glass columns filled with water—the first two show the current sea level at Vlissingen at IJmuiden, and the third, 5 meters above your head, the high-water mark during the disastrous floods in Zeeland in 1953. This plaque sets the standard for altitude measurements in Europe.
- Hear the **lunchtime concerts,** from 12:30 to 1pm, at the Muziektheater (Tuesday) and the Concertgebouw (Wednesday) every week from October through June.
- Sail on the **IJ ferry** across the channel from behind Centraal Station to North Amsterdam.
- Visit the **Floating Flower Market** on the Singel (see "Markets" in chapter 8)— enjoying the wonderful scents of the flowers is free, even though the flowers themselves are not.
- Tour Europe in a single street, Roemer Visscherstraat 20–30, where the **Seven Countries Houses** were built in 1894 in the styles of Germany, France, Spain, Italy, Russia, Holland, and England.
- Stand on the **Magere Brug (Skinny Bridge)** over the River Amstel between Kerkstraat and Nieuwe Kerkstraat, a narrow white-painted drawbridge that has spanned the river since 1672.
- Check out the **narrowest houses** in Amsterdam (see "Historic Buildings & Monuments" earlier in this chapter).
- Hear the music from four **17th-century carillons:** Westertoren (Tuesday noon to 1pm), Zuidertoren (Thursday noon to 1pm), Munttoren (Friday noon to 1pm), and Oude Kerkstoren (Saturday 4 to 5pm).
- Listen to the earthier performances of the **barrel organs** in the street (mixed with the rattle of money as the organ-grinder tries to "persuade" you to make a donation).

WALKING TOUR
The Golden Age Canals

Start: Herenmarkt (off Brouwersgracht).
Finish: River Amstel.
Time: 3 hours to all day, depending on how long you linger in museums or shops along the way.
Best Times: Begin in the morning.

Each of the three 17th-century Golden Age canals explored here—the Herengracht (Gentlemen's Canal), Keizersgracht (Emperor's Canal), and Prinsengracht (Princes' Canal)—deserves at least a morning or afternoon all to itself. Time being limited, we're going to combine them all in one monumental effort; but if you're not so rushed, by all means slice the tour up into two or three segments for a more leisurely experience. You'll see miles of tree-lined canals, and innumerable canal houses with classical facades or gables in a multiplicity of styles (bell, step, neck, and variations), as well as bridges, warehouses converted to expensive apartments, houseboats, museums, cafes, restaurants, boutiques and offbeat shops, and seagulls and herons.

I'm only going to mention the more special sights along the way (leaving out the seagulls and herons).

The jump-off point is:

1. West-Indisch Huis (West India House), at Herenmarkt, just off of Brouwersgracht. At the north side of this little square is the building that in 1623 became headquarters of the Dutch West India Company, which controlled trade with the Americas. In the courtyard is a bronze statue of Peter Stuyvesant, governor of Nieuw Amsterdam (later New York) from 1647 until the British took over in 1664, and a sculpture showing the first Dutch settlement at the tip of Manhattan island, founded in 1626.

Walk up Brouwersgracht (Brewers' Canal) to the point where it adjoins Prinsengracht. This is one of the most photogenic corners of Amsterdam. Brouwersgracht is lined with magnificent old brewers' warehouses that have been turned into apartments. Worth special attention are nos. 204 and 206, which are named "Het Kleine Groene Hert" (the Little Green Deer) and "Het Groote Groene Hert" (the Big Green Deer)—each has a gable crowned with a sculpted deer painted green.

On Prinsengracht, the first stop is:

2. Noordermarkt. On Saturday, there's a Bird Market here and a Farmers' Market for organically grown products; on Monday morning, there's a busy flea market. Stop for a while to look at the gables of the houses on the square (nos. 15–22). Each elaborate gable is decorated with an agricultural image—a cow, sheep, or chicken—left from the days when an agriculture and livestock market was held here. Hendrick de Keyser, who designed many of Amsterdam's churches, also designed the Noorderkerk (Northern Church), which dominates this old market square.

Continue along Prinsengracht to the bridge at Prinsenstraat, and cross over. A few steps back along the canal on this side is:

3. Zon's Hofje, at Prinsenstraat 159–171, a hidden almshouse surrounding a garden at the end of the passageway.

Head down Prinsenstraat to Keizersgracht. A short trip to the left at this point brings you to the:

4. Groenland Pakhuizen (Greenland Warehouses), at nos. 40–44, built in 1621 to store whale oil.

Cross the Keizersgracht bridge—note the houseboats tied up on either side—to Herenstraat, with maybe a detour to Keizersgracht 123 for the Huis met de Hoofden (House with the Heads), built in 1621 by Hendrick de Keyser. The heads in question on the facade represent, from left to right, Apollo, Ceres, Mars, Athena, Bacchus, and Diana. Glance into some of the interesting shop windows on Herenstraat before turning right onto Herengracht, for the:

5. Theatermuseum, at Herengracht 168. The museum occupies five adjacent canal houses, one of which, the Bartolotti House at no. 166, was built around 1617 by Hendrick de Keyser, and is famous for its redbrick gable. In the museum itself are costumes, maquettes, masks, puppets, photographs, paintings, theatrical backdrops, and other exhibits covering all forms of theater.

Backtrack a few steps to Leliegracht; then go up onto Prinsengracht and turn left to visit the

6. Anne Frankhuis, at Prinsengracht 263, where the young Jewish girl Anne Frank (1929–1945) hid from the Nazis and wrote her imperishable diary. The earlier you get to this house the better because the line to get in grows as the day progresses.

At this point, you may need a break for lunch, so pop into:

☕ **TAKE A BREAK   Rum Runners,** Prinsengracht 277 (☎ **020/ 627-4079**), a Caribbean restaurant where they serve a stiff margarita and a mean guacamole, along with other laid-back drinks and dishes. Afterwards, with miles and miles to go before you sleep, you may be tempted to stow away on a pedalo from the Canal Bikes moorings outside Rum Runners, but if you're staying with the program, continue a few steps to Westermarkt and its:

7. **Westerkerk.** The Renaissance-style church was begun in 1620, at the same time as the Noorderkerk, and was also designed by Hendrick de Keyser. Hendrick's son Pieter took over after his father's death, and the church was opened in 1631. At Westermarkt 6 is the house where Descartes lived in 1634, when he wrote his *Treatise on the Passions of the Soul.* At the time Descartes apparently thought himself in need of some nonphilosophical passion, so he had an affair with his maid, producing a child. Also on Westermarkt is a bronze sculpture of Anne Frank and the pink marble triangles of the Homomonument, dedicated to persecuted gays and lesbians.

   Continue along Prinsengracht to Reestraat, where you turn left. At Keizersgracht go right to:
8. **Felix Meritis,** Keizersgracht 324, built in 1788 as the headquarters of a Calvinist scientific society. The group's motto was "Happiness From Merit," and they invited such luminaries as Tsar Alexander and Napoléon to experience the philosophy. The building was later the home of the Dutch Communist Party, and still keeps faith with its free-thinking past by hosting offices for a variety of avant-garde theater and dance troupes.

   Backtrack to Breenstraat and its rightward continuation, Runstraat. Here the Knopen Winkel (Button Shop) at no. 16 is a button-fancier's dream, with a stock of 8,000 different kinds of buttons. At Herengracht go right to the:
9. **Bijbels Museum** (Bible Museum), at Herengracht 366, one of a group of four houses (364, 366, 368, and 370) with delicate neck gables built by Justus Vingboons in the 1660s. The museum, naturally enough, features Bibles and things biblical. Continue along Herengracht and across Leidsestraat to the:
10. **Golden Bend,** so named because of the magnificent homes here, which were built on double lots with double steps and central entrances. You can trace the development of the rich folks' wealth and tastes as you move along the Herengracht. This section was built with old money around the 1670s, in the fading afterglow of the Golden Age, when French-influenced neoclassicism was all the rage. The entrance to Nieuwe Spiegelstraat, a street lined with antiques shops, is also here. At the end of the street you can see the Rijksmuseum. Keep going to the:
11. **Museum van Loon,** at Keizersgracht 672. This museum gives you a rare glimpse behind the gables at a patrician house of the post–Golden Age. The house dates from 1672, and has been owned by the van Loon family since 1884. Its completely restored period rooms are filled with richly decorated paneling, stucco work, mirrors, fireplaces, furnishings, porcelain, medallions, chandeliers, rugs, and more. The garden has carefully tended hedges and a coach house modeled on a Greek temple.

   Cross Reguliersgracht and return to Herengracht, passing near little Thorbeckeplein, and then turn right to the:
12. **Willet-Holthuysen Museum,** at Herengracht 605, a patrician canal house dating from 1687, richly decorated in the Louis XIV style. In the dining salon,

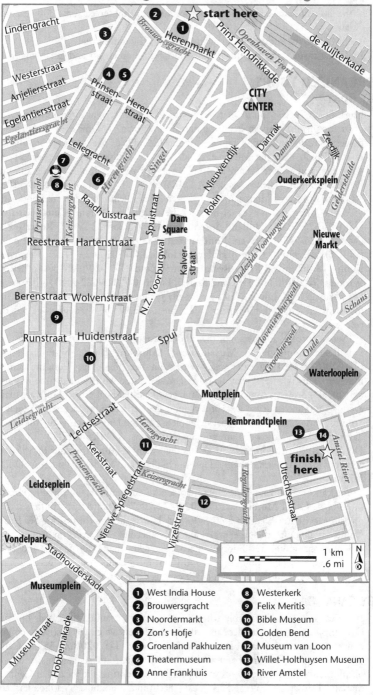

Walking Tour—The Golden Age Canals

☆ **start here**

Lindengracht

Brouwersgracht

Herenmarkt

Prins Hendrikkade

Openhaven Front

de Ruijterkade

Westerstraat

Anjeliersstraat

Egelantiersstraat

Egelantiersgracht

Prinsen-
straat

Heren-
straat

**CITY
CENTER**

Nieuwendijk

Damrak

Damrak

Zeedijk

Leliegracht

Singel

Herengracht

Prinsengracht

Keizersgracht

Raadhuisstraat

Reestraat

Hartenstraat

Berenstraat

Wolvenstraat

Runstraat

Huidenstraat

Spuistraat

N.Z. Voorburgwal

**Dam
Square**

Kalver-
straat

Rokin

Oudezijds Voorburgwal

Ouderkerksplein

Gelderskade

**Nieuwe
Markt**

Kloveniersburgwal

Groenburgwal

Schans

Oude

Waterlooplein

Spui

Leidsegracht

Leidsestraat

Herengracht

Kerkstraat

Prinsengracht

Keizersgracht

Nieuwe Spiegelstraat

Vijzelstraat

Muntplein

Rembrandtplein

Reguliersgracht

Utrechtsestraat

**finish
here** ☆

Amstel River

Leidseplein

Vondelpark

Stadhouderskade

Museumplein

Museumstraat

Hobbemakade

| 0 | 1 km |
| | .6 mi |

N

1 West India House
2 Brouwersgracht
3 Noordermarkt
4 Zon's Hofje
5 Groenland Pakhuizen
6 Theatermuseum
7 Anne Frankhuis

8 Westerkerk
9 Felix Meritis
10 Bible Museum
11 Golden Bend
12 Museum van Loon
13 Willet-Holthuysen Museum
14 River Amstel

the table under the chandelier is set for a meal being served some 300 years too late.

Walk to the end of Herengracht and finish the tour at the:

13. River Amstel, which at this point is thick with houseboats and canal barges.

ORGANIZED TOURS
By Boat

Canal-boat trips last approximately 1 hour and leave at regular intervals from *rondvaart* (excursion) piers in key locations around town. The majority of launches, however, are docked along Damrak or Prins Hendrikkade near Centraal Station and on the Rokin near the Muntplein and near the Leidseplein. Tours leave every 45 minutes in winter (10am to 4pm), every 15 to 30 minutes during summer (9am to 9:30pm). The average fare is Dfl 12 to 18 ($6 to $9) for adults, Dfl 10 to 12 ($5 to $6) for children age 4 to 13. Evening candlelit cruises are also popular.

Major operators of canal-boat cruises are **Amsterdam Canal Cruises** (☎ 020/626-5636), **Holland International** (☎ 020/622-7788), **Rederij Plas** (☎ 020/624-5406), **Meyers Rondvaarten** (☎ 020/623-4208), **Rederij Boekel** (☎ 020/612-9905), **Rederij Hof van Holland** (☎ 020/623-7122), **Rederij P. Kooij** (☎ 020/623-3810), **Rederij Noord-Zuid** (☎ 020/679-1370), **Rederij Wisman** (☎ 020/638-0338), and **Rederij Lovers** (☎ 020/622-2181)—despite its heart-shaped logo, Lovers is not necessarily for lovers, though not necessarily not for them either; it just happens to be the name of the man who started the company.

Ever resourceful and aware of the transportation possibilities of their canals, the Dutch have introduced **Museumboot (Museum Boat),** Stationsplein 8 (☎ **020/622-2181**), to carry weary tourists on their pilgrimages from museum to museum. This is an easy way to travel and, for those with limited time in Amsterdam, also provides some of the advantages of a canal-boat cruise. Stops are made every 45 minutes at seven key spots around the city, providing access to a total of 16 museums. The Museum Boat's complete package fare, which is for the whole day and includes a discount on museum admissions, is Dfl 25 ($12.50) for adults, Dfl 20 ($10) for children age 13 and under. A single round-trip tour on the boat costs Dfl 20 ($10) with no reductions for children; and a halfway tour costs Dfl 15 ($7.50).

You can even be your own captain aboard an environmentally friendly, electric motorboat. **Canal Motorboats** (☎ **020/422-7007**) operates two landing stages, one close to Centraal Station on the Oosterdokskade (next to the floating Sea Palace Chinese restaurant), the other where the Kloveniersburgwal meets the Amstel river (opposite the Hôtel de l'Europe). Each boat takes up to six people, and costs Dfl 65 ($32.50) for 1 hour, or Dfl 150 ($75) for 3 hours. You will need to leave identity plus Dfl 300 ($150) or a credit card as a deposit.

By Canal Bike

If the canal-boat cruise simply whets your appetite to ramble the canals on your own, there are sturdy paddleboats, called canal bikes, which (by a strange coincidence) you rent from **Canal Bike,** Weteringschans 24 (☎ **020/626-5574**). Canal bikes seat two or four and come with a detailed map, route suggestions, and a bit of information about the places you'll pedal past. Moorings are located at Centraal Station, Leidseplein, Westerkerk near the Anne Frankhuis, Stadhouderskade (between the Rijksmuseum and the Heineken Reception Center), and at Toronto Bridge on the Keizersgracht, near Leidsestraat. The canals can get busy with tour boats and other small craft, so watch out, particularly when going under bridges. Rental is Dfl 19.50 ($9.75) for a 1-hour jaunt for two people; a four-passenger water bicycle is Dfl 29.50 ($14.75) per hour.

BY BICYCLE

You're going to look pretty conspicuous taking one of the guided tours offered by **Yellow Bike,** Nieuwezijds Kolk 29, off Nieuwezijds Voorburgwal (☎ **020/ 620-6940**). Why? Because you'll be cycling on a yellow bicycle along with a dozen other people also on yellow bicycles, that's why. In partial compensation, you'll have a close encounter with Amsterdam or the nearby countryside.

BY BUS

For many travelers, a quick bus tour is the best way to launch a sightseeing program in a strange city, and although Amsterdam offers its own unique alternative—a canal-boat ride—you might want to get your bearings on land as well. A 3-hour tour costs Dfl 35 to 40 ($17.50 to $20); on most tours children 4 to 13 are charged half price. Major tour companies are **The Best of Holland,** Damrak 34 (☎ **020/623-1539**); **Holland International Excursions,** Dam 6 (☎ **020/551- 2800**); **Holland Keytours,** Dam Square 19 (☎ **020/624-7304**); and **Lindbergh Excursions,** Damrak 26 (☎ **020/622-2766**).

ON FOOT

Amsterdam Walking Tours (☎ **020/640-9072**) leads guided strolls through historic parts of Amsterdam on Saturday and Sunday morning at 11am. If you'd rather guide yourself around, try **Audio Tourist,** Oude Spiegelstraat 9 (☎ **020/ 421-5580**), whose map-and-cassette packages allow you to "see Amsterdam by your ears." You can choose among different tours lasting from 2 to 3 hours. Renting the cassette player, tape, and map costs Dfl 15 ($7.50) for adults, Dfl 6.50 ($3.25) for children age 13 and under; seniors and holders of a CJP under-26 pass get a 20% discount.

IN THE AIR

A 30-minute bird's-eye view of Amsterdam, the tulip fields, the beaches, and nearby Volendam will give you a different perspective on the city and its environs and also present quite graphically Amsterdam's all-important relationship with the sea. During summer months, **KLM Cityhopper,** KLM's domestic affiliate, offers Saturday- and Sunday-afternoon sightseeing flights from Schiphol Airport. If money is no object, you can also charter a chopper for an aerial tour of Amsterdam from **KLM Helikopters,** which operates big birds that more usually service North Sea oil rigs. For details, fares, and booking, call ☎ **020/474-7747.**

8 Sports & Recreation

RECREATION, LEISURE & OUTDOOR ACTIVITIES

BEAUTY SALONS   The **Body Tuning Clinic,** Jan Luykenstraat 40 (☎ **020/ 662-0909**), and **Vitalitae,** Nieuwezijds Voorburgwal 301 (☎ **020/624-4441**), will both take excellent care of the outer you.

BOATING & CANOEING   From March 15 through October 15 you can go to Loosdrecht, outside Amsterdam, to rent sailing equipment at **Ottenhome** (☎ **035/582-3331**). **Yacht Haven Robinson,** Dorpstraat 3, Landsmeer (☎ **020/ 482-1346**), rents rowing equipment. Canoes can be rented in the **Amsterdamse Bos,** south of the city, for use in the park only.

BOWLING If you find you just have to knock down a few pins, try **Knijn Bowling,** Scheldeplein 3 (☎ 020/664-2211).

CYCLING South of the city is **Amsterdamse Bos,** where you can rent bicycles (☎ 020/644-5473) for touring the woodland's paths. Of course, you can always do as Amsterdammers do and explore all those bridges and canals by bike (see "By Bicycle" under "Getting Around" in chapter 13 for rental information).

FISHING Anglers should try the **Bosbaan** artificial pond in Amsterdamse Bos, south of the city. You can get a license there at Nikolaswetsantraat 10 (☎ 020/626-4988), open Tuesday through Friday, or at any fishing supply store in the area.

FITNESS CENTERS If don't want to neglect your exercise routine, there are several centers you can try, including **Fitness Aerobic Center Jansen,** Rokin 109–111 (☎ 020/626-9366); **Sporting Club Leidseplein,** Korte Leidsedwarsstraat 18 (☎ 020/620-6631); **Garden Gym,** Jodenbreestraat 158 (☎ 020/626-8772); **Splash,** Looiersgracht 26 (☎ 020/624-8404).

GOLF There are public golf courses in or near Amsterdam at the **Golf en Conference Center Amstelborgh,** Borchlandweg 6 (☎ 020/697-5000); **Sloten,** Sloterweg 1045 (☎ 020/614-2402); **Waterland Golf Course,** Buikslotermeerdijk 141 (☎ 020/636-1010); and **Spaarnwoude Golf Course,** Het Hogeland 2, Spaarnwoude (☎ 020/538-5599). Call ahead for greens fees and tee times.

HORSEBACK RIDING Riding, both indoor and outdoor, is offered at **Amsterdamse Manege,** Nieuwe Kalfjeslaan 25 (☎ 020/643-1342); indoor riding only is available at **Nieuw Amstelland Manege,** Jan Tooropplantsoen 17 (☎ 020/643-2468). Horses rented at **De Ruif Manege,** Sloterweg 675 (☎ 020/615-6667), can be ridden in Amsterdamse Bos.

ICE-SKATING All those Dutch paintings of people skating and sledding—not to mention the story of Hans Brinker and his silver skates—will surely get you thinking about skating on Amsterdam's ponds and canals (see the box "Skating on the Dutch Canals," below). However, doing this won't be easy unless you're willing to shell out for a new pair of skates—there are very few places that rent them. One of those is **Jaap Eden Baan,** Radioweg 64 (☎ 020/694-9894). Here you can rent skates from November through February, and they'll even allow you to take them out of the rink. The Jaap Eden Baan's marvelous outdoor rink is popular in winter—but unless you're highly competent, watch out for the long lines of speed skaters practicing for the next Eleven Cities Race.

JOGGING The two main jogging areas are Vondelpark in the center and Amsterdamse Bos on the southern edge of the city. You can also run along the Amstel River. If you choose to run along the canals, as many do, watch out for uneven cobbles, loose paving stones, and dog poop.

SAILING Sailboats and sailboards can be rented at **Duikelaars** on the Sloterplas Lake, Sloterpark, Noordzijde 41 (☎ 020/613-8855).

SAUNA & MASSAGE **Sauna Deco,** Herengracht 115 (☎ 020/627-1773), and **Oibibio Thermen,** Prins Hendrikkade 20–21 (☎ 020/553-9311) are two places where, in Dutch style, you get down to the altogether in mixed facilities. At **Koan Float,** Herengracht 321 (☎ 020/625-4970) you can float away the stress of a hard day's sightseeing.

SWIMMING Amsterdam's state-of-the-art swimming facility is **De Mirandabad,** De Mirandalaan 9 (☎ 020/642-8080). This ultramodern complex features indoor and outdoor pools with wave machines, slides, and other amusements. **The**

Marnixbad, Marnixplein 5 (☎ 020/625-4843), is a glass-enclosed public pool. The **Zuiderbad,** Hobbemastraat 26 (☎ 020/679-2217), dates from 1911. Other public pools are the **Floralparkbad,** Sneeuwbalweg 5 (☎ 020/636-8121), and the **Sloterparkbad,** Slotermeerlaan 2 (☎ 020/611-4565).

TABLE TENNIS   Ping-Pong to your heart's content at **Tafeltennis Centrum Amsterdam,** Keizersgracht 209 (☎ 020/624-5780).

TENNIS & SQUASH   You'll find indoor courts at **Frans Otten Stadion,** Stadionstraat 10 (☎ 020/662-8767). For both indoor and outdoor courts, try **Gold Star,** Karel Lotsylaan 20 (☎ 020/644-5483), and **Amstelpark Tenniscentre,** Karel Lotyslaan 8 (☎ 020/644-5436), which has a total of 36 courts.

Squash courts can be found at **Squash City,** Ketelmakerstraat 6 (near Centraal Station) (☎ 020/626-7883).

SPECTATOR SPORTS

AMERICAN FOOTBALL   Yes, there's an American football league in Europe, and Amsterdam has its own franchise. The Amsterdam Admirals, complete with cheerleaders, are based at the Amsterdam ArenA (see "Soccer," below).

BASEBALL   Honk if you like baseball (the game is called *honkbal* in Holland). The Amsterdam Pirates aren't the greatest practitioners of the art, but they have their moments, as you can see at the **Sportpark,** Jan van Galenstraat 16 (☎ 020/684-8143).

SOCCER   Soccer (called football in Europe) is absolutely the biggest game in Holland. Amsterdam's world-famous team, Ajax, are the best in Holland, and quite often the best in Europe as well. They play their home matches in a fabulous new stadium, the **Amsterdam ArenA,** in Amsterdam Zuidoost (☎ 020/311-1333).

9 Shopping

Bargain-hunters won't have much luck here (except at the flea markets), but shopping in Amsterdam definitely has its rewards. Best buys include diamonds and traditional Dutch products, such as Delftware, pewter, crystal, and old-fashioned clocks. No matter what you're looking for, you're sure to be impressed with the range of possibilities Amsterdam offers.

Shopping can easily be integrated into your Amsterdam experience because the city center is small enough that shops and other attractions are often right beside each other. Rather than going on dedicated shopping expeditions, it may make more sense to simply drop into the nearest shops while you're involved in more weighty cultural matters.

Shoppers should know that, for the most part, prices are fixed in Holland, with all applicable taxes included in the amounts shown on tags and counter display cards. Although end-of-season and other special sales occur from time to time throughout the year, the practice of discounting as we know it is not yet part of the Dutch pricing system, so there's little use running from shop to shop trying to find a better price on ordinary consumer goods. When you see what you want, buy it then and there, secure in the knowledge that you won't find it cheaper elsewhere. One exception to this rule is Schiphol Airport's renowned **duty-free shopping area,** where some 40 shops offer luxury goods at a 20% to 30% discount. There's even a duty-free car and motorcycle showroom called **ShipSide,** across from the main terminal (☎ 020/653-3333 for information).

Skating on the Dutch Canals

In winter, the Dutch watch the falling thermometers with the same avidity as people in Aspen and Chamonix. When it drops low enough for long enough, the landscape becomes a big ice-maker; and rivers, canals, and lakes become sparkling highways through the countryside. This doesn't happen very often, but if you're lucky enough to be here at such a time, the best experience of your whole trip may be skating on the canals of Amsterdam. Classical music plays over the ice, and little kiosks are set up to dispense heart-warming liqueurs. Just be cautious when skating under bridges, and in general don't go anywhere that the Dutch themselves don't.

THE SHOPPING SCENE

Major shopping streets in Amsterdam, many of which are closed to traffic, include the following: **Kalverstraat,** from Dam Square to Muntplein (inexpensive and moderately priced shops); **Rokin,** parallel to Kalverstraat (quality fashions, art galleries, antiques shops); **Leidsestraat** (upmarket shops for clothing, china, gifts); **P. C. Hooftstraat** and **Van Baerlestraat,** near Museumplein (designer fashion, accessories, china, gifts); and **Nieuwe Spiegelstraat,** near the Rijksmuseum (art and antiques).

Major shopping malls are springing up throughout the city. **Magna Plaza** has filled a former post office, just behind Dam Square, with four floors of exclusive and useful shops. The newest shopping center is the **Kalvertoren,** whose award-winning building occupies a prime triangular site at the corner of Kalverstraat, Heiligeweg, and the Singel canal near the Munt. The cafe at the top offers a bird's-eye view of Amsterdam's rooftops.

SHOPPING HOURS   Regular shopping hours in Amsterdam are Monday from 11am to 6pm; Tuesday, Wednesday, and Friday from 9am to 6pm; Thursday from 9am to 9pm; and Saturday from 9am to 5pm. In recent years there has been something of a revolution in the previously restricted opening hours. Against the wishes of churches and other groups, many shops now stay open on Sunday as well, usually from noon to 5pm, and more and more supermarkets are staying open daily from 8am to 8pm (or even later, until 10pm).

SHOPPING A TO Z
ANTIQUES

Amsterdam's antiques shops rank among the finest in Europe. The best places to look for them are around **Nieuwe Spiegelstraat** and **Kerkstraat,** and in the **Jordaan** section of the city. The VVV can also provide a list of antiques street markets, which can offer a glorious mix of junk and treasure. The ✪ **Kunst- & Antiekcentrum de Looier** at Elandsgracht 109 (☎ **020/624-9038**) is an indoor antiques market spread through several old warehouses, where hundreds of individual dealers rent small stalls and corners to show their wares.

ART

In Amsterdam, paintings large and small, originals and reproductions, peer out of every other shop window. For good-quality reproductions of the masters, **museum shops** are your best bet.

✪ **ABK Gallery for Sculpture,** Zeilmakersstraat 15, on Bickers Eiland (☎ 020/625-6332), a cooperative gallery, is worth a visit. Call before you head out, since it's open only by appointment on Thursday through Sunday from noon to 6pm. Pick up your favorite cartoon characters at **Animation Art,** Berenstraat 39 (☎ 020/627-7600), open Tuesday through Friday from 11am to 6pm and Saturday from 11am to 5pm. **Art Rages,** Spiegelgracht 2a (☎ 627-3645) has interesting contemporary ceramics, glass, jewelry, and mixed-media pieces from all over Europe, as well as the United States and Canada; it's open Monday through Saturday from 11am to 6pm.

Books

For English-language publications, there's the **American Book Center,** Kalverstraat 185 (☎ 020/625-5537), open Monday through Wednesday and Friday and Saturday from 10am to 8pm, Thursday from 10am to 10pm, and Sunday from 11am to 6pm, which gives a 10% student discount; **Waterstone's Booksellers,** Kalverstraat 152 (☎ 020/638-3821), open Monday from 11am to 6pm, Tuesday and Saturday from 10am to 6pm, Wednesday and Friday from 9am to 6pm, Thursday from 9am to 9pm, and Sunday from 10am to 5pm; and **Athenaeum Booksellers,** Spui 14–16 (☎ 020/622-6248), which carries one of the city's most comprehensive selections of international magazines and newspapers, as well as books.

For secondhand book bargains, browse through the stalls that cover the Spui square on Fridays.

Cigars, Pipes & Smoking Articles

Amsterdammers treasure **P. G. C. Hajenius,** Rokin 92–96 (☎ 020/623-7494), almost as much as they treasure their pipes. Indeed, this elegant and gracious tobacco and pipe shop, run by the same family since 1826, is the sort that I, for one, thought had long vanished from the face of the earth. The warm, wood-paneled store is virtually a museum of antique tobacco humidors (not for sale), and has a beautiful selection of distinctively Dutch blends for sale. Pipes of all description are displayed for your selection, and fine Sumatra and Havana cigars are kept in a room-size glass humidor. The shop is open Monday through Wednesday, Friday, and Saturday from 9:30am to 6pm, Thursday until 9pm.

Clocks

Dutch clocks can be hard to resist. Traditional clockmakers turn out timepieces with soft-toned chimes in exquisite Old Dutch–style handcrafted cases, covered with tiny figures and mottoes, insets of hand-painted porcelain, and hand-painted Dutch scenes. ✪ **B. V. Victoria,** Prins Hendrikkade 47 (☎ 020/624-7314), is a happy hunting ground for these treasures. This small shop across from Centraal Station near the Victoria Hotel has a particularly good selection, reasonable prices, and friendly, personal service from Theo, one of the owners, and his staff. It also has a good stock of Delftware, chocolates, and quality gifts. You can even pay in U.S. dollars if you wish. Open daily from 10am to 6pm.

Crafts & Curios

The **Blue Gold Fish,** Rozengracht 17 (☎ 020/623-3134) has no real rhyme or reason behind the items for sale. The shop stocks a wide range of ceramics, jewelry, household items, and textiles, running the gamut of expression from kitsch to chic. Still, there's unity in its diversity and in the more-or-less fantastic design sensibility that goes into each piece. Open Monday through Saturday from 11:30am to

---

VAT & the VAT Refund

If you live outside the European Union, whatever your nationality, you're entitled to a refund of the VAT—value-added tax—you pay on purchases of Dfl 300 ($150) or more in one shop in 1 day. On high-ticket items, the savings of 13.5% can be significant. You must take the purchases home within 3 months. To obtain your VAT refund, ask for a **tax-free shopping check** from the shop when you're buying your goods. Then as you're leaving the EU, present this check, your purchases, and receipts to Customs. They will stamp the check. You can get the refund in cash at an International Refund Point (in Holland, this is the ABN-AMRO bank in the Schiphol Airport terminal lounge). Otherwise you can return the check to **Europe Tax-free Shopping,** Leidsevaartweg 99, 2106 AS, Heemstede (☎ **023/524-1909;** fax 023/524-6164), who will refund the tax, minus their commission, either to your credit card or by check.

6:30pm. The more traditional **'t Winkeltje,** Prinsengracht 228 (☎ **020/ 625-1352**), sells assorted knickknacks such as colored bottles and glasses, modern versions of old tin cars and other children's toys from the 1950s and earlier, big plastic butterflies, lamps shaped like bananas, and many other such useful things. Open Monday from 1 to 5:30pm, Tuesday through Friday from 10am to 5:30pm, and Saturday from 10am to 5pm.

DELFTWARE

By far the most ubiquitous items you'll see will be those in the familiar blue-and-white "Delft" colors that have almost become synonymous with Holland itself. Souvenir shops, specialty shops, and department stores feature "delftware" earthenware products in the widest variety of forms imaginable. If any one object has particular appeal, by all means buy it—but be aware that unless it meets certain specifications, you are not carting home an authentic piece of the hand-painted earthenware pottery that has made the Delft name famous.

It's true that delftware, which can also be red and white or multicolored, is the accurate name for much of what you see displayed. If, however, a piece carries the hallmark Delftware or Delft Blue (with a capital D), you may be certain it came from one factory only, in the city of Delft (see chapter 16). Of equal quality and value are those hallmarked Makkumware (with a capital M), the fine hand-painted earthenware, often multicolored, made only by one firm in the Frisian town of Makkum (see chapter 17). Technically, copies of each should be called delftware and makkumware (small d and small m). In most cases you'll immediately see the difference, but if you're doing serious shopping, you should learn to recognize the hallmarks of each. A wide selection of Delftware can be found at ✪ **De Porceleyne Fles,** Prinsengracht 170 (☎ **020/622-7509**), opposite the Anne Frank House, and **Focke & Meltzer,** P. C. Hooftstraat 65–67 (☎ **020/664-2311**).

DEPARTMENT STORES

De Bijenkorf ("The Beehive"), Dam 1 (☎ **020/621-8080**), is Amsterdam's largest department store, with a vast array of goods in all price ranges and a very good restaurant. Other well-stocked warehouses, as the Dutch call department stores, include **Vroom & Dreesmann,** Kalverstraat 201, near Muntplein (☎ **020/ 622-0171**); **Metz & Co.,** Keizersgracht 455, on the corner of Leidsestraat

(☎ **020/520-7020**); and **HEMA,** the Dutch Woolworth's, on the Nieuwendijk and in the Kalvertoren shopping mall near the Munt (☎ **020/626-8720**).

DIAMONDS

Amsterdam diamond cutters have an international reputation for high standards. When you buy from them, you'll be given a certificate listing the weight, color, cut, and identifying marks of the gem you purchase. The following shops are members of the Amsterdam Diamond Foundation, and offer diamond cutting and polishing tours, as well as sales of the finished product: **Amsterdam Diamond Center,** Rokin 1 (☎ **020/624-5787**), open Friday through Wednesday from 10am to 6pm, Thursday from 10am to 6pm and 7 to 8:30pm; **Coster Diamonds,** Paulus Potterstraat 2–4 (☎ **020/676-2222**), open daily from 9am to 5pm; **Gassan Diamonds,** Nieuwe Uilenburgerstraat 173–175 (☎ **020/622-5333**), open daily from 9am to 5pm; **Stoeltie Diamonds,** Wagenstraat 13–17 (☎ **020/623-7601**), open daily from 9am to 5pm; and **Van Moppes Diamonds,** Albert Cuypstraat 2–6 (☎ **020/676-1242**), open daily from 9am to 5pm.

FASHIONS

Alongside the standard designer emporia along the **Rokin** and the **P. C. Hooftstraat** are more exclusive, often home-grown designer clothes in the small streets running across the main canals. Try the **Herenstraat, Hartenstraat, Wolvenstraat,** and **Huidenstraat** for something that will be unique at home, and fairly unique in Amsterdam.

FLOWER BULBS

Gardeners will find it well-nigh impossible to leave Amsterdam without at least one purchase from the ✪ **Floating Flower Market,** on Singel Canal at Muntplein, open daily year-round. Just be certain that the bulbs you buy carry with them the obligatory certificate clearing them for entry into the United States.

FOOD & DRINK

Jacob Hooy & Co., Kloveniersburgwal 10–12 (☎ **020/624-3041**), opened in 1743 and operated for the past 130 years by the same family, is a wonderland of fragrant smells that offers more than 500 different herbs and spices and 30 different teas, sold loose by weight, as well as health foods, homeopathic products, and natural cosmetics. Open Monday from noon to 6pm, Tuesday through Friday from 8am to 6pm, and Saturday from 8am to 5pm. **H. Keijzer,** Prinsengracht 180 (☎ **020/622-8428**), was founded in 1839 and specializes in coffee as well as tea, offering 90 different kinds of tea and 22 coffees. Open Monday through Friday from 8:30am to 5:30pm and Saturday from 8:30am to 5pm. **H.P. de Vreng en Zonen,** Nieuwendijk 75 (☎ **020/624-4581**), has an extensive selection of special Dutch liqueurs and gins. To recover from the aftereffects of these fine distilled spirits, head for **De Waterwinkel,** Roelof Hartstraat 10 (☎ **020/675-5932**), a one-of-a-kind store that stocks a massive range of mineral waters from around the world.

JEWELRY

Marvelous contemporary designs and materials turn jewelry into an art form at **Galerie Ra,** Vijzelstraat 90 (☎ **020/626-5100**). Owner Paul Derrez specializes in stunning modern jewelry in gold and silver, and also goes a bit further, turning feathers, rubber, foam, and other materials into pieces that he describes as "playful." **BLGK Edelsmeden,** Hartenstraat 28 (☎ **020/624-8154**), is owned by four jewelry designers, who each produce and sell affordable designer jewelry. Some of their pieces represent a new and fresh spin on classic forms, while others are more innovative models. Open Tuesday through Friday from 10:30am to 6pm and Saturday from 11am to 5pm.

MARKETS

At the **Albert Cuyp Markt,** Albert Cuypstraat, you'll find just about anything and everything your imagination can conjure up. It's open Monday through Saturday from 9:30am to 5pm. Every Friday there's a **Book Market** held on the Spui. The **Farmer's Market,** also known as the Bio Market, takes place every Saturday from 8am to 2pm in the Noordermarkt; it caters to Amsterdam's growing infatuation with health foods and natural products. Thorbeckeplein hosts a **Sunday Art Market** from March through December, with local artists showing their wares. The daily **Waterlooplein Flea Market** is the classic market of Amsterdam, offering everything from cooking pots to mariner's telescopes to decent prints of Dutch cities. Open daily from 9am to 5pm. On Sunday in the summer (late May through the end of September), the junk goes away for a day and the antiques and books come in.

10 Amsterdam After Dark

Nightlife in Amsterdam, like an Indonesian *rijsttafel,* is a bit of this and a bit of that. The cultural calendar is full, but not jammed. There's a strong jazz scene, good music clubs, and enjoyable English-language shows at the little cabarets and theaters along the canals. The club and bar scene can be entertaining if not outrageous; the dance clubs may indeed seem quiet and small to anyone used to the flash of New York, L.A., or London. However, the brown cafes—the typical Amsterdam pubs—have never been better.

Prices for after-dark entertainment in Amsterdam tend to be modest. Many nightspots only charge for drinks, although others have a nominal cover charge.

ENTERTAINMENT ORIENTATION

INFORMATION   Before setting out for the evening, pick up a copy of *What's On in Amsterdam,* the VVV tourist office's monthly program guide in English, which costs Dfl 4 ($2). There is also the free, monthly, newspaper-style *Uitkrant,* available at many performance venues. It's in Dutch, but you should be able to decipher most of the listings information.

MAIN NIGHTLIFE AREAS   Nightlife is centered around the **Leidseplein** and **Rembrandtplein** areas, both of which have a massive and varied selection of restaurants, bars, and nightspots. The **Rosse Buurt (Red Light District)** serves up its own unique brand of nightlife, and adjoining this is **Nieuwmarkt,** which is rapidly becoming a popular, somewhat alternative hangout.

TICKETS   If you want to attend any of Amsterdam's theatrical or musical events (including rock concerts), make it your first task on arrival to get tickets. **Amsterdam Uit Buro (AUB) Ticketshop,** Leidseplein 26 (☎ **020/621-1211**), can book tickets for almost every venue in town; it also handles advance booking from abroad. The VVV tourist office also books tickets for a charge of Dfl 5 ($2.50). Most upmarket and many mid-level hotels will book tickets for you as well.

HOURS & PERFORMANCE TIMES   Concert, theater, opera, and dance performances generally begin at 8:15pm; jazz concerts begin at 11 or 11:30pm. Jazz clubs and music spots are usually open from 10pm to 2am on weekdays, and as late as 4am on weekends. Dance clubs open at 10 or 11pm and close at 4am during the week, 5am on weekends.

DRINK PRICES   With the exception of the dance clubs, nightclubs, and other high-ticket nightspots in Amsterdam, you can expect to pay Dfl 3 to Dfl 6 ($1.50–$3.00) for a beer or a Coke and Dfl 4 to Dfl 8 ($2–$4) for *jenever* (Dutch gin). Whisky and water will probably cost you at least Dfl 8 ($4), and a mixed cocktail can be as much as Dfl 20 ($10). But remember, these are average prices around town; the cost at a brown cafe (pub) could be less, and a hotel bar could be more.

SAFETY   Wherever you wander in Amsterdam after dark it's wise to be mindful of your surroundings. Fortunately, Amsterdam's less desirable citizens tend to congregate in the less desirable neighborhoods, and none of the nightspots described here is in a "problem area," although taxis are advised in a few cases. For safety in the Red Light District, see its description in "Attractions," above.

THE PERFORMING ARTS
CLASSICAL MUSIC

Amsterdam's top orchestra—indeed one of the world's top orchestras—is the famed **Royal Concertgebouw Orchestra,** whose home is the **Concertgebouw,** Concertgebouwplein 2–6 (☎ **020/671-8345** daily 10am to 5pm; 24-hour information line, ☎ 020/675 4411). World-class orchestras and soloists are only too happy to appear at The Grote Zaal (Great Hall) of the Concertgebouw because of its perfect acoustics. No matter where your seat, the listening is impeccable. Chamber and solo recitals, including a top-notch string quartet series, are also given in the Kleine Zaal (Little Hall). Tickets cost between Dfl 40 and 150 ($20 to $75), with orchestral concerts averaging Dfl 60 ($30). The main concert season is September through mid-June, but during July and August there is the Robeco Summer Series, also world-class but with a more friendly price tag—all seats cost just Dfl 30 ($15).

The city's other symphony orchestra, the **Netherlands Philharmonic Orchestra,** doesn't lag far behind its illustrious cousin. The orchestra's official home is the **Beurs van Berlage,** Damrak 213 (☎ **020/627-0466** for information and box office), formerly the Amsterdam Stock Exchange. This venue also hosts chamber music concerts and recitals in the large hall that was once the trading floor of the exchange.

Holland is a hotbed, and the originator, of authentic performance of early and baroque music. Little surprise that there are all manner of world-class baroque groups based here, including the **Amsterdam Baroque Orchestra** and the **Orchestra of the Eighteenth Century.** Many concerts of this ilk are held in intimate, historic churches, such as the **Engelse Kerk,** Begijnhof 48 (☎ 020/624-9665); **Oude Kerk,** Oudekerksplein 23 (☎ **020/625-8284**); and **Waalse Kerk,** Walenplein 157, at the corner of Oudezijds Achterburgwal and Doelenstraat, (☎ **020/623-2074**).

At the other end of the musical spectrum, lovers of contemporary classical music should head to **De IJsbreker,** Weesperzijde 23 (☎ **020/668-1805**), where you can savor the delights of electronic adventurism and contemporary use of the standard instrumentarium. The terrace of the cafe/bar here is one of the most idyllic in town.

OPERA & BALLET

In recent years, Pierre Audi has been building up the **Netherlands Opera** and its repertoire, and the house is starting to establish an international reputation for often daring productions. The company has just completed a daring production of Wagner's massive four-part *Ring* cycle that exploits all the possibilities offered by its modern, well-equipped house, the **Muziektheater,** Waterlooplein 22 (24-hour information line ☎ **020/551-8100;** box office ☎ 020/625-5455). This theater is also used by **Het Nationale Ballet** (The National Ballet), which performs large-scale classical ballet repertoire as well as more contemporary work, and by the **Nederlands Dans Theater** (Netherlands Dance Theater), which is based in The Hague but also visits Amsterdam and is famous for its ground-breaking contemporary repertoire. Most performances begin at 8:15pm, with opera tickets costing Dfl 40 to 110 ($20 to $55), and ballet tickets slightly less.

THEATER

Homegrown theater productions are almost always in Dutch, but because English is so widely spoken, Amsterdam is a favorite venue for road shows from the United States and England. Check *What's On* to see what's happening when you're in town. Theaters that often host English-language productions include: **Felix Meritis,** Keizersgracht 324 (☎ **020/626-2321**); **Frascati,** Nes 63 (☎ **020/626-6866**), which focuses on modern theater; the multicultural **Melkweg,** Lijnbaansgracht 234a, near Leidseplein (☎ **020/624-1777**); **Royal Théâtre Carré,** Amstel 115–125 (☎ **020/622-5225**); and **Nieuwe de la Mar,** Marnixstraat 404 (☎ **020/623-3462**). Show time is usually 8:15pm, and ticket prices vary widely.

COMEDY THEATER

For several years, ✪ **Boom Chicago,** Leidsepleintheater, Leidseplein 12 (☎ **020/530-7300**), has been bringing delightful English-language improvisational comedy to Amsterdam. *Time* magazine compared it to Chicago's famous Second City comedy troupe. Dutch audiences don't have much problem with the English sketches; they often seem to get the point ahead of the native English speakers in attendance. Tickets are Dfl 27.50 ($13.75). Spectators are seated around candlelit tables for eight people and can have dinner and a drink while they enjoy the show. The restaurant is open at 7pm, and meals cost Dfl 20 to 25 ($10 to $12.50) per person.

THE CLUB & MUSIC SCENE
JAZZ & BLUES

In Amsterdam, jazz and blues groups hold forth in bars, and the joints start jumping at around 11pm. You'll find listings in *What's On.* **Bimhuis,** Oudeschans 73–77 (☎ **020/623-1361**), is for the more serious contemporary jazz connoisseur; **Joseph Lam Jazz Club,** Diemenstraat 8 (☎ **020/622-8086**), is Dixieland; and

An After-Dark Tip

Because Amsterdammers take evening "culture"—in whatever form—as just another part of everyday living, dress tends to be more casual than in other cities. Though some people show up for a symphony concert in a tuxedo, you'll see many others in jeans and a T-shirt. There are also free outdoor concerts in summer, where jeans or shorts are expected.

Bourbon Street Jazz & Blues Club, Leidsekruisstraat 6–8 (☎ **020/623-3440**), hosts a mix of local and traveling talent. Also recommended is **Alto,** Korte Leidsedwarsstraat 115, off of the Leidseplein (☎ **020/626-3249**).

DANCE CLUBS

Amsterdam's disco scene embraces every type of ambiance and clientele, from the more sophisticated rooms in large hotels to underground alternative spots. The scene isn't wildly volatile, but places do come and go, so check the listings in *What's On* for current addresses. Today's leading discos include **Mazzo,** Rozengracht 114 (☎ **020/626-7500**), for trance and techno; **Akhnaton,** Nieuwezijds Kolk 25 (☎ **020/624-3396**), for African music and salsa; **Melkweg,** Lijnbaansgracht 234a (☎ **020/624-1777**), for a variety of live music plus dance events; **iT,** Amstelstraat 24, near Rembrandtplein (☎ **020/625-0111**), which is gay on Saturday and mixed Thursday, Friday, and Sunday; **Paradiso,** Weteringschans 6–8 (☎ **020/626-4521**), which has live music followed by dance parties; the hip **RoXY,** Singel 465–467 (☎ **020/620-0354**), where you should dress to kill; and **Soul Kitchen,** Amstelstraat 32, near Rembrandtplein (☎ **020/620-2333**), which usually has a relaxed, amicable crowd just out to swing.

THE BAR SCENE

Amsterdam has just about as many bars as it has tulips. Virtually every Amsterdammer has a "local," but all places welcome visitors. There are several different types of bars in the city, as listed below.

BROWN CAFES

You'll see brown cafes (*bruine kroegen*) everywhere: on street corners, at the canal intersections, and down narrow little lanes. They look as if they've been there forever, and they have, practically (rumor has it there's one that hasn't closed its doors since 1574, but I never found it). These are the favorite local haunts and are quite likely to become yours as well—they're positively addictive. Brown cafes will typically sport lace half-curtains at the front window and ancient Oriental rugs on table tops (to sop up any spills from your beer). Wooden floors, overhead beams, and plastered walls blend into a murky brown background, darkened by the centuries of smoke from Dutch pipes. Frequently there's a wall rack with newspapers and magazines, but they get little attention in the evening, when conversations flow as readily as *pils* (beer). *Jenever,* the lovely (and potent) Dutch gin, is on hand in several different flavors, some served ice cold—but never on the rocks. Excellent Dutch beer, as well as more expensive imported brews, are available as well.

Your hotel neighborhood is sure to have at least one brown cafe close at hand, and far be it for me to set any sort of rigid itinerary for a brown-cafe *kroegentocht* ("pub crawl"), but you just might want to look into the following: ✪ **Hoppe,** Spui 18–20 (☎ **020/623-7849**), a student and journalist hangout since 1670, which still has sawdust on the floor and is always packed and lots of fun; **Kalkhoven,** at Prinsengracht and Westermarkt (☎ **020/624-9649**), an atmospheric old bar that dates back to 1670; ✪ **Cafe 't Smalle,** Egelantiersgracht 12 (☎ **020/623-9617**), in the Jordaan district on the canal-side, a beautiful bar in a former distillery and tasting house that dates from 1786; **Café Chris,** Bloemstraat 42 (☎ **020/624-5942**), a tap house since 1624; **Gollem,** Raamsteeg 4 (☎ **020/626-6645**), which sells more than 200 different beers; **De Karpershoek,** Martelaarsgracht 2 (☎ **020/624-7886**), which dates from 1629 and was once a favorite hangout of sailors; and ✪ **Papeneiland,** Prinsengracht 2 (☎ **020/624-1989**), a 300-year-old

Smoking Coffee Shops

Tourists often get confused about "smoking" coffee shops and how they differ from "no-smoking" ones. Well, to begin with, "smoking" and "no-smoking" don't refer to cigarettes—they refer to hashish and marijuana.

"Smoking" coffee shops not only sell cannabis, most commonly in the form of hashish, but also provide a place where patrons can sit and smoke it all day long if they so choose. Not too long ago, before there was a small crackdown on soft drugs in Amsterdam, smoking coffee shops advertised their wares with a marijuana leaf sign. Though the practice of buying and smoking hashish in the coffee shops is still tolerated, the marijuana leaf advertisements are now illegal. Generally, these smoking coffee shops are the only places in Amsterdam called "coffee shops"—regular cafes are called cafes or eetcafes—so chances are, whether or not you want to smoke, you'll be able to find what you're looking without too much difficulty.

In recent years, Holland has given in to pressure from surrounding countries regarding its drug policy and is tightening the rules for these coffee shops. You are now allowed to possess only up to 5 grams of hashish or marijuana for personal use, and coffee shops are forbidden to sell more than this amount to each customer. In addition, each local authority can decide to impose stricter rules if it thinks they are needed. The current mayor of Amsterdam is campaigning against "immorality" in the city, and wants to close many coffee shops and subject the remainder to strict rules. Nonetheless, Amsterdam is still a mecca for the marijuana smoker and seems likely to remain that way.

Each coffee shop has a menu listing the different varieties of hashish and marijuana it stocks. Hash comes in two varieties: light pollen and oily black. Connoisseurs say the best stuff has a stronger smell and is soft and sticky. The bright green weed called Skunk has an extra high content of THC (the active ingredient in cannabis). Bags cost between Dfl 10 and 25 ($5 to $12.50), depending on the variety. Coffee shops also have joints (stickies) for sale, rolled with tobacco. Officially, coffee shops are not allowed to sell alcohol, so they sell coffee, tea, and fruit juices. You're even allowed to bring along and smoke your own stuff, so long as you buy a drink.

Some of the most popular smoking coffee shops are **The Rookies,** Korte Leidsedwarsstraat 145–147 (☎ **020/694-2353**); **Borderline,** Amstelstraat 37 (☎ **020/622-0540**); and the several branches of the **Bulldog** chain (the **Bulldog Palace** is at Leidseplein 15, ☎ **020/627-1908**).

establishment filled with character with a secret tunnel leading under the Brouwersgracht that was used by Catholics in the 17th century.

TASTING HOUSES

The decor will still be basically brown and typically Old Dutch—and the age of the establishment may be even more impressive than that of its beer-swilling brown cafe neighbors—but in a tasting house (or *proeflokaal*) you usually order *jenever* (Dutch gin, taken "neat," without ice) or another product of the distillery that owns the place. To drink your choice of spirit, custom and ritual decree that you lean over the bar, with your hands behind your back, to take the first sip from your well-filled *borreltje* (small drinking glass).

Tasting houses to look for include: **D'Admiraal,** Herengracht 319 (☎ **020/ 625-4334**); **De Drie Fleschjes,** Gravenstraat 18 (☎ **020/624-8443**), behind the Nieuwe Kerk; **De Ooievaar,** Sint Olofspoort 1 (☎ **020/625-7360**), on the corner with the Zeedijk near Centraal Station; and **Het Proeflokaal,** Pilsteeg 35 (☎ **020/622-5334**), a wonderful little place that undoubtedly still looks much as it did when it first opened its doors in 1680.

TRENDY CAFES

Every city has its hipper venues, where those out to impress can preen their feathers against a fitting backdrop. Amsterdam is no exception. The places listed below offer modern tastes, contemporary design, and often cocktails instead of beer. Some of them also function as grand cafés (see "Dining," above). **Café Dante,** Spuistrat 320 (☎ **020/638-8839**), is an artist hangout with an exhibition space, located close to the Spui; **Seymour Likely,** Nieuwezijds Voorburgwal 250 (☎ **020/627-1427**), behind the Royal Palace at the Dam, has a constantly changing decor; and ✪ **Café Schiller,** Rembrandtplein 36 (☎ **020/624-9864**), has enduringly attracted artistic and literary types to its stunning art nouveau setting.

15

North Holland (Noord-Holland) Province

The landscape surrounding Amsterdam offers a taste of the cultural and natural variety of the Netherlands—the dikes that have brought this improbable country into being, windmills, wooden shoes, tidy farms, tiny yacht-filled harbors overlooking the IJsselmeer lake, flower fields reaching to the horizon, and sandy beaches looking out to the North Sea. To the west of Amsterdam is the historic city of Haarlem, while to the east are picturesque remnants of strategic fortifications that protected medieval crossing points. In other places in the province, you can climb tall towers and view museums that re-create the local life of yesteryear, ride a steam train, eat fish by the harbor, and see giant locks and tiny canals.

Everything in the North Holland province is an easy day-trip from Amsterdam, but there's so much to see that you'll need to make several trips to do the region justice. The easiest and most convenient way to see the province's highlights is to make use of the excellent bus tours available from Amsterdam. I have also provided some overnight possibilities in case you'd like to spend some extra time in these delightful towns. My suggestion for those staying in Amsterdam is to alternate a day of touring the countryside with one in the city.

BUS TOURS FROM AMSTERDAM   The major Amsterdam-based sightseeing companies—all of which offer the same selection of tours at essentially the same prices—are **Best of Holland Excursions,** Damrak 34 (☎ **020/623-1539**); **Holland International Excursions,** Damrak 90 (☎ **020/551-2800**); **Keytours,** Dam Square 19 (☎ **020/624-7304**); and **Lindbergh Excursions,** Damrak 26 (☎ **020/622-2766**). Prices for half-day tours are Dfl 32.50 to Dfl 47.50 ($16.25 to $23.75), and for full-day tours, Dfl 67.50 to Dfl 87.50 ($33.75 to $43.75); children ages 13 and under are charged half fare, and children under 4 travel free.

1   Haarlem

20km (12 miles) W of Amsterdam

If you have only 1 day to travel beyond Amsterdam, spend it in Haarlem. This city of music and art is just 12 miles west of Amsterdam, a 15-minute journey by train from Centraal Station. It's the gateway to the reclaimed Haarlemmermeer polder land, near the beaches and the bulb fields, in the heart of an area dotted with

North Holland Province

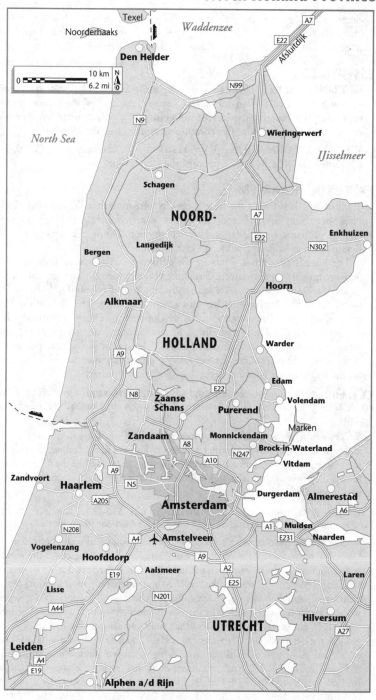

Texel
Noorderhaaks
Waddenzee
Den Helder
A7
E22
Afsluitdijk
N99
N9
North Sea
Wieringerwerf
IJsselmeer
Schagen
NOORD-
A7
E22
Langedijk
N302
Enkhuizen
Bergen
Hoorn
Alkmaar
A9
HOLLAND
Warder
N8
E22
Edam
Zaanse Schans
Volendam
Purerend
Marken
Zandaam
A8
Monnickendam
Brock-in-Waterland
A10
N247
Vitdam
Zandvoort
A9
Durgerdam
Almerestad
Haarlem
N5
A6
A205
Amsterdam
A1
Muiden
N208
E231
Naarden
Vogelenzang
A4
Amstelveen
Hoofddorp
A9
Laren
E19
Aalsmeer
A2
Lisse
N201
E25
A44
Hilversum
UTRECHT
A27
Leiden
A4
E19
Alphen a/d Rijn

elegant manor houses and picturesque villages. Haarlem is also home to two of Holland's finest museums. A trip to Haarlem can easily be combined with one to nearby Zandoort, which is on the same rail line (see below).

ESSENTIALS

GETTING THERE   There are trains departing at least every half hour from Amsterdam Centraal Station to Haarlem; journey time is 15 minutes. There are also buses every 15 minutes or so leaving from outside Centraal Station, but they take much longer than the train. By car from Amsterdam, take the N5 west.

VISITOR INFORMATION   VVV Haarlem is at Stationsplein 1 (☎ 0900/ 616-1600; fax 023/534-0537), opposite the train station.

EXPLORING HAARLEM

Traditionally, Haarlem is the little sister city of Amsterdam. It was where Frans Hals, Jacob van Ruysdael, and Pieter Saenredam were living and painting their famous portraits, landscapes, and church interiors during the same years that Rembrandt was living and working in Amsterdam.

The historic center is a 5-minute walk from the train station, most of it via pedestrian-only shopping streets. First-time visitors generally head straight for the **Grote Markt,** the central market square adjacent to the **Cathedral of St Bavo.** The monumental buildings around the square, which date from the 15th to the 19th century, are a visual minicourse in the development of Dutch architecture. The 14th-century **Town Hall** (Stadhuis), a former hunting lodge rebuilt in the 17th century, and the 17th-century **Meat Market** (Vleeshal), a Renaissance palace that is now one of the two annexes for temporary exhibitions of the Frans Hals Museum, are the two grandest buildings here, along with the cathedral.

✪ **Frans Hals Museum.** Groot Heiligland 62. ☎ **023/516-4200.** Admission Dfl 8 ($4) adults, Dfl 4 ($2) children 10–17, free for children under 10. Mon–Sat 11am–5pm, Sun 1–5pm.

This museum will be a high point of your trip to Holland. The galleries are the halls and furnished chambers of a former pensioners' home, and the famous paintings by the masters of the Haarlem school hang in settings that look like the 17th-century homes they were intended to adorn. This is a beautiful place to spend an hour or two at any time.

Cathedral of St. Bavo. Oude Groenmarkt 23. ☎ **023/532-4399.** Admission Dfl 2.50 ($1.25) adults, Dfl 1.50 (75¢) children age 14 and under. Mon–Sat 10am–4pm.

Walking to the town center from Haarlem station, you catch only glimpses of the Cathedral of St. Bavo (also known as the Grote Kerk) towering above the narrow streets. But the moment you reach the market square it is revealed in all its massive splendor. The cathedral was finished in 1520 after a relatively short building period (130 years), and therefore has a rare unity of structure and proportion. Its elegant wooden tower is covered with lead sheets and adorned with gilt spheres. The interior is light and airy, with tall whitewashed walls and sandstone pillars.

Look for the tombstone of painter Frans Hals, and for a cannonball that has been embedded in the wall ever since it came flying through a window during the siege of Haarlem in 1572–73. And, of course, don't miss seeing the famous Christian Müller Organ, built in 1738. Handel and Mozart both made special visits just to play this magnificent instrument. It has 5,068 pipes and is nearly 30 meters

(98 feet) tall, and when it's going flat out it sounds fit to blow your socks off. The woodwork was done by Jan van Logteren. Mozart played the organ in 1766 when he was just 10 years old—when you see it, you may be struck dumb at the thought of little Wolfie reaching for one of the 68 stops. You can hear it at one of the free concerts given on Tuesday and Thursday from April through October.

Teylers Museum. Spaarne 16. ☎ **023/531-9010.** Admission Dfl 10 ($5) adults, Dfl 3.50 ($1.75) children 15 and under. Tuesday–Saturday 10am–5pm, Sunday 1–5pm.

This is the oldest public museum in the country, established here in 1784 by a private collector. It contains a curious collection of displays: drawings by Michelangelo, Raphael, and Rembrandt (which are shown on a rotating basis); fossils, minerals, and skeletons; and instruments of physics and an odd assortment of inventions, including the largest electrostatic generator in the world (built in 1784) and a 19th-century radarscope.

CANAL BOAT TRIPS

As in Amsterdam, an ideal way to see Haarlem is by canal boat. These boats are operated by **Woltheus Cruises,** whose jetty is on the River Spaarne at the Gravensteenbrug (☎ **023/535-7723**). Cruises around the canals run from April through October, at 10:30am, noon, 1:30pm, 3pm, and 4:30pm. During the winter months, groups can be accommodated by appointment.

NEARBY SIGHTS

The little village of **Spaarndam,** 5 miles (8km) northeast of Haarlem, and reached by bus from outside Haarlem railroad station, is picturesque enough to warrant a visit just for the scenery, but its main claim to fame is a monument to a fictional character who has become an everlasting symbol of Holland and the Dutch people. You may remember Young Pieter (of *Hans Brinker or The Silver Skates* by Mary Mapes Dodge, 1865), who saved Haarlem from disaster when he plugged a hole in the dike with his finger and steadfastly refused to leave until help came at the end of a long night. Because this fictional boy's heroic act so captured the imagination of people around the world, the Dutch government erected a **memorial** in 1950, dedicating it to the courage of Dutch youth in general.

WHERE TO DINE

De Pêcherie Haarlem aan Zee. Oude Groenmarkt 10. ☎ **023/531-4848.** Main courses Dfl 30–40 ($15–$20). MC, V. Open Mon–Sat noon–midnight, Sun 5pm–midnight. SEAFOOD.

You can just about smell the fresh North Sea breeze at this fine seafood restaurant in the shadow of St. Bavo Cathedral. Diners sit in wooden booths on chairs that have brightly colored canvas backings, like deck chairs. The menu features oysters, crab, prawns, and various fish dishes, all of which go well with the crisp house white wine.

Jacobus Pieck. Warmoesstraat 18. ☎ **023/532-6144.** Main courses Dfl 15–28 ($7.50–$14); snacks from Dfl 6 ($3). AE, MC, V. Open Mon–Sat 10am–11pm, Sun noon–11pm. DUTCH/INTERNATIONAL.

This popular cafe-restaurant offers excellent food for reasonable prices and friendly, efficient service. There's a lovely shaded terrace in the garden for outside dining; the interior is bustling but crisply stylish. At lunchtime the place serves generous sandwiches and burgers, and excellent salads. Main dinner courses range from pastas and Middle Eastern dishes to warming wholesome Dutch standards.

2 Zandvoort

If you feel like drawing a breath of fresh sea air and you don't have much time for it, do what most Amsterdammers do: Head for Zandvoort, located on the North Sea coast just west of Haarlem. Zandvoort is a brash and brassy kind of resort in the summer, though it often has a forlorn look in the off-season. Yet even in winter it's a long-standing Amsterdam tradition to take the train here, walk up and down along the shore for an hour or so, and then head for one of the town's cafes. If you're in quick-look mode, Zandvoort can easily be combined with Haarlem as a day trip, as both are on the same railway line from Amsterdam.

ESSENTIALS

GETTING THERE   Zandvoort is best reached by rail from Amsterdam Centraal Station. Trains leave every hour and change at Haarlem (where the Zandvoort train is usually to be found waiting on the adjacent platform). In summer there are extra trains direct from Centraal Station. In either case, the total journey time is about 30 minutes. There are also buses every 30 minutes or so leaving from outside Amsterdam Centraal Station, but they take much longer than the train. You can also go by car via Haarlem, but beware of frequent traffic jams in summer.

VISITOR INFORMATION   **VVV Zandvoort** is at Schoolplein 1 (☎ 023/571-7947; fax 023/571-7003), opposite the bus station in the center of town.

EXPLORING ZANDVOORT

There is not very much more to Zandvoort than its **beach,** but what a beach! In summertime, this seemingly endless stretch of smooth sand is lined with beach cafes (no fewer than 39 of them) and discos. Holland's prurient picture magazines like to come out with summertime articles about the antics of the "Jongens van Zandvoort" (Kids of Zandvoort), which are not much more than an excuse to show as many topless girls as possible. Besides the mainstream beaches there are gay and nudist beaches, where the shocking sight of a clothed, or even partially clothed, individual can generate considerable moral outrage.

   Circuit Park Zandvoort, Burg van Alphenstraat 63 (☎ 023/574-0740) in the north of the town a short distance from the beach, used to be the venue for the Dutch Formula One Grand Prix auto race, but no longer, because of local protests over the nuisance it allegedly caused. Now the circuit hosts much smaller events. If you come on a summer weekend, you might find a Formula Three training session or a Porsche meeting underway.

   Equally racy, though less noisy, is **Holland Casino Zandvoort,** Badhuisplein 7 (☎ 023/571-8044), in the center behind the seafront promenade. It's one of only ten legal casinos in Holland, and offers roulette, blackjack, and more. The dress code here is "correct" (collar and tie for men), the minimum age is 18, and you'll need your passport to get in. Open daily from 1:30pm until 2am. Entry costs Dfl 6 ($3).

   More tranquil pursuits can be found by walking through the extensive dunes areas—the **Kennemer Duinen and Amsterdamse Waterleiding Duinen**—around the town. These protected reserves of rolling sand dunes and native vegetation play an important part in the sea defense system. You can have an active fresh-air experience here, strolling along the paths through the woods on the eastern side and across the dunes leading west towards the sea. You'll find quite a variety of flora in this relatively small area, and the beach is never far away if the call of the sea proves too strong.

In town, there's some beach-style shopping and a wide range of eating and drinking possibilities.

NEARBY RESORTS

At its northern end, beyond the slightly less crowded beach at **Bloemendaal-aan-Zee,** the coast eventually leads to the port of **IJmuiden,** easily identified by the Hoogovens steel plant's chimneys. Water quality in this stretch of the North Sea probably leaves something to be desired, and sand gives the water a muddy look. Here you can see the three great locks of the **North Sea Canal.** The **fish auctions** at Halkade 4 are held Monday through Friday from 7 to 11am.

Near IJmuiden, you'll find the graciously restored 18th-century manor house and country estate, **Beeckestijn,** in the town of Velsen-Zuid (open Wednesday through Sunday noon to 5pm); to get there from Haarlem, take bus 73 towards Heemskerk, or bus 5 towards IJmuiden. By car, take the A9 northbound, exiting at junction 8. The **Museum De Cruquius** is a steam-driven water mill and land-reclamation museum located at Heemstede (open March through October, Monday to Friday 10am to 5pm, Saturday and Sunday 11am to 5pm). To get there, take bus 174 from Haarlem towards Heemstede until the Cruquiusweg. By car, take the E19 towards Leiden and The Hague, and exit at junction 3, heading towards Haarlem on the N201. Cruquius is just after Hoofddorp.

3 The Tulip Trail

The first tulip bulbs were brought to Holland in 1592 by the botanist Carolus Clusius, who planted them at the Hortus Botanicus in Leiden, but never got to see the first plants flower—they were stolen by rivals. Tulips soon became highly popular, especially among the aristocracy. Trading in bulbs was a lucrative business and prices soared to ridiculous heights. Today, the bulbs are more affordable, but competition to produce new strains is still fierce. The place to see tulips in their full glory is the Keukenhof Gardens at Lisse, where vast numbers of these and other flowers create dazzling patches of color. Combine your visit with a trip through the bulb fields between Leiden and Haarlem, for which VVV offices provide a detailed "Bulb Route."

If you are interested in the original plants, a specialized tulip garden in Limmen, 30km (18 miles) northwest of Amsterdam, has re-created some of the older varieties. Here you can see the flowers that are so prominent in the floral displays painted by 17th-century artists. You'll find this garden, the **Hortus Bulborum,** at Zuidkerkerlaan 23 in Limmen. It's open in April and May. By car, follow the A8 from Amsterdam past Zaandam, then take the N203; Limmen is just a couple of miles past Castricum. By public transport, take the local train to Castricum, then bus 167 towards Alkmaar.

BULB FIELDS

The largest bulb growers are in the northern corner of the South Holland province and the southern part of North Holland, with the heaviest concentration along the 40km (25-mile) Haarlem–Leiden drive. The organized Dutch make finding the different growers easy with a signposted **Bulb District** (*Bollenstreek*) route that covers about 61.5km (38½ miles). It's best to drive the route during weekdays, when stalls along the roads sell flower garlands (do as the natives do and buy one for yourself, another for the car).

Flower Power

During the 17th-century's "Tulip Mania," a single tulip bulb could be worth as much as a canal house, complete with garden and coach house.

KEUKENHOF GARDENS AT LISSE

Flowers at their peak and the Keukenhof Gardens (☎ 0252/465-555) both have short but glorious seasons, but you'll never forget a visit to this park. It's a meandering 70-acre wooded green in the heart of the bulb-producing region, planted each fall by the major Dutch tulip growers (each plants his own plot or establishes his own greenhouse display). Come spring, the bulbs burst forth and produce not hundreds of flowers, or even thousands, but millions (almost 8,000,000 at last count) of tulips and narcissi, daffodils and hyacinths, bluebells, crocuses, lilies, amaryllis, and many others. The blaze of color is everywhere: in the park and in the greenhouses, beside the brooks and shady ponds, along the paths and in the neighboring fields, in neat little plots and helter-skelter on the lawns. The park is said to be the greatest flower show on earth—and it's Holland's annual spring gift to the world.

The Keukenhof Gardens are open late March through late May, daily from 8am to 7:30pm. Special trains and buses run via Haarlem and the town of Leiden (see chapter 16). Admission is Dfl 17.50 ($8.75) for adults, Dfl 15 ($7.50) for seniors, and Dfl 8.50 ($4.25) for children 4 to 12. There are four cafes where you can grab a quick lunch so you don't have to go running around looking for a place to eat when you'd rather be enjoying the flowers.

FRANS ROOZEN NURSERY

Just one of many bulb growers, the **Frans Roozen Nursery,** Vogelenzangseweg 49, Vogelenzang (☎ 023/584-7245), south of Haarlem, provides excellent guided tours that illuminate the ins and outs of growing tulips and getting them to market. Its **Tulip Show** is open daily from late March through late May from 8am to 7:30pm, and the **Summer Show** from July until early October, Monday to Friday from 9am to 5pm. Admission is free, but your hosts have no objection whatsoever to you buying some of their products.

AALSMEER FLOWER AUCTION

Growing flowers is a year-round business that nets more than a half billion dollars annually at the **Aalsmeer Flower Auction** (☎ 0297/393-939), held in the lakeside community of Aalsmeer, near Schiphol Airport. Every year, the auction sells 3 billion flowers and 400 million plants, coming from 8,000 nurseries. Get there early to see the biggest array of flowers in the distribution rooms, and to have as much time as possible to watch the computerized auctioning process, which works basically like the old "Beat the Clock" game on television—the first one to press the button gets the posies.

In keeping with a Dutch auctioneering philosophy that demands quick handling for perishable goods, the bidding on flowers goes from high to low instead of proceeding in the usual direction of bidding—up. Mammoth bidding clocks are numbered from 100 to 1. The buyers, many of whom are buying for the French and German markets, sit in rows in the four auditorium-style auction halls; they have microphones to ask questions and buttons to push to register their bids in the central computer (which also takes care of all the paperwork). As the bunches of tulips or daffodils go by the stand on carts, they are auctioned in a matter of seconds, with the first bid—which is the first bid to stop the clock as it works down from 100 to 1—as the only bid. About 600 lots change hands every hour. Whether or not its tactics are really for the sake of the freshness of the flowers, the Aalsmeer Flower Auction is smart Dutch business.

The auction is held Monday through Friday from 7:30 to 11am. The entrance fee to the auction is Dfl 5 ($2.50) for adults, free for children 12 and under. Aalsmeer lies some 16 kilometers (10 miles) south of Amsterdam, close to Schiphol Airport. To drive there, take the A4 (E19) south to the Hoofddorp junction, then go southeast on the N201. Bus 172 will take you there from Amsterdam Centraal Station.

4 The IJsselmeer Shore

Only in Holland could you say, "This place used to be a sea." Well, the big lake on Amsterdam's doorstep called the IJsselmeer actually used to be a sea, the Zuiderzee (as in the words of the song, "by the side of the Zuiderzee . . ."), until the Dutch decided they didn't want it to be a sea any longer because it was always threatening to flood Amsterdam (Amsterdammers don't like water in their *jenever*). So in the 1930s, they blocked off the mouth of the Zuiderzee with a massive dike, the Afsluitdijk (see "Enclosing Dike," below), which stretches from the tip of Noord Holland to Friesland. In the sea's place there is now a well-behaved freshwater lake called the IJsselmeer (pronounced "*Eye*-sselmeer"). The lake's long shoreline is a scenic and popular place of escape from Amsterdam.

The places described below are listed in the order you would encounter them going north along the western shore of the IJsselmeer from Amsterdam. For the eastern and southern shores of the IJsselmeer, which belong to the provinces of Friesland and Flevoland respectively, see chapters 17 and 18.

VOLENDAM, MARKEN & MONNICKENDAM

There are differences between Volendam and Marken—one is Catholic, the other Protestant; one is on the mainland, the other on a former island; one has women wearing white caps with wings, the other has women wearing caps with ribbons—but Volendam and Marken have been combined on bus-tour itineraries for so long that they seem to have contributed a new compound word to the Dutch language. Unfortunately, *volendammarken* will probably come to mean "tourist trap," or perhaps, "Packaged Holland and Costumes to Go." Nonetheless, it's possible to have a delightful day in the bracing air of these waterside communities, where residents go about their daily business in traditional dress.

ESSENTIALS

GETTING THERE   Volendam and Monnickendam are reached by separate buses every hour from outside Amsterdam Centraal Station; the Monnickendam bus continues to Marken. When driving to Marken, which was once an island, you cross a 2-mile-long causeway from Monnickendam. You must leave your car in the parking lot outside before entering the narrow streets.

VISITOR INFORMATION   VVV **Volendam** is at Zeestraat 37 (☎ **0299/ 363-747;** fax 0299/368-484); and VVV **Monnickendam/Marken** is at De Zarken 2, Monnickendam (☎ **0299/651-998;** fax 0299/655-268). Opening times for both are Monday through Friday 9am to 5pm, Saturday 9am to 4pm.

EXPLORING VOLENDAM

Volendam is geared for tourism in a big way, with lots of souvenir shops, boutiques, gift shops, and restaurants in full swing during summer months. Still, its boat-filled harbor, tiny streets, and traditional houses have an undeniable charm. If you simply must have a snapshot of yourself surrounded by fishermen in little caps and balloon-legged pants, this is the place to visit. Volendammers will gladly pose. You'll enjoy the day as long as you realize what the villagers understand quite well: Dutch costumes are a tradition worth preserving, as is the economy of a small town that lost most of its fishing industry when the enclosure of the Zuiderzee cut it off from the North Sea. Tourism isn't a bad alternative, they figure—it brings lots of people to town to see such attractions as the **fish auction,** the **diamond cutter,** the **clog maker,** and the **house** with a room entirely wallpapered in cigar bands.

EXPLORING MARKEN

✪ **Marken** used to be an island until a narrow causeway was built connecting it with the mainland, and it remains as insular as ever. This is a tiny green village of houses on stilts grouped around an equally tiny harbor. It's smaller and quieter than Volendam, and also more rural, with clusters of farmhouses dotted around the polders and a candy-striped **lighthouse** on the IJsselmeer shore. This town does not go gushy all over for the tourists; it merely feeds and waters them, and allows them to wander around its pretty streets. Occupants of Marken's green-and-white houses wear traditional dress, as much to preserve the custom as for the tourists who pour in daily. There's a typical **house** open as a sort of museum and a **clog maker,** who usually works in the parking lot in summer.

In case you feel a bit uncomfortable at seeming to gawk at "the picturesque locals" as they go about their daily routine of hanging out laundry, washing windows, and shopping for groceries, take comfort from knowing that your visit is not crass exploitation. This is a village that also lost its livelihood when access to the open sea was cut off (some of the fishing boats that now sail the IJsselmeer hoist dark-brown sails as a sign of mourning for their lost sea fishing), and tourism has become an alternative industry, with a tax levied on every tour, which goes directly into the village coffers. Gawking saved Marken's life.

EXPLORING MONNICKENDAM

In contrast to its two neighbors, **Monnickendam** doesn't pay much attention to tourists at all, but gets on with its own life as a boating center and with what's left of its fishing industry, as you can see in its busy **harbor.** Visit the **Town Hall,** at Noordeinde 5, which began life as a private residence in 1746, and step inside to admire the elaborately decorated ceiling. Then take a walk through streets lined with gabled houses, and make a stop to admire the 15th-century late-Gothic **Sint-Nicolaaskerk,** at Zarken 2.

WHERE TO STAY

If you want to overnight in Volendam or Monnickendam in traditional style, ask at their VVV offices about staying on one of the old wooden IJsselmeer *boters* (sailing ships) moored in the harbor (this option is not available in Marken). This makes for a romantic, if somewhat cramped, way to spend the night. Another good bet is listed below.

✪ **Hotel Spaander.** Haven 15–19 (north end of the harbor), 1131 EP Volendam. ☎ **0299/363-595.** Fax 0299/369-615. 81 rooms. TV TEL. Dfl 130–210 ($65–$105) double. Rates include breakfast. AE, DC, MC, V.

This old-fashioned hotel has a real harbor flavor to go with its waterfront location. The public spaces have an Old Dutch interior look; the rooms, however, are modern, brightly furnished, comfortable, and attractive. There's a heated indoor pool and a fitness center. The hotel's two dining rooms and outside terrace cafe are excellent restaurant choices. Meals average Dfl 45 ($22.50).

WHERE TO DINE

✪ **De Taanderij.** Havenbuurt 1, Marken. ☎ **0299/601-364.** Main courses Dfl 15–25 ($7.50–$12.50); snacks Dfl 6–12.50 ($3–$6.25). No credit cards. Apr–Sept daily 10am–10pm; Oct–Mar Tues–Sun 10am–10pm, Sun 6–10pm. DUTCH/FRENCH.

This little *eethuis* at the end of the harbor is great for lunch or a traditional Dutch treat of *koffie en appelgebak met slagroom* (coffee with apple pie and cream) or *poffertjes* (small fried pancake "puffs" coated with confectioner's sugar and filled with syrup or liqueur). Seafood dishes are also served. The interior is an elegant and cozy interpretation of old Marken style. When the weather is good, a terrace is spread onto the harborside, where you can absorb the sunshine, the tranquil view over the Gouwzee, and, of course, the luscious goodies on the menu.

EDAM

The town of Edam, a short way inland from the IJsselmeer and about 3 miles north of Volendam, has given its name to one of Holland's most famous cheeses. Don't expect to find it in the familiar red skin, however—that's for export. In Holland the cheese's skin is yellow. This pretty little town (pronounced "*Ay*-dam") is centered around canals you cross by way of drawbridges, with views on either side of lovely canal houses, beautiful gardens, and canal-side teahouses.

ESSENTIALS

GETTING THERE   Edam has no railroad station, but there are buses every hour or so from Amsterdam Centraal Station. By car from Amsterdam, drive via Volendam.

VISITOR INFORMATION   VVV **Edam** is at the Stadhuis, Damplein 1 (☎ **0299/315-125;** fax 0299/374-236). Open Monday through Friday 9am to 5pm, Saturday 9am to 4pm.

EXPLORING EDAM

Edam was once a port of some importance. A visit to the **Edam Museum,** Damplein 8, just opposite the Town Hall (☎ **0299/372-644**), not only gives you a peek at the town's history, but also at some of its most illustrious citizens of past centuries (look for the portrait of Pieter Dirksz, one-time mayor and proud possessor of what is probably the longest beard on record anywhere). The building dates from circa 1530, when it was built as a merchant's house. One intriguing feature is the cellar, which is actually a box floating on the ground water, constructed that way so the changing water levels wouldn't upset the foundations of the whole house. The museum is open from April through October, Monday to Saturday 10am to 4pm, Sunday 1 to 4:30pm.

You should also take a look at the lovely "wedding room" in the **Stadhuis** (Town Hall), as well as the summertime cheese-making display at the **Kaaswaag** (Weigh House). The **Carillon Tower** (Speeltoren) tilts a bit, and was very nearly lost when the church to which it belonged was destroyed. The carillon dates back to 1561.

WHERE TO STAY & DINE

Hotel-Restaurant De Fortuna. Spuistraat 3, 1135 AV, Edam. ☎ **0299/371-671.** Fax 0299/371-469. 30 rooms. MINIBAR, TV, TEL. Dfl 162–182 ($81–$91) double. AE, DC, MC, V.

Most of the modern, comfortable rooms in this hotel look out onto a quiet garden and the canal in back. In fine weather you can lounge on the canal-side terrace. The step-gabled main house, where you eat breakfast, features country-style furnishings and exposed beams. The restaurant here is open daily from 6pm and offers a regularly changing menu with specialties including game and fish. A three-course dinner costs Dfl 49.50 ($24.75).

HOORN

Hoorn (pronounced "Hoarn") is one of the IJsselmeer's emblematic places, a living reminder of the traders and explorers from Zuiderzee towns in the past. It was the home of Willem Cornelis Schouten, who rounded the southernmost tip of South America in 1616 and promptly dubbed it Kap Hoorn (Cape Horn).

ESSENTIALS

GETTING THERE   There are trains departing at least every hour from Amsterdam Centraal Station to Hoorn; the journey time is 1 hour. There are also buses every hour or so leaving from outside Amsterdam Centraal Station, but they take much longer than the train. By car from Amsterdam, take the E22 north.

VISITOR INFORMATION   VVV Hoorn is at Veemarkt 4 (☎ **0900/ 403-1055;** fax 0229/215-023), between the Hoorn railroad station and the town center. It can furnish information on Hoorn's many historic buildings and interesting houses, as well as a delightful "Walking in Hoorn" booklet. Open Monday through Friday 9am to 5pm, Saturday 9am to 4pm.

EXPLORING HOORN

Hoorn wears its history on its sleeve. The town takes good care of its old sailors' houses, gabled merchants' villas, Stadhuis (Town Hall), and churches. You can best appreciate these buildings by strolling around the beautiful inner harbor, the **Binnenhaven.** The harbor tower (Hoofdtoren) dates from 1532. Also, don't miss **Rode Steen square,** considered one of the most beautiful in the country.

Another top attraction is the **Westfries Museum,** Rode Steen 1 (☎ **0229/ 280-028**). This beautiful 1632 building holds 17th-century artifacts brought from Indonesia by the East India Company—armor, weapons, paper cuttings, costumes, toys, so-called naïve paintings (which embody a deliberately childlike style), coins, medals, jewels, civic guards' paintings, porcelain, and a second-floor exhibit on the town's maritime history. There are also tapestries and period rooms in original 17th- and 18th-century styles, as well as a collection of Bronze Age relics in the basement. The museum is open April through September, Monday to Friday 11am to 5pm, Saturday from 2 to 5pm, Sunday from noon to 5pm; October through March, Monday to Friday 11am to 5pm, Saturday and Sunday from 2 to 5pm. Admission is Dfl 6 ($3) for adults, Dfl 3 ($1.50) for seniors and children age 16 and under.

During July, there's an interesting craft market with demonstrations in the marketplace every Wednesday; and during the summer an **antique steam train** (☎ **0229/214-862**) takes tourists from Hoorn to **Medemblik,** a small IJsselmeer town nearby. The 8th-century **Radboud Castle** in Medemblik, which was fortified in 1288 against possible rebellion from those troublesome Frisians, has been restored to its original state and is well worth a visit. It's open every day from June through August, and on Sunday afternoons during other months.

WHERE TO DINE

De Waag (Weighing House). Rode Steen 8. ☎ **0229/215-195.** Open daily 10am–1am.

This grand cafe is located in the monumental weighing house dating from 1609. All around it are the beautiful 17th-century buildings of Rode Steen square. You can still see the antique weighing scales in the wood-beamed interior.

De Hoofdtoren (The Harbor Tower). Hoofd 2. ☎ **0229/215-487.** Main courses in upstairs restaurant Dfl 29.50–52.50 ($19.75–$26.25); downstairs grill main courses from Dfl 18.50 ($9.75); snacks from Dfl 6 ($3). AE, MC, V. Daily 10am–10pm. FRENCH/DUTCH.

Boat lovers will want to sit on the terrace of this cafe-restaurant in the midst of this busy harbor, filled with pleasure boats large and small. The tower dates from about 1500, and once protected the harbor entrance. The interior retains many antique features. Traditional Dutch fare and grilled specialties, both meat and fish, are served at dinner. During the day there is a smaller menu for lunch and snacks.

ENKHUIZEN

A great herring fleet of some 400 boats once sailed out of Enkhuizen harbor, and then came the Enclosing Dike, closing off the North Sea. Now Enkhuizen looks to tourism and pleasure boating for its livelihood. Its population has declined from 30,000 in its 17th-century heyday to a mere 13,000 today.

GETTING THERE   There are trains every hour from Amsterdam Centraal Station to Enkhuizen; journey time is 1¼ hours. There are also buses every hour or so leaving from outside Hoorn railroad station. By car from Amsterdam, take the E22 north.

VISITOR INFORMATION   VVV **Enkhuizen** is at Tussen Twee Havens 1 (☎ **0228/313-164;** fax 0228/315-531).

AN OPEN-AIR MUSEUM

From the Enkhuizen/Lelystad dike parking area you can take a ferry over to the open-air ✪ **Zuiderzeemuseum,** Wierdijk 12–22 (☎ **0228/351-111**), where old farmhouses, public buildings, shops, and even a church from around the Zuiderzee have been brought together and reconstructed to form a cobblestone-street village with real live inhabitants practicing traditional crafts. The museum is open from April through late October, daily from 10am to 5pm. Admission is Dfl 18 ($9) for adults, Dfl 15 ($7.50) for senior citizens, Dfl 12 ($6) for children age 3 to 18, and free for children under 3.

ENCLOSING DIKE

Its official name is the **Afsluitdijk,** and it's simply impossible to grasp just what a monumental work this is until you've driven its 29km (18-mile) length. The imagination boggles at the thought of what massive effort and backbreaking labor went into this 3000-foot dike that stands a full 21 feet above mean water level, keeps back the sea, and, through ingenious engineering, has converted the salty Zuiderzee into the freshwater lake IJsselmeer and has transformed large areas of its muddy bottom into productive (and dry!) land. The Enclosing Dike is a heroic achievement.

Midway along its length—at the point where the dike was completed in 1932—there's a beautiful **monument** to the men who put their backs to the task. Stop for a light lunch at the cafe in the monument's base and pick up an illustrated booklet that explains the dike's construction. Nondrivers will find both a biking and a pedestrian path along the dike.

Cycling Along the IJsselmeer Shore

It's possible to cycle to Hoorn and return to Amsterdam by train in a day, providing you're fit and healthy and ready for some vigorous exercise. Watch out for the wind—you may prefer to choose another day if it's blowing strongly in your face when you're ready to set out. You can turn back at various logical places on the route, but once you're beyond the half-way point, you're really committed to going all the way to Hoorn.

Still with me? OK, board the IJ ferry at the pier behind Centraal Station and cross to Amsterdam North. Take Durgerdammerdijk, the road that runs alongside the lakeshore, to **Durgerdam,** a lakeside village huddling below water level behind its protective dike, with its roofs sticking up over the top. You can either pedal beside the houses or venture up onto the dike-top path, past **Uitdam,** with a fine view over the polders to your left and the lake studded with the sails of old-style IJsselmeer sailing ships, *boters* and *skûtsjes,* to your right.

Beyond Uitdam, turn right onto the causeway that leads to **Marken** (see "The IJsselmeer," earlier in this chapter, for more detailed information about some of the places you will pass through). You can turn left towards Monnickendam instead, which bypasses Marken and means less cycling. In summer you can take a boat, the *Marken Express,* from Marken harbor across to Volendam, a half-hour trip, with boats leaving every hour. This, in turn, means bypassing Monnickendam. Or retrace your route back across the causeway and stay on the lakeside road to **Monnickendam.** Pass through, keeping to the shore, then on through **Katwoude** to **Volendam.** If you've had enough, this is a good place to take a break before cycling back to Amsterdam.

If you're still with the program, go inland a short way from the lakeside dike to **Edam,** famed for its Edammer cheese (see "Edam," above, for more details). Turn right at the canal bridge at Damplein in Edam, and back along the canal to regain the IJsselmeer shore.

Ahead of you is a straight run north on the lakeside road through the polders. The villages of **Warder, Eteresheim,** and **Scharwoude** are your "checkpoints" on the way to **Hoorn.** You may be ready to flop aboard a train going anywhere by now, but should you have some puff left, visit Hoorn's beautiful inner harbor, the Binnenhaven. Then follow the green-painted signs, pointing first to the VVV office, then to the station for the train ride back to Amsterdam. Speed racers might want to carry on to **Enkhuizen** and look at the Zuiderzee Museum, just before the N302 dike-top road across to Lelystad.

When you approach the dike from the town of Wieringerwerf, keep an eye out for the marker about 5.5km (3½ miles) to the east that tells of a heroic effort in 1945, when the dike was breached by the Nazis only 18 days before they surrendered. The indomitable Dutch repaired the dike, pumped the polder dry, and were growing crops in polder fields again by the very next spring!

5 The Zaanstreek

Just 16km (10 miles) northwest of Amsterdam is a district known as the Zaanstreek. Much of it is now taken up with shipping and industry, but also nestled here is the charm of the **Zaanse Schans,** a planned replica-village and open-air museum made up of houses moved to the site after industry took over their original locations. It

Get Your Clogs On

Clogs are still a staple in many farming areas, where they're much more effective against wetness and cold than leather shoes or boots. They're also, of course, a tourist staple, and if you plan to buy a pair, Zaanse Schans is a good place to do it. Traditionally, clogs with pointed toes are for women and rounded toes are for men. All must be worn with heavy socks, so when buying, add the width of one finger when measuring for size.

---

may all look familiar because you'll have seen pictures of windmills and green wooden houses in many a Holland brochure; but remember that until a century or two ago, not even the ground on which everything here was built existed.

ESSENTIALS

GETTING THERE   Trains depart at least every 20 minutes from Amsterdam Centraal Station to Koog-Zaandijk, from where the windmills and museums are only a short walk; the journey time is 15 minutes. In many cases, you will have to change at Zaandam to take a local train to Koog-Zaandijk. There are also buses every 15 minutes or so leaving from outside Amsterdam Centraal Station. By car from Amsterdam, take the E22 north.

VISITOR INFORMATION   VVV **Zaanstreek/Waterland** is at Gedempte Gracht 76, Zaandam (☎ 075/616-2221; fax 075/670-5381), just outside the railroad station. Opening times Monday through Friday 9am to 5pm, Saturday 9am to 4pm.

EXPLORING THE ZAANSTREEK

Although most of the traditional houses here are inhabited by the sort of Amsterdam expatriates who can afford and appreciate their historic timbers (and have the patience for the pedestrian traffic from the tour buses), a few can be visited as museums. **Het Noorderhuis** is an 18th-century merchant's home furnished in the old Zaanse style, at Kalverringdijk 17 (☎ 075/617-3237). You can also explore the **Albert Heijn Museum Shop,** Kalverringdijk 5 (☎ 075/659-2808), which commemorates the first ever grocery of this now giant supermarket chain, with late-19th-century products and packaging. Less industrial, but equally charming, is the small **Dutch Clockwork Museum** (Museum van het Nederlands Uurwerk) at Kalverringdijk 3 (☎ 075/617-9769). Other sights include the old-style **bakery** and the **clog shop,** where you can see how the wooden shoes called *klompen* are made. You can also take a **minicruise** on the River Zaan.

Most of the individual museums in the village are open daily from 10am to 5pm (tour buses full of visitors turn up all the time on organized day trips). Admission varies from Dfl 3 to 4 ($1.50 to $2).

Add a visit to four different kinds of **windmills** to the pleasure of just walking through the village—one windmill for lumber, one for paint, one for vegetable oil, and one for the renowned Zaanse mustard. At one time the industrious people of the Zaanstreek had almost 500 windmills working for them. Only 12 have survived, including these four. A short tour shows you just how these wind machines worked; the four are open for visitors at varying hours from late March through October. At **Koog-aan-de-Zaan,** on the short walk from the railway station to the Zaanse Schans, there's the **Windmill Museum** (Molenmuseum) at Museumlaan 18 (☎ 075/628-8968), with a superb collection of model windmills and exhibitions about the natural and industrial history of the region.

In nearby **Zaandam,** the main town of the Zaanstreek and an important shipbuilding center in the 17th-century, you can visit **Tsar Peter Cottage** (Het Peterhuisje), Krimp 23, where the Russian monarch lived under an assumed name in 1697. He was studying shipbuilding with craftsmen whom he—an avid nautical student—considered to be the world's best. In the marketplace you can see his statue, a gift from Tsar Nicholas II.

WHERE TO DINE

De Hoop op d' Swarte Walvis. Kalverringdijk 15. ☎ **075/616-5629.** Lunch Dfl 70 ($35), Dfl 97.50 ($48.75) for 5-course dinner. AE, DC, MC, V. Mon–Sat noon–2:30pm, 6–10pm. DUTCH/INTERNATIONAL.

This unique gourmet restaurant with a mouthful of a name sits amidst the green-painted Zaanse Schans houses. Its glass pavilion and terrace overlook the wide River Zaan and the waterside villas on the opposite bank. Here you can expect subtle mixtures of superior ingredients (the place is owned by the same company as the Netherlands's biggest supermarket chain). For a rich combination, try the duck liver with poached peach; or for lighter fare, try the sole with lemon butter. There are also vegetarian alternatives.

6 The Cheese Trail

This group of towns and villages has been a center for dairy produce for many centuries. The cheesemaker's guilds in Alkmaar are more than 400 years old. Both Edam (see above) and Alkmaar are filled with monumental buildings that give you a taste of local history.

ALKMAAR

30km (19 miles) N of Amsterdam

Every Friday morning during the long Dutch summer season there's a steady parade of tourists leaving Amsterdam to visit the ✪ **Alkmaar Cheese Market,** and it's quite a show they're on their way to see.

GETTING THERE　　Trains depart at least every hour from Amsterdam Centraal Station to Alkmaar, and buses every half hour or so. By car from Amsterdam, take the A8 and A9 north, via Zaanstad.

VISITOR INFORMATION　　VVV **Alkmaar** is at Waagplein 2–3 (☎ **072/ 511-4284;** fax 072/511-7513) in the town center. It's open Monday through Friday 9am to 5pm, Saturday 9am to 4pm.

EXPLORING ALKMAAR

On Fridays in summer, cheeses are piled high in the cobblestone market square, and the carillon in the **Waag** (Weigh House) tower drowns the countryside in Dutch folk music. Around the square dart the white-clad cheese carriers whose lacquered straw hats tell you to which of four sections of their medieval guild they belong: red, blue, yellow, or green. Carriers are so proud of their standards that every week they post the name of any carrier who has indulged in profanity or has been late arriving at the auction on a "shame board." The square is filled with sightseers, barrel organs, souvenir stalls, and a palpable excitement.

The bidding process is carried on in the traditional Dutch manner of hand-clapping to bid the price up or down, with a good solid hand clap to seal the deal. Once a buyer has accumulated his lot of cheeses, teams of guild members move in

Need a Refreshing Swim?

From Alkmaar it's only a short distance westward to the historic and picturesque town of **Bergen** and the nearby seaside resort of **Bergen aan Zee,** easily reached by bus from Alkmaar or by car or bike from Amsterdam (follow the A9 ringroad around Alkmaar, after which Bergen is signposted). The beautiful 15th-century **Ruïnekerk** (church ruin) is a focal point in the center of the old town, with friendly cafes and restaurants lining the square around it. By the main attractions of the area are the beach and the wooded dunes, which are protected by their nature reserve status.

You'll need a day pass, available from Bergen's **VVV,** (☎ **072 581-2124;** fax 072/581-3890), which is located in the middle of town next to the bus terminus, in order to walk or cycle across the dunes. Not surprisingly, the environment has attracted a large number of well-heeled or artistic residents—Bergen even has its own recognized art movement. The beach is popular but still has a wild feel to it that you can no longer find at resorts nearer Amsterdam. The gently undulating sea bottom means that the water warms up in little lagoons stretching along the beach, and the slow gradient makes bathing safe for children.

with their shiny, shallow barrows, or carriers, and, using slings that hang from their shoulders, carry the golden wheels and balls of cheese to the Weigh House for the final tally of the bill. The market is held on Friday from mid-April through mid-September, from 10am to noon.

While you're in Alkmaar, there are a few other attractions you may want to see, including the **Old Craft Market** (also held on Friday from 10am to noon); the **Huis met de Kogel** (House with the Cannonball), a 16th-century house retaining a cannonball, presumably a souvenir of the Spanish siege; and the **Remonstrant Church,** a clandestine 17th-century church in a former granary. There's also a **Cheese Museum** (☎ **072/511-4284**) housed in the Waag. It's open April through October, Monday to Saturday 10am to 4pm, Friday 9am to 4pm. Admission is Dfl 5 ($2.50).

BROEK-IN-WATERLAND
11km (7 miles) N of Amsterdam

This pretty little village behind the lake-side dike is worth a stop during the summer months to visit the **Jakob Wiedermeier & Son farmhouse,** where you can see Edam cheeses being made. Broek-in-Waterland has 17th-century wooden-fronted houses and a church with an original pulpit from 1685. The village is like an island amidst waterways and sub-sea-level polderlands that were pumped dry many centuries ago. It's ideal territory for a cycling day trip.

7 Den Helder & Texel Island
62km (39 miles) N of Amsterdam

DEN HELDER
Den Helder, at the tip of North Holland Province, is Holland's most important naval base and the site of its Royal Naval College. It also has the dubious distinction of being possibly the only port in the world that ever lost a fleet to a company

of horsemen. That unique event took place back in January 1794, when the Dutch fleet found itself stuck fast in the frozen waters between Den Helder and Texel Island—French cavalry simply rode out to the ships and captured them all. The embarrassing defeat was quite a fall from the heights of glory the navy had known a century earlier when Admirals de Ruyter and Tromp led Dutch ships to victory over a combined English and French fleet off this same coast in 1673.

During the summer months, you can take a pleasant, 30-minute ferry trip from Den Helder to Texel (see below), a quiet, family-oriented resort island in the Waddenzee.

ESSENTIALS

GETTING THERE   There are trains departing at least every half hour from Amsterdam Centraal Station to Den Helder; journey time is 1½ hours. By car from Amsterdam, take the E22 north.

VISITOR INFORMATION   VVV Den Helder is at Bernhardplein 18 next to the railway station (☎ 0223/625-544; fax 0223/614-888). Open Mon 1–6pm, Tues–Fri 9:30am–6pm, Sat 9:30am–5pm.

EXPLORING DEN HELDER

Visit the **Navy Museum** (Helders Marinemuseum), Hoofdgracht 3 (☎ 0223/616-704), which holds exhibits illustrating the Dutch Royal Navy's history, and take a look at the state shipyards. Among the ships on display is the steam-drive warship *De Schorpioen*, which was built in France for the Dutch Navy in 1868. Although it's now safely chained to the quayside, this impressive vessel was once a warship to be reckoned with. Its secret weapon was the ram below the waterline that could deal fatal blows to enemy ships. The steam engine still works, and you can visit the restored captain's cabin and crew's quarters. Another maritime attraction is the **National Lifeboat Museum,** Bernhardplein 3 (☎ 0223/618-320), which chronicles the history of the National Lifeboat service. The National Fleet Festival is held at Den Helder from Friday through Sunday on the second weekend in July.

TEXEL ISLAND

66km (41 miles) N of Amsterdam

Texel is the biggest and most populated of the Wadden Islands—that's not saying much—and the only one that can be reached directly from North Holland Province (although a tourist ferry operates from the north of Texel to Vlieland island from May through September). It has the serenity that seems intrinsic to islands, even allowing for the many visitors who pour in during the summer. Beaches, boating, cycling, and bird watching are the big attractions here, yet eating, drinking, and partying have their place too.

For the other populated Wadden Islands, which belong to Friesland Province, see chapter 17.

ESSENTIALS

GETTING THERE   The TESO company (☎ 0222/369-600) runs the car ferries *Molengat* and *Schulpengat* from Den Helder to 't Horntje on Texel—a half-hour trip. Ships sail every hour in both directions from 6:35am (8:35am on Sundays and public holidays) to 9:35pm; the last return from Texel is at 9:05pm. Reservations are not accepted. Passenger fares are Dfl 10 ($5) for adults, Dfl 5 ($2.50) for children, standard-size cars Dfl 48.50 ($24.25). There's a connecting bus service every hour from Den Helder railroad station to the ferry terminal. When buying your ferry ticket, if you need a ride to get to your destination on Texel, purchase a

TelekomTaxi ticket as well. For just Dfl 7 ($3.50) each way, the minibus will drop you wherever you want and pick you up in time for the ferry for your return.

VISITOR INFORMATION **VVV Texel** is at Emmalaan 66, Den Burg (☎ **0222/312-847;** fax 0222/314-129), just off the N501 main road into the centrally located town of Den Burg. Open Monday through Friday 9am to 6pm, Saturday 9am to 5pm.

EXPLORING TEXEL

Unlike some of the Wadden Islands, cars are allowed on Texel, but there's no doubt that the best way to get around and to keep faith with the island's environmental spirit is to go by bicycle. Bikes can be brought over on the ferry for Dfl 6 ($3), or rented from dozens of outlets, either at the ferry port, in the island's centrally located "capital" **Den Burg,** or in the other villages dotted around the coast.

The island's varied landscape, with tidal gullies, sand dunes, and rolling meadows, offers a temporary home to some 300 bird species, around 100 of which breed here. The cream of this avian crop includes oystercatchers, Bewick swans, spoonbills, Brent geese, avocets, marsh harriers, snow buntings, ringed plovers, kestrels, short-eared owls, and bar-tailed godwits. They can be seen in the three protected **nature reserves** that are open to the public: the **Schorren, Bol,** and **Dijkmanshuizen** reserves. Visitors can only enter on guided tours organized by the **Natuurmonumenten,** Polderweg 2, De Waal (☎ 022/312-590).

Nature trails through areas belonging to the **Staatsbosbeheer** (State Forest Authority) abound in the dunes and wooded areas, and can be freely visited so long as you stick to the marked paths. Guided tours of some of these areas are organized by **EcoMare,** Ruyslaan 92, De Koog (☎ **0222/317-741**). EcoMare's visitor center is one of the best places to start a nature tour of the island. The center is also a seal rehabilitation facility—the waters around Texel used to be rich in seals until their numbers were greatly reduced by a virus in 1988. EcoMare assists with their recovery by caring for weak and injured seals until they can be returned to the sea. From an underwater observation gallery you can watch the seals swimming happily and can also see some of the rich variety of life that lives in the tidal mud flats of the Waddenzee. There's also a bird rehabilitation scheme here.

WHERE TO STAY

If you want to overnight on Texel, there are a large number of hotels, holiday homes, apartments, and camping sites. Contact the VVV (see above) for reservations and an extensive list of possibilities.

WHERE TO DINE

Het Vierspan. Gravenstraat 3, Den Burg. ☎ **0222/313-176.** Dfl 55 ($27.50) for 3 courses, Dfl 77.50 ($38.75) for 4 courses. AE, MC, V. Wed–Mon 6–11pm. DUTCH/FRENCH.

Het Vierspan is located on a pretty corner occupied by the top restaurants on the island. The warm welcome here is complemented by a homely interior and well-prepared dishes based on local ingredients. Don't miss out on the local Texel lamb, succulent and salty from grazing the sea-sprayed grass. Other specialties here include game and mushrooms.

8 Castles, Moats & Art

The destinations below are all in a district east of Amsterdam known as **Het Gooi,** an area that has historically served as Amsterdam's back garden. For centuries the well-heeled have set up stately homes in this beautiful green area. In even earlier times, the Het Gooi was a place of strategic importance, as evidenced by the grand constructions still standing today, such as the 13th-century Muiderslot moated castle in Muiden and the star-shaped fortifications of Naarden.

MUIDEN
13km (8 miles) E of Amsterdam

ESSENTIALS
GETTING THERE Muiden stands on the banks of the River Vecht. By car from Amsterdam, take the Muiden junction of the A1 (E231), east of Amsterdam.

VISITOR INFORMATION There is no VVV office in Muiden.

MUIDEN'S CASTLE
The perfect starting point for a lovely day in the Middle Ages is the **Rijksmuseum Muiderslot,** on the edge of this small harbor town at Herengracht 1 (☎ **0294/ 261-325**). This turreted, fairy-tale castle lies on the banks of the river Vecht, surrounded by protective excavations and a moat. Go there to see where Count Floris V was living when he granted toll privileges to the small, new community of "Amstelledamme" in 1275, and where he was murdered just 20 years later. Muiderslot is also where Dutch 17th-century poet, P. C. Hooft, found both a home and employment—and, we suppose, inspiration for romantic images and lofty language—when he served as castle steward and local bailiff for 40 years. The castle is furnished essentially as it was in Hooft's time, with plenty of distinctly Dutch carved cupboard beds, heavy chests, fireside benches, and mantelpieces.

Muiderslot is open April through September, Monday to Friday from 10am to 5pm and Sunday from 1 to 5pm (last tours at 4pm); October through March, Saturday and Sunday only from 1 to 4pm (last tour 3pm). Admission is Dfl 10 ($5) for adults, Dfl 7.50 ($3.75) for seniors and children age 4 to 12, and free for children under 4.

NAARDEN
19km (12 miles) SE of Amsterdam

ESSENTIALS
GETTING THERE There are trains every hour or so to Naarden from Amsterdam Centraal Station. By car from Amsterdam, take the A1 (E231) east.

VISITOR INFORMATION VVV **Naarden (Gooi and Vechtstreek)** is at Adriaan Dortsmanplein 1b (☎ **035/694-2836;** fax 035/694-3424), inside the walls of the old town.

EXPLORING NAARDEN
Just beyond Muiderslot is the small, fortified town of Naarden, where, much in the manner of locking the barn door *after* the horse was gone, the local inhabitants erected their beautiful star-shaped double fortifications after the town was brutally sacked by Don Frederick of Toledo and his boys in the late 16th century. Beneath the Turfpoort Bastion, you can visit the casemates (the artillery vaults) at the **Nederlands Vestingsmuseum** (Dutch Fortifications Museum), Westwalstraat 6 (☎ **035/694-5459**), open from Easter through October 31, Monday to Friday from 10am to 4:30pm and Saturday, Sunday, and holidays from noon to 5pm; the rest of the year on Sunday only from noon to 5pm. Admission is Dfl 10 ($5) adults, Dfl 7.50 ($3.75) for children age 5 to 16, free for children under 5.

Also see the 15th-century **Grote Kerk,** on Marktstraat (☎ **035/694-5211**), renowned for its fine acoustics and annual performances of Bach's *St Matthew's Passion.* The Grote Kerk is open from April 30 through September 30, Saturday to Thursday from 2 to 4pm.

LAREN

26km (16 miles) SE of Amsterdam

ESSENTIALS

GETTING THERE   There are trains every hour or so from Amsterdam Centraal Station to Hilversum, from where buses leave every half hour or so to Laren. By car from Amsterdam, take the A1 (E231) east.

VISITOR INFORMATION   VVV **Laren** is at Tramstraat 4, Lochem (3 miles east of Laren on the N352) (☎ **0573/251-898;** fax 0573/256-885). Open Monday through Friday 9am to 5:30pm, Saturday 10am to 1pm.

EXPLORING LAREN

The Dutch legacy of impressive art was not a one-shot, Golden Age phenomenon, nor were the later 19th-century contributions solely the work of Vincent van Gogh. Visit the pretty little suburban town of Laren, 15 miles east of Amsterdam in the district of Het Gooi, and you'll discover a less well-known Dutch art center, where a number of important painters chose to live and work at the turn of the century. Among the town's star residents were Anton Mauve, the Dutch Impressionist who attracted other members of The Hague School, and the American painter, William Henry Singer, Jr., who chose to live and paint in the clear light of Holland rather than follow his family's traditional path to fame and fortune via the steel mills of Pittsburgh.

Today the principal attraction of Laren is Singer's former home, once called the Wild Swans and now simply called the **Singer Museum,** Oude Drift 1 (☎ **035/531-5656**). It houses both the works of the former occupant and also his collection of some 500 works by American, Dutch, French, and Norwegian painters. Open Tuesday through Saturday from 11am to 5pm and Sundays and holidays from noon to 5pm (closed January 1, April 30, and December 25). Admission is Dfl 15 ($7.50) for adults, Dfl 4.50 ($2.25) for children age 6 to 12, and free for children under 5.

To reach the Singer Museum by public transport from Amsterdam, take bus 136, which leaves the Amstel Bus Station in Amsterdam every half hour and takes you directly to the museum stop in Laren.

16

South Holland
(Zuid-Holland) Province

The province of South Holland occupies the southern half of the highly industrialized and densely populated western part of the Netherlands. A new term has been coined for the whole of the busy area from Amsterdam to Rotterdam and Utrecht—the *Randstad,* sometimes translated as the "Rim City." The area contains some two-thirds of the country's population, as well as much of its business activity. Here you'll find plenty of greenery and history along with many city attractions. Everything in the Ranstad is within about an hour's drive—traffic jams notwithstanding—or train journey from Amsterdam.

The Hague and Rotterdam are about as different as two cities could be, yet The Hague—stately and dignified—is quite at ease with its brash, modern neighbor. **The Hague** has seen the centuries come and go with scarcely a rumble in the foundations of its lofty perch. Technically it's not even a true "city," never having been granted a charter or city rights, but never has a "village" maintained such an imperial disdain for such a triviality. Secure in its regal position, The Hague goes serenely on its way as the seat of the Netherlands' government, even if not the country's capital. The coastal resort of **Scheveningen,** just a short tram-ride away, has a few attractions that are worth seeing year-round.

In contrast, **Rotterdam,** which sits on the delta where the Rhine and Maas rivers meet the North Sea, has been commercial to the core from the very beginning. Most of its historically significant buildings—along with most of the city—were destroyed in World War II bombings. Rebuilding was a remarkable feat of contemporary urban planning. High-rise office blocks, straight lines and right angles—features that are considered anathema in other parts of the country—mold an oddly attractive open cityscape. Rotterdam's port, a bit farther down river, boast the world's highest annual shipping tonnage.

The triangle formed by the historic towns of **Delft, Gouda,** and **Leiden** makes for leisurely sightseeing, with distances short enough to allow you to visit all three from a base in Rotterdam, The Hague, or Amsterdam. The roads here pass through a landscape straight out of a painting by one of the Dutch masters, with flat green fields ribboned with canals and distant church spires piercing a wide sky (admittedly, there's also the occasional clump of industrial smokestacks). For the most part, this is the Holland of your imagination.

South Holland Province

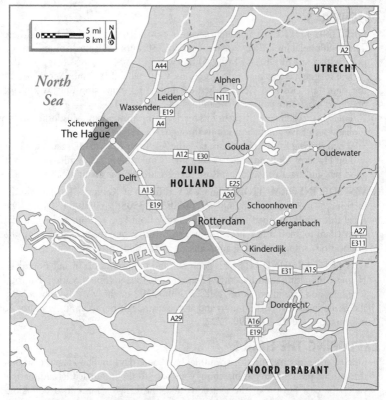

1 The Hague

63km (43 miles) SW of Amsterdam

The Hague is above all an elegant city of style and culture. It makes an easy day trip from Amsterdam, but many travelers actually prefer The Hague as a quieter, more relaxed sightseeing base.

In the beginning, a small village named *Haag* (hedge) was chosen by the counts of Holland as the setting for their hunting lodge, which was why the town was later called *'s Gravenhage* (the count's hedge), at least officially. By the time count Willem II was named King of the Romans in 1247, his father, Floris IV, had already begun construction on the Binnenhof, which Willem quickly appointed as the official royal residence. Willem's son, Floris V, added the massive Knights' Hall (*Ridderzaal*), expanding a complex that today is the heart of the country's administrative government.

As Holland's center of government, The Hague has grown into a cosmopolitan city; it's now the site of no fewer than three royal palaces, some 64 foreign embassies, and European headquarters for innumerable international engineering, oil, and chemical concerns. The lush greenery of its original hunting grounds remains in the large parks, gardens, and woods that continue to thrive within the city limits.

The nearby former fishing village of **Scheveningen** (see below) has blossomed into a popular seaside resort, a short tram or bus ride from the city center.

ESSENTIALS

GETTING THERE   The Hague is within easy reach of all major Dutch airports. The "Schiphol Line" offers fast train service (30 minutes) from Amsterdam's airport, with a fare of Dfl 14.50 ($7.25) one way.

The Hague has two major train stations: Centraal and Hollands Spoor. Most of the sights are closer to Centraal Station, but some trains stop only at Hollands Spoor, so make sure you're on the right track.

There is excellent and frequent bus service from Amsterdam. Most other areas of Holland also have good connections through The Hague.

When driving from Amsterdam, take the A4; from Rotterdam, take the A13.

The Hook of Holland sea-ferry terminal is only 20km (12.5 miles) away, with good bus and train connections; Rotterdam's Europoort is about a half-hour drive.

VISITOR INFORMATION   The **VVV office** is at Koningin Julianaplein, just in front of the Centraal Station (☎ **0900/340-3505;** fax 070/347-2102), open April through September, Monday to Saturday from 9am to 9pm and on Sundays from 10am to 5pm; it has shorter hours during other months. Pick up a copy of its publication "Info," which is a good guide to what's on at the moment.

GETTING AROUND   There is good bus and tram transport in and around The Hague, originating at both Centraal Station and Hollands Spoor Station. For route, schedule, and fare information, call ☎ **0900/9292** or the VVV (see above). Taxi stands are located at both stations and at many strategic points around the city. For information, call ☎ **070/390-7722.**

EXPLORING THE HAGUE

One of the great pleasures of spending 1 or more days in The Hague is walking through its pleasant streets, matching your pace to the unhurried leisure that pervades the city. Stroll past the mansions that line Lange Voorhout, overlooking a broad avenue of poplar and elm trees, and notice how these spacious, restrained structures differ from Amsterdam's gabled, highly ornamented canal houses. Window- shop or get down to serious buying in the covered shopping arcades or shop-lined pedestrian streets. And take time to loiter in the more than 430 square miles of parks and gardens within the city limits, or hop on a tram for the short ride out to The Hague's two seaside resorts, Scheveningen and Kijkduin, or even close-by Delft.

A tremendous help in your ramblings is the VVV publication "The Hague," which costs a mere Dfl 5.50 ($2.75), and offers a wealth of sightseeing and dining information, as well as a good city map.

✪ **Parliament (Binnenhof) & Hall of the Knights (Ridderzaal).** Binnenhof 8a. ☎ **070/364-6144.** Admission Dfl 6 ($3.00). Mon–Sat 10am–4pm (last tour begins at 3:45pm). Closed public holidays and special events. Tram: 3, 7, or 8.

This magnificent "Inner Court," the 13th-century hunting lodge of the counts of Holland, is the center of Holland's political life and the official seat of government. This complex of buildings is set in the oldest part of the city. In the center of the Binnenhof is the beautiful Hall of Knights, measuring 126 by 59 feet and soaring 85 feet to its oak roof. Since 1904, its immense interior—adorned with provincial flags and leaded-glass windows depicting the coats of arms of Dutch cities—has hosted the Queen's annual address (the third Tuesday in September), the opening of Parliament, official receptions, and interparliamentary conferences.

There are three entrances and four gates to the Binnenhof. The buildings on the left and right of the Ridderzaal are the former Stadtholders' Quarters, which now

The Hague Accommodations & Attractions

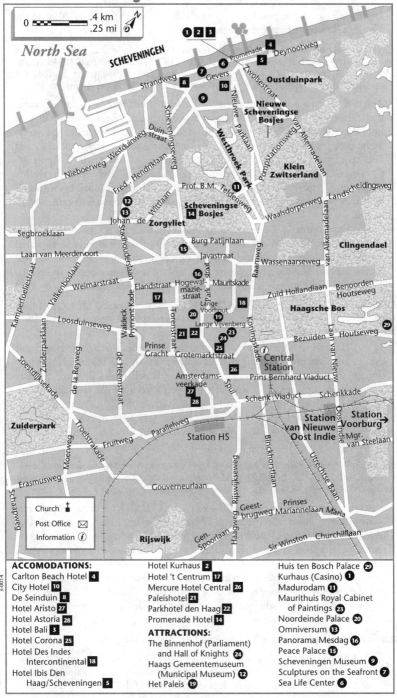

0 —■■■—■ .4 km
.25 mi

North Sea

SCHEVENINGEN

ACCOMODATIONS:
Carlton Beach Hotel 4
City Hotel 10
De Seinduin 8
Hotel Aristo 27
Hotel Astoria 28
Hotel Bali 3
Hotel Corona 25
Hotel Des Indes
  Intercontinental 18
Hotel Ibis Den
  Haag/Scheveningen 5

Hotel Kurhaus 2
Hotel 't Centrum 17
Mercure Hotel Central 26
Paleishotel 21
Parkhotel den Haag 22
Promenade Hotel 14

ATTRACTIONS:
The Binnenhof (Parliament)
  and Hall of Knights 24
Haags Gemeentemuseum
  (Municipal Museum) 12
Het Paleis 19

Huis ten Bosch Palace 29
Kurhaus (Casino) 1
Madurodam 11
Maurithuis Royal Cabinet
  of Paintings 23
Noordeinde Palace 20
Omniversum 13
Panorama Mesdag 16
Peace Palace 15
Scheveningen Museum 9
Sculptures on the Seafront 7
Sea Life Center 6

Church ✝
Post Office ⊠
Information ⓘ

3-0014

355

house the First and Second Chamber of the States General, the equivalent to the House of Representatives and Congress, respectively.

✪ **Municipal Museum (Haags Gemeentemuseum).** Stadhouderslaan 41 (bordering the Museum Gardens north of the city center). ☎ 070/338-1111. Admission Dfl 10 ($5) adults, Dfl 5 ($2.50) children 5–13 and senior citizens, free for children under 5. Tues–Sun 10am–5pm, Sun and public holidays midday–5pm. Closed Jan 1, Dec 25. Tram: 8 or 10.

This fine museum is housed in an early 20th-century building designed by Berlage, most famous for his redbrick Amsterdam Stock Exchange. The collection is divided into three separate departments. The modern art section focuses on early-19th-century Dutch romantic paintings, the Impressionist Hague School, and 20th-century art, including a fine collection of prints and drawings by K. Appel, M. C. Escher, O. Redon, and Toulouse-Lautrec. Top billing is reserved for the world's most comprehensive collection of works by Piet Mondrian, including his last work, New York Boogie Woogie, acquired by the Dutch National Bank for a princely $20 million.

The Department of Decorative Arts shows ceramics from China, the Middle East, and Delft; Venetian and Dutch glass; and silver; as well as interesting period rooms. The Music Department displays European and non-European musical instruments and also has an impressive music library, with scores, books, and prints. The new wing is currently used for an innovative fashion exhibition.

Madurodam. George Maduroplein 1. ☎ 070/355-3900. Admission Dfl 19.50 ($9.75) adults, Dfl 14 ($7) children. July–Aug daily 9am–11pm, Sept–Mar daily 9am–6pm. Tram: 1 or 9.

To see "Holland in a Nutshell," head to the wooded dunes linking The Hague and the coastal resort of Scheveningen. This amazing display of a miniature, fictitious city sprawls over 28,000 square yards. Typical Dutch townscapes and famous landmarks are replicated on a scale of 1:25—you'll feel a bit like Gulliver viewing Lilliput. The wonder of it all is that this is a working miniature city: trains run, ships move, planes taxi down runways, the barrel organ plays, there's a town fair in progress, and 50,000 tiny lamps light up when darkness falls. Children love it—but surprisingly, 75% of the 1.2 million annual visitors are adults!

Mauritshuis Royal Cabinet of Paintings. Korte Vijverberg 8 (next to the Binnenhof, overlooking Court Lake). ☎ 070/302-3435. Admission Dfl 12.50 ($6.25) adults, Dfl 6.50 ($3.25) children under 18. Tues–Sat 10am–5pm, Sun 11am–5pm. Tram: 7, 8, 9, or 12.

This was once the residence of Stadholder Frederik Hendrik's nephew, Maurits van Nassau-Siegen. Today the delightful 17th-century mansion houses a small but unsurpassed collection of paintings from Holland's "Golden Age." The intimate rooms make it seem as if you are visiting a private collection, and you can appreciate each painting at ease. The ground floor is devoted to works from the 15th and 16th centuries, mainly religious paintings by Dutch and Flemish artists and portraits by Holbein and Rubens. Works by Rembrandt, Vermeer, and Jan Steen are on the second floor, including such pieces as Rembrandt's *The Anatomy Lesson* and Vermeer's *The View of Delft*.

Huis ten Bosch Palace. Haagse Bos (Het Bos). Daily daylight hours. Bus: 4, 43, or 91.

When Queen Juliana abdicated the Dutch throne in 1980, her daughter, Queen Beatrix, moved her family and the official royal residence to the Paleis Huis ten Bosch, the "House in the Woods" Palace in the beautiful Haagse Bos. For many years, this palace was a summer residence for the royal families. Originally it was a small, rather plain structure consisting of several rooms opening from a domed central hall, but Prince Willem IV added the two large side wings in the 1700s. The palace can be only viewed from the park, not entered.

Het Paleis (Palace Lange Voorhout). Lange Voorhout 74. ☎ **070/362-4061.** Admission Dfl 10 ($5) for adults, Dfl 5 ($2.50) for children under 13. Tues–Sun 11am–5pm. Tram: 1, 9, or 12.

This small 18th-century palace in the heart of the old city was the home of Emma, the Queen Mother, from 1901 to 1934. Nowadays the Municipal Museum (Gemeentemuseum) (see above) organizes temporary exhibitions here, usually focusing on a single artist or movement.

Noordeinde Palace. Noordeinde (west of Lange Voorhout). Tram: 3, 7, 8, or 12.

Noordeinde is the "working palace" for Queen Beatrix and her staff. This splendid neoclassical town palace, which dates back to 1553, was quite elegantly furnished when William of Orange's widow was in residence, but became almost derelict by the beginning of the 19th century. In 1815 restoration brought it back to a state suitable for the residence of Willem I. In 1948, fire damage necessitated extensive renovation, and in the early 1980s further restoration was begun.

It is from this palace that Queen Beatrix and Prince Claus, on the third Tuesday of September each year, depart in a golden coach drawn by eight horses, escorted by military corps, bands, local authorities, and a blaze of street pageantry, to proceed to the Binnenhof, where the queen officially opens Parliament with an address to the States General and parliamentary members in the Ridderzaal.

Omniversum. President Kennedylaan 5. ☎ **070/354-5454.** Admission Dfl 17.50 ($8.75) adults, Dfl 13 ($6.50) children 4 to 12. Tues–Wed 11am–5pm, Thurs–Sun 11am–9pm. Tram: 10.

This globe-shaped construction contains a digital planetarium and various multimedia theaters that explain man, the universe, foreign cultures, and space travel. It's truly another world!

✪ **Panorama Mesdag.** Zeestraat 65 (just north of the city center). ☎ **070/310-6665.** Admission Dfl 7.50 ($3.75) adults, Dfl 4 ($2) children. Mon–Sat 10am–5pm, Sun and public holidays noon–5pm. Closed Dec 25. Tram: 7 or 8.

This panorama will, quite simply, take your breath away. It's the world's largest circular painting, with a total circumference of 395 feet. You'll walk through a dark passageway, up a stairway, and out onto a circular platform—and suddenly you're in the 1880 fishing village of Scheveningen. Its dunes, beach, fishing boats, and everything else in the village are three-dimensional, an illusion enhanced by the artificial dunes that separate you from the painting. The panorama is the work of Dutch artist Hendrik Willem Mesdag, with the assistance of his wife and two other prominent artists.

Peace Palace (Vredespaleis). Carnegieplein. ☎ **070/346-9680.** Admission Dfl 6 ($3.50) adults, Dfl 3 ($1.75) children. Guided tours Mon–Fri at 10am, 11am, 2pm, and 3pm. Tram: 7 or 8.

This imposing building—whose construction between 1907 and 1913 was largely due to donations made by Andrew Carnegie—houses the Permanent Court of Arbitration, the International Court of Justice, the International Law Academy, and an extensive library. Its furnishings have been donated by countries around the world. Guided tours are given four times a day.

ORGANIZED TOURS

Speedwell Travel B.V., Valeriusstraat 65 (☎ **070/365-4848**) conducts coach tours to the flower fields and Keukenhof Gardens, Delta Expo, Amsterdam, Delft, Rotterdam, Antwerp, Brussels, Alkmaar cheese market and Zaanse Schans, and the windmill district of Kinderdijk. There's also a Grand Holland tour. Prices range from Dfl 21.50 to 85 ($12.50 to $49.30) for adults. Tours run from April through November, with different destinations scheduled for different days of the week. Call for schedules and reservations.

SHOPPING

Interesting shopping areas in The Hague include Oude Molstraat and Denneweg in the city center, where you'll find a concentration of authentic Dutch shops. Connected to the Centraal Station, the Babylon shopping complex has two floors of over 60 shops, restaurants, and a luxury hotel. Several streets running off the Groenmarkt are pedestrian shopping streets.

WHERE TO STAY

The Hague has hotel accommodations of high standards in every price range, but for seaside accommodations, see "Scheveningen," below.

VERY EXPENSIVE

✪ **Hotel des Indes Intercontinental.** Lange Voorhout 54–56, 2514 EG The Hague. ☎ **070/363-2932.** Fax 070/345-1721. 83 units. MINIBAR TV TEL. Dfl 515 ($257.50) double; Dfl 1150 ($575) suite. AE, DC, MC, V. Tram: 1, 3, 7, 8, 9, or 12.

This elegant old-world hotel is highly recommended for both its elegant accommodations and its location in the center of the oldest part of the city. It began life as the residence of Baron van Brienen, and became a hotel in 1881. Since then it has welcomed royalty, diplomats, celebrities, and tourists, and has held a consistently prominent place in the social life of The Hague. The classically decorated guest rooms are the ultimate in comfort, with telephones in both bedroom and bathroom, and such extras as bathrobes and hair dryers. Some bathrooms contain a Jacuzzi. Public rooms are breathtakingly beautiful, with lots of marble, polished wood, chandeliers, and velvet upholstery. The gracious lobby lounge is a favorite place with for Hagenaars to meet for tea or other refreshments.

Dining/Diversions: Le Bar has the ambiance of a typical Hague bar, and the fine restaurant, called Le Restaurant, is a stylish setting for good eating (see "Where to Dine" below). Both of these imaginatively named places are as popular with locals as with visitors and guests.

Amenities: Indoor pool, concierge, 24-hour room service, twice-daily maid service, dry cleaning and laundry, in-room massage, baby-sitting, banquet and conference facilities, secretarial services, express checkout, courtesy car, health club with Jacuzzi, sauna, Turkish bath, massage, and solarium.

EXPENSIVE

✪ **Promenade Hotel.** Van Stolkweg 1, 2585 JL The Hague. ☎ **070/352-5161.** Fax 070/354-1046. 99 units. MINIBAR TV TEL. Dfl 425 ($212.50) double; Dfl 775–1785 ($387.50–$892.50) suite. AE, DC, MC, V.

This high-rise hotel is a bit removed from the city center, in a lovely wooded area just a short drive from city sightseeing as well as the beach. It features luxury guest rooms with balconies, modern and comfortable furnishings, and hair dryers.

Dining: There's an a la carte restaurant, The Gallery; an Italian restaurant, La Galleria; and the grand cafe Promenade.

Amenities: Concierge, 24-hour room service, gift shop, newsstand, hairdressing salon, conference and banquet facilities, wheelchair access.

MODERATE

Hotel Corona. Buitenhof 39–42, 2513 AH The Hague. ☎ **070/363-7930.** Fax 070/361-5785. 26 units. MINIBAR TV TEL. Dfl 310 ($155) double; Dfl 350 ($175) suite. Rates include buffet breakfast. AE, DC, MC, V.

This charming small hotel, once a lively coffeehouse, is centrally located opposite the House of Parliament and between the Binnenhof and the Passage, a large covered shopping center. Public rooms feature contemporary decor, with touches of handsome marble and mahogany in the lobby. The guest rooms are done in soft pastel colors, with graceful window drapes. The hotel's popularity dates back to the early 1900s. Politicians, antiques dealers, and gourmets still congregate here today. The elegant restaurant, full of French Provincial furnishings, soothing ecrus, and brushed blues, is a favorite retreat for the good and the great in government circles. In balmy weather, part of the restaurant becomes a sidewalk terrace. The hotel provides 24-hour room service.

✪ **Mercure Hotel Central.** Spui 180, 2511 BW The Hague. ☎ **070/363-6700.** Fax 070/363-9398. 162 units. MINIBAR TV TEL. Dfl 240 ($120) double; from Dfl 350 ($175) suite. AE, DC, MC, V.

This first-class hotel sits right in the heart of the city, no more than a 5-minute walk from both train stations. The public rooms are tastefully furnished; there's a spacious lounge, a Japanese restaurant Shirasagi, and a gift shop. The guest rooms, each outfitted with a hair dryer and trouser press, reflect the same good taste and comfort.

Paleishotel. Molenstraat 26 (next to Palace Noordeinde), 2513 BL The Hague. ☎ **070/362-4621.** Fax 070/361-4533. 20 units. MINIBAR TV TEL. Dfl 175–219 ($67.50–109.50) double. AE, DC, MC, V.

The Paleishotel has spacious and elegant guest rooms furnished with soft chairs and settees. The beds are very comfortable. Bathrooms are a bit small but fitted out beautifully. There's a lavish breakfast buffet, as well as a bar and a sauna. The location is excellent both for shopping (the pedestrian shopping promenade is nearby) and for sightseeing.

Parkhotel den Haag. Molenstraat 53, 2513 BJ The Hague. ☎ **070/362-4371.** Fax 070/361-4525. 113 units, 1 suite. TV TEL. Dfl 250–315 ($125–$157.50) double, Dfl 395 ($197.50) suite. Rates include continental breakfast. AE, CB, DC, MC, V.

This pleasant, centrally located, full-service hotel is on a quiet street. Its breakfast room overlooks the gardens of a former royal palace. The recently redecorated guest rooms are comfortable and attractive. There's also a cozy, attractive bar.

INEXPENSIVE

Hotel Aristo. Stationsweg 164–166 (a 5-minute walk from the station), 2515 BS The Hague. ☎ **070/389-0847.** 11 units. Dfl 90 ($52.20) double. Rates include continental breakfast. No credit cards.

This small hotel is nothing to rave about, but it has a friendly English-speaking staff and large, adequately furnished rooms.

Hotel Astoria. Stationsweg 139 (a short walk from Hollands Spoor Station), 2515 BM The Hague. ☎ **070/384-0401.** Fax 070/354-1653. 16 units (7 with bathroom). TV. Dfl 100 ($58) double. Rates include continental breakfast. No credit cards.

The furnishings here (such as the fake leather couches) are plain, but the owners are friendly, the rooms are clean, and the beds are comfortable. There's no restaurant, but plenty of eateries are around the corner.

✪ **Hotel 't Centrum.** Veenkade 6 (near the Nordeinde), 2513 EE The Hague. ☎ **070/346-3657.** Fax 070/310-6460. 10 units. TV. Dfl 125 ($72.50) double. Rates include continental breakfast. V, MC.

This small family hotel is a welcome addition to the accommodations in The Hague. Rooms are furnished with walnut cupboards and chairs and have comfortable box-spring beds. There's also a cozy bar. The Hague's lively center, with its sights and shopping streets, is but a pleasant walk away.

A NEARBY HOTEL

✪ **Golden Tulip Auberge de Kieviet.** Stoeplaan 27, 2243 CX Wassenaar. ☎ **070/511-9232.** Fax 070/511-0969. 25 units. A/C TV TEL. Dfl 235–385 ($117.50–$192.50) double, Dfl 410 ($205) suite. AE, DC, MC, V. Take the A44 highway 10 minutes from The Hague and follow the signs; it's 20 minutes from Schiphol Airport, Amsterdam.

This luxurious small hotel, about 1½ miles from the sea, is well worth the drive from The Hague, Amsterdam, or Scheveningen. The guest rooms are attractive, and there's 24-hour room service—something not always available in hotels in this category. There's also a bar and a brasserie and an excellent gourmet restaurant. The nearby woods and dunes provide lovely walking or cycling routes; golf, riding, swimming, and tennis are also close at hand.

WHERE TO DINE

Thanks to its wealth of international visitors, The Hague offers a wide range of restaurants, both in ambiance and cuisine. It also has a multitude of casual outdoor cafes, sandwich and coffee shops, and brown cafes, any one of which will give you good, fresh food for about Dfl 6 to 15 ($3 to $7.50). The VVV's booklet "The Hague" contains a comprehensive listing of restaurants and bars—it's well worth the small cost.

EXPENSIVE

✪ **Le Restaurant.** In the Hotel des Indes Intercontinental, Lange Voorhout 54–56. ☎ **070/363-2932.** Main courses Dfl 45–55 ($22.50–$27.50); fixed-price menu Dfl 70 ($35). AE, DC, MC, V. Mon–Fri noon–2:30pm (brunch on Sun from 11:30am); daily 6–10:30pm. CONTINENTAL.

The Des Indes's exquisite dining room is a beloved spot for locals, visiting dignitaries, and tourists. It's probably the most elegant and refined dining spot in The Hague. Menu items might include a smoked breast of duck salad as a starter, and guinea fowl with goose liver and "Des Indes" spices or turbot with truffles and chicory as main courses. For dessert, try the sinfully sweet chocolate parfait. There's also an extensive and very fine wine list.

MODERATE

Hotel Corona. Buitenhof 39–42 (opposite the House of Parliament). ☎ **070/363-7930.** Main courses Dfl 29.50–39.50 ($17.10–$22.90); fixed-price menus Dfl 44.50–49.50 ($25.80–$28.70). AE, DC, MC, V. Daily 11:30am–2:30pm and 5:30–10pm. FRENCH/CONTINENTAL.

When the Heineken family acquired this lovely old hotel in the city center, they set about transforming its restaurant into one of The Hague's top dining spots. That they have succeeded admirably is evident in the beautiful decor, widely spaced tables, and—most of all—the beautifully prepared food. Chef Marc Smeets has built on this restaurant's reputation as one of the city's most distinguished kitchens. Specialties include mullet with couscous, and *verjuice* and beef tenderloin braised in red wine with "Nicola" potatoes. There's also an outstanding wine cellar.

Le Bistroquet. Lange Voorhout 98. ☎ **070/360-1170.** Reservations required. Main courses Dfl 30–40 ($15–$20); fixed-price menus Dfl 65–85 ($32.50–$42.50). AE, CB, DC, MC, V. Mon–Fri noon–2pm and 6–10:30pm. FRENCH.

This small and very popular restaurant in the city center is one of The Hague's best, with lovely table settings in a quietly elegant setting. The menu is mostly French. Lamb, fish, and fresh vegetables are featured.

Restaurant Garoeda. Kneuterdijk 18A. ☎ **070/346-5319.** Reservations recommended for lunch. *Rijsttafel* Dfl 39.50–68.50 ($22.90–$39.70). AE, DC, MC, V. Mon–Sat 11am–11pm, Sun 4–11pm. INDONESIAN.

If it's *rijsttafel* you're hankering for, you couldn't find it any better than at this pleasant and very popular Indonesian restaurant in the city center. It's crowded at lunch, so reserve or come early or late.

✪ Restaurant Saur. Lange Voorhout 47. ☎ **070/346-2565.** Reservations required. Main courses Dfl 37.50–59.50 ($21.75–$34.50); fixed-price menus Dfl 45.50–65.50 ($22.75–$32.75). AE, DC, MC, V. Mon–Sat noon–2:30pm and 6–10:30pm. FRENCH/SEAFOOD.

The Saur, which overlooks a beautiful square in the city center, has been a favorite of Hagenaars for generations. The traditional French cuisine is superb, and the service is impeccable.

INEXPENSIVE

✪ Café-Restaurant Greve. Torenstraat 138. ☎ **070/360-3919.** Main courses Dfl 25–32 ($12.50–$16); fixed-price menus Dfl 35–52.50 ($17.50–$26.25). AE, DC, MC, V. Cafe open daily 10am–1am, restaurant open Sun–Wed 6–10pm, Thurs–Sat 6–11pm. MEDITERRANEAN/INTERNATIONAL.

What was once a car showroom is now a popular cafe-restaurant. The large windows of the cafe look out on the lively Torenstraat; the restaurant, however, is more intimate, with its low ceiling, candle lights, and wooden tables. You can choose a dish either as a starter or as a main course, which is an ideal solution for small appetites (or when you just want a taste of everything!). Fish and lamb dishes, such as *bouillabaisse* or lamb cutlets with feta cheese and ouzo sauce, are popular.

Eetcafé Valerius Inn. Valeriusstraat 18 (near President Kennedystraat). ☎ **070/346-1958.** Main course from Dfl 12.50 ($6.25); snacks Dfl 8–15 ($4–$7.50). AE, DC. Sun–Thurs 9:30am–1am, Fri–Sat 9:30am–1:30am. LIGHT MEALS/SNACKS.

This popular brasserie, just a few blocks away from Scheveningen, caters mainly to the younger crowd. It offers such budget-priced snacks as small pizzas, hamburgers, and ice cream.

Rhodos. Buitenhof 36. ☎ **070/365-2731.** Main courses Dfl 22.50–32.50 ($13.05–$18.85). AE, DC, MC, V. Daily 4–11pm. GREEK.

This large restaurant is one of several Greek places in town. It serves most of the traditional Greek specialties, such as *moussaka,* grilled veal, rabbit, *souvlaki,* mussels, and Greek salad. The dining rooms are decorated with colorful wood paneling and traditional pictures of the Acropolis and Rhodes.

✪ 't Goude Hooft. Groenmarkt 13. ☎ 070/346-9713. Main courses Dfl 27.50–39.50 ($15.95–$22.90); fixed-price menus Dfl 35–39.50 ($17.50–$19.75). AE, DC, MC, V. Mon–Sat 10am–midnight, Sun 11am–midnight. DUTCH.

There's a definite Old Dutch flavor to this large, happy restaurant overlooking the Market Square. The wooden beams, brass chandeliers, rustic chairs, and tables blend harmoniously with stained-glass windows and touches of whimsy. The large terrace cafe, which overlooks the "Green Market" square, is pleasant on sunny days. The long menu covers everything from snacks to light lunches to full dinners; there's also a budget-priced Tourist Menu. This is also a good place to drop by for nothing more than a beer or coffee.

WORTH THE SHORT DRIVE

✪ **Golden Tulip Auberge de Kieviet.** Stoeplaan 27, Wassenaar. ☎ **070/511-9232.** Reservations required. Fixed-price menus Dfl 49.50–59.50 ($24.75–$29.75) for 3 to 5 courses. AE, DC, MC, V. Daily noon–2:30pm and 6–10pm. Take A44 and follow the signs, about a 10-minute drive. CONTINENTAL.

A gourmet meal in this brasserie-style restaurant is definitely worth the short drive from The Hague. Indeed, such is its reputation that Amsterdammers often make the slightly longer drive to eat here. Specialties include cream of pumpkin soup with salmon and truffles, and rabbit with apricots.

THE HAGUE AFTER DARK

There's nearly always something going on culturally in The Hague; for a casino and other nightspots, head to nearby Scheveningen (see below). The Spui, just behind The Hague's Centraal Station, is the city's modern cultural square. Here you'll find the **Dr. Anton Philips Concert Hall,** Spui 150 (☎ 070/360-9810), home to the Residentie Orchestra; and the **AT&T Dance Theater,** Spui 152 (☎ 070/360-4930), where the three companies of the renowned Netherlands Dance Theater perform their virtuoso contemporary productions. If you're more into jazz and pop music, check out **'t Paard,** Prinsengracht 12 (☎ 070/360-1618). For 3 days during the second weekend in July, the **Nederlands Congresgebouw** (Congress Building), Churchillplein 10 (☎ 070/354-8000), hosts the world-famous North Sea Jazz Festival, which features star performances by internationally acclaimed musicians. The monthly **The Hague Info,** available at the VVV offices and many hotels and restaurants, lists up-and-coming concerts and other cultural events.

2 Scheveningen

4km (2¾ miles) NW of The Hague city center

Until about 1813, Scheveningen was a sleepy little fishing village. But as its beaches began to attract holiday crowds, the town evolved into an internationally known seaside resort, with accommodations in all price ranges, restaurants with international cuisines, a wide variety of shopping, and abundant nighttime entertainment. The magnificent Kurhaus Hotel draws Europe's crowned heads and celebrities from around the globe, and gamblers flock to the casino nightly. Businesspeople and diplomats often stay here as well, making the 10-minute drive into The Hague to conduct their affairs. Scheveningen is active year-round.

But even today, Scheveningen's little harbor is still crowded with fishing boats and lined with restaurants that feature just-caught seafood. This is where the Dutch

Code Name: Scheveningen

Just try to pronounce Scheveningen (Sgh-*ay*-vening-en) correctly! The name is so difficult to say that during World War II the Dutch underground used it as a code name for identification—not even the Germans, whose language is similar, could get it right.

herring fleet is launched with a colorful Flag Day celebration each year on the last Saturday in May. The fleet then returns with the first herring catch amid just as much fanfare, sending the first batch off to the queen and conducting a lively auction with leading restaurateurs for the rest.

ESSENTIALS

GETTING THERE   There is frequent service from The Hague on trams 1, 7, 8, and 9.

Driving from The Hague, take the A44 north and follow the signs.

VISITOR INFORMATION   The **VVV office** is at Gevers Deynootweg 1134, opposite the Europe Hotel, but shares the same phone service as The Hague's office (☎ **0900/340-3505;** fax 070/347-2102).

SPECIAL EVENTS   Each year, usually in late June or early July, jazz greats from around the world gather in Scheveningen for the North Sea Jazz Festival, 3 days of nonstop music during the second weekend of July. It's an exciting, energizing experience.

EXPLORING SCHEVENINGEN

In addition to its wide, sandy beach bordered by the 2-mile-long promenade, Scheveningen has the **Holland Casino Scheveningen** (in the Kurhaus, open 1:30pm to 2am daily); the **400-yard-long pier** with four entertainment "islands," one of which holds a replica of Jules Verne's submarine *Nautilus* of *20,000 Leagues Under the Sea* fame; and the seashore **Promenade** and the **Palace Promenade,** both with scores of interesting shops that are open 7 days a week.

The historical **Scheveningen Museum** at Neptunusstraat 92 (☎ **070/ 350-0830**), tells you all about life in this former fishing village. Open from Tuesday to Saturday 10am to 5pm, also Monday 10am to 5pm during school vacations and from April through September; admission is Dfl 5 ($2.50) for adults, Dfl 3.50 ($1.75) for children 14 and under.

The Sea Life Center, Strandweg (a.k.a. the Boulevard) 13 (☎ **070/354-2100**), takes you under the sea in an aquarium with a walk-through underwater tunnel, from where you can see the denizens of the deep, including sharks, swimming around above your head. The center is open daily from 10am to 6pm (8pm in July and August) and costs Dfl 15 ($7.50) for adults, Dfl 11.50 ($5.75) for seniors, Dfl 9.50 ($4.75) for children age 4 to 11, and free for children under 4.

A few hotel-blocks away from the Kurhaus you'll find a museum built inside the dunes, a surprisingly peaceful oasis amidst all the seaside entertainment. This museum, **Sculptures on the Seafront (Beelden aan Zee),** Harteveltstraat 1 (☎ 070/358-5857), is dedicated to sculptures of the human body. Here you'll find changing exhibitions by contemporary sculptors from all over the world, as well as an impressive permanent collection. The halls are all of a different shape and some of the exhibits are outside on the patios. But wherever you are in the museum, you'll be aware of the surrounding dunes and the wind playing in the grass. From the highest terrace you can even glimpse the sea. Open Tuesday through Sunday from 11am to 5pm; admission is Dfl 6 ($3).

Scheveningen's neighbor, **Kijkduin,** is a quieter, more family-oriented beach resort, where the main attractions are the sea and dunes. There's a covered shopping complex with 50 interesting shops open 7 days a week, year-round.

ESPECIALLY FOR KIDS

Duinrell Theme Park. Duinrell 1, Wassenaar (3 miles north of The Hague). ☎ 070/ 515-5155. Admission Dfl 26 ($13). Theme park: Apr–Oct daily 10am–5pm. Pool is open throughout year.

This theme park has rides galore—roller-coasters, carrousels, treetop cable cars— and the largest tropical water paradise in Europe. Waterbound activities include luge runs, a centrifugal "Waterspin," and floating frogs. In addition to the amusement park, there are covered tropical swimming pools, ideal for wet-weather days with kids. From September through March there's also an artificial ski slope.

WHERE TO STAY

Budget bed-and-breakfasts, family hotels with kitchenettes, modern high-rises with moderate rates, and the luxurious, incomparable Kurhaus all take part in the diverse accommodations scene in Scheveningen.

EXPENSIVE

Carlton Beach Hotel. Gevers Deynootweg 201, 2586 HZ Scheveningen. ☎ 070/ 354-1414. Fax 070/352-0020. 183 units. MINIBAR TV TEL. Dfl 300 ($150) double. Rates include buffet breakfast. AE, DC, MC, V. Tram: 1 or 9 from The Hague.

This modern seaside hotel, on the northern end of the Promenade, has recently been renovated. The guest rooms are well planned, attractive, and comfortable; hair dryers are provided.

Dining/Diversions: The hotel has a cozy bar and two restaurants.

Amenities: Health center with sauna, solarium, and swimming pool.

✪ **Hotel Kurhaus.** Gevers Deynootplein 30, 2586 CK Scheveningen. ☎ 070/ 416-2636. Fax 070/416-2646. 255 units. MINIBAR TV TEL. Dfl 338–388 ($169–$194) double, Dfl 950–1450 ($425–$725) suite. Rates include full breakfast. Admission to the casino and spa/recreation center is Dfl 40 ($20) for a day. AE, DC, MC, V.

The five-star Kurhaus, the undisputed grande dame of the North Sea coast, will give you a wonderful hotel experience. It began life in 1818 as a four-room wooden bathing pavilion in which bathtubs were filled daily with warm or cold sea water; guests at that time were transported to the sea in enclosed "bathing coaches" so as not to shock the public by their daring! The Kurhaus's Kurzaal concert hall has seen performances by leading musical artists as disparate as violinist Yehudi Menuhin and the Rolling Stones, and its casino rivals any in the world. Its leather-bound guest register, which opens with the signature of the 13-year-old Queen Wilhelmina, is filled with the names of the world's great and illustrated by leading artists who embellished their signatures with original drawings.

The luxury of this lovely place, in the words of one writer, goes beyond fantasy. The guest rooms, many with balconies facing the sea, are spacious and feature elegant decor and furnishings, including safes, hair dryers, and trouser presses.

Dining: The Kurzaal Restaurant and Kurzaal Café are both popular, and the splendid Kandinsky has earned an international reputation (see "Where to Dine," below).

Amenities: Concierge, 24-hour room service, twice-daily maid service, dry cleaning and laundry, newspaper delivery, in-room massage, baby-sitting, conference facilities, secretarial services, express checkout, direct access to the Kuur Thermen Vitalizee spa and recreation center, with indoor and outdoor swimming pools, sauna, and solarium.

MODERATE

✪ **Hotel Ibis den Haag/Scheveningen.** Gevers Deynootweg 63, 2586 BJ Scheveningen. ☎ **070/354-3300.** Fax 070/352-3916. 87 units. TV TEL. Dfl 161–196 ($80.50–$98) double. Rates include buffet breakfast. AE, DC, MC, V.

This bright, attractive hotel, just 1 block from the sea, has recently undergone a complete renovation. The decor is bright, and furnishings are comfortable. Most rooms have a balcony; many have sea views. There's also a restaurant, a terrace bar, and a cozy lounge.

INEXPENSIVE

City Hotel. Renbaanstraat 1, 2586 EW Scheveningen. ☎ **070/355-7966.** Fax 070/354-0503. 35 units (22 with bathroom). TV TEL. Dfl 145 ($72.50) double. Rates include continental breakfast. AE, DC, MC, V.

The rooms in this small, family-type hotel have recently been redecorated. The furniture has a walnut finish and bathrooms are brand new, equipped with either a shower or a bathtub. The rooms at the back look out over the large garden. The hotel serves a generous breakfast buffet and has a cozy bar. The sea is only a short walk (3 minutes) away.

De Seinduin. Seinpostduin 15, 2587 CA Scheveningen. ☎ **070/355-1971.** Fax 070/355-7891. 15 units. MINIBAR TV TEL. Dfl 135–145 ($67.50–$72.50) double. Rates include continental breakfast. AE, DC, MC, V.

This rather plain small hotel has clean, simply furnished guest rooms. Some large rooms are especially suitable for groups or families—the hotel offers a special group discount. The beach is just around the corner, and the beachfront is lined with cafes and restaurants where you can relax after a plunge in the sea.

✪ **Hotel Bali.** Badhuisweg 1, 2587 CA Scheveningen. ☎ **070/350-2434.** Fax 070/354-0363. 20 units. TV TEL. Dfl 110–125 ($55–$62.50) double. Rates include breakfast. AE, DC, MC, V.

"Exotic" is the word for this delightful, Indonesian-themed budget hotel. The guest rooms are plainly furnished, but very bright and comfortable, with wicker chairs and greenery (in some rooms) adding the Balinese touch. The small bar is inviting, and the restaurant is widely famed for its *rijsttafel* (see "Where to Dine," below). It's a short walk to the sea.

WHERE TO DINE

The square in front of the Kurhaus (the Gevers Deynootplein) holds a nest of international restaurants, and the wharf is lined with good seafood places on a street called Dr. Lelykade. The Promenade and Strandweg also have a variety of very good options.

La Galleria I & II. Strandweg 51–53 (on the square in front of the Kurhaus) & Gevers Deynootplein 120. ☎ **070/355-5006** (for the former) ☎ **070/352-1156** (for the latter). Main courses Dfl 15–35 ($7.50–$17.50); fixed-price dinner Dfl 47.50–52.50 ($23.75–$26.25). AE, DC, MC, V. Daily 9am–midnight. ITALIAN.

La Galleria is one of my personal favorites in Scheveningen. The warm, intimate room is the perfect setting for a relaxing dinner. The menu offers everything Italian from pizza to full dinners, at moderate prices. The staff is friendly and welcoming, and the service is good.

✪ **Kandinsky Restaurant.** In the Hotel Kurhaus, Gevers Deynootplein 30. ☎ **070/ 416-2636.** Reservations required. 3-course lunch Dfl 57.50 ($28.75), 5-course dinner Dfl 92.50 ($46.25). AE, DC, MC, V. Mon–Fri noon–3pm and daily 6–10:30pm. FRENCH/ MEDITERRANEAN.

Save your most special Scheveningen meal for this small exquisite restaurant on the beach. The dining room, which overlooks the sea, features signed lithographs by abstract artist Wassily Kandinsky. The cuisine here is classic French.

Also in the Kurhaus complex is the **Kurzaal Restaurant,** which offers a lavish buffet on weekdays for Dfl 35 ($26.10) for lunch and Dfl 55 ($27.50) for dinner, and an even more lavish buffet on weekends for Dfl 55 ($27.50) for lunch and Dfl 65 ($32.50) for dinner. Both buffets are spread in the gorgeous Kurzaal area, with after-dinner dancing on Friday and Saturday nights.

✪ **Restaurant Bali.** Badhuisweg 1. ☎ **070/350-2434.** *Rijsttafel* from Dfl 60 ($30). AE, DC, MC, V. Mon–Sat 5–10pm, Sun 4–10pm. INDONESIAN.

The Bali's *rijsttafel* has become widely recognized as the best in the region. In the adjoining Bali bar, international cocktails are served with expertise; try the Bali Mystery after dinner—and don't ask me its ingredients, all I know is that it's great. The place is located a short walk from the sea.

Visrestaurant Ducdalf. Dr. Lelykade 5. ☎ **070/355-7692.** Main courses Dfl 32–52.50 ($16–$26.75). Fixed-price dinner Dfl 52.50 ($26.25) for 3 courses; Dfl 75 ($37.50) for 4 courses; Dfl 85 ($42.50) for 5 courses. AE, DC, MC, V. Daily noon–10pm. SEAFOOD.

This pleasant place is located on a street along the wharf. You can rest assured that the fish you order is not long out of local waters. The menu lists an amazingly varied selection of main courses, including steak, veal, and chicken for non-seafood lovers. There's a very good mixed grill, and fillet of sole appears in no fewer than 11 different guises.

SCHEVENINGEN AFTER DARK

After dark, look for nightclubs at Gevers Deynootplein in front of the Kurhaus and theater productions at the **Circustheater,** which may include opera and ballet as well as musical theater—you might even find a smash-hit re-run of an Andrew Lloyd Webber show.

3 Rotterdam

75km (51 miles) S of Amsterdam; 23km (16 miles) SE of The Hague

Rotterdam is only a half hour from The Hague and an hour from Amsterdam, but it's centuries away from both in appearance and personality. Unlike Amsterdam and The Hague, Rotterdam retains traces of its ancient history in only one tiny section—Oude Haven (Old Harbor). World War II takes the blame for that. The city center was totally burned out by incendiary bombs in 1940, and in 1944 Nazi occupation forces sent demolition squads to finish off the entire harbor. By the end of the war, Rotterdam was utterly devastated.

But Rotterdam's city fathers, in a display of incredible efficiency and fortitude, quickly set in motion plans to rebuild their city. They were determined that it should adhere to modern standards and attempted to raise ancient styles from the still-smoldering ruins. The task of rebuilding consumed several years; the wonder is that it did not require decades.

Today Rotterdam is a bustling metropolis with the world's largest port, created when its several harbors were opened directly to the sea (some 20 miles away) by the dredging of a deep-water channel that accommodates even the largest oil tankers. The city's population numbers over one million, and more arrive annually. Indeed, Rotterdam is expanding at such a rate that many Dutch believe a few more decades will see it reach the outskirts of The Hague, swallowing up Delft on its way. What a megalopolis that would be!

ESSENTIALS

GETTING THERE   Rotterdam's airport is located at Rotterdam Airportplein 60 (☎ 010/446-3455); bus no. 33 will take you to or from the city center.

There's frequent rail service to Rotterdam from Brussels, Paris, and all around Holland. Trains arrive at Centraal Station, Stationsplein. From Amsterdam, there are two trains each hour around the clock; the trip takes 50 minutes. For information on train schedules, call ☎ **0900/9292.**

Driving from Amsterdam, take A4 to The Hague, then A13 to Rotterdam.

VISITOR INFORMATION   The **VVV office** is at Coolsingel 67, on the corner of Stadhuisplein (☎ **0900/403-4065;** fax 010/413-0124), reached by tram no. 1, or the Stadhuis stop of the Metro. The office is open Monday through Thursday and Saturday from 9am to 7pm, Friday from 9am to 9pm, and Sunday from 10am to 5pm. Pick up a copy of the VVV's publication **"Deze Maand"** ("This Month") for listings of current happenings. Staff can also arrange accommodations and provide a city map that shows major attractions.

GETTING AROUND   Rotterdam's sprawling size makes it a city to be explored on foot one area at a time, using public transport or taxi to move from one area to another.

Rotterdam has an extensive public transport network of **bus, tram,** and **metro** (which runs on north-south and east-west axes). The VVV can furnish a map of routes for all.

Taxis are expensive but save time in getting around. Taxi stands are sprinkled throughout the city, or you can call (☎ **010/462-6060**).

EXPLORING ROTTERDAM

Before setting out to experience Rotterdam, stop by the VVV to pick up the helpful brochure "Welcome to Rotterdam."

Rotterdam features some spectacular modern architecture. Just outside the Centraal Station you'll encounter the office of the **Nationale Nederlanden,** the highest skyscraper in the city at 165 yards. Down Coolsingel is the bottle-green **World Trade Center,** and east of this (on Overblaak) is a geometric chaos of quirky apartments known as the **Kijk-Kubus**—cubes turned on one corner, balancing on the tops of tall concrete stalks (one of them is open to the public March through December, daily from 11am to 5pm, and January and February, Friday to Sunday from 11am to 5pm; admission is Dfl 4 [$2]; ☎ 010/414-2285). Two prominent bridges span the Nieuwe Maas river, the dark red **Nieuwe Willemsbrug** and a new landmark, the single-span suspension bridge officially called the **Erasmusbrug** and nicknamed "The Swan" (or, if you're not quite charmed by its looks, "The Dishwashing Brush").

To see the only corner of Old Rotterdam that's left, take tram no. 6 or 9 to **Delfshaven,** which, many years ago, was the harbor of Delft. Of special interest to Americans is the old **Pilgrim Fathers Church** (on Voorhaven), in which the Pilgrims said their last prayers before setting off for the New World in the *Speedwell*. The *Speedwell* didn't prove to be very seaworthy, however, so after crossing the English

Rotterdam Accommodations, Dining & Attractions

Holland

Rotterdam

ACCOMMODATIONS:
Bienvenue **2**
Bilderburg Parkhotel **19**
Golden Tulip Barbizon
  Capelle **14**
Hotel Breitner **7**
Hotel New York **22**
Savoy **13**

DINING
Brasserie La Vilette **18**
De Pijp **4**
Henkes' Brasserie **8**
Parkheuvel **10**
Restaurant Engels **3**
The Old Dutch **5**

ATTRACTIONS
Biljdorp Zoo **1**
Euromast & Space
  Adventure **9**
Het Schielandhuis **16**
Holland Casino Rotterdam **11**
Kunsthal **21**
Museum Boymans van
  Beuningen **20**
National Schools Museum **12**
Netherlands Architecture
  Institute **6**
Prins Hendrik Maritme
  Museum **17**
Tropicana **15**

3-0015

Channel, the Pilgrims boarded another ship in Southampton—the *Mayflower*. The Pilgrims are remembered in special services every Thanksgiving Day.

MUSEUMS & OTHER ATTRACTIONS

Rotterdam's modern urban planning has resulted in an unusually effective use of city-center space. Particularly attractive are the shingle paths and lazy lawns in the landscaped **Museumpark,** which serves as a central focus for the first three museums mentioned below. Between visits you can stretch your legs or sit down and have a picnic.

Kunsthal. Museumpark, Westzeedijk 341. ☎ **010/440-0301.** Admission Dfl 10 ($5.80) for adults, Dfl 7.50 ($4.35) for children up to 15 years. Tues–Sat 10am–5pm, Sun and holidays 11am–5pm. Tram: 5.

The unusually designed Kunsthal (Art Hall) plays host to cutting-edge temporary exhibitions, sometimes several at the same time. These range from Warhol to automobile design, Indonesian court jewelry, and Chinese ritual gowns. Much attention is paid here to design and presentation, often resulting in an intriguing combination of exhibits and surroundings.

✪ **Museum Boymans Van Beuningen.** Museumpark 18–20. ☎ **010/441-9400.** Admission Dfl 7.50 ($3.75). Tues–Sat 10am–5pm, Sun and holidays 11am–5pm. Metro: Eendrachtsplein. Tram: 5.

Art lovers will find here a collection of works by Dutch and Flemish artists of the 16th and 17th centuries, such as Rubens, Hals, Rembrandt, and Steen. Other galleries have international modern art, applied arts, ceramics, sculpture, and regular exhibitions of prints and drawings. It's particularly enjoyable to walk among the modern sculptures in the gardens. The museum will be undergoing renovations in 1999.

Netherlands Architecture Institute. Museumpark 25. ☎ **010/440-1200.** Admission Dfl 7.50 ($3.75). Tues–Sat 10am–5pm, Sun 11am–5pm. Metro: Eendrachtsplein. Tram: 3, 6, or 7.

The national institute of architecture serves as an archive, study-center, and exhibition space, all housed in a remarkable building designed by Jo Coenen. Temporary exhibitions feature work from all around the world, as well as from centuries gone by.

✪ **"Het Schielandshuis" Historical Museum.** Korte Hoogstraat 31. ☎ **010/217-6767.** Admission Dfl 6 ($3) adults, Dfl 3 ($1.50) children. Tues–Fri 10am–5pm, Sat–Sun 11am–5pm. Metro: Beurs/Churchillplein. Tram: 3 or 6.

Lost between towering office blocks is the Schielandshuis, the city's sole survivor from the 17th century. The building has been gloriously restored and now shows off Rotterdam's cultural heritage. Period rooms are filled with furnishings rescued from mansions destroyed during World War II. The Atlas Van Stolk—a vast collection of prints and drawings relating to Dutch history—occupies a whole floor. On Voorhaven, in the old port district, is the affiliated Historical Museum "De Dubbelde Palmboom," which consists of twin converted warehouses. Entrance is included with admission to the Schielandshuis. Craftspeople work in the old Zakkendragershuisje (Grain Sack Carriers Guild House), using copies of 17th- and 18th-century molds to cast beautiful plates, bowls, tea-urns, and other utensils—their products make great gifts.

National Schools Museum. Nieuwe Markt 1A. ☎ **010/404-5425.** Admission Dfl 3.50 ($1.75) adults, free for children under 16, and Wednesday is free for everyone. Tues–Sat 10am–5pm, Sun 1–5pm. Metro: Blaak. Tram: 3 or 7.

This interesting museum traces the history of education in Holland from the Charlemagne era right up to the present. Six marvelous, fully furnished classrooms are populated by lifelike figures of teachers and pupils, as well as pictures, prints, and documents.

✪ **Prins Hendrik Maritime Museum.** Leuvehaven 1 (in the harbor area). ☎ **010/413-2680.** Admission Dfl 6 ($3) adults, children Dfl 3 ($1.50). Tues–Sat 10am–5pm, Sun and public holidays 11am–5pm. Metro: Beurs/Churchillplein. Tram: 1, 3, 4, 6, or 7.

This marvelous museum is devoted entirely to the history of the Rotterdam harbor. It consists of two sections: the main building, and De Buffel, a beautifully restored 1868 warship. The constantly changing exhibits will give you new insight into the close relationship between the Dutch and the sea. In the museum harbor basin, some 20 vessels dating from 1850 to 1950 are moored. There's also a bookstore and a coffee shop.

Organized Tours

One of the best things to do in Rotterdam is to take a **Spido Harbor Trip** (via Metro to Leuvehaven station; ☎ 010/413-5400). Departures are every 30 to 45 minutes from 9:30am to 5pm, April through September; and two to four times per day, October through March. The season of the year will determine how much of the vast port you'll be able to see, but it's an unforgettable experience. You'll feel dwarfed by the hulking oil tankers and container ships that glide like giant whales into their berths along the miles of docks. The basic harbor trip, offered year-round, is a 75-minute tour of the city's waterfront; between April and September, you can also take an extended 2¼-hour trip daily at 10am and 12:30pm; and on a limited schedule in July and August, you can make all-day excursions to the sluices of the Delta Works and along the full length of the Europoort. Prices vary according to the trip, but run from Dfl 14.50 to Dfl 45.00 ($7.25 to $27.50) for adults and Dfl 7.25 to Dfl 22.50 ($3.65 to $11.25) for children ages 3 to 11. There's also a music/dinner cruise offered from April through November that costs Dfl 99.50 ($49.75) and includes a welcome cocktail, a four-course meal, two glasses of wine, and coffee. A reservation is absolutely necessary.

From May through September, the VVV teams up with the RET (Rotterdam Public Transport) to give a 3-hour guided tour by open **double-decker bus.** This Rotterdam Tourist Hopper will take you past all the major sights, both historic and modern. Tours depart from the Stadhuis (City Hall), across from the VVV at 1:30pm, from Tuesday through Saturday in May, July, and August; and on Wednesday, Friday, and Saturday in June and September. Tickets are Dfl 15 ($8.70) for adults and Dfl 12.50 ($7.25) for children up to 12 years. For more information, call the VVV (☎ **0900/403-4065**).

Especially for Kids

✪ **Blijdorp Zoo.** Van Aerssenlaan 49. ☎ **010/443-1431.** Admission Dfl 22.50 ($11.25) adults, Dfl 15 ($7.50) children 4–9 and senior citizens, free for children under 4. Daily 9am–5pm, April–Sept daily 9am–6pm. Tram: 3.

The animals here feel right at home in this natural environment that re-creates their homes in the wild. A large enclosed plaza contains elephants, crocodiles, reptiles, amphibians, and tropical plants and birds. An Asian section houses Javanese monkeys, a bat cave, and exotic birds.

Euromast and Space Adventure. Parkhaven 20. ☎ **010/436-4811.** Admission Dfl 14.50 ($7.25) adults, Dfl 9 ($4.50) children 4–12. Mar–Sept, daily 10am–7pm; Oct–Feb, daily 10am–5pm. Metro: Dijkzigt. Tram: 6 or 9.

A Trip to Kinderdijk

There are three things that stir the soul of a true Hollander: the Dutch flag, the Dutch anthem, and the sight of windmill sails spinning in the breeze. Kinderdijk, a tiny community between Rotterdam and Dordrecht, has 19 water-pumping windmills; that means 76 mill sails, each with a 14-yard span, all revolving on a summer day. It's a spectacular sight and one of the must-sees of Holland. The mills are in operation on Saturday afternoons in July and August from 2:30 to 5:30pm; the visitors' mill is open April through September, Monday to Saturday from 9:30am to 5:30pm.

To get to Kinderdijk take the train to Rotterdam Centraal Station, and board a train going to Rotterdam Lombardijen Station. From here, Bus 154 takes you to Kinderdijk. If you're driving, take the N210 east from Rotterdam and then go south to Kinderdijk.

This slender tower, some 611 feet tall, is indisputably the best vantage point for an overall view of Rotterdam and its environs. More than that, however, the tower contains interesting exhibitions, a restaurant, and an exciting Space Cabin ride that emulates a rocket take-off.

✪ **Tropicana.** Maasboulevard 100. ☎ **010/402-0700.** Dfl 17.50 ($8.75) for adults, Dfl 13 ($6.50) for children aged 5 to 12, free for children under 5. Mon–Fri 10am–11pm, Sat–Sun 10am–6pm. Metro: Oostplein. Tram: 3 or 6.

This water-based amusement park simulates a luxuriant tropical setting, and features recreational facilities like a swimming pool and wave pool, a sauna, water slides, hot whirlpools, a wild-water strip, and a swimmers' bar.

WHERE TO STAY

Many visitors prefer to base themselves in either Amsterdam or The Hague, but Rotterdam also has a wealth of good accommodations choices. The VVV can provide a complete "Hotels" brochure, as well as arrange reservations for your stay.

EXPENSIVE

Bilderberg Parkhotel. Westersingel 70, 3015 LB Rotterdam. ☎ **010/436-3611.** Fax 010/436-4212. 189 units. MINIBAR TV TEL. Dfl 335–470 ($167.50–$235) double. AE, CB, DC, MC, V. Metro: Eendrachtsplein. Tram: 5.

For city-center convenience, you can't do better than this modern high-rise, set in its own private garden. The spacious guest rooms are the ultimate in classic luxury, furnished with soft couches and comfortable beds. Bathrooms are elegant and supplied with every convenience. Some of the rooms are air-conditioned; some are nonsmoking. The hotel has its own private parking.

Dining: The Empress restaurant is open for breakfast, lunch, and dinner.

Amenities: 24-hour room service, fitness center, sauna, solarium, wheelchair access.

MODERATE

✪ **Golden Tulip Barbizon Capelle.** Barbizonlaan 2, 2908 MA Capelle a/d IJssel. ☎ **010/456-4455.** Fax 010/456-7858. 101 units. MINIBAR TV TEL. Dfl 320 ($160) double. AE, DC, MC, V. Metro: Hesseplaats.

This spectacularly modern high-rise in a suburb of Rotterdam is the perfect escape from city chaos—and only a 10-minute drive from the city center and the airport.

The guest rooms, equipped with hair dryers and trouser presses, are superbly furnished, with a pleasant decor. Guests enjoy complimentary fruit and daily newspapers, as well as access to the convivial Luigi's Bar, and fine dining in the Rousseau restaurant. The hotel also offers 24-hour room service, valet service, laundry service, a gift shop, conference rooms, and wheelchair access.

Hotel New York. Koninginnenhoofd 1, 3072 AD Rotterdam. ☎ **010/439-0500.** Fax 010/484-2701. 71 units. MINIBAR TV TEL. Dfl 160–240 ($80–$120) double. AE, DC, MC, V. Metro: Wilhemina, then walk along the riverside.

This building, one of Europe's first skyscrapers, was constructed at the beginning of the century for the Holland-America passenger line to—you guessed it—New York. Many of the city's immigrants passed through these portals with their trunks. The reception rooms retain some of the original features. In the bright guest rooms, stylish furnishings combine the old and the new; some rooms have stunning balcony views. The cafe-restaurant downstairs has a great view over the river and docklands. It's open all day and serves tea-time treats as well as a three-course dinner for Dfl 35 ($17.50).

INEXPENSIVE

Bienvenue. Spoorsingel 24 (located behind Centraal Station), 3033 GL Rotterdam. ☎ **010/ 466-9394.** Fax 010/467-7475. 10 units (7 with bathroom). TV. Dfl 100 ($58) double without bathroom; Dfl 125 ($72.50) double with bathroom. Rates include breakfast. AE, DC, MC, V. Tram: 3, 5, or 9.

This small, budget-priced hotel is one of the best in its price range. The bright guest rooms have soft red carpets, comfortable beds, and clean showers (two rooms have baths). There's a canal in front of the hotel, and rooms at the back open onto the terrace. The hotel offers a tasty breakfast buffet.

✪ **Hotel Breitner.** Breitnerstraat 23, 3015 XA Rotterdam. ☎ **010/436-0262.** Fax 010/436-4091. 32 units (23 with bathroom). TV TEL. Dfl 100 ($50) double without bathroom; Dfl 140 ($70) double with bathroom. Rates include continental breakfast. AE, DC, MC, V. Bus: 38 or 45.

The Breitner is located near the picturesque Delfshaven historic area as well as Centraal Station. It's a friendly hotel with attractive, no-frills guest rooms. There's a good-size lounge and a garden with a terrace.

Savoy. Hoogstraat 81, 3011 PJ Rotterdam. ☎ **010/413-9280.** Fax 010/404-5712. 95 units. MINIBAR TV TEL. Dfl 180 ($90) double. AE, DC, MC, V. Metro: Blaak. Tram: 3 or 7.

Savoy is a modern hotel on the edge of the city center. Its spacious guest rooms are decorated in pastel colors and furnished with easy chairs and comfortable beds. Some bathrooms are fitted with a bathtub instead of a shower. Rooms on the second floor have balconies. All rooms have hair-dryers. In the morning you can serve yourself a delicious breakfast from the varied buffet.

WHERE TO DINE
VERY EXPENSIVE

Parkheuvel. Heuvellaan 21. ☎ **010/436-0766.** Main courses Dfl 57.50–70 ($28.75–$35); fixed-price lunch menu Dfl 72.50 ($35.75); 3-course dinner menus from Dfl 97.50 ($48.75). AE, DC, MC, V. Mon–Fri noon–2pm, Mon–Sat 6–10pm. FRENCH/INTERNATIONAL.

With two Michelin stars on his sleeve, patron-chef Cees Helder will amuse your palate with luxurious dishes made from the freshest ingredients. The seafood dishes are particularly astounding: try the starter of *carpaccio* of sea bass, or a lobster salad with sun-dried tomatoes and rucola. Main courses range from *turbot gratinée* to poached filet of beef with truffles.

MODERATE

Brasserie La Vilette. Westblaak 160. ☎ **010/414-8692.** Main courses Dfl 25–35 ($12.50–$17.50); fixed-price menu Dfl 55 ($27.50). AE, DC, MC, V. Mon–Sat noon–2pm and 6–9:30pm. FRENCH.

This plant- and flower-filled oasis in the city center is very elegant in appearance, with soft rose-colored walls and starched white table linen. The cuisine is classic French and the service is both polished and friendly. For starters, try the filet of beef *carpaccio*. The grilled sea bass with lobster sauce is a fine main course, and the *crème brûlée* with ice cream flavored with sweet Pedro Ximenez sherry is a tempting dessert. This member of the Alliance Gastronomique is much favored by leading business executives.

✪ **Henkes' Brasserie.** Voorhaven 17. ☎ **010/425-5596.** Main courses Dfl 27.50–37.50 ($13.75–$18.75); fixed-price menu Dfl 55 ($27.50). AE, DC, MC, V. Daily 11:30am–midnight; kitchen closes at 10pm. DUTCH/CONTINENTAL.

Henkes' Brasserie is an ideal place to appreciate the special atmosphere of old Delfshaven. The waterside terrace invites you to while away a sunny afternoon, interrupted only by a leisurely stroll down the harbor, then to return for dinner. Inside, the old Henkes' *jenever* (Dutch gin) distillery has been completely transformed; the interior now features the furnishings of a 19th-century Belgian insurance bank. The warm woodwork and brass chandeliers create a dining room on a grand scale. You can enjoy seafood and meat dishes or seasonal specialties like venison with a chocolate-port sauce.

✪ **The Old Dutch.** Rochussenstraat 20 (in the city center). ☎ **010/436-0344.** Main courses Dfl 32–45 ($16–$22.50); fixed-price menus Dfl 62.50–77.50 ($31.25–$38.75) for 5 courses. AE, DC, MC, V. Mon–Fri noon–midnight, Sat 6pm–midnight. DUTCH/FRENCH.

This atmospheric place, housed in what was once a traditional-style home, is one of Rotterdam's leading restaurants. It offers traditional Dutch dishes, as well as the best in French cuisine. The wild duck breast in elderberry sauce is an excellent main course; try the walnut parfait drizzled with honey for dessert.

INEXPENSIVE

De Pijp. Gaffelstraat 90 (in the city center). ☎ **010/436-6896.** Main courses Dfl 20–35 ($10–$17.50). No credit cards. Mon–Sat noon–midnight. INTERNATIONAL.

Steaks and a number of international dishes are prepared right in the middle of this delightful restaurant. The place attracts a mixed bag of regulars—students, bankers, business executives, and blue-collar workers—and has a real "Rotterdam" ambiance. Everything is cooked to bring out all the natural flavors: Steaks are simply fried and served in their own juices; fish is either fried or steamed.

✪ **Restaurant Engels.** In the Groothandelsgebouw (Business Center), next to Centraal Station, Stationsplein 45. ☎ **010/411-9550.** Main courses Dfl 20–37.50 ($10–$18.75); fixed-price menu in Don Quijote, Tokaj, and Sunday brunch in Restaurant Engels Dfl 42.50 ($21.25) for 3 courses. Carvery buffet in the Beefeater Dfl 29.50–45 ($14.75–$22.50). AE, DC, MC, V. Daily 8am–1am. INTERNATIONAL/LIGHT MEALS.

This marvelous restaurant is actually a complex of four, each dedicated to a different international cuisine: Don Quijote (Spanish), Tokaj (Hungarian), The Beefeater (British), and Restaurant Engels (British). Tokaj and Don Quijote offer live music. There's an à la carte menu (full dinners, light meals, sandwiches, omelets, snacks, etc.) and a vegetarian menu.

ROTTERDAM AFTER DARK

The world-class **Rotterdam Philharmonic Orchestra** plays at the **De Doelen** concert hall, at Kruisstraat 2 (☎ 010/217-1717). If you want to see a global pop star, take a ride to the **Ahoy** at Zuiderparkweg 20 (☎ 010/410-4204), a sports center often used by touring world bands.

Rotterdam is also home to one of the ten legal casinos in the country, the **Holland Casino Rotterdam,** Plaza Complex, Weena 624 (☎ 010/414-7799). Roulette, blackjack, punto banco, and gambling machines are featured. You must be 18 or over and show a passport or driver's license to get in. Admission is Dfl 6 ($3). Open daily 1:30pm to 2am (closed May 4, Dec 31). Metro: Centraal Station. Tram: 1, 3, 4, 5, or 7.

4 Delft

10km (6 miles) SE of The Hague; 14km (9 miles) NW of Rotterdam; 35km (22 miles) W of Gouda; 30km (19 miles) SW of Leiden

Delft is perhaps the prettiest little town in all of Holland. The facades of the Renaissance and Gothic houses here reflect age-old beauty, and tree-lined canals enhance the sense of tranquillity that pervades the air. Around every corner and down every street you'll walk into a scene that might have been composed for the canvas of a great artist. Indeed, it's easy to understand why Vermeer chose to spend most of his life surrounded by Delft's gentle beauty.

A good part of Holland's history is preserved in the tombs of Delft. William the Silent was assassinated in the Prinsenhof and now rests in a magnificent tomb in the Nieuwe Kerk, and every member of the House of Orange-Nassau since King Willem I has been brought here for burial as well. Delft is also the final resting place of someone named Karl Naudorff, who is suspected of being Louis XVII, Dauphin of France. And two of Holland's greatest naval figures, admirals Tromp and Heyn, are entombed in the Oude Kerk.

Of course, to many visitors Delft means just one thing—the distinctive blue-and-white earthenware still produced by the meticulous methods of old. Every piece of true Delftware is still hand-painted by skilled craftspeople.

ESSENTIALS

GETTING THERE   There are train and bus connections to Delft from Amsterdam, Rotterdam, and The Hague.

By car, Delft is just off of the A13, the main The Hague–Rotterdam expressway.

VISITOR INFORMATION   The **VVV office** is at Markt 83–85 in the center of town (☎ 015/212-6100; fax 015/215-8695). Open Monday through Friday from 9am to 5:30pm, Saturday from 9am to 5pm.

EXPLORING DELFT

The first thing to do here is park your car and walk! Although the town's layout allows easy driving, it's only by strolling the streets that you can absorb Delft's special ambiance. Supplement your walks with a leisurely tour of the canals via the numerous water taxis that operate during the summer.

Two church spires grace the Delft skyline. One belongs to the 14th-century ✪ **Nieuwe Kerk,** located at the market. Inside is the magnificent tomb of William the Silent, surrounded by 22 columns and decorated with figures representing Liberty, Justice, Valor, and Religion. The royal dead of the House of Orange-Nassau lie in a crypt beneath the remains of the founder of their line. There's a marvelous panoramic view of the town from the church tower.

The other, slightly leaning spire is attached to the ✪ **Oude Kerk** at Heilige Geestkerkhof. As the name implies, this is the oldest church in Delft, founded around 1200. The tower is embellished with four corner turrets, and inside are the tombs of the artist Jan Vermeer and Antoni van Leeuwenhoek, the inventor of the microscope.

Both churches are open Monday to Saturday, April through October from 9am to 6pm, and November through March 11am to 4pm. Admission is Dfl 4 ($2) for adults and Dfl 1.50 (75¢) for children, and the ticket is valid in both. Admission to the tower of the Nieuwe Kerk is Dfl 3 ($1.50) for adults and Dfl 1.50 (75¢) for children.

✪ **De Porceleyne Fles.** Rotterdamseweg 196. ☎ **015/256-0234.** Admission for tours Dfl 4 ($2). Mon–Sat 9am–5pm, Sun 9:30am–5pm. Closed Sun Nov–Mar.

The Delft Blue you came to town to find is made by a traditional and painstaking method at De Porceleyne Fles. Here you can watch the hand-painting of each item and see an audiovisual show that explains the entire process. Delft potters have been at it since they met the competition of Chinese porcelain imported by the East India Company. And if you thought the trademark blue-and-white colors were the only Delft, here is where you see exquisite multicolored patterns. Your purchases can be packed carefully and shipped home directly from this factory.

Lambert van Meerten Museum. Oude Delft 199. ☎ **015/260-2358.** Admission Dfl 3.50 ($1.75). Tues–Sat 10am–5pm, Sun 1–5pm.

You'll find the most fascinating collection of Delft earthenware, including lovely tiles, in this 19th-century mansion north of the market, near Prinsenhof.

Museum Paul Tétar van Elven. Koornmarkt 67 (just south of the market). ☎ **015/212-4206.** Admission Dfl 3.50 ($1.75) adults, Dfl 1.50 (75¢) children. Mid-Apr to Oct Tues–Sun 1–5pm. Closed Nov to mid-Apr.

The 19th-century artist, Van Elven (1823–96), lived and worked here, and the furnishings are still just as he left them. The 17th-century-style studio looks like it's ready for the artist to enter and pick up his brushes.

✪ **Prinsenhof Museum.** Entrance at St Agathaplein 1. ☎ **015/260-2358.** Admission Dfl 5 ($2.50). Tues–Sat 10am–5pm, Sun 1–5pm.

The Prinsenhof (Prince's Court), located on the banks of Delft's oldest canal, dates from the late 1400s and was originally a convent. This is where William the Silent elected to stay when in Delft, and where an assassin's bullets ended his life in 1584 (you can still see the bullet holes near the bottom of a staircase). Restoration has re-created the interior William would have known, and a museum preserves the record of Dutch struggles to throw off the yoke of Spanish occupation between 1568 and 1648. There are also impressive tapestries and paintings. This municipal museum also houses the **Nusantara Ethnographical Museum,** a stunning collection of ethnographical objects from Indonesia. Because Indonesia was a Dutch colony, Dutch academics have been specialists in this area for many years. The collection includes such beautiful objects as *wayang* shadow puppets and ceremonial attributes. It's a short walk north of the market, near the Oude Kerk, a 5-minute walk from the train station.

WHERE TO DINE

Food is served in the medieval manner—at moderate prices and in copious quantities—at **Stadsherberg De Mol,** Molslaan 104 (☎ **015/212-1343**), and

Delft

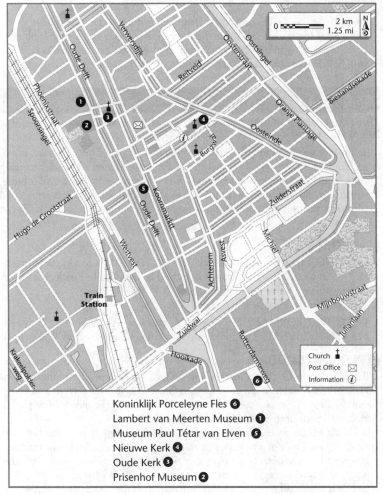

Koninklijk Porceleyne Fles ❻

Lambert van Meerten Museum ❶

Museum Paul Tétar van Elven ❺

Nieuwe Kerk ❹

Oude Kerk ❸

Prisenhof Museum ❷

there's live music with dancing as well. There's also good food at moderate prices, along with friendly, professional service at **Prinsenkelder,** Schoolstraat 11 (☎ **015/ 212-1860**), in the Prinsenhof. **La Fontanella,** Voldersgracht 8 (☎ **015/ 213-5929**), is a snazzy Italian cafe with inexpensive pizzas, omelets, and the like, as well as excellent coffee. These places are open from noon to 2pm and 6 to 10pm, and closed on either Monday or Wednesday.

✪ **Le Vieux Jean.** Heilige Geestkerkhof 3. ☎ **015/213-0433.** Main courses Dfl 29.50–39.50 ($14.75–$19.75); fixed-price menus Dfl 49.50–89.50 ($24.75–$44.75). Closed last 2 weeks in July, first week in August. AE, DC, MC, V. Tues–Fri noon–2:30pm, Tues–Sat 6–10pm. FRENCH.

The skillfully prepared dishes here draw from the provincial French tradition, using the freshest of top-quality ingredients. The setting is a historical churchyard, and you receive a warm and friendly welcome.

Spijshuis de Dis. Beestenmarkt 36. ☎ **015/213-1782.** Main courses Dfl 19.50–37.50 ($9.75–$18.75); fixed-price menu Dfl 32.50–52.50 ($16.25–$26.25). AE, DC, MC, V. Thurs–Tues 5–9:30pm. DUTCH.

Some of the best Dutch cooking in Delft is dished up in this atmospheric restaurant east of the market. Steaks are the specialty, but there's also a great lamb fillet. If you're feeling especially decadent, opt for the luscious dessert of vanilla ice cream with hot cherries, whipped cream, and cherry brandy.

5 Gouda

25km (17 miles) NE of Rotterdam; 25km (17 miles) E of The Hague; 24km (16½ miles) SE of Leiden; 25km (17 miles) E of Delft

You may know about its cheeses, but did you know that in Dutch its name is pronounced "Howdah" (with a guttural "h")? Try to come here on a Thursday morning (9am to noon) during July and August—that's when the lively cheese market brings farmers driving farm wagons painted with bright designs and piled high with round cheeses in their orange skins. It's an altogether different scene from the market in Alkmaar.

ESSENTIALS

GETTING THERE   There are train and bus connections to Gouda from The Hague, Amsterdam, Rotterdam, and Utrecht. The train and bus stations are north of the town center. For train information, call ☎ **06-9292.**

By car, Gouda is reached by A12 and A20.

VISITOR INFORMATION   The **VVV office** is at Markt 27 (☎ **0182/ 513-666;** fax 0182/583-210). Open Monday through Saturday from 9am to 5pm.

EXPLORING GOUDA

If you arrive on ✪ **cheese market day,** walk to the back of the **Stadhuis** (Town Hall), where you can sample of the famous Gouda cheese. This gray stone building, with its stepped gables and red shutters, is reputed to be the oldest Town Hall in Holland—parts of its Gothic facade date from 1449.

Gouda has been the center of a thriving **clay pipe industry** since the 17th century. One local style of pipe has a pattern on the bowl that's invisible when the pipe is new and only appears as the pipe is smoked and darkens—it's called a "mystery pipe," because the designs vary and the buyer never knows what the design will be. Gouda is also noted for its **candles.** Every year, from the middle of December, the Markt and the Town Hall are festively lit by candles.

✪ **Adrie Moerings Pottery and Pipemaker (Pottenbakkerij & Pijpenmakerij).** Peperstraat 76. ☎ **0182/512-842.** Free admission. Mon–Fri 9am–5pm, Sat 11am–5pm.

This interesting factory, just a 5-minute walk from Markt, presents fascinating demonstrations of the centuries-old craft of making beautiful pottery and clay pipes. You can watch the work going on and visit the pottery exposition and viewing room. This is a good place to pick up a uniquely Dutch memento of your visit.

Catharina Gasthuis Museum. Oosthaven 10. ☎ **0182/588-440.** Admission Dfl 4.50 ($2.25), ticket also valid in De Moriaan Museum. Mon–Sat 10am–5pm, Sun noon–5pm.

This 1665 mansion, a former hospital near Sint Janskerk, houses Gouda's municipal museum. The jewel of its collections is a gold chalice that Countess Jacqueline of Bavaria presented to the Society of Archers in 1465. Its whereabouts were unknown for over a century before it was recovered in the Town Hall's attic and

Gouda

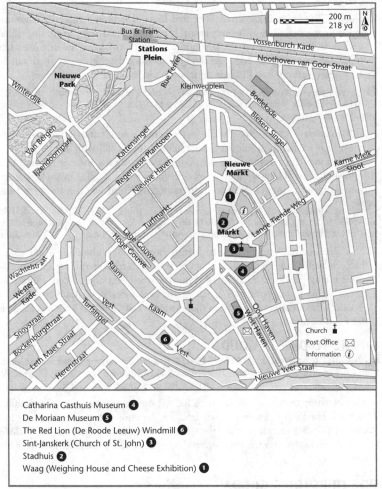

brought here. There are also colorful guild relics, antique furniture, and a terra-cotta plaque whose Latin inscription proclaims that the humanist Erasmus may have been born in Rotterdam but was conceived in Gouda. There's limited wheel-chair access here.

De Moriaan Museum. Westhaven 29. ☎ **0182/588-440.** Admission Dfl 4.50 ($2.25), ticket also valid in the Catharina Gasthuis Museum. Mon–Fri 10am–5pm, Sat 10am–12:30pm and 1:30–5pm, Sun and holidays noon–5pm.

During the 18th century, this was the home of a Gouda merchant who sold spices, tobacco, coffee, and tea. The interior of his shop remained unchanged over the centuries. Going through to the back rooms, you'll find a large and interesting pipe collection. Upstairs is Gouda's answer to Delftware: a beautiful display of *plateel*, a colorful local-made pottery.

✪ **The Red Lion (De Roode Leeuw) Windmill.** Vest 65 (west of Markt). ☎ **0182/522-041.** Admission Dfl 2.50 ($1.45). Thurs 9am–2pm and Sat 9am–4pm.

This 1727 grain mill, known as "The Red Lion," has been completely renovated and is now grinding away happily again. It's an impressive sight to see the mill at work—you can go out on the platform and watch the vanes swish past, while inside, the huge wooden cogwheels and beams work the millstones. There's also a shop where you can buy all kinds of flour ground in this mill.

✪ **Sint-Janskerk (Church of St John).** Achter de Kerk 16 (south of Markt). ☎ **0182/512-684.** Admission Dfl 3.50 ($1.75). Mar–Oct Mon–Sat 9am–5pm; Nov–Feb Mon–Sat 10am–4pm.

This majestic 15th-century church is Holland's longest, and it holds some of Europe's most beautiful stained-glass windows—64 in all, with a total of 2,412 panels. Some date back as far as the mid-1500s. To see the contrast between that stained-glass art of long ago and the work being carried out today, take a look at the most recent window, no. 28A, commemorating the World War II years in Holland.

✪ **Waag (Weighing House and Cheese Exhibition).** Markt 35–36. ☎ **0182/529-996.** Admission Dfl 5 ($2.90) for adults, Dfl 3.50 ($2) for children under 12, free admission for children weighing less than 40 pounds. Apr–Oct Tues–Sun 1–5pm, Thurs 10am–5pm.

This monumental Weighing House, dating from 1668, is the pride of the town. The exhibition inside tells the story of cheese using ultramodern interactive audiovisual media. You'll get to know all about the manufacturing process, from grass through cow through milk to cheese, as well as a chance to taste the finished product. The museum also explains the importance of Gouda as a center of Dutch dairy production.

WHERE TO DINE IN GOUDA

Mallemolen. Oosthaven 72. ☎ **0182/515-430.** Reservations recommended. Main courses from Dfl 37.50 ($18.75); fixed-price dinner Dfl 55 ($27.50) for 3 courses. AE, DC, MC, V. Tues–Fri midday–2pm, Tues–Sun 5pm–"until the last guest departs." FRENCH.

This excellent traditional restaurant is located on what's known as "Rembrandt's corner." There's even an ancient windmill on the same street. The restaurant has an Old Dutch atmosphere, although the cuisine is chiefly French. Dishes include fresh, homemade pasta with salmon, and tournedos with goose liver in a red-wine sauce.

SIDE TRIPS FROM GOUDA

There are a couple of places of interest within easy driving distance of Gouda that can be worked into a day's excursion.

OUDEWATER Only about 8 miles east of Gouda is a charming little village called Oudewater. You'd never guess that back in the 1500s it was the scene of some of Europe's most horrifying witch trials. During this time women were weighed on scales to determine whether or not they were witches—if they weighed little enough to fly through the air supported only by a broomstick, they were guilty. So many women were weighed and convicted of witchcraft that the town's reputation for having accurate scales was in serious jeopardy. To remedy that bad press, the town fathers devised a system of judging accused witches by having them stand on scales clad in nothing but a paper costume and paper broom. Present for this "trial" were the mayor, the alderman, the weighmaster, and the local midwife. When the weighmaster had finished juggling his weights and balancing the scales, he could then proclaim with confidence that the accused could not possibly be a witch, and a certificate was issued to that effect. For obvious reasons, Europe's accused witches flocked here in droves!

Nowadays, if you have some doubt about anyone in your party (or yourself!), between May and September you can step on the scales in the **Waag** (Weigh House) and—provided you're not too skinny—walk away with your very own certificate.

As you walk through the quaint streets of this village, take a look at the storks' nests on the **Stadhuis** (Town Hall) roof—the big birds, traditionally associated with the arrival of a new child, have been nesting here for over 3 centuries.

SCHOONHOVEN   This little town southeast of Gouda is where they make most of the silver objects and souvenirs you see around the country. The small workshops here welcome visitors, and it's fascinating to see the skill required to produce the delicate work. Demonstrations take place in the **Edelambachtshuis**, on the main canal.

When you're walking past the lovely old **Stadhuis** (Town Hall) dating from 1452, give a thought to the poor "witch" who never made it to those scales in Oudewater (see above) and was burned to death at the spot now marked by a circle of stones on the bridge nearby.

Also in Schoonhoven, the **Nederlands Goud, Zilver, en Klokkenmuseum** (Dutch Gold, Silver, and Clocks Museum), Kazerneplein 4 (☎ **0182/385-612**), has a wonderful collection of old clocks, as well as gold and silver objects of great beauty. Open Tuesday through Sunday from noon to 5pm; admission is Dfl 4.50 ($2.25).

6 Leiden

20km (12 miles) NE of The Hague; 44km (27 miles) N of Rotterdam; 32km (20 miles) NW of Gouda; 30km (19 miles) NE of Delft

A visit to Leiden is in the nature of a pilgrimage (pardon the pun) for Americans, for it was here that the Pilgrim Fathers found refuge during the long years they waited to sail to a fresh beginning in the New World. Their sojourn was, however, but one small incident in Leiden's long history.

For the Dutch, the high point in Leiden's history is surely its display of heroism during the 5-month siege by the Spanish in 1574. Thousands of its residents perished, and the food situation became so intolerable that the mayor offered his own body to be used as nourishment for the starving population—talk about sacrifice! His offer was not accepted, but his memory is honored by a town park in which his statue stands.

The Dutch fleet finally rescued Leiden on October 3, after a dramatic advance over flooded fields as dikes were broken to open up a watery route to the beleaguered citizens. From that terrible siege came one of Holland's most beloved national dishes, *hutspot* (hotpot), so named for the bubbling kettle of stew left behind by fleeing Spaniards (the kettle is now ensconced in the Lakenhal Museum). If you should be in Leiden on October 3, you'll see the anniversary of the Spanish defeat observed as *haring en witte brood* (herring and loaves of white bread) are distributed just as they were in 1574.

In recognition of Leiden's courage, William the Silent rewarded the city with a choice between freedom from taxation and the founding of a university in town. Perhaps to the consternation of some present-day residents, those 16th-century residents chose the university, Holland's first, which today is a leader in the fields of medicine and law.

Leiden is also known in artistic circles as the birthplace of Rembrandt, Jan Steen, and Lucas van Leyden.

ESSENTIALS

GETTING THERE   There are frequent train and bus connections to Leiden from points around Holland. Both stations are located to the northwest of the town center (about a 10-minute walk).

By car, Leiden is reached via A4 and N11.

VISITOR INFORMATION   The **VVV office** is just opposite the train station at Stationsplein 210 (☎ **0900/222-2333;** fax 071/512-5318). Open Monday through Friday from 9am to 5:30pm, Saturday from 10am to 2pm. Ask about guided tours during the summer months, as well as the self-guided walking-tour brochure.

EXPLORING LEIDEN

To touch base with those courageous but humble Pilgrim Fathers, pick up the VVV brochure **A Pilgrimage Through Leiden: A Walk in the Footsteps of the Pilgrim Fathers.** The walk starts at the **Lodewijkskerk,** which was used as a meeting place for the cloth guild. William Bradford, who later became governor of New Plymouth, was a member of this guild. The walk takes you past the house on William Brewstersteeg (formerly Herensteeg, marked by a plaque), where William Brewster's Pilgrim Press published the religious views that so angered the Church of England. Plaques at **Sint-Pieterskerk** (in a small square off Kloksteeg) also memorialize the Pilgrim Fathers, particularly the Rev. Jon Robinson, who was forced to stay behind because of illness and is buried in this church (an almshouse, the Jean Pesijnhofje, now occupies the house in which he died). Special Thanksgiving Day services are held each year in honor of the little band of refugees who worshiped here. Another notable monument in the city is **De Burcht,** a man-made fortified mound that provides a great view of the city center's rooftops.

✪ **American Pilgrim Museum.** Beschuitsteeg 9. ☎ **071/512-2413.** Dfl 3 ($1.50). Wed–Sat 1–5pm.

This museum occupies a 16th-century house where one of the Pilgrim families may have lodged. Here you can study a variety of documents relating to the Pilgrims' 11 years of residence in Leiden. The center also supplies a brochure that describes a self-guided walking tour of the city. The tour takes about an hour and leads you to the most important sites and monuments.

De Lakenhal Museum. Oude Singel 28. ☎ **071/516-5360.** Admission Dfl 5 ($2.50). Tues–Fri 10am–5pm, Sat–Sun noon–5pm; closed Jan 1 and Oct 3.

This fine 17th-century guild hall is now home to Leiden's municipal museum. Its collection of paintings by Dutch artists of the 16th and 17th centuries includes works by Lucas van Leyden, Rembrandt, Steen, and Dou. Temporary modern art exhibitions are also organized regularly. The cloth merchants guild (the original occupants of the building) is represented in historical exhibits; on the first floor you'll find the guild's splendid meeting hall.

Botanical Gardens (Hortus Botanicus). Rapenburg 73. ☎ **071/527-7249.** Admission Dfl 5 ($2.50) adults, Dfl 2.50 ($1.25) children under 12. Mon–Sat 9am–5pm, Sun and holidays 10am–5pm, except for the Christmas–New Year's period.

Leiden

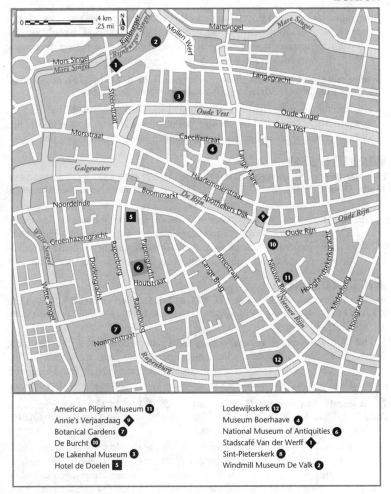

American Pilgrim Museum **11**
Annie's Verjaardaag **9**
Botanical Gardens **7**
De Burcht **10**
De Lakenhal Museum **3**
Hotel de Doelen **5**

Lodewijkskerk **12**
Museum Boerhaave **4**
National Museum of Antiquities **6**
Stadscafé Van der Werff **1**
Sint-Pieterskerk **8**
Windmill Museum De Valk **2**

The Hortus is located near the Weddesteeg, the small street where Rembrandt was born. This garden was established by students and professors of the University of Leiden in 1590. Researchers grew tropical trees and plants such as banana plants, ferns, and flesh-eating plants in greenhouses. Many of the old specimens are still thriving today. The original garden has been reconstructed in the Clusius Garden. There's also a minimalist Japanese-style garden.

✪ **National Museum of Antiquities (Rijksmuseum van Oudheden).** Rapenburg 28. ☎ **071/516-3163.** Admission Dfl 7 ($3.50). Tues–Fri 10am–5pm, Sat–Sun and holidays noon–5pm; closed Jan 1, Oct 3, and Dec 25.

No visit to Leiden is complete without seeing this museum, the most comprehensive of its kind in the Netherlands. It opened in 1818, and over the years has acquired an impressive collection of Egyptian, Near East, and Greek and Roman artifacts. It's still a center for archeological research. The first exhibit to catch your eye will be the magnificent Egyptian Temple of Taffeh from the 1st century A.D.—

the museum's pride and glory. Greek and Roman sculpture is well represented, and there are some beautiful examples of Greek decorated ceramics. The top floor provides an overview of the archaeological finds in the Netherlands from prehistoric times to the early Middle Ages.

✪ **Windmill Museum De Valk.** 2e Binnenvestgracht 1. ☎ **071/516-5353.** Admission Dfl 5 ($2.50) adults, Dfl 3 ($1.50) children. Tues–Sat 10am–5pm, Sun 1–5pm.

This small museum, located in a monumental windmill nicknamed "The Falcon," contains exhibits dedicated to various types of windmills. The focus is on the history of grinding grain and on the construction and workings of a corn mill.

WHERE TO STAY

Hotel de Doelen. Rapenburg 2, 2311 EV Leiden. ☎ **071/512-0527.** Fax 071/512-8453. 15 rms. MINIBAR TV TEL. Dfl 140–225 ($70–$112.50) double. Rates include buffet breakfast. AE, DC, MC, V.

This hotel is situated on one of the most beautiful and stately canals in old Leiden. Part of the building was formerly a patrician's house, dating from 1435. The higher-priced rooms have open hearths; with their high ceilings, they're grand as well as comfortable. There's a wonderful painted ceiling fresco in the breakfast room.

WHERE TO DINE

Annie's Verjaardag. Oude Rijn 1a. ☎ **071/512-6358.** Main courses Dfl 17.50–32.50 ($8.75–$16.25). No credit cards. Open Sun–Thurs 10am–1am, Fri–Sat 10am–2am. DUTCH/CONTINENTAL.

This lively restaurant is at canal-side level. Its vaulted cellars are a favorite dining spot for students and locals, who sometimes spill out onto the terrace in fine weather. The view is equally enchanting when the canals are frozen. The dinner menu is simple but wholesome. During the day you can order sandwiches or *tapas*.

✪ **Stadscafé Van der Werff.** Steenstraat 2. ☎ **071/513-0335.** Main courses Dfl 28.50–35 ($16.50–$20.30). AE, DC, MC, V. Open daily 10:30am–5pm and 6–10pm. CONTINENTAL.

This relaxed cafe-restaurant is located on the edge of the old town in a grand 1930s villa. It's popular with students and ordinary citizens. Main courses might include veal with apricots or roast lamb with hazelnuts. If you're not hungry, you can while away your evening just having a drink and reading a paper. The cafe section is open until 1am.

AN EXCURSION FROM LEIDEN

About 12km (7½ miles) east of Leiden, near the town of Alphen aan de Rijn, you'll find an unusual and fascinating theme park. To get there, take the train to Alphen aan de Rijn and then bus 197; or by car take the N11 from Leiden towards Bodegraven.

Archeon. Archeonlaan 1, Alphen aan de Rijn. ☎ **0172/447-744.** Admission Dfl 20 ($10) adults, Dfl 15 ($7.50) children 4–11, children under 4 free. Daily Apr–June Tues–Sun 10am–5pm; Sept–Oct Wed–Sun 10am–5pm; July–Aug 10am–6pm.

This archaeological theme park takes you through the history of the earth and humankind in a few hours. Your journey through time starts in the Expo building, where the story of the planet from its creation to the arrival of mankind is outlined. In the park itself you can follow the trail of human development and join people in their everyday activities through the ages. You'll find, for example, a stone-age settlement populated by hunter-gathers, and you can walk through a Roman-era village on your way to the amphitheater to watch a contest between gladiators. The last stop is a medieval town, where you can see artisans at work in their shops and be taken to the marketplace by a group of beggars and musicians to watch a farce unfold. The park is fun and educational for the whole family, not just the kids.

17

The Northern Provinces

The country's northern provinces—Friesland, Groningen, and Drenthe—were home to the Netherlands's earliest settlers. Friesland, in particular, is so ancient as to be almost another world, complete with customs and a language all its own. In the north, this province is dotted by *terpen,* huge earthen mounds that were used to escape from floodwaters before the discovery of dikes. Elsewhere, Friesland is a landscape of charming little villages and farmlands. In the west you'll find a cluster of lakes; in the southeast, woodlands and hilly moorland covered in heather. From its farms have come the world-renowned Frisian cattle and the lovely black Frisian horses, which are much sought after by circuses worldwide because they're so responsive to music.

Four of the string of Wadden Islands off of the Dutch coast belong to the province of Friesland: from southwest to northeast these are Vlieland, Terschelling, Ameland, and Schiermonikoog. The Dutch treasure these small islands as romantic getaways. The southernmost island, Texel, is part of the province of Noord-Holland (see chapter 15).

Groningen province may not be as varied as Friesland, but it also has its share of interesting historical sites, such as its own *terpen* and the sequential rows of dikes that gradually move seaward. The past is perhaps most eloquent at places like the Menkemaborg manor house in Uithuizen, or the fortress town of Bourtange. Groningen's eponymous capital city, on the other hand, is distinctly present day. It offers the spanking new Groninger Museum, as well as the vibrant atmosphere of a university town.

In lovely, sparsely populated Drenthe, 20th-century oil wells are hidden behind stands of trees to lessen their impact on the scenic beauty of lakes, forests, moors, and picturesque villages. The province is also home to prehistoric *hunebedden* (giants' beds), huge boulders that probably served early inhabitants as burial mounds.

1 Friesland

The major towns of Friesland are arranged so that you can tour the province with ease, stopping overnight in good, moderately priced hotels or selecting as a home base the beautiful château that is now a luxury inn, centrally located in Beetsterzwaag.

You can, of course, plot your own way from a map, but a much better idea is to go directly to the VVV office in Leeuwarden and pick up one of their carefully planned **tour guides.** The VVV office can even arrange do-it-yourself **car** or **bicycle** tours with prebooked accommodations each night. There is one route in particular that has made the province famous: the loop of the Elfstedentocht, or Eleven Cities' Race, a traditional skating race that follows the canals through 11 towns in the province. This race is still held whenever the canals freeze solidly enough (which isn't very often), but a more recent trend is to follow the same 200km (120-mile) course on bicycle—along the sides of the canals—in summer months. Special maps and accommodations recommendations are available from any VVV tourist office in the province. You'll receive a certificate for your efforts if you collect all the stamps at specified posts in each of the towns.

Road signs in Friesland are in two languages, one of which you will have not seen elsewhere—the ancient Frisian language. Frisian broke off from German long before the Dutch language followed suit, and is today still spoken by some 70% of the Frisian population. These fiercely independent people also have their own flag, their own coat of arms, and their own national anthem. Which is not to say they're not Dutch: They are, but *first* they are Frisian.

Friesland's independent spirit stood the United States in good stead. It was here, in the capital city of Leeuwarden, that documents were signed making Holland the first country to officially recognize the new nation overseas.

Boat Races in Friesland

During 2 weeks in July, Friesland comes under the spell of the skûtsje sailing races between traditional flat-bottomed barges. These boats, about 65 feet long, were originally used for transporting goods on inland waterways and across the IJsselmeer lake. The races are held on a different Frisian water body each day, sometimes on the "inland" lakes near Sneek, sometimes on the IJsselmeer from the port of Stavoren, and sometimes on the Wadden Sea off Harlingen. About 14 boats compete each time. They don't look very maneuverable, but the crews know how to handle their skûtsje and have an extensive arsenal of tricks designed to outwit their rivals. The competition is fierce and, especially when the wind is difficult, the races are a formidable spectacle. **VVV Friesland** (☎ **0900/3202-4060**) can provide information on dates and places, and you can also contact the race organizers directly: **Sintrale Kommisje,** J. van Huizumstraat 11, 8551 NM Woudsend (☎ **0514/596-666**).

EXPLORING FRIESLAND

The only sensible way to explore the province is by car or bike. The best plan is to make a circular swing through Friesland's most interesting towns and villages, beginning in the capital, Leeuwarden. From there, proceed to Franeker, Harlingen, Makkum, and Hindeloopen. As a side trip, or on the way back to Leeuwarden, consider heading to Bolsward to visit the Forefathers' Heritage Museum Route.

Exploring this sparsely populated province without a car is difficult. The train between Leeuwarden and Stavoren connects towns in southwest Friesland. Buses between towns often operate hourly, and generally connect with train services. For public transportation information call ☎ **0900/9292.**

LEEUWARDEN

168km (105 miles) NE of Amsterdam

ESSENTIALS

GETTING THERE   There are good **train** connections to Leeuwarden from around the country. Trains arrive every hour from Amsterdam Centraal Station. The train and **bus** stations in Leeuwarden adjoin each other at Stationsplein.

By **car** from Amsterdam, there are two alternative routes, both of which take about the same amount of time. Take the E231 east, then the A6 north through Flevoland to Heerenveen, then northwest to Leeuwarden on the N32; or travel through Noord-Holland province on the A8 from Amsterdam to Zaandam, then the E22 north across IJsselmeer on the Afsluitdijk, then northeast on the N31 and A31 to Leeuwarden.

VISITOR INFORMATION   The **VVV office** for both Leeuwarden and Friesland Province is next door to the train station at Stationsplein 1, Leeuwarden (☎ **0900/202-4060;** fax 058/215-3593). It's open Monday through Friday from 9am to 5:30pm, Saturday 10am to 2pm. The staff is very helpful and can provide directions for several interesting day trips from Leeuwarden, among them the *Terpen* tour to see the earthen mounds built to escape flood waters, the *Wouden* tour through Friesland's beautiful woodlands, the lakes tour, and the "Forefathers Heritage Route."

EXPLORING THE CITY

Before setting off to explore the rest of Friesland, take time to look around its capital city. Like most Dutch cities, Leeuwarden is best seen on foot. The VVV has an excellent walking-tour guide, **A Walk Through the Town of Leeuwarden,** that will take you to major points of interest.

✪ **Frisian Museum and Museum of the Resistance.** Turfmarkt 11. ☎ **058/212-3001.** Admission Dfl 7.50 ($3.75). Mon–Sat 11am–5pm, Sun 1–5pm.

Part of this fine museum occupies the Kanselarij, the seat of the Frisian High Court of Justice during the reign of King Philip II of Spain (1555–1581). Here you can trace the history of the Frisians by way of prehistoric artifacts dating back to the Ice Age, as well as medieval and Renaissance treasures. A subterranean tunnel takes you to the Eysinga House, the 18th-century home of a local nobleman, where the museum started in 1881. The rooms on the ground floor have been restored to their appearance when Mr. Eysinga lived here with his family. On the second floor is a series of stylized period rooms and costumes from the 19th century. The third floor holds a collection of colorfully painted traditional furniture from Hindeloopen. There's also a gallery of paintings, including Rembrandt's portrait of his Frisian wife, Saskia (they were married in the nearby village of St Anna Parochie in 1634). Finally, don't miss the new exhibit on the spy Mata Hari (see box below).

In the attics of the Kanselarij you'll find the very moving ✪ **Frisian Museum of the Resistance.** Its collection of photos and personal mementos documents the heroism of the Frisian people during the Nazi occupation in World War II. There's detailed information available in English about the Frisian resistance and the rigors of daily life during World War II. After a visit to this museum, you're sure to see the Frisian farmer in his fields in a different light.

Het Princessehof National Museum of Ceramics. Grote Kerkstraat 11. ☎ **058/212-7438.** Admission Dfl 6.50 ($3.25) adults, Dfl 3 ($1.50) children. Mon–Sat 10am–5pm, Sun and public holidays 2–5pm.

In the 18th century, this elegant neoclassical building in the town center was the home of Princess Maria Louise of Hessen-Kassel, William IV's mother; one of the rooms is preserved just as it was in her time. The museum also holds the largest collection of Dutch tiles in the world, as well as Spanish, Portuguese, and Persian work. There's a marvelous collection of Chinese porcelain and ceramics, too.

Provinciehuis (Provincial House). Tweebaksmarkt 52. Free admission. Visiting times vary: inquire at the VVV office (☎ **0900/202-4060**).

Here you'll find a bit of New York State, in the form of a bronze plaque that the DeWitt Historical Society of Ithaca, New York, presented to the people of Leeuwarden in 1909 in gratitude for their having been the first to vote for Holland's recognition of the United States in 1782. There's also a letter written by John Adams in 1783 expressing his personal thanks. Another document of interest to Americans relates to one Petrus Stuiffsandt—the same Peter Stuyvesant who had such an important role in America's beginnings. He was born in Scherpenzeel, a town in Friesland.

ESPECIALLY FOR THE KIDS

Aqualutra Otter Park. Kleine Wielen 4 (towards Dokkum, about 2.5 miles [4km] from Leeuwarden town center). ☎ **0511/431-214.** Admission Dfl 12.50 ($6.25) adults, Dfl 8.50

Mata Hari

The most famous figure in Leeuwarden's history was born here in 1876 as Margaretha Zelle, but became better known under the name Mata Hari. Margaretha grew up in a wealthy family, and at the age of 19 married an army officer and left for the Dutch East Indies. She returned to Holland in 1902.

With her marriage falling apart, Margaretha left for Paris, where she performed as an Oriental dancer. There she adopted the name "Mata Hari"—meaning "eye of the day" or "sun" in Malaysian. Her nude dancing became a sensation. Many of her affairs were with military officers and she eventually became a double agent, but her naïveté and yarn-spinning imagination led to her downfall. She was executed by the French for pro-German spying activities in 1917.

The **Frisian Museum** (see above) has devoted a new exhibition space to tracing the twists and turns of Margaretha's complex and mysterious life. The highlight is a re-creation of a Parisian salon from her day.

($4.25) children 4–11. Apr–Oct daily 9:30am–5:30pm, Nov–Mar daily 10:30am–4:30pm. By public transportation take bus 10, 13, 50, or 62 from the train station.

Otters are such adorable creatures that they delight both young and old. The Aqualutra Otter Park gives you the chance to observe north-European otters in their natural environment, in the water and on land. The park is in the middle of a recreation area where you can also enjoy water sports such as sailing and sailboarding.

WHERE TO STAY

The VVV office can supply names of town and country homes that welcome bed-and-breakfast guests. Rates start at Dfl 30 ($15) per person.

✪ **Bilderberg Oranje Hotel.** Stationsweg 4, 8901 BL Leeuwarden. ☎ **058/212-6241.** Fax 058/212-1441. 78 units. A/C TV TEL. Dfl 210 ($110) double. Breakfast Dfl 27.50 ($13.75). AE, DC, MC, V. Limited parking available on street.

You'd never suspect that this beautiful hotel is actually over a century old, so successful has its modernization been. It's located near the train station, and within an easy walk of everything you'll want to see in Leeuwarden. The management is genuinely friendly, and the staff goes out of its way to make you feel at home. The guest rooms are quite luxurious. Lots of locals come to the bright, moderately priced restaurant and cozy bar. There's also a formal gourmet restaurant (see "Where to Dine," below).

Hotel de Pauw. Stationsweg 10 (across the street from the train station), 8911 AH Leeuwarden. ☎ **058/212-3651.** Fax 058/216-0793. 30 units (none with private bathroom). Dfl 80–110 ($40–$55) double. MC, V. Limited parking available on street.

This old-fashioned budget hotel features Old Dutch lobby furnishings and a wood-paneled bar. Its basic rooms come with and without private showers (all toilets are down the hall). All the rooms are quite adequate, but of varying standards. There's a good restaurant on the premises that serves lunch and dinner at moderate prices.

A LUXURY CHÂTEAU NEARBY

✪ **Hotel Lauswolt.** Van Harinxmaweg 10, 9244 CJ Beetsterzwaag (28 miles [45km] from Leeuwarden). ☎ **0512/381-245.** Fax 0512/381-496. 58 units. TV TEL. Dfl 295 ($147.50) double. AE, DC, MC, V. Take the N31 from Leeuwarden to Drachten, then join the A7 expressway, heading towards Heerenveen, and take the Beetsterzwaag exit. Pass through the center of the village of Beetsterzwaag, and look for the Hotel Lauswolt on its outskirts, on the right.

I love this gracious three-story château. It's located on the edge of the typical Frisian village of Beetsterzwaag. Green lawns and huge shady trees surround the place. The grounds contain an 18-hole golf course, tennis courts, and any number of beautiful forest walks. The decor throughout the château, in both public rooms and guest rooms, is one of quiet elegance. The high level of service, swimming pool, and sauna add to the attractions of this lovely place. The restaurant enjoys a top reputation throughout this part of Holland and is a member of the prestigious Alliance Gastronomique Néerlandaise. The hotel offers wheelchair access.

WHERE TO DINE

Leeuwarden has several very good restaurants. The large student population here means that it's also packed with less expensive eateries. A ramble along the Nieuwestad canal is sure to reveal some tantalizing choices.

You'll find good Frisian specialties at moderate prices at **Onder de Luifel,** Stationsweg 6 (☎ **058/212-9013**), open Monday through Saturday from 9am to 8pm. The bistro **Herberg de Waag,** Nieuwestad 148B (☎ **058/213-7250**), in the atmospheric 16th-century Weigh House, has local specialties as well as more international fare, and in summer you can be served on the terrace overlooking the canal that runs along the main shopping street. The bistro is open Monday through Saturday from 10am to 9:30pm.

✪ **Restaurant l'Orangerie.** Stationsweg 4 (near the train station). ☎ **058/212-6241.** Main courses Dfl 29.50–46.50 ($14.75–$23.25); fixed-price menus Dfl 49.50–Dfl 59.50 ($28.90–$34.70). AE, DC, MC, V. Mon–Fri noon–3pm, daily 6–9:30pm. FRENCH.

The restaurant of the modern Bilderberg Oranje Hotel is sophisticated in both ambiance and service. Its dishes, which are mostly French, are beautifully prepared with the freshest ingredients. The presentation and the professional, friendly manner of the staff match the high standards of the food. Try the unusual salmon steak fried in sesame oil and served with squid ink tagliatelle, and finish your meal with the cooling melon sorbet floating in a plate of melon soup.

✪ **Hotel Lauswolt.** Van Harinxmaweg 10. ☎ **0512/381-245.** Reservations required. Fixed-price lunch Dfl 30–62.50 ($17.50–$36.40); dinner Dfl 75–115 ($43.75–$67). AE, DC, MC, V. Daily noon–2pm and 6:30–9:30pm. FRENCH.

This lovely château restaurant is well worth the drive. You'll dine by candlelight in a gracious paneled dining room overlooking a garden. The menu is mostly French. The mouth-watering dishes include a lasagna with black truffles and truffle sauce, and grilled sweetbreads with almonds and garlic. There's also an exceptionally good wine cellar.

To get to the hotel, take the N31 southeast from Leeuwarden to Drachten, then join the A7 expressway, heading towards Heerenveen, and take Exit 28 for Beetsterzwaag. Pass through Beetsterzwaag village, and about 200m (215 yards) after the sign indicating the end of the village, you'll find the hotel on the right. The distance from Leeuwarden is 32km (20 miles).

FRANEKER
17km (10.5 miles) W of Leeuwarden

In this enchanting little town, stop to visit the ✪ **Eise Eisinga Planetarium,** Eise Eisingastraat 3 (☎ **0517/393-070**). This simple house was the home of a woolcomber, who for 7 years in the late 1700s spent his leisure hours building a replica of the planetary system. Guides are on hand to explain his works, which are amazingly accurate. The place is open from May through September Monday to Saturday 10am to 12:30pm and 1:30 to 5pm, Sunday 1 to 5pm. Admission is Dfl 5 ($2.50).

HARLINGEN
29km (18 miles) W of Leeuwarden; 120km (18 miles) NE of Amsterdam

This picture-postcard-pretty little harbor town sits beside the Wadden Sea, which separates the mainland from the offshore barrier islands of ✪ **Terschelling** and **Vlieland.** These islands' wide beaches and wild natural beauty draw vacationers every summer, and bird sanctuaries attract a host of feathered visitors as well.

ESSENTIALS
GETTING THERE   By **car** from Amsterdam, take the A7 (E22) north via Hoorn and the Afsluitdijk (Enclosing Dike) across the mouth of the IJsselmeer, then the N31 from the Friesland shore to Harlingen. The distance is about 120km (75 miles).

Frequent **trains** to Harlingen run from Leeuwarden. Services coincide with **ferry** departures; shuttle **buses** operate between the train station and the ferry terminal.

VISITOR INFORMATION   VVV **Harlingen** is located at Voorstraat 34 (☎ **0800/919-1999;** fax 0517/415-176), in the town center.

EXPLORING HARLINGEN
Harlingen is a maze of tiny canals filled with fishing boats and lined with gabled canal houses. See the seafaring exhibits at the **Hannemahuis Museum,** Voorstraat 56 (☎ 0517/413-658). It's open April through June and mid-September through October, Monday to Friday 1:30 to 5pm; July through mid-September, Tuesday to Saturday 10am to 5pm, Sunday 1:30to 5pm. Also stop in at the **Harlinger Pottery and Tile Factory** at Voorstraat 84 (☎ **0517/415-362**) (open during shop hours throughout the year) for a taste of tile-painting in progress.

WHERE TO STAY & DINE
Hotel Anna Casparii. Noorderhaven 67–71, 8861 AL Harlingen. ☎ **0517/412-065.** Fax 0517/414-540. 15 units (10 with bathroom). MINIBAR TV TEL. Dfl 95 ($47.50) double without bathroom, Dfl 125 ($62.50) double with bathroom. AE, DC, MC, V. Limited parking available on street.

This charming little canal-house hotel on the edge of the harbor has comfortable and attractive guest rooms. Ask for one with a view of the sea. There's also a very good, moderately priced restaurant here, specializing in seafood fresh from the boats that come into this fishing village.

TERSCHELLING ISLAND
Terschelling is the most accessible and popular of the Wadden Islands. It occupies a thin strip of land, 30km (19 miles) long and an average of 3.5km (2 miles) wide. The ferry arrives at West-Terschelling, the island's capital.

ESSENTIALS
GETTING THERE   Rederij Doeksen (☎ 0562/442-141) runs three ferry crossings per day in each direction from Harlingen to Terschelling, with additional services in the summer. The trip takes 1½ hours and costs Dfl 41.25 ($20.65), half

Walking on the Wadden Sea

At low tide, the Wadden Sea, between the northern coast of Holland and the **Wadden Islands,** virtually disappears. The muddy seabed becomes visible, and sea birds feast on mollusks in the sand. At times like these, the Wadden Islands seem even closer to the mainland, and if you feel like walking the mud flats, you can join a Wadden Walking trip and plow your way across to one of the islands. **Don't attempt this without an official guide; with one it is perfectly safe.**

Several companies, both in Groningen and Friesland, organize guided trips from May through early October. These range from a relatively easy round-trip on the flats, to more difficult walks to the islands. Wear shorts and close fitting, ankle high shoes or boots. The trips are very popular; groups are often as large as 75 to 100 people, with about seven guides to look after you. Weather permitting, you start walking at ebb tide, which can be at the crack of dawn. Soon the safe mainland looks far away, and you may feel lost in the middle of a salty mire trying to suck your feet in deeper with every step. But you'll get used to it, and your attention will be drawn to the unusual landscape as you realize that this is actually the bottom of a sea that you're walking on, and that in a few hours all this will have disappeared under water again. If you're lucky, you might encounter some seals gallivanting in pools left by the retreating tide or sunbathing on the flats. When you finally reach the island, you'll have to wait for high tide to be able to go back by boat.

Advance booking is necessary, and prices range from around Dfl 15 to Dfl 45 ($7.50–22.50) per person. Longer trips can take about 8 hours (including the wait for the boat). For information and reservations, contact the **Wadloopcentrum Pieterburen** (☎ 0595/528-300) in Pieterburen (Groningen), or **Wadloopcentrum Friesland** (☎ 0518/451-491) in Holwerd (Friesland).

price for children aged 4 to 11. A faster hydrofoil crossing (subject to the weather) costs an additional Dfl 7.50 ($3.75) each way. Taking your car to any of these islands is possible but not encouraged; the cost is Dfl 27 ($13.50) per 50cm (20 inches) of car! If you're traveling by train, the most economical option is to buy an all-inclusive **Waddenbiljet** ticket from the NS (Dutch Railways), covering all transportation costs to the island of your choice and allowing stops on the outward and return journeys.

VISITOR INFORMATION   The **VVV office** at West-Terschelling overlooks the harbor at Willem Barentszkade 19a, West-Terschelling (☎ 0562/443-000; fax 0562/442-875). It's open Monday through Friday 9:30am to 5:30pm, Saturday 11am to 1pm and 4 to 5:30pm. The staff will supply walking and cycling maps, and information on guided tours and accommodation.

SEEING THE SIGHTS

There are many opportunities to enjoy Terschelling's natural assets—beaches, dunes, bird reserves, and woodlands. **De Boschplaat** nature reserve, an internationally recognized bird sanctuary, occupies almost half the island. During breeding times (mid-March through mid-August) access is limited.

In the third week of June, theater lovers throng to the island for the annual **Oerol Festival,** during which international theater companies exploit the island's natural forms as the settings for spectacular events. You may find yourself up to your ankles in water as the tide rises around you, or in the middle of the dunes with "lighting technicians" stoking fires. Hotels are fully booked well in advance for this unique event.

The **Behouden Huys Museum** at Commandeurstraat 30–32 (☎ **0562/ 442-389**) gives you a look at the lives of the islanders of yesteryear. It's located in the 17th-century houses of two seafaring captains. You'll find period rooms as well as displays about local activities. Admission is Dfl 5 ($2.50). Open from April through mid-June and September through October Monday to Friday 10am to 5pm; during July and August also on Saturday 1 to 5pm.

If you want to find out everything about local geography, wildlife, and plants, visit the **Nature and Countryside Center** at the Burgemeester Reedekkerstraat 11 (☎ **0562/442-390**). It's open April through October Monday to Friday 9am to 5pm, and from 2 to 5pm during weekends and holidays. One of the exhibitions is an aquarium re-creating the North Sea and Wadden Sea environments.

WHERE TO STAY

There are many different ways of staying on this island, with bungalows hidden away in the countryside, camping sites, bed-and-breakfasts, and hotels. It's best to contact the VVV and discuss your requirements with them.

VLIELAND ISLAND

Vlieland (pop.1,100) occupies a thin strip of land, 20km (12.5 miles) long and an average of 2.5km (1½ miles) wide. This is an almost ideal hideout for the world-weary, the only disturbances here being the cries of seabirds—and the occasional roar of Dutch air force F16s on exercises, which accounts for that "almost" caveat. The island also has what's said to be Europe's longest nudist beach, a visual distraction that must make it difficult for the pilots to concentrate on their targets. The only village on the island is Oost-Vlieland. There's not a lot to do on Vlieland; that is its main attraction.

ESSENTIALS

GETTING THERE **Rederij Doeksen** (☎ **0562/442-141**) runs three 1½-hour **ferry** crossings per day in each direction between Harlingen and Vlieland, with additional services in the summer. Passenger fares are Dfl 41.25 ($20.65), half price for children ages 4 to 11. A faster hydrofoil crossing in summer (subject to the weather) costs an additional Dfl 7.50 ($3.75) each way. **Cars** are not carried on either service. If you're traveling by **train,** your best bet is to buy an all-inclusive **Waddenbiljet** ticket from the NS (Dutch Railways), which covers all transport costs to Vlieland and allows stops on the outward and return journeys.

VISITOR INFORMATION **VVV Vlieland** is located at Hafenweg 10, 8899 BB Vlieland (☎ **0562/451-111;** fax 0562/451-361). Open Monday to Friday 9am–5pm, Saturday and Sunday when the ferry arrives. Consult the office for walking and cycling maps, guided tours, and accommodations.

SEEING THE SIGHTS

This car-free island is almost deserted, except in summer. Sunbathing, bird watching, cycling, and walking among the dunes and forests are the main activities. The 16th-century **Tromp's Huys,** Dorpstraat, Oost-Vlieland (☎ **0562/451-600**), named for the Dutch admiral Cornelis Tromp (though it never belonged to him), is now a local history museum, with a fine collection of antique clocks and other items. Open May through September Monday to Friday 10am to noon and 2 to

5pm; April and October Monday to Saturday 2 to 5pm; November through March Wednesday and Saturday 2 to 5pm. Admission is Dfl 3 ($1.50).

Also in Dorpstraat is the **Vistor's Center** (Bezoekerscentrum) (☎ 0562/451-700), which has displays on the island's flora and fauna, and can give advice on the best places for bird watching. Open from May through September daily 10am to noon and 2 to 5pm; October through April Wednesday and Saturday 2 to 4pm. Admission is Dfl 3 ($1.50).

WHERE TO STAY

There is a limited supply of small-scale accommodations on Vlieland. Contact the VVV for current information.

MAKKUM
ESSENTIALS

GETTING THERE   The only practical way to reach Makkum from Amsterdam is by car. The town is 8km (5 miles) south of the Friesland end of the Afsluitdijk (see "Harlingen," above). By public transportation, take the hourly local train to Sneek, then bus 98 from outside the train station to Makkum.

VISITOR INFORMATION   VVV Makkum is in the old Weigh House at Pruikmakershoek 2 (☎ 0515/231-422; fax 0515/232-920), in the town center.

EXPLORING MAKKUM

There have been tile makers and ceramics craftspeople in Makkum, 10 miles (16km) south of Harlingen, since the 1500s, and the craft is carried on today at the ✪ **Tichelaar Royal Makkum and Pottery Factory,** Turfmarkt 63 (☎ 0515/231-341), where you are taken through the entire process and can see the exquisite designs being painted by hand. Guided tours are given year-round. This interesting firm has been in operation for over 300 years, and the factory has used the same procedures since the 17th century. In 1960 the "royal" designation was conferred on their work. The Tichelaar's product is the only Dutch ornamental earthenware made from Dutch clay. At the salesroom you can buy anything from a simple tile to a larger piece with an elaborate design.

In the old **Waag** (Weigh House), dating from 1698, you'll find the **Frisian Earthenware Museum,** Pruikmakershoek 2 (☎ 0515/231-422). Its five rooms are filled with examples of Makkum, majolica, and earthenware tiles from the 17th to the 19th century. The building itself is a square, towerlike structure, built of brick and topped with an elegant steeple. The ground floor has quaint, oval windows; the upper floors have shuttered windows. The place was used for weighing cheese and butter. It's open from April through October Monday to Saturday 10am to 5pm; November through March Monday to Friday 10am to noon and 1 to 4pm. This building also houses the VVV office (see above).

HINDELOOPEN
20km (12 miles) S of Makkum

In this tiny little town on the IJsselmeer shore, talented craftspeople have for centuries adorned their homes, their furniture, their built-in cupboard beds, and even their wooden coat hangers with the vivid colors and intricately entwined vines and flowers that we associate with the Pennsylvania Dutch in America. It's thought that the designs were originally brought from Scandinavia by Hindeloopen sailors who sailed the North Sea in the days when the IJsselmeer was the Zuiderzee. Wherever it originated, this colorful decoration has reached its highest development in this little village.

A Museum Route

The little town of Bolsward, 6km (10 miles) from Hindeloopen via the town of Workum, is the starting point of one of Friesland's most intriguing attractions, the ✪ **Museumroute Aldfaers Erf** (Forefathers' Heritage Museum Route), which passes through a triangular area of restored buildings between the villages of Makkum–Workum–Bolsward. The route is well signposted along minor country roads. It leads you to Exmorra, with its 19th-century grocer's and schoolhouse; to Allingawier, where a bakery serves Frisian pastries and snacks and a slide presentation is given in an old church; and to Piaam, with its bird museum. The buildings are open April through October daily from 10am to 5pm. You can buy a map and a ticket for all sights, costing Dfl 15 ($7.50) for adults and Dfl 7.50 ($3.75) for children ages 5 to 14, at any one of the sights or at the **Aldfaers Erf Visitor Center,** Kerkbuurt 19, Allingawier, southwest of Bolsward (☎ **0515/575-681**). For further information contact the organizers at ☎ **0515/575-681**.

ESSENTIALS

GETTING THERE   Hindeloopen is 20km (12 miles) south of Makkum on minor roads. Hourly **trains** run from Stavoren or Leeuwarden to Hindeloopen station, just outside the village.

VISITOR INFORMATION   **VVV Hindeloopen** is at Nieuwstad 26 (☎ **0514/522-550;** no fax), in the village center.

EXPLORING HINDELOOPEN

The **Museum Hidde Nijland Foundation,** Dijkweg 3 (☎ **0514/521-420**), is a good place to view Hindeloopen's decorative designs. Each room presents a varied collection of period furniture and local costumes. There's a splendid selection of Dutch tiles, and every wooden surface in the museum seems covered in bright designs. The museum is open from March through October, Monday to Saturday 10am to 5pm, and Sunday 1:30 to 5pm.

Alternatively, you could visit one of the village workshops and see for yourself how the furniture is decorated. **Het Roosje,** Nieuwstad 19 and 44 (☎ **0514/521-251** or 0514/522-637), is a workshop established in 1894 that also specializes in wood carving. Admission is Dfl 4 ($2).

SCHIERMONIKOOG ISLAND

What more could you ask for than an island with a minimum of cars and a maximum of wilderness? Schiermonikoog Island is an internationally recognized nature reserve with fewer than 1,000 permanent residents. Cistercian monks established a monastery here in 1166. After the Reformation, the island was privately owned. It was returned to Dutch hands after World War II, and declared a National Park in 1982.

ESSENTIALS

GETTING THERE   You'll have to leave your **car** on the mainland at the ferry terminal at Lauwersoog, 42km (26 miles) northeast of Leeuwarden via the N361, and 42km (26 miles) northwest of Groningen, in the direction of Winsum. The **ferry** is run by **Wagenborg** (☎ **0519/349-050** during office hours). The trip takes about 45 minutes. There are 6 or 7 ferries per day in both directions, and the round-trip cost is Dfl 18 ($9) for adults, Dfl 10 ($5) for children ages 3 to 16.

By public transport, take the **train** to either Leeuwarden or Groningen, then **bus** 50 or 63 respectively to the ferry terminal. The cheapest public transport deal is the all-inclusive **Waddenbiljet,** a ticket good for transportation to the ferry terminal and then to the island.

VISITOR INFORMATION   The **VVV office** is on Schiermonikoog village's main street, at Reeweg 5 (☎ **0519/531-233;** fax 0529/531-325), and is open Monday to Saturday 9am to 5pm.

Exploring Schiermonikoog

Schiermonikoog village dates from the early 18th century, and life here doesn't seem to have changed much since then. The **Schiermonikoog Visitors Center** gives information about wildlife on the island and offers guided tours. It's housed in a lighthouse at Torenstreek 20 (☎ **0519/531-641**), just a short walk or ride from the village. Admission is Dfl 5 ($2.50) for adults, children free. Open mid-March through October, Monday to Saturday 10am to noon and 1:30 to 5:30pm; during winter, open Saturday 1:30 to 5:30pm.

Where to Stay & Dine

For such a small island, Schiermonikoog has a surprisingly wide range of accommodations. For more details contact the VVV office.

Hotel-Restaurant Van der Werff. Reeweg 2, 9166 PX Schiermonikoog. ☎ **0519/531-203.** Fax 0519/531-748. 55 units. TV TEL. Dfl 82.50 ($41.25) double. Rates include buffet breakfast. DC, MC, V.

This hotel has a certain stuffiness, which also somehow lends to its charm. In the lounge, you'll find games as well as sagging leather armchairs. Rooms are more modern, though they retain some elegant features. Taking breakfast in the restaurant/breakfast room is like stepping into a colonial officers' dining room. A three-course dinner here costs Dfl 60 ($30). Hotel guests can use the complimentary bus from the ferry terminal.

Graaf Bernstorff Hotel/Apartments. Reeweg 1, 9166 PW Schiermonikoog. ☎ **0519/532-000.** Fax 0519/532-050. E-mail: bernstor@globalxs.nl. 69 units. MINIBAR TV TEL. Dfl 225–295 ($112.50–$147.50) double; Dfl 995–1370 ($447.50–$685) per week for an apartment. Ask about lower prices during low season. AE, DC, MC, V.

This hotel and apartment complex opened in 1998. The brand-new rooms and apartments are luxuriously appointed. The restaurant downstairs has a more continental feel than the traditionally Dutch Van der Werff. Main courses start at Dfl 30 ($15). During the day you can get snacks on the terrace or at the bar.

2 Groningen

Groningen is one of Holland's most commercial and industrial provinces, and at the same time one of the most historic. Seagoing vessels sail up the 15-mile-long (24km) Eems Canal from the province's busy capital city—also called Groningen—to Delfzijl, the largest port. The town of Heiligerlee is an agricultural center, and also has famous bell factories that produce the smallest of dinner bells as well as massive carillons.

The province's long history, which stretches back beyond the 12th century, is reflected in the architecture of many buildings in the capital city, in numerous *terp* (mound) villages, in a 15th-century castle, in a 15th-century monastery, and in any number of picturesque villages. Groningen's most illustrious son was Abel Tasman, one of the greatest Dutch navigators, who was born in 1603 in the town of Lutjegast.

Most visitors base themselves in the city of Groningen and take day trips to the nearby towns.

GRONINGEN

182.5km (114 miles) NE of Amsterdam; 49km (35 miles) E of Leeuwarden

You'll want to spend some time in historic Groningen, a city that developed from a trading settlement at the confluence of two waterways, the Hoornse Diep and the Drentse Aa. The site has been settled since ancient times, but the town received its official charter in the 11th century. Its strategic location made it a successful trading center by the mid 13th century, after which, like so many other towns in the region, it became the embattled object of imperial rivalries through the centuries. Today the city is an important commercial and industrial center. Cars are banned from Groningen's picturesque historic center.

ESSENTIALS

GETTING THERE   There are **trains** every hour or so to Groningen from Amsterdam (journey time 3 hours). The train and bus stations adjoin each other south of the city center.

By **car** from Amsterdam, take the E22 north, cross the IJsselmeer on the Afsluitdijk to the Frisian shore, and then either continue on the E22 to Groningen, or switch to the A31 and N355 via Leeuwarden. Follow the well-placed signposts for car parking outside the pedestrians-only city center. Electronic information boards tell you where space is available.

VISITOR INFORMATION   The **VVV office,** Kattendiep 6 (☎ **0900/ 202-3050;** fax 050/311-0258), can supply information on both the city and the rest of the province, and can also reserve accommodations. The free booklet, "Rekreatiekrant," which lists current entertainment and cultural events, is available here.

SEEING THE SIGHTS

Groningen's highlights include its two beautifully designed central squares, the 15th-century **Martinikerk** (St Martin is Groningen's patron saint as well as the patron saint of hoteliers and travelers!), and the sparkling Renaissance **Goudkantoor** (Gold Office) just to the right of the neoclassical **Stadhuis** (town hall) in the Grote Markt.

During June, July, and August, there are regular ✪ **Canals of Groningen cruises.** Contact the VVV or call Rederij Kool, ☎ **050/312-8379** or 050/ 312-2713, for schedules, fares, and departure points.

✪ **Groninger Museum.** Museumeiland (opposite the train station). ☎ **050/ 366-6555.** Admission Dfl 10 ($5) adults, Dfl 6 ($3) children 16 and under. Tues–Sat 10am–5pm, Sun 1–5pm.

This museum makes an impressive introduction to the city. Italian architect Alessandro Mendini thought up a structure as quirky and varied as its contents. Four pavilions, one of which appears to be the victim of an exploded paint box, surround a golden tower. It's here that you'll find the main entrance. Once inside, your attention is drawn to more than the collection alone—the whole building can be experienced as a work of art. Each pavilion has a different theme: archaeological finds and the history of the city and province; Eastern ceramics; decorative arts; and paintings, prints, and sculpture from the 16th century to the present.

Northern Maritime Museum and Niemijer Tobacco Museum. Brugstraat 24–26. ☎ **050/312-2202.** Admission Dfl 6 ($3). Tues–Sat 10am–5pm, Sun 1–5pm.

This interesting museum traces the history of shipping in the northern provinces and the history of Holland's long involvement with the tobacco trade.

Prinsenhof Gardens. Prinsenhof (entrance on Turfsingel). Free admission. Apr to mid-Oct daily 10am–sundown.

This breathtaking garden was established in 1625. The hedges surrounding the herb beds and the rose garden are the result of more than 250 years of to piary. The Prinsenhof building has been the seat of the Bishops of Groningen since 1568.

WHERE TO STAY

A wide range of hotels are available in Groningen. The VVV can also provide a list of a limited number of private homes near the city that take paying guests; they charge about Dfl 35 ($17.50) per person per night.

De Doelen. Grote Markt 36, 9711 VL Groningen. ☎ **050/312-7041.** Fax 050/314-6112. 59 units. MINIBAR TV TEL. Dfl 185 ($92.50) double. AE, MC, V. Limited parking available on street.

De Doelen is about as centrally located as you can get, on the bustling Grote Markt square. The attractive guest rooms are done in muted colors, and feature soft carpets and a mixture of period and modern furniture. The Croissanterie Cave du Patron is a convenient drop-in spot for inexpensive sandwiches, salads, light meals, and snacks priced Dfl 15 ($7.50) and under. There's also a moderately priced steakhouse restaurant on the premises.

✪ **Family Hotel Paterswolde.** Groningerweg 19, 9765 TA Paterswolde (a 10-minute drive from Groningen). ☎ **050/309-5400.** Fax 050/309-1157. 71 units, 2 suites. MINIBAR TV TEL. Dfl 210–310 ($105–$155) double. AE, DC, MC, V. Free parking.

To get to this lovely lakeside hotel, take the A28 towards Assen, and then at the Haren intersection follow the signs for Paterswolde. From there the route to the hotel is signposted. The Paterswolde is set on 30 wooded acres and provides a restful respite from the city center. It offers spacious guest rooms, good wheelchair access, baby-sitting, a beauty salon, an indoor swimming pool, tennis courts, and bikes for hire. There's also a nice bar and good restaurant.

✪ **Hotel de Ville.** Oude Boteringstraat 43, 9712 GD Groningen. ☎ **050/318-1222.** Fax 050/318-1777. E-mail: hotel@deville.nl. 43 rooms, 2 suites. MINIBAR TV TEL. Dfl 195–275 ($97.50–$137.50) double; Dfl 375 ($187.50) suite. Breakfast included. AE, DC, MC, V. Limited parking available on street.

Three historic houses were converted into this stylish, up-to-date hotel in 1997. Many rooms overlook the quiet gardens at the rear of the block. The breakfast room/bar is in a glass conservatory. Next door to the hotel is the excellent brasserie-style restaurant Bistro 't Gerecht, which will even deliver dinner to your room. Main courses cost Dfl 20 to 35 ($10 to $17.50).

✪ **Schimmelpenninck Huys.** Oosterstraat 53, 9711 NR Groningen. ☎ **050/ 318-9502.** Fax 050/318-3164. 26 units, 6 suites. MINIBAR TV TEL. Dfl 170 ($85) double; Dfl 195–245 ($97.50–$122.50) suite. Breakfast Dfl 15 ($7.50). AE, DC, MC, V. Free parking.

This grand mansion was transformed from a derelict pile into an elegant hotel in the late 1980s, but it still retains many historical features. It's currently being further extended into neighboring buildings. The rooms are light and spacious, with the modern furniture blending in with the classical atmosphere. Room amenities include coffee- and tea makers. There is a snug bar in a 14th-century wine cellar, as well as a spacious and beautiful jugendstil lounge. There are plenty of dining facilities at this hotel, and they are well worth visiting even if you are not a guest here. The Empire Room is an elegant dining room serving high-quality Dutch/French food, with a French-style garden terrace in the summer.

WHERE TO DINE

Hotel-restaurants provide top-level dining (see "Where to Stay," above). Because of its large student population, Groningen has lots of moderately priced eateries, most of them around the Grote Markt. **Café De Stadlander,** Poelestraat 35 (☎ **050/312-7191**), offers an inexpensive à la carte menu. The following recommendations are at opposite ends of the price spectrum:

Muller. Grote Kromme Elleboog 13. ☎ **050/318-3208.** Fixed-price menu Dfl 75 ($37.50) for 3 courses, Dfl 95 ($47.50) for 4, Dfl 105 ($52.50) for the 6-course Menu Muller. AE, DC, MC, V. Tues–Sat 6–10pm. FRENCH.

For an exquisite experience amid classic French surroundings, come to Muller. Chef Jean Michel Hengge is the proud owner of a Michelin star. He uses local produce as often as possible, including game in season. The six-course chef's menu makes good use of the day's best market finds. Menu items include pumpkin soup, clams in cream sauce, and fillet of lamb en croûte. There's also a vegetarian option.

Binnenhof. Oosterstraat 7A (in a courtyard near the Grote Markt). ☎ **050/312-3697.** Main courses from Dfl 17.50 ($8.75). MC, V. Daily noon–1am. DUTCH/INTERNATIONAL.

This relaxed and friendly restaurant is part of an arts center in a former ballroom. It serves sandwiches and snacks throughout the day, and in the evening a range of entrees, including vegetarian options. In summer, you can take advantage of a quiet, shady terrace.

EXPLORING TOWNS NORTH & WEST OF GRONINGEN

The towns below can all easily be visited on day trips from Groningen.

WARFUM

25.5km (16 miles) N of Groningen

Warffum is typical of the "mound villages" that were built above flood level in past centuries. Before local people became expert at building dikes to hold back the water, they constructed mounds to provide places of safety for their families and livestock. These mounds are often the oldest settlements in the area and look like islands a few meters above the surrounding polders. **Openluchtmuseum Het Hoogeland** (Hoogeland Open-Air Museum) (☎ **0595/422-233**) holds fascinating relics from the mound settlements, as well as medieval costumes and other artifacts. It's open from April through October, Tuesday to Saturday from 10am to 5pm and on Sunday from 1 to 5pm. Admission is Dfl 5 ($2.50).

To get to Warffum from Groningen by **car,** take the N361 north. There are also local **trains** direct to Warffum.

UITHUIZEN

32km (20 miles) N of Groningen

Here, you'll find the **Menkemaborg,** Menkemaweg 2 (☎ **0595/431-970**), a double-moated fortified manor house that dates back to the 14th century. It was extensively rebuilt in the early 18th century, and its interior and much of its furnishings have changed little since then. The manor's formal gardens, which include a rose garden and a labyrinth, remain a star attraction. There's a pancake restaurant in the old carriage house. The manor is open April through September, Tuesday to Saturday 10am to noon and 1 to 5pm and on Sunday 1 to 5pm; October through December and February through March, Tuesday to Saturday 10am to noon and 1 to 4pm and Sunday 1 to 4pm; closed in January. Admission is Dfl 5 ($2.50).

To get to Uithuizen by **car,** take the N46 north from Groningen, then the N999. There are also direct **trains** from Groningen.

DELFZIJL

32km (20 miles) E of Groningen

The port town of Delfzijl overlooks German soil just across the estuary. Aside from its busy, colorful harbor, it has the ✪ **Museum Aquariom** (Aquarium and Shell Museum) at Zeebadweg 7 (☎ **0596/612-318**). Here you'll find North Sea aquatic life, corals, and a geological museum with fossils, minerals, and archaeological and maritime exhibits. The aquarium is open Monday through Saturday from 10am to 7pm; admission is Dfl 6 ($3) for adults and Dfl 4 ($2) for children.

To get to Delfzijl by **car** from Groningen, go northeast on the N360. There are also direct **trains** from Groningen.

Where to Stay & Dine in Delfzijl

Hotel Du Bastion. Waterstraat 78, 9934 AX Delfzijl. ☎ **0596/618-771.** Fax 0596/617-147. 40 units. TV TEL. Dfl 110 ($55) double. Rates include breakfast. AE, DC, MC, V. Limited parking available on street.

This small hotel is located in the town center. Its rooms are comfortable, clean, and bright, with whitewashed walls and period furniture. On the premises is a good moderately priced restaurant that features traditional Dutch dishes as well as a tourist menu.

SLOCHTEREN

24km (15 miles) E of Groningen

This little town is the source of the world's largest-known natural gas deposit (discovered in 1959) and supplies over one-third of the Netherlands's power requirements. Its star attraction is the lovely estate described below. To get there by **car** from Groningen, take the N360 towards Delfzijl, turn right onto the N986 just outside the city, and then take the N387. By public transportation, take bus 78 from Groningen bus station.

Fraeylemaborg. Hoofdweg 32. ☎ **0598/421-568.** Admission Dfl 6 ($3). Mar–Dec Tues–Sun and holidays 10am–noon, 1–5pm.

This 16th-century moated manor house is surrounded by attractive woods and gardens in the English landscape style. The interior has a wealth of richly decorated period rooms from the 18th and 19th centuries. You'll also find collections of Asian porcelain and an exhibition about the Royal House of Oranje-Nassau.

HEILIGERLEE

33.5km (21 miles) E of Groningen

Heiligerlee is known to every Dutch school child, as it was the scene of one of the most famous battles in the country's history. Here, on May 23, 1568, the Counts of Nassau defeated the allies of the Spanish King Philip II, in a battle that sparked the Eighty Years' War, which led to the formation of the free Republic of the

Netherlands. The modern **Slag bij Heiligerlee Museum** (Battle of Heiligerlee Museum) (☎ **0597/418-199**), just across the road from the Bell Foundry Museum (see below), has a multimedia exhibition that takes you back to the famous battle of May 1586 and the Eighty Years' War that ensued. The museum is open from April through September, Tuesday to Saturday 10am to 5pm, Sunday 1 to 5pm; October, Tuesday to Friday and Sunday 1 to 5pm. Admission is Dfl 5 ($2.50) for adults, Dfl 3.50 ($1.75) for children 6 to 13. Combination tickets for this and the Bell Foundry Museum cost Dfl 9 ($4.50) for adults, Dfl 6 ($3) for children 6 to 13.

✪ **Klokkengieterijmuseum (Bell Foundry Museum).** Provincialeweg 46. ☎ **0597/418-199.** Admission Dfl 5 ($2.50). Apr–Sept Tues–Sat 10am–5pm, Sun 1pm–5pm; Oct Tues–Fri and Sun 1pm–5pm.

This museum is housed in the former Van Bergen Bell Foundry, which received commissions from all over the world. It produced more than 10,000 bells for churches, carillons, and even dinner tables. The exhibits explain the history of bell casting. There are also casting demonstrations (by appointment only) and carillon concerts.

EXPLORING TOWNS SOUTH OF GRONINGEN
LEEK
22.5km (14 miles) SW of Groningen

The **Nationale Rijtuigmuseum** (National Carriage Museum) (☎ **0594/512-260**) here has a wonderful collection of antique horse-drawn carriages, sleighs, and the uniforms and accessories of their drivers. It's open from Easter through September, Monday to Saturday 9am to 5pm, Sunday 1 to 5pm. Admission is Dfl 6 ($3.50) for adults, Dfl 2.50 ($1.45) for children.

HAREN
5km (3 miles) S of Groningen

The premier attraction of the small town of Haren is the excellent botanical garden.

✪ **Hortus Haren.** Kerklaan 34, Haren. ☎ **050/537-0053.** Admission Dfl 15 ($7.50) adults, Dfl 5 ($2.50) children ages 4–11. Daily 9am–5pm.

Exotic flowers and plants of all climates, from alpine to tropical, are collected in Hortus Haren, the botanical gardens of Groningen University. Here you can visit the greenhouse complex, the different European gardens, and the Hidden Kingdom of Ming, a unique and mysterious re-creation of an imperial Chinese garden from the reign of the Ming dynasty (1368–1644). You can even sip Chinese tea in the Teahouse.

TER APEL
38.5km (24 miles) SE of Groningen

Near the little village of Ter Apel, hidden away in a peaceful forest of beech trees, is the tranquil ✪ **Monastery Museum** (☎ **0599/581-370**) at Boslaan 3. The cloister dates from the mid–15th century and is idyllically planted with rose bushes and 80 different herbs. Some of its leaded windows date from 1561. The museum was opened in 1990, and includes a collection of religious artifacts and church furniture. Take some time to walk into the surrounding woods. The museum is open March through October, Monday to Saturday 10am to 5pm and Sunday 1 to 5pm; November through February, Tuesday to Saturday 10am to 5pm and Sunday 1pm to 5pm. Admission is Dfl 6 ($3).

BOURTANGE

41.5km (26 miles) SE of Groningen

This unique fortress town has recently been restored to its former glory. It was constructed during the Eighty Years' War, and withstood many a battle over the centuries, only to fall into disrepair as the methods of warfare changed. Only two wooden drawbridges span the multiple star-shaped moat. Within the fortress you can visit the restored barracks, gunpowder storage rooms, a synagogue, and officers' lodgings. Various relics of military life are on display. The fort is open April through October Monday to Friday 10am to 5pm, Saturday and Sunday 12:30 to 5pm. Admission is Dfl 8 ($4) for adults, and Dfl 3.25 ($1.65) for children. Bourtange's **VVV office** is located at W. Lodewijkstraat 33 (☎ **0599/354-600**; fax 0599/354-554).

3 Drenthe

The Dutch call it *Mooi Drenthe,* which means "beautiful Drenthe." This is a land of deep forests, broad moors and peat bogs, small lakes, and picturesque villages. Its beauty and the traditional life of its peasant farmers and peat cutters drew Vincent van Gogh here for a 3-month sojourn early in his career. It was here that he painted his moody, moving canvases *The Potato Eaters* and *Weavers.*

Drenthe is also a land of prehistoric mysteries in the form of **hunebedden** (giants' beds). It is believed that these gigantic smooth stones were transported here from Scandinavia by Ice Age glaciers—legend has it that they were the home of a race of giants. Be that as it may, the Netherlands's earliest inhabitants apparently used them to mark tombs some 5,000 years ago, since the mounds have yielded stone axes, wooden vessels, and other relics.

Drenthe is idyllic holiday country, with a wealth of small hotels, cottages, and campgrounds. Since both Friesland and Groningen provinces can be toured from a base in Drenthe, this may be the place to combine a relaxing holiday with sightseeing. Drenthe Province VVV (see below) is the best contact point for reasonably priced accommodations, from campsites and hiker's huts to bungalow and farmhouse rentals in this sparsely populated, rural province.

Drenthe is also the site of large deposits of oil and gas, responsible for roughly one-third of the country's total production. The wells, however, are carefully landscaped, to prevent them from marring the lovely countryside.

EXPLORING DRENTHE

There are more than 50 *hunebedden* in the province, primarily around Borger, Rolde, Anlo, Emmen, Sleen, Vries, and Havelte. In Havelte, residents had to return their "giants' beds" to where they lay for centuries, since during World War II Nazi occupying troops dislodged the huge boulders to clear an airstrip and simply dumped them all into a large hole.

The province also includes two National Parks, the Dwingelderveld and the Drents-Fries Forest. You can find out more about accommodations, packages, and countryside tours by contacting the **Provincial VVV Drenthe** (☎ **0592/373-755**; fax 0592/371-410). Its mailing address is Postbus 10012, 9400 CA, Assen, but the office is not open to visitors. (*Note:* don't confuse this provincial VVV with the Assen VVV, which has a visiting address and deals with the Assen area.)

ASSEN

40km (25 miles) S of Groningen

Westerbork Camp—A Memorial

After the Germans annexed Holland in the beginning of World War II, the refugee camp that already stood in the middle of Drenthe province became a transit camp for the deportation of Jews and other "undesirables." A total of 102,000 people were transported via Westerbork to concentration camps, most never to return. In their memory, 102,000 stones have been laid out on the former parade ground. The camp now has a **Memorial Center** with exhibits and film footage that give an idea of the fate of those transported here. The displays are comprehensible to children without being graphic or bloody. The center is at Oosthalen 8, Hooghalen (☎ **0593/592-600**), and is open Monday to Friday 10am to 5pm, Saturday and Sunday 1 to 5pm. Entrance to the museum section costs Dfl 5 ($2.50) for adults and Dfl 2.50 ($1.25) for children aged 8 to 18 years.

To get here from Assen, take the minor road parallel to the A28 (E232) south to Hooghalen and then turn east for 4km (2.5 miles). From Emmen, take the N31 west to Beilen, turn north on the minor road parallel to the A28 (E232) to Hooghalen, and go east for 4km (2.5 miles). By public transportation, take the train from Zwolle or Assen to Beilen, then bus 22 from outside the station to the center of Hooghalen. The camp is a signposted, 15-minute walk. You can also go by *treintaxi* (combined train and taxi journey) from Assen train station; just buy the Dfl 12 ($6) return taxi ride from Beilen to Westerbork along with your train ticket between Assen and Beilen.

Assen is the capital of Drenthe, but unlike most other Dutch provincial capitals, it has little historical importance. Today it is an important inland shipping center. There are good **train** and **bus** connections from Groningen to the station on Stationsstraat, a short walk from the town center. By **car** from Amsterdam, take the E231 to Amersfoort, then the E232 north to Assen. From Groningen take the E232 south. There are also hourly trains from Amsterdam, which may involve a change at Zwolle.

The **VVV office** is located at Marktstraat 8–10 in the city center (☎ **0592/ 314-324;** fax 0592/317-306).

✪ **Drents Museum.** Brink 1. ☎ **0592/312-741.** Admission Dfl 7.50 ($3.75) for adults, Dfl 2.50 ($1.25) for children. Tues–Sun 11am–5pm.

This recently refurbished museum is a must-see for anyone with the tiniest interest in history. It's situated in the former Provinciehuis (Provincial House) and three other historic buildings. On display are Stone Age artifacts from Drenthe's *hunebedden* (large prehistoric stone graves), as well as weapons, pottery, and jewelry of Celtic and Merovingian origin. There are also Roman sarcophagi and other well-preserved items that have turned up in the peat bogs of Drenthe, including the mummified corpse of the girl Yde.

EMMEN

36.5km (23 miles) SW of Assen

Emmen, Drenthe's largest town, is a delightful mix of old buildings left from its village origins and new ones reflecting its prosperity in recent years. The star attraction here, however, is the town zoo. To get here from Amsterdam by **car,** take the E231 to Amersfoort, the E232 north to Hoogeveen, then the N37 east. From Groningen take the E232 south, then the N34. There are also hourly **trains** from Amsterdam, which may involve a change at Zwolle.

✪ **Noorder Dierenpark (Northern Zoo).** Hoofdstraat 18. ☎ **0591/618-800.** Admission Dfl 25 ($12.50) adults, Dfl 20 ($10) children. Daily 9am–4:30pm.

In this gigantic zoo animals roam freely in natural habitats. There are baboons, red kangaroo, penguins, white rhinoceros, and elephants, as well as a children's farm, totaling 500 different species. The complex also includes a magnificent butterfly garden, and "Biochron," an impressive depiction of the history of life on earth.

BARGER-COMPASCUUM
8km (5 miles) SE of Emmen

Set squarely in this town's surrounding peat moors is the extensive open-air museum called ✪ **Het Veenpark** (Peat Park), Berkenrode 4 (☎ **0591/324-444**). At this reconstructed peat cutters' village, you can see demonstrations of peat cutting, as well as butter churning, weaving, and clog making, as they were done at the end of the 19th century. There are also nostalgic shops and an antique barbers' shop. Open Easter through mid-October daily from 10am to 5pm. Admission is Dfl 17.50 ($8.75) for adults, Dfl 7.50 ($3.75) for children.

The town is located east of Emmen, on minor roads via Nieuw Dordrecht. By public transportation, take bus 45 from outside Emmen train station.

SCHOONOORD
24km (15 miles) NW of Emmen

Schoonoord's **De Zeven Marken Open-Air Museum,** Tramstraat 73 (☎ **0591/382-746**), includes sod huts, a smithy, a saw mill, an apiary (bee farm), and geological exhibits. Here you can see the living crafts and farming methods of yesteryear. The museum is open April through October, daily from 9am to 6pm. Admission is Dfl 5 ($2.50) for adults and Dfl 4 ($2) for children.

Schoonoord is located between Emmen and Assen, on the N376. By public transportation, take bus 21 from outside Assen train station.

THE LAKES
There are scores of lovely small lakes in Drenthe, and also two larger ones. ✪ **Lake Paterswolde,** some 12 miles (19km) northeast of Assen on the Groningen border, is a scenic sailing and water-sports center with a holiday village on its shores. To the southeast, **Lake Zuidlaren** and its eponymous village also attract water-sports enthusiasts; in October, this is the setting for one of Holland's largest horse fairs.

18

The Central Provinces— The Green Heart

Holland's central provinces spread before you a tapestry of history, scenic beauty, and incredible feats of engineering. Utrecht province—a center of learning and, formerly, of religion—is nearly 2,000 years old. Overijssel and Gelderland share a parklike landscape punctuated by historic towns, castles, industrial areas, and tranquil villages. Flevoland's polders, recently reclaimed from the IJsselmeer, are the country's newest; they're dotted with oddly integrated historical villages that were once islands.

1 Utrecht

Utrecht, the smallest of Holland's provinces, would come in a very close second to Gelderland if there were ever a contest for the *official* title of "royal." This is where Queen Juliana chose to live when she abdicated in favor of her daughter, Beatrix, and castles of one sort or another dot the landscape.

The provincial capital, also named Utrecht, is at least 2,000 years old, yet with its central location it is one of the country's most progressive commercial centers. Medieval centuries are recalled in Amersfoort and Oudewater, and Doorn was the home in exile of Kaiser Wilhelm II, of World War I fame. The interesting "witch city" of Oudewater, which lies in the province of Utrecht, is described in chapter 16.

Like most of the central Netherlands, Utrecht is usually toured from a base in Amsterdam or The Hague. I have, however, included in this chapter a few special lodgings for overnight stays.

UTRECHT
41.5km (26 miles) SE of Amsterdam

The capital city of Utrecht province is a good starting point for exploring the area. When the Dutch Republic was established in the late 16th century, Utrecht was one of its more powerful political centers, having been an important bishopric since the earliest centuries of Christianity in the Lowlands. As a result, this is a city of churches, with more restored medieval religious structures than any other city in Europe.

Unique to Utrecht is its bi-level, tree-shaded wharf along the Oude Gracht canal through the old center, where restaurants,

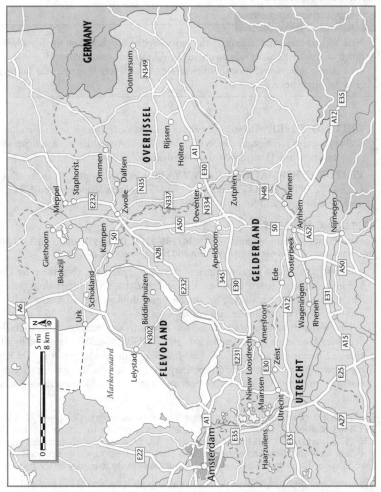

shops, and summer cafes have replaced the hustle and bustle of the wharfside commercial activity of former times, when Utrecht was a major port along the Rhine and these quays were used for offloading into the storage cellars.

Utrecht is renowned as the shopping center of the Netherlands, as you'll quickly realize if you arrive by train. Centraal Station is in the Hoog Catherijne (High Catherine)—a vast, multi-tiered, indoor shopping mall that spreads over a 6-block area and traverses both a multilane highway and the web of train tracks. However, the city has a thriving cultural life as well. The Hoog Catherijne also incorporates a modern concert hall that serves both classical and pop events. Every year, in the last week of August, Utrecht's churches are filled with the sound of Renaissance and baroque music during the Holland Festival of Early Music, an international event attracting the world's top performers. Another part of the Hoog Catherijne complex is the Jaarbeurs, a 40-room exhibition hall built especially to house the annual Utrecht Trade Fair, at which Dutch industry has presented its best products every year since 1916.

The Breukelen Bridge

New Yorkers may want to look up the tiny village of Breukelen, on the River Vecht north of Utrecht, a short ride north on the A2 towards Amsterdam. Here you can drive across the *original* Brooklyn Bridge—exactly 20 feet long and one car wide (and definitely not for sale!).

GETTING THERE   Because Utrecht is a central interchange point for Dutch Railways, **trains** arrive around every 15 minutes from Amsterdam Centraal Station.

By **car**, take to E35 southwest from Amsterdam.

VISITOR INFORMATION   The **VVV office,** at Vredenburg 90, in the Music Center (☎ **0900/414-1414;** fax 030/233-1417), is open Monday through Friday from 9am to 6pm, and Saturday from 9am to 5pm.

Exploring Utrecht

Central Museum. Agnietenstraat 1. ☎ **030/236-2362.** Dfl 6 ($3) adults, Dfl 3 ($1.50) children under 14. Tues–Sat 10am–5pm, Sun and holidays noon–5pm.

The emphasis here is on the contemporary and applied arts, but there are also historic exhibits such as a preserved Viking ship and a 17th-century dolls' house. The museum is worth visiting for the historical displays about Utrecht and the paintings by Utrecht's Golden Age artists.

On a more contemporary note, the museum also manages the **Rietveld Schröder House,** at Prins Hendriklaan 50 (☎ **030/236-2310**), designed by the architect Gerrit Rietveld in 1924. This building is the pinnacle of the De Stijl movement that so influenced contemporary art. To reach the house to see the exterior take bus 4 from Centraal Station, or contact the Central Museum about guided tours.

✪ Cathedral (Domkerk) and Cathedral Tower (Domtoren). Domplein. ☎ **030/ 231-0403** (Cathedral), or 030/233-3036 (Tower). Free admission to Cathedral; tower, Dfl 5.50 ($2.75) adults, Dfl 3 ($1.50) children under 12. Cathedral: Sun 2–4pm year-round; May–Sept Mon–Sat 10am–5pm; Nov–Apr Mon–Sat 10am–4pm. Tower: guided tours every hour, Mon–Sat 10am–4pm, Sun 12–4pm; Nov–Apr the weekday tours may be less frequent.

This magnificent cathedral in the city center was built between 1254 and 1517. Its 365-foot tower, which dominates old Utrecht's skyline, now stands across a square from its mother building—the nave collapsed during a storm in 1674, leaving the tower unharmed. In the paving on the square you can see the original outline of the church. One of the best views of Utrecht is from the top of the tower, a climb of some 465 steps (don't faint—about halfway up there's the 14th-century St Michael's Chapel where you can stop and ease the panting!). The climb goes past the 50 massive church bells you'll hear all through your stay in Utrecht. The cathedral cloisters are connected to the former Hall of the Chapter, where the signing of the 1579 Union of Utrecht took place.

Museum Het Catharijneconvent (St Catherine's Convent). Nieuwegracht 63. ☎ **030/231-3835.** Admission Dfl 7 ($3.50) adults, Dfl 5 ($2.50) children 6–18, free for children under 6. Tues–Fri 10am–5pm, Sat–Sun and holidays 11am–5pm. Bus: 2 or 22.

This museum houses extensive collections of paintings, religious relics, carvings, and church robes that help illustrate the development of Christian denominations in Holland from the 8th to the 20th centuries. The courtyard of the historic convent where the museum is housed has a cafe terrace where you can take a meditative pause.

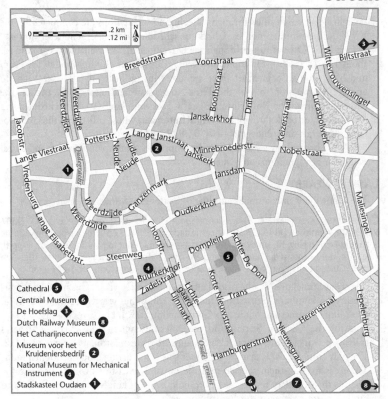

Legend:
Cathedral **5**
Centraal Museum **6**
De Hoefslag **3**
Dutch Railway Museum **8**
Het Catharijneconvent **7**
Museum voor het Kruideniersbedrijf **2**
National Museum for Mechanical Instrument **4**
Stadskasteel Oudaen **1**

✪ **Nationaal Museum van Speelklok tot Pierement (National Museum for Mechanical Musical Instruments).** Buurkerkhof 10. ☎ **030/231-2789.** Admission Dfl 9 ($4.50) adults, Dfl 5 ($2.50) children under 13. Tues–Sat 10am–5pm, Sun and holidays noon–5pm; guided tours on the hour. Bus: 2 or walk from Centraal Station.

Housed in a former church, this museum's delightful collection consists of mechanical music machines of all descriptions from the 17th century to the present, including those street organs you see on Dutch streets. There's also a player piano controlled by punched rolls. The most overwhelming exhibits are the music-hall organs of yesteryear, which you can dance along with at the end of your tour.

✪ **Nederlands Spoorwegmuseum (Dutch Railway Museum).** Maliebaanstation. ☎ **030/230-6206.** Admission Dfl 14 ($7) adults, Dfl 9 ($4.50) children. Tues–Fri 10am–5pm, Sat–Sun 11:30am–5pm. Bus 3 to Maliebaan.

You don't have to be a rail buff to be fascinated by this former train station and its marvelous collection of more than 60 steam engines, carriages, and wagons. There are also moving models, paintings, and films relating to train travel. The new multimedia project will have you and the kids stuck to your seats with presentations on the latest trains, such as the Thalys and TGV.

City Tours

Every Sunday from mid-May through mid-September, the VVV organizes ✪ **walking tours** of the city with different themes. Check for exact times and reservations. If you prefer a do-it-yourself walking tour, the staff can also supply an excellent **Walkman tour.**

Sightseeing coach tours through Utrecht and its environs are conducted by the VVV during summer months. Check for schedules, itineraries, and reservations.

One-hour ✪ **boat tours** through the Utrecht canals are available year-round for about Dfl 11 ($5.50) for adults and Dfl 7 ($3.50) for children under 13. From mid-May through September there are also trips by boat on the River Vecht to Loenen, with a stop to visit the Terra Nova estate and also a boat trip on the Kromme Rijn to the Rhijnauwen estate. Check with the VVV for schedules and reservations, or book through **Rederij Schuttevaer,** whose office is at the corner of Lange Viestraat and Oudegracht (☎ **030/272-0111**).

VVV Utrecht can also organize day trips, city walks, coach tours, and social events for private groups on request.

CASTLES NEARBY

The following is only a small sampling of castles near Utrecht.

✪ **De Haar.** Kasteellaan 1, Haarzuilens (about 3 miles west of Maarssen). ☎ **030/677-3804.** Admission Dfl 15 ($7.50) for castle and park; Dfl 5 ($2.50) for the park only. Castle open mid-Nov to Nov 30, Jan to mid-Mar Sun 1–4pm; mid-Mar to May 31 Tues–Sun 1–4pm; June to mid-Aug Mon–Fri 11am–4pm and Sat–Sun 1–4pm; mid-Oct to mid-Nov Tues–Sun 1–4pm. Guided tours every hour. Gardens open Mon–Fri 11am–4pm, Sat–Sun 1–4pm.

If you have time for only one castle jaunt, make it to De Haar. This imposing 15th-century castle suffered a disastrous fire in the 1800s, but was reconstructed in 1892 according to the designs of the neo-Gothic architect, P. J. H. Cuypers—also responsible for the Centraal Station and the Rijksmuseum in Amsterdam. Cuypers's craftsmen worked with medieval techniques to an extraordinary degree of detail. The only trouble now is that the weight of this construction atop the original foundations is making them subside into the moat! The castle's owners, who use the place as their primary residence, had to hold a sale of family heirlooms in 1998 to fund measures to prevent further subsidence.

You can still, however, take a look at the gorgeous furnishings and priceless paintings inside: precious Gobelin tapestries of the 14th and 15th centuries, Persian rugs, and Louis XIV, XV, and XVI furnishings. And don't miss the formal gardens, for which a whole village was transported down the road to afford a better view— they're magnificent.

Castle-Museum Sypesteyn. Nieuw Loosdrechtsedijk 150, Nieuw Loosdrecht (a few miles northeast of Maarssen). ☎ **035/582-3208.** Admission is Dfl 10 ($5). Apr–Oct Sat–Sun noon–5pm, May–Sept Tues–Fri 10am–5pm. Tours Tues–Fri at 11am, 12:30, 2, 3, and 4pm; Sat and Sun at 1, 2, 3, and 4pm. Train to Hilversum, then Treintaxi (a shared taxi that picks up train passengers).

Kasteel Sypesteyn is a castle turned art gallery and museum. It was rebuilt in the early 1900s on the foundations of a late-medieval manor house that was destroyed about 1580. Today it holds some 80 paintings from the 16th, 17th, and 18th centuries, representing the work of artists such as Moreelse, Maes, and Mierevelt. There are also collections of old weapons, glassware, silverware, pottery, porcelain, and furnishings dating from the 16th to the 18th centuries. The parklike grounds are laid out in 17th-century landscape style, and include a lovely rose garden.

Slot Zuylen. Tournooiveld 1, Oud-Zuilen, near Maarssen (5km, or 3 miles, north of Utrecht). ☎ **030/244-0255.** Admission Dfl 8 ($4). Mid-Mar to mid-Nov Sat 2–4pm, Sun 1–4pm; mid-May to mid-Sept Tues–Thurs 11am–4pm. Guided tours hourly. Bus: 36.

This is one of Holland's best examples of a medieval castle. It was built in the late 13th century and was inhabited until the early part of this century. Since 1952 the castle has been a museum. There are period rooms furnished in 17th- to 19th-century styles, along with family portraits. A special feature in the landscaped gardens is a so-called "snake wall" that creates a sun trap, thus protecting southern fruit trees from the harsher northern-European climate.

Shopping

The vast covered shopping mall, the **Hoog Catherijne,** sprawling from Centraal Station to the edge of the old city center, is a 6-block, multi-tiered shopper's paradise. It even encompasses a 40-room exhibition hall. Along the Oude Gracht (canal) there is a unique ✪ **bi-level wharf** filled with shops, restaurants, and sidewalk cafes, while much of Utrecht's old center has been transformed into a pedestrian-only zone, with many secondhand bookshops and antiques outlets.

✪ **Museum voor het Kruideniersbedrijf.** Hoogt 6. ☎ **030/231-6628.**

This grocery shop tucked away in a little courtyard is the place to head to satisfy your sweet tooth. The interior and equipment are original, and the ageless ladies behind the counter help you with old-fashioned friendliness. The aroma of cinnamon, ginger, and other spices pervades the air. It's difficult not to buy an ounce or two of each kind of sweet or cookie. There's also a tiny grocers' museum upstairs.

After Dark

The **Vredenburg Music Center,** in the Hoog Catherijne shopping center at Vredenburgspassage 77 (☎ **030/231-4544**), presents more than 450 concerts in both the classical and popular style each year—call ahead to find out what's on when you're there and to make reservations.

Where to Stay

Accommodations can be a problem in Utrecht, partly because of its proximity to Amsterdam. My best advice is to reserve as far in advance as possible.

✪ **Malie Hotel.** Maliestraat 204, 3581 SL Utrecht. ☎ **030/231-6424.** Fax 030/234-0661. 29 units. MINIBAR TV TEL. Dfl 190–210 ($107.30–$130.50) double. Rates include buffet breakfast. AE, DC, MC, V. Bus: 4 or 11.

Two 19th-century mansions in a quiet residential neighborhood near the university "Uithof" complex are the setting for this lovely small hotel. The small lobby is furnished with modern black-leather chairs. The guest rooms have large windows and are very bright. Both the breakfast room and bar overlook the peaceful garden at the back.

Park Plaza Utrecht. Westplein 50, 3531 BL Utrecht. ☎ **030/292-5200.** Fax 030/292-5199. 120 units. MINIBAR TV TEL. Dfl 325–365 ($162.50–$182.50) double. AE, DC, MC, V.

This centrally located hotel is as modern as tomorrow. Its decor is bright and attractive and its guest rooms are luxurious. Some rooms have air-conditioning. Amenities include a sauna, whirlpool, and fitness center. The Rhapsody restaurant here specializes in French cuisine, with a 3-course choice menu for Dfl 58 ($29). The hotel is within easy walking distance of Centraal Station and Industries Fair.

✪ **Tulip Inn Utrecht.** Janskerkhof 10, 3512 BL Utrecht. ☎ **030/231-3169.** Fax 030/231-0148. 45 units. TV TEL. Dfl 250 ($150) double. Rates include buffet breakfast. AE, DC, MC, V. Bus: 3.

This excellent hotel is literally in the shadow of the cathedral and also within a 2-minute walk of the canal, with its bi-level wharf, restaurants, and shops. The intimate guest rooms have comfortable wooden furniture and large beds. Some windows still retain the original early 20th-century stained glass. Breakfast is served in the adjacent Café-Restaurant Luden. The hotel has its own parking lot.

WHERE TO DINE

✪ **De Hoefslag.** Vossenlaan 28, Bosch en Duin (northeast of Utrecht). ☎ **030/ 225-1051.** Fixed-price menus Dfl 97.50–135 ($48.75–$77.50). AE, DC, MC, V. Mon–Sat noon–2:30pm, 5:30–9:30pm. SEAFOOD/GAME/FRENCH.

This beautiful dining spot on wooded grounds is considered by many to be Holland's top restaurant. Amsterdammers think nothing of driving the 20 miles down here for dinner. The lounge has a Victorian garden feel to it, while the dining room is reminiscent of an upscale hunting lodge, with lots of dark wood, an open hearth, and floor-to-ceiling doors opening to the terrace. The menu changes daily; specials are set only after the chef has returned from the market. The seafood is superb, as are the pork and lamb dishes, as well as the venison and other game dishes served in season.

There's also a 34-room hotel in this romantic wooded setting to save you driving back to town. Rooms cost from Dfl 300 to 550 ($150 to $275).

✪ **Stadskasteel Oudaen.** Oudegracht 99. ☎ **030/231-1864.** Main courses Dfl 35–45 ($17.50–$22.50); fixed-price menus Dfl 59.50–72.50 ($29.75–$36.75). AE, DC, MC, V. Cafe daily 10am–2am; restaurant Mon–Sat 5:30–10pm. DUTCH/CONTINENTAL.

This medieval town castle has been transformed into a culinary palace. Downstairs, in what once was the main hall, you can sit in the cafe and savor beer brewed on the premises according to medieval recipes. Upstairs is the restaurant "Tussen hemel en aarde" ("Between heaven and earth"), with its rustic tile floor and original fireplace. The menu changes weekly, according to what is freshest and in season. Seasonal specialties include roast of venison with wild mushrooms and a marjoram sauce and—using the home-brewed beer—poached pear in an "Alt"-beer *sabayon*.

AMERSFOORT

42.5km (26.5 miles) E of Amsterdam; 20km (12.5 miles) NE of Utrecht

GETTING THERE   **Trains** arrive every hour from Amsterdam Centraal Station and Utrecht.

Buses arrive every half-hour on average from Utrecht.

By **car,** take the E231 east from Amsterdam, and the E30 north from Utrecht.

VISITOR INFORMATION   The **VVV office** is at Stationsplein 9–11 (☎ **0900/ 112-2364;** fax 033/465-0108). Open May through September, Monday to Friday 9am to 5:30pm and Saturday 9am to 5pm; October through April, Saturday 10am to 2pm.

EXPLORING AMERSFOORT

This lovely medieval city has held onto its ancient character despite industrial development. Indeed, its medieval heart is guarded by a double ring of canals—the only city in Europe to have this feature.

On entering the town, you'll pass the oldest standing gateway, the **Kamperbin-nenpoort,** constructed around 1260. One of the two other surviving gates is the **Koppelpoort,** a land and water gateway. Look for examples of "wall houses" built into the ramparts and fortifications. Another impressive landmark is the tall

15th-century **Our Lady's Tower;** if you're there on a Friday, listen for its carillon concert between 10 and 11am. Other ancient religious buildings include the **St Joriskerk,** started in 1243 and completed round 1534, and the **Mariënhof Monastery,** where the Culinary Museum is located. If you visit on a summer Saturday, you may be lucky enough to encounter the colorful trumpeters who show up from time to time in the city center.

Culinair Museum Mariënhof (Mariënhof Culinary Museum). Kleine Haag 2. ☎ **033/463-1025.** Admission is Dfl 5 ($2.50) adults, Dfl 3 ($1.50) children under 14. Tues–Fri 10am–5pm, Sat–Sun and holidays 2–5pm.

This museum offers the visitor a playful journey through the history of the culinary vices and virtues of man from prehistoric times to the present day. A series of dioramas traces how man the hunter gradually transformed into the mass-production consumer. The museum is housed in the beautifully restored Mariënhof Monastery. You can sample some historical cooking in the restaurant.

Museum Flehite. Westsingel 50. ☎ **033/461-9987.** Admission Dfl 6 ($3) adults, Dfl 3 ($1.50) children under 15. Tues–Fri 10am–5pm, Sat–Sun 1–5pm.

The large collection of artifacts, models, and displays here illuminates the history of Amersfoort. Across the road, in the Sint Pietersgasthuis, a former pensioners' home from the late 14th century, there is a chapel and a medieval room.

ZEIST

10km (6 miles) NE of Utrecht

This village is a gem set in the green landscape of Utrecht province. It was once a fashionable country retreat for Utrecht city's wealthy nobility.

GETTING THERE There are frequent **buses** from Utrecht.

By **car,** take the E30 northeast from Utrecht.

VISITOR INFORMATION VVV **Zeist,** at Het Rond 1 (☎ **0900/109-1013;** fax 030/692-0017) has details on walking and cycling tours through the parks and forests surrounding Zeist. It's open Monday through Friday 9am to 5:30pm, and Saturday 10am to 1pm.

EXPLORING ZEIST

✪ **Slot Zeist.** Zinzendorflaan 1. ☎ **030/692-1704.** Admission Dfl 5.50 ($2.75) adults, Dfl 3 ($1.50) children. Guided tours year-round Sat–Sun 2pm and 3:30pm; July–Aug tours also Mon–Thurs 2:30pm. Hours may vary; call in advance.

This castle was built between 1677 and 1687 for Willem Adriaan van Nassau. The simple brick facade conceals a lavish interior designed by French architect Daniël Marot, who was also responsible for decorating Het Loo Palace (see below). Many of his baroque murals and ceiling paintings have survived, as well as the ornate gilded wood paneling and stucco. The grand drive is lined by elegant houses belonging to the Hernhutters, a religious order that had its origins in Switzerland in the first half of the 18th century. The vast formal gardens were relandscaped in the 19th century to create a pleasant park.

WHERE TO STAY & DINE IN ZEIST

Golden Tulip Hotel Figi. Het Rond 3, 3701 HS Zeist. ☎ **030/692-7400.** Fax 030/ 692-7468. 96 units. MINIBAR TV TEL. Dfl 350 ($175) double; Dfl 450 ($225) suite. AE, DC, MC, V.

Should you fall for the charms of Zeist, this modern, four-star hotel will ensure a pleasant stay. The rooms are decorated in a colorful, Mediterranean style. Four cinemas and the cozy "brown" Theatercafé are part of the hotel complex, accessible via the hotel and through their own street entrances. The hotel also has two restaurants.

2 Gelderland

Gelderland is in the province of the Rhine. Its large parks, nature reserves, and recreation centers are favorite holiday venues for the Dutch. Here you'll find the Hoge Veluwe, the largest nature reserve in Holland, located north of the Rhine, toward the sandy beaches of the Veluwemeer. The reserve offers all kinds of camping facilities, as well as bungalow and other holiday accommodations.

Nature is not the only reason to visit this province. Gelderland's cities beckon with attractions like the royal palace museum in Apeldoorn and Arnhem's Netherlands Open-Air Folklore Museum. The province also has many castles, some of which can be visited.

Most tourists visit Gelderland from an Amsterdam base, but you may prefer to move to a central location in Apeldoorn, which has some good hotels (see below).

APELDOORN

75km (47 miles) E of Amsterdam; 25km (15.5 miles) N of Arnhem

"Royal Apeldoorn" is a title often bestowed on this city, which has hosted the likes of Willem III in 1685, Louis Napoléon in 1809, Queen Wilhelmina from 1948 until her death in 1962, and Princess Margriet from 1962 to 1975. It's also a city of many parks and gardens.

Apeldoorn is the best place to base yourself for a visit to Hoge Veluwe National Park.

GETTING THERE There are **trains** every hour from Amsterdam Centraal Station and Arnhem.

Buses leave every half hour on average from the bus station in Arnhem.

By **car,** take the E30 east from Amsterdam, and the N50 north from Arnhem.

VISITOR INFORMATION The **VVV office** is at Stationsstraat 72 (☎ **0900/ 168-1636;** fax 055/521-1290). Open Monday through Friday 9am to 5pm and Saturday 9am to 4pm.

EXPLORING APELDOORN

✪ **Het Loo Palace.** Koninklijk Park 1. ☎ **055/577-2400.** Tues–Sun 10am–5pm. Admission Dfl 12.50 ($6.25) adults, Dfl 10 ($5) children.

Apeldoorn's 1685 palace has sheltered generations of royalty, being the favorite summer residence of Stadholders and the Dutch royal house of Oranje-Nassau until 1975. Since 1984 it has served as the magnificent home of this museum, which celebrates the history of the House of Orange. After a complete renovation, in which it was stripped of its 19th-century trappings to reveal the original paneling and colorful damasks, this splendid palace is now an ideal setting for paintings, furniture, silver, glassware, and ceramics, as well as memorabilia of the royal family. The vintage car and carriage collection in the stable block is also fascinating, but the jewel in the crown is the formal garden. The gardens were laid out during the renovation, using the original 17th-century plans and thus creating a small-scale Versailles.

EXPLORING THE NATIONAL PARK

This 5,750-hectare park lies between Apeldoorn and Arnhem, both of which have buses that go to the park every hour or so. If you drive to Hoge Veluwe, you'll find several places to park your car and pick up a free white bicycle. These include Hoenderloo, Otterlo, and Rijzenburg (near Schaarsbergen).

⊙ **Hoge Veluwe National Park.** Apeldoornseweg 250, 7351 TA Hoenderloo. ☎ **055/378-1441.** Admission Dfl 7 ($3.50) adults, Dfl 3.50 ($1.75) children aged 6–12 (park only); Dfl 14 ($7) adults, Dfl 7 ($3.50) children aged 6–12 (including the museum and hunting lodge). Additional Dfl 8.50 ($4.25) charged for cars. Daily 8am–sunset.

This beautiful park covers some 22 square miles in a setting flanked by Arnhem, Apeldoorn, and Ede, and shelters a wealth of nature's treasures. The gently rolling heathland and woodland here are home to all kinds of wildlife. One of the unexpected treasures in the middle of this nature reserve is the Kröller-Möller Museum, which is world famous for its collection of paintings by Van Gogh.

The park has solved its transportation issues in a unique way. It introduced about 800 white bicycles, which anyone can pick up from one of several convenient spots next to the perimeter car parks. The scheme has proved successful, and these bicycles are the perfect way to explore the park. You might have to overcome a certain moral barrier before you hop on a bike that isn't yours, but then again it isn't anybody else's either, and you'll be able to discover more of the park than on foot. Use of these bicycles is free.

⊙ **Museum Kröller-Möller.** In the Hoge Veluwe National Park, Houtkampweg 6, Hoenderloo. ☎ **0318/591-041.** Admission included in park entrance fee (see above). Open Tues–Sun and holidays 10am–5pm.

This major museum is where you'll find most of the Vincent van Gogh paintings that aren't in the Amsterdam Rijksmuseum. The collection also includes paintings by Braque, Mondrian, Picasso, Redon, and Seurat. A sculpture garden holds works by Rodin, Moore, and Lipchitz, among others, and there are exhibitions of Chinese porcelain and Delftware as well.

St Hubertus Hunting Lodge. In the Hoge Veluwe National Park. ☎ **055/378-1237.** Admission included in park ticket. Apr–Oct tours daily every half hour 11am–4:30pm (no tour at 1pm); Nov–Mar tours Mon–Fri at 2 and 3pm. Closed Jan.

This lodge was designed by H. P. Berlage for Mr. and Mrs. Kröller-Möller. Inside, stained-glass windows tell the story of St. Hubertus, the patron saint of hunters; the house is full of symbolic references to his life. You can stroll through the rose garden or sit on the banks of the swan-shaped lake.

WHERE TO STAY IN APELDOORN

⊙ **Bilderberghotel de Keizerskroon.** Koningstraat 7, 7315 HR Apeldoorn. ☎ **055/521-7744.** Fax 055/521-4737. 96 units. MINIBAR TV TEL. Dfl 275–335 ($132.50–$240) double; Dfl 435–555 ($217.50–$277.50) suite. AE, DC, MC, V.

This attractive hotel is set on the edge of town, adjacent to Het Loo Palace. Each of the spacious rooms is furnished with a writing desk; some have balconies overlooking the landscaped grounds. Restaurant De Keizerskroon provides classic gourmet fare. Amenities include a covered rooftop swimming pool, sauna, solarium, and fitness center.

Hotel Bloemink. Loolaan 556, 7315 AG Apeldoorn. ☎ **055/521-4141.** Fax 055/521-9215. 57 units TV TEL. Dfl 225 ($112.50) double; Dfl 280 ($140) suite. Rates include buffet breakfast. AE, DC, MC, V.

This hotel, also near the Het Loo Palace on the edge of town, offers spacious rooms decorated in different shades of brown and chestnut. Furnishings are modern and comfortable. Some rooms have a terrace; suites come with kitchenettes. There's also an indoor heated swimming pool.

Hotel-Pension Berg en Bos. Aquamarijnstraat 58, 7314 HZ Apeldoorn. ☎ **055/355-2352.** Fax 055/355-4782. 17 units. TEL TV. Dfl 120 ($60) double. Rates include continental breakfast. Dinner Dfl 27.50 ($13.75). AE, DC, MC, V.

This inexpensive little hotel has a quiet, peaceful setting near the Berg en Bos park and Het Loo Palace. The comfortable rooms are bright and airy. Some overlook the garden. There's also a bar and lounge.

WHERE TO DINE IN APELDOORN

✪ **Restaurant De Echoput.** Amersfoortseweg 86, Hoog Soeren/Apeldoorn, just off the N344. ☎ **055/519-1463.** Lunch Dfl 96.50 ($48.25) for 3 courses; dinner Dfl 97.50 ($48.75) 3 courses without wine, Dfl 145 ($72.50) for 5 courses with wine. AE, CB, DC, MC, V. Tues–Fri noon–2pm; Tues–Sat 6–9:30pm, Sun 1–9:30pm. DUTCH/CONTINENTAL.

This widely acclaimed restaurant is named after the old well at which travelers once watered their horses (the "echoing well"). It's located on the edge of the Royal Wood, about 6 miles west of Apeldoorn. From the outside it has the look of a modern hunting lodge, and the surprise comes when you enter the ultra-sophisticated lounge and dining room done up in shades of chocolate and pewter. Windows look out on pools and fountains and forest greenery. The specialty here is seasonal game (fall and winter), and summer specialties include lamb, beef, and poultry. No matter what the season, you can be sure your meal will be both classically superb and memorable.

ZUTPHEN

19km (12 miles) SE of Apeldoorn; 26km (16 miles) NE of Arnhem

GETTING THERE There are **trains** every hour from Apeldoorn and Arnhem.

Buses leave every half hour on average from the bus stations outside Apeldoorn and Arnhem train stations.

By **car,** take the N345 southeast from Apeldoorn, and the N48 northeast from Arnhem.

VISITOR INFORMATION The **VVV office** is at Wijnhuis/Markt (☎0575/519-355; fax 0575/517-928).

EXPLORING ZUTPHEN

The old town of Zutphen stands on the banks of the IJssel River. The ✪ **Walburgiskerk Library** is located in a magnificent church that also houses important works of art. Its medieval books and manuscripts are still in use, all chained to reading desks. Opening hours of both the church and library vary, so it's best to check with the VVV (see below) or ring the church vestry (☎ 0575/514-178) to make an appointment.

The VVV has mapped out several thematic walking tours of the city. One walk takes you to all the romantic courtyards in the city. During summer months a culinary tour is organized every Tuesday evening.

ARNHEM

80km (50 miles) E of Amsterdam

Arnhem is Gelderland's capital city. Its name became a household word during World War II, when it suffered from massive Allied air attacks against its Nazi occupiers. Today thousands make pilgrimages to its battlefields each year. On a less-somber note, Arnhem also offers many parks, a marvelous open-air museum, and the departure point for boat trips on the Rhine.

GETTING THERE   There are direct trains every hour from Amsterdam Centraal Station, via Utrecht. By car from Amsterdam, take the E35 south to Utrecht and east to Arnhem.

VISITOR INFORMATION   The **VVV office** is at Stationsplein 45 (☎ **0900/ 202-4075;** fax 026/442-2644).

EXPLORING ARNHEM

✪ **Netherlands Open-Air Museum and National Heritage Museum.** Schelmseweg 89. ☎ **026/357-6111.** Admission Dfl 17 ($8.50) adults, Dfl 11.50 ($5.75) children. Mid-Apr to Oct 31 daily 10am–5pm. By car take the A12/E35 and follow the signs to Arnhem-Noord/Openluchtmuseum; by bus take no. 3 from Arnhem Centraal Station to Alteveer.

If you see nothing else in Arnhem, don't miss this.

The 100 acres of this open-air museum provide a delightful minicourse in Dutch history, customs, dress, and architecture. Step-gabled town houses, windmills, colorful costumes of the past, farmhouses, and even ancient means of transport were gathered from all around the country. Today they bring together in one place much of Holland's history.

Other Arnhem Attractions

Contemporary and classic artworks, with an emphasis on contemporary Dutch painting and sculpture, can be found in the **Museum voor Moderne Kunst** (Museum for Modern Art), at Utrechtseweg 87 (☎ **026/351-2431**). It also has a sculpture garden, a coffee room, and open-air cafe. The **Historical Museum Het Burgerweeshuis,** Bovenbeekstraat 21 (☎ **026/442-6900**), contains archeological relics found in the province and an interesting topographical map of Holland. Both museums are open from 10am to 5pm Tuesday through Saturday and 11am to 5pm on Sunday and holidays; admission is Dfl 5 ($2.50) for adults, Dfl 2.50 ($1.25) for children.

Boat trips from Arnhem and Deventer by **Rederij Scheers** (☎ **026/322-9439**) include day-long excursions on the Rhine and IJssel rivers, waterways used by 200,000 boats a year. Some cruises cross the border into Germany, stopping at Emmerich; another visits the Dutch Hanseatic towns of Deventer, Doesburg, Zutphen, Zwolle, and Kampen (see box "The Hanseatic Towns," below). Trips are in July and August, and prices start at Dfl 22.50 ($11.25) for adults and Dfl 17.50 ($8.75) for children 11 and under for 1½-hour trips; for day-long cruises, including lunch and refreshments, prices are Dfl 52.50 ($26.25) for adults and Dfl 47.50 ($23.75) for children. Call for schedules, fares, and reservations.

NEARBY ATTRACTIONS

Oosterbeek, which adjoins Arnhem, traces its history back to the Roman era and is home to a few worthwhile attractions. Stop in the old Catholic church to see Jan Toorop's famous Fourteen Stations of the Cross, in addition to visiting the Airborne Museum (see below). The town of **Doorwerth,** just beyond Oosterbeek, is home to a number of interesting museums and parks. Just beyond Doorwerth is the zoo at **Rhenen.**

Airborne Museum. Utrechtseweg 232, Oosterbeek. ☎ **026/333-7710.** Admission Dfl 6 ($3) adults, Dfl 5 ($2.50) children. Mon–Sat 11am–5pm, Sun and holidays noon–5pm.

This museum is located in the former Hotel Hartenstein, the British Command Center during World War II. It has exhibits detailing the 1944 Battle of Arnhem, a pivotal and well-known conflict.

Museum for Game and Game Management. Doorwerth Castle, Fonteinallee, Door-werth. ☎ **026/333-5375.** Admission Dfl 8 ($4) adults, Dfl 3.75 ($1.85) children under 16. Apr–Oct Tues–Fri 10am–5pm, Sat, Sun and holidays 1–5pm; Nov–Mar Tues–Fri 1–5pm.

After sustaining heavy damage in World War II, this former residence of a Rhine baron was rebuilt in its original architectural style. The moated castle was started in the 13th century and extended during the 15th and 16th centuries. Today the south wing holds interesting exhibits on nature, game animals, and antique weapons. You can visit the rest of the castle as well during the summer months.

NIJMEGEN
85km (53 miles) SE of Amsterdam; 15km (9.5 miles) S of Arnhem

One of the Netherlands's two oldest cities (Maastricht is the other), Nijmegen dates back to A.D. 105. Its strategic position is clearly visible from the Valkhof, a park on the site of a fortress Charlemagne built here in the 9th century.

GETTING THERE   There are **trains** every hour from Amsterdam Centraal Station and Arnhem.

Buses leave every half hour on average from the bus station outside Arnhem train station.

By **car,** take the A52 south from Arnhem.

VISITOR INFORMATION   The **VVV office** is at St-Jorisstraat 72 (☎ **0900/ 112-2344;** fax 024/360-1429). It is open Monday through Friday 9am to 5pm, and Saturday 9am to 4pm.

EXPLORING NIJMEGEN

The **Valkof** is situated high on the south bank of the Waal river, and the views from this park of the surrounding region are magnificent. Here you'll find the ruins of the 12th-century **St Martin's Chapel** as well as a little 1030 chapel often called the Carolingian Chapel, because of the long-held, though erroneous, belief that it was built by Charlemagne (Nijmegen was a favorite residence for the emperor). There are more excellent views from the 15th-century **Belvedere watchtower.** Around the picturesque **Grote Markt,** look for the 1612 Weigh House (Waag), and the Kerk-boog vaulted passageway that dates from 1545.

✪ **Museum Het Valkhof.** Kelkensbos 59. ☎ **024/360-8805.** Admission Dfl 10 ($5) adults, Dfl 5 ($2.50) children under 18. Tues–Fri 10am–5pm, Sat–Sun 1–5pm.

This brand new art and historical museum, designed by Ben van Berkel and set to open in June 1999, integrates two older, smaller museums. Historic exhibits cover the prehistoric, Roman, and Frankish eras in the region; there's also an interesting array of contemporary art. The new glass structure accommodating the museum is worth seeing in its own right—a daring but successful project.

Liberation Museum 1944. Wylerbaan 4, Groesbeek (6 miles from Nijmegen). ☎ **024/ 397-4404.** Admission Dfl 7.50 ($3.75) adults, Dfl 4.50 ($2.25) children under 15. Mon–Sat 10am–5pm, Sun and holidays noon–5pm. Bus 5 from Nijmegen.

This museum is divided into three main sections. It starts with the rise of National Socialism between the two World Wars. Then a series of photographs, films, a slide show, and a model of the area evoke the period of occupation during World War II, leading up to the story of the 82nd Airborne Division that liber-ated Nijmegen from Nazi forces in 1944 in the impressive "Market Garden" oper-ation, the largest airborne operation in history.

Biblical Open-Air Museum. Profetenlaan 2 (southeast of town on the road to Groesbeek). ☎ **024/382-3110.** Admission Dfl 12.50 ($6.25) adults, Dfl 6 ($3) children under 14. Late Mar–Nov 9am–5:30pm; Christmas period, crib exhibition in main building.

This 120-acre museum holds life-size replicas of biblical scenes. The figurines leave a lot to be desired, but the sheer size of the place is impressive. The museum is run by the Heilig Landstichting (Holy Land Association).

3 Overijssel

The province of Overijssel is all too often passed over by visitors. And that's really a shame, because within its boundaries lie beautiful forests, lakes, and parks; steep-roofed, half-timbered farmhouses; the medieval town of Ootmarsum in Twente; the eastern region bordering Germany; the village of Giethoorn, called "The Venice of the North," because of its canals; and many more picturesque castles and towns, such as the strict Calvinist village of Staphorst and the Hanseatic towns of Kampen, Zwolle, and Deventer.

The province extends from the young Noordoostpolder in the northwest to the twisting border with Germany in the east, to the Salland district bordered by the Vecht and IJssel Rivers.

VISITOR INFORMATION   Contact the provincial **VVV office** in Almelo during normal office hours (☎ **0546/535-535;** fax 0546/535-549). There is no information desk for visitors.

WHERE TO STAY & DINE IN OVERIJSSEL

Because Overijssel is so easy to reach from major centers like Amsterdam, few tourists seek accommodations within the province itself. There is, however, one very special inn in Ootmarsum near the German border (in the Twente area; see below), and a fine restaurant in Blokzijl, 8 miles east of Zwolle.

✪ **Hotel de Wiemsel.** Winhofflaan 2, 7631 HX Ootmarsum (35 miles east of Zwolle). ☎ **0541/292-155.** Fax 0541/293-295. 49 units MINIBAR TV TEL. Dfl 430–495 ($215–$247.50) double, Dfl 550 ($225) suite. Rates include full breakfast. AE, DC, MC, V.

This country inn has the look of a traditional farmhouse, with timber and brick walls topped by a steeply sloping roof. Inside, all is graciousness, from the antique-filled lobby and lounges to the attractive dining room. Each of the spacious guest rooms has a heated towel rack, refrigerator, and terrace. Dividers separate the living room area from the bedrooms.

The setting lends itself to peaceful days of outdoor rambling, and the hotel can send you off via bicycle or horse (from its own stables) with a picnic lunch. On the grounds there are lighted tennis courts, an indoor swimming pool, a solarium, and a sauna. Nearby is the lovely village of Ootmarsum (see "Twente," below) and other sights. The restaurant serves gourmet meals, which cost about Dfl 95 to 130 ($42.50 to $65), without wine.

✪ **Kaatje Bij de Sluis.** Brouwerstraat 20, Blokzijl. ☎ **0527/291-833.** Fixed-price menus Dfl 105–165 ($52.50–$82.50). AE, DC, MC, V. Wed–Fri and Sun noon–2:30pm; Wed–Sun 6–9:30pm. Closed February. CONTINENTAL.

Its name means "Kate's by the Sluice," which is appropriate enough in this small fishing village that lost its port to the IJsselmeer project. The kitchen, awarded two Michelin stars, has earned a reputation fine enough to persuade Amsterdammers to make the 96 km (60-mile) drive across the polder just to have dinner. The menu changes daily—sometimes twice daily—according to what's available. Seafood, as you might expect, is high on the list of specialties, along with beef and wild duck. There are also eight comfortable double rooms here if you decide to stay overnight.

ZWOLLE

82.5km (51.3 miles) NE of Amsterdam; 35km (22 miles) N of Apeldoorn

Zwolle, the provincial capital, had its "Golden Age" during the 14th and 15th centuries. In that boom time, the city walls were fortified and many churches and civic buildings were enlarged or embellished. Zwolle became an important religious and cultural center, as well as a hub of trade. The renowned scholar Thomas à Kempis spent most of his life here and is buried in the small St Michael's Church.

GETTING THERE   There are **trains** every hour from Amsterdam Centraal Station, via Apeldoorn.

Buses leave every hour on average from Apeldoorn.

Drivers from Amsterdam should take the E231 east to Amersfoort, then the E232 northeast to Zwolle. From Apeldoorn, take the A50 north.

VISITOR INFORMATION   The **VVV office** is at the central Grote Kerkplein 14, Zwolle (☎ **0900/112-2375;** fax 038/422-2679). Open Monday through Friday 9am to 5:30pm, Saturday 9am to 4pm.

EXPLORING ZWOLLE

Much of Zwolle's original fortified wall is still standing. Following the walkways along the wall is a perfect way to discover the hidden charms of this city. Some of the gates are particularly impressive, such as the **Sassenpoort,** which dates from 1408 and is adorned with four octagonal towers. The Sassenpoort's building accommodates a **visitor information center** (☎ **038/421-6626**), which has information about Zwolle's history. Open Wednesday through Friday from 10am to 5pm, Saturday and Sunday noon to 5pm.

Grote Kerk (St Michael's Church). Grote Kerkplein. ☎ **038/421-7596.** June–Aug Wed–Sat 2–4pm; hours are variable, so check with VVV.

This church (not to be confused with the small St Michael's Church just outside the town center) dates from the early 1400s. It's interesting for its octagonal vestry and its massive 4,000-pipe Schnitger organ, which is often used for recordings.

Church of Our Lady. Ossenmarkt. ☎ **038/421-5491.** Admission Dfl 2 ($1) adults, Dfl 1 (50¢) children. Mid-May to mid-Sept Mon–Fri 1–4pm, Sat 11am–4pm; Mid-Sept to mid-May Mon–Sat 1:15–3:15pm.

This church's tower, affectionately called "The Peppermill," is Zwolle's primary landmark. You can climb it and treat yourself to the wide views over the IJssel valley. The church itself is a massive structure, with a high brick vaulted ceiling and some interesting medieval relics and statues.

Zwolle Museum. Melkmarkt 41. ☎ **038/421-4650.** Admission Dfl 7.50 ($3.75). Tues–Sat 10am–5pm, Sun and holidays 1–5pm.

This newly expanded museum features exhibits relating to Zwolle's past, including an authentically restored 16th-century kitchen and an interesting collection of French furniture. There are also contemporary art exhibits.

ESPECIALLY FOR KIDS

✪ **Ecodrome.** Willemstraat 19 (10 minutes on foot from the main train station). ☎ **038/421-5050.** Admission Dfl 13.50 ($6.75) adults, Dfl 11 ($6.50) children. Easter to mid-Oct daily 10am–5pm; mid-Oct to Dec 25 Tues–Sun 10am–5pm; Christmas–Easter restricted opening hours. By car, from A21 take Zwolle-Zuid exit.

This attraction is an educational theme park. The exhibits examine nature and the environment in the past and the future. You start in the Geology Pavilion, where you learn about the earth's muddy past, and then head into the Biology Pavilion, to see how plant and animal life started—and how people began to interact and exercise influence over nature. The Dinorama is a subtropical environment where you come face-to-face with dinosaurs—you can even help dig up the fossilized bones.

KAMPEN

16km (10 miles) W of Zwolle

Some ocean-going vessels still moor at Kampen (on the N331, west of Zwolle) on the River IJssel, continuing a tradition of trade that goes back to the Middle Ages. Stop in at the **Oude Raadhuis** (Town Hall) at Oudestraat 133 (☎ **038/ 331-7361**), for a look at the richly paneled **Schepenzaal** (Aldermen's Room), the great carved fireplace from the 1540s, and the most complete collection of portraits of the House of Oranje in the whole country. It's open Monday through Friday 10am to 4pm.

DEVENTER

25.5km (16 miles) S of Zwolle; 14km (9 miles) NE of Apeldoorn

Deventer had its beginnings in the 11th century, but has certainly kept up with the march of time. It's famous for its Deventer Koek (a delicious spicy gingerbread). You'll see some fine medieval houses along its streets.

GETTING THERE   There are **trains** every hour from Zwolle and Appeldoorn.
   Buses leave every half hour on average from Zwolle and Appeldoorn.
   By **car,** take the N337 south from Zwolle, and the N344 northeast from Apeldoorn.

VISITOR INFORMATION   The **VVV office** at Keizerstraat 22 (☎ **0570/ 613-100;** fax 0570/643-338) is open Monday through Friday 9am to 5:30pm, Saturday 9am to 4pm.

EXPLORING DEVENTER

The **Historical Museum** in the **Waag** (Weigh House) at Brink 56 (☎ **0570/ 693-780**), holds artifacts relating to the area and a marvelous collection of costumes. Open Tuesday through Saturday from 10am to 5pm, Sunday from 2 to 5pm; admission is Dfl 5 ($2.50) for adults, Dfl 3 ($1.50) for children. The **Stadhuis** (Town Hall), Grote Kerkhof 4, houses a large library of medieval books and manuscripts and is well worth a look. Open Monday through Friday from 10am to 4pm; free admission. Contact the VVV service for guided group tours (☎ **0570/649-959**).

   A few miles west of Deventer, residents of the lovely little villages **Rijssen** and **Holten** care tenderly for the graves in a Canadian war cemetery.

STAPHORST

16km (10 miles) N of Zwolle

Staphorst, located north of Zwolle on the Meppel road, is the Dutch village of your imagination, with colorfully dressed residents living as their ancestors did. This is no tourist act—you'll seldom get an enthusiastic welcome from these devout Calvinists, especially on Sunday, when the entire population observes a tradition that dates back centuries: With downcast eyes, separate lines of men and women form a silent procession to the churches. No automobiles are allowed into the village on the Sabbath—even bicycle riding is forbidden. Cameras are always

---

The Hanseatic Towns

The Hanze route runs along the IJssel river, once the quick way from the Rhine to the Zuiderzee (long before it was dammed in and turned into the freshwater IJsselmeer). The seven towns along this route played an important role in the international trade of yesteryear. Most of the traffic consisted of merchant ships plying goods from central Europe to the outside world and back. In order to improve the safety of their passage and to promote mutual trade, a league was formed by more than 150 towns and cities in north and north-west Europe. It was known as the Hanseatic League, and might well be compared to the European Community of today—though it had significantly less bureaucracy.

The Hanseatic League brought prosperity to most of its members. The seven Dutch towns along the 125km (85 mile) Hanze Route—Doesburg, Zutphen, Deventer, Hattem, Zwolle, Hasselt, and Kampen—profited handsomely, as you can tell today by their ancient gateways, churches, public buildings, and merchants' houses, many of which are still standing. Each of these towns' VVV offices can supply you with a cycling or walking route that incorporates the best of the sites along the Hanze Route.

---

frowned upon. Whenever you come to Staphorst—on Sunday or a weekday—be sure to respect the townspeople's conservative ways and keep cameras out of sight.

GIETHOORN
18km (11 miles) N of Zwolle

GETTING THERE   Buses leave every hour on average from Zwolle.
By **car,** take the N331, N375, and N334 north from Zwolle.

VISITOR INFORMATION   The VVV office is on a boat, at the southern end of the main canal at Beulakerweg 114a (☎ **0521/361-248;** fax 0521/362-281).

EXPLORING GIETHOORN
You wouldn't want to miss this Venice-like town northwest of Staphorst—it has no streets, only canals. The town is just off of the N334 as you head toward Steenwijk, so leave your car in one of the car parks, and follow a sign-posted path to the ✪ **main canal,** where motorboats and punts wait to take you past enchanting canal-side cottages.

Take the N340 going east toward the German border, and you'll come across the picturesque villages of **Dalfsen** and **Ommen,** both of which are nestled in some enchanting countryside.

TWENTE
This beautiful region covers the eastern third of Overijssel province. The northern part, known as Sagenland, is famous for its fairy-tale-like atmosphere: old Saxon farmhouses, castles and country estates, and unspoiled natural woodlands. Enschede is a good starting point for a cycling tour of the Dinkel River valley, with its peaceful wooded glades and country estates. **NS** (Dutch Railways) can provide guides to cycling tours of the area, with maps available at the station.

The **VVV office** in Enschede, in the town center at Oude Markt 31 (☎ **053/432-3200;** fax 053/430-4162), can provide more information about this out-of-the-way region. It's open Monday 10am to 5:30pm, Tuesday through Friday 9am to 5:30pm, and Saturday 9am to 2pm. To reach Enschede by car, take the E30 east-bound from Apeldoorn to Exit 29, then go southeast on the N35.

OOTMARSUM
55km (34.5 miles) E of Zwolle

This is the oldest town in Twente, dating back to 1300. The large Gothic **Westfaalse Kerk** and the rococo-style **Stadhuis** (Town Hall) are two focal points in the restored center, where there are also many craftsmens' houses and workshops.

The **VVV office** is at Markt 1 (☎ **0541/292-183;** fax 0541/291-884). Open Monday through Friday 9am to 5pm, Saturday 10am to 1:30pm, and Sunday 1:30pm to 4pm. To get to Ootmarsum by car, take the N35 and N349 east from Zwolle.

4 Flevoland

The creation of the polder towns of Flevoland was an awesome achievement—a triumph over the forces of the sea. Even the most world-weary traveler cannot fail to be amazed while riding Flevoland's straight roads through flat fields crossed with equally straight canals. The polder towns can easily be visited from a base in Amsterdam or The Hague, as a natural incorporation of a route to the northern provinces, or as part of a 1- or 2-day circle of the IJsselmeer.

For centuries the Dutch have been not only protecting themselves from an ever-encroaching sea, but snatching more land to accommodate their ever-expanding population. One of their most formidable opponents has always been the Zuiderzee, an incursion of the North Sea that washed over Frisian dunes to flood vast inland areas between A.D. 200 and 300. Over the centuries, the Zuiderzee continued to expand, and in the 1200s a series of storms drove its water all the way to the inland lake known as Flevo. The sleepy, picturesque villages that today line the Flevo's shores presented quite a different picture when their harbors were alive with great ships that sailed for the Dutch West and East India Companies, carrying Dutch navigators on voyages of exploration to the far reaches of the South Pacific and around Cape Horn. North Sea fishermen added to the maritime traffic as they returned to Zuiderzee home ports, and Amsterdam flourished as ships from around the world sailed to its front door.

Still, Holland needed to control the waterway, which had earned a reputation as a "graveyard of ships." As early as the 1600s there was talk of driving back the sea and reclaiming the land it then covered. Parliament—in the manner of governments since time began—only got around to authorizing the project in 1918, and in the 1920s work was begun. In 1932, in an unparalleled feat of engineering, the North Sea was sealed off with the 19-mile Enclosing Dike and the saltwater Zuiderzee became the freshwater IJsselmeer. Since then the Dutch have been pumping dry thousands of acres, and in the process, converting fishing villages into farming villages, joining island villages to the mainland, and transforming North Sea fishermen into freshwater fishermen.

LELYSTAD
49.5km (31 miles) NE of Amsterdam

This is the newest city in Holland's newest polder province, Flevoland. Should you visit on a Saturday, be sure to go by the town square to see vendors clad in traditional dress hawking everything from smoked eels to crafts to cheese—a delightful example of a people holding onto tradition in the middle of modern-day progress.

GETTING THERE   **Trains** arrive every hour from Amsterdam Centraal Station. **Buses** arrive every half hour on average from Amsterdam.

By **car,** take the A6 northeast from Amsterdam.

VISITOR INFORMATION   **VVV Lelystad** is at Stationsplein 186 (☎ **0320/ 243-444;** fax 0320/280218).

EXPLORING LELYSTAD

✪ **New Land Polder Museum.** Oostvaardersdijk 1–13, just off the Markerwaard dike approach road. ☎ **0320/260-799.** Mon–Fri 10am–5pm, Sat–Sun 11:30am–5pm. Dfl 8.50 ($4.25) for adults, Dfl 4 ($2) children.

This museum is a fascinating place that will send you off with a much deeper understanding of the area. The exhibits explain the Zuiderzee Project in great detail. You'll learn all about the construction of the dikes, the pumping process, and the final drying up operation. There are also relics of ships that went to a watery grave in the Zuiderzee, possibly at the very spot on which you stand. Appropriately, the museum is housed in a space-age construction that can be seen for miles across the flat landscape.

✪ **V.O.C. Ship *Batavia*.** Oostvaardersdijk 1–9. ☎ **0320/261-409.** Daily Sept–June 10am–5pm, July–Aug 10am–9pm. Dfl 17.50 ($8.75) for adults, Dfl 7.50 ($3.75) for children under 18.

Get aboard this faithful reconstruction of a 17th-century V.O.C. (Dutch East India Company) sailing ship and imagine yourself en route to the spice islands of the East. The original *Batavia* sank off the coast of Australia on its first trip to the Dutch East Indies. This replica was built using 16th- and 17th-century carpenters' manuals and without the help of any electrical equipment or modern construction techniques. The sail-making and rigging workshops and the carving studios are worth a visit as well, and you can also see a man-o'-war that is presently being constructed.

From June 1999, the Batavia wharf will also host the **National Museum for Maritime Archaeology** (Rijksmuseum voor Scheepsarcheologie), included in the admission to the *Batavia*. This museum exhibits ships that sank in the Zuiderzee (now the IJsselmeer) as far back as Roman times; the ships' remains were revealed as water was pumped out to make way for polderland.

A NEARBY ATTRACTION FOR FAMILIES

Harderwijk Dolfinarium. 20-mile drive south of Lelystad on N302. ☎ **0341/467-7400.** Admission Dfl 29.50 ($14.75) adults, Dfl 26.50 ($13.25) children ages 4 to 11. Late Feb–Nov daily 10am–6pm.

This is the largest dolphinarium in the world. It has both a dolphin research and rehabilitation station and entertaining performances by the resident dolphins. A visit here is a thrilling and interesting day out, especially for families. There is a series of open-air pools as well as underwater viewing galleries. Other sea animals at the center include walruses and seals.

Eel Selection

When buying smoked eels, you'll show yourself to be an expert by selecting only the skinny ones (the fat ones aren't as tasty).

Polder Men

When traveling in the polders (the reclaimed land), from time to time you'll come across groups of men working alongside the road, repairing damage to the roads and the dikes. These are the *polderjongens* (polder men), who travel from place to place, wherever there is a need for their special training.

URK

17.5km (11 miles) N of Lelystad

This quaint little fishing village 10 miles south of Stavoren was a Zuiderzee island for more than 700 years, its isolation undisturbed until the reclamation project joined it to the mainland in 1942. In 1948, a roadway to the village was constructed, but residents were so displeased that they promptly banned all automobiles, requiring them to park on the outskirts. In the end, practicalities (and the Dutch are nothing if not practical), such as getting the eels for which their fishing fleet is famous to market, forced them to reconsider and lift the restriction. So while you will certainly encounter automobiles in the narrow brick-paved streets of Urk, it's still a good idea to park outside and take to your feet.

GETTING THERE   **Buses** leave every hour on average from the bus stations outside Lelystad train station.

By **car,** take the A6 north from Lelystad.

VISITOR INFORMATION   **VVV Urk** is at Wijk 2/2 (☎ **0527/684-040;** fax 0527/686-180). Open April through October Monday to Friday 9am to 5pm, and Saturday 9am to 1pm; November through March open only Wednesday and Friday from noon to 3pm.

EXPLORING URK

As you walk past picturesque brick homes lining those tiny streets, notice the decorated wooden doors and elaborate wrought ironwork. At long piers in the harbor, you'll see the sturdy fishing boats that sail in search of eels. Smoked eel is sold everywhere in Urk.

Many of the women of Urk still wear traditional long dresses, light blue corsets with protective patches of chamois leather for longer wear, and a hand-embroidered *kraplap* (bodice cover), as well as garnet necklaces and bonnets with earflaps. Men sport baggy felt pants held up with silver buttons adorned with scenes from the Bible, and blue knit stockings with their hand-stitched shoes. Many residents do not speak English, and while they're quite cordial to outsiders like you and me (and provide plenty of souvenirs for sale), they still insist—actually, require—that we respect their traditional Sunday prohibitions against driving an automobile, sailing a boat, or riding a bicycle. If you can walk into town on a Sunday morning just after church services, you'll see most of Urk's citizens taking a ritual walk through the town and down to the harbor.

The small **Museum Het Oude Raadhuis,** the old Town Hall, at Wijk 2/2 (☎ **0527/683-262**), has exhibits about Urk's ancient and more-recent history, and displays of local costumes and architecture. Open Easter through September Monday to Friday 11am to 5pm, Saturday 10am to 6pm; limited opening hours during spring and autumn school holidays. Admission is Dfl 3.50 ($1.75) for adults, and Dfl 1.75 (85¢) for children ages 6 to 12.

19

The Southern Provinces

All too often, the southernmost provinces of Holland are merely entrance or exit routes for tourists rushing to or from Belgium, Luxembourg, and other European destinations. Yet from the watery islands of Zeeland to the forests and moors of Brabant to Limburg's wooded hill country, there is a rich vein of travel experience waiting to be mined here. History, recreational activities, and some of Holland's most beautiful scenery are all abundant in this southern region.

1 Zeeland

This "Sea Land" on Holland's western coast has often been likened to three fingers of land pointing out into the North Sea. Zeelanders cling to the firm Dutch belief that "he who cannot master the sea is not worthy of the land," and century after century they have cherished their precious group of islands and former islands, rescuing them each time the sea has roared in to claim them.

There have been plenty of close calls. In 1421 the St Elizabeth Flood came close to tipping the balance in favor of the North Sea, in 1944 it was bombs from Allied planes that loosed flood waters to flush out Nazi troops entrenched in bunkers along the coast, and in 1953 a fierce hurricane sent sea water crashing through the province and as far inland as Rotterdam, drowning more than 1,800 people. In between those disasters were numerous "little floods" that swamped "only" a few islands. Always, Zeelanders have pushed back the angry sea and reinforced protective measures in this ongoing, uncompromising battle. Today, with the completion of an ingenious system of dikes, storm-surge barriers, and sluice gates known as the Delta Project, it's more likely to be the North Sea that will finally have to concede defeat, acknowledging Zeeland's firm grasp on its cluster of islands.

At the center of Zeeland is Walcheren (often still called Walcheren Island even though polders have long connected it to South Beveland and the mainland). This region holds the provincial capital of Middelburg, a medieval city that has restored its historic landmarks so successfully that you'd think they have stood completely undisturbed through the centuries. North of Walcheren lie North Beveland and the islands of Schouwen-Duiveland, St Philipsland (now a peninsula), and Tholen. To the south of

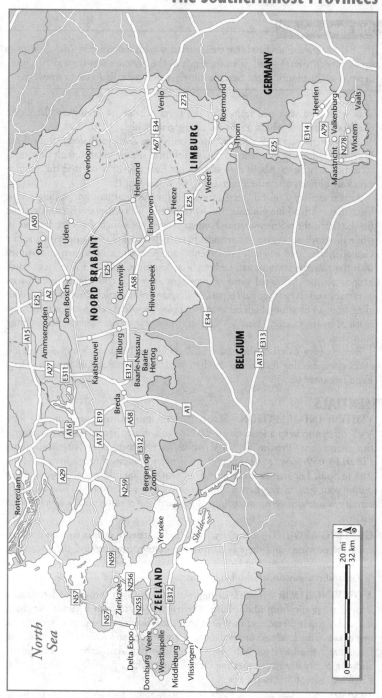

428 The Southern Provinces

Did You Know?

In 1810, Napoléon declared that the Zeeland was little more than "the silt thrown up by French rivers"—and in truth, much of the province was formed by alluvial deposits at the mouth of the Schelde, the river that controls access to Antwerp.

Walcheren, and separated from it by the River Schelde, is Zeeuwsch-Vlaanderen (Zeeland Flanders), which reaches to the Belgian border.

The western part of Walcheren (often called the Zeeland Riviera), from West-kapelle to Domburg, is a string of delightful small seaside villages, with all sorts of recreational facilities. About the only somber note along the coast at this point is struck by bunkers and other "mementos" of World War II.

As you explore Zeeland, keep an eye out for the local costume, a long simple black dress with a blue pinafore, still worn here in Walcheren and South Beveland (in the latter, the women wearing bonnets shaped like conch shells are Protestant, while those whose wearing trapezoidal bonnets with a light-blue underbonnet are Catholic). The gold-and-silver ornaments you see worn by both men and women with the national costume can be bought as souvenirs. Also, if you're lucky you'll happen on the traditional game of *ringsteken,* in which contestants ride on bare horseback and try, as they gallop past, to thrust a pointed stick through a ring dangling from a line strung high between two poles. Nowadays the horse is sometimes replaced by the tractor. The VVV can tell you where you can see the game during your visit.

Because it's so vital to the future of Zeeland and because it's one of the most exciting engineering feats of the modern world, no visitor should miss the **Delta Expo** (see box below).

ESSENTIALS

VISITOR INFORMATION   Scattered about the province are some 40 local VVV offices, so keep a lookout for the blue-and-white triangular sign that identifies them. The **Provincial VVV office,** at Nieuwe Burg 40, Middelburg (☎ **0118/659-965;** fax 0118/659-966), is open Monday through Saturday from 9am to 5pm. The staff here can provide information on bike rentals, special events during your visit, market days in the various villages, where to find 17th- and 18th-century windmills, accommodations along your travel route, and a host of other matters.

GETTING AROUND   Nondrivers will find a network of **bus** connections covering the province, and there is train transportation from around the country to Middelburg, Vlissingen, and Goes.

Zeeland is also wonderful biking country.

A DRIVING TOUR   If you're driving, virtually any of the provincial destinations is an easy day trip from Middelburg. Alternatively, begin from a Middelburg base, take a day trip to Veere, and then head south to Vlissingen and plan to stay over at one of the many lovely accommodations along the Zeeland Riviera (Westkapelle to Domburg), northwest of Vlissingen. The following day, drive to Stellendam, allowing plenty of time to tour the Delta Project, with a possible overnight stay at Zierikzee, a few miles to the east.

DINING   Your best meals in Zeeland will be in hotel dining rooms, but the locals or the local VVV offices can often recommend good small restaurants that are beginning to open with more frequency than in past years. Any seafood you order in this watery province will be fresher than fresh—right off of the local boats. *Special sweet-tooth note:* there's a Zeeland specialty called *bolus,* and when I asked my Zeelander friends to define it for me, all they could come up with was "they're these round things with sugar. . . ." I think its base is bread, but no matter what the ingredients, stop by a pastry shop or bakery and try one.

MIDDELBURG

184km (126 miles) SE of Amsterdam; 118km (81 miles) SE of Rotterdam

This provincial capital began as a 9th-century fortress, erected as a defense against the Normans. The fortifications expanded into a real settlement around 1150, when the abbey was established. Today the abbey is just one of the city's more than 1,000 historic buildings.

Middelburg's colorful **market day** is Thursday, when you can mingle in the Market Square with locals, some of whom wear native dress.

ESSENTIALS

GETTING THERE   There are trains every hour from Amsterdam Centraal Station, via Rotterdam and The Hague, to Middelburg, and from the nearby ferry terminal of Vlissingen.

By car, take the E19 south from Amsterdam. Pass by Rotterdam, and then, before Breda, take the E312 west toward Roosendaal and continue on to Middleburg.

VISITOR INFORMATION   The **VVV office** is at Nieuwe Burg 40 (☎ **0118/ 659-900;** fax 0118/659-940), open Monday through Saturday from 9am to 5pm. Among the mass of information and helpful literature, the office can supply an excellent walking-tour brochure. The VVV also conducts ✪ **guided walking tours** and organizes **coach tours** of the city, around Walcheren and to the Delta Expo (see below).

SEEING THE SIGHTS

Middelburg sights you really shouldn't miss include the **picturesque streets** of Spanjaardstraat (crowned by the monumental Oostkerk), Kuiperspoort, and Bellinkstraat; the 1559 **Vismarkt** (Fish Market), with its Doric columns and little auctioneers' houses (where summer Thursdays are **arts and crafts market** days); the **Blauwepoort** (Blue Gate); and the **Koepoort** (Cow Gate).

Town Hall. Markt. ☎ **0118/675-450.** Admission Dfl 4 ($2) adults, Dfl 3 ($1.50) children. Tours, Mar–Oct Mon–Sat 11am–5pm, Sun noon–5pm.

The Town Hall, another of Middelburg's miraculous reconstructions, consists of two distinct sections. The side facing the Markt is Gothic and dates from the 15th century, while the Noordstraat side, from the 17th and 18th centuries, is classic in style. Inside are such treasures as Belgian tapestries from the 1600s, a brass model of de Ruyter's flagship, 17th-century Makkum tiles, and the Middelburg coat of arms, originally located on the eastern facade of the building. The old tribunal hall is now known as the "wedding hall," and several ceremonies are held there each week. The banquet hall, originally the first cloth market in the Netherlands, is now used for official receptions, "welcome" evenings for new residents of Middelburg, and periodic concerts. The doors to the left of the main entrance open to the spacious vaulted Vleeshal (Meat Hall), which hosts intriguing contemporary art exhibitions.

✪ **Middelburg Abbey.** Abdijplein at Onder de Toren. Unrestricted admission to abbey courtyard.

This sprawling 13th-century abbey in the center of town had a life of traumatic ups and downs over the centuries, as it went from Catholic to Protestant to secular usages, all the while suffering from fires and careless alterations at the hands of whoever happened to be in charge. When 1940 bombings virtually leveled the structure, it would doubtless have passed into history as nothing but a dim memory had it not been for the dedication of Middelburg authorities and Zeeland citizens. At the close of World War II, they set about a restoration that amounted to a complete rebuilding—each brick had to be individually scraped and chipped smooth by hand before it could be put into place. The abbey you see today, a replica of the original, is an astonishing monument to all that work and dedication. As in medieval days, the abbey, with its magnificent courtyard and its tall Lange Jan Tower, serves as the very heart of Middelburg.

Nowadays, part of the abbey is occupied by the **Zeeuws Museum** and the **Abdij Historama** (see entries below)—both of which are very much worth a visit.

The courtyard is the ideal shady rest stop during sightseeing. It really pays to plan your day to include lunch here. The excellent restaurant, which has outdoor tables during good weather, serves everything from inexpensive snacks to complete three-course menus for about Dfl 40 to 52.50 ($20 to $26.25). It's open for lunch only.

Lange Jan (Long John) Tower. Middelburg Abbey, Abdijplein at Onder de Toren. ☎ **0118/675-450.** Admission Dfl 3 ($1.75) adults, Dfl 2.25 ($1.30) children. Easter–Oct Mon–Sat 10am–5pm.

Soaring 289 feet into the air, Long John can be seen from any point on the island, and of course there are magnificent panoramic views from its summit. The tower dates from the early 14th century. It was destroyed by fire several times but has been rebuilt.

✪ **Zeeland Museum (Zeeuws Museum).** Middelburg Abbey, Abdijplein 3. ☎ **0118/626-655.** Admission Dfl 8 ($4) adults, Dfl 2 ($1) children. Mon–Sat 11am–5pm, Sun noon–5pm.

There's a wonderful collection of antiquities in this museum. Highlights include a Roman altar to a pagan goddess recovered from the beach after a 17th-century storm, a medieval stone coffin that was used to water cattle before its origins were recognized, and 16th-century tapestries depicting the victory of Zeeland over the Spanish. National costumes are also displayed, with explanations of the differences in dress from one island or village to another.

Roosevelt Study Center. Abdij 9. ☎ **0118/631-590.** Free admission. Apr–Oct Mon–Fri 10am–12:30pm and 1:30–4:30pm; other times by appointment.

This research center was established in honor of Theodore, Franklin Delano, and Eleanor Roosevelt, whose ancestors emigrated to the New World in the 1640s from the Zeeland town of Tholen. The library here holds extensive research material on their modern American history, with audiovisual and slide presentations for use by European scholars. Since 1982, the annual Four Freedoms Medals (based on FDR's famous "four freedoms" speech in 1941, which named the four essential freedoms as freedom of speech and expression, freedom of worship, freedom from want, and freedom from fear) have been awarded in Middelburg in even-numbered years, and in Hyde Park, New York, in odd-numbered years.

Abdij Historama. Middelburg Abbey, Abdij 9. ☎ **0118/626-655.** Admission Dfl 6 ($3) adults, Dfl 2 ($1) children. Mon–Sat 11am–5pm, Sun noon–5pm.

The history of the abbey is revealed during a fascinating walk through the building. The tour here will take you through the cloisters, down to the cellars and the crypt,

Middelburg

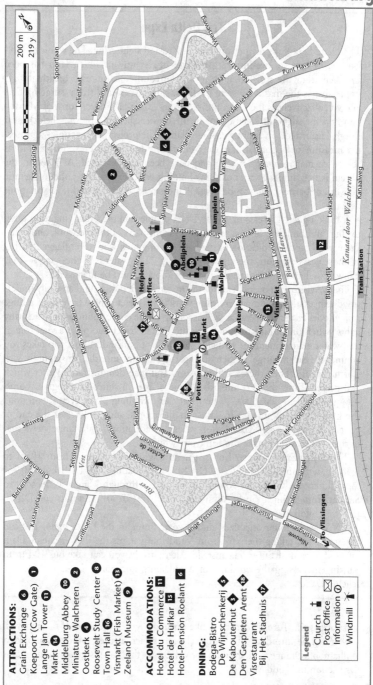

ATTRACTIONS:
Grain Exchange ⑥
Koepoort (Cow Gate) ①
Lange Jan Tower ⑪
Markt ⑭
Middelburg Abbey ⑩
Miniature Walcheren ②
Oostkerk ④
Roosevelt Study Center ⑧
Town Hall ⑯
Vismarkt (Fish Market) ⑬
Zeeland Museum ⑨

ACCOMMODATIONS:
Hotel du Commerce ⑪
Hotel de Huifkar ⑮
Hotel-Pension Roelant ⑥

DINING:
Bodega-Bistro
De Wijnschenkerij ⑤
De Kabouterhut ③
Den Gespleten Arent ⑱
Visrestaurant
Bij Het Stadhuis ⑰

Legend
✝ Church
☒ Post Office
ⓘ Information
✖ Windmill

431

The Delta Expo

The Delta Expo tops my personal list of Zeeland sightseeing. The whole of Holland is, of course, awe-inspiring because of the way in which land has been snatched from the sea, but nothing in the country is quite so breathtakingly impressive as the massive system of dikes, sluice gates, and storm-surge barriers known collectively as the Delta Project. It lies 20km (14 miles) north of Middelburg, on the island of Neeltje Jans in the Oosterschelde (Eastern Scheldt), near Burgh-Haamstede on Schouwen-Duiveland. The project was begun as a protective measure for Zeeland, but in the course of its development revolutionary ideas about sea management surfaced and have been implemented. As a result, the system is not simply a series of dams holding back the sea, but rather a gigantic network of barriers that can be opened and closed as storms and tidal variations demand.

It took a good 15 years of, as the Delta people told me, "dredging, dumping, towing, and building" to create the component parts of this network, and when I remarked on the dedication of the hardworking men who never flagged during all those years of effort, the reply was simply, "The water is in these men—they know it well and what it can do and they know it must be managed."

To give visitors an overall view of the massive undertaking and an easily understood explanation of how everything works, the Delta people have built a huge scale model of the complex, as well as a map of the entire country on which tiny lights switch on and off to show how the Delta Project also plays a vital role in freshwater management for virtually the whole of Holland. A boat trip takes you around the storm-surge barrier during the summer months; this tour is well worth the fare. Then there's a film history and map demonstration, after which you descend into the very innards of one of the 36 sluice-gate engine rooms. Allow yourself no less than 1½ hours at this intriguing place, even if you don't think you have any interest in dams, engine rooms, and the like. At the end of your tour there's a cozy coffee shop whose terrace affords panoramic views that in themselves would make the trip worthwhile.

The Delta Expo is open from April through October, daily from 10am to 5:30pm, with an admission fee of Dfl 20 ($10) for adults and Dfl 13.50 ($6.75) for children, including the boat tour; November through March Wednesday to Sunday from 10am to 5pm. Admission is Dfl 15 ($7.50) for adults and Dfl 10 ($5) for children.

VVV Middelburg organizes guided coach tours to the Delta Expo. You can also go by car, taking the N57 from Middelburg across the Oosterschelde Dam in the direction of Burgh-Haamstede. Alternatively, you can take bus 104 from Vlissingen, passing the outskirts of Middelburg and going across the Oosterschelde Dam.

and back again. Turning corners is like turning pages in the book of the abbey's history. You'll be introduced to historical figures such as the Norbertine monks and William of Orange and everyone involved in the abbey's renovation after the destruction in World War II.

ESPECIALLY FOR KIDS

✪ **Miniature Walcheren.** Molenwater Park, at Nieuwe Haven (near Middelburg Abbey). ☎ **0118/612-525.** Admission Dfl 11 ($5.50) adults, Dfl 8 ($4) children. Apr–Oct daily 10am–5pm. Closed Nov–Mar.

This marvelous one-twentieth-scale model of Walcheren is a faithful replication of more than 200 buildings, moving trains and ships, and windmills. This is a delight for both young and old, and a good place to visit before you leave Middelburg to explore the rest of Walcheren, where you'll see the real structures on which these models are based.

WHERE TO STAY

✪ **Hotel de Huifkar.** Markt 19, 4331 LJ Middelburg. ☎ **0118/612-998.** Fax 0118/612-386. 6 units. TV TEL. Dfl 135–185 ($67.50–$92.50) double, depending on whether with bathroom or shower. AE, DC, MC, V.

This pleasant little hotel overlooks the Market Square, right in the heart of the city. While not luxurious, the guest rooms are furnished in a modern style. Downstairs is a very good restaurant with moderate prices, serving its own tourist menu. In summer you can dine on the lively terrace spilling out onto the Market Square.

✪ **Hotel du Commerce.** Loskade 1, 4331 HV Middelburg. ☎ **0118/636-051.** Fax 0118/626-400. 46 units. MINIBAR TV TEL. Dfl 140–185 ($70–$92.50) double. Rates include breakfast. AE, MC, V.

This small canal-side hotel is just opposite the train and bus terminal and an easy walk from the town center, in one of the most convenient locations in town. The guest rooms are simply decorated. In the mornings you can treat yourself to a varied breakfast buffet. There's also a good restaurant serving French and Spanish specialties at moderate prices.

Hotel-Pension Roelant. Koepoortstraat 10, 4331 SL Middelburg. ☎ **0118/627-659.** Fax 0118/628-973. 16 units. TV TEL. Dfl 115 ($57.50) double. AE, MC, V.

This tranquil hotel is located in the oldest part of town. The rooms are simple and comfortable. There's a quiet back garden where you can have breakfast. The management offers special culinary arrangements that combine an overnight stay with dinner in the restaurant next door, Bodega-Bistro De Wijnschenkerij (see "Where to Dine," below).

WHERE TO DINE

Bodega-Bistro De Wijnschenkerij. Koepoortstraat 10A. ☎ **0118/633-309.** Fixed-price menu Dfl 41.50 ($20.75). Daily 6–11pm. FRENCH/PROVENÇAL.

This restaurant, in the cellars of Hotel-Pension Roelant (see above), serves original Provençal cuisine. There is always a choice between four menus that change regularly. Seasonal specialties include suckling lamb and green asparagus. The wine list is impressive.

De Kabouterhut. Oostkerkplein 8. ☎ **0118/612-276.** Pancakes Dfl 7.50–18 ($4.35–$10.45). Daily noon–7:30pm. DUTCH/PANCAKES.

The menu here offers more than 60 kinds of Dutch pancakes. The interior is crammed with little tables, each of them featuring a miniature garden gnome as part of the table setting. Try the traditional bacon and treacle pancake, or the more exotic cheese and ginger. In summer you can sit on the peaceful terrace facing the baroque Oostkerk.

✪ **Den Gespleten Arent.** Vlasmarkt 25 (near the Town Hall). ☎ **0118/636-122.** Main courses Dfl 28.50–39.50 ($14.25–$19.75); fixed-price menu Dfl 49.50 ($24.75). AE, DC, MC, V. Thurs–Mon 5:30–9pm. SEAFOOD.

Meals here, though a bit more expensive than at most local restaurants, are exceptionally good and still very good value nonetheless. The friendly owner has created a warm and intimate atmosphere in this patrician-house setting. Food is prepared with an imaginative use of ingredients. Specialties include lamb's tongues with fennel and pine nuts, and turkey stuffed with pancetta (Italian bacon).

Visrestaurant Bij Het Stadhuis. Lange Noordstraat 8. ☎ **0118/627-058.** Main courses Dfl 25–39.50 ($12.50–$19.75); fixed-price menu Dfl 36.50 ($16.25). AE, DC, MC, V. Wed–Mon noon–2:30pm and 5:30–10pm. SEAFOOD.

You'll find this cozy restaurant on a street next to the Gothic Town Hall. The place is full of small tables decked in yellow and brown. Besides serving almost any variety of fried and grilled fish, the restaurant's specialties include a succulent mussels au gratin Ste Marie topped by a cream sauce, and *waterzooï*, a delicious fish stew.

A Seafood Restaurant in Nearby Yerseke

✪ **Restaurant Nolet Het Reymerswale.** Jachthaven 5, Yerseke. ☎ **0113/571-642.** Fixed-price menus Dfl 90–125 for 4 courses ($45–$62.50). AE, MC, V. Thurs–Mon noon–3pm and 6–9pm. SEAFOOD.

This very special seafood restaurant—one of the best in Holland—is worth the 40km (25-mile) drive from Middelburg. The cozy place is located in the busy little port town of Yerseke, right at the waterfront. The owner and chef, Theo Nolet, has extensive training and experience behind him, and you may be sure that whatever lands on your plate has just come from fishing boats in the harbor below. Theo even angles for the sea bass himself. Try the decadent oysters and champagne, or a more restrained dish like grilled turbot with a béarnaise sauce.

VEERE

6km (4 miles) NE of Middelburg

This charming little village was an important port for Scottish wool from the 14th to the 18th centuries. Veere's streets are lined with houses and buildings straight out of the past, and its original fortifications are still intact, the ancient tower now housing an excellent restaurant.

GETTING THERE   There are no trains to Veere, but **buses** run every hour from Middelburg.

VISITOR INFORMATION   The **VVV office** is at Oudestraat 28 (☎ **0118/ 501-365;** fax 0118/501-792). Pick up the "Historical Walk Through Veere" booklet.

EXPLORING VEERE

You shouldn't miss the **Stadhuis,** at Markt 5, which dates from 1474—look outside for the *kaak,* an iron brace that locked around a wrongdoer's neck to hold him or her in place as townspeople threw refuse and spittle. Over the *kaak* hang the "stones of the law," which an offender was forced to drag through the town in penance. The Stadhuis is open June through mid-September, Monday to Saturday from 10am to 5pm.

The **Grote Kerk** (Great Church) took more than a century to construct (1405–1560). Later on, Napoléon turned it into a stable, barracks, and hospital. Although today the church is stripped to the bare bricks, its sheer size is awe-inspiring. In the tower, the slow sway of a Foucault pendulum gives proof of the earth's rotation. The church is open Monday through Saturday from 10am to 5pm, Sunday from 2 to 5pm.

Other sights include the step-gabled **Campveerse Toren** (Campveer Tower), which dates from 1500 and formed part of the town fortifications; and the **Schotse Huizen** (Scottish Houses) at Kade 25 and 27, 16th- and 17th-century waterfront mansions that belonged to Scottish wool merchants.

VLISSINGEN

6km (4 miles) S of Middelburg

> **GETTING THERE**   There are trains every hour from Rotterdam Centraal Station and Amsterdam Centraal Station to Vlissingen, via Middelburg, and there are frequent buses from Middelburg.
>
> By **car,** drive west on the E312 from Middelburg.
>
> **VISITOR INFORMATION**   The **VVV office** is at Nieuwendijk 15 (☎ **0118/ 412-345;** fax 0118/417-426).

EXPLORING VLISSINGEN

The port city of Vlissingen, which offers ferry service to England, is also a popular seaside resort. New Yorkers are sure to feel at home, since Vlissingen's name translates to Flushing.

Visit the ✪ **Stedelijk Museum** (Municipal Museum) for an overview of the region's maritime history, interesting ship models, and archaeological relics. Other interesting sites are the **Oude Markt,** the **Grote Kerk** (dating from the 14th century), and **St Jacobskerk.** Whatever you do, don't leave the city without at least one stroll down the **seafront promenade** that's named variously De Ruyter, Bankert, and Evertsen, in honor of those Dutch naval heroes.

ESPECIALLY FOR KIDS

✪ **Iguana Reptile Zoo.** Bellamypark 35. ☎ **0118/417-219.** Admission Dfl 9.50 ($4.75). Daily 2–5:30pm; June–Sept also Tues–Sat 10am–12:30pm.

This zoo is full of the animals that childhood nightmares are made of, but that kids seem to love just the same. It's a fascinating introduction to the life of reptiles, amphibians, and insects from all over the world. There are more than 500 specimens on display, from tiny, creepy scorpions to endless tiger pythons, but they're not all scary—you can also watch frogs, turtles, and salamanders. In the baby-room you can even see eggs hatching and young animals crawling out of their shells.

WHERE TO STAY

✪ **De Campveerse Toren.** Kade 2, 4351 AA Veere. ☎ **0118/501-291.** Fax 0118/ 501-695. 16 units. TEL. Dfl 125–225 ($62.50–$112.50) double; Dfl 275 ($137.50) suite. AE, DC, MC, V.

This delightful hotel is reputedly one of the oldest in the country. It offers simple but comfortable rooms with good light, wooden floors, and antique furniture. The Veerse Meer lake is right below the windows. The proprietors also run the adjoining restaurant (see below)—one of the best in Zeeland—so there are various gastronomic arrangements available. The breakfast and dining room have been furnished in a 17th-century style, with wooden floors, wainscotted walls, and a huge stone fireplace, creating an intimate atmosphere. You couldn't ask for a more romantic location than the 16th-century waterfront fortress of which it is a part. Just steps away are the equally ancient and historic buildings that make Veere so charming.

WHERE TO DINE

✪ **De Campveerse Toren.** Kade 2. ☎ **0118/501-291.** Fixed-price menus Dfl 69.50–99.50 ($34.75–$49.75). AE, DC, MC, V. Daily noon–2:30pm and 6–9:30pm; Nov–Feb closed Mon–Tues lunchtime. FISH/SEAFOOD.

This wonderfully atmospheric restaurant is a great place to bust the budget. It's perched in a 16th-century tower room overlooking the Veersemeer, a lake busy with the comings and goings of sailboats, yachts, and swans. The place has an interesting history and is filled with brass and copper antiques; it was a great favorite of Grace Kelly's (ask about the "parfait d'amour" created just for her). The atmosphere is not only gracious but also a lot of fun. Seafood dishes are specialties on the extensive menu. Seasonal specialties include Veerse Meer eel and mussels and oysters from the Oosterschelde.

THE ZEELAND RIVIERA

A few miles northwest of Vlissingen is the delightful little village of **Koudekerke,** starting point for a tour of what is often called the Zeeland Riviera because of its long stretches of wide, white-sand beaches. This is holiday country more than sight-seeing territory. Beaches are pollution free and safe for swimming. Several small villages along the route from Westkapelle to Domburg offer a variety of recreational facilities, including boating, golf, tennis, squash (in Domburg), fishing (inland or sea angling), and walks in wooded areas near the beaches. **Westkapelle** and **Domburg** are both family-oriented resorts, with activities aplenty for the younger set as well as their parents.

WHERE TO STAY & DINE IN THE ZEELAND RIVIERA

The area abounds with accommodations, including upscale hotels, bungalows, rustic cabins, and camping facilities. The listings below are only a small sample; any VVV office in this area or in Middelburg can help you find a good choice.

Hotel de Burg. Ooststraat 5, 4357 BE Domburg. ☎ **0118/581-337.** Fax 0118/582-072. 23 units. TV TEL. Dfl 100–135 ($50–$67.50) double. AE, MC, V.

You'll find this modern hotel on Domburg's main street, just a short walk from the dunes and the sea. Guest rooms are decorated in bright colors, with attractive wooden furniture and comfortable beds. Showers are small but clean. The hotel restaurant serves simple, hearty meals.

✪ **Hotel Zuiderduin.** De Bucksweg 2, 4361 SM Westkapelle. ☎ **0118/561-810.** Fax 0118/562-261. 67 units. MINIBAR TV TEL. Dfl 175–235 ($87.50–$117.50) double. AE, DC, MC, V. Closed first week in Jan.

A variety of accommodations is offered at this modern hotel set just behind the dunes. There are spacious rooms with private baths and kitchenettes, each with either a private balcony or a terrace, as well as complete apartments that can sleep up to five people. Facilities include a heated swimming pool, sauna, solarium, and an all-weather tennis court. The restaurant attracts locals as well as tourists, offering seafood and continental specialties at remarkably moderate prices.

ZIERIKZEE

42km (29 miles) NE of Middelburg; 58km (40 miles) SW of Rotterdam

This 11-centuries-old little town on the Oosterschelde is reputedly the best-preserved town in Holland. It's still guarded by the town walls built during the Middle Ages.

GETTING THERE   There are no trains to Zierikzee, but buses arrive every hour from Goes, the nearest station on the Amsterdam–Rotterdam–Vlissingen line.

By **car,** take the A29 and N59 south and west from Rotterdam, and the N255 and N256 north from Middelburg.

VISITOR INFORMATION   The **VVV office,** at Meelstraat 4 (☎ **0111/ 412-450;** fax 0111/417-273), can provide walking-tour information, as well as details and bookings on cruises on the Oosterschelde during summer months.

EXPLORING ZIERIKZEE

Strolling Zierikzee's narrow, cobblestone streets, you'll find it easy to imagine the everyday life of its citizens in medieval times, especially if you're there for a colorful Thursday market day. The **Stadhuismuseum** in the Town Hall traces its history through archaeological finds and other relics. It's open May through September, Monday to Friday from 10am to 5pm. Look for the **Sint-Lievens Monstertoren** (Great Tower) on the cathedral. This 199-foot-tall tower is actually incomplete, since townspeople lacked the funds to take it to its planned 680-foot height.

WHERE TO STAY

Hostellerie Schuddebeurs. Donkereweg 35, 4317 NL Zierikzee, 3km (2 miles) north of Zierikzee. ☎ **0111/415-651.** Fax 0111/413-103. E-mail: schuddebeurs@horecagids.nl. 24 units. MINIBAR TV TEL. Dfl 140–220 ($70–$110) double.

This hotel in the wooded countryside just outside the town is the only lodging of standing in the area, with a top-class restaurant to go with it. The bungalow-style farmhouse and its modern wings have some rooms on the ground floor with their own garden terrace. There are also three country houses close by. Golfers can take advantage of the nearby course. The restaurant serves dinners ranging from three to seven courses for Dfl 75 to 125 ($37.50 to $62.50). Ask about various gastronomic and golf arrangements.

WHERE TO DINE

Auberge Maritime. Nieuwe Haven 21. ☎ **0111/412-156.** Main courses Dfl 29.50–75 ($14.75–$37.50). Fixed-price menu Dfl 55 ($27.50). AE, MC, V. Sun–Thurs 11:45am–9pm, Fri–Sat 11:45am–10pm. SEAFOOD.

This informal bar-cafe-restaurant in the town center makes a pleasant stop for just a meal or just drinks and snacks. It overlooks the harbor and Zierikzee's fishing fleet. The atmosphere inside is reminiscent of high seas and boasting sailors. Meals are wonderfully cooked. In summer you can dine on the terrace. Try the sea bass in a pastry crust with dill sauce, or the lamb cutlets with thyme and honey. Oysters and lobsters are kept fresh in a special aquarium.

2 Brabant

Brabant—officially known as Noord-Brabant—is one of the Netherlands's most scenic provinces. There are the waterways and polders in the north and west; sand drifts, fir, and deciduous woods in the south and east; and picturesque villages and ancient towns are everywhere.

Residents of Brabant, which lies on the Belgian border, south of the rivers Rhine and Meuse, sometimes seem as much Belgian as Dutch; they have a more relaxed view of the world and place great emphasis on life's pleasures, such as the joys of eating well. There's even one town where the national border itself is blurred, with homes on one side of a street within Holland, and those on the other side in Belgium!

Accommodations standards are quite high and hotels numerous in Brabant, yet during July and August they tend to be especially tightly booked, making it highly advisable to make your reservations in advance.

GETTING AROUND   Train service runs to Den Bosch ('s Hertogenbosch), Tilburg, Breda, and Eindhoven, and there are **bus** connections from around the country. Drivers should consider exploring the province from a base in Den Bosch or Breda, making day trips to other points of interest.

DEN BOSCH

74km (51 miles) SE of Amsterdam; 80km (55 miles) E of Rotterdam

The full and difficult-to-say name of the capital of the province of Noord-Brabant is "'s Hertogenbosch," meaning The Duke's Wood, but the place is often referred to simply as "Den Bosch" (The Woods)—maybe the locals, too, have given up on trying to pronounce the longer version!

This cathedral town is more than 800 years old. Once it was heavily fortified. Parts of the town center have retained their medieval atmosphere, such as the crooked alleys leading up to the odd triangular market square. There's also a tiny river whose course is partly underground.

GETTING THERE   There are trains every hour at least from Amsterdam Centraal Station, via Utrecht, to Den Bosch. Similarly, there are frequent trains from Rotterdam and The Hague.

By **car,** take the E35 and E25 southeast from Amsterdam.

VISITOR INFORMATION   The **VVV office** is at Markt 77 (☎ **0900/ 112-2334;** fax 073/612-8930). Open Monday 11am to 5:30pm, Tuesday through Friday 9am to 5:30 pm, Saturday 9am to 4pm.

EXPLORING DEN BOSCH

Noordbrabants Museum. Verwersstraat 41. ☎ **073/687-7800.** Admission Dfl 10 ($5). Tues–Fri 10am–5pm; Sat, Sun, and holidays noon–5pm.

This 17th-century neoclassical building was the official residence of the Queen's Commissioner to Noord-Brabant from 1820 to 1983, but is now the stylish, centrally located setting for a museum. Exhibitions on local history focus on archaeological finds from the Noord-Brabant region, such as Roman remains, religious artifacts, manuscripts, maps, weapons, and coins. The paintings on display emphasize the Dutch still-life, with two rooms full of painted flowers from the 16th to 18th centuries. In the gardens there are contemporary sculptures.

☻ **St John's Cathedral (Sint-Janskathedraal).** Parade/Torenstraat 16. For info and guided tours, call VVV (☎ **0900/112-2334**). Daily (except during services) 8am–5pm; Nov–Easter daily 9:30am–4pm.

Parts of this magnificent cathedral date back to the 1200s, although most of the present Gothic structure was finished in 1529. The cathedral suffered considerable damage during a fire in 1584, when the cupola and its tower collapsed. Some of the original 15th-century frescoes were revealed during recent restoration. Beautiful examples are the *Joshua Tree* and *Saint James* in the ambulatory.

Also, have a look in the Chapel of the Holy Sacrament on the north side of the choir, where there is a 15th-century brass chandelier. This elegant structure, finished in 1497, is lavishly decorated and imbued with a soft light. Notice the little stone figures on the flying buttresses and up the copings—miniature copies of these delightful figures are on sale in local gift shops and make marvelous souvenirs to take home. The 50-bell carillon in the rump of the 13th-century, late-Romanesque tower is played every Wednesday, 11:30am through 12:30pm.

Het Zwanenbroedershuis. Hinthamerstraat 94. ☎ **073/613-5098.** Dfl 4 ($2). Guided tours: Sept–July Fri 11am, 12:15pm, and 2:30pm.

This neo-Gothic building is the house of the Brotherhood of Our Illustrious Lady, a charitable body founded in the 14th century that grew into an organization of considerable influence. Membership became a matter of prestige, attracting rich citizens and nobility, including Queen Beatrix and Crown Prince Willem-Alexander. The Brotherhood had its own chapel built in Sint-Janskathedraal, and music was especially commissioned for its choir. Some of these illuminated choir books are on display, as well as gifts from its members and other memorabilia documenting the Brotherhood's history.

NEARBY ATTRACTIONS

✪ **Ammersoyen Castle.** Kasteellaan 7, Ammersoyen (7 miles northwest of Den Bosch). ☎ **073/599-1270.** Admission Dfl 7.50 ($4.35) adults, Dfl 3.50 ($2) children. Mid-Apr to Oct Tues–Sat 10am–5pm, Sun 1–5pm; last tour at 4pm.

This is one of the best-preserved medieval castles in Holland. It has had a colorful array of inhabitants over the centuries, serving as a nunnery and later as a depot for a manufacturer of washing machines before being bought by the "Stichting Vrienden der Geldersche Kastelen" (Foundation of Friends of Castles in Gelderland) and restored to its former glory. Inside, the Foundation has re-created the plain, rather austere atmosphere the castle would have had in the 14th century. Outside, there's a moat and four sturdy towers connected to make a square, virtually impregnable building. You enter the castle through the cellar and go up staircases built inside the thick walls. Upstairs you'll find a magnificent hall and some smaller tower rooms. In the attic is a small exhibition of objects found during restoration on the grounds and in the moat.

ESPECIALLY FOR KIDS

Beekse Bergen Safari Park. Beekse Bergen 31, Hilvarenbeek. ☎ **013/549-0049.** Admission Dfl 23.50 ($11.75) adults, Dfl 20.50 ($10.25) children 3 to 11. Dec–Jan 10am–4pm; Feb and Nov 10am–4:30pm; July–Aug 10am–6pm; Mar–June and Sept–Oct 10am–5pm.

You can either stay in your own car or take a guided bus tour through this extensive open-air safari park. Some 125 different species live together here in a free, natural environment.

✪ **De Efteling Family Leisure Park.** Kaatsheuvel (a few miles north of Tilburg). ☎ **0416/288-111.** Admission Dfl 35 ($17.50), free for children 3 and under. Early Apr–end Oct daily 10am–6pm; July–Aug 10am–9pm. From Den Bosch take the A59 westbound, Exit 37.

This 700-acre recreational park just outside the town of Kaatsheuvel has amusements, restaurants, and facilities for boating. Most remarkable, however, is the miniature city, with towers, castles, and characters based on just about every fairytale that ever stirred a child's imagination, and slightly weirder and wackier figures dreamed up by the park's own creative team. Many of the characters are fully animated or played by an actor in costume—the kids will never forget the experience. Watch out for the exciting water rides. Organization is good, so queuing is kept to a minimum even in busy school-holiday periods.

WHERE TO STAY

Eurohotel. Hinthamerstraat 63, 5211 MG Den Bosch. ☎ **073/613-7777.** Fax 073/612-8795. 42 units. TV TEL. Dfl 140 ($70) double. Rates include breakfast. AE, DC, MC, V.

This small hotel in the city center has just been renovated. Downstairs is the reception; cream-colored, marble stairs lead to the restaurant and guest rooms. The rooms are attractive and intimate, decorated in pastels and print fabrics, and furnished with stylish chairs and comfortable beds. The restaurant looks out over a bustling pedestrian shopping street. The friendly owners have succeeded in making this a very convivial lodging.

Golden Tulip Hotel Central. Burg Loeffplein 98, 5211 RX Den Bosch. ☎ **073/692-6926.** Fax 073/614-5699. E-mail: info@hotel-central.nl. 121 units, 3 suites. MINIBAR TV TEL. Dfl 235 ($117.50) double; Dfl 395–570 ($197.50–$285) suite. AE, DC, MC, V.

You couldn't ask for a more romantic location than this, right on the city's medieval market square. The Central is large and modern, but somehow manages also to be cozy. The guest rooms are nicely appointed and include room safes for valuables, as well as hair dryers. There's also a coffee shop, a bar, an a la carte restaurant, and a 14th-century cellar restaurant (De Hoofdwacht).

✪ **Hotel-Restaurant De Swaen.** De Lind 47, 5061 HT Oisterwijk (9 miles southwest of Den Bosch). ☎ **013/523-3233.** Fax 013/528-5860. 18 units. A/C MINIBAR TV TEL. Dfl 325 ($162.50) double. Breakfast Dfl 32.50 ($16.25). AE, DC, MC, V. Closed 1 week in July.

De Swaen is located on the market square of the quiet little village of Oisterwijk. The exterior of this neat white two-story hotel, with its long verandah across the front and prim, blue-trimmed windows, calls to mind the coaching inn that preceded it here. Since its complete renovation, however, the hotel has become one of Holland's most popular, and its dining room has earned international renown (see "Where to Dine," below). The plush guest rooms feature baths done up in Italian marble, with such luxurious touches as gold-plated faucets. Tiny chocolates decorated with white swans appear on your pillow each evening.

✪ **Hotel-Restaurant "In den Verdwaalde Koogel."** Vismarkt 1, 5256 BC Heusden (12 miles west of Den Bosch). ☎ **0416/661-933.** Fax 0416/661-295. 13 units. MINIBAR TV TEL. Dfl 155 ($75) double. AE, MC, V. Follow the A59 motorway west to Exit 42, then take the N267 north.

Charming—this overworked word definitely applies to this 17th-century gabled town house that has been converted into an inn. Its name means "The Stray Bullet." The rooms here are small and the furnishings are modern; rooms on the upper floors sport some interesting decorative touches such as exposed beams or rafters. The largest room is the "honeymoon suite," which is furnished with antiques and has nice views (it's only slightly more expensive than other rooms).

The restaurant alone is sufficient reason for a detour through this picturesque little village. The cozy interior is decorated in Vermeer colors, with antique gray beams overhead and antique clocks among its decorations. The excellent menu choices might include Texel lamb or eel in a green sauce. Dinner costs Dfl 55 ($27.50) for three courses and Dfl 75 ($37.50) for five courses. The price/quality ratio is excellent, and the service is friendly.

WHERE TO DINE

Pilkington's. Torenstraat 5 (across from St. Janskathedraal). ☎ **073/612-2923.** Main courses Dfl 22–38 ($11–$19); 3-course daily special Dfl 42.50 ($22.25). AE, DC, MC, V. Mon 11:30am–5pm, Tues–Sun 10am–10pm. BRITISH/CONTINENTAL.

This lovely cafe-restaurant has the atmosphere of an English country home. As you come in, you'll see a display of luscious cakes, sandwiches, quiches, and homemade patés. People sit at small tables along the wall on wicker chairs. At the back is a roofed terrace overlooking a lovely garden, with clipped hedgerows and rosebushes, where you can have a romantic dinner in summer. Seasonal specialties include wild boar, venison, and hare, all with delectable sauces. Try the tasty *speculaas* pudding—made with traditional Dutch spicy biscuits—for dessert.

✪ **De Raadskelder.** Markt 1A. ☎ **073/613-6919.** Reservations not required. Main courses Dfl 32.50–40 ($16.25–$20); fixed-price dinner from Dfl 49.75 ($24.85) for 4 courses to Dfl

89.75 ($44.85) for 6 courses. AE, MC, V. Tues–Sat 10:30am–5pm and 5:30–10:30pm. Closed first 2 weeks in August, Christmas–New Year's. REGIONAL.

This huge, vaulted cellar restaurant under the Gothic Town Hall serves excellent meals at moderate prices. The interior is medieval in theme: lighting is provided by brass chandeliers and lanterns, and there are massive pillars and a grand stone fireplace. The imaginative menu includes fried pike perch with salsifies, black olives, and *beurre blanc,* as well as veal stewed in a sauce of Kriek Lambic (Belgian cherry beer) and celeriac root.

De Swaen. In the Hotel-Restaurant de Swaen De Lind 47, Oisterwijk (9 miles southwest of Den Bosch). ☎ **013/523-3233.** Reservations recommended. Main courses Dfl 42.50–95 ($21.25–$47.50); fixed-price dinner Dfl 115 ($57.50) for 4 courses. AE, DC, MC, V. Tues–Sun 6–9pm. Closed 1 week in July. CONTINENTAL/REGIONAL.

This hotel restaurant (see "Where to Stay," above) is the most widely recognized restaurant in Brabant. Its chef, Cas Spijkers, a native of this region, trained in leading kitchens throughout Europe before coming back to lead De Swaen to its current prestigious position. He selects the best of local products, travels to Brussels twice a month to shop in the excellent markets there, smokes his own fish, meat, and game, and bakes all breads and pastries right on the premises. The result is food that has earned De Swaen a Michelin star and a devoted following. A good choice would be the goose liver, lobster, and smoked-salmon salad, followed by the cockerel with truffle, steamed over herbs and served with a forest-mushroom sauce. All the desserts are wonderful.

BREDA
101km (69 miles) S of Amsterdam; 37km (25 miles) SW of Den Bosch

Historic Breda, on the main Rotterdam–Antwerp expressway, was granted its charter back in 1252. In 1625 the town withstood a 9-month siege before surrendering to superior Spanish forces. In 1660 England's exiled Charles II took refuge here, and in 1667 the Treaty of Breda (between England, France, the United Provinces, and Denmark) awarded the New World colonies of New Amsterdam and New Jersey to the English.

Today, life in Breda centers around the rectangular Grote Markt and the town's many fine parks.

GETTING THERE   Trains arrive at least every hour from Amsterdam Centraal Station, via Rotterdam and The Hague.

VISITOR INFORMATION   Check with the **VVV office,** located at Willemstraat 17–19 (☎ **076/522-2444;** fax 076/521-8530), for details on the ✪ **"Historical Kilometer"** walking tour that takes you to the **Castle of Breda** (dating from 1536, now a military academy), the **Great Church of Our Lady** (with its striking tomb of Count Engelbert II and his wife), and other historical sights.

EXPLORING BREDA

The **Breda Museum** in the former Chassé Barracks (Kazerne), Parade 12–14 (☎ **076/529-9300**), has an extensive collection focusing on the town's history and on products manufactured in the region. It also has a collection of religious artifacts belonging to the Bishop of Tilburg. Open from Tuesday through Sunday 10am to 5pm; admission is Dfl 5 ($2.50) for adults, Dfl 2.50 ($1.25) for children 12 and under.

Parks that offer open-air relief from city sightseeing include Valkenburg Park, Brabant Park, Sonsbeek Park, and Trekpot. Breda is also surrounded by beautiful

rural estates, many of which open their grounds to the public, and great **public forests** such as the **Mastbos** and **Liesbos,** whose ancient trees form peaceful retreats. Check with the VVV for directions and details.

Art lovers will want to stop by the village of **Zundert,** which is 14km (9 miles) south of Breda, on the N263. This is the birthplace of Vincent van Gogh. There's a touching statue here of the painter and his devoted brother, Theo, commissioned by the townspeople and sculpted by Zadkine.

TILBURG
20km (14 miles) SW of Den Bosch; 16km (10 miles) E of Breda

GETTING THERE   Local trains to Tilburg leave every half hour at peak times from Breda and Eindhoven. There are also frequent buses from Breda and Eindhoven.

By **car,** take the E312 east from Breda.

VISITOR INFORMATION   The **VVV office** is at Stadhuisplein 128 (☎ **013/535-1135;** fax 013/535-3795).

EXPLORING TILBURG
The town's heritage is based mostly on textile production in the Industrial Revolution. However, earlier history is preserved at the **Town Hall** (Stadhuis), Stadhuisplein 128, a 17th-century palace belonging to Prince Willem II of Orange, who lived here during most of his reign (1626–50).

The **Netherlands Textile Museum,** Goirkestraat 96 (☎ **013/542-2241**), in a former 19th-century textile factory, covers a century of textile production and use, and includes a contemporary art display in which textiles figure prominently. Open Tuesday through Friday 10am to 5pm, Saturday and Sunday noon to 5pm; admission is Dfl 7.50 ($3.75) for adults, Dfl 3.75 ($1.85) for children 7 to 13.

Scryption, Spoorlaan 434a (☎ **013/580-0821**), is another museum concerned with industrial development, this time in the form of written communication, especially typewriters and other office equipment. Open Tuesday through Friday 10am to 5pm, Saturday and Sunday 1 to 5pm; admission is Dfl 5 ($2.50) for adults, Dfl 4 ($2) for children 12 and under.

NEARBY ATTRACTIONS
De Biesbosch National Park. Visitor Center: Baanhoekweg 53, Dordrecht (☎ **078/630-5353**). Year-round, Tues–Sun 9am–5pm; May–June also Mon 1–5pm, July–Aug also Mon 9am–5pm. From the E31, take Exit 23, pass through Papendrecht, and then follow the signs. From Breda, take the A16 to Dordrecht, then the N3 toward Papendrecht, then follow the signs east across the River Merwede.

This unique natural park of marshland, meadows, and willow woods was formed during the St Elizabeth floods of 1421, when 16 villages were submerged and the former polders became an inland sea. Today, the area is a delta of creeks and inlets in and around the Maas (Meuse) and Waal rivers. One animal that has been reintroduced to the area in recent years is the beaver—last seen in the wild in 1826—which is once again breeding successfully. There's also a wide and varied selection of bird life. Activities include rowing, canoeing, and taking walking tours from the visitor center.

WHERE TO STAY & DINE
Hotel Breda. Roskam 20, 4813 GZ Breda. ☎ **076/522-2177.** Fax 076/522-3186. 50 units. TV TEL. Dfl 130 ($75.40) double. AE, DC, MC, V. Drive just southwest of Breda (exit at Rijsbergen from E19).

Canoeing in the Biesbosch

On the borders of the provinces of Noord Brabant and Zuid Holland, the Waal and the Maas rivers join in an estuary called the Biesbosch (Forest of Reeds). Once dry land, the area was drowned in the St Elizabeth Flood of 1421 and has since been shaped by the interplay between the rivers and the tides. Since the seaward Haringvliet Dam was built in 1970, the Biesbosch has been a freshwater zone and its marshes and islands are a favorite habitat for large flocks of geese and spoonbills. Making your way through the labyrinth of creeks, you may even encounter the recently reintroduced beaver. Start your trip in the village of Drimmelen, 17km (10.5 miles) north of Breda, where the Biesbosch Informatie Centrum, Biesboschweg 4 (☎ **0162/682-233**), can supply you with information on the history of this area and its unique flora and fauna. There's also a visitor center at Baanhoekweg 53, in the town of Dordrecht.

This large modern hotel has spacious and well-equipped guest rooms, decorated in colors that were fashionable in the 1970s—green, brown, and orange. Although it is near the highway, the hotel is surrounded by meadows and cows, giving it the air of a country inn. Its cozy bar and lounge features an open fireplace. There's an excellent a la carte restaurant nearby.

✪ **Hotel Mastbosch.** Kerstenslaan 20, 4837 BM Breda. ☎ **076/565-0050.** Fax 076/ 560-0040. 53 units. TV TEL. Dfl 175 ($87.50) double; Dfl 350 ($175) suite. Rates include full breakfast. AE, DC, MC, V.

This relaxing first-class hotel is located in a wooded site near the Mastbos forest on the outskirts of town. The guest rooms are large, modern, and airy, decorated in blue and gray and furnished with comfortable box-spring beds. Each room overlooks a sunny terrace and has a trouser press and hair dryer. There's also a good restaurant.

BERGEN OP ZOOM

23km (16 miles) SW of Breda; 38km (26 miles) N of Antwerp

Bergen op Zoom, near Zeeland and the Belgian border, would make a good alternative to Breda as a base for visiting the area. The influence of nearby ebullient, metropolitan Antwerp is unmistakable—the center of Bergen op Zoom is alive with many cafes and restaurants.

GETTING THERE   Bergen op Zoom lies on the Amsterdam–Vlissingen line, with trains every hour in both directions.

By **car,** take the E312 west from Breda and east from Middelburg.

VISITOR INFORMATION   The **VVV office** is at Beursplein 7 (☎ **0164/ 266-000;** fax 0164/246-031).

EXPLORING BERGEN OP ZOOM

The monumental **Stadhuis** (Town Hall), overlooking the Grote Markt, is a beautiful 14th-century castlelike structure. It can be visited in groups of 10 (contact the VVV office).

Het Markiezenhof (The Marquis' Court). Steenbergsestraat 8. ☎ **0164/242-930.** Admission Dfl 5 ($2.50) adults, Dfl 3.50 ($1.75) children under 13. Apr–Sept Tues–Sun 11am–5pm; Oct–Mar Tues–Sun 2–5pm.

Remnants of Bergen op Zoom's past as a small but powerful city state can be found all over the city center, and this unique town palace is perhaps the most impressive example. It was built between 1485 and 1525, and was once home to the Marquis of Bergen op Zoom. Behind the striped facade of red brick and yellow sandstone you'll find a museum dedicated to the city's history.

WHERE TO STAY & DINE

✪ **Hotel Mercure de Draak.** Grote Markt 36–38, 4611 NT, Bergen op Zoom. ☎ **0164/233-661.** Fax 0164/257-001. 45 units, 6 suites. MINIBAR TV TEL. Dfl 275 ($137.50) double; Dfl 395 ($197.50) suite. AE, DC, MC, V.

Modern comfort awaits you in Holland's oldest hotel, founded in 1397. The Mercure now occupies three adjacent buildings—which themselves date from the beginning of the 17th century—overlooking the lively Grote Markt square, the very heart of Bergen op Zoom. The guest rooms are luxuriously decorated, furnished with antiques and done up in flowery chintzes and stylish wallpapers. The hotel lounge is also a convivial bar; period furniture and a grand old fireplace lend it a medieval character. Golden-yellow curtains grace the windows in the hotel restaurant, which is furnished in a 17th-century style and specializes in refined French and Italian cuisine. Main courses average around Dfl 40 ($20); a three-course dinner costs Dfl 69.50 ($34.75). In summer you can dine on the large Grote Markt terrace.

BAARLE-NASSAU/BAARLE HERTOG
16km (10 miles) SE of Breda

This is the town that can't make up its mind whether to be in Belgium or in Holland, so it exists in both. Houses use colored number plates to identify their citizenship—if the figures are blue, the occupants are Dutch; if they're black on a white plate with a black, yellow, and red vertical stripe, the occupants are Belgian. Must get confusing!

To get to Baarle-Nassau and Baarle-Hertog, take the N268 from Breda to Turnhout (Belgium). You'll find the **VVV office** at Nieuwstraat 16, 5111 CW Baarle-Nassau (☎ **013/507-9921**).

EINDHOVEN
32km (22 miles) SE of Den Bosch; 120km (82 miles) SE of Amsterdam

Eindhoven, whose charter dates from 1232, limped along for centuries as not much more than a small village southeast of Den Bosch. Yet today it ranks as Holland's fifth-largest metropolis, with all the attributes of a modern industrial city. That transformation is due almost entirely to the Philips electronics company, which has been headquartered here for over 100 years.

Despite its industrialized face, Eindhoven has two fine museums and a water park.

GETTING THERE   There are trains to Eindhoven every half hour on average from Amsterdam Centraal Station, Rotterdam, The Hague, and Maastricht.

Eindhoven lies on the main north-south E35-E25 Amsterdam–Maastricht expressway.

VISITOR INFORMATION   The **VVV office** is at Stationsplein 17 (☎ **0900/112-2633;** fax 040/243-3135).

EXPLORING EINDHOVEN

Van Abbe Museum. Vonderweg 1. ☎ **040/275-5275.** Admission Dfl 6 ($3). Tues–Sun 11am–5pm.

This is one of the first museums in Holland to devote itself entirely to contemporary art. The museum's former home, at Bilderdijklaan 10, is currently undergoing extensive refurbishment and extension and will not reopen until 2001. But while the main building is being renovated, a small section of the permanent collection, combined with changing exhibitions by contemporary artists, can be seen at this address.

Kempenland Museum. St Antoniusstraat 5–7. ☎ **040/252-9093.** Admission Dfl 4 ($2). Tues–Sun 1–5pm.

This museum features exhibits depicting the history of this city and region. It's housed in an Italianate basilica that was constructed in 1917–19 and contains stained-glass windows. There's also a collection of 19th- and 20th-century art and sculpture by Dutch and Belgian artists.

✪ **De Tongelreep Swimming Paradise.** Antoon Coolenlaan. ☎ **040/238-1112.** Admission Dfl 6.50 ($3.75), free for children under 4. Wave pool: Mon–Fri 10am–10pm, Sat–Sun 10am–5:30pm; outdoor pool: May–Aug Mon–Fri 10am–6pm, Sat–Sun 10am–5:30pm.

This park on the southern edge of Eindhoven is the perfect place for a time-out from sightseeing. The park contains a subtropical wave pool, chute-the-chute, bubble pools, paddling pool, whirlpools, a 165-foot indoor swimming pool, and an outdoor pool with a sunbathing area. There's a large parking lot, and bus no. 7 takes you to the main entrance.

NEARBY ATTRACTIONS

War Museum (Oorlogsmuseum). Museumpark 1, Overloon, 40km (28 miles) NE of Eindhoven. ☎ **0478/641-250.** Admission Dfl 11 ($5.50). June–Aug daily 9:30am–6pm; Sept–May daily 10am–5pm.

In and around the little village of Overloon, tank corps met in fierce combat during September and October of 1944, towards the end of World War II, leaving some 300 tanks wrecked in the area. Today the 35-acre museum commemorates that battle with a vast collection of mechanized war vehicles, as well as an incredible display of antitank devices. There are also exhibits documenting the Nazi Occupation of Holland during World War II.

WHERE TO STAY

Dorint Hotel Eindhoven. Vestdijk 47, 5611 CA Eindhoven. ☎ **800/650-8018** or 040/232-6111. Fax 040/244-0148. 192 units. A/C MINIBAR TV TEL. Dfl 362.50 ($181.25) double; Dfl 600 ($300) suite. AE, DC, MC, V.

This large modern hotel is located in the city center, not far from the central train station. The guest rooms are spacious, with bright, attractive decor. Each room has a safe.

Dining: The hotel's restaurant, the Bruegel Brasserie, serves light lunch and dinner (see "Where to Dine," below).

Amenities: Indoor pool, health club (with Jacuzzi, sauna, Turkish bath, massage, and solarium), beauty parlor, concierge, 24-hour room service, dry cleaning and laundry, newspaper delivery, baby-sitting, conference facilities, secretarial services, express check-out.

Golden Tulip Hotel Geldrop. Bogardeind 219, 5664 EG Geldrop (on the outskirts of Eindhoven, on the A3 highway). ☎ **040/286-7510.** Fax 040/285-5762. 131 units. MINIBAR TV TEL. Dfl 260–285 ($130–$142.50) double. AE, DC, MC, V.

This modern hotel sits at the edge of the Strabrechtse heath, a restful retreat away from the bustle of the city streets. The large, nicely furnished guest rooms have in-house movies. Other amenities include a good restaurant, an indoor swimming pool, tennis and squash courts, a solarium, hair dryers in the rooms, and a sauna.

✪ Hostellerie van Gaalen. Kapelstraat 48, 5591 HE Heeze. ☎ **040/226-3515.** Fax 040/226-3876. 14 units, 1 suite. MINIBAR TV TEL. Dfl 150 ($75) double; Dfl 250 ($125) suite. Breakfast Dfl 22.50 ($11.25). AE, DC, MC, V. Closed first week in Jan, during Carnival (Feb 8 to 11), last week in July and first week in Aug. From Eindhoven take the A67 east, then Exit 34 south to Heeze (about a 20-minute drive).

This 18th-century coaching inn is situated in the little village of Heeze, directly across from a 17th-century château. The place has been redone with a curious Mediterranean touch that disavows its rustic heritage. Its guest rooms feature opulent furnishings and tasteful decor. The gourmet restaurant belongs to the illustrious Alliance Gastronomique Néderlandaise and serves delicious food with a Mediterranean accent (see "Where to Dine," below).

Motel Eindhoven. Aalsterweg 322, 5644 RL Eindhoven (south of the city, on the A67 expressway). ☎ **040/212-3435.** Fax 040/212-0774. 175 units, 2 suites. TV TEL. Dfl 100 ($58) single or double, Dfl 140 ($81.20) suite. AE, DC, MC, V.

The guest rooms at this motel are furnished in a modern style and decorated in pastel tints. All rooms have comfortable armchairs and beds; some have balconies. The motel offers a varied breakfast buffet, and there is a good restaurant on the premises. Facilities include sauna, fitness room, indoor swimming pool, and outdoor tennis court.

WHERE TO DINE

Bruegel Brasserie. In the Dorint Hotel, Vestdijk 47. ☎ **040/232-6111.** Main courses Dfl 25–45 ($14.50–$26.10); fixed-price menus Dfl 37.50–45 ($21.75–$26.10). AE, DC, MC, V. Noon–10:30pm. DUTCH.

The Bruegel (in the Dorint Hotel; see "Where to Stay," above) is a great centrally located restaurant, with good food, a stylish and casual ambiance, and good value for money. It serves the "Neerlands Dis" Old Dutch menu, as well as lunch and dinner buffets and snacks. You'll enjoy well-prepared dishes like grilled salmon with chives, or lamb cutlets with tagliatelle and a creamy mint sauce.

✪ De Karpendonkse Hoeve. Sumatralaan 3. ☎ **040/281-3663.** Reservations required. Fixed-price lunch Dfl 65 ($37.70) for 3 courses; fixed-price dinner Dfl 95 ($45) for 3 courses. AE, MC, V. Tues–Fri noon–2:30pm; Tues–Sat 6–9:30pm. Closed during Carnival (Feb 8 to 11), and first 2 weeks in Aug. INTERNATIONAL.

This first-class restaurant, a member of the prestigious Alliance Gastronomique Néderlandaise, specializes in game in season and always uses the best of local products. It's located on the outskirts of town, in an 18th-century farmhouse surrounded by trees and overlooking a small lake. Tables are decked stylishly in green and pink. The menu offers delicacies like a "triple quail fantasy": mousse, sautéed breast and an aspic of quail, or brill fillet topped with steamed carrot and cucumber, with a Noilly Prat sauce. In summer you can dine on the terrace overlooking the lake.

Hostellerie van Gaalen. Kapelstraat 48, Heeze. ☎ **040/226-3515.** Main courses Dfl 32–48 ($18.55–$27.85); fixed-price menus Dfl 57.50–97.50 ($23.75–$48.75). AE, DC, MC, V.

Mon–Fri noon–2:30pm; Mon–Sat 6–10pm. Closed first week in Jan, during Carnival, last week in July, and first week in Aug. MEDITERRANEAN.

Even if you're staying in Eindhoven, it's worth the 20-minute drive to this inn in Heeze (see "Where to Stay," above) for a meal created by patron Jules van Gaalen and his chef Toon Rumphorst. The cuisine is basically Mediterranean, with dishes like lamb *osso buco* and, the all-time favorite, *tiramisu*. In summer you can enjoy an outdoor dinner on the terrace. The menu changes regularly, with seasonal delights like asparagus in early summer and game in fall. This restaurant is also a member of the illustrious Alliance Gastronomique Néderlandaise.

3 Limburg

Of all Holland's provinces, Limburg is the least likely to fit any "Dutch" image you bring with you. Missing are the flat fields interlaced with canals, the windmills (although there are a few), and most of the other traditions we associate with Holland. It is, however, one of the most beautiful of the provinces—the Dutch themselves flock there in droves.

Limburg is surrounded on three sides by Germany and Belgium. Since Roman times it has been a well-trodden pathway for invaders, defenders, refugees, and just plain travelers. Its own cities draw liberally from the richness of other European cultures and cities.

Northern Limburg shelters holiday parks and villages in a landscape of wooded hills and broad heaths; its highlight is perhaps the town of **Thorn,** also known as the "White Village," because of its many whitewashed monumental buildings. Southern Limburg occupies the highest ground in Holland and hosts the province's capital city, Maastricht, an exuberant, joyful center of history, higher education, and smiling hospitality. For those of a gambling nature, Limburg provides the casino at Valkenburg, near Maastricht.

SEEING THE PROVINCE   Limburg offers a wealth of sightseeing—numerous castles and mansions, historic churches, picturesque villages, and mysterious caverns that tunnel into the heart of high cliffs. To all that, add the attractions of cities like Liège, Antwerp, Brussels, Cologne, Aachen, Düsseldorf, Bonn, and Luxembourg, all just a hop, skip, and a jump away. By no means, however, would I want to imply that Limburg is simply a province to pass through on your way elsewhere in Europe—this is a province so rich in holiday attractions that I urge you to make your base here.

You can reach Maastricht by air from Amsterdam with **KLM Cityhopper** (☎ 020/474-7747), which offers frequent daily flights. A single ticket costs about Dfl 160 ($80). **Drivers** to Maastricht should take A2 or E25. The province of Limburg is easily toured by car, of course, but nondrivers will also find it easy to get around by either **train** or **bus.** NS (Dutch Railways) has some handy arrangements for **cyclists** where you can pick up a bike at one station and drop it off at another. The scenic countryside also lends itself to hiking.

WHERE TO STAY   Limburg accommodations come in all shapes, sizes, locations, and price ranges. There are castle hotels, posh luxury establishments, homey small hotels with moderate rates, and bed-and-breakfast accommodations in private homes.

WHERE TO DINE   Maastricht, the capital of Limburg, is filled with good places to eat—it's not uncommon for people to drive from nearby Liège or Aachen just to have dinner here. Around the province are several more outstanding restaurants, and many others that serve excellent meals at moderate prices. In addition, many of the province's castles have been turned into restaurants.

MAASTRICHT

215km (147 miles) SE of Amsterdam; 124km (85 miles) SE of Den Bosch

Maastricht, the provincial capital, is the Netherland's oldest fortified city, tracing its roots back to a Roman settlement founded here in 50 B.C. on the rivers Meuse and Jeker at the foot of Mount St. Peter. The Romans and all those who came after them took from Mount St. Peter great chunks of marlstone, a type of limestone that's as soft to carve and chisel as soap; it gradually hardens when exposed to air. Many of Maastricht's buildings are constructed of marlstone. As more and more was extracted, Mount St. Peter became honeycombed with some 20,000 passages boring into its interior.

The Romans stayed for 4 centuries. When they finally departed, Maastricht became the seat of bishops for nearly another 400 years (Saint Servatius was the first, in about 380, and Saint Hubert was the last, in 722). From the early 1200s until the late 1700s, the city was under the feudal rule of the Dukes of Brabant. Maastricht was also the last earthly place seen by the hero of Alexandre Dumas's *The Three Musketeers:* It was here that d'Artagnan lost his life during King Louis XIV's siege of Maastricht in 1673 (the musketeers, of course, are fictitious characters, but the siege actually occurred). In 1795 French forces occupied the city and declared it the capital of a French province.

That changed with Napoléon's defeat at Waterloo in 1815, and when Belgium gained its independence from Holland in 1830, this little province stayed Dutch, with Maastricht as its capital. Over the years Maastricht sustained 21 sieges, as one ruler after another sought to control its strategic position. Today the city is a charming mixture of historic buildings and monuments (more than 1,450), cultural activities, a lighthearted carnival famous throughout Europe, and some of the finest restaurants to be found in any Dutch city of its size.

GETTING THERE   Maastricht has frequent train connections with Amsterdam, Rotterdam, and The Hague, with trains at least hourly to and from each of these cities.

VISITOR INFORMATION   The **VVV office,** Kleine Straat 1 (☎ **043/ 325-2121;** fax 043/321-3746) is one of the best equipped, most helpful, and friendliest in Holland. It's housed in a beautiful building called Het Dinghuis, which dates from 1470 and was formerly the seat of the local law courts. The office is open year-round from 9am to 6pm Monday through Saturday, and in July and August also from 11am to 3pm on Sunday. One special reason to contact the VVV before coming to Maastricht is to find out about their numerous culinary/hotel arrangements that will greatly reduce the cost of a gourmet stay. There's even a **reservation line** for these arrangements (☎ **043/321-7878**), dealing with last-minute requests during office hours.

EXPLORING MAASTRICHT

Keep your eye out for the little square called **Op de Thermen,** where you can still see the outline of a Roman thermal bath in the cobblestones; the **Markt** (Market square), where vendors gather on Wednesday and Friday mornings to open colorful stalls (some come from as far away as Belgium and Germany); the statue of the cheerful little **'t Mooswief** (Vegetable Woman) in the Markt square; the small, impish **Mestreechter Geis** statue in a tiny square at Kleine Stokstraat (he embodies

Maastricht

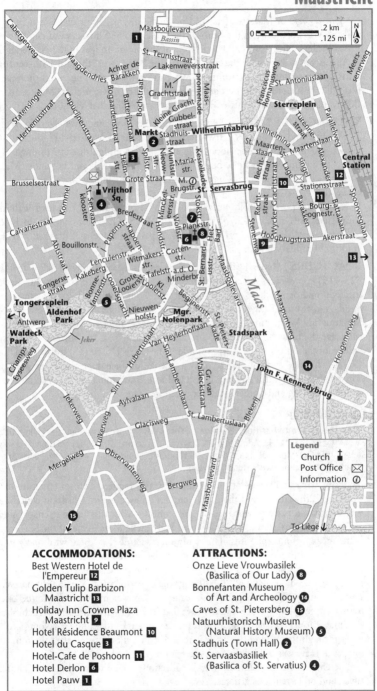

ACCOMMODATIONS:

Best Western Hotel de
l'Empereur **12**

Golden Tulip Barbizon
Maastricht **13**

Holiday Inn Crowne Plaza
Maastricht **9**

Hotel Résidence Beaumont **10**

Hotel du Casque **3**

Hotel-Cafe de Poshoorn **11**

Hotel Derlon **6**

Hotel Pauw **1**

ATTRACTIONS:

Onze Lieve Vrouwbasilek
(Basilica of Our Lady) **8**

Bonnefanten Museum
of Art and Archeology **14**

Caves of St. Pietersberg **15**

Natuurhistorisch Museum
(Natural History Museum) **5**

Stadhuis (Town Hall) **2**

St. Servaasbasiliek
(Basilica of St. Servatius) **4**

the *joie de vivre* of Maastrichters, and his name means "Spirit of Maastrichters"); and the **Vrijthof** square at the heart of the old city. The **Sint-Servaasbrug** (St Servatius Bridge) dates from 1280 and is one of the oldest bridges in the Netherlands.

And as you walk around the city, look for the 250 or so **17th- and 18th-century houses** with sculpted gable stones showing the name of the house and the year it was built. Some of the prettiest are on Hoogbrugstraat, Rechtstraat, Markt square, Boschstraat, Stokstraat Kwartier, Platielstraat, and Achter het Vleeshuis.

WALKING TOURS   To begin your tour of this lovely and lively city, go by the VVV office and pick up its "**Historic Walking Tour of Maastricht**" brochure. It guides you from the office, located in the busy shopping district, through city streets to a number of historic buildings and monuments. If you fall under Maastricht's spell as completely as I have, you'll keep the brochure with you during your entire visit.

From March through November, the VVV also conducts ✪ **guided walking tours** that cost Dfl 5.50 ($2.75) for adults, Dfl 3.25 ($1.65) for children. Included is a fascinating Maastricht Fortifications Walk past the remains of the medieval city and its old military buildings.

BOAT TOURS   **Rederij Stiphout River Cruises,** Maaspromenade 27 (☎ 043/325-4151), provides one of the most pleasant ways to see Maastricht. Easter through mid-September, every hour on the hour, and during the winter on Sundays, a riverboat leaves the landing stage on the River Meuse between the St. Servatius and Wilhelmina bridges for a 55-minute cruise past Mount St Peter (you can leave the boat, tour the caves, and catch the next boat to continue the cruise) and on to the sluices at the Belgian border. The fare is Dfl 10 ($5) for adults, Dfl 6 ($3) for children, and you should book a day ahead, since these cruises are popular. There's also a delightful daylong cruise to Liège and a romantic sunset cruise that includes dancing and dinner—call for schedules, fares, and booking.

SEEING THE SIGHTS

✪ **Onze Lieve Vrouwbasiliek (Basilica of Our Lady).** Onze Lievevrouweplein. Info from VVV (☎ **043/325-2121**). Admission Dfl 3.50 ($1.75) adults, Dfl 1 (50¢) children. Treasury: Easter to mid-Oct Mon–Sat 11am–5pm, Sun 1–5pm. Basilica: July–Aug daily 10am–5pm; Sept–June 10am–4pm, except during services.

The west wing and crypts of this medieval Romanesque cruciform structure date from the 12th century, and there's evidence of an even earlier Christian church, as well as a pagan place of worship, on this same site. But it is the side chapel sheltering the pilgrims' statue of Our Beloved Lady Stella Mare—Star of the Sea—that is the focus for most pilgrims. The richly robed statue is credited with many miracles, even during long years when it had to be hidden away because of religious persecution. It is said that in the early 1600s, when the Catholic religion was once more recognized, as many as 20,000 pilgrims came to worship at the shrine every Easter Monday. When the Calvinists came into power in 1632, the statue once more went into hiding, and legend has it that in 1699 Our Lady herself established the "prayer route" by stepping down from her pedestal and leading a devout parishioner through the muddy streets. It is recorded that the morning after the miraculous walk there was indeed mud on the hem of Our Lady's robe!

The church treasury contains a rich collection of tapestries, reliquaries, church silver, and other religious artifacts.

Bonnefanten Museum of Art and Archaeology. Avenue Ceramique 250. ☎ **043/329-0190.** Admission Dfl 10 ($5) adults, children under 13 free. Tues–Sun 11am–5pm. Bus 1, 5, 53, or 54 from train station.

This relatively new building, designed by Aldo Rossi in 1995, is elegantly restrained, the only extravagances being the grand staircase and the shining bullet-shaped tower in the courtyard. On display are archaeological finds dating from 250,000 B.C. to the Middle Ages, with emphasis on the Roman period. There's also artwork, ranging from the medieval to the modern. In a separate hall (the Wiebengahal) next to the museum are changing exhibitions by contemporary artists.

✪ **Caves of St Pietersberg.** Admission Dfl 5.50 ($2.75) adults, Dfl 3.25 ($1.65) children. Tours leave from 2 entrances—the Northern Caves and the Zonneberg Caves—at different times; check with the VVV office (☎ **043/321-7878**) for times and directions to reach the caves by city bus or boat.

If you do no other sightseeing during your Maastricht visit, you shouldn't miss these unique underground caves. From the Roman times to the days of medieval sieges to the months and years of enemy occupation during two world wars, these 20,000 passages have served as a place of refuge. Many people have left behind interesting drawings and signatures on the marlstone walls. During World War II the caves sheltered such Dutch masterpieces as Rembrandt's *Night Watch* and other treasures that were hidden away from the Nazis. You'll follow your guide's lantern through about 2 miles of what some say are nearly 200 miles (others say only 6 miles) of 20- to 40-foot-high tunnels. Stay close to that lantern—there are tales told in Maastricht of those who entered here and were never seen again (ask about the four monks). The temperature in the caves is about 50°F, so bring a cardigan or a coat to protect against the chill.

Natuurhistorisch Museum (Natural History Museum). De Bosquetplein 6–7 (in the city center, near the Music Conservatory). ☎ **043/350-5490.** Admission Dfl 5 ($2.50) adults, Dfl 4 ($2) children. Mon–Fri 10am–12:30pm and 1:30–5pm, Sat–Sun 2–5pm. Closed holidays.

You really should visit this museum after you've seen the Caves of St Pietersberg, for then you can more fully appreciate the fossils that have come from the walls of those caverns. In addition, there are other rocks, minerals, and gemstones. The courtyard contains a botanical garden, where you'll find some beautiful examples of the local flora.

Sint Servaasbasiliek (Basilica of St Servatius). Keizer Karelplein (in the city center). Info from VVV(☎ **043/325-2121**). Admission Dfl 4 ($2) adults, Dfl 1 (50¢) children under 13. Treasury and basilica, Mon–Sat 10am–5pm, Sun 1–5pm; July–Aug Mon–Sat 10am–6pm, Sun 1–5pm.

The oldest parts of this majestic medieval cruciform church date back to the year 1000, though the building was considerably enlarged in the 14th and 15th centuries. Saint Servatius, Maastricht's first bishop, is buried in the crypt. Over the centuries people have honored Saint Servatius with gifts, so the Treasury holds a collection of incredible richness and beauty, including two superb reliquaries fashioned by Maastricht goldsmiths in the 12th century. The southern tower of the cathedral's west wall holds Grandmère (Grandmother), the largest bell in Holland and a beloved symbol of the city.

SHOPPING

At Kesselskade 55, ✪ **Olivier Bonbons** (☎ **043/321-5526**) is a small shop that has been turning out chocolates and other sweets for more than 30 years. One of its specialties is a porcelain reproduction of the much-loved Bell of Grandmère (Grandmother) filled with luscious chocolates, a lovely gift to take home for friends or family (or yourself?).

The Maastricht Carnival

Although not blessed with the weather of places like Rio de Janeiro, Sydney, or New Orleans, Maastricht can surely compete with these cities in the way it celebrates Carnival. This celebration originates from the times when Catholics observed Lent with strict fasts from Ash Wednesday to Holy Saturday (the Saturday before Easter). The 3 days before Ash Wednesday, including Shrove Tuesday, or Mardi-Gras, were days in which the people stuffed their faces and drank themselves into a stupor, preparing for the lean time to come.

In some ways, nothing much has changed. On the Saturday before Ash Wednesday, the Mayor of Maastricht hands over the keys of the city to Prince Carnival, who will reign over the city and turn it completely upside-down over the next few days. The people dress up and prepare colorful floats for the parades that take place each day. When the sun goes down, everyone gradually disappears into the cafes and restaurants, continuing the party with more than enough wining and dining!

There are **souvenir shops** all through the shopping streets of Maastricht, but one with an exceptionally good selection at reasonable prices is **'t Klumpke,** Kesselskade 56 (☎ 043/325-1712), a small shop next door to Olivier Bonbons.

MAASTRICHT AFTER DARK

During the winter months Maastricht hosts frequent performances of theater, ballet, operettas, musicals, and cabaret. Check with the VVV for current happenings. Much of the after-dark action takes place in the more than 500 cozy bars and cafes. To get you started in the right direction, the VVV publishes a **"Pub Crawl"** booklet.

SIDE TRIPS FROM MAASTRICHT

Limburg sometimes calls itself the "Land Without Frontiers," and it would certainly seem so when you learn that it's possible to plan day trips by bus to Belgium (Liège, Antwerp, Brussels, the Ardennes), Germany (Moselle, Tuddern, Eifel, Aachen), Luxembourg (both the capital city and the small towns around the Grand Duchy), and France (Givet and Paris). The VVV can provide details on the many options and arrange bookings.

NS (Dutch Railways) also offers attractive routes and rates across borders as well as within Limburg itself, and there is a good bus service around the province. Inquire at the train station in Maastricht for schedules and fares.

WHERE TO STAY IN MAASTRICHT

Although accommodations are plentiful in Maastricht, they can fill up in the peak summer months or during trade fairs, so reserve ahead if possible and turn to the VVV office for help if you can't find anything. The VVV can also arrange a stay in a private home.

Expensive

Holiday Inn Crowne Plaza Maastricht. De Ruiterij 1, 6221 EW Maastricht. ☎ **043/ 350-9191.** Fax 043/350-9192. 111 units, 20 suites. A/C MINIBAR TV TEL. Dfl 410–465 ($237.80–$269.70) double; Dfl 510–735 ($295.80–$426.30) suite. AE, DC, MC, V.

This modern, deluxe, five-star hotel has a prime location overlooking the riverfront. Everything here is elegance, from top to bottom. Half the spacious guest rooms come with balconies or terraces, and all have hair dryers. There's a lively bar and lounge overlooking the river, a coffee shop, and three good restaurants.

Dining: Japanese steakhouse serving teppan-yaki, a newly decorated Mediterranean/Caribbean restaurant, and a waterside terrace.

Amenities: Concierge, 24-hour room service, twice-daily maid service, dry cleaning and laundry, newspaper delivery, baby-sitting, conference facilities, secretarial services, express checkout.

✪ **Hotel Derlon.** Onze Lieve Vrouweplein 6, 6211 HD Maastricht. ☎ **043/321-6770.** Fax 043/325-1933. 41 units, 3 suites. A/C MINIBAR TV TEL. Dfl 475–525 ($237.50–$262.50) double; Dfl 765 ($382.50) suite. AE, DC, MC, V.

This jewel of a four-star hotel sits on one of the loveliest of the city's small squares. In summer it operates a terrace cafe out under the trees. The hotel is built over ancient Roman ruins, and in its basement you can view excavated Roman foundations and artifacts. The guest rooms are bright and airy, and have a beautiful blending of classic and modern decor. There's a brasserie on the premises. The hotel is wheelchair accessible.

Amenities: 24-hour room service, dry cleaning and laundry, newspaper delivery, baby-sitting, conference facilities, secretarial services, express checkout.

Moderate

Best Western Hotel de l'Empereur. Stationsstraat 2 (across from the train station), 6221 BP Maastricht. ☎ **043/321-3838.** Fax 043/321-6819. 93 units. A/C MINIBAR TV TEL. Dfl 230 ($115) double. AE, DC, MC, V.

This lovely old turreted hotel has comfortable, attractive guest rooms, as well as apartments that can sleep up to four people. Some rooms feature trouser presses. There's a cozy lounge bar that draws a local clientele, and a brasserie/restaurant. Other amenities include an indoor swimming pool, sauna, solarium, and whirlpool.

✪ **Golden Tulip Barbizon Maastricht.** At the Maastricht Exposition and Congress Center, Forum 110, 6229 GV Maastricht. ☎ **043/383-8281.** Fax 043/361-5862. 180 units. A/C MINIBAR TV TEL. Dfl 345–365 ($172.50–$182.50) double. Special rates for sports package holidays. AE, DC, MC, V.

This luxurious modern hotel is about a 3-minute walk from Randwijck local train station. It offers deluxe rooms with luxury bathrooms. Amenities include hair dryers and trouser presses. There's also a gourmet restaurant specializing in French cuisine, an English-style pub that also serves Italian specialties at modest prices, and a sauna/fitness center. The hotel is wheelchair accessible.

✪ **Hotel & Résidence Beaumont.** Wijcker Brugstraat 2, 6221 EC Maastricht. ☎ **043/325-4433.** Fax 043/325-3655. 77 units, 2 suites. TV TEL. Dfl 197.50–250 ($98.75–$125) double, Dfl 295 ($147.50) suite. Breakfast Dfl 20 ($10). AE, DC, MC, V.

This well-established hotel is located halfway between the train station and the river, just a short walk from the town center. An extension planned for 1999 will add 40 rooms and a fitness suite. The Beaumont's decor is warmly classical, and the guest rooms are comfortable and attractive. The hotel's Restaurant Alsacien is a cozy but stylish restaurant serving moderately priced meals with Alsatian specialties and wines. Dinner costs from Dfl 49.50 ($24.75) for three courses, to Dfl 85 ($42.50) for five courses.

Hotel du Casque. Helmstraat 14, 6211 TA Maastricht. ☎ **043/321-4343.** Fax 043/325-5155. 38 units. MINIBAR TV TEL. Dfl 235–285 ($117.50–$142.50) double. Rates include breakfast. AE, DC, MC, V.

There's been an inn at this location since the 15th century. The present family-run hotel carries on the proud tradition, with modern facilities, comfortable rooms, and good old-fashioned friendliness. It faces the lively Vrijthof square and has its own private parking lot. The hotel was renovated in 1998.

Hotel Pauw. Boschstraat 27, 6211 AS Maastricht. ☎ **043/321-2222.** Fax 043/321-3432. 124 units. MINIBAR TV TEL. Dfl 225 ($112.50) double. AE, DC, MC, V.

The modern Hotel Pauw is on the edge of the city center, overlooking the old inner harbor (called *Bassin*). It couldn't be more convenient for sightseeing, shopping, dining, and just plain people-watching. The rooms are large and have wooden furniture and comfortable box-spring beds. The hotel offers a continental breakfast buffet, and there's also a restaurant and a convivial bar overlooking the covered winter garden. Drivers can use the private car park.

Inexpensive

Hotel-Café de Posthoorn. Stationsstraat 47 (near the train station), 6221 BN Maastricht. ☎ **043/321-7334.** Fax 043/321-0747. 14 units. TV TEL. Dfl 135 ($67.50) double. Rates include breakfast. MC, V.

At this small corner hotel, you register with the friendly owner in the ground-floor cafe. You needn't be afraid of being disturbed in your sleep—from the rooms you can hardly hear any of what's going on downstairs. The guest rooms aren't too large, but they're modern and stylish and have very comfortable beds. The cozy brown cafe on the premises specializes in foreign beers and also offers a simple menu; there's even a terrace on the sidewalk.

Where to Stay Outside of Town

✪ **Hotel Restaurant Berghoeve.** Julianastraat 20, 6285 AJ Epen (14 miles southeast of Maastricht). ☎ **043/455-1248.** Fax 043/455-2847. 18 units. TV. Dfl 145 ($72.50) double. Rates include continental breakfast. AE, MC, V. Take the N278 towards Vaals—the road to Epen is signposted.

This friendly, family-run hotel stands on one of the highest hills in Limburg—it almost looks like a Swiss chalet. It's ideal as a base for exploring the picturesque Geul river valley on foot or by bicycle. The guest rooms are simple, clean, and sparsely furnished, but quite spacious. All have magnificent views over the lush, green hills, and some even have balconies. The beds are very comfortable. The hotel offers a hearty Limburg breakfast buffet, and you can also stay on a half-board basis. In summer, you can relax on the terrace, shaded by a bright-red awning.

✪ **Kasteel Wittem Hotel.** Wittemerallee 3, 6286 AA Wittem (12 miles east of Maastrict). ☎ **043/450-1208.** Fax 043/450-1260. 12 units. MINIBAR TV TEL. Dfl 230–295 ($115–$147.50) double. AE, DC, MC, V.

If you're lucky, you'll draw one of the two tower rooms (one even has panoramic windows in the bathroom!) in this romantic 12th-century castle, where stately swans adorn an ancient moat. Castle guests over the centuries have included the Knights of Julemont, William the Silent, Charles V, other noblemen, and humble folk such as traveling monks. The guest rooms have a cozy charm with country-style decor and beautiful furnishings. The dining room boasts a Michelin star (see "Where to Dine Outside of Town," below), and the hotel offers a variety of gastronomic arrangements.

WHERE TO DINE

Because of Maastricht's renown as a gourmet paradise, many restaurants will be fully booked. If you just turn up without a reservation, it's almost a slight to the restaurant—you don't care enough about your food! Wander around looking in windows and at menus during the day, decide where you want to spent a gracious evening, and reserve.

Expensive

✪ **Toine Hermsen.** Sint Bernardusstraat 2–4, corner with Onze Lieve Vrouweplein. ☎ **043/325-8400.** Reservations required. Fixed-price menus Dfl 60 ($30) for 3 courses, Dfl 110 ($55) for 4 courses, Dfl 135 ($67.50) for 5 courses. AE, DC, MC, V. Tues–Sat noon–2pm, 6–11pm; no lunch on Saturday. Closed for 2 weeks during Carnival. REGIONAL/FRENCH.

One of the city's top restaurants is the proud possessor of a Michelin star. You can expect good portions of impeccable food and superb but relaxed service. The chef cooks up classics of French cuisine and also exploits more regional seasonal ingredients such as Limburg's famous asparagus and chicory. Spoil yourself!

Moderate

✪ **Au Coin des Bons Enfants.** Ezelmarkt 4. ☎ **043/321-2359.** Main courses Dfl 25–45 ($12.50–$22.50); fixed-price menu Dfl 55 ($27.50). AE, DC, MC, V. Wed–Mon noon–10pm. FRENCH/BELGIAN.

An open log fire adds to the elegant ambiance at this restaurant in the city center. In fine weather there's outdoor dining in a rustic courtyard. Fine French specialties include lovely asparagus and ham dishes in season, as well as lobster soup and veal with wild mushrooms and a béarnaise sauce. The wine cellar is exceptional.

Au Premier. 1st floor, Brusselsestraat 15. ☎ **043/321-9761.** Main courses Dfl 36–45 ($18–$22.50); fixed-price menus Dfl 49.50–89.50 ($24.75–$44.75). AE, DC, MC, V. Tues–Sun noon–2:30pm and 5:30–10pm. DUTCH/FRENCH.

Au Premier is a stylish, intimate restaurant in the city center. In summer, you can dine on the pretty garden patio. The cuisine features regional specialties utilizing fresh local produce, as well as provincial French dishes. Try the *Hemel en Aarde* ("Heaven and Earth"), a traditional Limburg stew combining apples, potatoes, black pudding, and goose liver. The restaurant's famous homemade ice-cream specialties include heavenly creations like honey-and-poppy-seed ice cream.

Brasserie De Kadans. Kesselskade 62. ☎ **043/326-1700.** Main courses Dfl 32.50–38.50 ($18.85–$22.30); fixed-price menus Dfl 49.50–57.50 ($28.70–$33.35). AE, DC, MC, V. Restaurant open daily 6–10pm; Cafe open daily 10am–2am. CONTINENTAL.

This modern brasserie is decorated in slick black and chrome, and populated by a lively clientele and friendly wait staff. In the upstairs restaurant you can sample inventive dishes such as pheasant with a delicate purée of celeriac root or braised veal in balsamic vinegar.

Corneille. Hoenderstraat 16. ☎ **043/325-0923.** Main courses Dfl 32.50–39.50 ($18.85–$22.90); fixed-price menus Dfl 49.50–75 ($28.70–$43.50). AE, DC, MC, V. Tues–Fri noon–3pm; Tues–Sun 5:30–10pm. SEAFOOD/CONTINENTAL.

This lovely little restaurant, located in a former mussels shop in the city center, is an intimate enclave with white walls, dark exposed beams, and an open fireplace. It's a warm and friendly place. The talented chef specializes in fish; he uses fresh catches to create memorable dishes like *carpaccio* of tuna or Victoria bass in a Riesling sauce.

't Plenkske. Plankstraat 6. ☎ **043/321-8456.** Main courses Dfl 27.50–45 ($13.75–$22.50); fixed-price menus Dfl 39.50–67.50 ($19.75–$33.75). AE, DC, MC, V. Mon–Sat noon–2:30pm and 6–10:30pm. REGIONAL/FRENCH.

't Plenkske, located in the beautifully renovated Stokstraat quarter in the city center, features regional specialties from Maastricht and Liège, with a number of French classics thrown in for good measure. Dishes include duck breast with lime sauce, and Limburg lamb with thyme and honey, garnished with garlic marmalade. This lovely restaurant, with its light, airy decor and outdoor patio overlooking the Thermen (site of ancient Roman baths), is a great local favorite.

Inexpensive

Café In den Ouden Vogelstruys. Vrijthof 15. ☎ **043/321-4888.** Snacks and light meals from Dfl 6 ($3). No credit cards. Daily 9:30am–2am. BAR FOOD/DUTCH.

This traditional cafe-bar in the city center is wonderfully atmospheric (there's a cannonball in its wall that lodged there in 1653—ask about the story). It sits diagonally across from a white house that supposedly hosted both Charlemagne and Napoléon. The bar's rustic interior and faithful local clientele make it a great place to stop for a light lunch or just for a drink.

Sagittarius. Bredestraat 7 (across from the Stadsschouwburg theater). ☎ **043/321-1492.** Main courses Dfl 32.50–45 ($16.25–$22.50). AE, MC, V. Tues–Sat 6–10pm. SEAFOOD/DUTCH/FRENCH.

This light, airy restaurant is on one of Maastricht's prettiest streets in the city center. Chef Jan van Werven prepares modern and classic variations of local and French cuisine as you watch in his open kitchen. The menu changes daily to feature the freshest ingredients. Among my personal favorites is the excellent *bouillabaisse et sa rouille,* a Provençal fish stew served with a spicy chili and garlic sauce. In summer there's pleasant garden dining.

Where to Dine Outside of Town

✪ **Kasteel Wittem Restaurant.** Wittemerallee 3, Wittem. ☎ **043/450-1208.** Reservations required. Fixed-price menus Dfl 110–145 ($55–$72.50). AE, DC, MC, V. Daily 6–9:30pm, Fri–Sun noon–2:30pm. FRENCH. From Maastricht take the N278 east towards Vaals for around 20km (12.5 miles), then exit left to Gulpen/Wittem. Turn left at the traffic lights; the Kasteel is about 500m (540 yards) farther on the left.

The beautiful dining room in this lovely castle about 18km (12 miles) east of Maastricht (see "Where to Stay Outside of Town," above) is paneled in French oak and has a warm, clubby atmosphere. You'll certainly be served an excellent meal here. Start with the duck *carpaccio* with ginger cream and a mushroom vinaigrette; then you can move on to the turbot, which is poached to perfection and served with fennel and a red-wine-and-aniseed butter sauce. Finish your meal with a sinfully luscious apple parfait with meringues and *calvados sabayon.*

✪ **Château Neercanne.** Cannerweg 800 (3 miles south of the center via Bieslanderweg). ☎ **043/325-1359.** Main courses Dfl 40–70 ($20–$35); fixed-price menus Dfl 95–120 ($47.50–$60). AE, DC, MC, V. Tues–Fri and Sun noon–2:15pm; Tues–Sun 6–9:15pm. FRENCH.

This gracious château is set on a high hill south of Maastricht's center, above the River Jeker. It was built in 1698 for a Dutch nobleman. Its wide stone terrace, where you can dine or have drinks in fine weather, affords views of the beautiful Jeker valley. Inside, tasteful renovations have created a classic, romantic ambiance, with baroque wallpaper, shades of beige and burgundy, and Venetian glass chandeliers. Marlstone caves extending back into the hillside serve as wine cellars. There's also a room with an arched ceiling, reserved for private candlelit dinner parties. Fresh herbs and vegetables straight from the restaurant's own gardens and the best of local ingredients assure top quality. Try the rack of lamb in a truffle gravy, or the cod in a simple tarragon butter sauce—both dishes are cooked to perfection. An unusual dessert is the locally produced Valdieu cheese in a caramel beer sauce. The menu changes almost daily, depending on what's available. The restaurant is a member of Alliance Gastronomique Néderlandaise.

VALKENBURG
13km (9 miles) E of Maastricht

When traveling from Maastricht to Valkenburg, you'll need to rethink your impression of the Netherlands as a country of flat polders and straight dikes. Valkenburg nestles in the midst of gently sloping hills where lush forests alternate with pastures unfolding towards the River Geul. Valkenburg's ruined fortress, up a steep hill, still seems to guard over this tranquil little town, which is best known for its spa and casino.

GETTING THERE   There is local train service from Maaastricht every hour, and buses twice an hour from outside Maastricht train station.

By **car,** take the A79 northeast from Maastricht.

VISITOR INFORMATION   The **VVV office** is in the Spaans Leenhof, Th. Dorrenplein 5, Valkenburg (☎ **043/609-8600;** fax 043/609-8608). Open Monday through Friday 9am to 5pm, Saturday 9am to 1pm.

Exploring Valkenburg

Some of Valkenburg's most intriguing sights are hidden. The rocks beneath Valkenburg are like a Swiss cheese—for centuries (beginning with the Romans), people have excavated the soft marlstone and used it as building material. Nowadays six of these caves are open to the public.

Gemeentegrot (Cauberg Caves). At the foot of the Cauberg (the main hill in town). ☎ **043/601-2271.** Admission Dfl 5.25 ($2.65) on foot, Dfl 6.75 ($3.35) by train. Guided tours daily every hour Apr–Oct 10:30am–4pm; July–Aug 9:30am–5pm; Nov–Mar Mon–Fri at 2pm, Sat–Sun 10:30am–4pm.

This cave can be visited on foot or in a little train. The interesting formations within the cave include a subterranean lake that has formed over the centuries. If you could return in about one million years you might see some stalactites and stalagmites.

Holland Casino Valkenburg. Kuurpark Cauberg 28. ☎ **043/609-9600.** Admission Dfl 6 ($3) per day, minimum age 18 years. Daily 1:30pm–2am. AE, MC, V.

In 1998, this state-operated casino moved to its current modernistic hilltop premises, just across the road from the Thermae 2000 spa. The place offers French and American roulette, blackjack, and mini punto banco. There's also a separate area with slot machines of all shapes and sizes, plus two restaurants, two bars, and reception rooms. For a whole evening's entertainment you can sit down to a spectacular dinner show. You should note that a dress code is observed (jacket and tie—or turtleneck—for men, dress or dressy pants suit for the ladies), and you'll need your passport to show you're over 18 years of age. Good luck!

Margraten Military Cemetery. 5km (3 miles) east of Maastricht on the N278 highway. ☎ **043/458-1208.**

This cemetery is the final resting place for American troops who died in Holland in World War II and whose remains were not repatriated. It's a place much revered by the Dutch, who tend the graves and often leave wreaths and flowers behind as symbols of gratitude for the sacrifices that liberated them from Nazi oppressors.

Drielandenpunt (Three-Country Point)

The little finger of Limburg is hemmed in between Belgium and Germany. Near the village of Vaals in the south-eastern corner of Limburg, those two countries and Holland meet. The elevation at this point is the highest in Holland, 1058 feet above sea level—a mountain for the Netherlands! The landscape offers a particularly excellent opportunity to look across miles of countryside in three different countries. The area is surrounded by extensive forest. Wealthy merchants built a number of grand homes here during the 18th century, including Vaalsbroek Castle and Bloemendal Castle.

For more information contact the **VVV Drielandenpunt office,** at Maastrichtenlaan 73a, Vaals (☎ **043/306-2918;** fax 043/306-4400). Office hours Monday through Friday 9am to 5pm, Saturday 9am to 1pm. Vaals is 30km (19 miles) east of Maastricht on the N278; the Three-Country Point is a farther 0.5km (1 mile) south.

Thermae 2000. Kuurpark Cauberg 27. ☎ **043/601-9419.** Admission Dfl 30 ($15) for 2 hours, Dfl 52.50 ($26.25) for a whole day. Daily 9am–11pm.

The waters that simmer below Valkenburg's mountains are the source for this futuristic health spa where you can relax completely in the soothing thermal baths, as well as have a stay in the sauna or a workout in the gymnasium. Extra pampering possibilities include getting a massage or floating in a warm bath amidst all the goodness of a herbal body-wrap. The entrance fee includes all services except massages, floats, and beautician and therapeutic treatments. There's also an excellent hotel here (See "Where to Stay & Dine," below).

WHERE TO STAY & DINE

✪ **Thermaetel.** Kuurpark Cauberg 27, 6300 AD Valkenburg. ☎ **043/601-9445** or 043/601-6050. Fax 043/601-4777. 69 units. TV TEL MINIBAR. Dfl 385 ($192.50) double; Dfl 475 ($237.50) suite. AE, DC, MC, V.

This is the place to stay overnight in Valkenburg. After checking in, you can just put on your bathrobe and walk to the pool! The price of a room includes admission to the health spa for the length of your stay, including on the day you arrive and the day you leave (so if you stay for 2 nights, for example, you can actually use the spa for 3 days). The water in your hotel room comes from the spa's spring. Each room has a hillside garden terrace. The restaurant offers a tasty array of health-oriented dishes—it's up to you to decide whether to load up on calories or try to lose some!

20

Getting to Know Luxembourg

The Grand Duchy of Luxembourg is such a tiny country—only 999 square miles—that it hardly seems possible that its borders could embrace so many worthy travel delights. Yet within this country are the remnants of a rich history and a landscape whose scenic beauty varies from wild highlands to peaceful river valleys to southern plains dotted with picturesque villages and farmlands. Luxembourg's people have emerged from a turbulent past to forge a prosperous present and build the framework for an optimistic future, not only for their own country, but also for the entire European Union.

1 The Physical Landscape

Geographically, the Grand Duchy consists of two very distinct regions. In the northern half lie the richly forested Ardennes hills; while to the south are rolling farmlands, woods, and the valley of the Moselle, with its famous vineyards. The mining district is tucked away in the extreme south.

Luxembourg City, which sits in the center of the southern region, is a marvelously contrasting mix of the old and the new. The old part of the city runs along a deep valley beneath brooding casemates that have lent themselves so readily to defense in times of war, while the more modern part of town crowns steep cliffs overlooking the old. In the northern Ardennes region, handsome castles are everywhere, with especially impressive examples at Clervaux and Esch-sur-Sûre. The area also has its share of holiday resort towns, perhaps most notably in medieval Vianden, the proud site of a huge restored fortress surrounded by beautiful forests.

For Americans, the Ardennes area holds another fascination, for it was here, in places like Berdorf, Clervaux, Ettelbruck, and Wiltz, that U.S. forces engaged German troops in the fierce Battle of the Bulge. Memorials to those who fell in these fierce encounters mark the route that finally led to Luxembourg's total liberation on February 12, 1945.

2 Luxembourg Today

Today the Grand Duchy of Luxembourg, a constitutional monarchy, has a population of about 400,000. Economically it has a strong iron and steel industry and a growing number of light industries. The strength of its banking and financial institutions has attracted some 220 foreign banks (which employ 1 out of every 23 Luxembourgers), including the headquarters of the European Investment Bank. Its economic strength attracts European immigrants—some 25% of the total population (65% of the work force) are foreigners.

Agriculture is still important, as are the vineyards of the Moselle Valley. And the enchanting Luxembourg countryside has become a favorite holiday destination for many Europeans, making tourism an important industry.

THE PEOPLE "We are very much a combination of what surrounds us," Prince Jean de Luxembourg (second son of Grand Duke Jean) is quoted as saying. This is undeniably true—in such a small country it could hardly be otherwise. But it's a strange sort of combination, one that results in a distinctive individuality that even extends to the national language, which is vaguely related to both French and German, yet quite different from both.

Luxembourgers have a personality that's hard to capture in words. They generally seem content to leave it simply at *"Mir woelle bleiwe wat mir sin"* ("We want to remain what we are") with no need to spell out "what we are" in detail. You'll see that national motto inscribed over old door frames, hear it echoed in songs, and recognize its essence in everyone you meet in the Grand Duchy.

But some of their character traits are easy to pin down. One thing they definitely are is hardworking. Foreign firms that open branches in Luxembourg will tell you that their productivity is far higher in the Grand Duchy than in other locations. One look at the country's well-tended farms or shops will reveal the industriousness of their owners. Go into a Luxembourg home and the cleanliness and order will speak more loudly than the proud homemaker ever could. And, of course, the swiftness with which Luxembourgers repaired the devastation from World War II in their country is ample testimony to their collective abilities.

The people of Luxembourg are also quite cosmopolitan. From their cuisine (a combination of the best from surrounding countries) to their culture and dress, they are at home in the world, eager to travel, and secure enough in their own uniqueness to appreciate the special qualities of others. But in addition to this openness, they are essentially proud and patriotic. Centuries of domination by foreign rulers could not kill their independent spirit.

Finally, to say that Luxembourgers are fond of eating is an understatement. If there's an important matter to discuss, decision to be made, or social crisis to resolve, Luxembourgers repair to the nearest cafe or pastry shop. It goes without saying, then, that they are also fond of cooking—don't go away without indulging in their luscious pastries, and forget the calories!

After you spend a little time with these proud and charming people, you may well find yourself silently echoing their motto, with the slight addition, "We want you to remain what you are!"

THE LANGUAGE *Letzebuergesch,* the national language, has a vaguely German base with overtones of French, yet is completely distinct from both of those languages. Luxembourgers learn and use their native tongue from earliest childhood, and then study German in their first school years and French shortly after.

As for anyone who isn't native born learning *Letzebuergesch,* forget it—it's a tongue twister. Not to worry, however; for while the native language is widely used among Luxembourgers, and although French is most often used in official and cultural activities and German is heard frequently—everyone speaks English. In other words, you'll encounter few, if any, language difficulties in the Grand Duchy.

Luxembourg

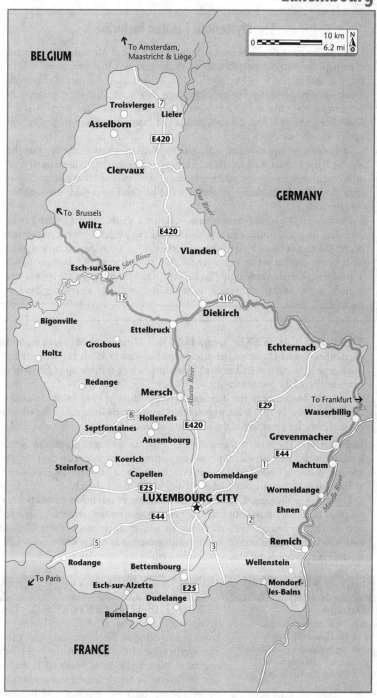

The Mysterious Maiden Mélusine

Luxembourg has a rich folklore tradition, and the tale of Mélusine the mermaid is perhaps the nation's most famous myth. Legend says that imprisoned within the rock that helped form Luxembourg City's tremendous defenses is a beautiful maiden named Mélusine. She passes the time by knitting, but she manages only one stitch each year—and it's a very good thing she's so slow. You see, should she finish her knitting before she's released, all of Luxembourg and its people will vanish into the rock with her!

Mélusine was imprisoned after Sigefroi married her without knowing that she was really a mermaid. At first, she kept her secret by reverting to her natural state only on Saturday, a day she told her husband was reserved for her personal privacy. But when his curiosity got the better of him and he peeked, she vanished into the rock.

Once every 7 years Mélusine returns, either as a serpent with a golden key in its mouth or as a beautiful woman. All it will take to win her freedom is for some brave soul to kiss the womanly vision or take the key from the serpent's mouth. That brave soul has yet to appear, and in the meantime all of Luxembourg (or at least that part of Luxembourg that believes in the legend) prays for her to drop a stitch or two so that whatever it is she's knitting will take a very long time to complete!

THE POLITICAL SCENE Grand Duke Jean of the House of Nassau succeeded his mother, Grand Duchess Charlotte, as head of state in 1964. Luxembourg has a one-house legislature, the Chamber of Deputies, which is made up of 60 members who are elected for 5-year terms.

Since the beginning of the Benelux Customs Union in 1948 (which became an economic union in 1958), Luxembourg has been actively involved in the affairs of its neighbors. It's a member of the UN, the Council of Europe, NATO, and the EU.

RELIGION The vast majority (some 95%) of Luxembourgers are Roman Catholic, although a significant percentage of those hasten to make it clear that they are nonpracticing Catholics. It is, however, rare to meet one who does not observe at least some of the customs, traditions, and mores of the church.

Despite their thorough Catholicism, Luxembourgers also follow a strict policy of religious freedom. Along with Catholic priests, the state supports the Chief Rabbi and the Official Protestant Pastor. There are also small clusters of other Christian and non-Christian faiths. While religious instruction is a part of the school curriculum, upper levels can choose instead an ethics-and-morality course.

3 History 101

Dateline

- 963 Count Sigefroi, founder of the House of Luxembourg, exchanges some of his lands for a Roman fortress called Lucilinburhuc and builds a small castle on a rocky outcrop called the

continues

BEFORE THE 12TH CENTURY B.C. Long before recorded history, the Grand Duchy was home to Magdalenian, Neolithic, and Celtic tribes. The Treviri tribe of the Celts, a fierce people who resisted invaders to the death, finally fell in the first century A.D. to Roman legions intent on bringing all of Europe under Caesar's rule. For almost 500 years afterward one Roman emperor after another put down numerous uprisings as the area's independent-minded inhabitants stubbornly refused to give up their worship of Druidism for the paganism of Rome.

As Rome suffered military defeats and Christianity became more widespread, the Roman hold on the region finally weakened. By the fifth century the only reminders of the Romans left in Luxembourg were the bits and pieces of their urban civilization, a network of bridges that marked their progress across the land, and place names such as Ettelbruck (Attila's Bridge), named for the Hun general who dealt the coup de grâce to the Western Roman Empire. Luxembourg was by then quite firmly in the Frankish camp.

Along with monasteries that sprang up and flourished with the support of the people came educational and cultural influences that helped form the foundation of today's Luxembourg. The great Frankish leader Charlemagne brought in Saxons to settle the Ardennes, thus adding another ethnic imprint to the face of the region.

In the 10th century, Sigefroi, the youngest of the counts of Ardennes, obtained a large land grant from the Abbey of Saint Maximin (the deed, dated April 12, 963, is still kept in the Pescatore Museum in Luxembourg). He built his castle on the ruins of Castellum Lucilinburhuc, an ancient Roman fort that had guarded the crossroads of two important Roman routes, from Paris to Trier and from Metz to Aix-la-Chapelle road. On that strategic spot grew a town and eventually a country by the name of Luxembourg.

THE 12TH & 13TH CENTURIES By the 12th century, the counts of Luxembourg were at the country's helm. They enlarged their territory by wars with other noblemen, fortunate marriages, and various diplomatic shenanigans. But soon they began to absent themselves for long periods; some of the nobility joined the forces of Godfrey of Bouillon to travel to the Holy City during the Crusades. Some never returned (having fallen in battle), and those who did found that much of their land had been confiscated by other overlords during their absence.

When Henry the Blind's daughter, the Countess Ermesinde, reached adulthood in the early 1200s, things were in disarray. But Ermesinde was able to restore some of Luxembourg's lost territory through a few marriages, as she inherited lands previously held by her ailing spouses; and when her last husband died in 1225, she boldly took charge

Bock, laying the foundation for the future city of Luxembourg.

- **1244** Countess Ermesinde grants personal freedom to the citizens of the town of Luxembourg and autonomy to its administration.
- **1288** Luxembourg suffers a crushing defeat in the Battle of Worringen, putting an end to its acquisition of land in Limburg and Brabant.
- **1308** Henry VII, Count of Luxembourg, is elected King of Germany, and in 1312 is crowned Holy Roman Emperor Henry IV. His son, the blind John of Luxembourg, becomes King of Bohemia in 1310, and is killed in action fighting for France against England at the Battle of Crécy in 1346.
- **1346** John of Luxembourg's son Charles becomes King of Germany and King of Bohemia in 1346, and in 1355 is crowned Holy Roman Emperor as Charles IV.
- **1354** Charles IV raises Luxembourg's status from a county to a duchy.
- **1378** Charles IV's son Wenceslas II succeeds him as Holy Roman Emperor.
- **1388** Wenceslas II gives the duchy to his nephew, Jost von Mahren, as a fiefdom, with disastrous results for Luxembourg.
- **1443** Philip the Good of Burgundy captures the fortress of Luxembourg and establishes French rule.
- **1506** Beginning of Spanish rule, which lasts until 1684.
- **1684** The fortress is recaptured and the country is once more under French rule.
- **1697** Start of the second period of Spanish rule, when France returns the duchy to

continues

Spain under the "Treaty of Ryswick."

- **1713** Beginning of the Golden Age of Luxembourg, when Philippe V forfeits his rule in favor of Charles VI and Maria Theresa of Austria.
- **1794** French lay siege to Luxembourg, gaining control when the Austrian garrison is starved out.
- **1814** The French garrison leaves the fortress.
- **1815** Treaty of Vienna partitions Luxembourg; lands east of the Moselle, Sûre, and Our are ceded to Prussia, and the remainder go to Holland's William of Orange.
- **1839** Under the Treaty of London, Luxembourg's Walloon districts are returned to Belgium; the duchy's independence is acknowledged in its first constitution.
- **1867** The Treaty of London guarantees Luxembourg's neutrality under the protection of the great powers; all fortifications are razed.
- **1914** German troops occupy the country.
- **1922** Agreement on economic union with Belgium signed in Brussels.
- **1940** German army invades Luxembourg on May 10; royal family and government go into exile.
- **1944** American troops begin liberation of Luxembourg.
- **1944–45** Battle of the Bulge. Hitler's last offensive brings destruction to much of the Grand Duchy. The German army is thrown back again by American troops and Luxembourg is liberated.
- **1948** Customs Union with Belgium and the

continues

of the affairs of state. By bringing noblemen who had always been at each other's throats together in a central governing body, she achieved such revolutionary reforms as the establishment of a court of justice and limited judicial rights for ordinary citizens. The tight rein of feudal lords was somewhat loosened. Countess Ermesinde also began to establish convents and monasteries to provide education and culture for her people. Her legacy to her people was a united nation with enlightened social standards.

THE 14TH THROUGH 18TH CENTURIES
In 1308 Henry VII of the House of Luxembourg became emperor of the Holy Roman Empire. He spent the rest of his life trying to unite all of Europe under his rule. His son, John the Blind, was a valiant warrior who perished at Crécy fighting the forces of Edward III of England, after ordering his men to lead him into the thickest part of battle. Today he is revered as Luxembourg's national hero. John's son, Charles IV, favored extending his domain through treaty and marriage; by the time his son, Wenceslas, gained the throne, the House of Luxembourg ruled a territory some 500 times the size of today's Luxembourg.

The glory days did not last long, however. King Wenceslas's son, Sigismund, proved to be far less capable than his ancestors. By the mid-1400s Luxembourg itself was a province ruled by the dukes of Burgundy. During the next 400 years that rule shifted among Spain, France, Austria, and Burgundy.

THE 19TH CENTURY One might have thought that the constant domination by foreign powers would crush the Luxembourgers' strong spirit of independence, but the stubborn sense of individuality born with their Celtic forebears and rekindled under Countess Ermesinde refused to fade. To quell the locals' growing unrest, each successive ruler found it necessary to further strengthen a capital city that was already one of Europe's best defended. Luxembourg, then, became a problem for the rest of Europe: Its position was too strategic and its fortifications too strong to allow it to be self-governing—or even to be controlled by any one nation. The answer seemed to be to divide Luxembourg among several nations; therefore, the Congress of Vienna handed over most of the country to Holland's William of Orange-Nassau, and the remainder to Prussia.

Then with the Treaty of London in 1839, more than half of Holland's piece of Luxembourg was given to Belgium (the resulting Belgian province still bears the name Luxembourg).

Since its boundaries were becoming smaller and smaller, the Grand Duchy of Luxembourg posed no real threat to anyone. Still, its many fortifications made it all but impenetrable, so in 1867 the European powers convened in London and decided that freedom would be granted the Grand Duchy on condition that its fortifications be dismantled. Luxembourgers were overjoyed. In October 1868 they affirmed a constitution that boldly proclaimed "The Grand Duchy of Luxembourg forms a free state, independent and indivisible." Today there are green parks throughout the capital city to mark the sites of mighty fortifications, now vanished, and tiny Luxembourg has led the way toward the peaceful economic unification of Europe's separate nations.

THE 20TH CENTURY   Since that momentous announcement of independence, Luxembourg has seen periods of prosperity (largely due to its important steel industry) and periods of decline that have prompted thousands to emigrate in search of work. Twice—in World Wars I and II—the country suffered the agonies of military occupation. The heroism of the Luxembourg underground resistance movement during World War II is legendary. Many of the younger men made their way to Allied countries to fight in their ranks, while those at home actually went out on strike when the Nazis imposed compulsory service in the Wehrmacht—a move that brought swift retribution from the Nazis. By the close of World War II in 1945, more than 60,000 homes and 160 bridges and tunnels in Luxembourg had been destroyed. But once more, determined Luxembourgers set about to rebuild

Netherlands takes effect (it becomes an economic union in 1958). Luxembourg's constitutional revision provides for the right to work, social security, and recognition of trade unions.

- **1949** Luxembourg joins NATO.
- **1952** As a founding member of the European Coal and Steel Community, Luxembourg is chosen as the seat of important European institutions.
- **1958** Luxembourg joins the European Economic Community.
- **1964** Head of State Grand Duchess Charlotte abdicates in favor of her son, Grand Duke Jean.
- **1966** Opening of the European Center in Kirchberg; Luxembourg's financial market and stock exchange gain outstanding reputation worldwide.
- **1992** The Chamber of Deputies ratifies the Treaty on European Union by an overwhelming majority vote.
- **1993** Luxembourg opposes efforts of other EU members to impose withholding tax on savings and investments in the Grand Duchy.
- **1999** Luxembourg joins ten other European Union countries in launching the new European currency, the euro.

their homeland, and within a remarkably short time, fields were once again plowed, highways and railways repaired, homes rebuilt, and everything restored to the orderly efficiency you see today.

4 The Active Vacation Planner

FISHING   The rivers of the Grand Duchy are an anglers' paradise. Licenses are issued by the district commissioners in Luxembourg City, Diekirch, and Grevenmacher, and by a few communal administrations, such as those in Ettelbruck, Vianden, and Wiltz—there's sure to be a source close by. A license to fish from the banks of eastern-border rivers and lakes costs 600 LF ($16.65) for a month. Fishing from boats requires a special license for 450 LF ($12.50) per week, 1,100 LF

($30.55) per month. There are several rather complex and changeable regulations governing fishing in frontier waters. For complete details on all types of fishing, contact the Administration des Eaux et Forêts, B.P. 411, 2014 Luxembourg.

GOLF The course maintained by the Grand-Ducal Golf Club in Luxembourg City is known throughout Europe for its difficult, narrow fairways. Visitors can arrange to play the course by contacting **Golf Club Grand-Ducal,** Senningerberg/Luxembourg (☎ **352/34-00-90**). The Hotel Association of Clervaux also offers attractive golf holiday packages at country hotels; contact the Clervaux Tourist Office, Clervaux Castle, 9701 Clervaux, Luxembourg (☎ **352/92-00-72**).

HORSEBACK RIDING—Riding is a favorite sport in Luxembourg, with several very good stables offering mounts at about 360 LF ($10) per hour. For a full list of stables and riding schools, contact **Tourisme Equestre,** rue de Schoenfels 16, Luxembourg (☎ **352/22-28-09**). The organization also puts together various horseback tours in Luxembourg City and in the countryside.

TENNIS & SQUASH Many of the resort areas offer tennis facilities, and squash courts are widely available as well. Contact the **Institute National des Sports** (☎ **352/478-34-00**) for details.

WALKING There are marked walking paths throughout the Grand Duchy. During the summer, organized walking tours of 6 to 25 miles are conducted from Luxembourg City. Contact the **Fédération Luxembourgeoise des Marches Populaires,** rue de Rollingergrund 176, Luxembourg (☎ **352/44-93-02**), for more information.

5 A Taste of Luxembourg

RESTAURANTS

Luxembourg City, because of its large number of international diplomatic and business visitors, has many fine restaurants offering international cuisine. It also has just as many small cafes and bistros featuring traditional dishes. In smaller towns and villages, hotel restaurants are often quite good, as are the small local cafes.

Note: Most restaurants are open for lunch from noon to 2:30pm and for dinner from 7pm to 10pm. The hours, however, are flexible.

THE CUISINE

Among the national favorites are some of the best pastries you're ever likely to eat; Luxembourg cheese (delicious); trout, crayfish, and pike from local rivers; hare (during the hunting season); and lovely small plum tarts called *quetsch* (in September). Other tasty treats include calf's liver dumplings (*quenelles*) with sauerkraut and boiled potatoes, black pudding (*treipen*) and sausages with mashed potatoes and horseradish, and smoked pork with broad beans. French cuisine also features prominently on restaurant menus, and a German influence is felt as well.

DRINK

WATER & SOFT DRINKS You need have no concerns about Luxembourg's water—it's clear, pure, and safe. As for soft drinks, they go by the name of "minerals," and most leading European brands are available, along with some from the United States.

BEER & WINE Although many of the fine beers of Belgium and Holland are available here, Luxembourg has its own that take a backseat to none—look for such brand names as Mousel (pronounced "*Mooz*-ell"), Bofferding, and Henri Funck. And of course the Moselle wines (mostly white) will top any list—look for the National Mark, which certifies that they are true Luxembourg wines.

In 1993 it was reported that Luxembourg had the highest worldwide per capita consumption of alcohol—the equivalent of about three beers a day for every man, woman, and child—so when you visit the local bars, don't feel compelled to keep up with the natives.

21

Planning a Trip to Luxembourg

Like the other two Benelux countries, Luxembourg is an easy country in which to travel. This chapter is designed to provide most of the nuts-and-bolts information you'll need before setting off for the Grand Duchy.

1 Visitor Information & Money

VISITOR INFORMATION

In the United States, the **Luxembourg National Tourist Office** is at 17 Beekman Place, New York, NY 10022 (☎ **212/935-8888;** fax 212/935-5896). In Britain, the Luxembourg National Tourist Office is at 122 Regent St., London W1R 5FE (☎ **0171/ 434-2800;** fax 0171/734-1205).

In Luxembourg, the administrative address of the Luxembourg National Tourist Office (Office National du Tourisme Luxembourgeois) is BP 1001, 1010 Luxembourg City (☎ **352/42-82-821;** fax 352/42-82-82-38). The office also operates a **Welcome Desk** (Bureaux d'Acceuil) at Gare Centrale (☎ **352/42-82-82-20;** fax 352/42-82-82-30), open from July through mid-September Monday to Saturday 9am to 7pm, Sunday 9am to noon and 2 to 6:30pm; mid-September through May daily 9am to noon and 2 to 6:30pm. There's a second Welcome Desk at Luxembourg Airport (☎ **352/42-82-82-21**), open from April through October Monday to Friday 10am to 2:30pm and 4 to 7pm, Saturday 10am to 1:45pm, Sunday 10am to 2:30pm and 3:30 to 6:30pm; November through March Monday to Friday 10am to 2:30pm and 4 to 7pm, Saturday 10am to 1:45pm.

Luxembourg City Tourist Office (Syndicat d'Initiative et de Tourisme), place d'Armes, 2011 Luxembourg City (☎ **352/ 47-96-27-09;** fax 352/47-48-18), is open January through March and October through December from Monday to Saturday 9am to 6pm; April through September Monday to Saturday 9am to 7pm, Sunday 10am to 6pm.

There are around 20 local tourist offices in towns and villages throughout the Grand Duchy.

The Luxembourg Franc

At this writing \$1 = approximately 36 francs (or 1 franc = 2.8¢) and £1 = approximately 55 francs (or 1 franc = 1.8 pence). These were the rates of exchange used to calculate the dollar and pound values given in this book and in the table below (rounded off).

LF	U.S. $	U.K. £	LF	U.S. $	U.K. £
1	.03	.02	500	13.89	9.09
5	.14	.09	750	20.83	13.64
10	.28	.18	1,000	27.78	18.18
20	.56	.36	1,250	34.72	22.73
25	.69	.45	1,500	41.67	27.27
30	.83	.54	1,750	48.61	31.82
40	1.11	.73	2,000	55.55	36.36
50	1.39	.91	2,500	69.44	45.45
75	2.08	1.36	3,000	83.33	54.55
100	2.78	1.82	3,500	97.22	63.64
125	3.47	2.27	4,000	111.11	72.73
150	4.17	2.73	4,500	125.00	81.82
200	5.56	3.64	5,000	139.89	90.91
250	6.94	4.55	6,000	166.67	109.09

What Things Cost in Luxembourg City   U.S. $

	U.S. $
Taxi from the airport to the city center	18.05
Bus from the airport to the city center (with luggage)	2.20
Local telephone call	.55
Double room at the Grand Le Royal (very expensive)	291.65
Double room at the Hôtel Français (moderate)	116.65
Double room at the Hôtel Carlton (inexpensive)	38.90
Dinner for one, without wine, at La Lorraine (expensive)	55.00
Dinner for one, without wine, at Chiggeri (moderate)	35.00
Dinner for one, without wine, at the Taj Mahal (inexpensive)	20.00
Glass of beer	1.50
Coca-Cola	1.30
Cup of coffee	1.65
Roll of ASA 100 color film, 36 exposures	5.00
Admission to the National Museum	2.80
Movie ticket	6.95
Concert ticket	15–100.00

MONEY

Luxembourg's currency is tied to the Belgian franc, and Belgian currency is freely accepted throughout the Grand Duchy. The **Luxembourg franc** (LF) is made up of 100 centimes, and notes are issued in 100-, 200-, 500-, 1,000-, 2,000-, 5,000-, and 10,000-franc denominations. Coins come in 50 centimes, and 1, 5, 20, and 50 francs, and it's a good idea to keep a small supply of 5- and 20-franc coins on hand for tips, telephone calls, and the like. For more information on the Belgian franc, see chapter 4.

Luxembourg is one of the first wave of 11 countries that are establishing the new European currency called the euro (see the box in chapter 4).

2 When to Go

"In-season" in Luxembourg, as in the rest of the Benelux countries, means mid-April through mid-October. The peak of the tourist season is July and August, when the weather is at its finest. The weather, however, is never really extreme at any time of year, and if you're one of the growing numbers who favor shoulder- or off-season travel, you'll find the Grand Duchy every bit as attractive during those months. Not only are airlines, hotels, and restaurants cheaper, less crowded, and more relaxed during this time, but there are also some very appealing events going on. Theater is most active during winter months in Luxembourg City, and outside the city, on the second weekend in September, Grevenmacher celebrates its Wine and Grape Festival with a splendid folklore procession.

CLIMATE   The Grand Duchy is blessed with a moderate climate, with less annual rainfall than either Belgium or Holland, since North Sea winds have usually wept their tears before they get this far inland. July and August temperatures average around 60°F; winter temperatures average around 37°F.

HOLIDAYS   Public holidays in Luxembourg are January 1 (New Year's Day), Shrove Monday (the Monday before Ash Wednesday), Easter Monday, May 1 (Labor Day), Ascension Day (40 days after Easter), Whitmonday (the Monday following the 7th Sunday after Easter), June 23 (Luxembourg National Holiday, the grand duke's birthday), Assumption Day (August 15), November 1 (All Saints' Day), December 25 (Christmas Day), and December 26 (Boxing Day).

LUXEMBOURG CALENDAR OF EVENTS

March

- **Carnival Parade,** Pétange. Mid-Lent Carnival. Contact **Pétange Tourist Office** (☎ **352/50-12-511**). Refreshment Sunday (3 weeks before Easter).

April

- **Easter Exhibition,** Grevenmacher. Agricultural products and handicrafts. Contact **Grevenmacher Tourist Office** (☎ **352/75-82-75**). Easter Saturday through the Thursday after Easter.
- **Folk Festival,** Luxembourg City. L'Emais'chen Festival, when young lovers buy pottery items for each other. Contact **Luxembourg City Tourist Office** (☎ **352/47-96-27-09**). Easter Monday.
- **Wine Fair,** Grevenmacher. Contact **Grevenmacher Tourist Office** (☎ **352/ 75-82-75**). Thursday after Easter.

- **Musical Spring.** Festival of music, including classical, jazz, and folk, at venues around Luxembourg City. Contact **Luxembourg City Tourist Office** (☎ **352/47-96-27-09**). April and May.

May

- **Grand Wine Tasting Day,** Remerschen. In the Cooperative Cellars. Contact **Caves Coopératives des Vignerons** (☎ **352/66-41-65**). May 1.
- **Octave of Our Lady of Luxembourg,** Luxembourg City and Diekirch. Grand religious processions in honor of the Virgin Mary. Contact **Luxembourg City Tourist Office** (☎ **352/47-96-27-09**) and **Diekirch Tourist Office** (☎ **352/80-30-23**). Fifth Sunday after Easter.
- **International Trade Fair,** Luxembourg City. Contact **Luxembourg City Tourist Office** (☎ **352/47-96-27-09**). Last week of May.
- **Flower Parade,** Wiltz. The Féerie du Genêt festival includes a street market. Contact **Wiltz Tourist Office** (☎ **352/95-74-44**). Monday after Pentecost (end of May or beginning of June).
- **Dancing Procession,** Echternach. Colorful and internationally renowned 1,200-year-old folk-dancing procession in honor of St. Willibrord. Contact **Echternach Tourist Office** (☎ **352/72-02-30**). Tuesday after Pentecost, beginning at 9am (end of May or beginning of June).

June

- **International Classical Music Festival,** Echternach. National and visiting orchestras play in the Basilica and the Church of Saints Peter and Paul. Contact **Echternach Tourist Office** (☎ **352/72-02-30**). Mid-May through end of June.
- **National Day,** Esch-sur-Alzette. Gala celebration with fireworks. Contact **Esch-sur-Alzette Tourist Office** (☎ **352/54-73-83-246**). June 22 to 23.
- **Luxembourg National Day,** Luxembourg City. Gala celebration featuring festival activities, the Grand Duke reviewing his troops, and fireworks. Contact **Luxembourg City Tourist Office** (☎ **352/47-96-27-09**). June 23.
- **Wine Festival,** Remich. Open-air celebrations and wine tasting. Contact **Remich Tourist Office** (☎ **352/69-84-88**). End of June through August.

July

- **Open-air Concerts.** Evening concerts in the place d'Armes, Luxembourg City. Contact **Luxembourg City Tourist Office** (☎ **352/47-96-27-09**). Throughout July.
- **Folkloric and Gymnastic Shows, Ballet, and Exhibitions.** Series of events spread among these small towns: Diekirch, Mersch, Echternach, Wiltz, Mondorf-les-Bains, and Vianden. Contact **Luxembourg National Tourist Office** (☎ **352/42-82-821**). July and August.
- **Remembrance Day,** Ettelbruck. Celebration in honor of U.S. General George S. Patton, who liberated Luxembourg in World War II. Contact **Musée Patton,** rue du Dr. Klein 5 (☎ **352/81-03-22**). Second weekend of July.
- **Old Diekirch Festival,** Diekirch. Folklore events, music, and street market. Contact **Diekirch Tourist Office** (☎ **352/80-30-23**). Second weekend of July.
- **International Open-Air Theater Festival,** Wiltz. Performances every Friday, Saturday, and Sunday. Incorporates a music program at the Château de Wiltz. Contact **Wiltz Tourist Office** (☎ **352/95-74-44**). Mid-July.
- **Beer Festival,** Diekirch. A popular event in this beer-brewing town. Contact **Diekirch Tourist Office** (☎ **352/80-30-23**). Third Sunday in July.

- **Pottery Festival,** Nospelt. The center of Luxembourg's pottery industry opens its workshops and hosts a street market for pottery and handicrafts. Contact **Musée de la Potterie,** rue des Potiers 12a (☎ **352/30-01-99**). Last Sunday in July.
- **Folklore Festival,** Wellenstein. Contact the **Musée Folklorique et Viticole** (☎ **352/69-73-53**). End of July.

July and August

- **Riesling Day,** Wormeldange. Wine tasting at Cooperative Wine Cellars. Contact the **Caves Coopératives des Vignerons,** route du Vin 115 (☎ **352/76-82-11**). July 31, 1999; August 5, 2000.

August

- **Agricultural Fair,** Ettelbruck. Contact **Ettelbruck Tourist Office** (☎ **352/81-20-68**). First weekend in August.
- **Jumping CSI,** Mondorf-les-Bains. International riding tournament. Contact **Casino 2000** (☎ **352/66-10-101**). Mid-August.
- **Schobermesse,** Luxembourg City. Big amusement fair and market. Contact **Luxembourg City Tourist Office** (☎ **352/47-96-27-09**). Two weeks, beginning next-to-last Sunday in August.

September

- **Liberation Remembrance Day,** Pétange. Ceremony in front of American soldier monument. Contact **Pétange Tourist Office** (☎ **352/50-12-511**). September 9.
- **Wine and Grape Festival,** Greiveldange. Contact **Caves Coopératives des Vignerons** (☎ **352/69-83-14**). Third weekend of September.

3 Getting Around

BY TRAIN & BUS

Luxembourg National Railways (Chemins de Fer Luxembourgeois) operates fast and frequent schedules throughout the Grand Duchy, with good connecting bus service to those points it doesn't reach. Travelers over 65 are eligible for a 50% reduction in both first and second class except when traveling to or from a frontier point. In addition, special half-fare weekend and holiday round-trip tickets are offered throughout the system except from frontier points. A **1-day network ticket,** good for unlimited travel by train and bus, costs 160 LF ($4.45); for 5 days, the cost is 660 LF ($18.35), and travel may be for any 5 days within a 1-month period.

Porters (available only at Luxembourg City station) charge a flat fee of 50 LF ($1.40) per bag. For **train and bus information,** call ☎ **352/49-90-49-90** daily from 7am to 8pm.

In addition to frequent bus service to all points in the Grand Duchy, there are several well-planned bus tours from Luxembourg City that cover the most scenic countryside locations (see chapter 22).

BY TAXI

During the day taxis charge 100 LF ($2.80) when the meter starts and 32 LF (90¢) per kilometer, with a 10% surcharge after 10pm and 25% on weekends and holidays. Waiting time is charged at the rate of LF 8.30 (25¢) per minute.

BY CAR

Roads within the Grand Duchy are kept in very good repair and are well sign-posted, although some roadways are narrow, with many curves, especially in the Ardennes region.

To park in the city, you may need a **parking disc.** These are cardboard or plastic discs with a revolving hour scale. When you park, you set your arrival time by turning the disc to the appropriate hour, displayed in a slot in the card, so that the parking inspectors know when you have overstayed your welcome. The discs—which are available in stores and banks at no charge—are required in "blue zones" in Luxembourg City, Esch-sur-Alzette, Dudelange, Remich, and Wiltz. In many other places, there are parking meters or half-hour parking-ticket dispensers.

The **Automobile Club du Grand Duché de Luxembourg** is at route de Longwy 54, Luxembourg-Helfenterbruck (☎ **352/450-04-51**).

RENTALS   If you plan to rent a car after your arrival in the Grand Duchy, you'll need a driver's license valid in your own country, and you'll be required to purchase insurance when you book the car. Car-rental rates begin at about 2,200 LF ($61.10) per day and 2,600 LF ($72.20) for a weekend. Leading car-rental firms in Luxembourg City are: **Budget Rent a Car,** rue de Longwy 300 (☎ **352/44-19-38**) and Luxembourg Airport (☎ **352/43-75-75**); **Avis,** place de la Gare 17 (☎ **352/48-95-95**) and Luxembourg Airport (☎ **352/43-51-71**); and **Hertz,** Luxembourg Airport (☎ **352/43-46-45**).

GASOLINE   Gas (*benzine* in these parts) will run about 27 LF (75¢) per liter; diesel fuel costs 23 LF (64¢) per liter.

DRIVING RULES   Speed limits are 50kmph (31 m.p.h.) in built-up areas, 90kmph (57 m.p.h.) on rural roads, and 120kmph (75 m.p.h.) on expressways. The use of seatbelts is compulsory, and horn blowing is permitted only in case of imminent danger.

ROAD MAPS   An excellent road map of the Grand Duchy, which shows camping grounds, swimming pools, and tourist attractions in addition to main roads, is available at no cost from the Luxembourg National Tourist Office in Luxembourg City. Other good road maps include the Ordnance Survey maps (two sheets) and Michelin map no. 215, both available at local bookstores and newsstands.

BREAKDOWNS/ASSISTANCE   The Automobile Club du Grand Duché de Luxembourg, route de Longwy 54, Luxembourg-Helfenterbruck (☎ **352/450-04-51**), offers a 24-hour emergency road service.

HITCHHIKING

Hitchhiking is generally quite safe but, as in most countries, it pays to have a companion along. It's illegal to hitchhike on highways, but you should be fine along country roads and on entry ramps.

BY BICYCLE

The Luxembourg countryside lends itself to cycling, and while you're free to ramble down any road that strikes your fancy, there are also several cycling tracks leading through some of the most scenic regions. Local tourist offices can provide suggestions for cycling tours on these tracks or on less-traveled roadways. Also, tourist offices in Luxembourg City, Diekirch, Echternach, Mondorf-les-Bains, Reisdorf,

and Vianden can arrange **bike rentals.** Bicycles can be transported by train for a
very small set fee, regardless of distance traveled, but this is subject to space availability (which is not usually a problem).

ON FOOT

If ever the Almighty planned a country especially for the walkers of the world, it
must have been the Grand Duchy of Luxembourg! Walking is perhaps the best way
of all to travel through this beautiful land. Great walkers themselves, Luxembourgers have set out some 20 walking paths (one of the densest networks of any
country in the world), most of them signposted. Bookshops carry maps of some
142 walking routes, and many local tourist offices have brochures of walking tours.
The Luxembourg Youth Hostels Association, rue du Fort Olisy 2, 2261, Luxembourg (☎ **352/22-55-88;** fax 352/46-39-87), issues Ordnance Survey maps on
which walking paths are marked in red. All youth hostels are linked by walking
paths designated by white triangular signs.

SUGGESTED ITINERARIES

With 3 days in the Grand Duchy you can get a good impression of Luxembourg
City and make a quick foray into the countryside; with a week you can get the same
view of Luxembourg City and do better justice to the rest of the country, fully
taking in one or maybe two of its regions. If you have less than 3 days, either stick
to Luxembourg City, or take a tour, preferably by car, of a single region; with more
than a week, you'll just about be able to shake every Luxembourger individually by
the hand.

If You Have 3 Days

Days 1 and 2   Start with a visit to the Luxembourg City tourist office in the place
d'Armes, then take a leisurely stroll around the immediate area, including the Palace
of the Grand Dukes, and the warren of narrow streets in the old city. In the afternoon, take one of the excellent city and countryside tours. On the second day, visit
those attractions that have sparked your interest during the above tour; you might
choose the network of cliffside casemates or the impressive cathedral fortress
remains (but unless you're an enthusiast for big modern office blocks, forget the
European Center).

Day 3   Head out of town, either behind the wheel or by way of a full- or half-day
coach tour. Choose either the Luxembourg Ardennes (see "Days 4 and 5" below) or
the Moselle Valley wine district (see "Days 6 and 7" below), shortening the itineraries in each case.

If You Have 1 Week

Days 1 and 2   Luxembourg City (see "Days 1 and 2" above).

Days 3   Tour the Valley of the Seven Castles, northwest of Luxembourg City.

Days 4 and 5   Tour the Luxembourg Ardennes, visiting Ettelbruck, Wiltz, Clervaux, Vianden, and Diekirch, all of which were important sites of World War II's
Battle of the Bulge, but which also have plenty of peace-related things to see and
do. Even without a car it's possible to do some or all of this itinerary by a combination of train and bus transportation. Sports enthusiasts can take some time out
for angling or boating on the rivers and lakes.

Days 6 and 7   Switch to the Sûre and Moselle river valleys east of Luxembourg
City, visiting Echternach, Grevenmacher, Remich, and points between, including

one of the wineries of the Moselle. On the evening of the last day, take a trip to the Casino 2000 at Mondorf-les-Bains (although this could also have made an evening excursion from Luxembourg City).

FAST FACTS: Luxembourg

American Express   The Amex office is at Forum Royal, rue des Bains 25, 1212 Luxembourg City (☎ 352/470281; fax 352/471721).

Business Hours   Banks are open Monday through Friday from 8:30am to noon and 1 to 4:30pm. Currency-exchange offices are open daily at the airport and the central station in Luxembourg City. Shops generally stay open from 10am to 6pm Monday through Saturday, and many also open on Sunday for shorter hours.

Drugs   Possession or use of drugs is illegal in Luxembourg, with severe penalties imposed on offenders.

Electricity   Electricity in Luxembourg is 220 volts AC, 50 cycles, but you should pack a European-style transformer, adapter, and several different styles of plugs, since the outlet style and voltage strength can vary.

Embassies   The **U.S. Embassy** is at bd. Emmanuel-Servais 22, 2535 Luxembourg (☎ 352/46-01-23; fax 352/46-14-01). The **British Embassy** is at bd. Roosevelt 14, 2450 Luxembourg (☎ 352/22-98-64; 352/22-98-67). The **Irish Embassy** is at route d'Arlon 28, 1140 Luxembourg (☎ 352/45-06-10; fax 352/45-88-20). Australia, Canada, and New Zealand do not have embassies in Luxembourg; the closest embassies for these countries are in Brussels (see "Fast Facts: Belgium" in chapter 4).

Emergencies   Call ☎ 113 for the police; ☎ 112 for fire and ambulance.

Gay and Lesbian Organizations   The gay men's organization is **Rosa Letzebuerg,** bd. Patton 94, 2316 Luxembourg City (☎ 352/091/31-00-37—this is a cell phone); the lesbian organization is **Rosa Lila,** rue Beck 14, 1222 Luxembourg City (☎ 352/24-10-97).

Fax   If your hotel does not make fax machines available to guests, you'll find fax facilities at the downtown branch of the **post office,** rue Aldringen 25, open Monday through Saturday from 7am to 7pm.

Mail   The post office at place de la Gare 1 in Luxembourg City is open daily for letters from 6am to 10pm, but packages are not accepted for mailing after 5pm. At the airport post office, hours are 7am to 8pm daily. Postage charges are 17 LF (47¢) for postcards or letters under 20 grams (.7 oz.) mailed to European addresses, 36 LF ($1) outside Europe.

Pharmacies   Each one has a list of after-hours pharmacies posted on the door.

Police   For emergency police assistance, call ☎ 113.

Safety   Luxembourg might be the safest country in Europe, but as is the case in any unfamiliar place, the usual warnings apply. Be aware of your immediate surroundings. Wear a moneybelt and keep a close eye on your possessions. Be particularly careful with cameras, purses, and wallets, all favorite targets of thieves and pickpockets.

Telephone   The entire country of Luxembourg is in the same local dialing area, so no **area codes** are used (I have provided the country code with all

Luxembourg numbers in this book for consistency and to avoid confusion, but you only need to dial it when calling from outside the country). To phone Luxembourg from within Europe, dial **00** (which gets you into the European long-distance network), **352** (the country code for Luxembourg), and then the five-, six-, or even eight-digit local number; from North America, dial **011** (for AT&T international service, or the access code for your long-distance company), **352** (the country code for Luxembourg), and then the local number.

Direct dialing to other European countries in addition to overseas (including North America) is available in most hotels. To avoid hotel surcharges on calls placed from your room, use a pay phone. You'll save money on calls to the United States if you request AT&T's **USA Direct** (☎ 0800/022-9111) service, but you must call collect or use an AT&T calling card. Similar services are offered by **MCI CallUSA** ☎ 0800/022-9122; **PhoneUSA** ☎ 0800/022-0224; **Sprint Express** ☎ 0800/022-9119; **Canada Direct** ☎ 0800/022-9116; and for **British Telecom** ☎ 0800/022-9944.

Coin telephone boxes that display stickers showing flags of different countries can also be used to place international calls with operator assistance. Almost all public telephones now accept plastic phone cards; these cost 250 LF ($6.95), 500 LF ($13.90), and 1,000 LF ($27.80), and are sold at post offices and newsstands. Coin telephones accept 5 LF (14¢), 20 LF (55¢), and in some cases 50 LF ($1.40) coins, and it's advisable to have a good supply of these coins when you place a call.

Time Luxembourg is 6 hours ahead of eastern standard time in the United States (when it's 3pm in Luxembourg, it's 9am in New York, 8am in Chicago, 7am in Denver, and 6am in San Francisco). Clocks are moved ahead 1 hour each year at the end of March and back 1 hour at the end of September.

Tipping Restaurants and hotels will almost always include a 16% service charge and the 15% value-added tax (VAT) on the bill. If you've had really exceptional service, you may want to add a little more, but it isn't necessary. Porters at Luxembourg's Central Station charge a fixed 50 LF ($1.40) per bag.

Luxembourg City 22

Luxembourg City was for many years a thorn in Europe's flesh. Its location is a natural fortress in the first place, and the immensely powerful fortifications built here gave warmongers and peacemakers alike sleepless nights. But today the city is an attractive mixture of the reminders of Europe's constant battles for power, Luxembourgers' own equally vigorous determination to create a comfortable lifestyle for themselves, and modern Europe's search for peaceful cooperation between nations.

Luxembourg City grew up around Count Sigefroi's 10th-century fortifications on the Bock promontory. The count's choice of location was particularly astute—the 48-meter-high (156-foot) cliffs overlooking the Pétrusse and Alzette valleys were persuasive obstacles to invading forces. In time there came to be three rings of battlements around the city, including the cliff bastions, some 15 forts surrounding the bastions, and an exterior wall interspersed with 9 more forts, 3 of them cut right into the rock. Even more impressive than these above-ground fortifications were the 25km (15.5 miles) of underground tunnels that sheltered troops by the thousands, as well as their equipment, horses, workshops, artillery, arms, kitchens, bakeries, and even slaughterhouses. Legend says that within these tremendous rocky walls of the fortress sits a beautiful maiden named Mélusine, whose knitting needles control the fate of Luxembourg (see chapter 20, "Getting to Know Luxembourg").

Over the centuries, Burgundian, French, Spanish, Austrian, and German Confederation forces managed to take control of these strategic fortifications, each in turn adding to the already formidable defenses. Europe's fears of the city's strength stood in the way of Luxembourg's very freedom and independence. Finally, in 1867, the Treaty of London ordered the dismantling of all these battlements, and what you see today represents only about 10% of the original works. The beautiful parks that so distinguish the face of today's city now cover ground once occupied by forts.

Today, it is fitting that the European Union's Council of Ministers meets here, since Luxembourg was the birthplace of Robert Schuman, often called the "Father of Europe" because of his role in bringing together the original European Economic Community. But despite the banks and Euro-office blocks, the city has retained plenty of its small-scale, almost provincial, ambiance.

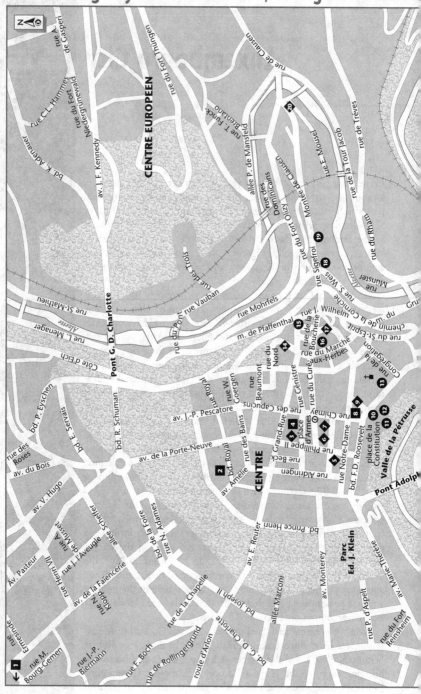

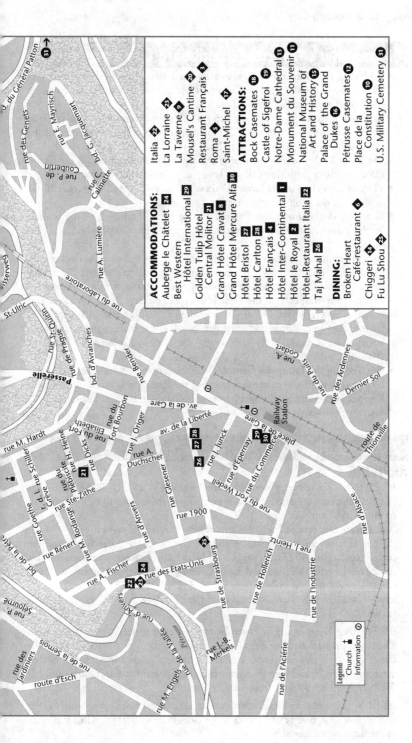

ACCOMMODATIONS:
Auberge le Châtelet **24**
Best Western
 Hôtel International **29**
Golden Tulip Hôtel
 Central Molitor **21**
Grand Hôtel Cravat **8**
Grand Hôtel Mercure Alfa **30**
Hôtel Bristol **27**
Hôtel Carlton **28**
Hôtel Français **4**
Hôtel Inter-Continental **1**
Hôtel le Royal **2**
Hôtel-Restaurant Italia **22**
Taj Mahal **26**

DINING:
Broken Heart
 Café-restaurant **6**
Chiggeri **7**
Fu Lu Shou **25**

Italia **22**
La Lorraine **23**
La Taverne **9**
Mousel's Cantine **20**
Restaurant Français **3**
Roma **5**
Saint-Michel **17**

ATTRACTIONS:
Bock Casemates **18**
Castle of Sigefroi **19**
Notre-Dame Cathedral **13**
Monument du Souvenir **11**
National Museum of
 Art and History **15**
Palace of the Grand
 Dukes **16**
Pétrusse Casemates **12**
Place de la
 Constitution **10**
U.S. Military Cemetery **31**

Legend
 Church
 Information

1 Frommer's Favorite Luxembourg City Experiences

- **Exploring the Luxembourg Casemates.** For a tour of medieval Luxembourg, head to the impressive Pétrusse Casemates and Bock Casemates of Luxembourg City's mostly dismantled fortifications.
- **Taking a Trip on the Pétrusse Express.** This *petit train touristique* (a "little tourist train" on rubber wheels) takes the weight off your feet when you tour the city. Don't worry: You don't have to be a "little tourist" to board it.
- **Dining at Le Normandy.** A meal at this haute cuisine restaurant at the Grand Hôtel Cravat might be the culinary height of your Benelux vacation.
- **Visiting the Palace of the Grand Dukes.** This magnificent palace evokes all the opulence of the Grand Duchy's medieval splendor.
- **Watching the National Day Parade.** The big parade on June 23 is a gala affair in which the Grand Duke reviews his guards with all the pomp and ritual of centuries past.
- **Bargain Hunting at place Guillaume.** The bustling and colorful market days (Wednesday and Saturday) in place Guillaume will have you pitting your bargain-acquisition skills against the money-making instincts of wily traders.
- **Paying Your Respects at the U.S. Military Cemetery.** At this peaceful and beautiful cemetery 5km (3 miles) east of the city you can pay your respects to General George S. Patton and more than 5,000 of the soldiers and airmen who liberated the Grand Duchy and fought the terrible Battle of the Bulge in 1944–45.
- **Not Visiting the European Center.** The ultramodern Euro-zone on the Kirchberg plateau northeast of the city, home to the European Council of Ministers, European Commission, European Investment Bank, and related institutions, is a desert with windows. Don't fail to miss it.

2 Orientation

ARRIVING

BY PLANE   Luxembourg's modern **Findel** airport (☎ 352/47-98-50-50) is 6km (4 miles) outside Luxembourg City. Regular flights arrive from all major European countries and North America.

A **Luxair** bus service from the airport into the central station costs 120 LF ($3.35). City bus service line 9 to or from the city center, the youth hostel, and the central station costs 40 LF ($1.10) plus 40 LF ($1.10) per piece of luggage, but this service can be refused during peak hours (around noon) to those carrying a mountain of luggage. For bus information, call ☎ 352/47-96-29-75. Taxi fare from the airport into the city is 650 LF ($18.05) until 10pm, and thereafter 715 LF ($19.85).

BY TRAIN   Luxembourg is linked by train to most major European countries. The city **train station,** place de la Gare 9, in the southern part of town, is also the terminus for all city bus lines, and has a national tourist information center, currency exchange, and luggage-storage facilities. For train or bus information, call ☎ 352/49-90-49-90 daily from 7am to 8pm.

BY BUS   Luxembourg is well connected by bus to the rest of Europe, with further connections to virtually every corner of the Grand Duchy. The main **bus station** is in the train station (see above).

Who, Us?

Can you say "bloated plutocrat?" If not, practice the term before coming here because you may need it. Luxembourg (pop. 120,000) is a city of banks, zillions of them, mostly foreign owned, taking advantage of Luxembourg's favorable—to them—laws on banking secrecy. Everywhere you go you'll trip over great marble-and-tinted-glass palaces, the plush repositories of all kinds of money from all kinds of places. You don't have to be Che Guevara's grandson to be suspicious. Luxembourg's European Union partners, particularly its immediate neighbors, have been leaning on the Grand Duchy for years in an effort to reduce the flood of tax-dodging money through these shining portals. "Who, us?" in a tone of injured innocence, is a rough paraphrase of Luxembourg's answer.

BY CAR   Highways A31/E25, E44, N6, and N4 provide direct motor access to Luxembourg City.

VISITOR INFORMATION

Luxembourg City Tourist Office, place d'Armes, 2011 Luxembourg City (☎ **352/47-96-27-09;** fax 352/47-48-18), is open January through March and October through December from Monday to Saturday 9am to 6pm; April through September Monday to Saturday 9am to 7pm, Sunday 10am to 6pm.

CITY LAYOUT

MAIN SQUARES & STREETS   The heart of Luxembourg City revolves around two main squares in the old city center. The smaller **place d'Armes** was once a parade ground, and this is where you'll find the tourist office, lots of outdoor cafes, and marvelous band concerts during summer months. The much larger **place Guillaume** is the setting for the town hall and statues of William II and Luxembourg poet Michel Rodange; it also hosts morning markets on Wednesdays and Saturdays during the summer months.

Main arteries bordering the old city center are **bd. Grande-Duchesse Charlotte** to the north, and **bd. Franklin D. Roosevelt** to the south. The principal shopping street is **Grand Rue.** The **promenade de la Corniche** is a pleasant walkway connecting the Bock casemates to the Citadelle du St-Esprit fortifications. There are steps, in addition to an elevator, from **place St-Esprit** down to the **Grund** neighborhood in the valley below.

STREET MAPS   The tourist office on place d'Armes provides a free, detailed city map that lists the main attractions; it's not a very sturdy item, so you may need a second one as a backup. Or buy the bigger and sturdier "Bonjour Luxembourg" tourist map for LF 80 ($2.20) from the tourist office and most bookshops.

3 Getting Around

BY BUS

Because of the city's small size, you may have little need to use the **bus** network. Bus service is extensive but not always frequent. The fare (valid for 1 hour) is a standard 40 LF ($1.10). There's also a money-saving **day ticket** for 160 LF ($4.45), in addition to a 10-ride ticket for 320 LF ($8.90).

BY TAXI

During the day taxis charge 100 LF ($2.80) when the meter starts and 32 LF (90¢) per kilometer, with a 10% surcharge after 10pm and 25% on weekends and holidays. For 24-hour taxi service, call **Benelux Taxis,** place Virchow 2 (☎ **352/40-38-41**).

BY CAR

Driving in Luxembourg City is not difficult, but my best advice is to park your car and save it for day trips outside the city. You'll find that most attractions here are within easy walking distance. For information on car rental and driving rules, see "Getting Around" in chapter 21.

PARKING   Street parking can present a problem in Luxembourg, but there are many parking garages. The detailed street map supplied by the tourist office (see above) has parking areas clearly marked. The three most centrally located underground parking lots are just off bd. Royal near the post office, just off rue Notre-Dame, and at place du Théâtre.

BY BICYCLE

Luxembourg City is not the best place to cycle. However, if you plan to make day trips around the city's environs, a bike is a delightful mode of transport. **Bike rentals** run about 400 LF ($11.10) per day. If you cycle out of the city, then return by train, you can take your bike on board for just 40 LF ($1.10) from anywhere in the Grand Duchy. The tourist office can supply addresses of bike-rental agencies, in addition to preplanned cycling routes.

ON FOOT

Luxembourg is a city made for walking—that's really the only way to do it justice. Few attractions are more than an easy walk through picturesque streets, and the many green spaces and parks invite either a soul-refreshing sit-down or a leisurely stroll to slow your sightseeing pace.

FAST FACTS: Luxembourg City

American Express   The Amex office is at av. de la Porte-Neuve 34 (☎ **352/ 22-85-55;** fax 352/22-85-50).

Area Code   Luxembourg's country code is **352;** to call Luxembourg from within Europe, you must dial **00-352,** then the five- or six-digit local number. The Grand Duchy is small enough not to have area codes; to call a number in Luxembourg from another Luxembourg number, you do not need to dial the country code, just the subscriber number.

Baby-Sitters   Most hotels can recommend reliable baby-sitters.

Bookstores   Two good sources of English-language publications are **Chapter One,** rue Astrid 42 (☎ **352/44-07-09**), and **Librairie Ernster,** rue du Fossé 27 (☎ **352/22-50-77**).

Dentist/Doctor   Dial ☎ **112** for referrals to English-speaking dentists and doctors.

Emergencies   Call ☎ **113** for the police; ☎ **112** for fire and ambulance.

Hospitals   The most centrally located hospital is the **Clinique Ste-Elisabeth,** av. Emile Reuter 19 (☎ **352/45-11-21**).

Newspapers/Magazines   The English-language *Luxembourg News* is published weekly, and English-language newspapers and magazines are available at the newsstand in the train station.

Police   Central police headquarters is at rue Glesener 58–60 (☎ **352/ 40-94-01**).

Post Office   The main post office, av. Monterey 8a (☎ **352/4-76-51**), is open Monday through Friday from 7am to 8pm and on Saturday from 7am to 1pm. The branch just opposite the train station, place de la Gare 38a, is open daily from 6am to 8pm.

4   Accommodations

Luxembourg has some of the best luxury hotels anywhere in the world. The city also offers many comfortable and attractive small hotels in the more moderate price ranges, some with rooms above excellent ground-floor restaurants. One note of caution: If you plan a late arrival, be sure to notify your hotel—otherwise your booking may be canceled. Unless otherwise stated, all the recommended accommodations come with private bathroom, and service and tax are included in the price.

VERY EXPENSIVE
✪ **Hotel Le Royal.** bd. Royal 12, 2449 Luxembourg City. ☎ **352/241-61-61.** Fax 352/ 22-59-48. www.hotelroyal.lu. E-mail: reservations@hotelroyal.lu. 210 units. A/C MINIBAR TV TEL. 10,500–14,500 LF ($291.65–$402.80) double; suites from 17,500 LF ($486.10) and way up. Rates include buffet breakfast. AE, DC, JCB, MC, V. Free airport shuttle service. Parking 400 LF ($11.10).

The Royal fully deserves its recognized status as one of the Leading Hotels of the World. There isn't much that this hotel doesn't offer in the way of luxury service. It's located on Luxembourg City's main financial street in the old city center, across from a park. The rooms are big and tastefully modern in style; some have balconies overlooking the park. All rooms have hair dryers.

Dining/Diversions: There are two top-notch restaurants, the international La Pomme Canelle, and the Mediterranean-style Le Jardin, with terrace dining in summer. The Piano Bar features live music after 6pm.

Amenities: Concierge, 24-hour room service, laundry and dry-cleaning service, baby-sitting, secretarial services, express checkout, heated indoor pool, health club, Jacuzzi, sauna, solarium, beauty salon, business center, conference rooms, boutique.

EXPENSIVE
✪ **Grand Hotel Cravat.** bd. Roosevelt 29, 2450 Luxembourg City. ☎ **352/22-19-75.** Fax 352/22-67-11. 60 units. MINIBAR TV TEL. 6,200–7,200 LF ($172.20–$200) double; 18,000 LF ($500) suite. Rates include buffet breakfast. AE, DC, MC, V. Parking 400 LF ($11.10).

The Hôtel Grand Cravat has stood for almost a century at this central location overlooking the Pétrusse Valley and place de la Constitution. The hotel has retained much of its old-world charm, high standards, and friendly hospitality. It's a classy place, but not in-your-face classy. The guest rooms are beautifully furnished and have hair dryers, among other amenities. Some have balconies overlooking place de la Constitution and the Gelle Fra monument.

Dining/Diversions: Restaurant Le Normandy serves fine French and seafood cuisine. In the gracious Le Trianon Bar, you often see Luxembourg's leading businesspeople gathered at the end of the day. Inexpensive meals are served in the traditional restaurant La Taverne (see "Dining" later in this chapter).

Amenities: Concierge, 24-hour room service, laundry and dry-cleaning service, baby-sitting, secretarial services, express checkout, health club.

Best Western Hôtel International. place de la Gare 20–22. ☎ **352/48-59-11.** Fax 352/49-32-27. 53 units. MINIBAR TV TEL. 4,120–4,950 LF ($114.45–$137.50) double; 7,250–7,750 LF ($201.40–$215.30) suite. Rates include buffet breakfast. AE, DC, MC, V. Parking nearby 400 LF ($11.10).

The stylish, modern International is about as close to the train station as you can get without sleeping in the waiting room. All rooms are tastefully though not lavishly decorated and have hair dryers in the notably well-equipped bathrooms. The owner, Madame J. Klein-Sutor, provides a personal touch.

Dining: The Am Inter restaurant serves French cuisine in a formal setting; the more relaxed La Terrasse has an international menu and a long, well-lit room beside the street.

Amenities: Limited hours room service, laundry service, secretarial services, conference rooms.

MODERATE

✪ **Auberge Le Châtelet.** bd. de la Pétrusse 2 (near the Pétrusse Valley on the edge of the new city center), 2320 Luxembourg City. ☎ **352/40-21-01.** Fax 352/40-36-66. 39 units. TV TEL. 2,800–4,500 LF ($77.80–$125) double. Rates include breakfast. AE, DC, MC, V. Parking 300 LF ($8.35).

This small hotel, owned and operated by the friendly and gracious Mr. and Mrs. Ferd Lorang-Rieck, is a longtime favorite of visiting academics and businesspeople. Its rooms are divided between two lovely old Luxembourg homes; all have hair dryers and modern, comfortable, and attractive furnishings. The rustic restaurant, a local favorite, serves traditional Luxembourg specialties and a nice variety of fish and meat dishes at very moderate prices.

Golden Tulip Hotel Central Molitor. av. de la Liberté 28, 1930 Luxembourg City. ☎ **352/48-99-11.** Fax 352/48-33-82. E-mail: molitor@pt.lu. 36 units. MINIBAR TV TEL. 4,500 LF ($125) double. Rates include buffet breakfast. AE, CB, DC, MC, V. Parking 200 LF ($5.55).

This handsome traditional hotel is not far from the train station, and convenient to good shopping, restaurants, and nightspots. Its rooms are not exactly big or extensively furnished, but all are pleasantly outfitted and comfortable and have coffee-makers and hair dryers.

Dining: The curved hotel restaurant serves local and international dishes.

Amenities: Laundry service, secretarial services, express checkout, business center, conference rooms.

Grand Hotel Mercure Alfa. place de la Gare 16 (opposite the train station), 1616 Luxembourg City. ☎ **800-MERCURE** or 352/49-00-11. Fax 352/49-00-09. 155 units. MINIBAR TV TEL. 3,450–4,200 LF ($95.85–$116.65) double. Rates include buffet breakfast. AE, DC, MC, V. Parking nearby 400 LF ($11.10).

The Alfa is easily identified by its cast-iron balconies and rooftop turrets. It served a tour of duty as General Patton's headquarters during the Battle of the Bulge. Its rooms, spread over six floors, are unusually large and have all been fully refitted in a restrained, modern style. All have hair dryers. The Marie Louise dining area comprises a brasserie, rotisserie with terrace, and a bar.

Hôtel Français. place d'Armes 14 (in the old city center), 1136 Luxembourg City. ☎ **352/47-45-34.** Fax 352/46-42-74. 28 units. TV TEL. 4,200 LF ($116.65) double. Rates

> ### ⓕ Family-Friendly Hotels
>
> **Hôtel Inter-Continental** *(see p. 485)* You can't go wrong with an Inter-Continental. Children are sure to love the heated indoor swimming pool.
>
> **Hôtel Alfa** *(see p. 484)* This excellent hotel welcomes younger guests. They might be excited to learn that this was General George S. Patton's Third Army headquarters during the Battle of the Bulge.

include breakfast. AE, DC, MC, V. Limited parking available on nearby street (the place d'Armes is a pedestrian zone).

The small, conveniently located Hôtel Français is one of the nicer moderately priced hotels in town. The guest rooms have all been recently refurbished and redecorated in a bright, modern style; although some are on the small side, they are all well laid out. The hotel is located in a pedestrian-only zone, but cars and taxis are allowed to drop off and pick up people and baggage. On the ground floor is a popular French/Italian brasserie-restaurant called the Restaurant Français, with a terrace on the square in summer (see "Dining," later in this chapter).

Hôtel-Restaurant Italia. rue d'Anvers 15–17, 1130 Luxembourg City. ☎ **352/48-66-26.** Fax 352/48-08-07. 20 units. TV TEL. 2,950–3,900 LF ($81.95–$108.35) double. Rates include continental breakfast. AE, DC, MC, V. Limited parking available on street.

This lovely small hotel is not far from the central train station in a quiet location in the new city center. The attractive and comfortable guest rooms are located above one of the city's best Italian restaurants.

INEXPENSIVE

Hôtel Bristol. rue de Strasbourg 11, 2561 Luxembourg City. ☎ **352/48-58-29.** Fax 352/48-64-80. 30 units (most with bathroom). TV TEL. 1,500–2,000 LF ($41.65–$55.55) double without bathroom, 2,300–3,000 LF ($63.90–$83.35) double with bathroom. Rates include buffet breakfast. AE, DC, MC, V. Parking 300 LF ($8.35).

The guest rooms in this conveniently located hotel are attractive and comfortable. The rooms without private bathrooms are a great value for those who don't mind a short trip down the hall. Some rooms have balconies.

✪ **Hôtel Carlton.** rue de Strasbourg 9, 2561 Luxembourg City. ☎ **352/29-96-60.** Fax 352/29-96-64. 45 units (36 with bathroom). 1,400 LF ($38.90) double without bathroom, 1,700 LF ($47.20) double with bathroom. Rates include continental breakfast. V. Limited parking available on street.

The Carlton is one of the best deals in its category in Europe, particularly, but not exclusively, for young travelers. It has bright public areas and rather plain guest rooms, though all are clean and not lacking in comfort. The manager is Mr. Gianni, a multilingual man who seems as comfortable with English, German, and Chinese as with his native Italian, and who may be his hotel's strongest asset. He will serve you an orange juice on checking in, bring the *Herald Tribune* to your breakfast table, and treat you like a person, not a number.

A NEARBY PLACE TO STAY

Hôtel Inter-Continental. rue Jean-Engling 12, 1466 Luxembourg-Dommeldange. ☎ **352/4-37-81.** Fax 352/43-60-95. E-mail: luxembourg@intercontinenti.com. 337 units. A/C MINIBAR TV TEL. 9,000 LF ($250) double. AE, DC, MC, V. Free parking.

This bastion of luxury is located on the outskirts of the city center, in a wooded setting to the northwest. It caters mainly to a business and EU clientele. The decor is smartly sophisticated.

Dining/Diversions: There are two restaurants, the elegant French Le Continent and the less formal Le Casse Stischen, in addition to the La Véranda bar.

Amenities: Concierge, 24-hour room service, laundry and dry cleaning, newspaper delivery, secretarial services, express checkout, heated indoor pool, health club, outdoor tennis courts, business center, conference rooms.

5 Dining

Some of my greatest dining pleasures in Luxembourg have come on balmy summer evenings in one of the sidewalk cafes in place d'Armes, a band playing in the square in front of me, an obvious appreciation for the food, and the accompanying ambiance reflected in every face around me. If there's a more relaxing pastime in Luxembourg, I have yet to find it. There are, however, many other very fine—and more formal—restaurants down quiet little streets, in old and elegant buildings.

High-end restaurants in Luxembourg City often have a few dishes, notably ones involving lobster, caviar, truffles, and such like, that skew their price ranges misleadingly upwards.

EXPENSIVE

La Lorraine. place d'Armes 7. ☎ **352/47-46-20.** Main courses 580–1,680 LF ($16.10–$46.65); fixed-price menus 1,400–2,000 LF ($38.90–$55.55). AE, DC, MC, V. Mon–Fri 11:30am–2pm, daily 6–10pm. SEAFOOD/FRENCH.

The popular, atmospheric La Lorraine excels in its preparation of seafood specialties. There are two dining sections here: Downstairs is a casual and airy brasserie-style room, with an oyster bar in the corner whose wooden roof models the underside of a fishing boat's hull; upstairs, formal elegance reigns in the art deco–style main salle. Bouillabaisse is a standout, and there's also a gigantic selection of Breton oysters, but the menu is not limited to fish; there's a deft French touch to the duck with honey-vinegar sauce and the succulent lamb. *Cuisine de nos grand-mères,* says the menu ("Just like grandma used to make").

Saint-Michel. rue de l'Eau 32. ☎ **352/22-32-15.** Reservations required. Main courses 600 –1,500 LF ($16.65–$41.65); fixed-price menus 1,750–3,300 LF ($48.60–$91.65). AE, DC, MC, V. Mon–Fri noon–2pm and 7–10pm, Sat 7–10pm. FRENCH.

Bare stone and wooden beams mark this cozy place in the Old City, down a narrow side street near the Palace of the Grand Dukes. Flawless service and classic French cuisine combine to make this family-run restaurant one of Luxembourg's most highly regarded. Seafood occupies a prominent place on the menu, but look out also for meat dishes such as game poultry with truffles in season. The contents of the dessert "chariot" will make true believers of even the most waistline aware. The wine list has some 330 fine performers.

✪ **Speltz.** rue Chimay 8 (in the old center). ☎ **352/47-49-50.** Main courses 850–1,200 LF ($23.60–$33.35); menus du marché 1,450–1,650 LF ($40.30–$45.85); menu dégustation 2,350 LF ($65.30). AE, MC, V. Mon–Fri 11:45am–2pm and 6:45–10pm. LUXEMBOURG/FRENCH.

Speltz, set in an atmospheric, wood-paneled town house, is both refined and renowned. It serves traditional Luxembourg favorites, such as game, in addition to superb fish and lobster dishes. The desserts are excellent, and there's a good wine list as well. Owners Isabelle and Carlo Speltz-Jans are food enthusiasts, and it shows in their delicious cuisine and friendly service. You can dine outdoors on the terrace in good weather. On Saturday and Sunday, the restaurant is open for prebooked banquets and receptions only.

MODERATE

✪ Chiggeri. rue du Nord 15. ☎ **352/22-99-36.** Main courses 680–940 LF ($18.90–$26.10); fixed-price menus 1,280–1,880 LF ($35.55–$52.20); Sunday brunch 850 LF ($23.60). AE, DC, MC, V. Mon–Fri noon–2pm and 7–10:30pm, Sat–Sun noon–2pm and 7–11pm. INTERNATIONAL/VEGETARIAN.

"Chiggeri" is Letzebeurgisch for chicory, and also refers colloquially to the pleasant state of well-being induced by a glass of wine too many. This unusual place has two levels. The main dining room upstairs employs African-influenced decorative motifs (including a ceiling-mounted dugout canoe), and has a notably laid-back and friendly style. Grab the bay-window table, if you can, for a view over the Alzette valley. Downstairs, there's a cafe and raclette-fondue space. The menu changes seasonally, but the food is always fine and fresh. There's a strong vegetarian slant. The wine list won a *Wine Spectator* Award for Excellence in 1998.

Broken Heart Café-Restaurant. rue de Louvigny 10. ☎ **352/22-88-85.** Main courses 480–580 LF ($13.35–$16.10); fixed-price menus 1,200–1,400 LF ($33.35–$38.90). AE, MC, V. Cafe 7am–1am; restaurant Mon–Sat noon–2pm and 6–10:30pm, Sun 6–10:30pm. MEDITERRANEAN.

The dark, southern-European ambiance of this place brings a certain zest to the often traditional-to-the-point-of-stuffy approach common in the Old City. The downstairs cafe serves snacks as well as drinks, and there are several other dining rooms scattered around the building. You might dine on seafood or a fine steak to the strains of Puccini, and there's a wide choice of wines as well.

Italia. rue d'Anvers 15–17. ☎ **352/48-66-26.** Main courses 590–790 LF ($16.40–$21.95); fixed-price menus 950–1,800 LF ($26.40–$50). AE, DC, MC, V. Daily noon–2:30pm and 6–10:30pm. ITALIAN/CONTINENTAL.

Italian and other continental dishes are featured at this pretty restaurant in the small hotel with the same name (see "Accommodations," above). There's a long à la carte menu, with outstanding specialties such as scampi al ferri and entrecôte ala peperonata.

La Taverne. In the Grand Hôtel Cravat, bd. Roosevelt 29. ☎ **352/22-19-75.** Main courses 500–760 LF ($13.90–$21.10); fixed-price menus 950–1,250 LF ($26.40–$34.70). AE, DC, MC, V. Daily 10am–11pm. LUXEMBOURG.

This casual ground-floor restaurant is in a leading hotel in the old city (see "Accommodations" above). Menu items include some marvelous traditional dishes; a wide range of fish, meat, and chicken selections; and light salads and snacks such as herring, smoked salad, shrimp cocktail, and escargots. Try the luscious chicken pie in its light-as-a-feather pastry and cream-and-mushroom sauce. This is a popular lunchtime spot for local businesspeople, but since it has continuous service, you can plan lunch early or late to avoid a possible wait. It's less crowded at dinner. There's also a very good late-breakfast menu, in case you missed out at your hotel.

Mousel's Cantine. Montée de Clausen 46 (next to the Mousel Brewery, beside the Alzette stream). ☎ **352/47-01-98.** Main courses 480–650 LF ($13.35–$18.05); plat du jour 340 LF ($9.45). MC, V. Mon–Sat noon–10:30pm. LUXEMBOURG.

The Cantine is an excellent place to sample regional treats. It was recently renovated, but it's still rustic in decor, with plain wooden tables and oil paintings in the back room. The front room overlooks the quaint street outside. The friendly staff

---

ⓕ Family-Friendly Restaurants

Cheminée de Paris The food is good at this none-too-stuffy restaurant at Rue Michel-Rodange 38—even the homemade pizzas and burgers.

Roma *(see p. 488)* The excellent spaghetti dishes at this Italian restaurant are just the thing for kids with no interest in Luxembourg's favorite pâté de foie gras.

---

serves up large portions of Luxembourg favorites such as sauerkraut with sausage, potatoes, and ham. To wash down this hearty fare, try a stein of the unfiltered local brew.

Restaurant Français. In the Hotel Français, place d'Armes 14. ☎ **352/47-45-34.** Main courses 480–840 LF ($13.35–$23.35); fixed-price meals 1,150 LF ($31.95). AE, DC, MC, V. Daily 10am–11pm. FRENCH/ITALIAN.

You can dine a little or a lot at this pleasant restaurant, with its extensive à la carte menu. Stop in for light refreshments, a salad plate at lunch, or one of the excellent fixed-price meals. In summer the place has a fine open-air terrace on the pedestrians-only place d'Armes.

INEXPENSIVE

Fu Lu Shou. rue de Strasbourg 56 (a few minutes' walk from the train station). ☎ **352/ 48-57-20.** Main dishes 340–480 LF ($9.45–$13.35); menu du jour 320 LF ($8.90). AE, DC, MC, V. Daily noon–2pm (except Saturday) and 5:30–11pm. ASIAN.

This restaurant serves several different types of Asian food: Chinese, Thai, and Vietnamese. It has a dining room decorated with red dragons, colored lamps, and bamboo curtains. Dishes include deep-fried chicken wings, garlic prawns, tofu, fish-ball soup, dumplings stuffed with vegetables or meat, shredded pork, and cashew chicken.

✪ Roma. rue Louvigny 5. ☎ **352/22-36-92.** Main courses 360–750 LF ($10–$20.85). AE, CB, DC, MC, V. Tues–Sun noon–2:30pm; Tues–Sat 7–10:30pm. ITALIAN.

This cheerful, attractive place in the city center is the oldest Italian restaurant in Luxembourg (it opened in 1950). It has an amazingly extensive menu, featuring both classic and regional (especially Umbrian) dishes. There are more than 20 homemade pasta dishes. Other specialties include veal escalope with either white wine or marsala wine sauce, and osso bucco with vegetables.

Taj Mahal. rue de Strasbourg 19 (near the train station). ☎ **352/40-59-41.** Main courses 385–710 LF ($10.70–$19.70); plat du jour 350 LF ($9.70); fixed-price menus 825–875 LF ($22.90–$24.30). AE, DC, MC, V. Wed–Mon noon–2pm and 6:30–11pm. INDIAN.

This place serves decent Indian food. It has a wide-ranging menu of subcontinental staples, with the emphasis on north Indian specialties, including curry and tandoori dishes. This is a good choice for vegetarians. Service in the long and atmospheric room is bright and friendly, and a selection of Indian beers makes a welcome addition to the local Mousel brew.

LATE-NIGHT EATERIES

The **Café Um Bock,** rue de la Loge 4–8 (☎ **352/46-17-15**); the **Hôtel Walsheim restaurant,** place de la Gare 28 (☎ **352/48-47-98**); and **L'Académie,** place d'Armes 11 (☎ **352/22-71-31**), all stay open until midnight 7 days a week.

6 Attractions

Luxembourg City is a delight for the sightseer. Most of its attractions are in a compact, easily walked area, and there are inexpensive coach tours to take you to those sites of interest farther afield. My best advice, in fact, is to stash the car in a garage and use it only when you head out to see the rest of the Grand Duchy.

THE TOP ATTRACTIONS

The **place de la Constitution** (across from rue Chimay on bd. Franklin D. Roosevelt) affords a marvelous view of the Pétrusse Valley and the impressive Adolphe Bridge that spans it. The tall **Monument du Souvenir** (Remembrance Monument) in the center of the square is a memorial to those who have perished in Luxembourg's wars—a bronze plaque at its base declares in four languages, "This is to remind us of the brutal act of the Nazi occupant who, in destroying this monument on October 21, 1940, turned it into a symbol of our freedom, thus sparking off the desperate resistance of a deeply humiliated nation whose only weapon was its bravery." The monument, known affectionately as the **Gelle Fra** (Golden Lady), was erected in 1923. In 1958 it was partly rebuilt, but it wasn't until 1985 that it was finally restored to its original form, a gold-plated female figure on a tall stone obelisk. Luxembourgers who remember those bitter years give an involuntary shudder when they pass the villa at bd. de la Pétrusse 57; it now houses the Ministry of Public Health, but from 1940 to 1944 it was the dreaded Gestapo headquarters.

The ruins of the once-mighty **Castle of Sigefroi** are at Montée de Clausen.

Casemates. place de la Constitution/bd. Roosevelt and Montée de Clausen. ☎ **352/22-28-09.** Admission 70 LF ($1.95) adults, 40 LF ($1.10) children. Mar–Oct daily 10am–5pm.

You can enter the casemates from two points: The place de la Constitution entrance takes you to the Pétrusse casemates, and the Montée de Clausen entry leads to the Bock casemates. These vast, hollowed-out strong points in the city's fortifications are extremely moving when you realize how many people they sheltered over the centuries. In the Bock Casemates is the **Archaeological Crypt** (Crypte Archéologique), in which an audio-visual presentation runs through the highlights of the history of the Luxembourg fortress.

✪ **National Museum of Art and History (Musée National d'Histoire et d'Art).** marché-aux-Poissons. ☎ **352/47-93-30.** Admission 100 LF ($2.80) adults, 50 LF ($1.40) children 12–18, free for children 12 and under. Tues–Sun 10am–5pm.

This museum in the oldest part of the city holds fascinating archaeological, geological, and historical exhibits, in addition to the exquisite Bentinek-Thyssen Collection of works of art by 15th- to 18th-century Low Countries artists, including Rubens, Van Dyck, Breughel, Rembrandt, and others.

Notre-Dame Cathedral (Cathédrale de Notre-Dame). bd. Roosevelt (entrance on rue Notre-Dame). Free admission. Daily 10am–noon, 2–6pm.

This magnificent Gothic structure was built between 1613 and 1621. It holds the royal family vault and the huge sarcophagus of John the Blind, in addition to a remarkable treasury (it can only be viewed on request, so ask the sacristan, whose office is on the right as you enter). This is also the scene of the **Octave of Our Lady of Luxembourg,** a lovely annual ceremony on the fifth Sunday following Easter, when thousands of pilgrims arrive to pray to the miraculous statue of the Holy

Virgin for protection. They then form a procession to carry the statue from the cathedral through the streets to an alter covered with flowers in the av. de la Porte Neuve, north of place d'Armes

Palace of the Grand Dukes (Palais Grand-Ducal). rue du Marché-aux-Herbes. ☎ **352/ 22-28-09.** Admission 200 LF ($5.55) adults, 100 LF ($2.80) children. July–Aug Mon–Fri 2:30–5pm, Sat 10–11am.

The oldest part of this interesting and newly renovated building dates back to 1572 (its "new" right wing was built in 1741 and renovated in the 1890s). Next door is the Chamber of Deputies (Luxembourg's Parliament).

OTHER ATTRACTIONS

Among other museums worth visiting are the following: the **National Museum of Natural History** (Musée National d'Histoire Naturelle), rue Münster 25 (☎ **352/46-22-331**), open Tuesday through Friday 2 to 6pm, Saturday and Sunday 10am to 6pm; admission 100 LF ($2.80) adults, 50 LF ($1.40) children 6 to 18; and the **Luxembourg City Historical Museum** (Musée d'Histoire de la Ville de Luxembourg), rue du Saint-Esprit 14 (☎ **352/47-96-30-61**), open Tuesday, Wednesday, and Friday through Sunday 10am to 6pm, Thursday 10am to 8pm. Admission is 200 LF ($5.55) for adults, 150 LF ($4.15) for seniors and children.

The suburban areas of **Clausen, Grund,** and **Pfaffenthal,** south of the Pétrusse Valley, are among the oldest, most picturesque sections of Luxembourg, and each merits at least an hour's visit, although be warned—you'll probably want to loiter at least half a day. Take a stroll alongside the River Alzette, and look up at the for-tifications on the hills. There are many nightlife possibilities here, as well as cafes and restaurants, often with open-air terraces in good weather.

Belts of dense greenery ring the city of Luxembourg, giving the visitor an easy, close-at-hand escape from the rigors of city sightseeing. Take your pick: **Bambesch,** to the northwest, contains more than 8,000 acres of play areas for children, tennis courts, and footpaths through the **Grengewald** forest; **Kockelscheuer,** to the south, holds a campsite, ice rink, tennis courts, and a pond for fishing.

A TRIP TO THE U.S. MILITARY CEMETERY

The peaceful U.S. Military Cemetery is 5km (3 miles) east of Luxembourg City. This is the final resting place of some 5,076 of the 10,000 American troops who fell in Luxembourg during World War II. There are 101 graves of unknown soldiers and airmen, and 22 sets of brothers buried side by side. The identical graves are arranged without regard to rank, religion, race, or place of origin, the only excep-tion being the grave of General George Patton (because of the many visitors to his gravesite). The moving inscription "Here is enshrined the memory of valor and sac-rifice" hangs over the doorway of the nondenominational chapel. About a mile away is the German Military Cemetery, which has 11,000 graves.

To get to the U.S. Military Cemetery, take bus no. 5 from Gare Centrale; by car, take bd. Général Patton east, which becomes the E42 outside town.

TOURS OF THE CITY

WALKING TOURS   The Tourist Information Office has an excellent brochure entitled **A Walk Through the Green Heart of Europe** to guide you through Lux-embourg City. The tour can be covered in an hour, 1½ hours, or 2½ hours, depending on your route and how long you choose to tarry.

TRAIN TOURS   One of the city's best tours is on the brightly painted miniature train on tires that leaves twice each hour from Constitution Square. The train, called the ✪ **Pétrusse Express** (☎ **352/42-22-881**), travels paved pathways through the Pétrusse and Alzette Valleys, and on through some of the oldest sections of town to one of the original city gates. You can simply sit back and enjoy the passing scenery, or don earphones and listen to a historical commentary (given in English, French, German, Dutch, Spanish, and Letzebuergisch). The train runs from April through September between 10am and 6pm. The 50-minute ride costs 230 LF ($6.40) for adults, 160 LF ($4.45) for children 4 to 12, free for children under 4.

BUS TOURS **Sightseeing Luxembourg** operates coach tours of the city every morning from June through September. Tours start at 10am and finish at 11:30am, and take you to the cathedral, the Grand Duke's Palace, the remains of the fortress, the European Center, the U.S. and German cemeteries, Radio Television Luxembourg, and some of Luxembourg's most important avenues. Adults pay 350 LF ($9.70); children, 230 LF ($6.40). Book tickets at Sales Lentz, rue du Curé 26 (☎ **352/46-18-18**), the day before. There are several pickup points—the staff can tell you which is closest to your hotel.

A 2¼-hour ✪ **afternoon coach tour** covers much of the same territory as the tour above, and also adds a foray to several outlying destinations, including a restored castle, the Grengewald forest, and the airport. The tour operates Tuesday to Sunday from April through mid-November, leaves at 2:15pm, and costs 400 LF ($11.10) for adults, 250 LF ($6.95) for children. Book at Sales Lentz, rue du Curé 26 (☎ **352/46-18-18**).

SPECIAL EVENTS

Wednesday and Saturday are ✪ **market days** in Luxembourg City, when place Guillaume is awash with the color and exuberance of country folk tending stalls filled with brilliant blooms, fresh vegetables, and a vast assortment of other goods.

If you're lucky enough to hit town during Lent, you'll find plenty of **street carnivals** and general festivity to keep you entertained. A more solemn—but still colorful—seasonal celebration is the **Octave of Our Lady of Luxembourg** procession on the fifth Sunday after Easter (see the Notre-Dame Cathedral listing in "Attractions," earlier in this chapter).

On Luxembourg's ✪ **National Day,** June 23, it's great fun to watch as the Grand Duke reviews his troops. City streets continue to ring with festive sounds until well after dark, when the celebration concludes with spectacular fireworks over the Pétrusse Valley.

7 Outdoor Activities

GOLF There's an excellent course about 4-miles northeast of Luxembourg City. Visiting members of other clubs are welcomed. Arrangements to play should be made through the Golf Club Grand-Ducal de Luxembourg, Senningerberg (☎ **352/34-00-90**).

HORSEBACK RIDING Riding is popular in Luxembourg. Visitors can arrange riding time through the Hohenhof Riding School, in Findel (☎ **352/34-84-56**), about 4 miles outside the city.

TENNIS & SQUASH For addresses and hours of play at the numerous tennis courts in Luxembourg, contact the Sports Ministry (☎ **352/43-10-14**). Squash players looking for a game should contact the Squash Club Luxembourgeois, rue de la Gare 25 (☎ **352/35-71-80**).

Band Concerts

From June through October, place d'Armes hosts some excellent open-air band concerts, performed by the Grand Ducal Big Band for Military Music or bands from other towns around Luxembourg. The program ranges from classical to light classics to show tunes. The concerts usually take place on Sundays at 11am and 8:30pm.

8 Shopping

For a comprehensive guide to shopping in Luxembourg City and around the Grand Duchy, pick up *Les Rues de la Mode et du Shopping au Luxembourg,* a glossy publication available from bookshops and some newsstands.

In the old city, upmarket shops are clustered around the **Grand Rue** and adjacent streets and **rue de la Poste.** Many of Europe's leading designers are represented in boutiques in this area, and there are good art galleries as well. In the station area, **avenue de la Gare,** which joins the Passerelle (bridge) to the new city, is lined with shops, most in the moderate price range.

Luxembourg City is filled with souvenir shops selling attractive **handcrafted items, clocks, pottery,** and miscellaneous objects. **Paintings** by artists from the Grand Duchy, in addition to the rest of Europe, are also featured at many fine galleries in the city. **Porcelain plates,** decorated with painted landscapes of the Grand Duchy, and **cast-iron wall plaques** produced by Fonderie de Mersch, depicting castles, coats of arms, and local scenes, are excellent mementos of a Luxembourg visit. The best place to find all these items is in the streets leading off of place d'Armes.

9 Luxembourg City After Dark

Luxembourg City stays up late, and there are numerous nightspots, jazz clubs, theater performances, concerts, and other after-dark activities to choose from. Clubs come and go rather frequently, however, so it's a good idea to stop by the Tourist Information Office on place d'Armes and pick up a copy of *La Semaine à Luxembourg* (The Week in Luxembourg) to see what's happening during your visit. Also, pick up a copy of the *Luxembourg News,* an English-language newspaper (published every Friday) that carries listings of current events. *City Luxembourg Agenda* also lists leading entertainment venues in addition to restaurants.

THE PERFORMING ARTS

CONCERTS, MUSIC & DANCE   From May through October, the **Municipal Theater** (Théâtre Municipal), rond-point Robert Schuman (☎ **352/47-08-95**), presents major concert artists from around the world, in addition to concerts by the local Orchestre Symphonique RTL. There are also dance (ballet and modern) performances and musical revues by visiting artists year-round. Admission varies according to what's on, but on average you can expect to pay around 750 LF ($20.85). Local **dance** and **jazz** school students have periodic performances at Théâtre des Capucins (see below).

THEATER   The ✪ **Round Tower Players** present high-caliber productions (in English) at **Théâtre des Capucins,** place du Théâtre 9 (☎ **352/22-06-45**). Admission is usually around 450 LF ($12.50).

THE CLUB & MUSIC SCENE

Many of the deluxe hotels (such as the Royal and Inter-Continental) offer night-time entertainment in lounges. Musical entertainment, however, thrives in the city's convivial bars and discos.

DISCOS   The numerous establishments concentrated in the station area tend to be a bit—sometimes quite a bit—sleazy, so you'll have to use your judgment about exploring them. A cool disco popular with students is ✪ **Melusina,** rue de la Tour Jacob 145 (☎ **352/43-59-22**), which alternates between rock and jazz groups; it's open on Friday and Saturday from 11pm to 3am. For techno and house, head for **Pulp,** bd. d'Avranches 36 (☎ **352/49-69-40**), which will give you as much of both as you can handle; it's open Wednesday, Friday, and Saturday from 11pm to 3am. If Latino is more your style, there's the hot-blooded **Cuba Libre,** place des Bains 5 (☎ **352/47-27-08**); it's open Monday to Thursday 9pm to 1am, Friday and Saturday 9pm to 3am.

THE BAR SCENE

Two lively, youthful, interesting pubs in the old city are **Um Piquet,** rue de la Poste 30, and **Club 5,** rue Chimay 5, a trendy bar with a good upstairs eatery. Down in the valley, Grund is blessed with several good pubs: **Scott's,** Bisserwée 4 (☎ **352/22-64-74**), which serves Guinness and English ale to a mostly expatriate crowd; ✪ **Am Häffchen,** Bisserwée 9 (☎ **352/22-17-02**), a popular watering hole across the street from Scott's, in an atmospheric old building; **Pygmalion,** rue de la Tour Jacob 19, a typical Irish pub; and ✪ **Malou,** rue de la Tour Jacob 57, a favored hangout for locals and visitors.

GAY BARS   **Café-Club David,** av. Emile Reuter 30 (☎ **352/45-32-84**), used to be a famous gay bar called Chez Mike. After extensive renovation, it reopened as a not-only-but-also kind of place, and now attracts a wider clientele than before. **Le Conquest,** rue du Palais de Justice 7 (☎ **352/22-21-41**), is more outrageous than purely gay, and a lot less tranquil than Café-Club David.

CINEMA

FILMS   Luxembourg cinemas show films in their original language, with subtitles in French and German where appropriate. American and other English-language first-run movies are often showing. Cinemas include **Utopia,** av. de la Faïencerie 16 (☎ **352/22-46-11**), with five screens; and the ultramodern **Utopolis** complex, av. John F. Kennedy 45 (☎ **352/42-95-95**), in the European Center on the Kirchberg plateau, with ten screens. Admission to movies is around 250 LF ($6.95).

23 Around the Grand Duchy

Once outside Luxembourg City, you'll find yourself in a magical fairyland countryside. It's as though Mother Nature drew together her most sparkling scenic beauties—high hills, rushing rivers, and broad plains—and plunked them all down in this tiny corner of Europe. Mankind then came along and sprinkled her stunning landscape liberally with lovely little medieval villages, picture-book castles, wineries, and idyllic holiday retreats. The best of romantic Europe can be found within the borders of the Grand Duchy.

1 Exploring the Grand Duchy

Any one of the regions detailed in this chapter can be covered in a day trip from a base in Luxembourg City. However, spending a few days on a circular tour of the Grand Duchy is also an easy matter and provides more leisurely sightseeing. Good train and bus connections, in addition to a wealth of walking and cycling paths, make it easy for the non-driver to ramble through all parts of the Grand Duchy. Drivers will find good roads and more-than-adequate road signs.

If time is limited, however, or your own interests dictate that you spend more time in Luxembourg City itself, there are excellent full- and half-day **coach trips** that provide tantalizing glimpses of the Grand Duchy. For example, one 9:30am-to-5pm tour takes you to the Valley of the Seven Castles, the Ardennes, Vianden, and a good portion of the Moselle Valley; another visits the Ardennes, the Upper Sûre Valley, Clervaux, and Vianden; and still another covers Little Switzerland, Echternach, and the Moselle Valley. Full details and reservations are available at the **Tourist Information Office** in place d'Armes in Luxembourg (☎ **352/22-28-09**), at most hotels, and at **Sales Lentz,** rue du Curé 26 (☎ **352/46-18-18**), in Luxembourg.

Independent travelers can make their own route through Luxembourg by car or bicycle. The best route is as follows: Beginning at Luxembourg City, go northwest through the Valley of the Seven Castles. At Mersch turn north, passing through Ettelbruck, Diekirch, Wiltz, and Clervaux, a route which takes you through Luxembourg's beautiful Ardennes region. From Clervaux turn south through Vianden and continue along the Moselle River Valley. Each of these areas can also easily be toured from a Luxembourg City base.

2   Valley of the Seven Castles

Its real name is the Valley of the Eisch River, but somehow that just doesn't have the same panache as "Valley of the Seven Castles," which is what Luxembourg tourist literature calls it. This little triangular area holds one of Europe's most scenic and spectacular concentrations of castles.

VISITOR INFORMATION   There's a **tourist office** in the Mersch town hall (Mairie), 7501 Mersch (☎ **352/32-50-23**); it's open Monday through Friday from 8:30 to 11:30am and 1:30 to 5pm. In July and August, another office operates in St. Michael's Tower (Tour St-Michel) (☎ **352/32-50-23**) in town during the same hours.

TIPS ON DINING & ACCOMMODATIONS   Try to have lunch at one of the outstanding hotels listed below in Eischen-Gaichel, even if you plan to return to Luxembourg City. Failing that, if it's fine weather, take along a picnic (or stop and buy the makings in one of the villages you pass through) and eat at Hunnebour, a spring in a beautiful spot between Hollenfels and Mersch. The word "Hunnebour" means "Huns' Spring"—the story is that Attila's army pitched camp here.

EXPLORING THE VALLEY

Leave Luxembourg City on the N4 heading west to Steinfort—a distance of about 20km (12.5 miles)—which is the entry point to the valley. Thereafter your route is east to **Koerich,** and its ruined medieval castle. As you continue, following the course of the river (which is really no more than a stream), the castles are seldom more than 10km (6 miles) apart.

Next up is **Septfontaines,** a highly situateded village dominated by its ruined 13th-century castle. Below the castle are the seven springs (*sept fontaines*) that give the village its name.

From here the valley road turns east to **Ansembourg,** which has two castles, a 12th-century one with later modifications high on a hill, and a 17th-century one in the valley. A little way north is **Hollenfels,** an 18th-century castle built around a 13th-century keep and dramatically situated on a cliff top. It is now a youth hostel. From there you go northeast on a minor road to the castle at **Schoenfels.**

Go north now, to **Mersch,** the geographical center of the Grand Duchy. In addition to the early-feudal Pettingen Castle, you'll also find here the remains of a Roman villa that exhibits mosaics, sculpture, and wall paintings. From Mersch, you can head north to tour the Ardennes Region.

WHERE TO STAY AND DINE IN THE VALLEY: EISCHEN-GAICHEL

19km (12 miles) NW of Luxembourg City

Before starting out on the first leg of the Valley of the Seven Castles tour, it may make sense to get accommodations in Eischen-Gaichel, a tiny twin village with only a few houses and no street names. The exceptional accommodations listed below make the few miles' detour west of the Steinfort–Septfontaines road well worthwhile.

To get to Eischen-Gaichel by car, go west on the N5 from Luxembourg City to Steinfort, then north on the country road. There are also buses every hour from Luxembourg City via Steinfort.

✪ **Hôtel-Restaurant de la Gaichel.** 8469 Eischen-Gaichel. ☎ **352/39-01-29.** Fax 352/39-00-37. E-mail: gaichel@pt.lu. 13 units. MINIBAR TV TEL. 4,750–5,550 LF ($131.95–$154.15) double. Rates include full breakfast. AE, CB, DC, MC, V. Free parking.

This small hotel is a gracious old home in the town center surrounded by green lawns and shady trees. All the rooms have recently been fully renovated. There's a terrace for outdoor dining in good weather. The guest rooms are attractively arranged. Some have good views of the surrounding countryside; all have hair dryers. Other amenities include golf and tennis facilities and a sauna. The lovely restaurant specializes in seafood, and also makes expert use of meats in such dishes as veal with rhubarb. You can expect dinner without wine to be about 3,000 LF ($83.35).

Hostellerie La Bonne Auberge. House 7, 8469 Eischen-Gaichel. ☎ **352/39-01-40.** Fax 352/39-71-13. 18 units. TV TEL. 2,750 LF ($76.40) double. Rates include continental breakfast. AE, DC, MC, V. Free parking.

This delightful, unusually shaped small hotel lies on the edge of town. It's owned by two related families and offers exceptional extended-family hospitality. Its rooms are gracefully decorated and generally have good views. Some rooms have hair dryers. In the excellent restaurant, wild boar in wine sauce is a specialty in season, while fish and local meats star the rest of the year. Menu prices run 1,550 to 2,250 LF ($43.05 to $62.50).

3 The Ardennes Region

This region, which spills over from the Belgian Ardennes, is a treat for the nature lover and a gift for those in search of a quiet holiday. It also bears more visible scars of World War II than any other part of Luxembourg because of the fierce fighting that took place here during the Battle of the Bulge in the winter of 1944–45, when Allied troops valiantly pushed back von Rundstedt's forces.

While easily explored from a base in Luxembourg City, the Ardennes also rewards more extended visits. The region offers excellent country inns and small hotels in all price ranges.

EXPLORING THE ARDENNES

From **Mersch,** drive north to **Ettelbruck.** Make a short side trip east to **Diekirch** before continuing northwest to **Wiltz;** from there you can head northeast to **Clervaux,** then southeast to **Vianden,** and farther southeast to **Echternach.** To the south lies the Moselle Valley.

TIPS ON ACCOMMODATIONS & DINING   Book accommodations as far in advance as possible because the Luxembourg Ardennes is a popular summer holiday spot, and hotel rooms can be hard to come by.

Restaurants in the hotels listed (indeed, in most hotels in the Ardennes) are excellent, and you'll find that prices are a bit lower than in Luxembourg City.

ETTELBRUCK

25km (15.5 miles) N of Luxembourg City; 11km (7 miles) N of Mersch

The first thing Americans may note about this crossroads of tourist routes is **Patton Square,** on the edge of town in Patton Park. The square holds a 9-foot statue of the general; nearby is a Sherman tank similar to the ones that arrived to liberate Ettelbruck in 1944.

GETTING THERE   There are **trains** and **buses** every hour or so from Luxembourg City.

By **car,** take the N7 north from Luxembourg City.

Valley of the Seven Castles

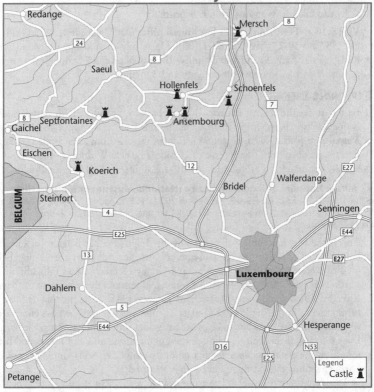

VISITOR INFORMATION The **tourist office** is at place de la Gare 1, 9044 Ettelbruck (☎ **352/81-20-68;** fax 352/81-98-39). Open July and August Monday to Friday 9am to noon and 1:30 to 5pm, Saturday and Sunday 10am to noon and 2 to 4pm; September through June Monday to Friday 9am to noon and 1:30 to 5pm.

EXPLORING ETTELBRUCK

General George Patton Memorial Museum. rue Dr. Klein 5, 9054 Ettelbruck (☎ **352/81-03-22**). Admission 80 LF ($2.20) adults, 40 LF ($1.10) children. July to mid-Sept 10am–noon and 1–5pm; mid-Sept to June Sun 2–5pm.

This museum is dedicated to the hard-driving commander of the U.S. Third Army, whose troops liberated Ettelbruck and did so much to turn the tide in the Battle of the Bulge. More than 1,000 photographs and other documents here portray the war years in Luxembourg. There are also displays of military equipment, some of it excavated from the battlefield in recent years.

DIEKIRCH

4.5km (3 miles) E of Ettelbruck

Diekirch was a Celtic stronghold in the days before recorded history. Ask the tourist office for directions to the town's prehistoric **dolmen,** also known as the "Devil's Altar."

GETTING THERE There are **trains** and **buses** every hour or so from Luxembourg City, via Ettelbruck.

By **car,** take the N15 east from Ettelbruck.

VISITOR INFORMATION   The **tourist office** is at Esplanade 1, 9227 Diekirch (☎ 352/80-30-23; fax 352/80-27-86). Open July to mid-August Monday to Friday 9am to 6pm, Saturday and Sunday 10am to noon and 2 to 4pm; mid-August to June Monday to Friday 9am to noon and 2 to 5pm.

EXPLORING DIEKIRCH

Be sure to see the ancient **church**—it dates back to the 7th and 9th centuries and is open at no charge from 10am to noon and 3 to 5pm daily. The **Municipal Museum** in place Guillaume contains Roman mosaics from as far back as the 4th century. It's open from Easter through October Friday to Wednesday 10am to noon and 2 to 6pm; admission is 50 LF ($1.40) for adults, 10 LF (30¢) for children.

✪ **Musée National d'Histoire Militaire (National Museum of Military History).** Bamertal 10. ☎ **352/80-89-08.** Admission 200 LF ($5.55) adults, 100 LF ($2.80) children 10–18, free for children under 10. Jan–Mar and Nov–Dec daily 2–6pm; Apr–Oct daily 10am–6pm.

This is the best museum of the Battle of the Bulge in either Belgium or Luxembourg, better even than the big museum at Bastogne. It displays a series of superb life-size dioramas depicting American and German military forces, in addition to wartime civilians; perhaps the best is the one that portrays the crossing of the Sauer River by Allied forces near Diekirch in January 1945, an event that marked a turning point in the Battle of the Bulge. The dioramas all give an eerie glimpse of what it might have been like to be there, struggling and fighting through the battle. Even veterans of the Bulge—who see things among the hills and forests and hear sounds in the crisp Ardennes air that no other visitor ever will—are impressed by Diekirch's museum, and there can be no higher praise.

This incredibly realistic and moving display is augmented by artifacts such as military equipment, uniforms, weapons, maps, and several large items such as a tank, artillery pieces, and tracked vehicles. Besides the events of the Bulge, the museum also covers the occupation and liberation of Luxembourg and the history of Luxembourg's army.

WHERE TO DINE

✪ **Hiertz.** Clairefontaine 1, 9220 Diekirch. ☎ **352/80-35-62.** Fixed-price menus 1,500–2,000 LF ($41.65–$55.55). AE, DC, MC, V. Daily noon–2pm and 7–9:30pm. REGIONAL.

This small hotel in the town center has won wide recognition for the excellence of its kitchen, which has won it a coveted chef's toque in the Gault-Millau rating system. Local produce is featured in creative Luxembourg specialties. The hotel also has seven guest rooms for rent, at a cost of 2,800 LF ($77.80) per double, buffet breakfast included.

WILTZ

40km (25 miles) NW of Luxembourg City; 18km (11 miles) NW of Ettelbruck

Wiltz is split right down the middle, with a 150m (500-foot) difference in height between "uptown" and "downtown." This popular holiday town lies in a beautiful and heavily wooded setting and offers many excellent sports facilities. It's a great place for leisurely walks in the woods or other outdoor pursuits.

GETTING THERE   There are **trains** and **buses** every hour or so from Luxembourg City, via Ettelbruck.

By **car,** take the N15 northwest from Ettelbruck.

VISITOR INFORMATION   The **tourist office** is in the Château de Wiltz, 9501 Wiltz (☎ **352/95-74-44;** fax 352/95-75-56). Open July and August daily 10am to 6pm; September through June Monday to Friday 10am to noon and 2 to 5pm.

EXPLORING WILTZ

Just as the town itself is divided geographically, the town's attractions are divided historically between the medieval and the modern. Witness the **1502 stone cross** at whose feet the powerful lords of Wiltz once meted out justice and the **1944 battle tank** that sits at the bend of the approach road. The 12th-century **castle** ("modernized" in the 1600s) perhaps best represents the town's dual traditions, since its ancient left wing houses a museum commemorating the 1944–45 fighting.

The town also contains a memorial to those who were killed following a general strike protesting military conscription during the Nazi occupation (the Nazi response to the general strike was predictably brutal—participants were killed both during the strike and in reprisals after it had been crushed). The **Niederwiltz Church,** a Romanesque and Renaissance marvel, holds richly ornamented tombs of the counts of Wiltz, and also a beautiful 1743 Renaissance altar made by a local artist in the Oberwiltz church.

A good side trip to make is southeast along the scenic wooded Wiltz Valley for 11km (7 miles) to **Kautenbach.**

ESCH-SUR-SÛRE
6km (4 miles) S of Wiltz; 14km (9 miles) NW of Ettelbruck

The scenically situated town, which stands beside a bend in the River Sûre, has a ruined medieval castle, floodlit on summer evenings. But it's the fishing, boating, hiking, and other outdoor sports that bring tourists here in large numbers.

GETTING THERE   There are **buses** every hour or so from Wiltz and Ettelbruck.

By **car,** take the N15 south from Wiltz and northwest from Ettelbruck.

VISITOR INFORMATION   The **tourist office** is at rue de l'Eglise 6 (☎ **352/ 8-93-67**). Open July through mid-September Tuesday to Sunday from 10am to noon and 2 to 6pm.

EXPLORING ESCH-SUR-SÛRE

✪ **Parc Naturel de la Haut-Sûre (Haut-Sûre Natural Park).** Visitor Center (Maison du Parc), route de Lultzhausen 15, Esch-sur-Sûre. ☎**352/89-93-31.** Free admission. Visitor Center Mon–Fri 10am–noon and 2–6pm, Sat–Sun 2–6pm.

This recently established natural park, though tiny by North American standards, occupies a significant chunk of Luxembourg's real estate. More important, it occupies a protected and very scenic part of the Grand Duchy, in the hills and forests around the artificial Upper Sûre Lake and on the water itself. This is the place for fishing, boating, hiking, horse riding, and other outdoor sports, including cross-country skiing in winter. There's also good bird watching here. Visit the Visitor Center for full details.

CLERVAUX
48km (30 miles) N of Luxembourg City; 13km (8 miles) NE of Wiltz

GETTING THERE   There are **trains** and **buses** every hour or so from Luxembourg City, via Ettelbruck.

By **car,** take the N7 north from Luxembourg City.

VISITOR INFORMATION   The **tourist office** is in the Château de Clervaux, 9712 Clervaux (☎ **352/92-00-72;** fax 352/92-93-12). Open from mid-April through June daily 2 to 5pm; July and August daily 9:45 to 11:45am and 2 to 6pm; September daily 9:45 to 11:45am and 1:30 to 5:30pm; and October daily 9:45 to 11:45am and 1 to 5pm.

EXPLORING CLERVAUX

Dominating this little town is its 12th-century **Castle** (Château) (☎ **352/ 92-96-57**), which has been restored after suffering heavy damage in World War II. The castle houses scale models of several other medieval fortresses, uniforms and arms from World War II, and Edward Steichen's moving *Family of Man* photographic essay. It's open from March through December Tuesday to Sunday 10am to 6pm. Admission is 150 LF ($4.15) for adults, 50 LF ($1.40) for children.

WHERE TO STAY

✪ **Grand Hôtel du Parc.** rue du Parc 2, 9701 Clervaux. ☎ **352/92-06-50.** Fax 352/ 92-10-68. 7 units. TV TEL. 2,500 LF ($69.45) double. Rates include full breakfast. MC, V. Free parking.

This lovely old manor house is on the outskirts of town, surrounded by a beautiful wooded park. Its interior has been completely modernized. The attractive and comfortable guest rooms eschew a determinedly modern look in favor of something a bit more timeless. The restaurant and lounge have a refined old-world charm. Outside terraces overlook the picturesque little town. An excellent chef presides over the restaurant, which is also graced with a good wine list. Other hotel amenities include a sauna and solarium.

Hôtel Koener. Grand-Rue 14, 9701 Clervaux. ☎ **352/92-10-02.** Fax 352/92-08-26. 48 units. TV TEL. 2,500 LF ($69.45) double. Rates include buffet breakfast. AE, DC, V. Free parking.

This century-old hotel faces Clervaux's central town square. The guest rooms are comfortable and attractive; some have hair dryers. There's a good restaurant on the ground floor.

VIANDEN

34km (21 miles) NE of Luxembourg City; 18km (11 miles) SE of Clervaux

In 1871 an exiled writer-resident of Vianden—Victor Hugo by name—described this town as a "jewel set in its splendid scenery, characterized by two both comforting and magnificent elements: the sinister ruins of its fortress and its cheerful breed of men."

GETTING THERE   There are **trains** every hour or so from Luxembourg City to Diekirch, which connect with **buses** to Vianden.

By **car,** take the N7 north from Luxembourg City to Ettelbruck, then go northeast on the N19 and N17.

VISITOR INFORMATION   The **tourist office** is in the **Victor Hugo House,** rue de la Gare 37, 9420 Vianden (☎ **352/8-42-57;** fax 352/84-90-81). Open July and August daily 9:30am to noon and 1 to 6pm; September through June Monday to Friday 9:30am to noon and 2 to 6pm. You can tour the house for 45 LF ($1.25) for adults, 25 LF (70¢) for children.

EXPLORING VIANDEN

For the best view of Vianden's narrow, winding streets, castle, and the river valley, take the **chair lift** that operates daily 10am to 6pm in July and August and daily 10am to 5pm in April, May, June, and September. Round-trip fare is 160 LF ($4.45) for adults and 80 LF ($2.20) for children; one-way fare is 90 LF ($2.50) for adults and 50 LF ($1.40) for children.

Vianden also has a charming **Folklore and Dolls Museum** (Musée d'Art Rustique et Musée des Poupées et des Jouets), Grand-Rue 98 (☎ **352/8-45-91**). It's open Easter through October Tuesday to Sunday 10am to noon and 2 to 6pm. Admission is 100 LF ($2.80) for adults, 80 LF ($2.20) for children.

✪ **Château de Vianden.** ☎ **352/8-41-08.** Admission 120 LF ($3.35) adults, 40 LF ($1.10) children. Mar and Oct daily 10am–5pm; Apr–Sept daily 10am–6pm; Nov–Feb daily 10am–4pm.

This mighty 9th-century fortress castle perched on a hill above town draws most of Vianden's visitors. It has been restored to its original plans, so you can now see the 11th-, 12th-, and 15th-century additions that are even more impressive than the earlier sections.

WHERE TO STAY

Hôtel Heintz. Grand-Rue 55, 9410 Vianden. ☎ **352/83-41-55.** Fax 352/83-45-59. 30 units. TV TEL. 2,000–2,500 LF ($55.55–$69.45) double. Rates include continental breakfast. AE, DC, MC, V. Free parking.

The Hôtel Heintz is in one of the Grand Duchy's oldest buildings, a former Trinitarian monastery—but you needn't worry about bare cells and being woken up for prayers at 3am. This lovely place has thoroughly modernized rooms, which still manage to keep some old character and ambiance. Twelve of the rooms face south and have large balconies. Facilities include a cozy bar, a good restaurant, and a private parking lot.

ECHTERNACH

30km (19 miles) NE of Luxembourg City

GETTING THERE   There are **buses** every hour or so from Luxembourg City.
By **car,** take the E42 northeast from Luxembourg City.

VISITOR INFORMATION   The **tourist office** is at St Willibrord Basilica (☎ **352/72-02-30;** fax 352/72-75-24). Open July and August daily from 9am to noon and 2 to 5pm; September through June Monday to Friday 9am to noon and 2 to 5pm.

EXPLORING ECHTERNACH

This little town is a living open-air museum, from its patrician houses and picturesque market square to its medieval walls and towers, its beautiful 1444 **town hall** (Mairie), and its 18th-century **abbey** and **basilica.** Echternach has been the repository of the ages since St Willibrord arrived from Northumberland in 658 and established the abbey that made this one of the area's earliest centers of Christianity. Allow yourself enough time in this enchanting town to soak up the medieval atmosphere that permeates the very air.

If you arrive on Whit Tuesday (the sixth Tuesday after Easter), you'll encounter the spectacular and unique Dancing Procession. Pilgrims from all over Europe come to join this parade, during which they march, chant, sing, and dance to an ancient tune performed by bands. This event mixes religious solemnity with a liberal dose of native gaiety. The procession forms at 9am and ends at the basilica.

WHERE TO STAY

✪ **Hôtel Bel-Air.** route de Berdorf 1, 6409 Echternach (one-half mile outside town). ☎ **352/72-93-83.** Fax 72-86-94. 32 units. MINIBAR TV TEL. 3,800–5,900 LF ($105.55–$163.90) double. Rates include buffet breakfast. AE, DC, MC, V. Free parking.

This luxury hotel is a member of the Relais & Châteaux hotel chain, which is composed exclusively of converted manor houses and châteaux. It lies in its own park overlooking the Sûre Valley. Hotel features include lovely terraces, glass-walled restaurants, attractive lounges, tennis courts, and serene wooded walking paths just outside the door. All rooms have hair dryers.

WHERE TO DINE

Melickshaff. rue Melick 2, Eternach (one-half mile from town). ☎ **352/72-02-05.** Main courses 360–580 LF ($10–$16.10). V. Easter–Sept Thurs–Tues noon–2pm and 6–9pm; Oct–Easter weekends only. LUXEMBOURG/FRENCH.

The talented chef and owner of this attractive farmhouse is Paul Weber. He uses his culinary expertise to create excellent local specialties at good prices.

4 The Moselle Valley & Southern Luxembourg

This vineyard and winery region of Luxembourg is set in a landscape quite different from that of the Ardennes. A tour of the area will take you along the flat banks of the broad Moselle River, with the gentle slope of low hills rising on both sides of the river. For miles, these slopes are covered with vineyards. The riverbanks themselves are alive with campers, boaters, and anglers. Several wineries open their doors to visitors. They'll take you on a guided tour, explain just how their still or sparkling wine is made, and top off your visit with a glass of what comes out of their vats.

Luxembourg's only casino and a widely recognized health spa are located at Mondorf-les-Bains, at the southern end of the wine district. To the west, almost on the French border, are Bettembourg, the mining towns of Dudelange, Kayl, and Rumelange, and also Esch-sur-Alzette, a major trade and industrial center and Luxembourg's second-largest city.

EXPLORING THE REGION

To explore the Moselle Valley, begin at Echternach, and follow the well-marked *Route du Vin* (Wine Route) south through Wasserbillig, Grevenmacher, Machtum, Wormeldange, Ehnen, Remich, and Wellenstein to Mondorf-les-Bains.

Exploring Luxembourg's southern industrial and mining district is a matter of easy driving along this suggested route: From Mondorf-les-Bains, head west to Bettembourg, south to Rumelange, north to Kayl, then west to Esch-sur-Alzette.

TIPS ON ACCOMMODATIONS & DINING   Most tourists make the Moselle Valley tour a day trip from Luxembourg City. If you find yourself beguiled by this peaceful part of the country, however, there are plenty of accommodations along the route. As is the case elsewhere in the Grand Duchy, your best meals will probably be in hotels, although small local restaurants can be excellent as well.

WASSERBILLIG
28km (17.5 miles) NE of Luxembourg City

The best attraction here is the delightful ✪ **Aquarium,** promenade de la Sûre (☎ **352/74-82-69**), open from June to mid-July and mid-September to October Saturday 2 to 6pm, Sunday 10am to noon and 2 to 6pm; mid-July through mid-September daily 10am to noon and 2 to 6pm. Admission is 80 LF ($2.20) for adults and 60 LF ($1.65) for children.

To get to the town by **car,** take the N1 northeast from Luxembourg City. There are also **trains** and **buses** every hour or so from Luxembourg City. Wasserbillig doesn't have a tourist office.

GREVENMACHER
6km (4 miles) SW of Wasserbillig

GETTING THERE   There are regular **buses** from Wasserbillig.
By **car,** take the river-side road southwest from Wasserbillig.

VISITOR INFORMATION   The **tourist office** is at route du Vin 10, 6701 Grevenmacher (☎ **352/75-82-75;** fax 352/75-86-66). Open Monday through Friday 8am to noon and 2 to 5pm.

EXPLORING GREVENMACHER

In this town you'll find the **Cooperative Wine Cellars** (**Caves Coopératives des Vignerons**), rue des Caves 12 (☎ **352/75-01-75**). They're open to the public May through August, daily from 9am to 5pm (by appointment other months). The tour is 70 LF ($1.95) for adults and 40 LF ($1.10) for children.

Interesting tours of the sparkling wine cellars of ✪ **Bernard-Massard,** rue du Pont 8 (☎ **352/75-05-45**), are given April through October, daily from 8am to noon and 1 to 5pm, with a charge of 80 LF ($2.20) for adults and 50 LF ($1.40) for children.

The tourist cruiser MS *Princesse Marie-Astrid,* which has an onboard restaurant, plows a furrow up and down the scenic River Sûre from its base at Grevenmacher from Easter through the end of September. For details of the timetable and fares, contact the tourist office.

WHERE TO STAY
✪ **Hôtel-Restaurant Mühlbach.** rue de Trèves, 6793 Grevenmacher. ☎ **352/75-01-57.** Fax 352/7-52-85. 11 units. TV TEL. 1,860 LF ($51.65) double. Rates include buffet breakfast. AE, DC, MC, V. Free parking.

This picturesque old-style hotel (a turn-of-the-century manor house) is centrally located near several leading wineries and makes an ideal touring base. The modern guest rooms are nicely done. An outdoor swimming pool is minutes away from the hotel—a refreshing option at the end of a day of sightseeing. There's a very good restaurant on the premises.

A NEARBY RESTAURANT
Chalet de la Moselle. Route du Vin 35, 6841 Machtum. ☎ **352/75-91-91.** Main courses 440–1,040 LF ($12.20–$28.90). AE, DC, MC, V. Fri–Wed noon–3pm; Fri–Tues 6–11pm. SEAFOOD.

This charming chalet restaurant on the Wine Route between Grevenmacher and Ahn specializes in fish and seafood dishes—and, of course, it prides itself on its wine list! The best choices on the extensive seafood menu are *moules au Riesling* (mussels in a Riesling sauce), *sole meunière,* and the wonderful *cassolette de crustaces et de fruits de mer* (seafood casserole) for two. The Chalet also offers two lovely upstairs guest rooms for modest rates.

WORMELDANGE & EHNEN
8km (5 miles) SW of Grevenmacher

GETTING THERE   By **bus** and **car,** it's a quick trip on the riverside road from Grevenmacher.

EXPLORING WORMELDANGE & EHNEN

The **Caves Coopératives des Vignerons** (Cooperative Wine Cellars), Route du Vin 115 (☎ **352/76-82-11**) at Wormeldange, are open April through October, Monday to Friday from 8am to noon and 1 to 5pm. There's a fee of 80 LF ($2.20) for the tours.

Half a mile farther on is the town of **Ehnen,** which has a noted Wine Museum.

✪ **Wine Museum (Musée du Vin).** Route du Vin 115. ☎ **352/76-00-26.** Admission 120 LF ($3.35) adults (includes glass of wine), 50 LF ($1.40) children (no glass of wine!). Apr–Oct Tues–Sun 9:30–11:30am, 2–5pm.

This museum is set in a beautiful old winegrower's mansion that has been lovingly restored. It serves as an information center for the region's wineries. A comprehensive exhibit explaining viniculture processes now occupies what was once the fermenting cellar.

WHERE TO STAY & DINE

✪ **Bamberg's Hôtel-Restaurant.** Route du Vin 131, 5416 Ehnen. ☎ **352/76-00-22.** Fax 352/76-00-56. 12 units. TV TEL. 3,000 LF ($83.35) double. Rates include buffet breakfast. AE, MC, V. Free parking.

This lovely, small, traditional hotel overlooking the river is also known for its very good restaurant. The guest rooms are beautifully decorated and nicely furnished, and the public rooms have a relaxed, homey feel. The restaurant, which draws locals in addition to visitors, has an old-world atmosphere, with a fireplace, dark wainscoting, and exposed rafters. The cuisine is French, supplemented by Luxembourg specialties. Prices are in the moderate range, with main courses averaging about 700 LF ($19.45). This is a good place to stop for lunch or dinner, even if you're not staying in the hotel.

REMICH
18km (11 miles) SE of Luxembourg City; 6km (4 miles) S of Ehnen

GETTING THERE   There are **buses** every hour from Luxembourg City and Grevenmacher.

By **car,** take the N2 southeast from Luxembourg City, and the riverside road south from Grevenmacher.

VISITOR INFORMATION   The **tourist office** is at the bus station on the Esplanade, 5533 Remich (☎ **352/69-84-88**). It is open in July and August daily from 10am to 5pm.

EXPLORING REMICH

The **St-Martin Wine Cellars** (Caves St-Martin), route de Stadtbredimus 53 (☎ **352/69-97-74**), offer an interesting and informative tour. They are open from April through October daily 10am to noon and 1:30 to 6pm. Admission is 90 LF ($2.50) for adults and 70 LF ($1.95) for children.

WHERE TO STAY

Hôtel Saint Nicolas. Esplanade 31, 5533 Remich. ☎ **352/69-88-88.** Fax 352/69-90-69. www.lohengrin.lu. E-mail: hotel@pt.lu. 40 units. TV TEL. 3,300 LF ($91.65) double. Rates include buffet breakfast. AE, DC, MC, V. Limited parking available on street.

Overlooking the Moselle on a broad promenade beside the river, with a view across the water to Germany, this large terraced hotel has tastefully modern guest rooms. Other amenities include a sauna, Turkish bath, solarium, and fitness center, a mini-bar on each floor, and Jacuzzi in some rooms. All rooms have hair dryers. The fine French-style Lohengrin restaurant has fixed-price menus for 950 to 1,750 LF ($26.40–$48.60), in addition to à la carte selections. There's also a nice bar and lounge.

WELLENSTEIN

4km (2.5 miles) SW of Remich

GETTING THERE   By **car,** drive southwest.

VISITOR INFORMATION   The **tourist office** is at Heenegässel 4, 5470 Wellenstein (☎ **352/69-98-58;** fax 352/69-98-59), but is open minimally with irregular hours.

EXPLORING WELLENSTEIN

Wellenstein's **Cooperative Wine Cellars** (Caves Coopératives des Vignerons), rue des Caves 13 (☎ **352/69-83-14**), offer guided tours. They are open from May through August Tuesday to Friday (Monday by appointment only) from 10am to noon and 1 to 6pm, and on weekends from 11am to 6pm. Admission is 70 LF ($1.95) for adults, 40 LF ($1.10) for children.

ESCH-SUR-ALZETTE

16km (10 miles) SW of Luxembourg City

It's claimed that the history of this trade and industrial center can be traced back some 5,000 years. Before it evolved into a quiet rural village during medieval times, it was a Celtic settlement—that's a past totally at odds with its modern incarnation. It was not, in fact, until the mid–19th century that the discovery of a rich iron-ore seam brought prosperity and growth at a phenomenal speed. Recent years have seen a decline in the town's steel industry, and attention is once more being directed to the past, with significant renovations going on in the "old city"—Nei Wunnen and Al Esch. "It's worth living in old Esch" goes the oft-repeated and increasingly relevant town motto.

GETTING THERE   There are **trains** and **buses** every hour from Luxembourg City.

By **car,** take the N4 southwest from Luxembourg City.

VISITOR INFORMATION   The **tourist office** is at the Town Hall (Mairie), 4004 Esch-sur-Alzette (☎ **352/54-73-83-246;** fax 352/54-26-27). It is open Monday to Friday 7:30 to 11:30am.

EXPLORING ESCH-SUR-ALZETTE

✪ **Musée National de la Résistance (National Resistance Museum).** place de la Résistance. ☎ **352/54-73-83-481.** Free admission. Thurs, Sat, Sun 3–6pm; call to arrange a visit at other times.

A trip to this museum is almost certain to be a highlight of your visit. You'll recognize it by the impressive monument at the entrance—it commemorates the courage of Luxembourgers during the World War II occupation. Exhibits inside cover the period from just before war broke out right up to the country's liberation.

Index

FROMMER'S® COMPLETE TRAVEL GUIDES

Alaska
Amsterdam
Arizona
Atlanta
Australia
Austria
Bahamas
Barcelona, Madrid & Seville
Belgium, Holland &
  Luxembourg
Bermuda
Boston
Budapest & the Best of
  Hungary
California
Canada
Cancún, Cozumel &
  the Yucatán
Cape Cod, Nantucket &
  Martha's Vineyard
Caribbean
Caribbean Cruises & Ports
  of Call
Caribbean Ports of Call
Carolinas & Georgia
Chicago
China
Colorado
Costa Rica
Denver, Boulder &
  Colorado Springs
England
Europe
Florida

France
Germany
Greece
Greek Islands
Hawaii
Hong Kong
Honolulu, Waikiki & Oahu
Ireland
Israel
Italy
Jamaica & Barbados
Japan
Las Vegas
London
Los Angeles
Maryland & Delaware
Maui
Mexico
Miami & the Keys
Montana & Wyoming
Montréal & Québec City
Munich & the Bavarian Alps
Nashville & Memphis
Nepal
New England
New Mexico
New Orleans
New York City
Nova Scotia, New Brunswick
  & Prince Edward Island
Oregon
Paris
Philadelphia & the
  Amish Country

Portugal
Prague & the Best of the
  Czech Republic
Provence & the Riviera
Puerto Rico
Rome
San Antonio & Austin
San Diego
San Francisco
Santa Fe, Taos &
  Albuquerque
Scandinavia
Scotland
Seattle & Portland
Singapore & Malaysia
South Pacific
Spain
Switzerland
Thailand
Tokyo
Toronto
Tuscany & Umbria
USA
Utah
Vancouver & Victoria
Vermont, New Hampshire
  & Maine
Vienna & the Danube Valley
Virgin Islands
Virginia
Walt Disney World &
  Orlando
Washington, D.C.
Washington State

FROMMER'S® DOLLAR-A-DAY GUIDES

Australia from $50 a Day
California from $60 a Day
Caribbean from $60 a Day
England from $60 a Day
Europe from $50 a Day
Florida from $60 a Day

Greece from $50 a Day
Hawaii from $60 a Day
Ireland from $50 a Day
Israel from $45 a Day
Italy from $50 a Day
London from $75 a Day

New York from $75 a Day
New Zealand from $50 a Day
Paris from $70 a Day
San Francisco from $60 a Day
Washington, D.C.,
  from $60 a Day

FROMMER'S® PORTABLE GUIDES

Acapulco, Ixtapa &
  Zihuatanejo
Alaska Cruises & Ports of Call
Bahamas
California Wine Country
Charleston & Savannah
Chicago

Dublin
Las Vegas
London
Maine Coast
New Orleans
New York City
Paris

Puerto Vallarta, Manzanillo
  & Guadalajara
San Francisco
Sydney
Tampa & St. Petersburg
Venice
Washington, D.C.

FROMMER'S® NATIONAL PARK GUIDES

Family Vacations in the
   National Parks
Grand Canyon

National Parks of the
   American West
Yellowstone & Grand Teton

Yosemite & Sequoia/
   Kings Canyon
Zion & Bryce Canyon

FROMMER'S® GREAT OUTDOOR GUIDES

New England
Northern California

Southern California & Baja
Pacific Northwest

FROMMER'S® MEMORABLE WALKS

Chicago
London

New York
Paris

San Francisco
Washington D.C.

FROMMER'S® IRREVERENT GUIDES

Amsterdam
Boston
Chicago

London
Manhattan

New Orleans
Paris

San Francisco
Walt Disney World
Washington, D.C.

FROMMER'S® BEST-LOVED DRIVING TOURS

America
Britain
California

Florida
France
Germany

Ireland
Italy
New England

Scotland
Spain
Western Europe

THE COMPLETE IDIOT'S TRAVEL GUIDES

Boston
Cruise Vacations
Planning Your Trip to Europe
Hawaii

Las Vegas
London
Mexico's Beach Resorts
New Orleans

New York City
San Francisco
Walt Disney World
Washington D.C.

THE UNOFFICIAL GUIDES®

Branson, Missouri
California with Kids
Chicago
Cruises
Disney Companion

Florida with Kids
The Great Smoky &
   Blue Ridge
   Mountains

Las Vegas
Miami & the Keys
Mini-Mickey
New Orleans

New York City
San Francisco
Skiing in the West
Walt Disney World
Washington, D.C.

SPECIAL-INTEREST TITLES

Born to Shop: Caribbean Ports of Call
Born to Shop: France
Born to Shop: Hong Kong
Born to Shop: Italy
Born to Shop: New York
Born to Shop: Paris
Frommer's Britain's Best Bike Rides
The Civil War Trust's Official Guide
   to the Civil War Discovery Trail
Frommer's Caribbean Hideaways
Frommer's Europe's Greatest Driving Tours
Frommer's Food Lover's Companion to France
Frommer's Food Lover's Companion to Italy
Frommer's Gay & Lesbian Europe

Israel Past & Present
Monks' Guide to California
Monks' Guide to New York City
New York City with Kids
New York Times Weekends
Outside Magazine's Guide
   to Family Vacations
Places Rated Almanac
Retirement Places Rated
Washington, D.C., with Kids
Wonderful Weekends from Boston
Wonderful Weekends from New York City
Wonderful Weekends from San Francisco
Wonderful Weekends from Los Angeles